D1567999

ANTONI VAN LEEUWENHOEK,

LID VAN DE KONINGHLYKE SOCIETEIT IN LONDON,

Geboren tot Delft. A°. 1632.

Daer leeft een aerdigh Man, een vaerdigh Man en gauw,
Die wisse wondren teelt; en heeft Natur' in't nauw,
Doorkruypt all' haar geheim, en opent all haer Sloten.

Syn Glase Sleuteltiens en is'er geen ontschoten,
Noch kan ontschieten, dit's die duppre Man niet: maer
Siet scherp toe, die hem soeckt; 't gelyckt hem of hy 't waer.

J. Verkolje pinx fe. & exc. A. 1686. CONSTANTER.

GABB COLLECTION. LONDON.

A COLLECTION OF WRITINGS BY THE FATHER OF PROTOZOOLOGY AND BACTERIOLOGY

Antony van Leeuwenhoek And His "Little Animals"

BEING SOME ACCOUNT OF
THE FATHER OF PROTOZOOLOGY AND BACTERIOLOGY AND HIS MULTIFARIOUS DISCOVERIES IN THESE DISCIPLINES

COLLECTED, TRANSLATED, AND EDITED FROM HIS PRINTED WORKS, UNPUBLISHED MANUSCRIPTS AND CONTEMPORARY RECORDS

BY

CLIFFORD DOBELL

DOVER PUBLICATIONS, INC.
NEW YORK

Published in Canada by General Publishing Company, Ltd., 30 Lesmill Road, Don Mills, Toronto, Ontario.

Published in the United Kingdom by Constable and Company, Ltd., 10 Orange Street, London WC 2.

This Dover edition, first published in 1960, is an unabridged republication of the work originally published by John Bale, Sons & Danielsson, Ltd., in 1932. This work has been published by special arrangement with Mrs. Dobell and is corrected according to the author's notes.

International Standard Book Number: 0-486-60594-9
Library of Congress Catalog Card Number: 60-2548

Manufactured in the United States of America
Dover Publications, Inc.
180 Varick Street
New York, N. Y. 10014

FRATRI CARISSIMO

D'ARCY WENTWORTH THOMPSON

SCOTO

HAEC ACTA MORTVI BATAVI

D.D.D.

EDITOR ANGLVS

ANIMALCVLVM ELEPHANTI

NECNON

FRATERCVLO AEQVE CARO NOTHOQVE

PAUL DE KRUIF

AMERICANO

ANIMALCVLVM ANIMALCVLO

Dedicated to the memory
of my husband

CLIFFORD DOBELL, F.R.S.
(1886–1949)

CONTENTS

CHRONOLOGICAL NOTE

The Gregorian correction of the Julian Calendar was not made simultaneously in England and the Netherlands, and during Leeuwenhoek's lifetime two different systems of dating—known as "Old Style" and "New Style"—were current in these countries.

"New Style" dating was adopted in the Provinces of Holland (wherein Delft is situated) and Brabant on 5 December 1582, which was called the 15th of the month—thus advancing the Calendar by 10 days: though other Provinces of the Netherlands (Gelderland, Utrecht, Overyssel, Groningen, Friesland) did not recognize the new system until 1700. But in England the change was made even later, for it was not until 1752 that the "Old Style" was abolished by Act of Parliament. The discrepancy between the Julian and the Gregorian systems having become 11 days in the year 1700, the English Calendar was corrected by calling the 3rd of September (1752) the 14th. At the same time, the old Anglican method of commencing the year on March 25 (instead of January 1) was ended. Good Friday was New Year's Day in Delft before 1575, but not afterwards.

All Leeuwenhoek's own dates are therefore "New Style", and agree with modern reckoning. English dates of his period are, however, usually "Old Style", and consequently to be understood as 10 days (from 1632 to 1700) or 11 days (from 1700 to 1723) later in actual time. In the present work all dates of importance are given, as far as possible, in present-day form (N.S.) unless old-style dating (O.S.) is indicated.

LIST OF PLATES

Antony van Leeuwenhoek
And His "Little Animals"

THE AUTHOR'S EPISTLE TO THE READER:

Introducing Mynheer ANTONY VAN LEEUWENHOEK of Delft in Holland, Fellow of the Royal Society of London in England.

DEAR READER: *I know full well that you and everyone else must have met Mr* van Leeuwenhoek *many a time before; but please let me reintroduce him to you, for he is a man worth knowing more intimately. Though he was born exactly 300 years ago he is still very much alive, and would be glad to make your better acquaintance—provided only that you are "a true lover of learning" (as of course you are). But as his fleshly body ceased to work and dissolved in dust about a century before your grandfather came into the world, and as he himself knows no language but very old-fashioned Dutch, I think you will agree that an introducer and interpreter may not be superfluous and might even be helpful? So please let me tell you how I first met Mr* Leeuwenhoek, *and why I now presume to take these onerous offices upon myself without any obvious call or qualification. Let me tell you why I, an almost unknown living Englishman, wish to make you more nearly familiar with a famous old Hollander who wrought and died long before we were born.*

When I was a very young man I began to study, for my own amusement, the microscopic creatures in organic infusions; and in the course of some desultory reading I then, to my surprise, discovered—a thing I ought, naturally, to have known—that these "little animals" had originally been observed more than two centuries earlier by somebody called, more or less, Leeuwenhoek. (*I say "more or less" because I found his name spelled in a great variety of ways: and being then only some 20 years of age, and having no knowledge of Dutch, I could not tell which way was right.*) *On looking into the matter, I found of course that this man with the strange patronymic was really a well-known figure in the History of Biology—notwithstanding my teachers had never told me of him (possibly, I now think, because they were unable to utter his name). I found that he was honourably mentioned as a pioneer in many different fields of scientific research—his discovery of the Protozoa in infusions being only one of his many noteworthy achievements. An odd circumstance, which (I remember) struck me forcibly at the time, was that this old Hollander—for some reason unexplained—apparently made a practice of publishing his observations in English in our* Philosophical Transactions, *and was himself actually a* Fellow *of our own* Royal Society *of London. This then seemed to me very queer and inexplicable: yet had it not so happened, the present book would never have been written.*

After this my first meeting with Leeuwenhoek, *it chanced that my studies led me away from the protozoa in infusions to those living inside frogs. I spent two or three painful years in their pursuit; and in reading up the writings on the subject, I found again, to my astonishment, that the earliest observations on these organisms too had been made by the same person—* Leeuwenhoek *once more. This revived my interest in him, and caused me to look into his publications anew. But I made little progress in my inquiries, because his original records were at that time inaccessible; and the second-hand sources of information then at my disposal were mostly worthless and contradictory—different authors supplying different references and statements, most of which turned out to be so incorrect that they led me nowhere. When I tried to find out something about the man himself, I met with no better success. Most writers agreed in calling him "well-known" or even "celebrated", and many called him "microscopist" or "naturalist" (all excellent epithets, as I now know). But some people said that he was "a maker of lenses" and even "the inventor of the microscope" (which even then I knew to be wrong), while others said he was a "physician": and had I then looked further, I should have found that still others called him "surgeon" and even "Doctor" and "Professor." Yet all writers seemed to be in agreement on one point, expressed or implied: and that was that they knew next to nothing about* Leeuwenhoek *himself, despite his alleged celebrity. No two writers gave the same account of him—even when copying one another.*

My own next researches (forgive me, dear Reader, *for obtruding myself in this fashion: it is unfortunately necessary for the present narrative) were largely concerned with the Bacteria—*

including those in the human mouth, and more especially the Spirochaetes. And here again I found—this time to my amazement—that all these organisms also had first been seen and described by Leeuwenhoek. *It seemed impossible; so again I attempted to ascertain who this person really was, and what precisely he had discovered in this connexion. But I failed once more.*

Somewhat later, I turned my attention particularly to the intestinal protozoa of man—only to find that their first observer was, incredible though it seemed, again Leeuwenhoek . . . *To make a long story short, I continually found that whatever protozoa or bacteria I worked at, I was always forestalled and led back to the same mysterious and elusive individual who had somehow succeeded in registering the first observations on almost every kind of microbe I attempted to investigate.*

It is now some 25 years since I first began to try and find out something about Leeuwenhoek *and his discoveries in protozoology and bacteriology. The task has always been hard, but because of my personal interest it has never been irksome. My interest has, indeed, grown with my knowledge; and the more I have found out, the more I have ever wanted to find out about this truly marvellous man and his works. From the very beginning, I have been able to get little or no help from the writings of others (most of whom merely led me astray), so that I have always had to do the best I could for myself. Consequently, the first few years of my labours were woefully barren: they yielded me little else than imperfect copies of* Leeuwenhoek's *publications in Latin, and their garbled English version—the* "Select Works" *of Hoole. As I soon detected the shortcomings (also the merits) of the latter, I applied myself at first to the study of the "original" Latin texts.*

I had barely begun to read the Latin letters of Leeuwenhoek, *however, when I met with a serious setback. I found that these letters were not written in the Latin which I learnt at school, but in a language I could scarcely understand—a language bristling with difficulties for a man like myself, whose "Latin" was little more than a fading recollection of the dialect used by writers of the Augustan age. Yet long before I had mastered Leeuwenhoekian Latin I received a far worse shock: I discovered that* Leeuwenhoek *himself knew no Latin at all (of any kind or sort), and that all his own writings were really in Dutch. Profoundly discouraged, I therefore began a new search for the Dutch originals.*

When I finally succeeded in obtaining a copy of the Dutch edition of Leeuwenhoek's *works, it was only to find that I could make out hardly anything of what he had written: for if the instructors of my youth had taught me a Latin inadequate to my needs, they had never even pretended to teach me one single word of the languages spoken in the Netherlands. So I made a foolhardy attempt to learn Dutch by myself—using* Leeuwenhoek's *printed Dutch letters as a text, and checking my interpretations by the Latin editions of the same letters and the old* Dutch Bible. *When I had made some little progress in this study, and had got a smattering of seventeenth-century Dutch and Latin, I made the worst (and the best) discovery of all: I discovered that* Leeuwenhoek's *own original Dutch letters—written by his very own hand, and many of them even now unpublished—are still, for the most part, extant among the manuscripts belonging to the* Royal Society *in London. I therefore went, all excited, to consult them . . . and found that nearly all those most important for my purpose were inscribed in a script which, for all I could make of it, might just as well have been Hebrew or Arabic. I could not read a single word.*

This was a blow which staggered me completely: and as we were then in the midst of the Great War, and my time was more than fully occupied with other and more urgent duties, I momentarily gave up all hope of ever being able to read Leeuwenhoek *in the original.*

But after the War, when my own work was temporarily at a standstill, I returned one day—"merely out of curiosity" (as he would say)—to the library of the Royal Society, *and puzzled over those tantalizing manuscripts. After a bit, I found that I could make out a word here and there: in a few days I could even read, now and then, a whole sentence. So I became—almost unconsciously—an amateur palaeographer, and at last attempted to find and decipher and copy all the passages which specially interested me in* Leeuwenhoek's *letters. To an unprepared and wholly inexperienced person like myself it was a task nearly as great as that which faced the first readers of the Rosetta Stone, and it was accomplished by similar methods. You may laugh,* dear Reader, *but it is true. You, who are doubtless familiar with Dutch and Latin and English of all periods, and for whom the deciphering of ancient manuscripts holds no terrors, must please try to put yourself in my ignorant position and consider my handicaps. I knew—to my shame and sorrow—little Latin, less Dutch, and not much more English of* Leeuwenhoek's *time. I had nobody to help me, and therefore made the most pitiable mistakes. But I persevered, and ultimately attained my object (more or less). I also learnt afresh the truth contained in the Dutch-Latin proverb* nil volentibus arduum—*or, as we say in English, "where there's a will there's a way."*

When I had finally discovered where to look for Leeuwenhoek, *my serious work began. Having possessed myself—after long search and many bitter disappointments—of perfect copies of the Dutch and Latin editions of his writings, and with all the* Royal Society's *manuscripts and* Transactions *available for study, I began my real hunt for the man himself and his protozoological and bacteriological knowledge. Whilst reading the various versions of his numerous letters, in quest of passages relating to protozoa and bacteria, I learnt much about himself and his multifarious other activities. In addition, naturally, I ransacked every accessible book and paper and manuscript for further information. And at last, after encountering obstacles at every turn, and surmounting difficulties which often seemed at first insuperable, I met Mynheer* Antony van Leeuwenhoek *his very self; and he told me all—or nearly all—that he knew about the Protozoa and the Bacteria. To my surprise and delight I found not only that he knew no language but Dutch, but also that he knew no "science"; for he was merely an ordinary shopkeeper, holding a few minor municipal appointments, in the little old town of* Delft. *In the world of science he was no better than an ignorant and bungling amateur—self-taught but otherwise uneducated. He did everything by himself, alone and unaided: so that when he wished to make a microscopical discovery, he had first to make himself a microscope; and when he wished to describe this discovery, it often turned out to be something so novel that he had no words wherewith to express it. Consequently, though we both strove hard, I often found it very difficult to understand what he kept trying to tell me: for he was terribly short of words, and could only talk in the commonest and most ungrammatical and old-fashioned language—often using expressions which are not in any modern Dutch-English dictionary (or if they are, have now a different meaning). How such a man ever became famous as a "scientist," and even a* Fellow *of the* Royal Society *of London, is a curious story which I shall retell you presently.*

My own chief interest in Leeuwenhoek *has always been in his observations on protozoa and bacteria—as I have already told you. But this is because these "little animals" (as he called them) have engaged my own attention all my life, being the favourite objects of my own researches. His own tastes were more catholic: indeed, he studied almost everything that can be looked at through a lens, and thereby found out something new about it too. His inquisitiveness was insatiable, and his discovery of the Protozoa and the Bacteria was merely an incident in a life crowded with discoveries—real and imaginary. For example,* Leeuwenhoek's *observations on insects, rotifers, and a host of other "animalcules," are equally remarkable; his researches on blood-corpuscles and the capillary circulation are already classics; his comparative studies of spermatozoa now stand as a landmark in the History of Biology; his discovery of parthenogenesis (in aphids) and of budding in an animal* (Hydra) *are too notorious almost for comment: while his other investigations in anatomy, histology, physiology, embryology, zoology, botany, chemistry, crystallography, and physics, only await editors for their proper appreciation. He made the maddest experiments, and attempted to see things that nobody would now even dream of seeing. I imagine, for instance, that nobody before (or after)* Leeuwenhoek *ever thought of watching the explosion of gunpowder under the microscope: yet he devised an apparatus for this purpose, and though he nearly blinded himself he succeeded in seeing what he wanted. And he actually discovered protozoa and bacteria in organic infusions in the course of a crazy attempt to find out, by the microscopic examination of macerated peppercorns,* why *pepper is hot!*

But these are only a few of Leeuwenhoek's *astonishing doings, and I need say nothing further about them here. In the pages which follow I merely attempt to assemble and edit all his observations on protozoa and bacteria. Originally I collected—simply for my own information and pleasure—everything that I could find on these matters, both published and unpublished, in his extant writings. I had no thought of making a book for others to read. Yet after a time I found that I had amassed a body of records which seemed to me so surprisingly great and original, that I felt it my duty to share my findings with other protozoologists and bacteriologists: so my own private notes gradually grew into the work now before you.*

At first I thought merely to print or reprint all the relevant passages in Leeuwenhoek's *writings in the languages (Dutch, Latin, or English) in which they now survive: but on second thoughts I realized that this would be futile. I realized that it would be useless, for example, to reprint the Dutch and Latin words already accessible to everybody, and by everybody still unread or misunderstood. So I resolved to put everything into English, in order that every man who can read my mother-tongue shall henceforth be able to read and understand what* Leeuwenhoek *himself recorded in his own language. My translations of his words are, I know, imperfect: but they are to be excused as a first attempt to reduce all his protozoological and bacteriological knowledge to a uniform and intelligible modern system, and in every case they are accompanied by exact references to original sources, so that you can—if you have the time and patience—verify my own words for yourself. A certain amount of editing and rearrangement has been unavoidable, and indeed essential to my plan; but I have, I hope, reduced my* apparatus criticus *to a minimum.*

The difficulties which I have encountered in translating Leeuwenhoek *into modern English—or, at least, into English sufficiently modern to be nowadays intelligible—have been very great. I could have rendered his words much more easily in the English of his own period—interlarded as it was with Capitals and italics and irregular and curious spellings and the queerest punctuation. But this, while superficially presenting an old-world appearance, would have been nowise satisfactory to You,* dear modern Reader. *Rather would it have recalled the false ancientry of William Morris, whose "Old English" was often no better than anachronism: for I imagine that many of Morris's "translations"—such as his version of* Beowulf*—are written in a language which no other Englishman ever employed. They remind me unpleasantly of* "Ye Olde Englishe Petrole Pumpe," *from which (I am told) motorists can now fill their tanks within 20 miles of London Town.*

All my translations of Leeuwenhoek *(as you will soon observe) are compromises between ancient and modern. I adopt old words and old phrases (used by his own English contemporaries) whenever they are understandable at the present day, but I eschew—on principle—all unfamiliar expressions. I want you,* dear English Reader, *to read* Leeuwenhoek *in his own words—as nearly as possible—but above all I want you to understand him; and I do not forget the warning issued to the translators of the* Targums (*the Aramaic versions of the old Hebrew testament*): "He who translates quite literally is a liar, while he who adds anything is a blasphemer." *The Rev. Dr Pusey hit the nail on the head, I think, when he said* (*introducing his English rendering of St Augustine*) *that a translation of an author should be* "a re-production" *in another language*, "with as little sacrifice as may be of what is peculiar to him": *adding feelingly that* "it is very difficult to avoid introducing some slight shade of meaning, which may not be contained in the original." *This, and more than this, I discovered for myself many years ago. Long ago I realized the truth of the Italian saying* "traduttore traditore"—*a translator is no better than a traitor. Instinctively I dislike and distrust translations, and it is only by the irony of fate that I now appear before you in the garb of a translator myself. I would also add, in the words of another interpreter of St Augustine* (*the Rev. Marcus Dods*): "*That the present translation also might be improved, we know; that many men were fitter for the task, on the score of scholarship, we are very sensible; but that anyone would have executed it with intenser affection and veneration for the author, we are not prepared to admit.*"

In making my translations for you I have always tried—with what success you must judge—to preserve the flavour of Leeuwenhoek's *own writings, yet at the same time to satisfy the requirements of the most up-to-date protistologist: and when I have had to translate the words of other authors, or of old documents, I have always tried to preserve their individual peculiarities in a like manner. My ideal has not* (*I know*) *been attained, but it is probably unattainable: nevertheless, you will* (*I hope*) *perhaps allow me some small credit for possessing, in these uninspired times, even an ideal, towards which I have ever striven. No similar attempt has ever been made by another—despite its crying need. No protozoologist or bacteriologist has ever before so much as read, or even pretended to read, all* Leeuwenhoek's *extant writings on these subjects; and those authors who have previously offered to interpret his discoveries have usually gone ludicrously astray themselves* (*whereof I shall give you many instances*). *Almost everything that has yet been written about* Leeuwenhoek's *work on protozoa and bacteria is glaringly inaccurate. His fame has consequently suffered, though the reputations of his translators and traducers are bound to suffer far more in the end. If I succeed only in showing you his own immeasurable superiority over all his commentators (including, of course, myself), my work will not have been wholly wasted.*

And now, dear Reader, *after prejudicing my case with these disparaging remarks, I must cast myself upon your mercy. I am forced to confess that, had I fully understood the difficulties of my present undertaking at the outset, I would never have embarked upon it: for it is a work suited to a linguist, historian, antiquary, and man of leisure, and unhappily I possess none of these necessary qualifications. The only qualification which I can justly claim is that I have spent all my time and energies, all my life, in studying the micro-organisms which* Leeuwenhoek *discovered; and consequently I imagine that I know the subject-matter of his writings on protozoa and bacteria as no mere scholar or philologist can ever hope to know it. I freely admit that my knowledge of Dutch, Latin, Greek, French, German, Italian, and even English, is unscholarly and defective: but I venture to assert that nobody, however skilled he may be in these tongues, can ever comprehend* Leeuwenhoek's *writings on protozoology and bacteriology unless he be himself a working protozoologist and bacteriologist. And this I conceive to be the primary and indispensable qualification for anybody who would rightly interpret his discoveries in these disciplines. But no man can do everything: and a modern protozoologist has little time for studying the classics or for learning languages. He has not even time to read all the current literature on his own subject. I can but plead, therefore, that my knowledge of Dutch and Latin and English would (I hope) have been greater if I had not applied all my chief energies, all day and every day, to the practical study of protozoa and bacteria. The study of* Leeuwenhoek *is really an occupation—to use his own words—"for a whole man, which my circumstances did not allow of: and I have devoted only my spare time to it".*

Yet very seldom, dear Reader, *in the course of my working life have I had anything that you could fairly call "spare time". For many years I have had to work for seven days in every week and for fifty weeks in every year at my own researches: consequently, I have had little opportunity to edit* Leeuwenhoek's*—or even to read his voluminous writings. Most of the lines* *which I now offer for your indulgent perusal have been written at odd moments in the course of other studies of my own. Weeks, months, and even years, have often elapsed between sentences and paragraphs which now run consecutively in the following pages—long periods filled with most concentrated work on subjects but distantly related. I beg you, therefore, to bear this ever in mind, but especially when you detect inconsistencies (whereof there are, I fear, many) in the several sections of this book: it has been some 20 years a-writing, and I am not now the same person that I was 20 years ago.*

If you are disposed (which is like enough) to find fault with my poor scholarship, I intreat you to consider kindly what I have already published of my own researches (which is but a small fraction of what I have done), and to remember that the present publication of Leeuwenhoek's *work has been an additional charge upon these my own most exacting labours. The whole of this book has been written at irregular intervals and under very great difficulties—mostly at the dead of night (between midnight and 3* a.m.) *after a hard day's work at my own researches, and with another similar day in the laboratory before me. If you find that I have done my task badly, please remember that it has been almost impossible for me to do it at all. I cannot even tell you now how I have achieved it: but to show you the shifts to which I have been put in order to carry out this undertaking, however ill, I may tell you that one of the following translations (and that, I think, not the worst) was made during several long and interrupted nights in the Great War, when German airplanes were trying to drop their bombs on London. Any one of these random missiles might well have fallen upon Burlington House and utterly destroyed all* Leeuwenhoek's *priceless original letters (not to mention myself). . . . But he said himself prophetically that he "never trusted people, especially Germans"; though he also said more generously elsewhere, in another connexion, "yet they're to be forgiven, for they know no better".*

I know that I cannot paint you a true picture of Leeuwenhoek's *protozoology and bacteriology without framing it with some authentic account of himself. This also I have therefore attempted. But almost every veridical record of his life is buried in obscurity: almost every biographer of this great discoverer seems to have taken delight in burying his own findings in almost inaccessible places, where others could discover them only by chance or inspiration. Consequently, much still remains to be unearthed. I have only scraped the surface here and there—through lack of opportunity to delve more deeply—and must reluctantly leave the rest of the work to others. You will therefore please remember,* dear Reader, *that my present "life" of our great Delvenaar makes no pretence to be more than a preliminary collection of materials for the use of some more competent future historian.*

About Leeuwenhoek *himself the greatest ignorance still prevails—not only in England but even in his native country. Only one full-length biography (by Haaxman) has yet been printed; though Boitet, van Haastert, Halbertsma, Harting, and more recently Bouricius, Schierbeek, and others, have published many valuable data. To Haaxman's booklet all students will forever be deeply indebted: but none can suppose that the Rotterdam apothecary, writing more than half a century ago, was in a position to say the last word about* Leeuwenhoek, *or to appraise his scientific achievements at their true worth. Outside of Holland little has been written about him which is not almost comically inaccurate. The biographical dictionaries are stuffed with ridiculous statements, and most historians of biology have hitherto been content to misprint their mistakes.*

Leeuwenhoek *himself is, indeed, now almost unknown—notwithstanding his celebrity. If you doubt it,* dear Reader, *go to his native town of* Delft, *and make inquiries for yourself. Ask any man in the street about him, and he will probably direct you to a modern road which now bears his name—a road outside the old town in which he lived, and leading to the railway station. Or your informant will possibly send you to a spot where a bronze effigy of our hero now hangs on the railings surrounding the playground of a girls' school.* "Here", *you may read,* "Leeuwenhoek, the discoverer of the Infusoria, lived and worked in the year 1675"*—the year (presumably) of the discovery. Yet he never lived in that street, nor was the discovery made in that year. The whole memorial is mistaken and misplaced. If you still doubt my words (when I say that* Leeuwenhoek *is comparatively unknown, even to his own countrymen), let me tell you a story for whose truth I can vouch. A few years ago, a party of Dutch physicians visited the Institute where I work. One of them, on hearing from a colleague that I had been studying* Leeuwenhoek's *letters,* *expressed a desire to meet me: and on being introduced he said "I am glad to make your acquaintance, as I also am interested in* Leeuwenhoek; *I understand that you knew him personally?"* . . .

To appreciate Leeuwenhoek *properly, it is (I submit) needful to know not only the particular history of many sciences but also the general history of his own times: and to see him in his true perspective it is even necessary to understand the relations of* Holland *and* England *in his day, and the peculiar circumstances which led to the founding of the* Royal Society *and to his connexion with that learned assembly. I confess I do not fully comprehend any of these things myself, so I can here do no more than indicate a few sources of my own imperfect information.*

Most men of my acquaintance seem to know little more of the history of Holland *than is contained in those ever-popular English classics written by John Motley (an American), whose great stories end where* Leeuwenhoek*'s life begins. Yet* Leeuwenhoek*'s period is well documented on the English side: for it is covered by such deservedly famous and widely read records as the* Diaries *of gay Samuel Pepys and gentle John Evelyn; John Ray's unadventurous but instructive* Travels*; dear Dorothy Osborne's entrancing* Letters *to her future husband William Temple; the entertaining* Epistles *of the Welsh scholar James Howell; Gilbert Burnet's solid* History of his own Times*; and the indiscreet Scottish-French* Memoirs *of Count Grammont written by Anthony Hamilton. (I may perhaps remind you that Pepys, Evelyn, Ray, and Howell all travelled in Holland: that Sir William Temple was once our Ambassador at The Hague: and that Bishop Burnet not only lived in Holland but even married a Dutchwoman—of noble Scottish descent. Pepys, Evelyn, Ray, and Burnet were, as of course you know, once distinguished* Fellows *of the* Royal Society.) *What little I have been able to learn of life in* England *and* Holland *in* Leeuwenhoek*'s day has been derived from these and other contemporary writers, rather than from professional modern historians. Nevertheless, I have not neglected to study (I hope with profit) the excellent works of Motley and Edmundson and Bense and others, and the well-known* Histories *and* Record *of the* Royal Society *compiled by Sprat, Birch, Thomson, Weld, and the rest. I have even learned something from the scribblings of men like Ned Ward,* *the London publican and sinner, who left us the common man's view of the* Royal Society *and its* Fellows *at the time when* Leeuwenhoek *was in his prime. I regret that space will not allow me to quote at length Ned's description of a typical* Fellow *of his period, who "could see as far into a millstone as another:" or of the Society's museum at* "Wiseacres' Hall" *[Gresham College]—a "warehouse of Egyptian mummies, old musty skeletons, and other antiquated trumpery . . . skeletons of men, women and monkeys, birds, beasts, and fishes; abortives put up in pickle, and abundance of other memorandums of mortality."*

Tempora mutantur, nos et mutamur in illis—*the times are changed, and with them we ourselves: 'tis a hackneyed phrase,* dear Reader, *and as you know a misquotation, but none the less true. Today an Englishman must almost apologize for reintroducing an ancient Hollander to his own countrymen, and for presuming to revive and interpret his long-forgotten words. Yet England and Holland were once more closely joined—both geographically and spiritually. Only 250 years ago the links of language and spiritual endeavour needed no emphasis: it would then even have been unnecessary to explain the manifest connexions between certain bits of Holland (such as* Delft *and* Leeuwenhoek) *and allied bits of England (such as* London *and its* Royal Society). *Today, alas! we are apt to forget our common heritage of race, language, religion, and even science. . . . The times are changed indeed.*

You will doubtless exclaim that I exaggerate the affinities between the Dutch *and* English *nations: and you will (with some show of justice) oppose my statements with familiar arguments from certain memorable wars—both old and new. But please do not forget that those old contests for naval and colonial supremacy were fought in the days before we had learned to express our rivalry in the form of tennis and football: and if you should perchance remind me of South Africa, pray remember also that* Christianity *was originally implanted in* Holland *herself chiefly by monks from* Britain, *and that the struggle for religious freedom—and its ultimate success—ran sympathetically parallel in both countries. Even when* England *and* Holland *were at war, Englishmen and Scotsmen (as you know) once fought on both sides against the common enemy: it was once no inconsistency, during an Anglo-Dutch war, for British troops to fight simultaneously side-by-*

side with Hollanders against Spain or France or Germany. You will remember too, I hope, that an English nobleman (Dudley, Earl of Leicester) was once Governor-General of Holland—after his mistress, our good Queen Elizabeth, had been offered (and had refused) the sovereignty of the States. Had Cromwell's dream—a little later—come true, Englishmen, Scotsmen, Irishmen, Welshmen, Hollanders, Zealanders, and Frieslanders, might even now be living together in the first "United States". Just think of that! And of more personal and private relations, let me recall the beautiful friendship of Erasmus and Thomas More—a Dutchman and an Englishman who were true brothers. Let me remind you also that the first President of the Royal Society (Sir Robert Moray) was formerly a soldier in the Netherlands, where he had many friends, and could speak the language; that a very celebrated Hollander (Christiaan Huygens) was among the first Fellows; and that the Royal "Patron and Founder" of our Society was himself an exile in Leeuwenhoek's land during his lifetime.

But you will ask (very properly) what all this has got to do with Leeuwenhoek himself and with this book? I will tell you. In reintroducing plain Mr van Leeuwenhoek, the Dutch draper and amateur micrographer, I want also to impress upon you that there are still blood-brothers in every different nation. Barriers erected by birth and prejudice and education are blown sky-high before the fire of common human aims and interests. Language and land and lineage are no bars to mutual and native understanding. An honest man in any country is linked to all other honest men in all other countries. When a true man like Antony van Leeuwenhoek is born, the heavens are opened. Even when he dies he is not dead: his spirit glows with the divine light forever, and will forever be seen and understood—somewhere, sometime, by somebody. No Princes, Popes, politicians, or even prophets, can unite mankind in universal brotherhood; but the disinterested and simple men everywhere can (and perhaps eventually will) unknowingly draw warring nations together, and may ultimately save humanity from the fate of the Triassic reptiles. As surely as Leeuwenhoek, the old Dutch draper, has—after centuries of misunderstanding—established connexion with me, a modern English biologist, and has awakened my sympathy with himself and his countrymen; just as surely will other men of other nations and other interests be drawn together by the endearment *engendered by common enterprise and common human endeavour. This is the real* League of Nations—*the only one that can ever succeed or survive.*

Therefore, dear Reader, *meet Mr* van Leeuwenhoek (*a simple and ordinary dead Dutchman*) *and shake him by the hand and hearken to what he has to say. When you have done that, you will not only know the true meaning of that misused term "scientific research", but you will also realize* (*I hope*) *that you have already gone further along the path of peace and progress than some of the more sophisticated people now sitting solemnly at Geneva or at the meetings of the most learned and modern and Royal and scientific societies* (*God bless and prosper them all!*).

For my own part, I will only add—though it must now be obvious—that the making of this book has been to me a labour of love: and as such it is offered with all its manifest imperfections to You, good Reader, *and to all other lovers of* Leeuwenhoek *and of his "little animals" and of all else that such love implies.*

Farewell.

MEMORABILIA

Philips v. Leeuwenhoek married Margriete Bel v.d. Berch	30 Jan. 1622
Their son **Antony van Leeuwenhoek** born at Delft	24 Oct. 1632
baptized	4 Nov. 1632
Father buried	8 Jan. 1638
Mother remarried	18 Dec. 1640
Apprenticed to draper in Amsterdam	1648
Draper and haberdasher in Delft	*circa* 1654
Married Barbara de Meij	29 July 1654
Maria his daughter born	22 Sept. 1656
Appointed Sheriffs' Chamberlain of Delft	26 Mar. 1660
Mother buried	3 Sept. 1664
First wife (Barbara) died	11 July 1666
Appointed Surveyor	4 Feb. 1669
Married Cornelia Swalmius	25 Jan. 1671
Addressed first letter to Royal Society of London	Apr. 1673
Discovered the Protozoa	1674
and the Bacteria	1676
Executor of Vermeer's estate	30 Sept. 1676
Wine-gauger of Delft	15 Aug. 1679
Fellow of the Royal Society	29 Jan. 1679/80 *O.S.* [= 8 Feb. 1680 *N.S.*]
Second wife (Cornelia) buried	6 Jan. 1694
Correspondant de l'Académie des Sciences, Paris	4 Mar. 1699
Died at Delft	26 Aug. 1723
and buried in the Old Church	31 Aug. 1723
Tomb erected	1739
Maria died	25 Apr. 1745
Microscopes sold	29 May 1747

PART I

LEEUWENHOEK

A very civil complesant man, & douptless of great natural Abileties; but contrary to my Expectations quite a stranger to letters, . . . which is a great hindrance to him in his reasonings uppon his Observations, for being ignorant of all other Mens thoughts, he is wholy trusting to his own.—Dr *Thomas Molyneux* (1685).

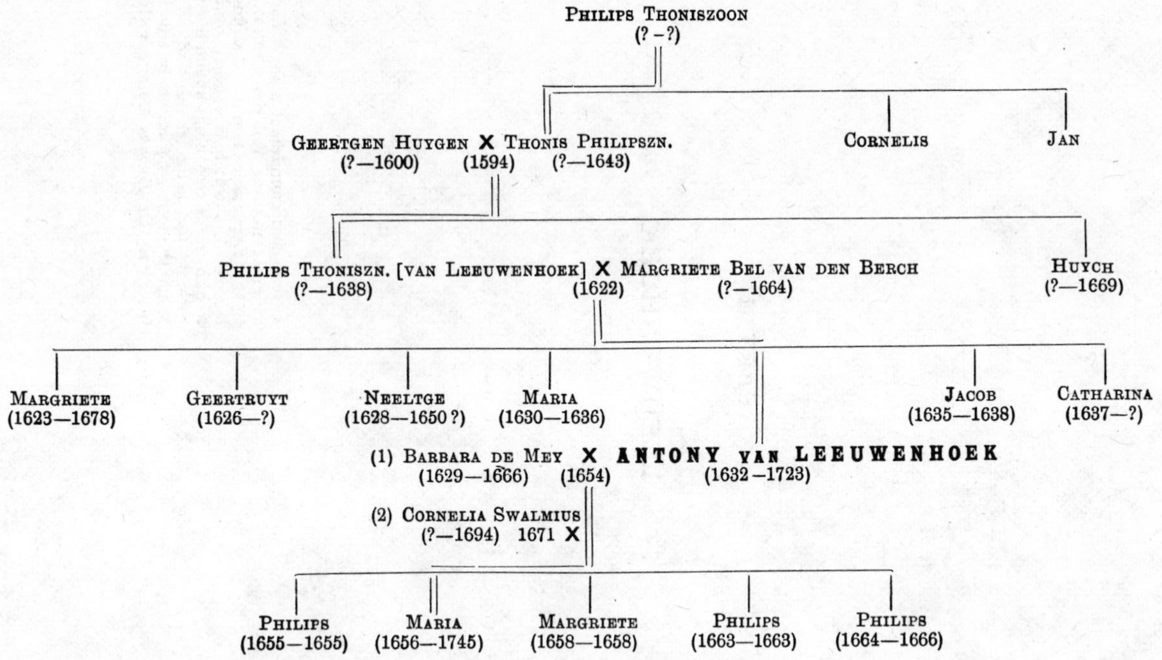
PHILIPS THONISZOON
(? –?)
GEERTGEN HUYGEN X THONIS PHILIPSZN.
(?—1600) (1594) (?—1643)
CORNELIS
JAN
PHILIPS THONISZN. [VAN LEEUWENHOEK] X MARGRIETE BEL VAN DEN BERCH
(?—1638) (1622) (?—1664)
HUYCH
(?—1669)
MARGRIETE
(1623—1678)
GEERTRUYT
(1626—?)
NEELTGE
(1628—1650 ?)
MARIA
(1630—1636)
JACOB
(1635—1638)
CATHARINA
(1637—?)
(1) BARBARA DE MEY X ANTONY VAN LEEUWENHOEK
(1629—1666) (1654) (1632—1723)
(2) CORNELIA SWALMIUS
(?—1694) 1671 X
PHILIPS
(1655—1655)
MARIA
(1656—1745)
MARGRIETE
(1658—1658)
PHILIPS
(1663—1663)
PHILIPS
(1664—1666)

FAMILY TREE

THE LIFE OF ANTONY VAN LEEUWENHOEK

ANTONY VAN LEEUWENHOEK,[1] the hero of the following pages, was born at Delft in Holland on 24 October 1632. He died in his native town on 26 August 1723; being then aged—as his epitaph informs us, with appropriate numerical particularity—"90 years, 10 months, and 2 days."

The year of Leeuwenhoek's birth is memorable, to Englishmen and Hollanders alike, as that in which several of our other great men—of widely different genius—were also born: our philosophers John Locke (1632—1704) and Baruch de Spinoza (1632—1677); the architect Christopher Wren (1632—1723); and the famous painters Jan Vermeer of Delft (1632—1675) and Nicolaes Maes (1632—1693). It is also remembered by historians as the year of the Siege of Maestricht, which marks approximately the middle of the Thirty Years' War. The unhappy Charles I was then King of England; the great Prince of Orange Frederik Hendrik, whose period is called a "golden age" by Dutch writers, was Stadholder of the United Netherlands: and for both Holland and England the times were big with coming developments in politics, religion, and commerce—no less than in science, philosophy, and art. Verily a strange hour for the birth of one who, while leading in the midst of wars the peaceful life of a provincial tradesman, was to win immortal fame by his amateur activities as a man of science.

Of Leeuwenhoek's parents not much is certainly known. His father was named Philips Antonysz. van Leeuwenhoek[2],

---

[1] For orthography, derivation, and pronunciation of the name, see p. 300.

[2] *i.e.*, Phillip, son of Antony v. L. The name is sometimes given as Philips (or Philippus) Antony, but this is a mistake. Cf. Boitet (1729), Haaxman (1875), and Soutendam (1875). In an old genealogical tree—which I have seen—in the possession of the Haaxman family, the name is written as given above: but in the archives of Delft he is styled simply "Philips Thonisz." (Bouricius, 1924, 1925.)

and was a basket-maker living in the East-End (*Oosteinde*) of Delft—near the now long-vanished Leeuwenpoort[1]. He appears to have been a craftsman of good Dutch stock, but of no personal or social distinction. His own father (Antony Philipszn.) was likewise a basket-maker[2].

Leeuwenhoek's mother was Margaretha, daughter of Jacob Sebastiaanszoon Bel van den Berch[3], a Delft brewer[4]. She belonged to a good family, and was related to other Dutch families of equally good standing[5]. The brewers then, as now, were no inconsiderable folk in Holland; and it thus seems clear that any claims which our Antony may have to gentle birth must rest upon his mother[6].

Philips van Leeuwenhoek and Margaretha Bel van den Berch were married in 1622. Their betrothal (*ondertrouw*) was formally announced on January 15, and the marriage took place on the 30th of the same month—as Bouricius has now

---

[1] Cf. p. 338 *sq.*, *infra.* The house in which he is believed to have lived, and in which L. was born, is shown in Plate II.

[2] *fide* Bouricius. The Leeuwenhoeks, for several generations at least, were consistently named Phillip and Antony alternately. (Cf. the family tree, p. 18.) This system of alternate nomenclature seems to have been common in Dutch families at that period. (L. himself made three unsuccessful attempts to rear a son called Phillip—as will be evident in the family tree.)

[3] *alias* Berg, or Bergh. The name is spelled variously. Margaretha's forename is also given as Margriete (cf. Schierbeek, 1930) and Grietge (cf. Plate III).

[4] Cf. Boitet (1729), Soutendam (1875), Haaxman (1875), and Bouricius (1924, 1925). L. himself tells us (*Send-brief* XXII, 16 May 1716) that his grandfather and great-grandfather were brewers, and that his grandmother was the daughter of a brewer. But his grandfather on the father's side (another Antony) was, as just noted, only a basket-maker.

[5] Namely, the families of Hoogenhouk, Bleiswijk, Swalmius, and Mathenesse. Cf. Boitet (1729), Halbertsma (1843), and Haaxman (1875).

[6] Boitet (1729), only six years after L.'s death, records that he came from "*zeer deftige en eerlyke ouders*"; but this was perhaps merely a euphemistic way of saying that he was born of respectable parents. It can hardly be taken to prove that he belonged to the aristocracy. Although it would be unusual to call a basket-maker "*zeer deftig*" at the present day, such hyperbolic expressions were as customary in Holland as they were in England at the date when Boitet's book was published. It must be remembered, also, that his book was not issued with the object of belittling Delft and her burghers.

THE HOUSE IN WHICH LEEUWENHOEK WAS BORN (1632)

in the East-End (*Oosteinde*) of Delft: as it appeared in November, 1926. [Identified by Mr L. G. N. Bouricius. Now demolished.]

facing p. 20

REGISTRATION OF LEEUWENHOEK'S BAPTISM

(New Church, Delft ; 4 November 1632). The entry reads :

VOLCHT DE MAENT NOVEMBER. 1632

4. dito. 1. kint *Thonis*, vader Philips thonis zn, moeder Grietge Jacobs, getuijges Thonis philips zn, Huijch thonis zn, Magdalena, en Catharina Jacobs d^r^.,

---

[Translation] *Followeth the Month of November*, 1632

4th ditto. 1 child *Tony*; father Phillip, son of Anthony; mother Maggie, James's daughter. Witnesses: Tony Phillip's son [L.'s paternal grandfather], Hugh Tony's son [L.'s paternal uncle], Madeleine and Catherine daughters of James [L.'s maternal aunts].

ascertained definitively.[1] Antony, their first son and fifth child, was born to them ten years later. He was born on 24 October, and was baptized in the New Church at Delft on 4 November[2], A.D. 1632. (See Plate III.)

It is recorded that Antony had four[3] surviving sisters—Margriete, Geertruyt, Neeltge, and Catharina—though very little is now known about any of them. We know,[4] however, that Margriete [Margaret] the eldest (born 1623), married one Jan Molijn,[5] and herself bore five children; and one of these, named Maria (like Leeuwenhoek's own daughter), married a certain Cornelis Haaxman from whom Leeuwenhoek's biographer, P. J. Haaxman, claimed descent. Geertruyt [Gertrude] was born in 1626, and Catharina in 1637[6], and

---

[1] See Bouricius (1924, 1925). The date "5/30 Jan." given by Schierbeek (1930) is incorrect, and should read "15/30."—It has recently been alleged by Naber that L.'s father had previously tried to marry one of the daughters of the adventurer Cornelis Drebbel (1572—1633), who is regarded by some admirers as the inventor of the microscope. Naber even avers (p. 32) that L.'s father was "one of Drebbel's lens-grinders"; and would insinuate apparently that what L. himself knew about lenses was learned from his father, who in turn derived it from Drebbel. But this story is apocryphal. We now know that L.'s father was not a lens-grinder but a basket-maker, and that he died when Antony was only 5 years old: and we now know also—thanks largely to Jaeger (1922)—a good deal about Drebbel. Dr Schierbeek, who first drew my attention to Dr Naber's statements, wrote to ask for his evidence: and as a result of this correspondence (which Dr Schierbeek kindly allowed me to read) and of my own inquiries, I can only conclude that no evidence exists. Cf. Jaeger (1922, especially p. 7) and Bouricius (1924).

[2] Schierbeek (1923), Bouricius (1924, 1925). Schierbeek (1930), through a misprint, wrongly gives the date of baptism as Nov. 14.

[3] Haaxman (1875), Schierbeek (1930). Two other children—a sister (Maria) and a brother (Jacob)—died in infancy. Haaxman mentions only 3 sisters, but Bouricius has since discovered the existence of the fourth (Neeltge), who apparently attained maturity. The names of Margriete and Geertruyt are spelled "Margaretha" and "Geertruida" by Haaxman.

[4] Haaxman (1875), Bouricius (1924).

[5] This Jan Molijn (*alias* du Molyn), who married L.'s sister Margaret on 10 May 1643, was himself the son—by an earlier marriage—of the Jacob Molijn whom L.'s mother (also named Margaret) married after the death of her first husband (L.'s father): *fide* Bouricius, *in litt.*

[6] According to Bouricius (1924) and Schierbeek (1930).—Catharina, who was married to Claes Jansz. van Leeuwen in 1655, is referred to by L. himself in unpublished postscripts to *Letter* 13*a* (22 Jan. 1676) and *Letter 39* (17 Sept. 1683), in both of which he requests that the *Phil. Trans.*

both married subsequently. Neeltge [Nellie] apparently died young. (See the Family Tree, p. 18.)

All the trustworthy evidence now available thus shows that Antony was a true Hollander of decent though not of aristocratic descent—a child of fairly well-to-do tradespeople. Richardson's statement (1885)—unhesitatingly accepted by Locy (1901, 1910), Plimmer (1913), and others—that he was of "Jewish Saxon" extraction, is nothing but a wild speculation[1]: and the evidence against the guess that Leeuwenhoek was a Jew, or of Jewish origin, is overwhelming. Mr Bouricius assures me[2] that "there were practically no Jews in Delft" at that date: and if there were any, they certainly did not then engage in basket-making or in brewing, nor did they hold any municipal appointments (from which they were debarred). Moreover, the baptisms and marriages and burials of all members of the families concerned (whose names are obviously not Jewish) were entered in the registers of the Reformed Church; while Leeuwenhoek was, of course, himself baptized in the New Church and buried in the Old Church at Delft. Mr Bouricius, who speaks with authority, says: "*In geen geval was van Leeuwenhoek een jood*"—Leeuwenhoek was no Jew anyway.

When our Antony was only five years old, his father Philips died,[3] leaving his mother in sole charge of their little family. But soon afterwards (18 December 1640) she married again—her second husband, Antony's stepfather, being a painter named Jacob Jansz. Molijn, who died in 1648. Antony's mother herself died 16 years later, and was buried in the Old Church at Delft on 3 September 1664.[4]

---

may be forwarded to him through "Mistress Catharine Leeuwenhoek, widow . . . living in the High Street at Rotterdam." She had no children (*fide* Bouricius).

[1] Richardson's ridiculous statement had no other foundation than his own imagination. The "Jewish" and "Saxon" ancestors were divined by inspection of L.'s portrait!

[2] *in litteris.*

[3] He was buried in the Old Church at Delft on 8 January 1638 (Bouricius, 1924). The exact date of his death I have been unable to ascertain. Cf. Schierbeek (1930).

[4] The foregoing facts—imperfectly noted by earlier biographers—are recorded in part by Bouricius (1924, 1925), and additional confirmatory details have been kindly sent me by him in personal communications. Cf. also Schierbeek (1929, 1930).

Somewhere about the time of her second marriage, Antony's mother put him to school at Warmond, a townlet a few miles north of Leyden. After receiving his earliest education here, he went—at what age is not exactly known—to live with an uncle who was an attorney, and also town clerk, at Benthuizen.[1] It has been said that young Antony was at this time contemplating a similar career, and that he went to his uncle to prepare himself for it.[2] But there appears to be very little foundation for such a supposition ; and it has been judiciously remarked[3] that, as he was never even taught Latin, it is unlikely he was ever destined either for the law or for the university.

But whatever his own or his family's intentions may have been at this date, we know certainly that Antony neither progressed far in the study of the law nor did he prepare himself for a university career. We may suppose, however, that his education was not wholly neglected during his residence with his uncle : and it was, perhaps, at this time that he acquired those rudiments of mathematics and physical science in which he so delighted to indulge himself in his later life. Yet it is certain that he received no instruction in languages, for to the end of his days he knew none but his own.[4]

In 1648[5] (the year in which his stepfather died) Antony, being 16 years of age, was sent to Amsterdam—then, as now, one of the great commercial cities of the world. He was there placed in a linen-draper's shop, in order to learn the business ; and in a very short time he qualified himself as a draper and rose to the position of book-keeper and cashier[6]—a post which he held for several years at least. How long he remained in the shop at Amsterdam is not known, and nothing is known with certainty regarding his other doings at this period. But it seems probable that during his sojourn in the capital he

---

[1] Cf. Boitet (1729) and Haaxman (1875).—Benthuizen is a small place some 9 miles N.E. of Delft.

[2] Boitet (1729), followed by v. Haastert (1823).

[3] Halbertsma (1843).

[4] Cf. p. 305 *infra*.

[5] Schierbeek (1929) gives the year as 1638 : but this is obviously a misprint.

[6] According to Boitet (1729), who is copied by later biographers. There are no known records extant relating to L.'s apprenticeship.

made the acquaintance of Swammerdam,[1] and perhaps of other young men with congenial interests.

I may remind the reader that in 1648—the year in which Antony went to serve in the shop at Amsterdam—the Treaty of Münster, which ended the Thirty Years' War, was signed. This reminder will recall the posture of Europe at the moment—a moment when "Holland had taken her place in the very front rank in the civilised world, as the home of letters, science and art, and was undoubtedly the most learned state in Europe."[2]

About six years after his first apprenticeship in Amsterdam, Leeuwenhoek returned to his native town: and here, for the rest of his days, he remained. For nearly 70 years—from 1654 until the day of his death in 1723—he lived and worked in Delft; so that when, in the fullness of time, he became famous, he also became enduringly identified with his habitation. During his later lifetime he was regarded as one of the sights of the place–hardly less conspicuous than the Old Church, and almost as permanent a fixture.

As Delft forms the background of all the scenes displayed in this book, I must here say a little more about this fine old town. There are several descriptions and many pictures of the place as it was in Leeuwenhoek's day. We have, for example, not only the compendious and valuable Dutch accounts by Dirk van Bleyswijck (1667) and Reinier Boitet (1729)—enriched with numerous engravings—but also various shorter and less particular records contained in works such as the earlier Latin "*Batavia*" of Junius (1588) and "*Batavia Illustrata*" of Scriverius (1609), and in the anonymous but once popular French guide-book called "*Les Délices de la*

---

[1] That L. was acquainted with Swammerdam we know from his own statements (*e.g.*, he refers to visits which Swammerdam paid him in *Letter 6*, 7 Sept. 1674). Haaxman has gone so far as to suggest (1875, p. 10 *seq.*) that it was Swammerdam who, during L.'s residence in Amsterdam, first aroused his interest in microscopic studies. But this appears improbable: for, as Pijzel (1875, p. 108) points out, Swammerdam was only 11 years old when L. went there, and not more than 16 or 17 when he left: and we can hardly suppose, therefore, that L. received much guidance from so youthful and junior a mentor.

[2] Edmundson (1922), p. 186. This is an indisputable fact which many people nowadays—in many different countries—are all too apt to forget.

PLATE IV

OUDE DELFT:

the main thoroughfare of the town, looking northwards. On the left, the East-India Company's house: in the distance, the tower of the Old Church. From an old engraving.

facing p. 25

Hollande."[1] All old histories of Holland and of the House of Orange[2] also contain repeated references to Delft—the family's stronghold in the Netherlands. Here William the Silent was assassinated (you can still see the hole made by the murderer's bullet in the wall of the staircase of the Prince's Court): and here, in the New Church, is the mausoleum wherein many of the most distinguished sons and daughters of the House lie buried. Delft, in the time of Leeuwenhoek, also forms the subject of one of the world's pictorial masterpieces.[3] But the best and shortest description of the town at the time when Leeuwenhoek was in his prime—when Holland and England were at settled peace under William III of Orange and Great Britain—is, I think, that left to us by an obscure Englishman, William Mountague, *Esq*., who once spent a holiday in Holland and afterwards wrote a lively description of what he saw. From his little book (1696) I may quote the following lines[4]:

> *Delft* is a fair and populous City, very clean, well built, and very pleasant; well seated in a Plain of Meadows, which may be laid all round under Water, if they open their Sluces, when the Wind is East-North-East. At the Entrance of it stands a general Magazine of Warlike Stores (but no Powder[5]) for the Publick Service. This City was burnt to Ashes *Anno* 1536, but soon re-built, and now in greater Glory than ever. The *East-India* Company of this Place have here a very good House and large Ware-Houses; as also an eighth part of the Great or General Stock, this being the Third Town of *Holland*, having the Third Voice in the *States*, whither it sends Deputies, as also to all the other Colleges. Here are very

---

[1] Pepys (*Diary*, 10 Dec. 1663) mentions that he bought a copy of this work. I have read only the revised version of 1710.

[2] As examples I may mention the early Dutch histories of William and Maurice (see *Anonymus*, 1662), and the *Historia Nostri Temporis* by Brachelius (1666).

[3] See Plate VII, opp. p. 35. My small reproduction gives but a poor idea of the splendour of the original painting.

[4] Mountague (1696), p. 18 *sq*.

[5] Cf. footnote 3 on p. 55 *infra*.

fine Buildings, and amongst them the Town-House,[1] with these two Verses on the Front.

> *Haec domus odit, amat, punit, conservat, honorat,*
> *Nequitiam, Pacem, Crimina, Jura, Probos.*[2]

Here is a spacious Market-Place between this House and the great Church,[3] in which stands *William*[4] the First Prince of *Orange* (Great Grand-Father to his Sacred Majesty King *William*[5]) at full length, in Armor, in Copper Effigie . . . 'Tis the most Magnificent Tomb in all the *Seventeen Provinces.* Here that Prince kept his Court, and here was that brave Prince assassinated in the 51st Year of his Age . . .

In the t'other Church[6] is a Monument of Admiral *Trump*'s[7] inrich'd with Miniature, and a fine Inscription . . . In the same Church is *Myn Heer Pithin*'s Tomb[8], a very handsome one. . . . The Churches here, and in all the Seven *United-Provinces,* are generally bigger than ours in *England*, but fewer in Number.

Here is a large and neat Market, or Flesh-Hall (as they call it) for all sorts of Butchers Meat, which they have very good . . . They have also a good Fish-Market here, and another of Fruits, Roots, and Herbs.

The People in this City are rich, trade much to Sea, and make much Porcelain, or fine Earthen Wares, to a great Perfection, tho' far short of *China,* which they pretend to resemble, and brew good Beer here . . . yet it tastes

---

[1] The *Stadhuis* or Town Hall. See Pl. VI, opp. p. 32.

[2] "This House hates, loves, punishes, keeps, honours; Wickedness, Peace, Crimes, Oaths, the Righteous." This inscription is no longer to be seen—having been removed in the process of subsequent "restoration."

[3] The New Church.

[4] William I, the Silent (1533-1584); Stadholder.

[5] William III of England and Orange (1650-1702).

[6] The Old Church, where L. himself now also lies. See Pl. XIV, opp. p. 100.

[7] Admiral Maarten Tromp (1598-1653).

[8] Admiral Piet Hein (1572-1629).—All the tombs and places mentioned by Mountague can still be seen.

> insipid, and indeed is but weak, compar'd to the *English*, having little or no relish of the Mault.[1] . . .

Mountague forgot, however, to mention the trees and the waterways which are still so typical of the town; so I would complete his picture by adding a few touches from a modern historian[2] who wrote of a time still earlier than Leeuwenhoek's:

> It was a quiet, cheerful, yet somewhat drowsy little city, that ancient burgh of Delft. The placid canals by which it was intersected in every direction were all planted with whispering umbrageous rows of limes and poplars, and along these watery highways the traffic of the place glided so noiselessly that the town seemed the abode of silence and tranquillity. These streets were clean and airy, the houses well built, the whole aspect of the place thriving . . . .

And writing of the same period, the Earl of Leicester—Queen Elizabeth's favourite, who was once, by a strange freak of fortune, Governor-General of the Netherlands—even describes Delft as "*another London almost for beauty and fairness.*"[3]

But to return to our subject proper. On 29 July 1654[4]

---

[1] Delft was always famous for her beer: but the author of *Batavia* (1588) agreed with Mountague that it was inferior to the English—"*Cerealis potus prima post Britannicum zythum laude,*" etc. (p. 260). Dr Hadrianus Junius (*alias* Adriaen de Jongh) doubtless knew what he was talking about, for he was at one time resident family physician to the Earl of Norfolk (cf. Bense, 1925, p. 198).

[2] Motley, *Dutch Republic:* last chapter *ad init.*

[3] Quoted by Motley, *United Netherlands* (1869), Vol. I, p. 352. The words are from a letter written by Robert Dudley, Earl of Leicester (1532?-1588), to Lord Walsingham on 26 Dec. 1585. He adds (*fide* Motley) "the other towns I have passed by are very goodly towns, but this is the fairest of them all."

[4] Haaxman (1875, p. 16) gives the date as 26 July 1654. Bouricius (1924) says 29 June 1654: but in a letter he informs me that this is a misprint, and that the date given above is correct. According to Mr Bouricius the archives of Delft show that the marriage was formally announced on 11 July 1654, and registered on the 29th of the same month. Schierbeek (1930) correctly gives the date as "11/29 Juli 1654"—July 11 being the date of the *ondertrouw* (corresponding roughly with "calling the

when he was not quite 22 years old, Leeuwenhoek married Barbara, the daughter of Elias de Mey[1] and Maria Virlin[2]—a young woman three years his senior.[3] The marriage took place at the New Church in Delft. From this union five children were born—three sons and two daughters—all but one of whom died in early infancy.[4] The one who survived was Maria, the second child, born on 22 September 1656. She lived to a great age, but never married. She stayed with her father Antony all his life, and ultimately buried him in the Old Church of Delft—in a tomb wherein she was herself interred in 1745, aged close upon 89 years[5]. Maria van Leeuwenhoek was no "scientist," but she was a good daughter: we shall meet her again later. She kept house when her father was at work, she kept himself when he was weak, and she housed his body when he was dead. She will not be forgotten while her father is remembered.

The year of Leeuwenhoek's marriage (1654) was long recollected in Delft: for this was the year of the terrible explosion of the powder-magazine—a disaster which wrecked the whole town, and killed untold hundreds of the inhabitants[6]. The Queen of Bohemia[7], writing to Sir Edward Nicholas[8] from The Hague a week later (19 October 1654), says:[9]

---

banns" in an English church), and July 29 that of the actual marriage ceremony (*huwelijk*).

[1] It may be of interest to English readers to note that Elias was at one time a cloth-merchant in Norwich (*fide* Bouricius).

[2] Maria's surname is given as "Viruly" by Haaxman, but Mr Bouricius assures me that this is incorrect. She came from Utrecht—not Delft.

[3] Barbara de Mey was born 20 Dec. 1629 (*fide* Haaxman and Bouricius; and *cf*. Schierbeek, 1930).

[4] The three sons—all named Philips—were born in 1655, 1663, and 1664. The daughter who died (1658) shortly after birth was named Margriete. See the Family Tree, p. 18.

[5] Maria died on 25 April 1745. The dates of her birth and death, as here given, are those graven on the tomb.

[6] Cf. Boitet (1729), p. 564 *octies*. The explosion involved some 80 or 90 thousand pounds of gunpowder and happened at 11.30 a.m. on Monday 12 Oct. 1654. The event is not mentioned—so far as I know—by L. Among those who perished was Karel Fabritius, the famous painter—supposed by some (on very slender evidence) to have been Vermeer's master.

[7] Elizabeth Stuart (1596-1662), sister to Charles I of England.

[8] Edward Nicholas (1593-1669), Secretary of State to Charles I and Charles II.

[9] Published in Bray's edition (1827) of Evelyn's *Memoirs*, Vol. V, p. 204.

> I was at Delft to see the wrack that was made by the blowing up of the powder this day seuenight, it is a sad sight, whole streets quite razed; not one stone vpon another, it is not yett knowen how manie persons are lost, there is scarse anie house in the toune but the tyles are off.

A happier event which occurred in the same year, however, was the conclusion of peace—for a time—between Holland and England.

At about this date Leeuwenhoek bought a house and shop in Delft, and set up in business as a draper. For these premises he paid altogether—including interest on the money, which he had to borrow—5000 florins[1]. His house was situated[2] in a street still called the *Hippolytusbuurt*, running parallel to the *Oude Delft* (the main canal and thoroughfare of the town), and within sight of the Old Church and the New Church[3], and near to the Fish and Meat Markets and the Town Hall—all which places are mentioned by Leeuwenhoek and can still be seen by the inquiring traveller. But Leeuwenhoek's house itself is no longer there. According to Bouricius, to whom the identification of the site is due, it was the second one from the *Nieuwstraat* (which connects *Hippolytusbuurt* with *Oude Delft*) and was called "The Golden Head" (*Het Gouden Hoofd*). A few further details regarding it can be gathered from certain passages in the Letters. Leeuwenhoek lived in this house for the rest of his life, and there can be little doubt that it was here he made most of his discoveries[4].

By great good fortune, two of the bills which Leeuwenhoek made out for his customers have recently been recovered. They prove conclusively that he carried on business as a

---

[1] Cf. Schierbeek (1929*a*). The facts were ascertained by the late Mr Bouricius.

[2] This was forgotten until quite recently, when it was rediscovered by Morre (1919) and Bouricius (1924). Cf. p. 338 *infra*.

[3] These Churches are still called "Old" and "New," as they were in L.'s day. The "New" one, however, is not very new, as it was built between 1391 and 1496; while the "Old" Church was probably built about 1240. Cf. Boitet (1729) and Wildeman (1903).

[4] Cf. p. 338 *infra*.

draper and haberdasher, and are the earliest known examples of his handwriting. The shorter of these bills is here reproduced[1] in Plate V: the longer and earlier shows similar items (silk, cloth, buttons, tape, ribbon, braid, etc.) sold to Johannis Heijnsbroeck in 1658. In view of its singular interest I give a complete translation of the bill exhibited in the Plate:

Praise be to God! the 19th day of December 1659. In Delft.

Mr. Pieter Heijnsbroeck *debtor*

To **Antony Leeuwenhoeck** for the following

— Shop-wares —

	$4\frac{1}{4}$ ells[2] red kersey - - - @ 26 stivers th'ell - - -	5.	10.	8.[3]
	$2\frac{1}{2}$ dozen buttons and button-loops - - - - - - - - -	—	6.	—
	1 ell white bombazine @ 9 stivers - - - - - - - -	—	9.	—
	To raw silk -	—	6.	—
24th *ditto*	2 ells wide filoselle [?] ribbon - - - - - - - - - - - -	—	6.	—
	Total	6.	17.	8.

The contents hereof paid unto me
this 15th day of June in the year 1660.
Antony Leeuwenhoeck

Leeuwenhoek's wife Barbara died on 11 July 1666,[4] when they had been married twelve years: and not long afterwards —on 25 January 1671[5]—he contracted a second marriage with

[1] This little document has already been printed by Morre (1919), who discovered it among the estate-papers relating to the Delft "court of chancery" (*Boedelpapieren der Delftsch Weeskamer*, dossier No. 105). It has also been referred to by Mr Bouricius, to whose widow and Dr A. Schierbeek I am indebted for the photograph from which my plate has been made.

[2] The Dutch ell at this period was approximately a modern metre, and therefore less than an English ell (45 inches).

[3] The columns stand respectively for *florins* (guilders), *stuivers* (stivers), and *pennings*. 16 pennings = 1 stuiver; and 20 stuivers = 1 florin (about 1/8 in modern English money).

[4] *fide* Haaxman. She was buried on July 14 in the Old Church (Schierbeek, 1930).

[5] *fide* Bouricius.

FACSIMILE (REDUCED) OF A BILL MADE OUT BY LEEUWENHOEK FOR ONE OF HIS CUSTOMERS, AND RECEIPTED BY HIMSELF. It reads as follows:

Laus Deo adij 19^{en}. Xmb. a^{o}: 1659. In Delff

S^{r}. Pieter Heijnsbroeck Debitt

Aen Antonj Leeuwenhoeck over volgende

—Winckelwaren—

	$4\frac{1}{4}$ el Root carsaij - - à. 26. st. d'el	*F* 5 : 10 : 8
	$2\frac{1}{2}$ dosijn Knoopen en Knooplussen -	*F* - : 6 : -
	1. el Wit Bombasijn à. 9 st. - - - -	*F* - : 9 : -
	Aen Roo Sij - - - - - - - - - -	*F* - : 6 : -
24^{en}. ditto.	2. el breet Fijasel Lint - - - - -	*F* - : 6 : -
		S^{a}. *F* 6 : 17 : 8

Den Inhout deses mij voldaen

Adij 15. Junij a^{o}: 1660

Antonj Leeuwenhoeck

a kinswoman of hers named Cornelia Swalmius.[1] It is said that she bore him another child, who died in infancy:[2] and Bouricius states that Cornelia herself died in 1694.[3]

It is probable that Leeuwenhoek carried on his drapery business for many years—from the time of his first marriage (1654) onwards. We have no direct information about him again, however, until six years later, when he was made Chamberlain to the Sheriffs of Delft. He held this post for 39 years; and thereafter, till his death, continued to draw the salary attaching to it. At the date of his nomination Leeuwenhoek was only 27 years old: for according to an entry in the town archives he was appointed—retrospectively, as it appears—on 26 March 1660, in succession to one Jan Strick (otherwise unknown). The full title of this office[4] was "Chamberlain of the Council-Chamber of the Worshipful Sheriffs of Delft,"[5] and the terms of appointment were as follows:[6]

---

[1] *alias* Kornelia Zwalmius (*seu* van der Swalm). The name is spelled variously. According to van Bakkenes (1873) and van der Baan (1874) she was the daughter of Johannes Swalmius (1621-1661), a clergyman of Valkenburg. The date of her birth is apparently unknown, but she must have been much younger than L., as her father was only 11 years his senior.

[2] Boitet (1729), Haaxman (1871, 1875), and Bouricius (1924). It is said by van Bakkenes (1873), however, that L.'s second marriage was childless. In any case, no child of this marriage survived.

[3] Buried 6 Jan. 1694; *fide* Schierbeek (1930). That she was alive in 1677 can be inferred from a passage in a letter written in this year (*Letter 22*, Nov. 1677. *Phil. Trans.* (1678), Vol. XII, No. 142, p. 1040): and that she was dead in 1700 is directly attested by L. himself, who then refers to her as "my late wife" (*Letter 130*, 27 June 1700).

[4] Curiously enough, L.'s civil appointments are not mentioned in Boitet (1729); and it is perhaps for this reason that Banga (1868, p. 610) refers to him—incorrectly—as "a simple citizen of Delft, holding no office." L.'s appointment as Chamberlain was first reported by van Haastert (1823), who quotes no authority for his statement.

[5] "*Camerbewaarder der Camer van Heeren Schepenen van Delft.*" The *Schepens*, or Sheriffs, were important civil dignitaries at this period. But *Schout* and *Schepen* have no exact English equivalents, so I can translate such words only approximately.

[6] This entry was extracted from the town records by Mr J. Soutendam, sometime Town Clerk and Archivist (*Archivaris en Secretaris*) of Delft. It has already been published in full by Haaxman (1871, p. 14 *sq.*; 1875, p. 20 *sq.*) and by Soutendam (1875), from whose printed Dutch transcriptions I translate. The information on this subject which Richardson (1885),

Their Worships the Burgomasters and Magistrates of the Town of Delft have appointed and do hereby charge *Antony Leeuwenhoek* to look after the Chamber wherein the Chief Judge the Sheriffs and the Law Officers of this Town do assemble: to open and to shut the foresaid Chamber at both ordinary and extraordinary assemblies of the foresaid Gentlemen in such wise as shall be required and needful: *item* to show towards these Gentlemen all respect honour and reverence and diligently to perform and faithfully to execute all charges which may be laid upon him and to keep to himself whatever he may over hear in the Chamber: to clean the foresaid Chamber properly and to keep it neat and tidy: to lay the fire at such times as it may be required and at his own convenience and carefully to preserve for his own profit what coals may remain unconsumed and see to it that no mischance befall thereby nor from the light of the candles: and he shall furthermore do all that is required of and that pertaineth to a good and trusty Chamberlain. For the which service the foresaid Antony Leeuwenhoek shall enjoy such wages benefits and emoluments as the foresaid lamented Jan Strick his predecessor in office did enjoy and shall enter into his duties upon the morning of the 24th of January 1660 and his wages shall be paid upon the same terms as those whereon the foresaid Jan Strick's were paid. Ordered by all the Burgomasters in Council assembled this 26th day of March 1660 and signed by

J. Camerling, *Pensionary.*

Locy (1901, 1910, 1925), and Plimmer (1913) give, and which is stated by them to have been derived from the researches of Dr A. Wynter Blyth [a writer on toxicology and food-analysis, and Medical Officer of Health for St. Marylebone, London], is evidently nothing but a garbled version of Haaxman. There is no evidence to support Locy's statements (1910, p. 78; 1925, p. 207) that Wynter Blyth himself examined the town archives—which seems to be merely a mistaken inference from Richardson's loose expressions.

THE TOWN HALL OF DELFT

Eastern (front) aspect, viewed from the Market Place. The Sheriffs' Chamber was in the second storey, on the north side (right in picture). From an old engraving.

From the treasurer's accounts it appears that the emoluments attaching to this appointment amounted, in all, to 314 florins *per annum*.[1] Later entries show, however, that by 1699 Leeuwenhoek's grant had been increased to 400 florins yearly; while a still later entry,[2] in 1711, shows that at that time he was receiving an additional salary of 50 florins for his services as "*generaal-wijkmeester*"—an office resembling that of an English alderman. Both these municipal appointments were probably sinecures, and their menial obligations performed by proxy. I note this in order not to convey the impression that Leeuwenhoek was really—as Richardson and Plimmer would have us believe—a sort of village beadle.[3] It is hardly necessary to add that 450 florins represented a much larger sum of money in the XVII Century than they do today.

To preserve the historic perspective I must here venture once more to remind the reader of contemporary affairs in the world at large. In 1664, when Leeuwenhoek was 32 and had been Chamberlain for some 4 years, his mother—as we have already heard—died: but in this same year another memorable event also occurred. England and Holland were then again at war; and our Admiral Holmes[4] attacked and captured the Dutch colony of New Amsterdam on Manhattan Island in North America, and changed its name to New York in honour of his chief—the Duke of York, afterwards our King James II. Englishmen, Hollanders, and Americans—not to mention men of other nations—therefore have good reason to remember this epoch. But we must return to our real hero, who wisely took not the least notice of politics or warfare.

It has recently come to light that Leeuwenhoek was not only a draper and sheriffs' chamberlain but also a qualified

---

[1] The sum was made up as follows: For acting as Chamberlain, 260 florins; for cleaning the Chambers of the Sheriffs, Council, etc., and on account of expenses necessarily incurred thereby, 54 florins. (Haaxman, 1875.)

[2] Quoted by Haaxman (1875).

[3] *Bedellus immortalis* Richardson (1885)—unblushingly borrowed by Plimmer (1913)—is not only an unsuitable designation for L. but is in addition (under the Rules of Nomenclature) an invalid synonym of the more adequate name *Homo sapiens* Linnaeus.

[4] Sir Robert Holmes (1622-1692), a great but now almost forgotten warrior who distinguished himself on many other occasions.

surveyor.[1] This discovery illuminates various passages in his letters, where he enters into arithmetical calculations regarding areas, volumes, heights, magnitudes of organisms, and so forth. The act of his admission as surveyor (*landmeter*) in 1669 is extant in the Dutch State Archives, and seems sufficiently interesting to quote. It runs as follows:[2]

> FORASMUCH AS ANTONY LEEUWENHOECK,[3] burgher and denizen of the town of Delft, hath made petition unto the Court of Holland, saying that he hath for some while heretofore exercised himself in the art of Geometry, and advanced so far that he deems himself capable to fulfil henceforth the office of surveyor, and perform the service and duty thereof, wherefore he humbly intreateth that the Court be pleased to permit him to exercise the office of surveyor, after previous examination and trial of his ability: ACCORDINGLY, the said Court, having heard the report of the commissioner appointed thereunto, in whose presence the applicant was examined by the mathematician Genesius Baen[4] as to his aptness for the performing the foresaid office of surveyor, wherein he was found competent, hath allowed the application and hereby authorizes the applicant to perform the office and duty thereof, within the jurisdiction of the Court; and hath administered unto him the statutory oath, that he acquit himself well and truly therein, by the hands of Mr. Pieter Ockers,[5] councillor

---

[1] Ascertained by the late Mr Bouricius, though not published by him. It appears that Dr Baart de la Faille, archivist of Haarlem, supplied him with the reference to the relevant entry in the Archives. Cf. Schierbeek (1929*a*, 1930).

[2] Extract from 12*de memoriaalboek van mr. Adriaens Pots*, fol. 17. Rijksarchief: *fide* Schierbeek (1929*a*, 1930). Dr Schierbeek first published the entry from Mr Bouricius's MS. remains; and the above is my English translation of his printed versions, checked by a photographic copy of the Dutch original which he has kindly sent me.

[3] The name is so spelled in the original.

[4] *Paen* Schierbeek (1930): a misreading.

[5] *Ochers* according to Schierbeek (1930); but this is also an obvious misreading or misprint.

Mauritshuis VIEW OF DELFT *The Hague*

from the south : after the oil-painting by Jan Vermeer (1632-1675).

at Court, and commissioner appointed therefor. Ordered in Council the 4th day of February 1669.

There is at least one direct reference to surveying in Leeuwenhoek's writings, and it now acquires new significance in the light of the foregoing record. In the postscript to a letter written in 1713—containing some celebrated remarks on whales—he wrote: [1]

> The height of the Tower of our New Church [2] was measured many years ago by me and the late Surveyor *Spoors*, each with his own quadrant, and found to be 299 feet high . . .

For the year 1676 there is an entry in the Archives of Delft which illuminates Leeuwenhoek from an entirely different angle. Under date 30 September it is there recorded: [3]

> Their Worships the Sheriffs of the Town of Delft do hereby appoint Anthonij Leeuwenhouck [4] to be Trustee [5] for the estate and property of Catharina Bolnes, widow of the late Johannes Vermeer (in his lifetime Master Painter) and petitioner for a writ of insolvency, [6] for what he remained possessed of . . . Ordered the 30th of September 1676.

Now the incomparable artist Jan Vermeer was born at Delft in the same year as Leeuwenhoek himself (1632), their

---

[1] *Send-brief* IV, 14 March 1713. To Jan Meerman, Burgomaster of Delft. Published (Dutch) in *Brieven*, Vol. IV, p. 38; (Latin) *Op. Omn.* Vol. IV, p. 38. (No MS. and not in *Phil. Trans.*)

[2] Visible in Vermeer's view (Plate VII)—in the distance, to the right of the middle line.

[3] *Kamerboek der Stad Delft*, 1671-1684: *fide* Obreen (1881-2), who has published the entry (p. 295) and from whose printed Dutch version I translate.

[4] So spelled in original, *fide* Obreen.

[5] *Curateur* orig.

[6] *Impetrante van mandement van cessie* orig. These legal terms have no exact equivalents in modern English, though their meaning seems plain. According to Meijer's *Woordenschat* (1745), *impetrante = verkrijgster* and *mandement = bevel*: while "*mandement van cessie*" is there explained as "*om zyne inschulders te mogen dagen*", and "*Brieven van cessie*" are defined as "*Brieven van Boedel afstand te mogen doen.*"

baptisms[1] being entered on the very same page of the Register of the New Church: and he married Catharina Bolnes (*alias* Bolenes) on 5/20 April 1653. He was buried in his native town on 15 December 1675 at the early age of 43, leaving his widow with eight children (all under age), an insolvent estate, and some of the world's finest pictures. To meet her creditors Catharina Vermeer was forced to file a petition in bankruptcy and realize her assets: whereupon—as we see—the Sheriffs nominated Leeuwenhoek to act as "curator" or "official receiver". Everything regarding this affair now ascertainable from the Delft Archives has already been extracted and published by Obreen (1881-2) and Bredius (1885); and as the incident has but little present interest, I must refer readers seeking further information to their publications.[2]

Obreen has inferred[3] that Leeuwenhoek's appointment as administrator of Vermeer's estate was one of the "pickings" to which he was entitled by virtue of his office as Chamberlain. Obreen may be right: but it seems hardly likely that Leeuwenhoek derived any profit from his trusteeship of the affairs of an insolvent family, and the extant records (as published) show only that he met with worries and legal difficulties in the discharge of his duty. To me the incident appears rather to indicate that Leeuwenhoek may have been a personal friend of the Vermeers, though it also shows clearly that he himself must have held a solid position as a citizen of Delft at that date; since it is inconceivable that the Sheriffs could have nominated anybody but a respected fellow-townsman to disentangle Vermeer's involved finances. For Vermeer—though soon forgotten and only recently rediscovered—was then rightly regarded as a great artist and ornament of the Town, and his wife apparently had well-to-do connexions.

---

[1] Vermeer's was registered on 31 Oct. 1632: so this was not the date of his birth—as many writers state. The date of his birth is actually unknown.

[2] I have had considerable difficulty in ascertaining the above particulars about Vermeer and his relations to Leeuwenhoek, because most biographers of both these great Delvenaars give little or no trustworthy information on the subject. On Vermeer cf. also Plietzsch (1911), Vanzype (1921), Lucas (1922), Chantavoine (1926).

[3] Obreen (1881-2), p. 295.

One other municipal function which Leeuwenhoek is now known to have discharged is that of wine-gauger (*wijnroeijer*).[1] He was elected to this post on 15 August 1679, and apparently occupied it (partly by proxy) for the rest of his life. The terms of this office are too long to print here *in extenso*. It must suffice to note that the wine-gauger had to assay all wines and spirits entering the town, and to calibrate the vessels in which they were contained; while he was himself debarred from engaging in any trade connected with liquor.[2] This appointment again throws some light upon our Leeuwenhoek: for his personal knowledge of wines—including their effects and antidotes—will be evident to all attentive readers of his letters.

From the date of his appointment as Chamberlain in 1660 nothing was heard of Leeuwenhoek outside of Delft for thirteen years, though we may be sure that he was not idle during this interval. But in 1673 we hear of him again in an altogether unexpected connexion. Our Dutch Draper-Chamberlain is now suddenly discovered to us as an amateur of science—offering a paper, containing some modest original observations, for publication in the *Philosophical Transactions* of the Royal Society of London.

How this came about is soon told. The Royal Society, then but recently founded,[3] was eager to get into communication with all men—no matter what their rank or nationality—who were working for "the promotion of natural knowledge":[4] and in this endeavour it was successful, in no small measure, through the efforts of its energetic secretary Mr Oldenburg

---

[1] First recorded by Morre (1919) and Bouricius (1925). The latter has kindly supplied me (from the archives of Delft) with full particulars—partly given above—relating to the functions of a wine-gauger.—There is, I find, an early Dutch work on gauging by Cornelis van Leeuwen (1663), with which L. was probably familiar and which describes the technique fully.

[2] Since these lines were written Schierbeek (1929) has published the regulations regarding the office of wine-gauger in greater detail.

[3] Readers desirous of knowing more about this historic event may be referred specially to the works of Sprat (1667) and Weld (1848); and also to the more recent *Record of the Roy. Soc.* (1912) and the posthumous publication of Miss Ornstein (1928).

[4] "They [the Royal Society] exact no extraordinary praeparations of *Learning*: to have found *Senses* and *Truth*, is with them a sufficient Qualification" (Sprat, 2 ed. (1702), p. 435).

(Plate VIII). His foreign correspondence was enormous, as can be gathered from the manuscript letters to and from him still preserved by the Society. Among the *Roy. Soc. MSS.* (to mention no others) are drafts of more than 400 letters—apart from numerous translations and many other documents—written by Oldenburg to various more or less celebrated and scientific persons between the years 1657 and 1677 : while the extant letters addressed to him well exceed 1200 in number.

Henry Oldenburg (1615 ?—1677),[1] first Secretary of the Royal Society,[2] was a remarkable man. He was a German of good family—a native of Bremen—who came to England about 1640 and afterwards played a prominent part in contemporary English scientific life. He is now chiefly remembered, however, as a translator and as the first editor of the *Philosophical Transactions* and as a correspondent with nearly all outstanding "philosophers" and "virtuosi" of his day. Curiously enough, no adequate biography of this influential figure in the History of Science has ever yet been published.

It may be noted in passing that several scientific letters written to Oldenburg—including some of Leeuwenhoek's—are addressed to "Mr. Grubendol". He sometimes used this anagram when corresponding with foreigners, apparently, in order to avoid suspicion through receiving too many communications from abroad in his proper name. It was a transparent subterfuge which reflects no discredit upon him: but that his fears were well founded is clear from the fact that he was actually imprisoned, as a suspected spy, towards the end of June, 1667. Pepys,[3] in his *Diary*, under the date 25 June 1667, notes: "I was told, yesterday, that Mr. Oldenburg, our Secretary at Gresham College, is put into the

---

[1] For his life see Birch, Vol. III, p. 353 ; Rix (1893) ; and the *Dict. Nat. Biogr.* The date of his birth is not certainly known ; but it was not 1626, as usually stated.

[2] Jointly with John Wilkins (1614-1672), D.D. ; Master of Trinity College, Cambridge (1659) ; later Bishop of Chester (1668). Wilkins was also a man of considerable parts. A collective edition of his "mathematical and philosophical works" appeared in 1708 (with a portrait and the author's life prefix'd).

[3] Samuel Pepys (1633-1703) was elected Fellow of the Royal Society in 1665 and President in 1684.

Royal Society *London*

HENRY OLDENBURG (1615?-1677)

First Secretary of the Royal Society, 1663-1677

From an oil-painting by Jan van Cleef (1646-1716) made in the year 1668.

Tower, for writing newes[1] to a virtuoso in France, with whom he constantly corresponds in philosophical matters; which makes it very unsafe at this time to write, or almost do anything." Weld,[2] who has given a more circumstantial account of this incident, calls it "a very remarkable event which seems to have had so much influence upon the Society as to cause a suspension of the Meetings from the 30th May to the 3rd October". Yet the event appears less remarkable when we remember that the citizens of London—already severely shaken by the Great Plague and the Great Fire of the two previous years—were listening, for the first time, to the guns of a foreign fleet advancing up the Thames at the moment when they clapped Oldenburg in jail. Evelyn says[3] "The alarme was so greate that it put both Country and Citty into a paniq, feare and consternation, such as I hope I shall never see more." But the Londoners were then feeling far more afraid of the fierce Dutch Admiral de Ruyter than of the mild German-English scientist, and poor Oldenburg was soon exonerated. On his release from the Tower he wrote to Boyle (3 September 1667): "I hope I shall live fully to satisfy his majesty and all honest Englishmen of my integrity, and of my real zeal to spend the remainder of my life in doing faithful service to the nation to the very utmost of my abilities": which he did.

Among Oldenburg's innumerable correspondents was the youthful but already famous Dutch physician Reinier de Graaf,[4] a friend and fellow-townsman of Leeuwenhoek. (See

---

[1] Cf. also Evelyn (*Diary*, 8 Aug. 1667): "Visited Mr. Oldenburg, a close prisoner in the Tower, being suspected of writing intelligence."

[2] Weld (1848), I, 201 *sq.*

[3] *Diary*, 18 June 1667. John Evelyn (1620-1706) was an original Fellow of the Royal Society, and Secretary in 1672.

[4] Reinier [*seu* Regnerus] de Graaf (1641-1673) was born at Schoonhoven, studied under Sylvius at Leyden, and practised (and died) at Delft. His anatomical researches—especially upon the organs of generation—are still well known. The "Graafian follicle" of the ovary (which he regarded as an egg) enshrines his memory. His *Opera Omnia* were first published posthumously at Leyden in 1677. (L. has left it on record that his untimely death was hastened by his embittered controversy with Swammerdam over the priority of their anatomical discoveries.) He did not live to be elected a Fellow of the Royal Society, but died at the age of 32, after a brief but brilliant career, in the very year in which he introduced L.

Plate IX.) During the silent period preceding the year 1673 Leeuwenhoek was evidently engaged—in his spare time, when he was not selling buttons and ribbon—in making lenses, and mounting them to form "microscopes" of simple pattern: and after he had acquired much skill in the manufacture of these curious instruments,[1] and had taught himself how to grind and polish and mount lenses of considerable magnifying power, he began to examine all manner of things with their aid. Dr de Graaf was personally acquainted with Leeuwenhoek's work, and had had opportunities of inspecting various objects through his glasses.

In the *Philosophical Transactions* for 1668 the editor had published[2] an extract from the *Giornale dei Letterati*, containing an account of a new microscope made by Eustachio Divini in Italy. With this instrument, it was claimed, he had been able to discover "*an animal lesser than any of those seen hitherto*." It was doubtless as a counterblast to this sweeping assertion, and with pardonable patriotism, that de Graaf (28 April 1673) addressed himself to Oldenburg in the following words:[3]

> That it may be the more evident to you that the humanities and science[4] are not yet banished from among us by the clash of arms,[5] I am writing to tell you that a

---

[1] Cf. p. 313 *sq.*, *infra*.

[2] *Phil. Trans.* (1668), Vol. III, No. 42, p. 842—then edited by Oldenburg. Divini's portrait can be seen in the work of Manzini (1660).

[3] The original letter, from which I here translate a part, is still preserved by the Royal Society (MS. No. 1168; *G.1.* 11). It is written in Latin, and an extract—in English—was published in *Phil. Trans.* (1673), Vol. VIII, No. 94, p. 6037. The letter was read at the meeting of the Society held on 7 May 1673 [O.S.], when L.'s first observations were also communicated. Cf. Birch, Vol. III, p. 88.

[4] *studia humaniora et philosophica* MS.

[5] I may remind the reader that a European war was being waged at this time, and that England was actually at war with Holland. Peace was not concluded between us until February, 1674; but communications apparently remained unbroken throughout—probably because "the Nations had been at War without being angry; and the Quarrel had been thought on both Sides rather of the Ministries than the People" (Sir William Temple (1709), *Memoirs* [1672-1679] p. 3). Contemporary writers, both in England and in Holland, afford numerous other gratifying instances of the lack of personal enmity between our two peoples. For example, the Earl of Castlemain

REINIER DE GRAAF (1641-1673)

From the unsigned engraving prefixed to his posthumous *Opera Omnia.*

facing p. 40

certain most ingenious person here, named *Leewenhoeck*,[1] has devised microscopes which far surpass those which we have hitherto seen, manufactured by Eustachio Divini and others. The enclosed letter from him, wherein he describes certain things which he has observed more accurately than previous authors, will afford you a sample of his work: and if it please you, and you would test the skill of this most diligent man and give him encouragement, then pray send him a letter containing your suggestions, and proposing to him more difficult problems of the same kind.

The enclosed specimen of Leeuwenhoek's work consisted of various rather crude observations on Mould; on the sting and mouth-parts and eye of the Bee; and on the Louse. It was published in English in the *Philosophical Transactions*[2] with some comments by Oldenburg, who wound up by remarking (somewhat sardonically, I fear) "*So far this observer*: who doubtless will proceed in making and imparting more Observations, the better to evince the goodness of these his Glasses"—a prophecy which was actually fulfilled more amply during the next fifty years than anybody could then have thought possible. Yet the Fellows evidently liked the observations, and Oldenburg was instructed to communicate with their author. To his letter Leeuwenhoek sent the following characteristic answer from "*Delff in Hollant*":[3]

(1671, p. 97) remarks "We have now finisht a sharp and bloody War, which nevertheless leaves not the least rancor (that I know) in the heart of any English man; and the reason of it is, because we have generally an affection for these our neighbors [the Dutch], esteeming them an industrious and sober people".

[1] So spelled in original.

[2] *Letter 1.* See *Phil. Trans.* (1673), Vol. VIII, No. 94, p. 6037. The original MS. has not been preserved by the Society, and is presumably no longer extant.

[3] Translated from *Letter 2* (15 August 1673). MS.Roy.Soc. The original is in Dutch. Cf. Plate X. The drawings were engraved and published in *Phil. Trans.* (1673), Vol. VIII, No. 97, but their originals are lost. The part of this letter here translated has not been published previously, but some extracts from the remainder were printed—in English, in two parts—in *Phil. Trans.* (1674), Vol. IX, No. 102, pp. 21-25.

> I have oft-times been besought, by divers gentlemen, to set down on paper what I have beheld through my newly invented *Microscopia*: but I have generally declined; first, because I have no style, or pen, wherewith to express my thoughts properly; secondly, because I have not been brought up to languages or arts, but only to business; and in the third place, because I do not gladly suffer contradiction or censure from others. This resolve of mine, however, I have now set aside, at the intreaty of Dr Reg. de Graaf; and I gave him a memoir on what I have noticed about mould, the sting and sundry little limbs of the bee, and also about the sting of the louse. This memoir he (Mr de Graaf) conveyed to you; whereupon you sent me back an answer, from which I see that my observations did not displease the Royal Society, and that the Fellows desired to see figures of the sting and the little limbs of the bee, whereof I made mention. As I can't draw, I have got them drawn for me, but the proportions have not come out as well as I had hoped to see 'em; and each figure that I send you herewith was seen and drawn through a different magnifying-glass. I beg you, therefore, and those Gentlemen to whose notice these may come, please to bear in mind that my observations and thoughts are the outcome of my own unaided impulse and curiosity alone; for, besides myself, in our town there be no philosophers who practise this art; so pray take not amiss my poor pen, and the liberty I here take in setting down my random notions.[1]

Exactly a week before Leeuwenhoek dispatched the foregoing letter to the Royal Society, some further information about himself had been sent to one of the Fellows by Constantijn Huygens[2]—the once celebrated diplomatist and

---

[1] *gedachten, die ick als overhoop hier onderstel* MS. It is difficult to render these words exactly in modern English.

[2] Constantijn Huygens (1596—1687), statesman, poet, musician, and man of letters—" the most brilliant figure in Dutch literary history. Other statesmen surpassed him in political influence . . . but his talents

LAST LINES OF LEEUWENHOEK'S SECOND LETTER (15 Aug. 1673) TO OLDENBURG

This is his earliest extant epistle to the Royal Society, and is a good sample of his early handwriting and signature.

poet who is now best known to men of science as father of Christiaan Huygens the mathematician and astronomer. On 8 August 1673, Sir Constantijn wrote (in English, as here given) to Robert Hooke:[1]

> Our honest citizen, Mr. Leewenhoeck—or Leawenhook,[2] according to your orthographie—having desired me to peruse what he hath set down of his observations about the sting of a bee, at the requisition of Mr. Oldenburg, and by order, as I suppose, of your noble Royal Society, I could not forbear by this occasion to give you this character of the man, that he is a person unlearned both in sciences and languages, but of his own nature exceedingly curious and industrious, as you shall perceive not onely by what he giveth you about the bee, but also by his cleere observations about the wonderfull and transparent *tubuli* appearing in all kind of wood . . . His way for this is to make a very small incision in the edge of a box, and then tearing of it a little slice or film, as I think you call it, the thinner the better, and getting it upon the needle of his little microscope—a *machinula* of his owne contriving and workmanship—brass[3] . . . I trust you will not be unpleased with the confirmations of so diligent a searcher as this man is, though allways

---

were more varied, and his general accomplishments more remarkable than those of any other person of his age, the greatest age in the history of the Netherlands. Huygens is the *grand seigneur* of the republic" (Edmund Gosse). He was also the friend and confidant of L. King James I knighted him in 1622—ten years before L. was born.

[1] The original letter is preserved among the MSS. in the Royal Academy at Amsterdam, and has been recently printed by J. A. Worp (1917), *Briefwisseling van Const. Huygens*, Vol. VI; No. 6909, p. 330. A part has been copied—not too accurately—by Vandevelde (1924*a*, p. 289), who wrongly dates the letter Aug. 3.—On Hooke see note 1 on p. 47 *infra*.

[2] Cf. p. 304 *infra*.

[3] This word (*brass*, following a dash) occurs thus in the MS. but is omitted from the printed letter by the modern editor (Worp), who says it is "unintelligible". To me, however, it appears very easy to understand: Huygens meant that L.'s little microscope was "made of brass"—as so many of his instruments were.

modestly submitting his experiences and conceits about them to the censure and correction of the learned. . . .

The foregoing extracts show clearly how Leeuwenhoek's relations with the Royal Society originated: and they disprove, I think, a statement which has been made elsewhere[1] that he owed his introduction to Sir Constantijn Huygens.

From the time when his words quoted above were written until the day of his death, fifty years later, Leeuwenhoek continued to send letters to the Royal Society. They cover an immense field, and contain observations on matters zoological, botanical, chemical, physical, physiological, medical, and miscellaneous (unclassifiable). They are mostly—but not entirely—concerned with observations and discoveries made with the microscope. But this is not the place to speak of their contents in detail: and I shall only add here that many of them—but not all—were published, more or less curtailed, in English (or occasionally in Latin) in the *Philosophical Transactions* from 1673 to 1723; and that many of them—but not all—were issued fully in Dutch and Latin,[2] as separate publications, in his lifetime. He himself spoke and wrote and understood Dutch only,[3] and versions of his views in any other tongue suffer from the inevitable defects of translation and interpretation. Consequently, one must be able to read old-fashioned Dutch to read Leeuwenhoek: and for my own part

---

[1] In the *Œuvr. Compl. de Chr. Huygens*, Vol. VII, p. 316 (footnote)—published in 1897—it is averred (I know not by whom) that MS. letters at Amsterdam, which passed between L. and Constantijn Huygens (*pater*), and between the latter and Robert Hooke and Oldenburg, show that L.'s first relations with the Royal Society were established through the intermediation of Const. Huygens: but the documentary and other evidence at my disposal seems to show incontrovertibly that the statements made above are correct.

[2] It is not now known who translated L.'s letters into Latin for the editions of his works in that language. It is obvious—from the Latin styles, and the period of time covered—that the translations were made by more than one hand; but all my attempts to solve this problem have hitherto been fruitless. At one moment I thought I had discovered the name of one of his translators: for in an English MS. version (unpublished) of one of his later letters there is a reference to the translator as "Mynheer Aalder". But on consulting the original, I found that this was merely a misreading of the words "*de Heer vertaalder*" [= the translator] in the Dutch manuscript!

[3] See p. 305 *sq.*, *infra*.

I would say that it is well worth the trouble of learning this admirable language merely for the pleasure of reading this admirable man's admirable letters.

All Leeuwenhoek's recorded observations were described in letters. He never wrote a book or a scientific paper—only letters, and still more letters, addressed to all manner of people. His letters were all written by himself in his own old-fashioned Dutch, though they were often translated by others into other languages, published in many different ways, and collected in various volumes at divers dates by different editors. All his own original writings are distinguished by a certain businesslike formality, but almost total lack of coherence. After presenting his compliments, he just wrote down what he wanted to say at the moment—recording now perhaps a few experiments, with his speculations about their significance, then adding a few personal remarks, and winding up with a mass of further observations and thoughts on some totally different topic. He wrote much as he must have spoken, so that his letters have an extraordinarily colloquial and familiar flavour which conveys—to me, at least—a strange sense of intimacy. He wrote as loosely and discursively as other people usually speak—just as though he were talking to a friend who obviously understood his common everyday speech: and he was always so intent on telling what he had seen or thought that he had no time to worry about grammar or the niceties of literary composition. Consequently, his writings are more like conversations than formal letters. He would certainly have agreed with his sweet English contemporary, Dorothy Osborne,[1] when she said: "All letters, methinks, should be free and easy as one's discourse; not studied as an oration, nor made up of hard words like a charm. 'Tis an admirable[2] thing to see how some people will labour to find out terms that will obscure a plain sense . . . ." And he would also have agreed with James Howell[3] that "we

---

[1] Dorothy Osborne (1627-1695); afterwards wife of Sir William Temple, sometime English Ambassador to Holland. I quote from *Letter 33* of Parry's edition of her letters to Temple. The words quoted were written at some unknown date in 1653.

[2] Meaning, of course, "wonderful" or "marvellous"—not "admirable" (=to be admired or approved) in the modern sense.

[3] James Howell (1594?-1666), celebrated author, linguist, and letter-writer. I quote from the 1705 edition of his *Epistolae*, p. 1 (letter dated 25 July 1625).

should write as we speak; and that's a true familiar Letter which expresseth one's Mind, as if he were discoursing with the Party to whom he writes in succinct and short Terms." But whether serious scientific work should be published in so plain and unceremonious a fashion is, of course, debatable nowadays.

Yet there can be no doubts in the mind of anyone who seriously studies his writings that Leeuwenhoek—as he so often tells us—worked entirely by himself. He received no help from contemporary microscopists,[1] and was wholly inspired by his own inborn genius. Indeed, he disliked and resented interference, and distrusted the knowledge—and sometimes the purpose—of people who went to see him or who offered him advice: and for this he evidently had good reasons. Writing to Oldenburg as early as 1675 he remarked:[2]

> Your Excellency recommends me to make use of the services of other people, who are in a position to form a proper judgement of such things. Sir, I must say that there be few persons in this Town from whom I can get any help; and among those who can come to visit me from abroad, I have just lately had one who was much rather inclined to deck himself out with my feathers, than to offer me a helping hand.

It was not until 1680, after Oldenburg had died and when he himself was in his 48th year, that Leeuwenhoek was elected a Fellow of the Royal Society. As the date and other details are frequently given wrongly by biographers I must here briefly chronicle the relevant facts. For his election

---

[1] Carbone (1930) has recently tried to show that L. was inspired by the Italian workers of his time. But Carbone's only evidence for this is a letter (attributed by him to L.) which he has "discovered" among the Magliabechi MSS. at Florence. It is certain, however, that this letter (dated 2 May 1692) was not written by Leeuwenhoek but by Leibniz. (It is in Latin, and unsigned: but it bears Leibniz's seal, much internal evidence of his authorship, was written from Hanover, and had previously been published as an authentic Leibniz letter by Targioni-Tozzetti in 1746.)

[2] From *Letter 12*. 14 August 1675. To Oldenburg. MS. Roy. Soc. Incompletely abstracted in English in *Phil. Trans.* (1675), Vol. X, No. 117, p. 380. Not published elsewhere.

was, to him, an event of the first magnitude, and an unfailing source of encouragement for the rest of his life.

From letters still extant it appears that Hooke [1] wrote to Leeuwenhoek early in 1680, and expressed surprise that his name was not upon the list of Fellows of the Society: and he also then offered, apparently, to propose him for election. To this letter Leeuwenhoek replied [2] that he had "never had a thought of pretending" to such a distinction, though he would "thankfully have acceded if Mr Oldenburg, in his lifetime,[3] had afforded any opening": and he would regard election to the Fellowship, he says, as "the greatest honour in all the world".

This letter was written on 13 February 1680 [N.S.] in reply to Hooke's dated 23 January 1680 [O.S.]; but the election actually took place on 29 January [O.S.]—before Leeuwenhoek's answer could have been received in England. Moreover, Hooke was not the proposer: for it is recorded by Birch [4]—and accurately, as reference to the minutes shows—that on 29 January 1679/80 [O.S.] "Dr. Heusch,[5] Mr. Firmin [6] and

---

[1] Dr Robert Hooke (1635-1703), an original Fellow of the Royal Society, was also an original and eccentric genius and inventor. His contributions to science are too well-known and numerous to mention; though his influence on his contemporaries, and the part he played in the early days of the Society, are only just beginning to receive their due recognition. Inadequate accounts of his life will be found in Waller (1705) and the *Dict. Nat. Biogr.*—also in some more recent publications. It is impossible and unnecessary to discuss this remarkable man and his work here.

[2] *Letter* 29*b*. 13 February 1680 [N.S.] to R. Hooke. MS. Roy. Soc. Unpublished. This letter was translated by Francis Aston, and read at a meeting of the Society held on 12 Feb. 1680 [O.S.]. Cf. Birch, Vol. IV, p. 11.

[3] Oldenburg died, it will be recalled, in 1677. Hooke and Grew were appointed Secretaries in the same year, while Gale succeeded to this office in 1679.

[4] Birch, Vol. IV, p. 6.

[5] Johann Christian Heusch, M.D., principal physician to the Elector Palatine but otherwise apparently undistinguished. He attended a meeting of the Society on 22 Jan. 1680, and subsequently signed his name in the register. Cf. Birch, Vol. IV, pp. 5, 7.

[6] Thomas Firmin (1632-1697), citizen of London, remembered only as a philanthropist. Though a Fellow of the Society he was not a man of science. See *Dict. Nat. Biogr.* and life by Cornish (1780).

Mr. Houghton[1] were elected; as was also Mr. Leewenhoeck upon the motion of Dr. Croune,[2] and Dr. Gale[3] was desired to draw up a diploma to be sent to him."

There is thus ample documentary evidence to prove that Leeuwenhoek was elected a Fellow of the Royal Society—a full Fellow, and not a Foreign Member,[4]—on 29 January 1679/80 [O.S.]; that is, on 8 February 1680 according to present-day reckoning [N.S.].[5] He was proposed by Croone—not by Hooke—and his election was unanimous.[6]

At the gathering of the Society on 12 February [O.S.] 1680, "Dr. Gale was called upon for the diploma directed at the meeting of January 29 to be sent to Mr. Leewenhoeck; and it was ordered, that the society's seal should be affixed to it, and that a silver box should be provided for it."[7] Later, at the same meeting, "Dr. Gale produced his draught of a diploma for Mr. Leewenhoeck"[8]: and on February 19, "it was ordered, that the arms of the society be ingraved on the silver box."[9] Finally, at a meeting of Council on February 23, it was directed "That Mr. Hunt[10] prepare a silver box for the diploma to be sent to Mr. Leewenhoeck;"[11] and on the 28th

---

[1] John Houghton (?—1705), now imperfectly known as a writer on husbandry (especially on potatoes) and trade. See *Dict. Nat. Biogr.*

[2] William Croone [*seu* Croune] M.D. (1633-1684), educated at Emmanuel College, Cambridge, was an original Fellow of the Royal Society and a well-known physician in his day. The "Croonian Lectures" still serve to perpetuate his memory. See Birch, Vol. IV, p. 339 and *Dict. Nat. Biogr.* for further details of his life and legacies.

[3] Thomas Gale, D.D. See p. 193, note 2, *infra*.

[4] "Foreign Members" were an invention of a much later date. Cf. Nuttall (1921) and Dobell (1923).

[5] Boitet (1729, p. 766) wrongly gives the date as 26 February 1679, and has been copied by Soutendam (1875) and others.

[6] So Hooke informed him. See *Letter* 31*a*, 13 May 1680. To R. Hooke. MS. Roy. Soc. Unpublished. Cf. also p. 87 *infra*.

[7] Birch, Vol. IV, p. 11.

[8] Birch, Vol. IV, p. 13.

[9] Birch, Vol. IV, p. 13.

[10] Henry Hunt was the Society's "operator," who assisted at demonstrations and in other ways. He filled the offices of laboratory attendant, assistant secretary, and general factotum—for £40 a year (when he could get it)—and left the Society a legacy on his death.

[11] Birch, Vol. IV, p. 16.

PLATE XI

Rijksmuseum *Amsterdam*

ANTONY VAN LEEUWENHOEK (1632-1723)

From the oil-painting made in 1686 by Johannes Verkolje (1650-1693).

"The president[1] took with him the diploma for Mr. Leewenhoeck, and presented the Society with a screw-press for sealing such diploma's."[2]

Unfortunately the "diploma," though safely delivered[3] in Delft, is now lost; but it is portrayed in Verkolje's oil-painting of Leeuwenhoek,[4] wherein it is shown as a vellum scroll with a pendent red seal. Curiously enough, it was apparently engrossed in Dutch[5]—not in Latin—in deference to the recipient's ignorance. On receipt of this document, with its big red seal and in its engraved silver box, Leeuwenhoek returned the following acknowledgement:[6]

Delft, 13th May 1680.

To the President, Council,
& Fellows of the Royal Society.

Gentlemen,

I was quite taken aback to hear that the members of the Roy. Society had been pleased to confer upon me, all undeservedly, so much honour and dignity as to admit me a Fellow of the same most worthy College; as I first learnt from a letter written by Mr Secretary Thos. Gale, and a bit later through the receipt of a sealed Diploma; whereof both were full of expressions on my behalf that

---

[1] Sir Joseph Williamson (1633-1701), statesman.

[2] Birch, Vol. IV, p. 21.

[3] Halbertsma (1843, p. 19) says he had heard ["*ut audivi*"—no authority quoted] that L. received the diploma from the British Ambassador at The Hague. This seems likely enough; but I have sought in vain for any confirmation of the statement.

[4] Now in the Rijks-Museum (see Plate XI). It is not shown in Verkolje's mezzotint (see Frontispiece).

[5] Several words are clearly legible in the painting.

[6] *Letter* 31*b*. 13 May 1680 [N.S.]. To the Royal Society. MS.Roy.Soc. Unpublished. The original is in Dutch, and the above is my translation: but I confess my inability to convey to the modern English reader the extraordinary mixture of formal and familiar, colloquial and commercial, and above all genuine and sincere phraseology of the ancient original. A similar letter (No. 31*a*, also unpublished) was sent to Robert Hooke personally at the same time (dated 13 May 1680 [N.S.] MS.Roy.Soc.). Both letters were communicated to the Society by Hooke on 13 May [O.S.]. Cf. Birch, Vol. IV, p. 37.

my merits must fall far short of. Under which protest I notwithstanding hold myself most straitly pledged hereby, by unalterable intent and promise, to the Fellows of the said Society, for the signal favour they have shown me, to strive with all my might and main, all my life long, to make myself more worthy of this honour and privilege.

Wherewith commending you, most noble Gentlemen, one and all, to the merciful protection of Almighty God,

I remain, Gentlemen,

Your most humble servant

Antony Leeuwenhoek.

An amusing sidelight is thrown upon Leeuwenhoek at this moment in his career by a passage in a letter to Christiaan Huygens from his brother Constantijn.[1] Writing on 13 August 1680 he says[2]:

> Everybody here is still rushing to visit Leeuwenhoek, as the great man of the century. A few months ago the people of the Royal Society in London received him among their number, which gave him some little pride; and he even seriously inquired of *Sir Father*[3] if, being now invested with this dignity, he would be obliged in future to take a back seat in presence of a doctor of medicine!

Leeuwenhoek never came to London to sign the Register of Fellows or attend any meeting of the Royal Society. He was a busy man, and seldom went far from home—though he tells us of occasional short excursions from Delft in some of his letters. For example, in those here translated there are

---

[1] Constantijn Huygens *filius* (1628-1697), son of Constantijn *pater*—the "*grand seigneur*" and English knight—and elder brother of Christiaan.

[2] Printed in *Œuvres Compl. de Chr. Huygens* (1899); No. 2226, Vol. VIII, p. 295. The original MS. is in the University Library at Leyden, and is written in French—from which I translate.

[3] *al Signor Padre* orig.—meaning Sir Constantijn, their father. Constantijn *jun.* sometimes lapsed thus into Italian when writing in French to his brother—whom he called occasionally "*fratello caro*".

references to holidays spent at the seaside (Scheveningen) and "in Brabant and elsewhere." But he once, before his election, visited London—though this is not generally known—and recorded the circumstance in an unpublished passage in an early letter (1674). What he there says is so interesting, in more ways than one, that I must quote his words. In the course of describing some microscopic observations on the composition of chalk and clay, he unexpectedly adds [1]:

> About six years ago, being in England, out of curiosity, and seeing the great chalk cliffs and chalky lands at Gravesend and Rochester, it oft-times set me a-thinking; and at the same time I also tried to penetrate the parts of the chalk.[2] At last I observed that chalk consisteth of very small transparent particles [3]; and these transparent particles lying one upon another, is, methinks now, the reason why chalk is white.

It is clear from his own words that Leeuwenhoek spent a holiday in England sometime during the year 1668.[4] He came to London—sailing up the Thames by way of Harwich, Rochester, and Gravesend (after embarking probably at Rotterdam)—and brought a microscope with him. From this it seems legitimate to infer, therefore, that he was already engaged in his microscopic studies in 1668—at least five years before his first communication with the Royal Society. These

---

[1] From *Letter 6*, 7 Sept. 1674. To Oldenburg. MS.Roy.Soc. Incompletely translated into English in *Phil. Trans.* (1674), Vol. IX, No. 108, pp. 178-182 [misprinted 821]. From this translation the passage here given was entirely omitted: and in the following paragraph (p. 181), where L. speaks of the colour of the English soil, "*die ick aldaer tusschen Harwits en Londen gesien heb*", his words have been altered to an impersonal statement about "that, which *is found* between Harwich and London" [my italics].

[2] *de deelen van het krijt te penetreren* MS. By this L. evidently means that he attempted to study the microscopic structure of chalk. No other interpretation—if the context be considered—appears to me possible.

[3] *clootgens* MS. It is hardly possible to doubt that some, at least, of these "transparent particles" were fossil shells of Foraminifera.

[4] England and Holland were then temporarily at peace. The second Anglo-Dutch War was concluded in July, 1667, and the third was not declared until March, 1672.

observations on chalk are, so far as I have yet ascertained, the earliest dated microscopic investigations recorded by Leeuwenhoek: and they dispose of a recent suggestion[1] that he began his career as a microscopist under the influence of his second wife—the "blue-stocking" Cornelia Zwalmius. He did not marry this supposedly learned lady[2] until 1671; but the foregoing extract shows that he was already engaged in making microscopic observations at least three years earlier, and when we remember that he made all his microscopes and lenses with his own hands it seems certain that he must have begun his studies whilst his first wife was still alive.[3]

By the end of the XVII Century, when he had been demonstrating the scientific possibilities of the microscope for more than 25 years, Leeuwenhoek was actually the only earnest microscopist in the whole world. It is a remarkable fact that in all his later life he had no rivals and hardly a single imitator. His observations excited the greatest interest—but that was all. Nobody seriously attempted to repeat or extend them. The superexcellence of his lenses, combined with the exceptional keenness of his eye, killed all competition. As early as 1692, Robert Hooke, discoursing on "the Fate of Microscopes",[4] says that they "are now reduced almost to a single Votary, which is Mr. *Leeuwenhoek*; besides whom, I hear of none that make any other Use of that Instrument, but for Diversion and Pastime":[5] and he adds later that the microscope at that

---

[1] Schierbeek (1929).

[2] The only evidence that Cornelia was a highly-educated female appears to be (1) that her father was a clergyman; (2) that her brother was a doctor; and (3) that she once signed her name "Swalmia" (instead of Swalmius) on a legal document—which has been taken to prove that she knew Latin. There is no evidence, however, to show that she changed the gender of her patronymic on her own initiative: and it seems to me unlikely that women were less dependent on their male relatives and friends 250 years ago than they are today.

[3] It is not known with certainty when L. began making "microscopes." The recent statements by Garrison (1921, p. 835) in a learned work ("1673. Leeuwenhoek makes microscopes"), and by Mrs Williams-Ellis (1929, p. 13) in a juvenile broadcast ("1660. Leeuwenhoek has made hundreds of microscopes"), are equally misleading and gratuitous guesses at the date.

[4] Published by Derham (1726) in Hooke's *Phil. Expts. & Obss.*

[5] *Ibid.*, p. 261.

date "is become almost out of Use and Repute: So that Mr. *Leeuwenhoek* seems to be the principal Person left that cultivates those Enquiries. Which is not for Want of considerable Materials to be discover'd, but for Want of the inquisitive Genius of the present Age."[1] These remarks were not due to the circumstance that Hooke was growing an old man, and therefore *laudator temporis acti*: they are supported by all scientific publications of the period.

It is often stated[2] that Leeuwenhoek was elected a Fellow not only of the Royal Society but also of the *Académie des Sciences* of Paris. The date of his election is variously given (usually 1697), and it is also sometimes stated that he wrote a number of letters (usually said to be 26) to this other learned and royal Society. But no authority is ever quoted for such statements, and Leeuwenhoek's name is not included—so far as I have been able to ascertain—in the lists of *Membres de l'Académie* published prior to the reconstitution of this body (1699).[3] Moreover, all the "Letters from Leeuwenhoek" in the *Journal des Sçavans* appear to be merely extracts or quotations in French from the *Philosophical Transactions*. I must confess, however, that I have not searched all the early publications of the *Académie* properly—the task appearing somewhat unprofitable.

As I have not had access to the archives of the *Académie des Sciences*—the only present source of authoritative information—I have sought the help of my friend Professor F. Mesnil, *Membre de l'Académie*, who has very kindly instituted inquiries on my behalf. As a result he tells me in a recent letter:[4] "I have had the Archives of the Academy of Sciences searched for information about Leeuwenhoek, and I have been shown

---

[1] *Ibid.*, p. 268.

[2] *e.g.* by Richardson (1885), De Toni (1923), etc. No reference to the subject is made by Halbertsma, Harting, Haaxman, or any reliable Dutch author.

[3] Cf. Fontenelle (1709). Ornstein (1928) gives the history of the old Academy (p. 139 *sq.*) and enumerates the early members (pp. 146, 156, 159). Christiaan Huygens was the only original foreign member, though several associate members (including Hartsoeker) were appointed later (1682). In Godin's *Table Alphabétique* the name of L. does not occur, nor is it included in the elaborate tabulation of De Candolle (1885, p. 224 *sq.*).

[4] Letter dated 21 November 1930 (translated).

the manuscript record of the proceedings of the meeting held on *4 March 1699*, at which each member 'nominated his correspondents' (*correspondant* in the etymological sense of the word). A physician, Burlet, nominated Leeuwenhoek—'well known by virtue of what he had been able to observe by the use of the microscope.' One may therefore say that Leeuwenhoek was a 'correspondant' of the old *Académie des Sciences*: his name also figures in some printed lists. Was he informed of this officially? No letter of thanks from him is in existence, nor is there any manuscript of his elsewhere in our Archives."

I conclude, therefore, that Leeuwenhoek was "nominated" as a "corresponding member"—but never elected a full Member—of the *Académie* in 1699, and probably without his knowledge: for I can find no reference to the subject in any of his own letters, and there appear to be no extant letters of his, either published or in manuscript, addressed to Burlet or to the Academy or to any other member thereof (except Huygens). In any case, the event was without influence upon his activities. No scientific society except the Royal Society enrolled him as a member during his lifetime, though many have honoured him since his death.[1] His name is forever linked to the Royal Society of London, and to that Society alone.

As soon as his discoveries became famous, Leeuwenhoek was visited by all manner of people who wanted to look through his glasses. The list of celebrities who went to see him is a long one, and has been drawn up more or less completely and accurately by various writers.[2] I need not give it here: for nobody believes nowadays that scientific truth depends upon literary or political authority or royal assent. Leeuwenhoek himself—being a common man—naturally felt flattered when a King or Queen of England, an Emperor of Germany, or a Tsar of Russia called upon him. It impressed his fellow-citizens and advanced his reputation, but he frankly confessed (in one of his letters to Magliabechi) that he was bored by such interruptions, and preferred to be left in peace to carry on his work.

---

[1] Cf. Harting (1876). The statement that L. was a Fellow of "the Royal College of Physicians in London" (Nieuwenhuis, 1859) is an error due, apparently, to confusion of this body with the Royal Society.

[2] *e.g.* Halbertsma (1843), Haaxman (1875), etc.

As a sample of the recorded royal visitations I will only mention the famous interview with Peter the Great—which took place in 1698, and is noted by all biographers of this renowned Russian monarch.[1] The circumstances were recorded by van Loon in the following words:[2]

> The Tsar's departure from The Hague was made in a canal-yacht passing by Delft, where he inspected with very great attention the fine arsenal of the States of Holland, and caused the boat to be stopped before the powder-magazine[3] of the States-General, nearby Delft: and he sent two gentlemen of his retinue to the celebrated Antoni van Leeuwenhoek, to bid him come to see him, with his incomparable magnifying-glasses, on one of the freight-ships in his train: and the Tsar would gladly have gone himself to see him at his own house, had it not been that he was apprehensive of the crowds, which he desired to avoid. Leeuwenhoek repaired to His Majesty, and had the honour of showing him among other remarkable discoveries, through his particular glasses, the marvellous circulation in the tail of an eel; which so delighted the Prince, that in these and other contemplations he spent no less than two hours, and on taking his leave shook Leeuwenhoek by the hand, and assured him of his special gratitude for letting him see such extreme small objects.

Peter I spoke Leeuwenhoek's language fluently (if not grammatically)—having picked it up by fraternizing with Dutch seamen and shipbuilders. He mixed with all classes of people whilst in Holland and England, and had an insatiate curiosity to see things for himself. (It is recorded that the words which fell from his lips most frequently were "*Dat wil*

---

[1] *e.g.* Barrow (1896), p. 67.

[2] Translated from van Loon (1731). This description is trustworthy; for van Loon knew L. personally, and may well have heard the story from his own lips.—On v. Loon see p. 80, note 2, *infra*.

[3] After the dreadful explosion of the former magazine inside the town (in 1654), it was rebuilt well outside the walls—in the direction of Rotterdam (*i.e.* to the south): so Peter must have passed through Delft before he sent back to summon L. into his presence. Cf. p. 28 *supra*.

ik zien".[1]) Consequently, we may suppose that his interview with Leeuwenhoek in the canal-yacht on the outskirts of Delft was somewhat informal, and more satisfactory both to the exhibitor and to his audience than some other like meetings which required the presence of an interpreter. It is probable that Leeuwenhoek, on this occasion, presented the Tsar with some of his microscopes[2]—including his instrument for examining the circulation in the tail of an eel: for at a later date some similar apparatus of his manufacture was brought back to Holland from Russia.[3]

What manner of man was this "celebrated Leeuwenhoek"? Unfortunately we get little direct information from the writings of his contemporaries. Kings and princes, philosophers and physicians and men of science, statesmen and clergymen, and even common men, went to see him and looked through his wonderful glasses: but few indeed left any written record of what they saw, or of their impressions of the man himself. Nevertheless, there are some extant descriptions of Leeuwenhoek by people who actually interviewed him, though only two are of any real importance. One of these is contained in a manuscript letter written by a young Irish doctor, Thomas Molyneux, who waited upon him early in 1685 on behalf of the Royal Society; the other is a lengthier printed account by one von Uffenbach, a German, who paid him a visit in 1710 when he was already a very old man. But all the records are interesting, and I shall therefore give them at length. Here is the first—that of Molyneux,[4] whose autograph letter is still preserved by the Royal Society. I give it word for word, as he wrote it, though I take the liberty of expanding

---

1 "I want to see that." Tsar Peter was evidently the father of "the man from Missouri."

2 As he did to our Queen Mary II (cf. p. 317 *infra*).

3 Discovered and recorded by Haaxman (1875), p. 35. L. never sold or gave away microscopes to ordinary people.

4 Thomas Molyneux (1661-1733), physician and zoologist, was brother of William Molyneux the mathematician and writer on dioptrics. Thomas was at Trinity College, Dublin, where he took his M.D. degree in 1687. He became a Fellow of the Royal Society in 1686, President of the College of Physicians of Ireland in 1702, Professor of Medicine at Dublin University in 1717, and was made a Baronet in 1730. For further details of his life see the *Dict. Nat. Biogr.* (art. by Norman Moore).

the contractions in the original manuscript for typographical reasons and for the convenience of the modern reader:[1]

> I have hitherto delay'd answering your last, because I could not give You any account of Myn Heer Leeuwenhoeck, but last week I was to wait uppon him in Your name: he shew'd me several things through his Microscopes, which 'tis in vain to mention here, since he himself has sent You all their descriptions at large. as to his Microscopes themselves, those which he shew'd me, in number at least a Dozen, were all of one sort, consisting only of one smal Glas, ground, (this I mention because 'tis generaly thought his Microscopes are blown at a Lamp, those I saw I'm sure were not) placed between two thin flat Plates of bras, about an Inch broad & an Inch & ½ long; in thees two Plates there were two Apertures one before, the other behinde the Glas, which were larger or smaler, as the Glas was more or less convex, or as it magnify'd; just opposite to thees Apertures on one side was placed sometimes a Needle, sometimes a slender flat body of glas or opaque[2] mater as the occasion requir'd, uppon which, or to it's apex, he fixes whatever object he has to look uppon, then holding it up against the Light by help of two smal scrues he places it just in the Focus of his glass and then makes his observations. Sutch were the Microscopes which I saw, and thees are they he shews to the Curious that come and vizite him, but besides thees he told me he had an other Sort, which no Man living ever look'd through setting aside himself, thees he reserves for his own

---

[1] MS.Roy.Soc., No. 2445; *M.1.* 103, dated from Leyden, 13 February 1685 [N.S.]. This letter has been printed previously, with slight inaccuracies and amended spelling, by Birch (Vol. IV, p. 365). It was addressed to Francis Aston, then Secretary of the Royal Society, and was read at the meeting held on 11 February 1685 [O.S.]—not Feb. 4 (an impossible date) as it appears in Birch, who here wrongly combined the proceedings of two different meetings.

[2] In translating this letter—from Birch—Haaxman has made a slip. He renders "opaque" as "*doorschijnende*"—instead of *ondoorschijnende*, as he should have done. See Haaxman (1875), p. 13, *lin. penult.*

private Observations wholy, and he assur'd me they perform'd far beyond any that he had shew'd me yet, but would not allow me a sight of them, so all I can do, is barely to belive, for I can plead no experience in the mater. as for the Microscopes I looked through, they do not magnify, mutch, if any thing, more, then several Glasses I have seen both in England & Ireland: but in one particular I must needs say they far surpas them all, that is in their extreme clearness, and their representing all objects so extrordnary distinctly. for I remember we were in a dark rome[1] with only one Window, and the sun to, was then of a that,[2] yet the Objects appeerd more fair and clear, then any I have seen through Microscopes, tho the Sun shone full uppon them, or tho they receved more then ordnary Light by help of reflectiv Specula or otherwise: so that I imagine tis chiefly, if not allone in this particular, that his Glasses exceeds all others, which generaly the more they magnify the more obscure they represent the Object; and his only secret I belive is making clearer Glasses, and giving them a better pollish then others can do. I found him a very civil complesant man, & douptless of great natural Abileties; but contrary to my Expectations quite a stranger to letters, master neither of Latin French or English or any other of the modern tongues besides his own, which is a great hindrance to him in his reasonings uppon his Observations, for being ignorant of all other Mens thoughts, he is wholy trusting to his own, which I observe now and then lead him into extravagances, and suggest very odd accounts of things, nay sometimes sutch as are wholy irreconsilable with all truth. You see Sir how freely I give You my thoughts of him because You desired it.

---

[1] *i.e.*, room.

[2] "of a that" = off of that, *i.e.* off the window—not on, or shining through it.

A little later Molyneux wrote again to the Society, and gave a few further particulars—evidently in reply to a request for additional information. From this letter, dated from Leyden, 16 March 1685, I extract the following[1]:

> The Glasses Mr Lewenhoeck shew'd me magnified Objects no more then several other glasses I have seen before, & therefore discover nothing but what may easily be seen by help of other Microscopes, so an account of them would be no ways satisfactory; 'tis only his owne privat Glasses which make those more then ordnary discoverys. I never heard he sold those glasses of his more common sort; but I sha'nt returne suddenly into England, for I designe, to have stayd some while in France, & perhaps visite Italy before that time, so I ca'nt serve You in this particular.[2]

When Thomas Molyneux visited Leeuwenhoek in 1685 he was probably accompanied by his elder brother William[3]: for the latter has left a record of a similar visit—buried in a book on optics, and consequently not generally known—which affords some confirmation of the foregoing account. William Molyneux's words are as follows[4]:

> The *Heer Lewenhoeck* of *Delft* in *Holland*, had lately apply'd himself with great Diligence to the use of Microscopes: of which Instrument he thinks he has a better kind than was ever yet known. When I visited

---

[1] MS.Roy.Soc., No. 2446, *M.1.* 104. Printed by Birch, Vol. IV, p. 384. The letter was read at the meeting of the Royal Society on 1 April 1685 [O.S.]. I expand the contractions again, but otherwise give the exact words of the original.

[2] I take it that "this particular" was a request to Molyneux that he should endeavour to buy some of L.'s glasses for the Society.

[3] William Molyneux (1656-1698). He was B.A. of Trinity College, Dublin, and a "philosopher" and mathematician. Elected F.R.S. in 1686—the same year as his brother (though owing to the confusion of "old style" and "new style" dating, apparently a year earlier): entered Middle Temple, 1675: M.P. for Dublin University, 1692 and 1695. For his life see the *Dict. Nat. Biogr.* (in which the dates of election to the Roy. Soc. are given wrongly for both brothers).

[4] W. Molyneux (1692), p. 281.

> this Gentleman at *Delft*, he shew'd me several that indeed were very curious; but nothing more than what I had ordinarily seen before; being composed only of one single, very minute Glass-Sphere or Hemisphere,[1] placed between two very thin pierced *Laminae*, or Plates of Brass, and the Object was brought to its due distance before the Glass by a fine Screw: But for his *best* sort, he beg'd our Excuse in concealing them. The Observations he has made with his Glasses are Printed in several Letters of his in *Dutch*; but for the most part, they are to be found dispers'd in the *Philosophical Transactions*.

There is a more illuminating reference to Leeuwenhoek in a letter written by Constantijn Huygens *jun.* to his brother Christiaan in the year of Molyneux's visit: and as it illustrates Leeuwenhoek's extraordinary jealousy in guarding his microscopes, it may be quoted here. Constantijn *junior*, in this epistle, tells his brother that he has just seen one Willem Meester[2] (a skilled Dutch mechanic), who had recently been with the Landgrave of Hesse[3] to interview Leeuwenhoek. Says Constantijn:[4]

> He [Meester] had been with him [the Landgrave] to Leeuwenhoek's, who wouldn't show him any of his microscopes except those which he shows to everybody; whereof the little glasses had, at least, a focal distance equal to the width of the back of a knife. And when the Landgrave had asked him whether he could obtain some, of his manufacture, he answered with much pride that he

---

[1] This is an error: for L.'s glasses were neither spherical nor hemispherical, but ground biconvex lenses—as Thomas Molyneux correctly observed.

[2] There are many other references to Meester in the Huygens correspondence. He appears to have accompanied the Prince of Orange in his campaigns. Cf. *Œuvr. Compl. de Chr. Huygens*, Vol. VII, p. 439 *note*.

[3] Karl, Landgrave of Hesse-Cassel (1654-1730), an amateur of science.

[4] Printed in *Œuvr. Compl. de Chr. Huygens*, Vol. IX, p. 38, No. 2408. 5 Nov. 1685. The original MS. is in the Leyden Library, and is in French—from which I translate. Constantijn Huygens *jun.* (1628-1697) was elder brother of Christiaan (1629-1695), both being sons of Constantijn *sen.* (1596-1687).

never gave any to anybody, nor did he intend to do so: and that if he were ever to submit to that, he would then soon be the slave of everybody; with other expressions of the like sort. When he had shown two or three of his microscopes, he took them away, and went to look for as many others; saying that he did this for fear lest any of them might get mislaid among the beholders, because he didn't trust people, especially Germans: and he repeated this two or three times. *O what a brute!*[1]

Another person who has left a brief contemporary account of Leeuwenhoek and his microscopes—professedly from personal knowledge—is the Rev. Jean Cornand de la Crose. This gentleman was a French protestant refugee, who fled to Holland after the revocation of the Edict of Nantes and later settled in England, where he was received into the Anglican Church.[2] In the year 1693 he published in London a curious monthly magazine[3] in imitation of the *Philosophical Transactions*: and in its May number he presented his readers with an English translation[4] (neither complete nor accurate, though written in a language which gives no cause for complaint) of Leeuwenhoek's famous letter[5] on the capillary circulation of the blood—the first version to appear in English. At the end of this he added:[6]

> Mr. *Leeuwenhoek* being so deservedly famous in the learned World, the Ingenious will undoubtedly be glad to

---

[1] These final words are in Italian in the original. Cf. note 3 on p. 50.

[2] But little is now known of de la Crose (*alias* Croze *seu* Lacroze). His own *Memoirs* etc. supply some information regarding his career, however, and a few further details may be found in Agnew (1886), Vol. II, p. 270, and the *Nouv. Biogr. Gén.* (Hoefer), Vol. XXVIII [*s.v.* Lacroze].

[3] *Memoirs for the Ingenious* [etc.]. 1693. This work is now extremely rare. Only one volume appeared: and an attempted continuation (*The Universal Mercury*) expired with its first number in January, 1694.

[4] *Ibid.*, Letter XIX, p. 145.

[5] *Letter 65.* To the Royal Society. 7 Sept. 1688. Published (complete) in Dutch and Latin works: not in *Phil. Trans.* A full modern English translation (with Dutch original reprinted) will be found in *Opuscula Selecta Neerlandicorum*, Vol. I, p. 38 (Amsterdam, 1907), and a mutilated bit of this in Fulton (1930).

[6] *Mem. Ing.*, p. 152.

have an account of him. He is about 50 years of age,[1] but has already imployed 15 or 20 years in Observations as curious as these, which I have here related. His Parents designed him for a Chyrurgeon, which Profession he has exercised some time with Honor.[2] And as he rightly conceived, that Anatomy was the foundation of that useful Art, and that Microscopes were highly serviceable to acquire the knowledge of it, he applied himself not only to perfect those that were already in use, but even to invent new ones, in which he has succeeded to admiration, having discovered amongst other things more kinds of invisible Animals, than the World before him knew there were visible ones: and withal made an anatomical description of many of them. The perfection to which he has brought his Microscopes, has afforded him great light. For they are not big and cumbersom tools, as the ordinary ones; but light and portable, consisting only of a glass or two at the end of a small and short tube,[3] so that he may manage them, and apply them to the object, as easily as his own Eyes. And what is still more wonderful is, That tho his Glasses magnify the Objects far beyond any I have seen, yet they do not darken it.[4] To which if it be added, that he is an able Surgeon, and has made it his chief business during many years to dissect and view little Animals, Plants, Seeds, Eggs, Saps, and the like, his surprizing discoveries will become more credible. I know some are apt to imagine, that this curious Observer of Nature imposes at least upon himself, in several things

---

[1] In May 1693 L. was, of course, in his 61st year. Perhaps de la Crose was reporting his recollection of the time when he was himself resident in Holland.

[2] This is an extraordinary mistake: but no more remarkable or inexplicable than that made by one of L.'s own distinguished modern fellow-countrymen (de Groot, 1910), who calls our hero "physicist and surgeon of Haarlem"! (cf. p. 352 *infra*).

[3] An evident error.

[4] These words confirm what T. Molyneux wrote in 1685. Cf. p. 58 *supra*.

which appear to them undiscernible. But as to the matter of fact he relates, I dare answer for his sincerity, having myself tried his Microscopes, viewed several things through them, and found them conformable to his relations. Besides, he is very free to let Objects be viewed through his Glasses, and to communicate his Observations to Gentlemen of Learning and Credit, especially Travellers: but he has made so many of them at all seasons and times of the year, that the Thousandth part cannot be examined by those that repair to him on that account. There is a Volume of his Observations printed in Latin, some of which are inserted in the *Philosophical Transactions*, and I have by me some other[1] very curious, which I shall publish in due time.[2]

The last important contemporary record is Uffenbach's[3] well-known account of his visit to Leeuwenhoek in 1710. It is entertaining enough; but chiefly because of the fatuous comments of this complacent German diarist, who was so satisfied of his own superiority that he would be horrified if he could hear that his condescending notes on our poor Dutch draper are now the chief thing of interest in his tedious memoirs. This is what he wrote:[4]

On the 4th December [1710] we[5] went in the morning

---

[1] From other references, it appears that de la Crose possessed a copy of the Dutch edition of L.'s letters of that period.

[2] A few further observations on the circulation of the blood were published by de la Crose, but nothing else.

[3] Zacharias Conrad von Uffenbach (1683-1734) was a German jurist, town-councillor of Frankfort, and a keen collector of books, coins, and "curiosities". His *Travels* were published posthumously in 1753-54 (*ed.* Schelhorn), and much of his insignificant correspondence has also appeared in print. His life is prefixed to his memoirs, and will also be found in the *Allg. Dtsch. Biogr.*

[4] Translated from the German of Uffenbach (1754), Vol. III, pp. 349-360, with immaterial omissions which are duly indicated. The full description is too long-winded to give here in its entirety. In my translation I have left the Latin words as Uffenbach gave them, in order to preserve his pedantic style of expression. His mistakes are too evident for comment.

[5] "We" apparently denotes Uffenbach and his brother.

to see the famous *observator microscopicus*, Leeuwenhoek,[1] by whom . . . we were most courteously received. The only daughter that he has, a person of about forty,[2] led us first into an antechamber, and told us that her father, though he had discovered many new things with his *microscopia* in recent years, did not wish to publish any more of his observations during his lifetime, because of the affronts he had suffered, presumably in the writings of others; for he has now and then been ridiculed for the odd views expressed in his own writings, and has been accused of seeing more with his imagination than with his magnifying glasses. Mr. Leeuwenhoek is a man of seventy-eight, but still hale and hearty, save that he cannot much use his feet. We were surprised to find him not at all shaky, and he still has almost incomparable eyesight, though he taxes his eyes greatly with his observations. He showed us the following experiments: First, the circulation of the blood, very fine and clear, in the tail of a quite little flounder (which is one of the greatest delicacies among sea-fish). He was not only of opinion that where the blood runs upwards, these are the arteries, and where it runs downwards, the *venae* (of which I justly doubted whether such a sweeping assumption were allowable?), but also he maintained that it is the *venae* and not the *arteriae* which pulsate. He also insisted that he could see with the naked eye that the pulse at the wrist beats downwards rather than upwards. Methinks, however, that herein Mr. Leeuwenhoek does but show his ignorance of anatomy; for the structure of the arteries sufficiently proves that the *valvulae* in them undoubtedly cause the pulse-beat, whereas the blood merely flows along and

---

[1] His name is spelled "Leuwenhoeck" by Uffenbach throughout—a mistake which I have taken the liberty of correcting wherever it occurs in his narrative.

[2] Maria was really aged 54 at this time; and consequently Uffenbach's statement is an unintentional compliment on her personal appearance.

through the *venae*, which have no *valvulae*. Besides, it is surely impossible to distinguish whether the pulse at the wrist beats downwards or upwards? But this by the way.—Mr. Leeuwenhoek then cut off with a knife a small bit from a mussel,[1] such as they are here wont to eat, and showed us that all its parts were in a continuous motion; just as a snake apparently continues to move itself for a long time when freshly hacked to pieces with a switch. In both cases this is due to the vital spirits, which seek to escape, and so bring about the movements. Afterwards Mr. Leeuwenhoek cut a mussel in two through the middle, in order to show us how the eggs and young mussels are generated. He also showed us certain black dots, which he maintained were young mussels in their black shells; but we couldn't take them for such, being unable to distinguish them. He also cut the gut of a mussel in two, and showed us, by means of his *microscopium*, a great mass of sand in it, which the mussels presumably take in with the slime in which they live. Mr. Leeuwenhoek considered, and not unjustly, that this sand serves for the formation of the shells of their young ones, just as hens and other birds readily eat sand and lime for the sake of their egg-shells. He wished also to show us the circulation of the blood in an eel, only the creature was too big and black. Mr. Leeuwenhoek makes this experiment with an instrument which . . . is simple, large, and not at all convenient. The one made by Mez in Amsterdam, with a *camera obscura*, is better; with this one you are dazzled by the light and the glass. . . . Mr. Leeuwenhoek showed us the circulation of the blood very well with this machine, though it was somewhat troublesome to manipulate, and would be even worse for making observations lasting over a long time, because you have to put the side of the *microscopium*, where the lens is, against your forehead, and look

---

[1] No doubt L. showed the ciliary motion on a portion of the gill of *Mytilus*—as he well knew how.

upwards through the tiny glass; which, after some time, would become tiresome. Mr. Leeuwenhoek afterwards fetched some cases, in each of which were two *microscopia*[1] . . . likewise of quite a simple structure. . . . Each of these *microscopia* had a particular curiosity stuck before it; but we saw the following: First, *in tubulo capillari*, upwards of thirty small young oysters *in spiritu vini*. These could be seen quite clearly, and had the perfect form and structure of old and big oysters. . . . We inquired how he introduced these young oysters into his capillary tubes, which he explained in the following fashion: He cuts off the gut of an oyster, takes some of the stuff that is in it on a pen-knife, and smears it on his thumb-nail; he then pours a drop of spirits of wine upon it, and applies the capillary tube thereto, whereupon the spirit runs up the tube of itself, through the pressure of the air, and takes the little oysters along with it, they being commonly present in the substance that is in the beard or the gut of the old oysters. He uses spirit for this purpose in order that they may not so easily become foul, which, being fish, they only too readily do, as happened indeed formerly with him, when he used only water. This experiment is one of the finest and most curious that we saw at Mr. Leeuwenhoek's. He showed us further a "maggot", as they are called, supposed to grow in the *pori* of the nose. . . . Through another *microscopium* he showed us a sand-grain, which looked like the finest crystal with facettes. . . . In another *microscopium* he had, on a bit of glass, a particle of gold, which he had previously dissolved in *aqua regia* and then precipitated: this appeared just like a little gold tree, and exceeding pretty. . . . Next, Mr. Leeuwenhoek showed us, through another *microscopium*, the scale of a fish, whose structure

---

[1] These may have been the silver instruments bequeathed to the Royal Society. Cf. p. 96 *infra*.

was certainly wonderful. . . . At this point Mr. Leeuwenhoek remarked that he must show us that men also have scales. Accordingly, he took a pen-knife, and scratched his arm several times; then took a glass tube and with it scraped several times the place that he had scratched. He then let us look at this tube through his *microscopium*, whereupon many little particles, like scales, were visible lying upon it. These the good man takes to be scales, which a human being is provided with in order that the extremities of the nerves may not be injured, as also to prevent his sensations being too strong; for if the nerves were not so guarded, he would be unable to stand pain, or irritation, nor could he do any work. It is surely quite sufficient, however, that man is clothed with several skins, as is known from anatomy, and he has no need of scales like a fish: and what the good Mr. Leeuwenhoek takes for scales are really only the particles, or scurf, from the outermost skin, which are commonly present, especially in persons of a dry habit, and particularly on the head, and which are cast off from the *cuticula* as it dries up and peels off under the influence of the external air, but chiefly through the internal heat of the body, though it always forms anew underneath. Mr. Leeuwenhoek showed us further the eye of a fly, which appeared very remarkable under the *microscopium*, and had the appearance of veritable *hexagona* lying alongside one another; which Mr. Leeuwenhoek considers actually are eyes, and consequently makes flies into something better than so many *Arguses*; for he is of opinion that a fly, according to his view, has more than a hundred, nay, more than a thousand, eyes; which is only one of this good man's extraordinary notions, which seem wont to have more of ingenuity than foundation. Further, he showed us the wing of a fly, which also appeared very wonderful . . . The sting of a fly appeared also very singular . . . Finally, Mr. Leeuwenhoek showed us his cabinet, in which he had at least a dozen little lacquered boxes, and in these quite a hundred and fifty of the little cases before mentioned, in each of which there lay two microscopes of the small sort. As we marvelled at this large store, we asked him whether he never sold any? as we would gladly have possessed ourselves of some: but he said no, he would sell none in his lifetime. He was also very secret about his work, and how he did it: but we drew one thing and another out of him with all manner of questions. Thus, when we asked him whether all these *microscopia* were identical? he said they were all ground in the same grinding-cup, but nevertheless there was a difference between the various lenses, and as regards those ground last in any cup, indeed, a great difference. . . . . When we further inquired of Mr. Leeuwenhoek whether he ground all his lenses, and did not blow any? he denied this, but displayed great contempt for the blown glasses. He pointed out to us how thin his *microscopia* were, compared with others, and how close together the *laminae* were between which the lens lay, so that no spherical glass could be thus mounted; all his lenses being ground, contrariwise, convex on both sides. He also had some *microscopia* with double glasses, which, though they were double, and the lenses separated inside at their proper distance, presumably by another *lamina*, were nevertheless not much thicker than the simple ones. Notwithstanding that these are pretty troublesome to make, they yet are not much better than the simple ones, excepting that they magnify a little more; but only a little, as Mr. Leeuwenhoek himself confessed. As regards the blown glasses, Mr. Leeuwenhoek assured us that he had succeeded, after ten years' speculation, in learning how to blow a serviceable kind of glasses which were not round. My brother was unwilling to believe this, but took it for *a Dutch joke*[1]; since it is impossible, by blowing, to form anything but a sphere, or rounded end. Yet one cannot sufficiently marvel at Mr. Leeuwenhoek's great

[1] A pleasing German expression for a falsehood.

diligence and industry, both in the making of observations and in the grinding of lenses, as also in the manufacture of the mechanical parts for his *microscopia*; albeit the latter are simple, and badly worked, and for the most part roughly fashioned, even the silver not being filed smooth in a single one of them. We much wanted to ask him why he made so many *microscopia*, though he would not sell any; but we feared we might get only *a Dutch answer*.[1] Presumably jealousy lest anybody should get hold of microscopes of his pattern, during his lifetime, is chiefly at the bottom of this; but there is also some self-interest, in that his daughter will one day be able to sell them so much dearer, if they cannot be got during his own lifetime.[2] As we were going, both this extraordinary man and his daughter earnestly intreated us to tell no one that we had been to see him, or seen anything there; for the reason that he is old, and tired of being pestered, especially by people who are not true lovers of learning. . . . We were told not only in Delft, but also by many foreigners who had waited upon him in vain, that he would see no one, still less show people anything: and we were therefore greatly rejoiced that we saw so many curious things at the house of this extraordinary old man.

One final account of Leeuwenhoek by a man who met him must, unfortunately, be mentioned. It was given by Hartsoeker,[3] an envious fellow-countryman, and was obviously

---

[1] *i.e.* none: another German pleasantry.

[2] As a comment on this unjust remark, it may be recalled that L.'s microscopes were not put up for sale until 1747—two years after Maria's death. Cf. p. 320.

[3] Nicolaas Hartsoeker (1656-1725), physicist, astronomer, and mathematician: son of Christiaan Hartsoeker (1626-1683), a minister of the reformed Church. He had a variegated career, which is recorded in *Dict. Sci. méd.* (1822), V, 85; *N. Ned. Biogr. Woordenb.* (1924), VI, 718; and elsewhere. In *Œuvres Compl. de Chr. Huygens* (VIII, 58*n*) it is stated that Hartsoeker was born on 25 March 1654: but this is contradicted by his own statement in the *Ext. crit.* (1730), p. 43, where he himself gives the date as 26 March 1656.

inspired by dislike and jealousy. I shall not quote his words,[1] as they have already been repeated by Haaxman (1875) and others, and are not worthy of further consideration. It is now abundantly evident that Hartsoeker had wronged Leeuwenhoek, and therefore hated him; while on his side Leeuwenhoek despised Hartsoeker and treated him with contempt. All this can be read in their various references to one another.[2] When he was very young, Hartsoeker—who had visited Leeuwenhoek with his father, and had been shown or had heard of the discovery of the spermatozoa—went to Paris, and there tried to palm off this discovery as his own. He did not succeed—though there are still credulous or ignorant writers who accept his claims[3]—and when the facts became known he was reduced to silence. More than forty years later, when Leeuwenhoek had at last died, Hartsoeker attempted to blacken his character and reasserted his own priority[4]: but he himself died before his malicious remarks were published (1730), so that he was denied the final satisfaction of kicking Leeuwenhoek's corpse in public. Hartsoeker was a man of undoubted ability, but quarrelsome and arrogant and in every way the very antithesis of Leeuwenhoek. He attacked and found fault with everybody he envied—not only Leeuwenhoek, but also Newton, Leibniz, and even Christiaan Huygens (who had befriended him)—and his foolish criticisms and personal complaints are now best consigned to the oblivion which they deserve. On his own confession he was virtually turned out of the house by Leeuwenhoek when he last attempted, by a subterfuge, to visit him. I shall therefore treat Hartsoeker likewise here,[5] and give him

---

[1] See Hartsoeker (1730), *Extrait critique*, passim.

[2] See L.'s letters and Hartsoeker's publications *passim*: also *Œuvres Compl. de Chr. Huygens*—especially Vol. VIII.

[3] Cf. Martin (1764), Launois (1904), etc.

[4] Hartsoeker's claims to the discovery of the spermatozoa have recently been critically considered and correctly assessed by Cole (1930).

[5] I must add, however, that I have carefully and impartially read all the available evidence concerning Hartsoeker's relations with L. Consequently I am well aware that much already written on this subject is incorrect, though it seems to me unnecessary to discuss all the data here. French writers especially—doubtless influenced by Fontenelle—have, in general,

no further publicity. Leeuwenhoek's own last comment on him was[1]:

> It has come to my ears that Hartsoeker hasn't much of a reputation among the learned: and when I saw that he laid claim to untruths, and was stuck up, I looked into his writings no further.

The foregoing quotations show what some of Leeuwenhoek's contemporaries thought about him: but the best description of himself is that unconsciously written by his own hand. His own letters are filled with autobiography. On almost every page he tells us of his thoughts, his feelings, his everyday actions: so that we can now form a very clear and probably correct picture of his personality. But it was all done quite naturally and ingenuously; for he had no thought, when he was writing, that he was often revealing himself rather than some "mystery of nature". He sets down his views—frequently quite mistaken and even ridiculous views—with childish and charming simplicity, and he has no feeling of embarrassment in telling the Royal Society the most intimate details about his blood, his sweat, or his urine; or about his sicknesses or his habits or his little vanities: because he always imagines that he is recording matters of scientific interest, and he knows by instinct that in registering his observations he ought not to withhold any data which may possibly have a bearing upon his findings. Yet he always presents his results in a way which, despite the imperfections of his language and his lack of scientific education, is a model for all other workers. He never confuses his facts with his speculations. When recording facts he invariably says "I have observed . . .", but when giving his interpretations he prefaces them with "but I imagine . . ." or "I figure to myself . . ." Few scientific workers—or so it seems to me—have had so clear a conception of the boundary between observation and theory, fact and fancy, the concrete and the abstract.

---

given Hartsoeker far more credit than he deserves: Dutch writers are better informed. (Fontenelle's *Eloge* of Hartsoeker will be found reprinted at the beginning of the latter's posthumous *Cours de Physique*, 1730.)

[1] *Send-brief* XVIII, 28 Sept. 1715, to Leibniz (*Brieven*, Vol. IV, p. 170).

But every reader of Leeuwenhoek's letters must form his own opinion of the man himself. Some have been—and will be—revolted by his "grossness" and "vulgarity": others will continue to delight in his very "commonness", and will even find in it something meritorious. For my own part, I confess that I enjoy his most commonplace sayings, because they satisfy my own craving for simplicity and common sense in all things—especially in those called "scientific". When Leeuwenhoek makes casual "asides" about the most trivial affairs of his life, it does not offend me: it rather helps me to understand him. I like to hear that he generally drank coffee for breakfast and took tea in the afternoon, or that he shaved himself twice a week and got a rash on his hands when he sat in the sun: and I even laughed uproariously when I first read the letter in which he gravely told the Royal Society—evidently giving it as a tip to the Fellows—that he found it advisable to drink a great many cups of extremely hot tea on rising if he had had a drop of wine too much the night before with a friend. But when he speaks of his little white long-haired pet dog, or of his parrot "which is moulting," or of his horse "which is a mare", or incidentally remarks that he was wont to throw bread to the sparrows when the snow was on the ground, I feel that I really know the sort of man he was. Little touches such as these bring the heavy-featured blue-eyed Hollander of Verkolje's painting very vividly before my mind's eye, and explain—in an inexplicable and inexpressible manner—his crude but inspired discoveries in protozoology and bacteriology. They make me want to find excuses for all his many mistakes. It is so obviously his works—not his words—which count. I do not suppose that he ever read any writings of his great contemporary John Bunyan: but had he done so he would certainly have understood what Bunyan meant when he wrote: "*Yea, if a man have* all *knowledge, he may yet be nothing, and so consequently be no child of God. When Christ said,* Do you know all these things? *And the Disciples had answered, Yes*: *He addeth,* Blessed are ye if ye do them."[1]

---

[1] John Bunyan (1628-1688), the immortal English tinker. I quote from the first edition of the *Pilgrim's Progress* (1678), p. 113—written in Bedford jail.

Our Leeuwenhoek was manifestly a man of great and singular candour, honesty, and sincerity. He was religiously plain and straightforward in all he did, and therefore sometimes almost immodestly frank in describing his observations. It never occurred to him that Truth could appear indecent. His letters, accordingly, are full of outspoken thoughts which more "scientific" writers would hesitate to put on paper: and to the modern reader this is, indeed, one of his particular charms—for he is far more childlike and innocent and "modern" than any present-day writer. In his own similar language he must often have said the beautiful prayer of Thomas More: "Our Lorde kepe me continuallye true faithfull and playne, to the contrarye whereof I beseche hym hartelye never to suffer me live."[1]

But Leeuwenhoek—like all honest workmen—took a pride in his work. He jealously guarded what he believed to be true, though always willing to change his opinions when cogent arguments were advanced against them. All studious readers of his letters will be able to call to mind a score or more of places where he confesses his scientific faith. It is impossible to quote all these passages here, but a few extracts—taken at random—will illustrate this aspect of his personality. Writing to the Royal Society in 1692 he says[2]:

> I well know, Most Noble Sirs, that the propositions I come to make, and which I've sent you from time to time, do not all agree with one another, but contradictions are to be found among them: so I will only say once more that 'tis my habit to hold fast to my notions only until I'm better informed, or till my observations make me go over to others: and I'll never be ashamed thus to chop and change.

---

[1] In one of Sir Thomas More's letters written in prison to his daughter Margaret. See More's *Utopia* etc., ed. Sampson (1910) p. 281. More was born in 1478 and beheaded on 6 July 1535. His *Utopia* was first published at Louvain in 1516. It is unlikely that L. had ever read it, though the first Dutch translation appeared in 1553.

[2] *Letter 74*, 12 August 1692. MS.Roy.Soc. Cf. *Brieven*, Derde Vervolg, p. 507. Not published in *Phil. Trans.*

A little later, in a letter to the Rev. George Garden[1] he wrote[2]:

> I must say to you, as I've oft-times said already, that 'tis not my intention to stick stubbornly to my opinions, but as soon as people urge against them any reasonable objections, whereof I can form a just idea, I'll give mine up, and go over to the other side: and especially because my efforts are ever striving towards no other end than, as far as in me lieth, to set the Truth before my eyes, to embrace it, and to lay out to good account the small Talent that I've received[3]: in order to draw the World away from its Old-Heathenish superstition, to go over to the Truth, and to cleave unto it.

The following characteristic passages[4] are all from the last published series of Letters—the *Send-brieven*, written by Leeuwenhoek to various people at various dates:

> I have said before now, that, if ever I came to err in my discoveries, I would make open-hearted confession thereof.[5]
>
> . . . .
>
> In the observations aforesaid I have spent a lot more time than many people would believe: yet I made them with pleasure, and paid no attention to people who say to me "Why take so much pains?" and "What's the use

---

[1] George Garden (1649-1733), a Scottish divine, and minister at Aberdeen till 1701—when he was deposed for writing an "*Apology*" for Antoinette Bourignon, the religious fanatic who assisted in Swammerdam's downfall. Garden was not a Fellow of the Royal Society.

[2] Quoted in *Letter 81*, to the Royal Society. 19 March 1694. Cf. *Brieven*, 4de Vervolg, p. 671-2. There is no extant MS. of this letter, which was sent to the Society by L. in the form of a printed proof-sheet and was not published in the *Phil. Trans.*

[3] The reference is obviously to *Matth.* XXV, 25 *sq.*—the parable of the talents. L. does not here use the biblical words, but his own have a strong flavour of the Bible—as was only meet, in writing to a clergyman.

[4] I translate from the Dutch versions, as nearly as I can: for the flavour of the originals is almost wholly lost in the more formal Latin translations.

[5] *Send-brief* II, p. 16.

of it ?" because I don't write for such folks, but only for Philosophers.[1]

. . . .

Hereupon I must remark that it don't seem strange to me that there are still some who won't accept of my propositions regarding generation : for novelties oft-times aren't accepted, because men are apt to hold fast by what their Teachers have impressed on 'em.[2]

. . . .

A certain very understanding Gentleman in our Town, who had been reading my printed Letters, said to me: "Leeuwenhoek, you've got the truth, but it won't be received in your lifetime". And therefore it doesn't strike me as odd, that I meet with contradictions during my life.[3]

. . . .

Yet how the *Tuba Fallopiana* can perform any kind of sucking is to me inconceivable : and though I must confess I've often heard Doctors and Physicians talk about things that seem to me to have no rhyme or reason, yet of nothing worse than generation by an eggstock and the Fallopian tube. 'Twould have been better if they'd said "it's a secret quality" : for of course it would have been too silly for learned people just to say "we don't know".[4]

. . . .

I see well that I can't bring many learned gentlemen to believe in my true discoveries and also in my propositions : but herein I find more to comfort me than for

---

[1] *Send-brief* II, p. 22.

[2] *Send-brief* XVIII, p. 166.

[3] *Send-brief* XVIII, p. 168.

[4] *Send-brief* XXIII, p. 211.

quarrel, if I have but the luck (as I have) that many great men also do accept of my discoveries.[1]

. . . .

I'm well aware that these my writings will not be accepted by some, as they judge it to be impossible to make such discoveries: but I don't bother about such contradictions. Among the ignorant, they're still saying about me that I'm a conjuror, and that I show people what don't exist: but they're to be forgiven, they know no better.[2]

. . . .

I well know there are whole Universities that won't believe there are living creatures in the male seed: but such things don't worry me, I know I'm in the right.[3]

These sayings are typical of Leeuwenhoek, though they are but random samples: I will not rob his readers of the pleasure of finding for themselves many another equally good. Almost every letter he ever wrote contains some remark which throws light upon his character—especially his last letters, written when he was very old. These, as might be expected, are crammed with the reminiscences of a lifetime spent in the solitary contemplation and interrogation of Nature. All his long life he kept on asking questions of Nature—whose own favourite child he was—in common colloquial old-fashioned Dutch, and trying in his simple way to understand her answers made in a pure and perfect language which we still cannot interpret correctly. But it is for the poet—not for the scientist or historian—to portray our Child of Nature in communion with his Mother. I cannot even attempt the task, and must now merely chronicle the last chapters in a prosaic life packed with the stuff of scientific and artistic dreams. . . .

In 1707, when he was in his 75th year, the Royal Society sent to ask after Leeuwenhoek's health—being anxious because

---

[1] *Send-brief* XXX, p. 304.

[2] *Send-brief* XXXII, p. 317.

[3] *Send-brief* XLI, p. 405.

LEEUWENHOEK IN 1707, AGED 75 YEARS

Enlarged from a miniature portrait by J. Goeree (1670-1731), inset in the engraved title-page of the last volume of the *Letters* (1718).

they had received no letters from him for nearly a twelvemonth. (He had evidently ceased to write merely because the Society had not acknowledged his three previous communications.) To their inquiries he returned the following reply, addressed to John Chamberlayne[1]:

> I received your acceptable Letter of the 20th of March, deliver'd by your Nephew the 29th of April last, wherein you are pleased to say, that the Honble. Royal Society are very much concerned that they have had no account of my health for a great while, and that you had commanded your Nephew to wait upon me and desired me to let you know how I did.
>
> Your Nephew delivered your Letter to my Daughter, but I was not at home, and since that time I never saw him again. I am thankfull for your Civilities.
>
> . . . .
>
> As to my health, thanks be to God, as long as I sit still I am without any pain, but if I do but walk a little I have pains in my leggs,[2] but that is, I think, caused by former colds and because they have carried my body so long.

In other letters of this period we hear of various other visits paid to Leeuwenhoek in his old age by Fellows of the Royal Society and other people. Most of these visitors—notwithstanding Uffenbach's statement[3]—seem to have been kindly received, and entertained with divers microscopical sights (especially the capillary circulation in the tail of a little eel). His reasons for refusing to see people occasionally were given by himself; and in this connexion the following unpublished passages from two otherwise published letters are

---

[1] From *Letter dated 17 May 1707.* To J. Chamberlayne, F.R.S. MS. Roy. Soc. Unpublished. This interesting letter is peculiar in that the original is in English. As no Dutch or Latin version accompanies it, and as it is apparently written on L.'s own gilt-edged letter-paper (such as he used at that time), I infer that the translation was made in Delft, by a friend, and that the letter was sent in the form in which it now survives. I transcribe the words of the MS. exactly, merely expanding a few contractions in the original.—For Chamberlayne, see p. 270, note 2, *infra.*

[2] Cf. Uffenbach's statement, p. 64 *supra.*

[3] Cf. p. 69 *supra.*

worth quoting. Writing to the Royal Society early in 1710 Leeuwenhoek remarks [1]:

> I have received by the hands of Mr Stuart [2] the six several *Transactions*, for which gift I am most deeply thankful, and wish I had the ability to do the Honourable Society some service in return.
>
> Mr Hans Sloane [3] recommended Mr Stuart to me, in his letter, as a curious Gentleman who has travelled through many countries; and the same Gentleman had two other Scottish gentlemen in his company, all of whom I gladly received, and so will I do all those who have an introduction from Mr Sloane. But if I should receive everyone who comes to my house, or tries to come, I should have no freedom at all, but be quite a slave.

The second letter was written to James Petiver,[4] who unsuccessfully attempted to see Leeuwenhoek in 1711. The passage in question reads as follows [5]:

---

[1] Translated from *Letter dated 14 January 1710.* MS.Roy.Soc. Original in Dutch. The rest of this letter, in English translation, appeared in *Phil. Trans.* (1709 [1710]), Vol. XXVI, No. 323, p. 444: not published in Dutch or Latin collective works.

[2] Alexander Stuart, M.D.; born about 1673, and died in 1742. He was elected F.R.S. in 1714. As a young man he journeyed to the Far East as a ship's surgeon. He entered the University of Leyden, being then 36 years old, on 14 Dec. 1709, and graduated M.D. there on 22 June 1711. Afterwards he settled in London, where he attained a position of considerable eminence in the medical profession. For these and other biographical details about Stuart—who is not mentioned in the *Dict. Nat. Biogr.*—I am indebted to Dr W. Bulloch, F.R.S.

[3] Sir Hans Sloane, M.D. (1660-1753): Secretary of the Royal Society from 1693 till 1712, and President from 1727 to 1741. His varied scientific and other activities are too well known to require further notice here. For his life see the *Dict. Nat. Biogr.*

[4] James Petiver (1663?-1718), a London apothecary. He was elected F.R.S. in 1695, and wrote much on plants, shells, and other subjects. His vast collections were purchased by Sloane, and incorporated in his own. His life will be found in the *Dict. Nat. Biogr.*, where it is recorded that "in 1711 he went to Leyden, mainly to purchase Dr Hermann's museum for Sloane". Cf. also Green (1914), who speaks highly of some of Petiver's work.

[5] Translated from *Letter dated 18 August 1711.* MS.Roy.Soc. Original

I have received your Letter of the 2nd of August *anno* 1711, wherein you are displeased at not being welcomed at my house. I beg you please not to take it ill, seeing that we send off everyone who tries to visit me, unless they have some sort of introduction.

I willingly received Mr Alexander Stuart *Medicina*[1] *Doctor*, who presented me with the dissertation for his degree,[2] and had with him your *Transactions*, and a letter from Mr Hans Sloane, and brought with him also two other Gentlemen; and I let them see sundry observations of mine. Since that time I would gladly have received you on divers days; and if you had kept by you the letter from Mr Hans Sloane, you would not have missed a friendly entertainment at my house. And you were sent away especially because you were not known, and because some 8 or 10 days earlier no less than 26 people came to see me within four days, all of them with introductions (except a Duke and a Count, with their Tutor): which made me so tired, that I broke out in a sweat all over. This being so, I beg that you will not take it amiss in me, that, to my great sorrow, you were turned away. If my poor old legs could have stood it, I would have looked you up in Rotterdam.

In 1716, when he was in his 84th year, the University of Louvain officially honoured Leeuwenhoek by sending him a medal in recognition of his work. This incident—which corresponds roughly, at the present time, with the conferring of an honorary degree—is not uninteresting, and may therefore be noted here with Leeuwenhoek's own comments.

---

in Dutch. The rest of this letter was published (in English) in *Phil. Trans.* (1711), Vol. XXVII, No. 331, p. 316. It is not in the Dutch or Latin collective works.

[1] So in original: "*medicina*" (for *medicinae*) is not a *lapsus calami* but a mistake on L.'s part—for he knew no Latin, and makes similar mistakes elsewhere.

[2] Stuart's thesis for his medical degree at Leyden was entitled "*De structura et motu musculari*"—a subject which greatly interested L. It was published in 1711 (4°. Leyden), and afterwards reprinted more than once.

Among the minutes of Mr J. van der Werff, onetime notary public of Delft, the following entry has been found[1]:

> Upon this day the 3rd of June 1716 appeared before me, *Jacob van der Werff*, notary within the Town of Delff, in presence of the witnesses hereinafter named, Mr. *Gerard van Loon*,[2] brewer at the Brewery called *This Cross-grained World*, within this town; and declared that by him present was duly received an epistle bearing the superscription: *To the Highly-honoured and Far-famous Mr.* ANTHONY LEEUWENHOEK, *etc. at Delff*, under cover; together with a little silver medal, having graven upon the obverse thereof the likeness of the said Mr. *Leeuwenhoek* encircled by the words "ANTHONY LEEUWENHOEK *Reg*: *Societ*: *Angl*: *Membr*:" and upon the reverse thereof the Town of Delff in the background,[3] with the subscription "*in tenui labor, at tenuis non gloria*" (from Virgil[4]): being enclosed in a little horn box, lined inside with velvet, and in a little bag of woven gold, sent to the appearant (as he explained) by Mr. ANTHONY CINK,[5] *Pro-*

---

[1] Quoted by Servaas van Rooijen (1904, p. 381), from whose transcript I translate. I have not seen the original.

[2] Gerard van Loon (1683-1758), born at Delft: historian, lawyer, and numismatist, as well as brewer. He is now best known for his monumental work on Dutch historical medals (4 vols. folio, 1723-1731). Cf. *N. Nederl. Biogr. Woordenb.* (1930), VIII, 1070. L.'s *Send-brief* XXII (16 May 1716) was addressed to v. Loon, and deals with hops—a subject of mutual interest, as L. indicates: for he notes that v. Loon's mother owned a brewery, while his (Leeuwenhoek's) grandfather and great-grandfather were brewers, and his grandmother the daughter of a brewer, "so that my forefathers handled much hops." Cf. p. 20, *supra*.

[3] And in the foreground, I may add (since this explains the motto), a beehive with bees actively at work collecting honey from a plant bearing flowers.

[4] *Georg.* lib. IV, v. 6—the famous poem on the oeconomy of bees. The application to L. is both obvious and apt.

[5] Antony Cinck (1668-1742), a Hollander born at 's-Hertogenbosch (Bois-le-Duc), was a remarkable man; and in addition to his qualifications noted above was also sometime professor of pedagogics at Louvain, and of rhetoric at Liége. Being a Jansenist, he was later excommunicated by the Archbishop of Mechlin and fled back to Holland, where he died (at Dordrecht). Cf. *N. Nederl. Biogr. Woordenb.* (1924), VI, 300; and S. van Rooijen (1904).

fessor of Philosophy, Canon of Liège, Prebendary of St. Peter's at Louvain, President of the College of Cranendonck,[1] etc. etc., with written accompaniment and urgent request that the appearant should be pleased to take upon himself the charge of delivering the foresaid letter, medal, box, and bag, to the said Mr. *Leeuwenhoek*, on behalf of Mr. *Cink* and the other Professors of Medicine and Philosophy at Louvain, as an honourable gift and recognition of their appreciation of his (Mr. Leeuwenhoek's) never yet properly appreciated and celebrated discoveries in Natural Philosophy: which foresaid letter, medal, box, and bag, according to the charge aforementioned, on receipt thereof from the appearant, hath been handed over to Mr. *Leeuwenhoek*.

Appeared likewise before us, notary and witnesses, the oft-mentioned Mr. *Anthony Leeuwenhoek*, who declared that he had received each several article, furthermore thanking Mr. *van Loon*.

This document was signed by van Loon, Leeuwenhoek, the two witnesses, and the notary. The silver medal itself can still be seen in the Municipal Museum at Delft, and has been depicted by van Loon[2] and by Haaxman.[3] The former, in his description of it, mentions that he himself handed it over to Leeuwenhoek in person "in a ceremonious manner."

Leeuwenhoek's own acknowledgement of this honour is contained in a letter[4] which he addressed on 12 June 1716 to

---

[1] One of the 43 colleges at Louvain: cf. Ray (1673), p. 13.

[2] G. van Loon (1731), Vol. IV, p. 223.

[3] Haaxman (1875), p. 116. The reproduction is not good, and the Latin motto contains a misprint.

[4] *Send-brief* XXV. Printed in *Brieven* (1718), Vol. IV, p. 220: and in Latin in *Op. Omn.* (*Epist. Physiol.*), Vol. IV, p. 219. [The Latin version of the passage here quoted is not a good translation of the original.] A previous communication with Cinck (through van Loon) is to be found in *Send-brief* IX, 24 Oct. 1713.

"Professors Cink, Narrez,[1] Rega,[2] and other Gentlemen of the College of *The Wild Boar*".[3] In this letter he wrote:

By the hand of Mr. Gerard van Loon, the advocate, I have received an obliging letter from Your Excellencies, dated 24 May last, and a purse made of cloth-of-gold; wherein lieth, in a little black box, a silver medal showing my bust on one side of it, and an emblem with the Town of Delft in the distance on t'other.

Along with this, in further explanation and as a dedication, was enclosed a certain Latin Poem of praise,[4] overflowing with elegant expressions; but notwithstanding my praises be therein sung very high, yet the poet's cleverness deserveth still higher praise for screwing them up to such a pretty pitch: and when I think on the flatteries expressed in your letter, and in the poem, I don't only blush, but my eyes filled with tears too, many a time: especially because my work, which I've done for many a long year, was not pursued in order to gain the praise I now enjoy, but chiefly from a craving after

---

[1] Ursmer Narez (1678-1744), M.D. Louvain (1718), in his day a distinguished man. After devoting himself to religious studies in his youth, he became lecturer on philosophy in the University; and after qualifying as licentiate in medicine (1706) was successively professor of botany, anatomy and surgery, and institutes of medicine. He was also head of the hospital at Louvain. Cf. *Biogr. Nat. Belg.* (1899), XV, 471.

[2] Henri-Joseph Réga (1690-1754), M.D. Louvain (1718). Entered the University of Louvain—where he was born and died—in 1707, and became licentiate in medicine in 1712. He was afterwards professor of chemistry (1716), anatomy (1718), and clinical medicine (1719), and is an influential and outstanding figure in the history of medicine in Belgium. Cf. *Biogr. Nat. Belg.* (1903), XVII, 842.

[3] *'t wilt Swijn* (= *Het wilde Zwijn* or *Het Varken*). There were formerly four principal schools of philosophy in the University of Louvain—each having a particular name and symbol. The members of "The Wild Boar" or "*Collège du Porc*" took theirs from a sign-board opposite the house where they first assembled in 1430. Cinck and van Loon (who was his pupil) both belonged to this "college" or "pedagogy", whose fellows were known by the apparently uncomplimentary title of "Porkers" (*Porcenses*). Cf. Ray (1673, pp. 15-17), and S. v. Rooijen (1904).

[4] Composed by J. G. Kerkherdere: *vide infra*.

knowledge, which I notice resides in me more than in most other men. And therewithal, whenever I found out anything remarkable, I have thought it my duty to put down my discovery on paper, so that all ingenious people might be informed thereof.

In conformity with the foregoing sentiments, our octogenarian microscopist here proceeds to record still further discoveries which need not now detain us. But in his next published letter, which was addressed to the writer[1] of the panegyric poem just mentioned, he makes a remark which is worth quotation. In this letter, after giving thanks for the Latin verses in his honour, Leeuwenhoek adds[2]:

> I always know myself well enough to realize that I'm not worthy of the hundredth part of the expressions you make about my poor work: for it springs only from an inclination I have to inquire into the beginnings of created things, in so far as 'twas ever possible for me to do so. . . . .

And he then delivers to the uninterested Kerkherdere a lengthy disquisition (occupying some 18 printed pages) on his latest botanical observations.

Another letter, written a few months later in the same year, gives some particulars of Leeuwenhoek's health at this period (1716). This letter was sent not to the Royal Society nor to Louvain but to Dr Abraham van Bleys-wyk[3]

---

[1] "*Den Heere J: G: Kerkherdere, syner Keyserlyke en Koninglyke Majesteyts Historicus.*"—Jan Gerard Kerkherdere (1677-1738) of Louvain was a theologian, grammarian, and classical scholar. By all accounts he possessed a special aptitude for writing Latin verses, which he was able to produce with great facility on all ceremonious occasions. He was appointed historiographer to the Emperor Joseph I in 1708. See *N. Nederl. Biogr. Woordenb.* (1924), VI, 878; and *Biogr. Nat. Belg.* (1886-7), IX; also *Nouv. Biogr. Gén.* (Hoefer), *sub voce* "Kerckherdère."

[2] Translated from *Send-brief* XXVI. 22 June 1716. Published in *Brieven* (1718), Vol. IV, p. 232; and in Latin in *Op. Omn.* (*Epist. Physiol.*), Vol. IV, p. 230.

[3] Abraham van Bleyswijk [*alias* Bleiswijk, Bleyswijck, etc.] was M.D., and *lector anatomicus* at Delft—as L. himself informs us. (Cf. *Send-brief* XXXVI. 26 May 1717.) He was a pupil of Boerhaave, and took his

of Delft — whom he calls his "nephew"[1] — and is as follows[2]:

> When I had the honour of being visited by yourself and Professors Boerhaave[3] and Ruysch,[4] who took delight in some of my discoveries; as Mr Boerhaave was taking his leave, and wishing me health and long life, I made objection to him that I couldn't go on much longer; because, in view of my advanced age, my insides (meaning the guts) were just about worn out. But as it was time for the Gentlemen to be off, my further reasonings were interrupted: wherefore I now take the liberty of explaining my last attack to you.
>
> 'Tis now above a sennight ago that I was very short of breath, which was accompanied by a tightness of the chest,[5] pain (as I imagine) in the diaphragm and in the stomach, and a rising of the gorge. Accordingly, I ordered them to fetch me some warm water, to help me

---

degree at Leyden with a dissertation "*qua in praxi felicitas mechanicorum vindicatur*" (4°. Lugd. Bat. 1708). Little else now appears to be known about him: he is not mentioned in *N. Nederl. Biogr. Woordenb.* or by Hirsch. Banga (1868, pp. 614, 869) who also notes the foregoing particulars adds that Bleyswijk helped L. in his anatomical studies—a statement for which he gives no evidence, and which may be questioned. It seems probable that Abraham was a kinsman of Dirk Evertsz. v. B. who published the well-known description of Delft (1667).

[1] *Neef*—a term which (like "cousin" in English) did not at that date necessarily denote the relationship now implied. It was commonly bestowed on any kinsman.

[2] *Send-brief* XXVII, 17 Sept. 1716. Printed in *Brieven* (1718), Vol. IV, p. 254: *Op. Omn.* (*Epist. Physiol.*), Vol. IV, p. 250. No MS. and not in *Phil. Trans.* I translate the whole letter—relying chiefly on the Dutch printed version.

[3] Herman Boerhaave. See p. 296, note 6, *infra*.

[4] Frederik Ruijsch (1638-1731), the celebrated anatomist and injector: Professor at Amsterdam. For his life see Banga (1868, p. 514 *sq.*), Scheltema (1886), and *N. Nederl. Biogr. Woordenb.* (1914), III, 1108. He was elected F.R.S. in 1715 (not 1720, as stated by Banga).

[5] *benautheyt* Dutch ed. *pectoris angustia* Lat.—The "shortness of breath" and "tightness of the chest" here mentioned in the originals are vulgar expressions usually denoting *asthma*. Cf. Blankaart (1748) and Gabler's *Woordenboek*.

to be sick: and no sooner had I drunk the warm water, than I vomited, and that very easily. Soon after I was sick again with great violence, so that the food I brought up (as they told me) came out of my mouth and nose: but I knew not what I was doing. When I came to myself, I examined the stuff I had cast up: and I found it was not only the food I'd taken the evening before, but even what I'd had the previous mid-day.

When I let my thoughts run regarding this, I imagine that the cause of my attack was as follows: The membranes, whereof the coats of the guts are composed, are so made that they have divers motions, in order to push the chyle, that's in them, onwards towards the outfall[1]: to bring which about, a continual increase of contraction[2] of the guts is needful, as long as there remaineth any chyle in 'em: and if there be no chyle in the guts, they stay at rest. And in promoting this pushing-on of the chyle, the bile, which is poured into the gut, helps not a little: for the bile congeals in the gut into sharp particles.

During this attack I was very costive, just as I had been for a good month previous, notwithstanding I was taking only bland food: and a full three days passed ere the chyle brought me to stool.[3]

I'm therefore sure there was no proper motion in my guts, and that the gut lying next the stomach was stuffed with food, or chyle; wherefore the stomach was also stopt with food: for if the guts don't lie still, the stomach strives to unburden itself of the food that's entered it, by squeezing itself together: so that I'm sure the stomach,

---

[1] *afgang* orig. [=*evacuatio intestinorum*]. The Latin translator evaded the word, merely saying that the chyle is pushed "*deorsum*". Chyle = chyme: see note 5 on p. 284 *infra*.

[2] Meaning *peristalsis*.

[3] This paragraph is so paraphrased in the Latin version that its import is rather obscure. The Dutch is particularly frank.

in a well set-up body, must so contract, that how little food soever be in it, 'tis ever full.

The stomach being now overladen with food, and unable to get rid of it because the gut is full of chyle; and these long strainings of the stomach being against its natural shape: it arouses, by its strivings, a pain in the midriff (which they call the *Diafragma*), which is thereby hindered in its continual motion; which also stirs up a second pain. The midriff accordingly presseth on the lung; and thereby, the lung is prevented from performing its office. And this being so, there must follow a great tightness and a great vomiting: and such violence is done to the body, to the stomach as well as to the guts, that the chyle in the gut is thereby pushed onwards; so that there followeth a motion in the gut itself. And, as I imagine, when the gut is full up, the gall-bladder can't empty its bile into the gut, yet with these onpushings of the chyle it pours a great quantity of bile into the guts; therefore on the day when this happens, four or five stools are brought off, whereas on the other days there ensueth a constipation.

You have here the feeble notions I've hammered out of my last distemper. Pray take it not amiss that I take upon myself to argufy about it.

The foregoing lines are not only an interesting record of Leeuwenhoek's bodily condition in his 84th year, but also a typical example of his own particular system of physiology.

References to his age and his infirmities become more numerous with advancing years. He continues to make and record observations and speculations, and to promise more: but he often begs the Royal Society to make allowance for his senescence, and sometimes qualifies his promises with expressions such as "if my health permits".[1] At the end of 1717 Leeuwenhoek thought his own end was near; and he therefore inscribed a "last letter" to the Society, as an envoy to the

---

[1] *met gesondheijt*, etc.

final collective edition of his works. Concluding this letter he wrote[1]:

> Methinks these will be the last observations I shall be able to send to you honourable Gentlemen; because my hands grow weak, and suffer from a little shakiness, which is due to my far advanced years, a good 85 having passed by me. And so I send you with this my deep thankfulness, because in the year 1679[2] you were so kind as to elect me, quite beyond my competence, a Fellow of the most worthy College of the Royal Society; and to send me a Diploma, together with two letters from the Secretaries of the Society, which likewise made known to me my election, by all the votes of the Fellows, then gathered together at a very full meeting.[3]
>
> I thank you also for the *Philosophical Transactions*, which Your Excellencies have been so good as to send me from time to time.
>
> For all these honours and gifts aforesaid, I herewith convey to you my gratitude once more.

But the end was not yet. After writing the foregoing lines, Leeuwenhoek lived for nearly six years more; and during this period he sent the Society no less than 18 more letters (including 2 posthumous epistles), containing a variety of new microscopical discoveries. In a postscript to one of these letters he says[4]:

---

[1] From *Letter dated 20 November 1717*. To the Royal Society. There is no MS. of this letter in the Roy. Soc. collection. It was not published in the *Phil. Trans.*, but was printed in both Dutch and Latin: *Send-brieven* (1718), No. XLVI, p. 451; *Opera Omnia* [*Epist. Physiol.*] (1719), Vol. IV, No. XLVI, p. 437. I translate from these published versions.—It is remarkable that Miall (1912, p. 201) and several other students of L. have assumed that this was really his last letter.

[2] 1680, according to present-day reckoning (N.S.). Cf. p. 48 *supra*.

[3] Cf. p. 48, note 6, *supra*.

[4] From *Letter dated 24 January 1721*. To the Royal Society. MS. Roy. Soc. (The postscript is in L.'s own hand, but the letter itself is in different handwriting.) Original in Dutch—from which I translate. An English version of this letter was published in *Phil. Trans.* (1721), Vol. XXXI, No. 367, p. 134. It is not in the Dutch or Latin collected works.

> I humbly beg that you will make some allowance for me, my years having mounted to a great height. A certain Gentleman, visiting me a few months ago, besought me to make some further discoveries; adding, that those fruits which ripen in the autumn last the longest.[1] And this is now indeed the Autumn of my days, for they have today mounted up to 88¼ years.

Yet only three months later he wrote with characteristic confidence—after describing some observations on the structure of peas:[2]

> 'Tis my intention to inquire into these marvellous structures more narrowly, just for my own amusement.[3]

Next year, after communicating other discoveries, Leeuwenhoek sent the Society still further observations together with the following unpublished personal remarks[4]:

> The learned Dr James Jurin, Secretary of the Royal Society,[5] writes to me from London in your name, on 22 Feb. 172½, with so many expressions of satisfaction at my discoveries, which I sent to your Fellows, that I stood all abashed when the letter was read to me; nay, my eyes filled with tears at all the great expressions, and

---

[1] The same remark is made by L. in his *Send-brief* XXXII, 2 March 1717, to Abraham v. Bleyswijk (printed in Dutch and Latin works): cf. *Brieven*, IV, 317.

[2] From *Letter dated 11 April 1721*. To the Royal Society. MS. Roy. Soc. Printed (in English) in *Phil. Trans.* (1721), Vol. XXXI, No. 368, p. 190. Not in Dutch or Latin collected works.

[3] *alleen voor mijn plaijsier* MS.

[4] Translated from *Letter dated 21 April 1722*. To the Royal Society. MS. Roy. Soc. Partially published (in English) in *Phil. Trans.* (1722), Vol. XXXII, No. 371, p. 72. Not in Dutch or Latin collective works. Original in Dutch, in L.'s own hand—showing evident signs of senility.

[5] *De seer geleerde Heer Jacob Jurin, Secretaris van Hare Hoog Edele Heeren Vergadering* MS. It is impossible to translate these merely formal expressions into literal English without making them appear rather ridiculous, and so spoiling their intention: I therefore paraphrase.—James Jurin (1684-1750) was a physician—sometime Fellow of Trinity College, Cambridge, and President of the Royal College of Physicians of London. He was elected F.R.S. in 1717, and became Secretary on 30 Nov. 1721. His life will be found in the *Dict. Nat. Biogr.*

respect that they have for my work, which I accomplish alone by my own impulse and inclination. For no money could ever have driven me to make discoveries, and I'm only working out as 'twere an impulse that was born in me, and I imagine I never meet with any other people who would spend so much time and work in searching into the things of Nature. And withal I had great pleasure too at hearing that the learned and curious Mr James Jurin's investigations have made him eye-witness of my discoveries.[1]

The same Gentleman also said, that your Fellows very earnestly desired, if 'twere possible, that my observations should be confirmed and cleared up by repeating them, so that the mouth of the unbelieving might be stifled.

On this matter I would reply to your Honourable Fellows, that I have indeed inquired into many things of one and the same nature, but not thought it needful to describe them all, because the one must imply the others. And those things that are not easy to believe, I have left standing for days, nay years, before the magnifying-glass, to let them be seen by as many people as possible; like the vessels in the nerves, which have lain so long before the magnifying-glass, that they have been all eaten up by that little creature the Mite.[2]

By this time Leeuwenhoek was an old and sick and dying man. But despite his age and his infirmities he still continued to make observations and send letters to the Royal Society. In two letters, written in March and May 1723, he even gave the Society an account of the illness from which he suffered in the last year of his life. Both letters were translated into Latin, and they were the last he lived to sign: their Dutch originals are now lost. As the relevant passages are of great personal interest, I shall quote them at length. On 19 March

---

[1] The whole of this paragraph is ungrammatical and very loosely constructed in the original.

[2] The two foregoing paragraphs were paraphrased—not translated—in the *Phil. Trans.*, though their sense is there conveyed correctly.

1723, after discussing the dimensions of blood-corpuscles, he wrote:[1]

> This also I have to add: that notwithstanding my advanced age cannot but hinder my sight, yet my right eye, to my great annoyance, groweth somewhat dim. I think this comes to pass for the reason that sundry blood-corpuscles, floating in the crystalline humor,[2] stray in front of my sight; some whereof being joined together in no or only an irregular order, with others floating separately, cause an appearance of little clouds[3] in my eye. Moreover, as I generally use my right eye, I readily shut my left eye whilst making observations, wherefore my eyesight is dimmer than 'twas wont to be.
>
> Not so long ago, to wit this last January, I was seized with a violent motion about that great and necessary organ we call the diaphragm: indeed, 'twas such that those present were not a little alarmed at it. When the motion abated, and I sought to know the name of this distemper, the Physician who was at hand replied that it was *a palpitation of the heart*. But I thought the

---

[1] To Dr James Jurin, *Sec. R.S.* MS.Roy.Soc. Printed in *Phil. Trans.* (1723), Vol. XXXII, No. 377, p. 341; not printed in Dutch or Latin collected works. I translate from the original Latin MS.—inscribed in an unknown hand (not Hoogvliet's).

[2] *humor crystallinus*—the old name for what is now called the "crystalline lens" (cf. Blankaart, 1748, *sub voce*). This structure was described in detail, in many animals, by L.; and he knew that it was solid and stratified and that it contained no blood-vessels or corpuscles. Consequently, I cannot help thinking that in his original words—here mistranslated (?) into Latin—he must really have referred to the *vitreous* humor: which would obviously be nearer the truth.

[3] *mibeculae* Phil. Trans. *nubeculae* MS. The printed word is meaningless, and greatly puzzled me until I discovered that it was merely a misreading of the original. L. was here referring, of course, to the familiar entoptic phenomena called *muscae volitantes*—now known to arise from shadows cast on the retina by strands in the vitreous humor. (Cf. Brewerton, 1930.) These appearances were first described by L. in his *Letter 41*, 14 Apr. 1684, to F. Aston (*Ondervind. & Beschouw.*, 1684, p. 19; also in Latin editions; incomplete English translations in *Phil. Trans.* XIV, 790 [=780], and Hoole, I, 241).

Physician was wrong; for whilst the motion lasted, I oft put my hand on my pulse, and could feel no quickening of its beat. This violent motion, returning at intervals, lasted for about three days; during which time my stomach and guts ceased to perform their office and motion, so that I was verily persuaded I stood at death's door.

In my opinion there was some obstruction, not less than a crown piece in bigness,[1] stopping my diaphragm.

On 31 May 1723 Leeuwenhoek actually sent the Royal Society a description of the histology of the diaphragm, which he had meanwhile studied (in sheep and oxen) in order to support the opinions expressed in the foregoing letter. And at the end of his account of the various muscles and tendons and vessels observable in the midriff he added:[2]

Accordingly, the oftener I recall the foresaid distemper which seized me last winter, and which I attributed mostly to my diaphragm, the more am I of opinion that our Physicians are mistaken when they call that commotion, which we sometimes feel in the region of our chest, a *palpitation of the heart.* For my part, I am persuaded that such palpitations arise from a disorder of the Diaphragm; howbeit this may be brought about either by a deficiency of diet, or by obstruction of those blood-vessels which run through the diaphragm in great plenty. Such an obstruction can easily excite convulsive motions in the tendons aforesaid; and I believe this was the very cause of my own complaint.

Towards the middle of August, 1723, Leeuwenhoek had another seizure; and now he was indeed—as he himself

---

[1] *non minorem nummo imperiali* MS. I take *nummus imperialis* to mean a *rijksdaalder* (= 2½ florins), which was roughly of the size and value of an English 5-shilling piece.

[2] From *Letter dated 31 May 1723.* To the Royal Society. MS.Roy.Soc. Printed in full in *Phil. Trans.* (1723), Vol. XXXII, No. 379, p. 400. Not in Dutch or Latin collective editions. Original MS. in Latin, from which I translate.

realized—at death's door. Yet even Death's proximity could not abate his scientific zeal. Boitet the publisher—who cannot always be trusted, but who here probably wrote from recent personal knowledge—has left it on record that he continued his researches to the very end. He says:[1]

> Our Leeuwenhoek, who had a sound mind in a sound body, felt however about a year before his death that his bodily powers were getting noticeably weaker, owing to an asthmatical chest and other symptoms: nevertheless, he continued his course cheerfully to the end of his life along the track of Science, to win a deathless name at last, though forsooth he had won the race long before during his lifetime. Six-and-thirty hours before his death, when his limbs were already growing numb, the fire of his ardour glowed still so bright, that, with lips stammering and well-nigh stiff, he directed his thoughts to be set down on paper regarding a kind of sand which a certain distinguished gentleman, a director of the East-India Company, had handed over to him, to find out whether any gold were concealed therein.

And this account is supported from another quarter. As he lay dying, Leeuwenhoek summoned his friend Dr Jan Hoogvliet[2] to his bedside, and requested him to translate a couple of letters[3] into Latin and send them to the Royal Society as a parting gift. The good doctor did so, and dispatched

---

[1] Boitet (1729), p. 768—translated.

[2] Little seems to be now known about Johannes Hoogvliet, who is not mentioned by Banga or Hirsch or in the *N. Nederl. Biogr. Woordenb.* or any other available works of reference. I have been able to ascertain only that he was a surgeon practising at Delft, and that he once published a work on wounds (*Konst om wonden te schouwen*, etc. 8°. Rotterdam, 1749). He was probably a kinsman (? brother) of the poet Arnold Hoogvliet (1687-1763) of Vlaardingen, who wrote the panegyric poem prefixed to the *Send-brieven*, and whose father—a shipowner and sheriff—was also called Johannes.

[3] On "corpuscles in the blood and in the dregs of wine" and "the generation of animals and palpitation of the diaphragm." Published posthumously in *Phil. Trans.* (1724), Vol. XXXII, No. 380, pp. 436-440: not in Dutch or Latin collective works.

them with the following covering note from himself to the Secretary[1]:

> Our venerable old Leeuwenhoek, being already in the throes of death, though none the less mindful of his art, ordered me to be called to him; and raising his eyes, now heavy with death,[2] kept asking me in half-broken words if I would translate these two letters out of our native tongue into Latin, and send them, most distinguished Sir, to you. In obedience, therefore, to these commands of so great a man, with whom I had been for some years on terms of most intimate friendship[3], I can do no less than send you, most learned Sir, this final gift of my dying and most dear friend: hoping that these his last efforts will prove acceptable to you.
>
> I pray that the Supreme Judge of all things may long bless Your Excellency, and the Royal Society: Farewell.

Leeuwenhoek's death was first made known to the Fellows of the Royal Society by a letter from the minister of his church—the Rev. Mr Peter Gribius.[4] His communication

---

[1] MS. Roy. Soc., No. 1413; *H. 3.* 112. Joannes Hoogvlietius to J. Jurin, *Sec. R.S.*, 4 September 1723. Printed fully (except last sentence) in *Phil. Trans.* (1724), XXXII, 435. My translation is made from the original MS. (very clearly written in good classical Latin), whose endorsement shows that the letter was read at a meeting of the Society on 7 Nov. 1723 [O.S].

[2] *attollensque oculos jam gravatos morte* MS. "*mij met reeds half gebroken oogen aanstarende*" Haaxman (1875, p. 122)—a mistranslation.

[3] *quo abhinc jam aliquot annos usus fueram familiarissime* MS. Haaxman, *loc. cit.*, also misconstrues these words, which do not imply that Hoogvliet had been accustomed to translate L.'s letters into Latin for several years. The expression "*utor aliquo*" means "I enjoy the friendship of someone": cf. Cicero—*His Fabriciis semper est usus Oppianicus familiarissime* (*pro Cluentio*, XVI, 461, 46). Moreover, no other known letters of L. are extant in Hoogvliet's handwriting.

[4] He styled himself "*Petrus Gribius, Ecclesiae Delphensis pastor senex.*" Gribius [*alias* Grybius] was born at Middelburg in 1651, and died at Delft in 1739. He was educated in the Latin Schools of Amsterdam, Utrecht, and Leyden, and before taking holy orders visited Oxford and Cambridge. He became minister of the New Church at Delft in 1681 (Boitet, 1729, p. 441), and retired in 1734. Some of his sermons and essays have been published, and his portrait was painted by Thomas v. d. Wilt (cf. p. 345). Further details of his life will be found in an article contributed by F. S. Knipsheer to the *N. Nederl. Biogr. Woordenb.* (1924), VI, 634.

has never been published, and even its existence has hitherto been overlooked. Yet it is a document of the greatest interest: for it not only announced Leeuwenhoek's death, but also recorded the exact date thereof, and gave a few particulars regarding his last illness and the cause of his decease—as determined by his medical advisors. I shall therefore give this letter in its entirety. The original is written in Latin, and addressed to Dr James[1] Jurin, Secretary of the Royal Society. Dated from Delft, 30 August 1723, it runs as follows:[2]

> I venture to interrupt you, most distinguished Sir, in your very urgent engagements and duties, solely because I am moved thereto by the tears of Maria, the only daughter of her great father Antony van Leeuwenhoek; who, while he neither feared nor desired his last day, peacefully concluded it upon the 26th of August; being then over ninety, and thus, having reached a rare old age, neither unripe nor half-ripe, though verily more than mature. For 'tis with man as with pear or apple, on a tree laden with fruits, some whereof it letteth fall thickly and perforce, while others, when they be more than ripe, drop singly of their own accord.[3] As the Poet[4] elegantly saith:
>
> —— *Κῆρες ἐφεστᾶσιν θανάτοιο*
> *Μυρίαι, ἅς οὐκ ἔστι φυγεῖν βροτὸν, οὐδ' ὑπολῆξαι.*[5]

---

[1] Gribius wrongly addressed him as "John" (*Nobilissimo Viro Joanni Jurin Regiae Societati a secretis Illustrissimo*).

[2] MS. Roy. Soc., No. 1214; *G.2.* 3. The translation of this letter has been by no means easy: for it contains several classical quotations and veiled allusions, and some unusual words and expressions—designed, apparently, to show off the writer's scholarship. Nevertheless, its latinity seems not altogether irreproachable. In tracing the references to Homer and Statius I have been greatly assisted by Prof. D'Arcy Thompson, F.R.S.

[3] The foregoing lines in the MS. are apparently a paraphrase of Cicero: "*quasi poma ex arboribus, cruda si sunt, vi avelluntur, si matura et cocta, decidunt*" (*de Sen.* lib. XIX, § 71 *ad finem*). Some modern texts read "*vix evelluntur*," but Gribius's words indicate that he was familiar with the older version.

[4] Homer, *Ilias* XII, 326-7.

[5] "Ten thousand fates of death do every way beset us, and these no

Yet 'tis our duty to submit to the wise dispensations of God, Whom we wrongfully defraud of His rights unless we humbly suffer each one of ours to live and die according to His will.

The notion possessed our good old man that he lay a-dying of a distemper of his diaphragm, though in fact 'twas of his lungs; and their gradual obstruction, turning slowly into a suppuration, reached such a pitch that he cast up purulent sputa and died when the lung had festered, on the sixth day after he took to his bed.[1] So at least say our Physicians, who are highly skilled in such matters: for my part, I know nought of diseases; a cobbler should stick to his lasts.[2]

A little cabinet, furnished with some most select glasses (commonly called Μικροσκόπια[3]), to be given after his death to the Royal Society, will be sent to you within six or seven weeks by his daughter, as she hath informed me.

Amongst us he has left a reputation truly good, and enshrined in the Temple of Memory, by virtue of his indefatigable inquiries into Nature. To you, most noble Sir, who hold an honorable office, and one worthy of your deserts, I wish many a long year of life, that for the

---

mortal may escape nor avoid" (translation of Lang, Leaf, and Myers). The last word of the quotation is given wrongly by Gribius: it should be ὑπαλύξαι. (Cf. *Ilias* ed. Doederlein, Lips.-Lond. 1863.)

[1] As the foregoing lines constitute the only known record of the cause of L.'s death, the reader will doubtless desire to see the original words. The MS. says: *Bonum senem tenuit opinio se moriturum diaphragmatis vitio, sed pulmonum fuit, eorumque lenta obstructio sensim in suppurationem vergens, adeo ut phlegmata purulenta ejecerit, et suppurato pulmone obierit, sexto postquam decubuit die.* It is clear that L. died of broncho-pneumonia: and there is much evidence (largely unpublished) in his later letters to show that he had suffered for many years from chronic bronchitis.

[2] *ne sutor ultra crepidas* MS. This familiar proverb occurs in several forms, and according to Pliny originated in a saying of the painter Apelles. Pliny's version is "*ne supra crepidam sutor judicaret*" (*Hist. Nat.* XXXV, [10] 36. Fol. Genevae [1582] p. 629).

[3] = Microscopes. To write the word thus in Greek—even at that date—was a ridiculous bit of pedantry.

public benefit you may live to equal, or even excel, those grand old men of Troy.[1]

The cabinet of microscopes bequeathed to the Royal Society—referred to in the foregoing letter--had been briefly described by Leeuwenhoek himself twenty-two years earlier. In an unpublished passage in an otherwise published letter to the Society he had written[2]:

I have a very little Cabinet, lacquered black and gilded, that comprehendeth within it five little drawers, wherein lie inclosed 13 long and square little tin cases, which I have covered over with black leather; and in each of these little cases lie two ground magnifying-glasses (making 26 in all), every one of them ground by myself, *and mounted in silver, and furthermore set in silver*, almost all of them in silver that I extracted from the ore, and separated from the gold wherewith it was charged; and therewithal is writ down *what object standeth before each little glass.*

This little Cabinet with the said magnifying-glasses, as I may yet have some use for it, I have committed to my only daughter, bidding her send it to You after my death, in acknowledgement of my gratitude for the honour I have enjoyed and received from Your Excellencies.

On 4 October 1723, Leeuwenhoek's bequest was duly and dutifully dispatched to the Royal Society by his daughter

---

[1] *ut . . . Iliacos aequare senes aut vincere possis* MS. This is apparently borrowed from the hexameter of Statius: "*Iliacos aequare senes, et vincere persta*" (*Silvae*, lib. II, iii, 73). I take it that by these words Gribius meant to say that he hoped Dr Jurin would live long enough to rival, by his scientific performances, the doughty deeds of the heroes of ancient Greece in the field of battle: but the comparison seems somewhat forced, to say the least.

[2] From *Letter 140*. 2 August 1701. MS.Roy.Soc. Printed (Dutch) in *Sevende Vervolg der Brieven* (1702), p. 375; and (Latin) in *Opera Omnia* (*Contin. Arc. Nat.*), Vol. III, p. 355. I translate from the Dutch MS. (Words here italicized were underlined by L. himself in the original.) Although this Letter was not published in the *Phil. Trans.*, the passage here given was translated into English and entered in the Society's Letter-books (Vol. XIII, p. 183), and this entry was long afterwards extracted and printed by Weld (Vol. I, pp. 244-5).

Maria along with two covering letters. One of these was a formal notification in Latin from the Rev. Mr Gribius; the other was a simple Dutch letter from Maria herself. I shall give them both.

Gribius wrote[1]:

In our present scientific age, ὁ Μακαρίτης[2] Antony van Leeuwenhoek considered that what is true in natural philosophy can be most fruitfully investigated by the experimental method, supported by the evidence of the senses; for which reason, by diligence and tireless labour he made with his own hand certain most excellent lenses, with the aid of which he discovered many secrets of Nature, now famous throughout the whole philosophical World: of which sacred apparatus he bequeathed no contemptible a share, inclosed by himself in this little cabinet, to the Royal Society, with no other object than to afford those ingenious and most erudite men a token of his veneration, and as a mark of his gratitude for having been enrolled among their learned Company.

His Daughter (a spinster of excellent repute, who has preferred a single life to matrimony, in order that she might ever continue to attend her father) earnestly begs this one favour: that you disdain not to send back word that this little present hath not gone astray, but is come safe into your hands; which I likewise fully trust was the lot of my own letter[3] written to you, in no joyful spirit, five weeks ago.

I pray God, most illustrious Sir, that He suffer you long to continue shining as a great and singular light and star of the first magnitude to Philosophy.

---

[1] Translated from MS.Roy.Soc., No. 1215; *G.2.* 4. Petrus Gribius, *Eccl. Delph. pastor senex*, to J. Jurin, *Sec. R.S.*; 4 Oct. 1723. Original in Latin: unpublished.

[2] = The blessed (*i.e.* in heaven).

[3] Referring to his communication of 30 August 1723—p. 94 *ante*. From this remark it must be inferred that the Secretary of the Royal Society had neglected to acknowledge Gribius's first epistle.

Maria's letter was very different from the foregoing. It made no pretensions to scientific knowledge or classical scholarship, and was written not in Latin but in homely, illiterate, and even ungrammatical Dutch. It was apparently dictated—not written by herself—for it is inscribed in a handwriting different from the somewhat shaky signature.[1] (Maria was then 67 years of age.) But for all that it is one of the most beautiful and pitiful letters I have ever read—breathing sincerity and filial devotion in every word, and eloquently testifying to Leeuwenhoek's own qualities as a man and father. Maria wrote[2]:

Most excellent Sirs

Instantly upon the sad death of my beloved father Anthonij van Lewenhoek,[3] I took care to have this my[4] loss made known to you by our reverenced and most learned pastor, Peterus Griebius[5]; adding thereto, that after the space of six weeks would be sent to the noble and far famed Royal Society, at London, a little cabinet with magnifying-glasses, made of silver wrought out of the mineral by my dear departed father his very self; which same is now sent to Your Excellencies, even as my late father made it up, with six-and-twenty magnifying-glasses in their little cases: truly in itself a poor present to so celebrated a Royal Society, but meant to betoken my father's deep respect for such a learned Society, whereof my most beloved and dear Father, of blessed

---

[1] Cf. Plate XIII.

[2] MS.Roy.Soc., No. 2137; *L.6.* 38. Maria van Leeuwenhoek to the Royal Society, 4 Oct. 1723. Original in Dutch, from which the above is a translation—and a poor one: for I confess myself incompetent to turn the pathetic but unscholarly expressions of Maria into intelligible modern English faithfully.

[3] So spelled in MS.

[4] In the MS. the words "this my" are reiterated: "*dit mijn mijn dit mijn*"—the second *dit* being scored out. Maria apparently hesitated, in dictating the letter, between saying "*mijn*" or "*dit mijn*": and in her agitation she failed to notice that the word *mijn* was finally left written thrice.

[5] So spelled in MS.

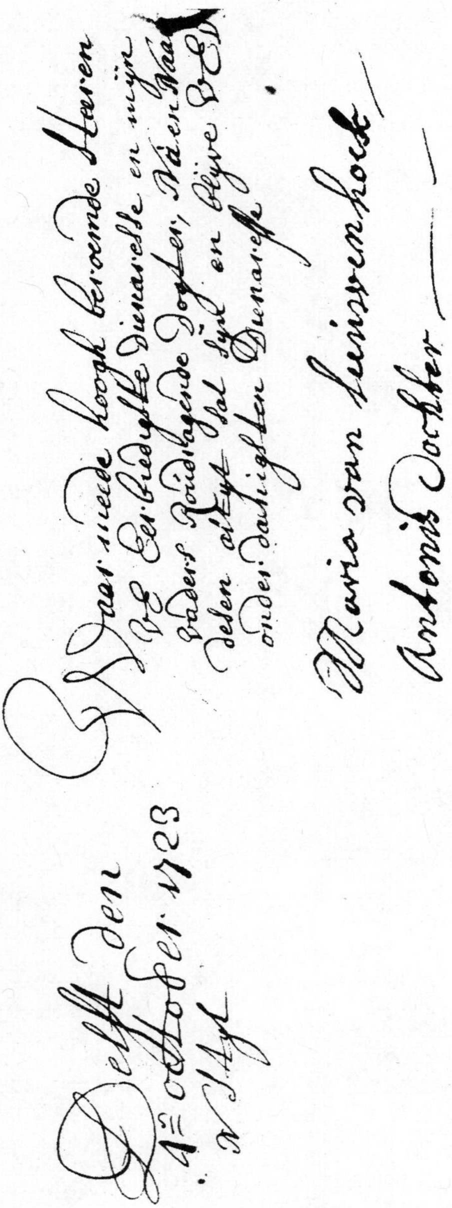

PLATE XIII

Delft den 4en October 1723
n Styl

Waar mede hoogh beroemde Heeren
UE Eerbiedighste dienaresse en mijn
vaders Rouwdragende Dogter, Nä en Vaa
deden altyt sal syn en blyve UEd
onderdanighsten Dienaresse

Maria van Leeuwenhoek

Antonis Dochter

LAST LINES OF MARIA'S LETTER TO THE ROYAL SOCIETY
(4 Oct. 1723): showing her signature—the sole example known.

memory, hath had the honour to have been a fellow-member. Your most humble servitress now begs Your Excellencies, please to be so good as to let me have word whether this trifling gift is come safe into the hands of the far famous College, that I may rest content I have fulfilled my Father's wish.

Wherewith, most famous Gentlemen,
your most respectful Servitress
and my father's Grief-stricken
Daughter now and hereafter
will ever be and remains
Your humble Servant
Maria van Leeuwenhoek
Antoni's daughter

Delft, the
4th October 1723
New Style

This letter needs no comment: it speaks for itself. I need only add here that the little cabinet of microscopes was safely received by the Royal Society: that it was examined and reported upon by the Vice-President, and by one of the Fellows at a later date: that it was treasured by the Society for a century—and then lost.[1] In return for the bequest, the Council in 1724 sent Maria "a handsome silver bowl, bearing the arms of the Society."[2]

Leeuwenhoek was buried in the Old Church of Delft on Sunday the 31st of August 1723—"with 16 pall-bearers and with coaches and tollings of the bell at 3 intervals"[3]—and his grave was finally closed two days later (2 September).[4] He was first laid to rest at a spot in the north church (section 19, grave 12) where his second wife had previously been interred (1694)[5]: but in 1739 his daughter Maria erected a monument

---

[1] Cf. p. 314 *infra*.

[2] Weld (1848), Vol. I, p. 245. This also has disappeared.

[3] "*met 16 d^rs. en met koetsen en 3 poose luijens*" (Begrafenisregister Oude Kerk. No. 138 Archief Delft). I am indebted to Dr Schierbeek and Mevr. Bouricius for this extract. From other entries in the Archives it appears that L. was actually entitled to have 18 pall-bearers.

[4] This accounts for the different dates of burial given by Schierbeek (1930)—31 Aug. and 2 Sept. 1723—as he informs me in a letter.

[5] Discovered by Jhr. mr. E. A. van Beresteijn, and communicated to Dr Bouricius—from whose posthumous papers the details given above have been published by Dr Schierbeek (1930).

to his memory—on the north side of the tower, in the north transept—and the two bodies were then transferred to its foot (section 22, graves 14 and 15), where they now lie. Maria was buried in the same sepulchre[1] on 30 April 1745.

The tomb of Leeuwenhoek is shown in Plate XV, which is reproduced from an old engraving.[2] It is little altered at the present day.[3] On the stone pedestal, which rests upon two plinths and is surmounted by a white marble skull and crossbones flanked by two spheres, is the inscription:

PATRI CHARISSIMO HOC MONUMENTUM FILIA
MARIA A LEEUWENHOEK MOERENS P.[4]

On the obelisk rising from the pedestal there rests a white marble urn supporting a gilt torch; and a circular plaque of similar marble, surrounded by decorative ribbon-work, is affixed to the front. The plaque bears a profile portrait of Leeuwenhoek. On the front of the obelisk is inscribed:

PIAE ET AET. MEM.
ANTONII A LEEUWENHOEK
REG. ANGL. SOCIET. MEMBRI
QUI NATURAE PENETRALIA ET PHYSICES ARCANA
MICROSCOPIIS AB IPSO INVENTIS ET MIRABILI ARTE FABRICATIS
ASSIDUO STUDIO ET PERSCRUTATIONE DETEGENDO ET IDIOMATE BELGICO
DESCRIBENDO DE TOTO TERRARUM ORBE OPTIME MERUIT.
NAT. DELPH. XXIV OCT. Aº. MVIᶜXXXII
IBIDEMQUE DENAT. XXVI AUGUSTI Aº MVIIᶜXXIII.[5]

---

[1] This tomb was purchased by L. himself on 8 June 1686 (*fide* Schierbeek, 1930).

[2] Supplement to Boitet (1729)—not found in all copies of this work.

[3] The only recent description of the tomb is that of Harris (1921), who appears to have visited it under unfavourable conditions and was consequently displeased. But his knowledge of L. was obviously very superficial, and his paper—in a popular journal—cannot be taken seriously.

[4] P. = *posuit.* "To her most beloved Father this monument his daughter Maria van Leeuwenhoek mourning has erected."

[5] "To the fond and everlasting memory of Antony van Leeuwenhoek, Fellow of the English Royal Society, who, by detecting through diligent application and scrutiny the mysteries of Nature and the secrets of natural philosophy by means of microscopes invented and marvellously constructed by himself, and by describing them in the Dutch dialect, has earned the

THE OLD CHURCH OF DELFT
West Front—viewed from *Oude Delft*.
From an engraving by P. Smith after C. Decker, published by Boitet (1729).

facing p. 100

T.J. del.
GRAFNAALD van den heer ANTHONI van LEEUWENHOEK
IN DE OUDE KERK TE DELFT.

LEEUWENHOEK'S TOMB IN THE OLD CHURCH

From an engraving by J. C. Philips (1740) after a drawing by the designer, T. Jelgersma.

facing p.

The monument is set in an arched niche, doubly recessed, the pilasters of the inner arch bearing two stone lamps and its apex the veiled head of a woman. The whole is protected by a decorative[1] iron railing. On the floor, in front of the railing, is a stone slab covering the tomb. Upon this is cut:

HIER RUST
ANTHONY VAN LEEWENHOEK,
OUTSTE LIT VAN DE KOONINCKLIJKE SOSYTEYT IN LONDE,
GEBOOREN BINNEN DE STADT DELFT OP DEN 24STEN OCTOBER 1632,
EN OVERLEEDEN OP DEN 26STEN AUGUSTY 1723,
OUT SYNDE 90 JAAR, 10 MAANDE EN 2 DAGEN.[2]

This is followed by some verses "to the reader" composed by Leeuwenhoek's young friend and fellow-townsman Hubert Poot (1689-1733)—the rustic poet who has been called the "Bobbie Burns of Holland" (see Plate XVI)—which run thus:

HEEFT ELK, O WANDELAER, ALOM
ONTZAGH VOOR HOOGEN OUDERDOM
EN WONDERBARE GAVEN,
SOO SET EERBIEDIGH HIER UW' STAP:
HIER LEGT DE GRYSE WEETENSCHAP
IN **LEEWENHOEK** BEGRAVEN.[3]

---

highest approbation of the whole world. Born at Delft 24 October 1632, and died in the same place 26 August 1723."—The final words "*de toto* . . . *meruit*" are curiously mistranslated "by which he astonished the whole world" by Wildeman (1903, p. 48).

[1] Morre (1912), following Wildeman (1903), describes this as "elegant": but Harris (1921) regards it as particularly nasty. I call it "decorative" in a descriptive sense: the reader can form his own estimate of its artistic merits from the illustration.

[2] "Here lieth Anthony van Leewenhoek, oldest Fellow of the Royal Society in London, born within the town of Delft on the 24th of October 1632, and deceased on the 26th of August 1723, being aged 90 years, 10 months, and 2 days." Note the spelling of L.'s name and the rest of the inscription—which has been "corrected" by every previous transcriber.

[3] "Since everyone, O traveller,
Great age respecteth, everywhere,
And gifts of wondrous merit:
So here all reverently tread,
Where Science old and gray of head
In LEEWENHOEK lies buried."

At the foot of the tombstone has been added an inscription stating that along with her father lies "Maria van Leeuwenhoek, his daughter, born at Delft the 22nd of September 1656, and passed away the 25th of April 1745." There is also a carved flying eagle, clutching a shield on which the coat-of-arms of the Leeuwenhoeks was probably once emblazoned.[1]

The following entry[2] relating to Leeuwenhoek's tomb is to be found in the Archives of Delft, from which it was extracted and published by Soutendam (1875)[3]:

> In the North Transept of the Old Church of Delft, against the wall of the tower, was erected in the year 1739, at the expense of Mistress *Maria van Leeuwenhoek*, in memory of her late father the world-famed Mr. *Anthony van Leeuwenhoek* (son of Phillip van Leeuwenhoek, Anthony's son, and of Margaret Bel van den Bergh, James's daughter), under the supervision and care of Mr. *William van der Lely*, at that time Councillor and Treasurer of the town of Delft, an Obelisk, simply but bravely and elegantly designed by the artist *Taco Jelgersma*, at Haarlem, and wholly wrought by the stone-mason *Gerrit van der Giesen*.

There is little more to add: but after recording the handiwork of Mr Gerard van der Giesen, the good Dutch mason, I should like to recall a few lines left by the more sensitive hand of an Englishman, Martin Folkes[4] *Esq., Vice-President of the Royal Society*, in his report on the microscopes bequeathed to the Society by Leeuwenhoek. Folkes's account of these

---

[1] See p. 305 *infra*.

[2] I translate Soutendam's transcription—not having seen the original. It is not unlikely that our famous "English" artist Sir Peter Lely was a kinsman of the Willem van der Lely, sometime Burgomaster of Delft, whose signature was appended to this document.

[3] I give it in full, because the information supplied by Boitet (1729, supplement), Haaxman (1875), Morre (1912), and others, is incomplete.

[4] Martin Folkes (1690-1754) was an antiquary, and a distinguished man in his day. He studied in France (Saumur) and later at Cambridge. He was elected F.R.S. in 1714, Vice-President of the Society in 1723, and was President from 1741 to 1753: he was also President of the Society of Antiquaries (1750) and a member of the *Académie des Sciences* (1742). Cf. *Dict. Nat. Biogr.* and *Rec. Roy. Soc.*

HUBERT POOT (1689-1733)

Who wrote Leeuwenhoek's epitaph, and addressed several panegyric poems to him in his lifetime.

From an engraving by J. Houbraken after an oil-painting by Thomas van der Wilt (who probably drew some of Leeuwenhoek's illustrations), prefixed to Poot's *Poems* (1722).

instruments will be considered later [1]: I shall here give only what he says about their maker, because it shows how Leeuwenhoek was regarded by the Society at that date and will serve as a funeral oration—for want of any other or better. In the *Philosophical Transactions* for November and December, 1723, Folkes wrote [2]:

> It is now above 50 Years, since the late *Mr. Leeuwenhoek* first began his Correspondence with the Royal Society; when he was recommended by *Dr. Regnerus de Graaf*, as a Person already considerable by his Microscopical Discoveries, made with Glasses contrived by himself, and excelling even those of the famous *Eustachio Divini*, so much talk'd of in the learned World: And as he has ever since that Time apply'd himself, with the greatest Diligence and Success, to the same Sort of Observations, no Doubt can be made of the Excellency of those Instruments he so long us'd, so much improv'd, and upon the fullest Experience so often commended in his Letters; great Part of which, at his Decease, he thought fit to bequeath to this Society, for whom he ever express'd the greatest Esteem and Respect.
>
> He had, indeed, intimated this Design in several of his Letters, and in his last Will and Testament [3] gave Orders, that the Glasses should be delivered as soon as conveniently might be after his Decease; which was accordingly done, by the Directions of his surviving Daughter, *Mrs.*[4] *Maria Van Leeuwenhoek*, to whose great Care we are oblig'd, for the safe and speedy Delivery of this very curious and valuable Present.[5]
>
> . . . .

---

[1] See p. 314 *sq.*, *infra.* [2] See Folkes (1724).

[3] According to Servaas v. Rooijen (1904, p. 384), L.'s will is still extant in the protocols of the notary Jan de Vries at Delft. I have not seen this document—executed jointly by Antony and Maria, "both being sound of mind and body," on 30 November 1721.

[4] = Mistress: a title applied at that date, of course, to unmarried women.

[5] Here follows an account of the cabinet of microscopes, and a list of the objects placed before them. See p. 314 *sq.*, *infra.*

It were endless . . . . to give any Account of *Mr. Leeuwenhoek*'s Discoveries ; they are so numerous as to make up a considerable Part of the *Philosophical Transactions*, and when collected together, to fill four pretty large Volumes in Quarto, which have been publish'd by him at several Times : And of such Consequence, as to have opened entirely new Scenes in some Parts of *Natural Philosophy*, as we are all sensible, in that famous Discovery of the *Animalcula in Semine Masculino*,[1] which has given a perfectly new Turn to the Theory of Generation, in almost all the Authors that have since wrote upon that Subject.[2]

. . . .

But however excellent these Glasses may be judg'd, Mr. *Leeuwenhoek*'s Discoveries are not entirely to be imputed to *their* Goodness only: His own great Judgment, and Experience in the Manner of using them, together with the continual Application he gave to that Business, and the indefatigable Industry with which he contemplated often and long upon the same Subject, viewing it under many and different Circumstances, cannot but have enabled him to form better Judgments of the Nature of his Objects, and see farther into their Constitution, than it can be imagined any other Person can do, that neither has the Experience, nor has taken the Pains this curious Author had so long done.

Nor ought we to forget a Piece of Skill, in which he very particularly excell'd, which was that of preparing his Objects in the best Manner, to be view'd by the Microscope ; and of this I am perswaded, any one will be

---

[1] The discovery was announced in a letter written to the Royal Society in November 1677—at the very moment when the marriage of William and Mary was being celebrated in London.

[2] Some further particulars of the microscopes themselves follow here: cf. p. 317 *infra*.

satisfied, who shall apply himself to the Examination of some of the same Objects as do yet remain before these Glasses; at least, I have my self found so much Difficulty in this Particular, as to observe a very sensible Difference between the Appearances of the same Object, when apply'd by my self, and when prepared by Mr. *Leeuwenhoek*, tho' view'd with Glasses of the very same Goodness.

I have the rather insisted upon this, as it may be a Caution to us, that we do not rashly condemn any of this Gentleman's Observations, tho' even with his own Glasses, we should not immediately be able to verify them our selves. We are under very great Disadvantages for want of the Experience he had, and he has himself put us in Mind, more than once, that those who are the best skill'd in the Use of Magnifying-Glasses, may be misled, if they give too sudden a Judgment upon what they see, or 'till they have been assured from repeated Experiments. But we have seen so many, and those of his most surprizing Discoveries, so perfectly confirm'd, by great Numbers of the most curious and judicious Observers, that there can surely be no Reason to distrust his Accuracy in those others, which have not yet been so frequently or carefully examin'd.

Upon the whole, it is to be hoped, some of the Society will pursue those Enquiries, the late Possessor of these Microscopes was so deservedly famous for; and that as we have lost in Mr. *Leeuwenhoek* a most worthy Member, and a most valuable Correspondent, this last Piece of his Respect to the *Royal Society* will not only enrich our Repository, but both encourage and enable some other diligent Observer to prosecute the same curious and useful Discoveries.

PART II

THE "LITTLE ANIMALS"

> While ruder heads stand amazed at those prodigious pieces of nature, as Elephants, Dromidaries, and Camels ; these I confesse, are the Colossus and Majestick pieces of her hand ; but in these narrow Engines there is more curious Mathematicks, & the civility of these little Citizens, more nearly sets forth the wisdome of their Maker.—Sir *Thomas Browne* (1642).

CHAPTER 1

THE FIRST OBSERVATIONS ON "LITTLE ANIMALS" (PROTOZOA AND BACTERIA) IN WATERS

(Letters 6, 13, 13*a*, 18, 18*b*)

LEEUWENHOEK'S observations on the free-living Protozoa probably began with his discovery of certain "very little animalcules" which he saw in fresh water in the year 1674. He described his findings in a letter addressed to Mr. Oldenburg,[1] and dated from Delft, 7 September 1674. This letter deals with other matters also, and the passage in which the Protozoa are mentioned is quite short. (See Plate XVII.) Here it is, in its entirety[2]:

About two hours distant[3] from this Town there lies an inland lake, called the Berkelse Mere, whose bottom in

---

[1] Henry Oldenburg, Secretary of the Royal Society. See p. 38.

[2] From *Letter 6*. 7 September 1674. MS.Roy.Soc. [Not in Dutch or Latin collected works.] Part of this letter was translated and printed in *Phil. Trans.*, Vol. IX, No. 108, pp. 178—182 [misprinted 821], 23 Nov. 1674. It is numbered "[10] Brief Tr. 7" by Vandevelde (1922, p. 344), who gives an abstract of it in Flemish (from the *Phil. Trans.* version—not from the MS.). The important passage given above has been generally overlooked by protozoologists—possibly because the letter was omitted, apparently by an oversight, from the table of contents at the beginning of the number in which it was printed. The passage here given begins on p. 181; and I have followed the original translation pretty closely, because it is so lively and faithful. I have a strong feeling—but no direct evidence—that it was not the work of Oldenburg himself: but I do not know who the translator was. The English MS. has not been preserved.—I find since writing the above that attention was directed to this passage—as fixing the date of L.'s earliest observations—by Schill (1887), who reprinted the original English version. His note has seemingly been overlooked by all later writers.

[3] John Ray, in his *Journey through the Low-countries*, notes (*anno* 1663) as a peculiarity that "they reckon or measure their way in these Countreys, by the time they spend in passing it" (Ray, 1673; p. 23).

many places is very marshy, or boggy. Its water is in winter very clear, but at the beginning or in the middle of summer it becomes whitish, and there are then little green clouds floating through it; which, according to the saying of the country folk dwelling thereabout, is caused by the dew, which happens to fall at that time, and which they call honey-dew. This water is abounding in fish, which is very good and savoury. Passing just lately[1] over this lake, at a time when the wind blew pretty hard, and seeing the water as above described, I took up a little of it in a glass phial; and examining this water next day, I found floating therein divers earthy particles, and some green streaks, spirally wound serpent-wise, and orderly arranged,[2] after the manner of the copper or tin worms, which distillers use to cool their liquors as they distil over. The whole circumference of each of these streaks was about the thickness of a hair of one's head. Other particles had but the beginning of the foresaid streak; but all consisted of very small green globules joined together: and there were very many small green globules as well. Among these there were, besides, very many little animalcules,[3] whereof some were roundish, while others, a bit bigger, consisted of an oval. On these last I saw two little legs near the head, and two little fins at the hindmost end of the body.[4] Others were somewhat longer than an oval, and these were very slow a-moving, and few in number.[5] These animalcules had divers colours, some being whitish and transparent; others

[1] *nu laest* MS. The date of the observation is not more precisely stated, but it seems clear that the discoveries must have been made in the late summer (end of August or beginning of September ?) of 1674.

[2] The common green alga *Spirogyra*: the earliest recorded observations on this organism. The size of the filament negatives the suggestion that L. could have been referring to *Arthrospira* or *Spirulina*.

[3] It can hardly be doubted that some, at least, of these animalcules were Protozoa.

[4] Probably Rotifers—seen under a low magnification.

[5] Probably Ciliates.

EXTRACT (REDUCED FACSIMILE) FROM LEEUWENHOEK'S LETTER NO. 6

(7 Sept. 1674: leaf 3 *recto* = p. 5), showing the original of the passage here translated. Holograph MS. The concluding words are on the *verso* of the page, and read: " . . . *int tarwen meel, in schimmel, en etc. heb gesien.*" Apart from this unavoidable omission, the passage is complete.

> with green and very glittering little scales; others again were green in the middle, and before and behind white[1]; others yet were ashen grey. And the motion of most of these animalcules in the water was so swift, and so various, upwards, downwards, and round about, that 'twas wonderful to see: and I judge that some of these little creatures were above a thousand times smaller[2] than the smallest ones I have ever yet seen,[3] upon the rind of cheese, in wheaten flour, mould, and the like.

No further observations on these "little animals" appear to have been reported until more than a year later. But in a letter written in December, 1675, Leeuwenhoek again alludes to them briefly, in the following words:[4]

> In the past summer I have made many observations upon various waters, and in almost all discovered an abundance of very little and odd animalcules, whereof some were incredibly small, less even than the animalcules which others have discovered in water, and which have been called[5] by the name of Water-flea, or Water-louse.

This passage is important as establishing the date when some of Leeuwenhoek's earliest observations were made—the summer of 1675. At this time, however, he gave no more detailed account of his discoveries: but he kept a careful record, and a month later the following passage occurs in a further note to Oldenburg:[6]

---

[1] Probably *Euglena viridis*. The peculiar arrangement of the chromatophores in this species gives the flagellate this appearance under a low magnification. The identification seems to me almost certain; and, if correct, this is the first mention of *Euglena*, whose discovery is usually attributed to Harris (1696).

[2] *i.e.*, in volume—not in linear dimensions.

[3] *i.e.*, mites.

[4] From *Letter 13*. 20 December 1675. MS.Roy.Soc. Unpublished. Original in Dutch.

[5] By Swammerdam. See note 1 on p. 118.

[6] From *Letter* 13*a*. 22 January 1676. MS.Roy.Soc. Unpublished. Original in Dutch.

> The living creatures discovered by me in water, were in ordinary rain-water, that was caught from a pantile roof[1] in stone troughs under the ground, or in tubs; also in well or spring water, coming up through well-sand; likewise in the canal water, that runneth through this Town and through the country. Upon these I have made divers notes, concerning their colour, figure, the parts whereof their body is composed, their motion, and the sudden bursting of their whole body; of which notes I keep a copy by me, which I shall send you at the earliest opportunity.

The promised "notes" were sent in due course: they form the celebrated letter (*Letter 18*) which protozoologists have long regarded as the first paper ever written upon the objects of their special study. Moreover, this letter also contains the first account ever written of the Bacteria, as well as many other original observations. In view of its unique interest, therefore, I must say a few further words of introduction at this point.

Leeuwenhoek's 18th Letter.

The famous "Letter on the Protozoa" is a truly amazing document. According to my reckoning it is Leeuwenhoek's eighteenth scientific epistle to the Royal Society, and I shall therefore refer to it henceforward simply as *Letter 18.* The original Letter itself is preserved among the Royal Society's manuscripts, and is still—except for a few slight mutilations—intact. It is in Dutch, and covers 17½ folio pages, closely written in a neat small hand which is not Leeuwenhoek's own, though the manuscript has been carefully corrected by him throughout (in a different ink), and bears his autograph signature at the end. It seems likely that he wrote the letter himself, with his notebook before him, and then caused his

---

[1] The water so collected was probably very clean water: for Dutch houses then—as now—were wont to be kept clean both inside and out. John Ray, in the diary of his *Travels*—writing in 1663—notes that, in the Netherlands, "all things both within and without" were "marvellously clean, bright, and handsomly kept: nay some are so extraordinarily curious as to take down the very Tiles of their Pent-houses and cleanse them." *Vide* Ray (1673), p. 52.

Obſervations, communicated to the Publiſher by Mr.* Antony van Leewenhoeck, *in a Dutch Letter of the 9th of* Octob. 1676. *here Engliſh'd: Concerning little Animals by him obſerved in Rain- Well- Sea- and Snow water; as alſo in water wherein Pepper had lain infuſed.

IN the year 1675. I diſcover'd living creatures in Rain water, which had ſtood but few days in a new earthen pot, glaſed blew within. This invited me to view this water with great attention, eſpecially thoſe little animals appearing to me ten thouſand times leſs than thoſe repreſented by Monſ. *Swamerdam*, and by him called *Water-fleas* or *Water-lice*, which may be perceived in the water with the naked eye.

The *firſt* ſort by me diſcover'd in the ſaid water, I divers times obſerved to conſiſt of 5, 6, 7, or 8 clear globuls, without being able to diſcern any film that held them together, or contained them. When theſe *animalcula* or living Atoms did move, they put forth two little horns, continually moving themſelves: The place between theſe two horns was flat, though the reſt of the body was roundiſh, ſharpning a little towards the end, where they had a tayl, near four times the length of the whole body, of the thickneſs (by my Microſcope) of a Spiders-web; at the end of which appear'd a globul, of the bigneſs of one of thoſe which made up the body; which tayl I could not perceive, even in very clear water, to be mov'd by them. Theſe little creatures, if they chanced to light upon the leaſt filament or ſtring, or other ſuch particle, of which there are many in water, eſpecially after it hath ſtood ſome days, they ſtook intangled therein, extending their body in a long round, and ſtriving to diſintangle their tayl; whereby it came to paſs, that their whole body lept back towards the globul of the tayl, which then rolled together Serpent-like, and after the manner of Copper- or Iron wire that having been wound about a ſtick, and unwound again, retains thoſe windings and turnings. This motion of extenſion and contraction continued a while; and I have ſeen ſeveral hundreds of theſe poor little creatures, within the ſpace of a grain of groſs ſand, lye faſt cluſter'd together in a few filaments.

I alſo diſcover'd a *ſecond* ſort, the figure of which was oval; and I imagined their head to ſtand on the ſharp end. Theſe were a little bigger than the former. The inferior part of their body is flat, furniſhed with divers incredibly thin feet, which moved very

FIRST PAGE (FACSIMILE) OF OLDENBURG'S TRANSLATION OF LETTER 18 (9 Oct. 1676) published in *Phil. Trans.* (1677), Vol. XII, No. 133, pp. 821-831. Compare with Plate XIX.

rough draft to be copied out in a fair hand before sending it to the Society. The letter is dated from "Delft in Holland, 9th October, 1676" [New Style], and is addressed to Henry Oldenburg in person. From an endorsement which it bears[1] it appears that he received it 10 days later, and sent back an acknowledgement of its receipt through Leibniz. The letter was read at the meetings of the Royal Society held on 1, 15, and 22 February 1677 [O.S.].[2]

A part of this letter was published (in English) in the *Philosophical Transactions* in March, 1677,[3] under the heading "*Observations, communicated to the Publisher*[4] *by Mr.* Antony van Leewenhoeck, *in a Dutch Letter of the 9th of* Octob. 1676. *here English'd: Concerning little Animals by him observed in Rain- Well- Sea- and Snow-water; as also in water wherein Pepper had lain infused*". (See Plate XVIII.) This English version was the work of Oldenburg himself, as is evident from the manuscript translation—in his hand—still preserved with its Dutch original.

Oldenburg's English rendering is the only version of *Letter 18* which has hitherto been printed. It is, on the whole, good: but it is not perfect, and most people will be surprised to learn that it is a condensed translation of less than half of the original, and that the part which Oldenburg did not print has never yet been published in any language. Why the letter has never been published, in its entirety, I do not know. I can only suppose that no protozoologist or bacteriologist has ever yet seen the original manuscript; or, having seen it, has had the courage and diligence to decipher

---

[1] The endorsement—in Oldenburg's hand—is as follows: "*receu le 9. Octob. st. v.* [=style vieux] *1676. resp*[ondu]. *le 16 Oct. d'avoir receu cette lettre, par M. Leibnitz, mais non pas encor consideré*".—It was in the autumn of 1676 that Leibniz paid his now well-known (but formerly hushed-up) visit to Spinoza at The Hague (cf. Pollock, 1899; p. 37). Perhaps Oldenburg, knowing this interview to be imminent, requested Leibniz to send word to L.—only a few miles distant at Delft—of the safe receipt of his letter. I can find no evidence to show that Leibniz visited Leeuwenhoek on this occasion.—The well-known correspondence between L. and Leibniz took place, of course, at a much later date, and has been already reviewed by Ehrenberg (1845).

[2] Cf. Birch, Vol. III, pp. 332, 333, 334.

[3] *Phil. Trans.* (1677), Vol. XII, No. 133, pp. 821-831.

[4] "Publisher" = Editor (*i.e.* Oldenburg).

it. It certainly is not very easy to read; but considering its supreme interest and importance, I am astonished that nobody hitherto appears to have made the attempt—nobody, that is, since Oldenburg: for Oldenburg evidently read the whole letter, and, though he published but a part, translated most of it—after a fashion. I have been through his manuscript translation carefully, but I have made no use of it in the preparation of my own: for it is much too abbreviated and confused for my purpose, and it is not free from errors. Oldenburg seems to have had a fair knowledge of Dutch, but the objects which Leeuwenhoek was endeavouring to describe were, of course, at that time entirely outside the experience of everybody but himself: and to understand his words, and to appreciate his efforts at description, it is necessary to be familiar with the things that he was studying as well as with his way of writing.

Many protozoologists have, no doubt, read Oldenburg's curtailed English version of *Letter 18* in the *Philosophical Transactions*, but probably many more are acquainted with it through the work of Saville Kent. This author copied a considerable part of the letter into his well-known book on the "Infusoria"[1]; but I must remark that his quotations from Oldenburg's translation do not altogether bear out his own statement that they were transcribed "with a faithful reproduction of their original quaint style of diction". Kent's version is, indeed, by no means faithful to its prototype, and even contains several bad mistakes. For example, in one place Leeuwenhoek says that he put some water in a glass "*op mijn comptoir*"—meaning "in my closet," *i.e.* the office or study[2] in which he worked and wrote (probably the counting-house in his shop). This frequently recurring phrase is usually rendered "*in musaeo meo*" by the Latin translators, and appears—concordantly—as "*dans mon cabinet*" in the

---

[1] *Manual of the Infusoria* (1880). Vol. I, pp. 3-7.—I may also note here that what purports to be another reproduction of the same letter, published recently by Knickerbocker (1927), is nothing more than a reprint of the garbled and condensed version printed in 1809 by Hutton, Shaw, and Pearson in their *Abridgement* of the *Phil. Trans.* It has no value either as a historical document or as an illustration of L.'s work.

[2] *Comptoir* = *reekenkamer*, *schrijfkamer*, etc. (Meijer, *Woordenschat* p. 56). Some particulars regarding L.'s "*comptoir*" are given in *Letter 18* (p. 125 *infra*).

short French version of Chr. Huygens.[1] Oldenburg rightly translated it "in my Counter[2] or Study"—evidently being at a loss for the exact English equivalent of the Franco-Dutch word. But Kent, by "copying" Oldenburg, ultimately gives us "on my counter of study"—an unintelligible expression which he perhaps imagined to mean "on my laboratory bench".[3]

On 7 November 1676, a month after he had sent his long letter to the Royal Society, Leeuwenhoek wrote a much shorter account of the same observations to his old friend Sir Constantijn Huygens—the statesman-poet father of Christiaan, the famous astronomer and mathematician. This letter[4] is preserved at Leyden, and has recently been published by Vandevelde and van Seters (1925). At Leeuwenhoek's request it was translated into French by Christiaan Huygens—then at Paris—whose MS. translation is also now in the Leyden University Library along with its Dutch original. This French version was evidently intended for presentation to the Paris Academy: but another French abstract or summary of Leeuwenhoek's observations was printed in the *Journal des Sçavans* some two years later,[5] and the translation made by Huygens has only recently been published in Holland.[6] These various abstracts give but a poor idea of

---

[1] See note 6 below.

[2] *i.e.* Counting-house (*reekenkamer*).

[3] I regret to say that at least one modern Dutch translator and one Flemish commentator have fallen into the same error. They should both have known better.

[4] *Letter* 18*b*, according to my numeration. Referred to by Haaxman (1875), p. 135. Snelleman (1874) has printed a part of this letter, in the original Dutch, but his version contains several manifest misreadings which Vandevelde and van Seters have rectified. I have carefully compared the (published) letter of 7 Nov. 1676 with *Letter 18*, and it is obvious that it is merely a very condensed account (not half the length) of the latter. It contains nothing that is not more fully given in the original (*Letter 18*, 9 Oct. 1676) addressed to the Royal Society. The comparison instituted by Vandevelde and van Seters between the French and Dutch abstracts and Oldenburg's short English version seems somewhat unprofitable, since they never consulted the Dutch original *in extenso* (Letter 18).

[5] *Journ. d. Sçav.*, Vol. IX. 1678 (pp. 55 and 68 of *nouv. éd.*, 1724).

[6] *Œuvres Complètes de Chr. Huygens* (1899), Vol. VIII, pp. 22-27 (No. 2100).

the extensive investigations described in the original Dutch epistle (*Letter 18*).[1]

The greater part of this very long letter—one of the longest Leeuwenhoek ever wrote—is in an unusual form. At the very end of it he remarks that "these my observations" are "taken from the diary which I keep from time to time;" and accordingly we find that he generally gives, in order, the observations as he made them from day to day—without making any attempt to summarize or correlate them. In his letter to Constantijn Huygens (7 Nov. 1676) he explains that he sent these details from his notebook "merely so as to make my observations more credible in England and elsewhere; and especially because Mr Secretary Oldenburg had formerly written to me that there are a number of philosophers at Paris and elsewhere who don't allow of the truth of what I describe"[2]. The subject-matter falls naturally, as will be seen, into various sections, dealing with the divers creatures found in the several sorts of water or infusions which he examined. Some of these sections are provided, by himself, with appropriate headings, while others are not: and I have therefore, for the sake of uniformity, interpolated such headings where they are lacking in the original.[3]

Leeuwenhoek's 18th Letter opens (cf. Plate XIX) with a few personal remarks, of no particular interest in the present connexion, and then drops abruptly into the description of his discoveries: and at this point I have begun my translation, which now follows.[4]

---

[1] Another French translation (or a copy of one of the two mentioned above?) was published later in a work called *Collection Académique de Dijon*, Vol. II, pp. 454-461, 1755: but this I have not been able to consult. Cf. Konarski (1895, p. 251 note) and Vandevelde (1922, p. 349).—No account of these observations appears to have been published in the *Acta Eruditorum*, which only began publication in 1682: but a reference to L., and the discovery of animalcules in infusions (attributed ambiguously to Butterfield), will be found in the note by Elsholz (1679) in *Miscellanea Curiosa*, Vol. IX.

[2] See Vandevelde and van Seters (1925), p. 20: and *Œuvres Compl. de Chr. Huygens* (1899), Vol. VIII, p. 22, footnote 3.

[3] These additions, wherever they occur, are indicated by being inclosed between square brackets.

[4] *Letter 18*. 9 October 1676. To Oldenburg. MS. Roy. Soc. I have not thought it necessary to mark all the places where my translation differs

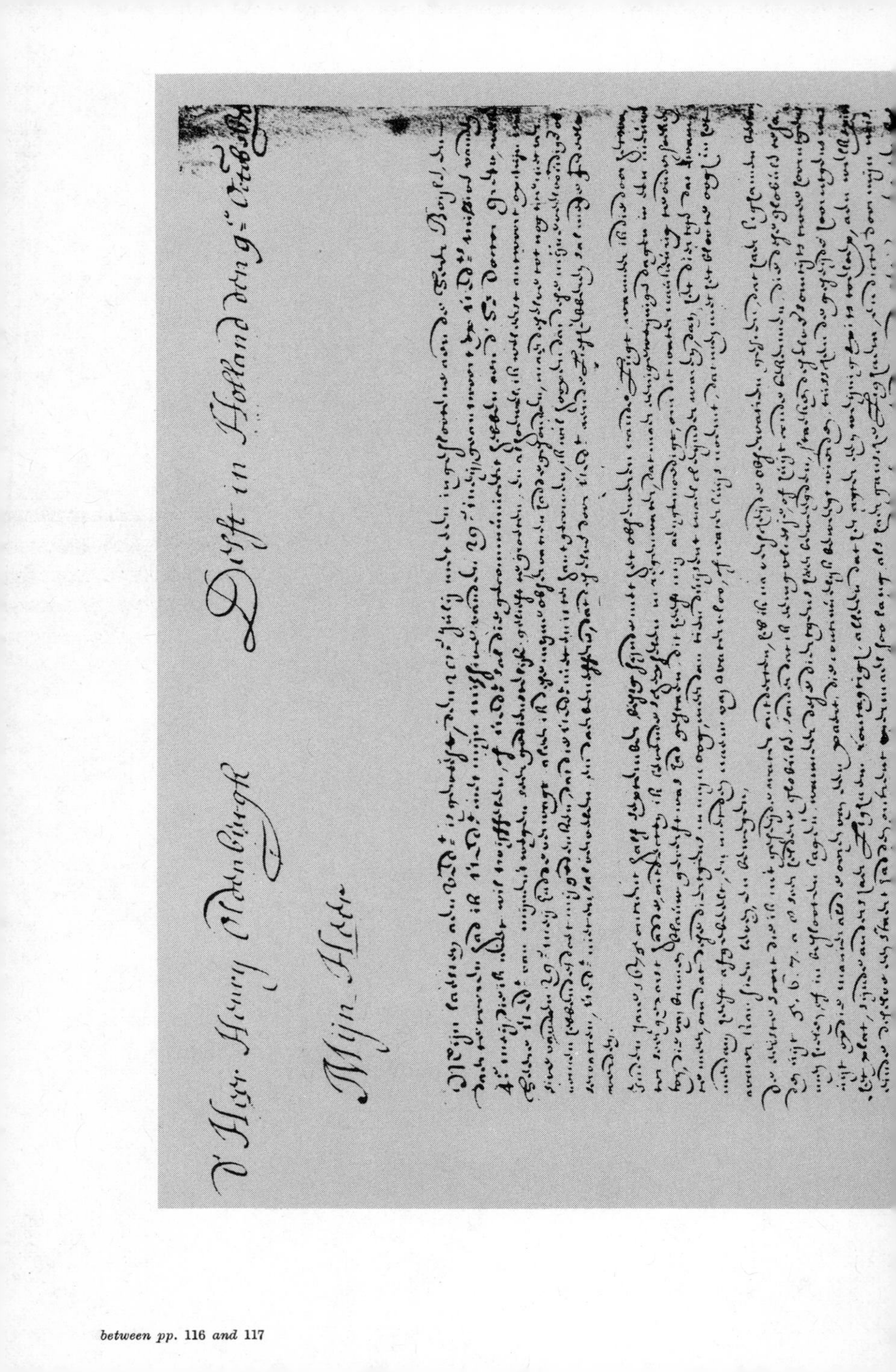

Mr. Henry Oldenburgh Delft in Holland den 9:en October

Mijn Heer

between pp. 116 and 117

FIRST PAGE (FACSIMILE) OF MS. OF LEEUWENHOEK'S LETTER NO. 18
(9 Oct. 1676)

The translation here given begins at the 2nd paragraph—"*Inden jare 1675 ontrent half september* . . . ." (The handwriting is not Leeuwenhoek's.) Compare with Plate XVIII.

[*1st Observation on Rain-water.*]

In the year 1675, about half-way through September [1] (being busy with studying air, when I had much compressed it by means of water [2]), I discovered living creatures in rain, which had stood but a few days [3] in a new tub, that was painted blue within.[4] This observation provoked me to investigate this water more narrowly; and especially because these little animals were, to my eye, more than ten thousand times smaller [5] than the animalcule which Swammerdam [6] has portrayed, and called by the name of

---

from Oldenburg's, nor yet to point out all his many minor omissions. These will be manifest to anybody who will take the trouble to compare this rendering with that in the *Phil. Trans.* Only important errors, interesting variants, or vital omissions, are indicated in my notes.—Vandevelde (1922, p. 348) numbers this letter " [15] Brief Tr. 11," but it certainly cannot be called " Letter 11 " or " 15 " in any sense.—The letter is not to be found, of course, in either the Dutch or the Latin edition of the collective works.

[1] *In den jare 1675 ontrent half September* MS. "In the year 1675" *Phil. Trans.* By neglecting to translate the latter part of the original statement, Oldenburg left the precise date of the discovery in doubt; and a controversy arose later between Ehrenberg and Haaxman in consequence—the former alleging that the observations were made in April, while the latter, on evidence furnished by the MS. letter from L. to Const. Huygens, believed the correct date to be mid-September. Cf. Haaxman (1875). It is now obvious that Haaxman was right.

[2] Some account of L.'s experiments "on the compression of the air" had already appeared in *Phil. Trans.* (1673), Vol. IX, p. 21. (*Letter 2*, 15 August 1673. MS. Roy.Soc.)

[3] " four days " Saville Kent (Vol. I, p. 3). This is merely due to careless copying, and is not in the originals.

[4] *in een nieuwe ton, die van binnen blauw geverft was* MS. " in a new earthen pot, glased blew within " *Phil. Trans.* Oldenburg here mistranslated L.'s words, which were quite plain and were rendered concordantly by Chr. Huygens "*dans un tonneau peint en huile par dedans*". The vessel was obviously not of Delft porcelain.

[5] *i.e.*, in bulk—not in diameter. This expression means, with L., that he judged the animalcules to have roughly one twenty-fifth of the diameter of the bigger creatures.

[6] Jan Swammerdam (1637—1680). For his life see especially his *Biblia Naturae* (1737) and Sinia (1878).

Water-flea, or Water-louse,[1] which you can see alive and moving in water with the bare eye.

Of the first sort[2] that I discovered in the said water, I saw, after divers observations, that the bodies consisted of 5, 6, 7, or 8 very clear globules, but without being able to discern any membrane or skin that held these globules together, or in which they were inclosed. When these animalcules bestirred 'emselves, they sometimes stuck out two little horns,[3] which were continually moved, after the fashion of a horse's ears. The part between these little horns was flat, their body else being roundish, save only that it ran somewhat to a point at the hind end; at which pointed end it had a tail, near four times as long as the whole body, and looking as thick, when viewed through my microscope, as a spider's web.[4] At the end of this tail there was a pellet, of the bigness of one of the globules of the body; and this tail I could not perceive to be used by them for their movements in very clear water. These little animals were the most wretched creatures that I have ever seen; for when, with the pellet, they did but hit on any particles or little filaments[5] (of which there are many in water, especially if it hath

---

[1] Swammerdam's "*watervlooy*" was *Daphnia*—as all students of the *Biblia Naturae* are well aware (cf. *B.N.* Vol. I, p. 86, Pl. XXXI). But as this work was not published until 1737—long after his death—it is clear that L. here alludes to his earlier Dutch publication (Swammerdam, 1669), in which the water-flea is shown on Pl. I. Swammerdam himself called it "the branched water-flea", and attributed the name "water-louse" to Goedaert.

[2] *Vorticella* sp. The following admirable description makes the identification certain.

[3] The optical section of the wreath of cilia round the peristome—so interpreted by most of the early observers.

[4] *i.e.*, as thick as a spider's web looks to the naked eye.

[5] *maer quamen aen eenige deeltgens of veseltgens* MS. "if they chanced to light upon the least filament or string, or other such particle" *Phil. Trans.* These words of Oldenburg are amusingly mistranslated by Nägler (1918, p. 7) "*Wenn man diese kleinen Kreaturen zufällig belichtete.*" (He apparently supposes that "to light upon" means "to illuminate"!)

but stood some days), they stuck intangled in them; and then pulled their body out into an oval, and did struggle, by strongly stretching themselves, to get their tail loose; whereby their whole body then sprang back towards the pellet of the tail, and their tails then coiled up serpent-wise, after the fashion of a copper or iron wire that, having been wound close about a round stick, and then taken off, kept all its windings.[1] This motion, of stretching out and pulling together the tail, continued; and I have seen several hundred animalcules, caught fast by one another in a few filaments, lying within the compass of a coarse grain of sand.[2]

I also discovered a second sort[3] of animalcules, whose figure was an oval; and I imagined that their head was placed at the pointed end. These were a little bit bigger than the animalcules first mentioned. Their belly is flat, provided with divers incredibly thin little feet, or little legs,[4] which were moved very nimbly, and which I was able to discover only after sundry great efforts, and wherewith they brought off incredibly quick motions. The upper part of their body was round, and furnished inside with 8, 10, or 12 globules: otherwise these animalcules

---

[1] Apparently it never occurred to L., at this time, that the contraction and extension of the stalk ("tail") of *Vorticella* could have any other significance than that here attributed to them. The idea of a *stalked* and normally *sessile animal* probably never entered his head; and consequently he jumped to the incorrect conclusion that the animals were endeavouring to "get their tails loose"—which, of course, was a mistake, though a very natural one. L. published pictures of Vorticellids later, in *Phil. Trans.*, Vol. XXIII (Letter dated 25 Dec. 1702): and still later he arrived at a more correct interpretation of the function of the "tail," and of the organization of these remarkable animals (*Send-brief* VII, dated 28 June 1713). See Chapter 4, below.

[2] *inde spatie van een grof sant* MS. "within the space of a grain of gross sand" *Phil. Trans.* This is a very common expression with L., and Oldenburg fully understood its meaning; but Nägler (1918, p. 9) mistranslates his words "*in der Höhlung eines grossen Sandkorns*"—as though L. had seen the animalcules lying in a cavity in an actual grain of sand!

[3] Not identifiable with certainty, but undoubtedly a ciliate.

[4] *i.e.* cilia.

were very clear. These little animals would change their body into a perfect round, but mostly when they came to lie high and dry. Their body was also very yielding: for if they so much as brushed against a tiny filament, their body bent in, which bend also presently sprang out again; just as if you stuck your finger into a bladder full of water, and then, on removing the finger, the inpitting went away. Yet the greatest marvel was when I brought any of the animalcules on a dry place, for I then saw them change themselves at last into a round, and then the upper part of the body rose up pyramid-like, with a point jutting out in the middle; and after having thus lain moving with their feet for a little while, they burst asunder, and the globules and a watery humour flowed away on all sides, without my being able to discern even the least sign of any skin wherein these globules and the liquid had, to all appearance, been inclosed; and at such times I could discern more globules than when they were alive. This bursting asunder I figure to myself to happen thus: imagine, for example, that you have a sheep's bladder filled with shot, peas, and water; then, if you were to dash it apieces on the ground, the shot, peas, and water would scatter themselves all over the place.[1]

Furthermore, I discovered a third sort[2] of little animals, that were about twice as long as broad, and to my eye quite eight times smaller[3] than the animalcules first mentioned: and I imagined, although they were so small, that I could yet make out their little legs, or little fins. Their motion was very quick, both roundabout and in a straight line.

---

[1] The foregoing graphic account of the bursting of the "little animals" is of great interest, as it shows clearly that L. was really observing protozoa. An animal whose body consisted entirely of soft "protoplasm"—without any skeletal parts or obvious skin—was, of course, a considerable novelty at this date.

[2] Not identifiable. Probably a small ciliate.

[3] *i.e.*, having a diameter equal to about half that of the *Vorticella*.

The fourth sort[1] of animalcules, which I also saw a-moving, were so small, that for my part I can't assign any figure to 'em. These little animals were more than a thousand times less than the eye of a full-grown louse[2] (for I judge the diameter of the louse's eye to be more than ten times as long as that of the said creature), and they surpassed in quickness the animalcules already spoken of. I have divers times seen them standing still, as 'twere, in one spot, and twirling themselves round with a swiftness such as you see in a whip-top a-spinning before your eye[3]; and then again they had a circular motion, the circumference whereof was no bigger than that of a small sand-grain; and anon they would go straight ahead, or their course would be crooked.[4]

Furthermore, I also discovered sundry other sorts of little animals; but these were very big, some as large as the little mites on the rind of cheese, others bigger and very monstrous.[5] But I intend not to specify them; and

---

[1] Probably—from the ensuing description—a species of *Monas*. Certainly not bacteria of any kind.

[2] This makes the diameter of the protozoon here described about 6-8 μ, and is agreeable with its interpretation as *Monas vulgaris*.

[3] If the description applies to *Monas*—as I strongly suspect—then the "spinning" here described was an illusion. I fancy L. saw a *Monas* attached by its caudal filament, and mistook the swirl of the water at its anterior end (occasioned by the movements of the small accessory flagellum) for a motion caused by the rotation of the body as a whole.

[4] *en dan weder soo regt uijt, als crom gebogen* MS. These words are hard to understand. The above seems to me to be L.'s meaning: but Oldenburg translates "and then extending themselves streight forward, and by and by lying in a bending posture" (*Phil. Trans.*). It is hardly likely that L. could have observed "a bending posture" in an organism so small that he could discern "no figure" in it: and as the "circular motion" just mentioned evidently refers to the orbit described by the organism—not to the animalcule itself—I imagine that "*regt uijt*" and "*crom gebogen*" likewise refer to the path traversed. I should point out, however, that L. elsewhere (*Letter 38*) applies precisely the same words to the *shape* of the spermatozoa of a frog.

[5] Some of these were doubtless protozoa, but the "monsters" were perhaps rotifers. Much later, when describing these animals, L. mentions that he had previously discovered them in rain-water, in which he had steeped pepper and ginger. See *Letter 144*, 9 Feb. 1702.

will only say, that they were for the most part made up of such soft parts, that they burst asunder whenever the water happened to run off them.

The 2nd Observation. [*Rain-water.*]

The 26th of May,[1] it rained very hard. The rain abating somewhat, I took a clean glass and got rain-water, that came off a slate roof, fetched me in it, after the glass had first been swilled out two or three times with the rain-water. I then examined it, and therein discovered some few very little animals[2]; and seeing them, I bethought me whether they might not have been bred in the leaden gutters, in any water that might erstwhile have been standing in them.

The 3rd Observation. Rain-water.

On the same date, the rain continuing nearly the whole day, I took a big porcelain dish, and put it in my court-yard, in the open air, upon a wooden tub about a foot and a half high: considering that thus no earthy particles would be splashed into the said dish by the falling of the rain at that spot. With the water first caught, I swilled out the dish, and the glass in which I meant to preserve the water, and then flung this water away: then, collecting water anew in the same dish, I kept it; but upon examining it, I could discover therein no living creatures, but merely a lot of irregular earthy particles.

The 30th of May, after I had, since the 26th, observed this water every day, twice or thrice daily, I now first discovered some (though very few) exceeding little animalcules,[3] which were very clear.

---

[1] *Anno* 1676.

[2] Unidentifiable. The animalcules from L.'s gutters were described by himself later. (Cf. p. 263 *infra.*) They include flagellates, ciliates, bacteria, and rotifers.

[3] From the description which follows, these were probably the same as the "very little animalcules" already described—*i.e.*, a species of *Monas*.

On the 31st *ditto*, I discovered more little animals in the water, as well as a few that were a bit bigger; and I imagine that ten hundred thousand of these very little animalcules are not so big as an ordinary sand-grain.[1] Comparing these animalcules with the little mites in cheese (which you can see a-moving with the bare eye), I would put the proportion thus: As the size of a small animalcule in the water is to that of a mite, so is the size of a honey-bee to that of a horse; for the circumference of one of these same little animalcules is not so great as the thickness of a hair on a mite.

The 4th Observation. Rain-water.

On June 9th,[2] collected rain-water betimes in a dish, as aforesaid, and put it at about 8 o'clock in the morning in a clean wine-glass, and exposed it to the air at about the height of the third storey of my house, wondering whether the little animals would appear sooner in water thus standing in the air.

The 10th *ditto*, observing this water, I fancied that I discovered living creatures; but because they were so few, and not so plainly discernible, I could not accept this for the truth.

On the 11th *ditto*, seeing this water, with the naked eye, stirred in the glass by a stiff gale of wind (which had now blown from the same quarter for 36 hours; the weather being so cold withal, that it did not irk me to wear my winter clothes), I had no thought of finding any living creatures in it; but upon examining it, I saw with wonder quite 1000 living creatures in one drop of water.

---

[1] This means that he estimated their diameter at something less than $\frac{1}{100}$ of the diameter of an "ordinary" (or large) sand-grain. Taking this as $\frac{1}{30}$ of an inch, their diameter would thus be of the order of $\frac{1}{3000}$ in., or roughly 8·5 μ. This is a very close guess at the size of *Monas vulgaris*. On sand-grains cf. p. 334 *infra*.

[2] *Anno* 1676.

These animalcules were of the smallest sort[1] that I had as yet seen.

The 12th of June, in the morning (the wind being west, with both sunshine and an overcast sky), observing again, I saw the foresaid animalcules in such great numbers in the water which I took from the surface, that now they did not amount to merely one or two thousand in one drop.

The 13th *ditto*, in the morning, examining the water again, I discovered, besides the foresaid animalcules, a sort of little animals that were fully eight times as big[2] as the first; and whereas the small animalcules swam gently among one another, and moved after the fashion of gnats in the air, these large animalcules had a much swifter motion; and as they turned and tumbled all around and about, they would make a quick dart.[3] These animalcules were almost round.[4]

On the 14th of June I did perceive the very little animalcules in no less number.

On the 16th *ditto*, the animalcules seen as before; and the water (which had been, in all, about ⅙ of a pint) being now more than half dried up, I flung it away.

5th Observation. Rain-water.

The 9th of June,[5] I put some of the last-collected water, likewise in a clean wine-glass, in my closet; and

---

[1] *i.e.*, probably *Monas* sp. again.

[2] On L.'s system this means "twice as long".

[3] *namen deselve een snelle scheut* MS. "and then making a sudden downfall" *Phil. Trans.* L.'s meaning seems clearly to be that given above (*i.e.*, they sometimes made sudden shoots or darts forward). Oldenburg renders his words as though *scheut* = Fr. *chute*.

[4] It seems to me almost certain that the animalcule here described was the common ciliate *Cyclidium*. This is the only likely organism—of this order of magnitude—which makes sudden springs (hence its name of "flea-animalcule"). The only objection to this interpretation is the statement that it was "almost round": but it must be remembered that L. made his observations under a very inadequate magnification.

[5] *Anno* 1676.

PLATE XX

Rijksmuseum *Amsterdam*

A HOUSE IN DELFT

From the picture by Jan Vermeer (1632-1675). This three-storey house is probably very like the one in which Leeuwenhoek lived. The picture shows the casement windows, with their leaded panes and wooden shutters, and an alleyway leading to the yard at the back (where the well was situated): only the canal in front of the house is not shown below the cobbled pavement in the foreground.

on examining it, I descried no animalcules. (*Note.* My closet standeth towards the north-east,[1] and is partitioned off from my antechamber with pine-wood, very close joined, having no other opening than a slit an inch and a half high and 8 inches long, through which the wooden spring of my lathe passeth. 'Tis furnished towards the street with four windows, whereof the two lowermost can be opened from within, and which by night are closed outside with two wooden shutters; so that little or no air comes in from without, unless it chance that in making my observations I use a candle, when I draw up one casement a little, lest the candle inconvenience me; and I also then pull a curtain almost right across the panes.)

The 10th of June, observing this foresaid rain-water, which had now stood about 24 hours in my closet, I perceived some few very little living creatures,[2] to which, because of their littleness, no figure can be ascribed; and among others, I discovered a little animal that was a bit bigger, and that I could perceive to be oval.[3] (*Note.* When I say that I have observed the water, I mean I have examined no more than 3, 4, or 5 drops thereof, which I also then throw away; and in narrowly scrutinizing 3 or 4 drops I may do such a deal of work, that I put myself into a sweat.)

---

[1] From the situation of the house, this indicates that the "closet" was at the front, looking on to the canal in the *Hippolytusbuurt*.—Plate XX is inserted here to show the sort of house which L. probably lived in, and to illustrate what he means by *four* windows with *two* wooden shutters over the *lowermost*. (This picture may *conceivably* have been painted from L.'s own house—or Vermeer's!) Although the original painting (formerly in the Six Collection, now in the Rijksmuseum) is now known as *Het Straatje* (= The Little Street), it appears to have been more correctly described as "A View of a House in Delft" in the catalogue of the sale of Vermeer's pictures at Amsterdam in 1696.

[2] Probably *Monas* (or *Cercomonas*): see below.

[3] From the observations recorded later, it appears probable that the organism was a ciliate; but its very small size is against this interpretation. It may have been a *Cyclidium*.

The 11th *ditto*, observing this water again, I saw the foresaid small animalcules, though very few in number.

The 12th *ditto*, I saw the very small animalcules, as yesterday; and besides these, a little animal[1] that had nearly the figure of a mussel-shell, lying with its hollow side downwards. 'Twas of a length anigh that of a louse's eye.[2]

The 13th *ditto*, in the morning, I found the said very small animalcules in greater number, and I saw also one bigger animalcule, like that just spoken of.[3] The same day, in the evening, I perceived the said very small animalcules again in no less number; and I could now see that they had a clear or transparent projection at the hind end of their body.[4] Moreover I discovered animalcules which were somewhat longer than an oval.[5] These were about 6 times as long as the foresaid very small animalcules; and their head, which was somewhat long drawn out, they oft-times pulled in, and then looked to be almost round. There were also animalcules[6] which appeared perfectly round, their diameter being twice as long as that of the smallest animalcules of all. These two large sorts were very yielding, so that their body did bend before the least little filament which they chanced to brush against in the water.

The 14th *ditto*, I perceived the oval animalcules in greater number.[7]

---

[1] Traditionally—and doubtless with justice—identifiable as *Stylonychia mytilus* (O.F.M.) Ehrbg., a common hypotrichous ciliate.

[2] That is, about 70 μ. See p. 336.

[3] *i.e.*, *Stylonychia*.

[4] Probably *Monas* again—or perhaps a *Cercomonas*.

[5] From the description which follows it seems probable that these were *Dileptus* sp., but it is impossible to identify them with certainty.

[6] Perhaps *Cyclidium* again — similarly described on June 13 (4th observation).

[7] This apparently refers to the oval animalcules seen on the 10th (? *Cyclidium*).

The 16th *ditto*, I perceived the oval animalcules in yet greater numbers; and they were flat beneath, and round above: and besides these, there were very small animalcules that were three times as long as broad,[1] together with divers other sorts which it would take all too long to specify. In the evening of the same day, I discovered little paws on the foresaid oval animalcules,[2] which were many in number, in proportion to the animalcule; and also a much bigger animalcule[3] of the same figure, that was likewise furnished with little legs. And at this point, I stopped my observations upon this water.

6th Observation anent Rain-water.

On the 17th *ditto*,[4] it rained very hard in the forenoon, and I collected water, as before related, in a new Delft porcelain dish, which had never been used before; but I found therein no living creatures, only many earthy particles, and, among others, bits which I imagined came from the smoke of coals[5]; and some very thin threads, at least ten times thinner than the thread of a silk-worm. They seemed to be made up of globules; and when they lay rather thick one upon another, they had a green colour.

The 26th *ditto*, having been eight days out of town on holiday, and my closet having stood tight shut up; being come home, and observing the water afresh, I discovered divers animalcules, which were very small.[6]

---

[1] Unidentifiable, as no further details are given. Possibly *Bodo caudatus*.

[2] ? *Cyclidium*. The "paws" were obviously *cilia*.

[3] A ciliate; but not determinable, as this is all that is ever said about it.

[4] June, 1676.

[5] *vande rook van smits coolen* MS. "from the smoak of Smiths-coals" *Phil. Trans.* "*Smits coolen*" means ordinary (or stone) coal, as distinguished from "*houts coolen*", or charcoal. The "globules" present in smoke are described by L. elsewhere.

[6] Unidentifiable. It is not clear from his words whether L. here refers to the "very small animalcules" (*Monas*?) previously mentioned or not.

Thereupon I put my observations upon rain-water on one side for the time being.

[*Observations on River-water.*]

This town of Delft is very well off for water, and in summer we get fresh water into the town with all the floods seaward from the river Maas; wherefore the water within the town is very good, and river fish are caught every day by children with fishing-rods in the waterways inside the town. This water being divers times examined by me, I discovered in it some exceeding small animalcules (so small, indeed, that I could scarce discern their figure) of sundry sorts and colours, and therewithal some that were much bigger; though were I to specify the motion and the make of every one of 'em, 'twould take all too long a-writing. But all these animalcules are very scanty in this water, compared with those that I saw in the rain-water; for if I discovered 25 animalcules in one drop of it, that was quite a lot.[1]

[*Observations on Well-water.*]

I have in my yard,[2] standing in the open air, a well, which is about 15-foot deep before you come to the water. It standeth at the south, but so encompassed with high walls, that even when the sun is in the sign of Cancer, the coping of the well is not shone upon. This water cometh out of the ground, which is well-sand, with such force, that whenever I have tried to empty the well there was always about a foot of water still left in. On a summer's day this water is so cold that 'tis not feasible to keep your hand in it for long. Having no thought that there would be living creatures in it (for 'tis very

---

[1] No identification of these "animalcules" can be attempted, though they must have been protozoa or bacteria. As some of them were coloured, it may be inferred that they included Phytoflagellates.

[2] *op mijn plaets* MS. "In the open Court of my house" Oldenburg *dans ma cour* Huygens.

National Gallery — *London*

THE SHORE AT SCHEVENINGEN
as it appeared in Leeuwenhoek's time.

After the oil-painting by Jacob van Ruisdael (1628 ?-1682).

palatable and clear), I examined it in September of last year,[1] and discovered therein a great number of very small animalcules, which were very clear, and a bit bigger than the very smallest animalcules that I've ever seen. And I imagine (having aforetime weighed a grain of water), that there were commonly more than 500 living creatures in one grain of this water. These animalcules were very sedate, moving without any jerks.[2]

In the winter[3] I perceived no little animals, nor did I see any of them this year before the month of July, and then not in such great plenty; but in the month of August, their number was much increased.

[*Observations on Sea-water.*]

The 27th of July, 1676, I betook myself to the seaside, hard by the village of Scheveling[e].[4] Finding myself upon the shore (the wind coming off the sea, with very warm sunshine), and observing the sea-water as well as I could, I discovered in it divers living animalcules. I gave to a certain person, who went into the sea to bathe himself, a

---

[1] *i.e., anno* 1675.

[2] *dese diertgens waren seer sedig, sonder eenige horten in haer beweginge* MS. " . . . were very quiet and without motion" *Phil. Trans.*—Oldenburg's translation is clearly wrong, and entirely changes the meaning of this passage. The organisms were probably very small flagellates (? *Cercomonas* sp.): and I imagine that L. is here contrasting their even (creeping) movements with the jumping motions of the *Cyclidium* which he had previously seen in rain-water.—According to Sewel (1708), *hort* means "*a Hunch, push, jog, tug*": and to do a thing "*met horten en stooten*" signifies to do it "by fits and starts", as we now say.

[3] Presumably 1675-1676.

[4] Now called *Scheveningen*—the well-known sea-side resort near The Hague: but the name is so spelled by L. here and elsewhere (cf. *Send-brief* XLII, 10 Sept. 1717), as it is in some old Dutch maps which I have examined. Pepys, in his *Diary*, also calls the place "Scheveling," while Temple (1693), our Ambassador to Holland in 1668, writes "Skeveling"; and Professor Beijerinck informs me further that the spelling "Schevelingen" was sometimes used formerly. The appearance of the "Shore at Schevelinge" in L.'s day is shown in the well-known picture by Jacob van Ruisdael (1628-1682) in the National Gallery (No. 1390). See Plate XXI.

new glass phial (which I had bought on purpose) and besought him that, when he was in the sea, he would rinse it out twice or thrice and then fill it up with water. This having been carried out according to my orders, I tied the phial up tight with a clean bit of bladder : and on reaching home and examining the water, I perceived therein a little animal[1] that was blackish, having a shape as if 'twere made of two globules. This little animal had a peculiar motion, after the manner of a very little flea, when seen, by the naked eye, jumping on a white paper; yet 'twas only displaced, at every jump, within the compass of a coarse sand-grain, or thereabouts. It might right well be called a water-flea; but 'twas not so big, by a long way, as the eye of that little animal which Swammerdam calls the Water-flea.[2]

I did also discover animalcules which were clear, of the same bigness as that first mentioned; but they had an oval figure, and their motion was snake-wise.

Furthermore, I perceived yet a third sort, which were very slow in their motion. Their body was mouse-colour; and they were also a bit on the oval side,[3] save that a sharp little point stuck out (sting-fashion)[4] in front of the head, and another at the hind end. This sort was a bit bigger.

And there was besides a fourth sort, rather longer than an oval. Yet all these animalcules were few in number, so that in a drop of water I could make out but 3 or 4, nay, sometimes but one.

---

[1] I am unable even to hazard a guess at the identity of this organism; but, judging from its estimated size, it may well have been a protozoon.

[2] *i.e.*, *Daphnia*. Cf. p. 118, note 1.

[3] *mede hellende na de ovale kant* MS. "clear towards the oval-point" *Phil. Trans.*—an evident mistranslation. L. means that *their shape tended to be oval*—not that they were clear at one end. I translate his colloquial old Dutch into its equivalent in modern conversational English.

[4] *angels gewijs* MS. "angle-wise" *Phil. Trans.* *Angel* means a sting (*e.g.*, that of a bee), not an angle (=*hoek*). L. was probably thinking of the mouth-parts of a mosquito—which he also called (as the man-in-the-street still does) its "sting".

The 31st *ditto*, having examined this water every day since the 27th, and perceived no little animals in it; upon this date I did now see a good hundred of 'em where at first I had seen but one: but they were now of another figure, and not only smaller, but also very clear. They were like an oblong oval, only with this difference, that they tapered somewhat more sharply to a point at what I imagined to be the head end. And although these were at least a thousand times smaller than a very small sand-grain, I saw, notwithstanding, that whenever they lay high and dry out of the water they burst asunder, and flowed apart or scattered into three or four very small globules and some watery matter, without my being able to discern any other parts.[1] (In the above, I took the water out of the phial from the surface: and at this time, too, I was no longer able to see the animalcules of the sort first spoken of.)

The 2nd of August I could discern nought but an abundance of the foresaid animalcules.

The 4th *ditto*, saw 'em as heretofore, without any difference.

The 6th of August, looking again, perceived nowhere near as many little animals.

The 8th *ditto*, I again discovered a very few of the foresaid animalcules; and I now saw a few so exceeding small that, even through my microscope, they well-nigh escaped the sight. And here I stopped my observations.[2]

[*Observations on Pepper-water. 1st Observation.*]

Having made sundry efforts, from time to time, to discover, if 'twere possible, the cause of the hotness or power whereby pepper affects the tongue (more especially because we find that even though pepper hath lain a

---

[1] This observation indicates that the organisms were protozoa.

[2] Beyond the obvious fact that they were probably protozoa and bacteria, I cannot offer any guess at the identity of the various organisms which L. saw in sea-water.

whole year in vinegar, it yet retaineth its pungency); I did now[1] place anew about $\frac{1}{3}$ ounce of whole pepper in water,[2] and set it in my closet, with no other design than to soften the pepper, that I could the better study it. This pepper having lain about three weeks in the water, and on two several occasions snow-water having been added thereto, because the water had evaporated away; by chance observing this water on the 24th April, 1676, I saw therein, with great wonder, incredibly many very little animalcules, of divers sorts; and among others, some that were 3 or 4 times as long as broad, though their whole thickness was not, in my judgement, much thicker than one of the hairs wherewith the body of a louse is beset.[3] These creatures were provided with exceeding short thin legs in front of the head (although I can make out no head, I call this the head for the reason that it always went in front during motion). This supposed head looked as if 'twas cut off aslant, in such fashion as if a line were drawn athwart through two parallel lines, so as to make two angles, the one of 110 degrees, the other of 70 degrees. Close against the hinder end of the body lay a bright pellet, and behind this I judged the hindmost part of all was slightly cleft. These animalcules are very odd in their motions, oft-times tumbling all around sideways; and when I let the water run off them, they turned themselves as round as a top, and at the beginning of this motion changed their body into an oval, and then, when the round motion ceased, back again into their former length.[4]

---

[1] The exact date is not recorded; but it will be seen from the next sentence that the pepper was laid in water during the first few days of April, 1676.

[2] Unfortunately L. omits to state what kind of water he used. Had he done so, it would have afforded some help in attempting to determine the organisms which he found in it later.

[3] About 3μ. See p. 337 *infra*.

[4] From the foregoing description I think it highly probable that the animal observed was *Bodo caudatus* (Duj.) Stein,—one of the commonest protozoa found in organic infusions. The description, as far as it goes, fits this animal almost exactly.

The second sort of animalcules consisted of a oval.[1] They had no less nimble a motion th animalcules first described, but they were in much greater numbers. And there was also a third sort, which exceeded both the former sorts in number. These were little animals with tails, like those that I've said were in rain-water.[2]

The fourth sort of little animals,[3] which drifted among the three sorts aforesaid, were incredibly small; nay, so small, in my sight, that I judged that even if 100 of these very wee animals lay stretched out one against another, they could not reach to the length of a grain of coarse sand[4]; and if this be true, then ten hundred thousand of these living creatures could scarce equal the bulk of a coarse sand-grain.

I discovered yet a fifth sort,[5] which had about the thickness of the last-said animalcules, but which were near twice as long.

2nd Observation [*on Pepper-water*].

The 26th of April,[6] I took 2½ ounces of snow-water (which was a good three years old, and which had stood throughout either in my cellar or in my closet in a glass bottle, well stoppered), wherein I was able to discover no living creatures. Having poured this same water into a porcelain tea-cup, with half an ounce of whole pepper, I set it likewise in my closet. I examined this water every day until May the 3rd, but could discover therein no living creatures; and by now the water was so far evaporated away and absorbed by the pepper, that some

---

[1] Perhaps a *Cyclidium*—equally common in infusions of all sorts.

[2] *Vorticella* sp. Cf. p. 118 *supra*.

[3] Evidently bacteria.

[4] L.'s "coarse sand-grain"=approximately $\frac{1}{30}$ inch in diameter. Cf. p. 334 *infra*.

[5] Probably bacilli.

[6] *i.e.*, *anno* 1676.

of the pepper-corns began to lie dry. And this water was now so thick with particles, that you might almost imagine you were looking at the spawn of very wee fish, what time the fish discharges its roe, when the roe-corns are very soft, and as 'twere hang together. Thereupon I added snow-water to the pepper once more, until the pepper-corns lay under about half an inch.

The 4th and 5th of May, examined it again, but perceived no living creatures.

The 6th *ditto*, I discovered very many exceeding small animalcules.[1] Their body seemed, to my eye, twice as long as broad. Their motion was very slow, and oft-times roundabout.

The 7th *ditto*, I saw the last-mentioned animalcules in still greater numbers.

On the 10th *ditto*, I added more snow-water to the pepper, because the water was again so diminished that the pepper-corns began to lie dry.

The 13th and 14th *ditto*, the animalcules as before.

The 18th of May, the water was again so dried away, that I added snow-water to it once more.

The 23rd of May, I discovered, besides the foresaid animalcules, living creatures that were perfectly oval, like plovers' eggs.[2] I fancied that the head was placed at the pointed end, which at times was stuck out a bit more. Their body within was furnished with some 10, 12, or 14 globules, which lay separated from one another. When I put these animalcules on a dry place, they then changed

---

[1] Probably bacilli.

[2] *de Kievits eijeren gelijk* MS. "like Cuckow-eggs" *Phil. Trans.* *Kievit* means the Peewit or Lapwing (*Vanellus cristatus*), not the Cuckoo (*Cuculus canorus*). The eggs of the former are, of course, those which are known commercially as "Plovers' eggs". The distinction is not without importance here, as the "Plover's egg" is conspicuously pointed—that of the Cuckoo being much more rounded.—The organism was probably *Colpidium* or an allied ciliate. L.'s remarks a little later support the view that he was observing the "small variety" of *C. colpoda*—a very common inhabitant of such infusions.

their body into a perfect round, and thereupon oft-times burst asunder; and the globules, together with some watery humour, flowed out on all sides, without my being able to discern any other remains. These globules, which, in the bursting asunder, flowed apart from one another, were of about the bigness of the first-mentioned very little animalcules. And albeit I could as yet distinguish no feet on the said animalcules, none the less I imagined that they must be furnished with many very little ones; for the very smallest animalcules (whereof I have already said there were a great many in this water, and of which more than 100 sometimes lay around one of the little oval creatures) were driven away from the bigger ones by the motion which these made in the water (even when the big animalcules themselves seemed to me simply to lie still, without stirring at all), just as if you were to blow a feather from your mouth.[1] Of these oval animalcules I could never discover any very little kind,[2] how diligently soever I sought them.

The 24th *ditto*, examining this water again, I found the oval animalcules in a much greater number. *Ditto*, in the evening, looking again, I perceived so great a plenty of the oval animalcules, that 'twas not a mere thousand that I saw in one drop; while there were several thousands of the very small animalcules in the same drop.

The 25th *ditto*, I saw still more of the oval animalcules, and some most exceeding thin little tubes,[3] which I had also seen many a time before this.

The 26th *ditto*, I saw such a great many of the oval creatures, that I believe there were more than 6 or 8 thousand in one drop, not counting the multitude of very little animalcules, whereof the number was far greater.

---

[1] This is obviously a description of a ciliate (e.g. *Colpidium*), with actively vibrating cilia, lying among bacteria.

[2] *i.e.*, any young ones.

[3] *pijpjes* MS. Probably thread-bacteria.

But I took this water from the surface, and in the water that I took from underneath there were nowhere near as many. Seeing these little animals increase to so vast a number, but therewithal not being able to detect that they did wax in bigness, nor yet to espy any like creatures drifting in the water, I bethought me whether these animalcules might not well be put together in an instant (so to speak)[1]: but this speculation I leave to others.[2]

The 26th *ditto*, in the evening, I perceived almost none of the little animalcules; but I now saw divers creatures with tails (whereof I have said heretofore that I saw 'em in rain-water).[3] And furthermore I saw one animalcule that was three times as long as broad. Through all the water floated numberless particles, like thin little hairs off men who haven't been shaved for a fortnight[4]; but with this difference, that many had a kink in them.

The 27th *ditto*, I perceived none at all of the very little animalcules, but the large creatures in greater number.

The 28th *ditto*, almost all the animalcules in the pepper-water were become somewhat scantier.[5]

The 30th *ditto*, I discovered very few animalcules in the water, and I saw there now but one where some days before I had seen a good hundred. And as the water was

---

[1] *of deselvige niet wel in een moment des tijts* (*om soo te spreeken*) *en waren te samen gestelt* MS. He means that it crossed his mind that these animals might possibly come into existence, on a sudden, by a fortuitous concourse of inanimate particles in the water. As a rule, of course, L. strongly opposed the doctrine of spontaneous generation.

[2] *dog ik geef dit aen anderen over* MS.

[3] *i.e.*, *Vorticella* sp.

[4] By this quaint simile L. means to convey the idea that the particles, if magnified in diameter to the size of human hairs, would be about as long, in proportion, as those forming the beard of a normally clean-shaven man who had not shaved himself for about a fortnight.

[5] *wat dunder* MS., lit. = somewhat thinner. I take L. to mean that the water itself was now not so full of animalcules—not that the animalcules had themselves grown thinner. But Oldenburg seems to have taken the latter view, for he translates (*Phil. Trans.*) "all sorts of those living creatures in this peppery water were grown thinner." The ensuing paragraph supports the above reading.

now so dried away, that the pepper began again to lie above the surface, I filled up the tea-cup with snow-water once more.

On June the 1st, the animalcules were again in as great numbers as I had ever before seen, though I can't say that I saw any of the very little ones. But now I could see very plain that the animalcules were furnished with very thin little legs,[1] which was a very pretty sight to see.

The same day, I discovered some few very little round animalcules,[2] that were about 8 times as big as the smallest animalcules of all. These had so swift a motion before the eye, as they darted among the others, that 'tis not to be believed. The big creatures, which were about 8 times smaller than the eye of a louse,[3] were in no less number.

My further observations on this water I have made no note of.

3rd Observation [*on Pepper-water*].

On May the 26th, I took about ⅓ of an ounce of whole pepper, and pounded it small, and then put it in a tea-cup in which there was about 2½ ounces of rain-water, stirring this water about in order that the pepper might mix itself with the water and then sink to the bottom. And after letting it stand thus an hour or two, I took some of the forementioned water in which the whole pepper lay, and which contained a multiplicity of little animals, and mixed it with this water wherein the pounded pepper had now lain for one or two hours: and

---

[1] *i.e.*, the cilia on the ciliates (? *Colpidium*).

[2] Probably larger bacteria.

[3] This is the first indication which L. gives of the size of his ciliates. "About 8 times smaller" means "having a diameter of about a half": and this therefore agrees with the supposition that the "oval animalcule" was the small species (or variety) of *Colpidium* so commonly found in such infusions.

I observed that when I added rather much of the water containing the pounded pepper, it came to pass that the foresaid animalcules died forthwith; but when I added somewhat less of the same water, then the little creatures remained alive.

On June 2nd, in the forenoon, after I had made divers observations since the 26th *ultimo*, but without being able to discover any living creatures, I now saw a few particles which had, indeed, the figure of some of the little animals, although I could distinguish no life in them, how attentively soever I looked. On the 2nd again, at night, about 11 o'clock, I discovered a few very little living animalcules.

The 3rd *ditto*, I discovered therein many more animalcules, which were all very small, and about 2 or 3 times as long as broad.[1] All through this water little bubbles kept rising, as if 'twere fresh beer that stood fermenting.

The 4th *ditto*, in the morning, I found therein a great many animalcules. The same day, in the afternoon, examining the water again, I saw such a great many living creatures in one drop of it, that they amounted to at least 8 or 10 thousand; and to my eye they were, when viewed through my microscope, like ordinary sand-grains to the naked eye.

On the 5th *ditto*, I discovered, besides the multifarious very little animalcules aforesaid, some few (but not above 8 or 10 in one drop of water) little oval animals,[2] whereof some exceeded the others quite 8 times in bigness,[3] whilst the biggest of them were in shape like the oval animalcules that I have made mention of before (those that were in the water wherein the whole pepper lay).[4]

---

[1] *soo lang als breet* MS. "as broad as long" *Phil. Trans.*—an obvious mistake.—The organisms were evidently bacilli.

[2] Probably *Colpidium* again.

[3] *i.e.*, were twice as long.

[4] *i.e.*, they resembled the organisms previously identified as *Colpidium*.

On the 6th *ditto*, the animalcules were as before.

On the 8th *ditto*, the little oval animals[1] were multiplied, swimming among the foresaid very numerous little animalcules[2]; and now they[3] were very nearly all of one and the same bigness.

The 9th of June, the oval animalcules were in yet greater number, but the very little animalcules were now less. And now, using again a particular method in observing, I saw the little feet or legs[4] (wherewith the animalcules were provided underneath their body, which was flat) moving very plainly; and with such a swiftness, that 'tis incredible. And methinks that ever and anon I could make out that each of the globules, whereof, as I have said, their body was for the most part composed, was not perfectly round, but every one of them stuck out in a point, in the same fashion as the shields or plates on the sturgeon or thornback do.[5] The said animalcules were, to my eye, 8 times smaller than the eye of a louse.[6]

On the 10th *ditto* I took a little of the last-mentioned water, and mixed it with a little water wherein 36 cloves had now lain for about 3 weeks; and I perceived that, no sooner did the multifarious little animals aforesaid come into this mixed water, than they were dead.

On the 12th *ditto*, the said animalcules seen in no less number; and as the water was now so evaporated away and sucked up by the pepper, that the pepper itself began

---

[1] *Colpidium.*

[2] Bacteria.

[3] *i.e.*, the colpidia. L. cannot have meant that the ciliates and bacteria were now equal in size.

[4] *i.e.*, the cilia (on the *Colpidium*).

[5] *i.e.*, like the "placoid scales" of some Ganoid and Elasmobranch fishes, such as the sturgeon (*Acipenser*) and the thornback (*Raja clavata*).

[6] This estimate accords with that given for the "oval animalcules" under date June 1 (2nd observation).—Oldenburg's translation in the *Phil. Trans.* terminates at this point. All that follows has never previously appeared in print.

to lie dry, I threw the latter away, after first of all tasting it on my tongue, and finding it as strong as if it had just been pounded.

4th Observation [on Pepper-water].

The 14th of June, a certain quantity of whole pepper put in well-water.

The 16th *ditto*, in the morning, on examining the same, I discovered, in a tiny drop of water, incredibly many very little animalcules, and these of divers sorts and sizes.[1] My further observations I have not made note of, save that on the 17th of July still more animalcules were seen, and among them many of the little oval creatures[2] many times mentioned already.

Examining the water again on July 20th, I now saw, with very great wonder, that some very long and very thin particles (which I imagine had come to my notice in various waters before) were alive. These most wonderful living creatures seemed, when viewed through my microscope, thinner than a very fine hair of one's head, and about as long as the back of a bread-knife,[3] others quite twice as long. Their whole body appeared of one and the same thickness throughout, without my being able to make out a head or any bodily parts; and therewithal their body was very clear, and 'twas thus very troublesome to succeed in seeing 'em alive in the water. They moved with bendings, as an eel swims in the water; only with this difference, that whereas an eel always swims with its head in front, and never tail first,

---

[1] Bacteria—various sorts.

[2] *Colpidium.*

[3] Another of L.'s homely similes. He means that the "animalcules" were very long, and uniformly thin—their proportions being similar to those of the blunt edge, or back, of a large knife such as is used for cutting bread; though their thickness actually appeared not so great, but even less than that of a human hair as seen by the naked eye. It is a peculiar comparison, but on the whole conveys a tolerably accurate notion of the appearance of the long thread-bacteria which he was evidently observing.

yet these animalcules swam as well backwards as forwards, though their motion was very slow.[1] And were I to contrast these creatures with the eels or worms which are in vinegar,[2] I imagine the proportions would be thus:

As a worm of the bigness of a big pin, is to an eel of the thickness of one's wrist: So are these very little living creatures or eels in the pepper-water, to the size of the eels in vinegar.

5th Observation [*on Pepper-water*].

On August the 2nd, in the evening about 7 o'clock, I again examined my well-water, which was very clear (especially when it stood in a kettle or pot; but standing in a clean glass, alongside of clean rain-water, the rain-water outdid the well-water in clearness). In this well-water I saw living a great many of the oft-mentioned very little animalcules[3]; some thousands, indeed, in one drop of water. I then poured some of this water into a porcelain tea-cup, adding thereto a quantity of coarsely pounded pepper; and I stirred round the pepper in the water, deliberating whether the said animalcules would remain alive in the peppery water, or whether they would die. This water and pepper having been stirred up, I examined it, and saw the animalcules living: after the lapse of half an hour I examined it again, and saw the animalcules still alive, but their motion was not so quick as when they were in plain well-water. After the lapse of two hours more, examining the water again, I saw the

---

[1] A remarkably shrewd observation, which proves conclusively that L. was here dealing with bacteria. The organisms were evidently the long flexible thread-bacteria (*Pseudospira* C.D.) so common in infusions.

[2] Of these more anon. The "vinegar-eel" (*Anguillula aceti*) was described by L. in an earlier letter, dated 21 April 1676. See *Phil. Trans.*, Vol. IX, p. 653 (1676). Power, Kircher, Borel, and others had, however, discovered this organism at a still earlier date, though L. was apparently unaware of their observations. L. gives figures of the eel in a later letter (No. *43*, 5 Jan. 1685).

[3] *i.e.*, bacteria, in all probability.

animalcules even yet alive, though in much less number than heretofore.

On the 3rd of August, about 7 o'clock in the morning, I saw some few animalcules still alive; while the water was fermenting, as if it had been beer that stood and worked. In the afternoon, about 4 o'clock, examining it again, I still saw a few animalcules alive. In the evening, at about 9 o'clock, however, I saw very few animalcules living.

On the 4th *ditto*, about 6 o'clock in the morning, I could discover no living animalcules, how attentively soever I looked; but I thought I saw some floating dead. The evening of the same day, about 9 o'clock, I discovered 4 or 5 very little animalcules, and among them one somewhat bigger, and very round. Such an animalcule I have never seen in well-water.

The 5th *ditto*, in the morning, I saw again 4 or 5 very little animalcules, among them one that exceeded the others a bit in length: and amidst the very many particles, I judged that I could distinguish little forms which agreed in their shape with the foresaid living animalcules, but I could discern no life in them. On the afternoon of the same day, about 3 o'clock, I saw several most extraordinarily small animalcules (nay, even smaller than those in the well-water), together with many animalcules that were somewhat bigger. These last [1] were well-nigh round, and their motion was mostly all a-rolling, wherewithal they didn't much hurry themselves. Together with these was a sort [2] that were of the same size, but they were somewhat elliptical. And lastly, I also saw some[3] (though very few) which were a good 20 times bigger than the biggest sort spoken of above. These were

---

[1] Probably small flagellates (? *Monas* sp.).

[2] Unidentifiable. Perhaps more elongated specimens of the same *Monas*.

[3] Perhaps *Euplotes* or an allied hypotrichous ciliate. (The movements described indicate that it cannot have been a *Cyclidium*.) "A good 20 times bigger" means "having about thrice the diameter" of the former sort.

long, and bent crooked, the upper part of the body round, but flat beneath, looking much after the fashion of an $\frac{1}{8}$ part of the peel of a large citron. Their motion was all a-wallowing, on their back as well as on their belly. I could discern no little feet or legs on them; and after this time, moreover, I never saw them any more. In the evening, about 10 o'clock, I saw the very little animalcules,[1] and the round ones,[2] in much greater numbers; together with a little animal that was 3 or 4 times as long as broad [3]; and besides these, many little worms, or little eels [4], which were even smaller than the very tiny eels spoken of before.

On the 6th *ditto*, about 6 o'clock in the morning, I discovered a very great many (indeed, incredibly many) exceeding little animalcules, to which, because of their littleness, no shape can be given [5]; and with these a very great number of round animalcules,[6] which to my eye seemed quite eight times as big as the first animalcules (in which I have just said I could make out no shape). These round animalcules I imagine to be more than 50 times smaller than the eye of a louse. And besides these there was a third sort,[7] that were twice as long as broad, and which had about the length of the round animalcules. The fourth sort [8] was the very tiny eels; but now I could not see their bending, when they moved, so very plainly as I had seen it before: and at this time too I saw some (though very few) animalcules, which had very nearly the length of the eye of a louse, and which were in shape very

---

[1] Bacteria.

[2] ? *Monas* sp.

[3] Unidentifiable; ? a small flagellate. (Had it been large, L. would doubtless have supplied some further details.)

[4] Bacteria, probably *Spirillum* sp.

[5] Bacteria.

[6] Larger bacteria? (" 8 times as big " = of twice the diameter.)

[7] Unidentifiable.

[8] Spirilla.

much like (only much smaller) that animalcule which I have previously likened to a piece of citron-peel. Moreover, I could not convince myself that I now saw, among the sorts of animalcules described, those creatures which I have said I saw in the well-water, although I examined the well-water also.

The same day, about 3 o'clock in the afternoon, I saw still more animalcules, both the round ones and those that were twice as long as broad; and besides these, a sort which were still smaller; and also incredibly many of the very little animalcules whose shape, this morning, I could not make out. I now saw very plainly that these were little eels,[1] or worms, lying all huddled up together and wriggling; just as if you saw, with the naked eye, a whole tubful of very little eels and water, with the eels a-squirming among one another: and the whole water seemed to be alive with these multifarious animalcules. This was for me, among all the marvels that I have discovered in nature, the most marvellous of all; and I must say, for my part, that no more pleasant sight has ever yet come before my eye than these many thousands of living creatures, seen all alive in a little drop of water, moving among one another, each several creature having its own proper motion: and even if I said that there were a hundred thousand animalcules in one small drop of water which I took from the surface, I should not err. Others, seeing this, would reckon the number at quite ten times as many, whereof I have instances; but I say the least. My method for seeing the very smallest animalcules, and the little eels, I do not impart to others; nor yet that for seeing very many animalcules all at once; but I keep that for myself alone.

The same day, about 11 at night, the animalcules were as before. The sort in which I could hitherto discern no shape, I now fancied to be round, rather than long.

---

[1] Spirilla.

On the 7th *ditto*, about 8 o'clock in the morning, the animalcules were as heretofore. The little eels or worms were a bit bigger, but the very smallest animalcules I could not now make out. *Ditto*, in the evening about 8 o'clock, I now saw again the smallest animalcules of all, but few in number. The round animalcules very plentiful; and the animalcules which were twice as long as broad, together with the little eels, I saw in numbers unspeakably vast, for the amount of water.

The 8th *ditto*, about 8 in the morning, the animalcules as before. The same day, afternoon and evening, the animalcules seen in no less number.

The 9th *ditto*, in the morning, the animalcules as before. *Ditto*, in the afternoon, the animalcules in no less number, excepting that the round animalcules now seemed fewer to my eye.

Having been, from the 10th to the 17th of this month, in Brabant and elsewhere for a holiday, I now observed that the water was very small in amount, and thick with all manner of very small particles; and I saw that the animalcules lay alongside one another in great plenty, without any motion, save 2 or 3 animalcules which I saw moving feebly. Thereupon I again added a little well-water to the pepper and the water that remained over: and I then viewed the water, but notwithstanding could perceive no further movement in it, after several observations.

The 18th *ditto*, in the morning, examining this water again, I saw the animalcules alive and moving in as great numbers as ever heretofore, though their motion was not so quick; excepting only the little eels, none of which I could discern. *Ditto*, in the evening, the motion in the animalcules was as quick as ever before.

The 19th *ditto*, the animalcules as before.

The 20th *ditto*, the animalcules as before.

The 21st *ditto*, the animalcules aforesaid, that were almost round, were in incredibly great plenty, and more than ever before; the animalcules that were twice as long as broad were fewer in number than hitherto, and now I could discern that before and behind they ran somewhat to a point; and 'twas pretty to behold the motion, all a-quivering and a-shivering, that such very little creatures made in going forward. No others than these two sorts could I discover. Among other particles, there drifted through the liquid a multitude of short straight little tubes, several times (yea, 3 or 4 times) shorter than the foresaid very thin little eels or worms, so that they were only to be made out by very curious inspection.

The 21st *ditto*, in the afternoon, the animalcules in abundance, as before. The long animalcules are clear; the rounded ones appear encircled with a dark streak, and having at the hindmost part of their body a little dark spot or point.

The 22nd *ditto*, the animalcules as before. The short and very small tubules were in greater numbers.

The 3rd of September, the animalcules being as before, without my being able to espy any notable change in them, I again poured well-water (in which there were many living animalcules) upon the pepper, and at the same time put also two eggspoonfuls of coarsely pounded pepper into the water; considering whether the animalcules might not then die.

[1] (I have, moreover, well-water containing whole pepper still standing in my closet; but I have sent no notes of the observations made thereon. I have seen in it, besides divers animalcules, a great many little eels or little worms, together with a sort of little animals that were a bit smaller than the oval creatures already oft-times referred to. These were rounded like an oval at the hind end of the body, but their foremost part had, at its end, a crooked bend, like a parrot's beak.[2]

[1] The whole of this passage is thus put in parenthesis in the MS., and was perhaps meant for a footnote.

[2] Probably *Chilodon.*

The animalcules which I have throughout called "oval animalcules", are not really oval, unless you look upon them on the back or upper part of their body; and as the making of observations is well-nigh a study in itself, I have only just now exhibited them to myself very prettily in side-view, and have demonstrated not only their little feet, but also their head, and their very short and pointed little tail. At such perfection in this tiny creature I did greatly marvel[1]: and were it not that the multiplicity of solid particles (which are present in plain water) hindered me, I could describe the little animals even more distinctly.)

The 4th of September, the animalcules were seen in such great abundance as never before; but whether the animalcules which were at first present in the well-water were yet alive, I still can't say for certain.

The 5th *ditto*, the animalcules in an incredible number, much greater than hitherto; but they consisted of only two sorts, to wit: the roundish animalcules, and the animalcules that were twice as long as broad, albeit some few somewhat exceeded the others in length. The long animalcules were a bit thicker than the hair of a louse, and the round ones about twice as thick.

The 6th *ditto*, the animalcules in as great abundance as heretofore. I now imagined that the long animalcules consisted of two sorts: and I imagined, furthermore, that I saw animalcules of such extreme littleness as I had never up to this date seen in pepper-water.

The 7th *ditto*, the animalcules in even greater number than before this date.

The 8th of September, besides the foresaid long animal-

---

[1] L. was always carried away with delight at beholding the "perfections" of "little animals". So also, it appears, was his draughtsman: for L. tells us elsewhere that in making drawings of a flea he was repeatedly provoked to exclaim (his words being given by L. in large capitals) "*Lieve God wat sijnder al wonderen in soo een kleyn schepsel!*" (*Letter 76*, 15 Oct. 1693.) Cf. also p. 279 *infra*.

cules and roundish animalcules, I discovered three which had the figure of a pear, only with this difference, that on the underside of their body they were flat.[1] Such a sort I had not seen till now in any water. And I had such a hunt for these creatures, because they were so few, that I gave no heed to the very smallest ones.

The 9th *ditto*, I perceived but one of the animalcules that had the figure of a pear, in four several observations. And though there was still quite a lot of water with the pepper, yet I added more well-water to it, because the pepper-water was become rather thick. *Ditto*, in the afternoon, about 4 o'clock, I could see none at all of the animalcules that had been in great plenty in the well-water ere I poured it on the pepper; neither could I discover any of the animalcules that had the figure of a pear.

The 10th *ditto*, in the morning, the roundish and the long animalcules were now in such inexpressibly great crowds, that they far exceeded in number all the animalcules that I had ever seen up to this date in any waters. Moreover, I could discern no other sort.

On the 14th *ditto*, I could remark no change since the 10th, save only that I now saw again animalcules which had the figure of a pear; and I saw there besides an animalcule with a tail.[2]

The 15th *ditto*, I saw more animalcules that had the figure of a pear, and two or three animalcules with tails. And I perceived at this time that the pear-shaped animalcules kept not against the surface of the water, like the other creatures, but that they swam a bit deeper under water. Their thickness was about that of a single small thread of a silk-worm,[3] and they were about 1½ times

---

[1] Evidently a hypotrichous ciliate.

[2] *i.e.*, *Vorticella*.

[3] Cf. *Letter 146*. 20 April 1702. To the Landgrave of Hesse. Printed fully in Dutch and Latin collective editions.

as long as broad. The smaller nearly round animalcules, and the long ones, were present in no less number.

The 16th *ditto*, the animalcules that had the figure of a pear, as before: the animalcules with tails were increased to a greater number: the small round animalcules, and the animalcules that were twice as long as broad, were now diminished in number.

[1] [The 16th *ditto*, the animalcules that had the figure of a pear, as before: the animalcules with tails were even more numerous than formerly: the long and the round small animalcules were even more reduced in number.] On this occasion I discovered three animalcules[2] that were equally thick throughout, but which tapered to rounded ends before and behind, very like the fruit that we call dates.[3] The thickness of them was about that of a very fine sheep's hair.[4] Their motion was very curious, with a rolling about and a tumbling and a drawing of themselves together into a round.

The 17th *ditto*, the animalcules that had a figure like a pear, as before: the animalcules with tails in greater number: the long and the round animalcules were decreased still further, and therewithal very slow a-moving. The animalcules that were equally thick throughout were somewhat more plentiful; and now I could make out

---

[1] The passage here placed in square brackets is in the MS., but it is obviously a repetition—with slight differences in wording—of the preceding paragraph. L. seems to have paraphrased the same entry in his notebook (for Sept. 16) twice over, by mistake.

[2] Evidently a large ciliate—probably *Oxytricha*.

[3] *dalen* MS. I have been unable to find this word in any dictionary—ancient or modern. Oldenburg (MS. *ined.*) translated the word thus, and may have had some authority for so doing. Elsewhere, however, L. speaks of the date by its usual Dutch name, *dadel* : cf. *Letter 47*, 12 Oct. 1685. The description is consistent with the above rendering : and Dr E. P. Snijders informs me that candied dates are still sometimes called "*confijte dalen*", in popular speech, in Holland.

[4] Elsewhere (*Letter 80*, 2 Mar. 1694) L. shows that sheep's wool consists of a number of "fine hairs" stuck together. By "a fine sheep's hair" he here means, apparently, one of these component filaments.

that they were a bit flat in front, furnished with divers little legs, which during motion stuck out a bit beyond the body; and at the hind end of the body there was a round spot, running out headwards in a dark streak, looking very much like the guts or the blood in the body of a louse,[1] as seen with the naked eye.

The 19th of September, the numerous long and roundish little animalcules were much slower in their motion, and amany of them lay without any motion at all. The animalcules with tails were increased to yet greater numbers: the animalcules equally thick throughout, and those that had the figure of a pear, were in number as before.

My further observations I have not recorded: I can only say this, that in the course of a day or two the water again got so thick, that all the animalcules that were still in it moved themselves very slow; and 2 or 3 days after I had poured in well-water once more, I perceived the small animalcules in as vast a number as ever heretofore.

[*Observations on Vinegar.*]

For the last 2 or 3 years I have not been able to find any little worms, or eels,[2] in the vinegar that I keep in a cask in my cellar, for my household. I now[3] drew off ⅓ pint of this vinegar into a glass, and set it in my closet, covering it over with a paper to keep off the dust: and after the lapse of 11 days, I did perceive therein little eels, which multiplied from day to day. I have divers times put a little vinegar into a little pepper-water, and have always seen that as soon as the pepper-water

---

[1] A more particular description of this phenomenon was given by L. in an earlier letter (7 April 1674) published—in part only—in *Phil. Trans.*, Vol. IX, p. 23. The more famous description of the "blood and guts in the louse" by Swammerdam was not published until long after this date.

[2] See note 2 on p. 141.

[3] No date is here recorded.

was mixed with the vinegar, the animalcules that were in the pepper-water died instantly; albeit that I was unable to perceive that the little eels, which were in the vinegar, suffered any hurt from the pepper-water.

At another time I took some 10 parts of the pepper-water last spoken of (at the time when the living creatures were most plentiful in it), and added to it about $\frac{1}{10}$ part[1] of vinegar, containing living eels, or little worms. This vinegar I put in at the bottom, and not on the surface, of the pepper-water: and I took note that, the moment the vinegar was added to the pepper-water, the multifarious very little animalcules that were next the bottom, where the vinegar was, lay without any motion; and those animalcules lying further from the bottom became slower in their motion; and after the lapse of a little while, all the very little animalcules were dead: yet the motion of the little eels was no less in this water than when they were in the vinegar alone. This pepper-water and vinegar, which together equalled in quantity one big drop of water, I observed almost from day to day: and after the lapse of about 2 or 3 weeks, I saw that the little eels in this mixed water were greatly increased; for where at first I had seen but 10 eels, I now saw fully 200 of 'em. And among the rest I saw a great number of very little eels, near of one and the same bigness as one another, whose length, to my eye, equalled about $\frac{1}{4}$ or $\frac{1}{5}$ part of the biggest eels of all; but notwithstanding the further observations that I made, I was able to discover no smaller eels, nor yet any particles that looked like the foresaid very little animalcules[2]; but they seemed all gone, without any remains being left over. Seeing this multitude of little eels (in the mixture of 10 parts pepper-water and 1 part vinegar), I imagined that surely they were not

---

[1] As becomes evident later, L. means that he took 1 part of vinegar to 10 parts of pepper-water—not, as he apparently says, one-tenth of a part of the former to 10 parts of the latter.

[2] *i.e.*, bacteria.

generated from any particles which might have been in the pepper-water, nor yet from such as might have been in the vinegar, as this, mixed with pepper-water, would have become unfit for the production of living creatures: but I felt firmly persuaded that the said little eels had become thus increased by procreation. I then made use of certain means, in order to throw more light on these very little animalcules; and first of all, after I had broken asunder or pulled apart some of the biggest sort (corresponding to those that I had seen originally in my wine), I saw that they were provided inside with a long structure, which had about ⅓ of the thickness of the eel itself. I imagined that this was the gut of the little animal. In some, moreover, I saw still much thinner long structures, which I imagined might well be small eels: otherwise the body of this creature was very soft, and streamed away on all sides in many big globules of various sorts, and others that were very little (in proportion to the animalcule). These globules did not consist of watery matter, but were, in fact, oil: for just as clearly as you can, by the eye, distinguish oil floating on water, from the water itself, so clearly could I see the oily particles, among which were some so small that they well-nigh escaped the sight. These curiosities of mine I divers times followed up further; and at last I saw very plainly, among other things, that from an eel which I had broken across the middle, there came out four distinct small eels, each twisted on itself, very nice and pretty, and each bigger than the one following: and the biggest, which came out first, lay and lived, and wrenched itself loose, and remained alive a little while.[1] I have more than once been able to see a small eel, out of an eel which I

---

[1] All these exact observations can be very easily confirmed. The vinegar-eel is viviparous; and L. was evidently here dealing with large pregnant females, whose larval young drop out and behave just as he says when they are torn in two.—These were the first observations ever made on the reproduction of *Anguillula*.

had broken in pieces, lie a-writhing, and remain alive so long, that it wearied me to keep my eye upon it. I have also seen two small living eels come forth from an eel after I had cut it in pieces: and they moved themselves, and swam, and were in bigness like the smallest sort. To sum up, the more observations I made on this matter, the clearer did I demonstrate that the small living eels come out of eels: and I conceive also that 'tis certain I have seen the little eels alive in the big eels; but this came to my notice only when I had taken the big eels out of the vinegar, and when they lay a-dying.[1]

. . . .

[*Observations on Ginger-water.*]

The 6th of May, 1676, I put into a porcelain tea-cup, which holds a little more than 2½ ounces of water, three of the ordinary large pieces[2] of ginger, after I had first of all bruised them a bit with a hammer; merely with the idea of seeing if the snow-water which I poured on the ginger would bring forth living creatures with it.

The 14th *ditto*. I observed this water almost every day, but till now I could perceive no living animalcules; and by this time the water was so dried up, or drawn into the ginger, that I poured fresh water upon it.

The 29th *ditto*, having again examined this water almost from day to day since the 14th, I now discovered

---

[1] L. at this point enters upon a long digression (about one whole page), in which he describes and discusses the structure of the peppercorns themselves and attempts to explain why they have a hot taste. This leads him further to discuss the constitution of wheat and other kinds of grain, and several physiological problems suggested by his observations. After this he suddenly returns to his experiments with infusions, and at this point I have resumed my translation. The observations here omitted have no interest from a protistological standpoint.

[2] *clauwen* MS. L. evidently means the broken pieces of the dried rhizome of the plant, as commonly sold by apothecaries.—I am informed that the irregularly branching pieces of rhizome are known in the trade as "hands" of ginger: and I take it that L.'s "claws" were the broken-off "fingers" of such "hands".

some very little animalcules, a bit longer and bigger than the small animalcules seen by me in the pepper-water. Nevertheless, these had a different form and motion; for while the animalcules in the pepper-water went forward all winding-wise, these animalcules all advanced in jumps, hopping like a magpie: yet were they very few in number.[1]

The 30th of May, observing the ginger-water anew, I discovered at least 25 times more animalcules therein than previously. Among them were some quite three times as long as broad, and I fancied I saw that their fore and hind ends were fashioned aslant; that is, with an acute angle and an obtuse angle, as I have said before[2] of a like sort that were bigger. *Ditto*, about 10 o'clock at night, the said animalcules seen in greater number.

The 31st *ditto*, the foresaid animalcules seen in still much greater number, amounting to several thousand in one drop of water: and some of them exceeded the others in length.

The 1st of June, the animalcules seen in still greater number.

The 3rd *ditto*, the animalcules seen in such a vast number (in the water that I took from above, off the surface of the water), that were I to declare, according to my own judgement, how many thousands there were in one drop of water, 'twould not be believable.

The 4th of June, the water was again so evaporated away, that the bits of ginger began to lie dry; so I poured on rain-water at this time.

The 10th *ditto*, upon the water lay a thick film, which I took off: and I then saw some oval animalcules,[3] in size and shape like those that I have said were in the pepper-water.

---

[1] From the description of its jumping movements, this was probably a *Cyclidium*—noted earlier.

[2] See p. 132, 1st observation on pepper-water. ? *Bodo* sp.

[3] Ciliates, but otherwise unidentifiable.

The 11th *ditto*, the oval animalcules were in greater number, mostly swimming at the top, against the thin film that had come again over the water. On this occasion I marvelled to see the violence that the first-mentioned little living creatures[1] exercised, whenever they came out of the water on to a dry place, ere they fell a-dying.

The 12th *ditto*, the oval animalcules were now in great plenty, as well as the other animalcules: and because the film that lay upon the water had grown in thickness, I poured the water and ginger away.[2]

. . . .

[*Observations on Clove-water.*]

On the 17th of May, 1676, I placed 36 cloves in some 2½ ounces of rain-water, after I had first of all examined the rain-water and found nought therein (so far as animalcules are concerned), save a very few creatures that were roundish, and which looked to my eye, through my microscope, no bigger than a coarse sand-grain doth to one's naked eye.

The 25th of May. Up to this date I could perceive no living creatures, notwithstanding the many observations I had made since the 17th of this month. I now added more rain-water (wherein I could discern no animalcules) to the cloves.

The 12th of July. After I had made divers observations on this water, and between-times had filled up the tea-cup with water once more; and having no thought that I should discover living creatures in this water, so

---

[1] *i.e.*, those seen on May 29 (? *Cyclidium*).

[2] L. again digresses at this point in order to describe the structure of the macerated ginger itself. After a long description and discussion—occupying more than one whole page of the MS.—he returns to the subject of animalcules, and at this point my translation is resumed. Nothing of protozoological or bacteriological importance is contained in the lines which I have omitted.

that I did not examine it from day to day, and kept no note of when I last added water thereunto: on this date I discovered very many living creatures, which displayed themselves, through my microscope, as no bigger than an ordinary sand-grain to the naked eye. These were very clear, and seemed to be about twice as long as broad. Along with them were some few animalcules which looked as big as ordinary ant-eggs[1]; the upper part of their body being round and raised, the under part flat, like unto tortoises in shape. Their whole body seemed to be made up of no other parts than big and little globules, which were all very glittering, so long as the animalcules were alive: but when I brought them into a dry place (whereupon they oft-times burst asunder), the glittering went off; and the globules became smaller, and flowed away on all sides, together with some watery humour in which these globules lay. These animalcules were provided underneath the body with divers little legs, whereof 5 or 6 stuck out in front of the head during motion.

The 14th *ditto*, I discovered many more animalcules than heretofore, but most of them were very small.

The 19th *ditto*, I discovered, besides the said creatures, many animalcules with tails,[2] along with many long animalcules that were fashioned aslant in front; and if I saw aright, their hindmost part was somewhat cloven, their body flat below and round above, their length well anigh that of the little oval animals.

The 4th of August, I did not perceive the long animalcules, but exceeding many very little animalcules, and some few that were a bit bigger. The water being now almost evaporated away, I added well-water to it.

---

[1] *i.e.*, they appeared, through the microscope, about as big as "ant-eggs" appear to the naked eye. (In a later letter L. showed that the structures commonly called "ant-eggs" are not really the ova of the ant, but its pupae. Cf. *Letter 58*, 9 Sept. 1687.) From the description which follows, they were obviously hypotrichous ciliates: but it is impossible to identify them more precisely.

[2] *i.e.*, some species of *Vorticella*. Cf. p. 118.

The 8th *ditto*, I saw very many animalcules whose figure was like an oval, and these were to my eye, through my microscope, like coarse sand-grains to the naked eye; and there were some few animalcules with tails; likewise some little animalcules, and plenty that were bigger, and had the length of the eye of a louse. These were bent a bit crooked, the underneath part flat; and therewithal looking much like an eighth part of a preserved citron-peel. Their motion was all turning about, so that I am persuaded that they had no little legs; and though they were a bit smaller, they resembled very closely the little animals previously likened to a piece of citron-peel. So great was their number, that it did not amount to a mere thousand or two in one drop.

The 17th of August, the animalcules found as before; but their motion was very slow: and as over a half of this water was evaporated away, I added well-water to it again.

The 18th *ditto*, the animalcules as before, and now their motion was a bit quicker again; and I now saw again more animalcules with tails.

The 20th *ditto*, the animalcules with tails were so multiplied, that by now they were the most plentiful.

The 21st and 22nd *ditto*, the animalcules with tails were now less, and their motion, too, was very slow. Furthermore, these animalcules with tails, whenever they got themselves stuck by the tail in any bit of dirt, stretched 'emselves out somewhat longer than the animalcules with tails which I have seen in pepper-water. The little animalcules were now also less; and here and there I discovered one of the animalcules that I have likened to an eighth of a citron-peel.

The 3rd September, I took one or two cloves out of the water, and they were now become so soft that one could rub them to bits between one's fingers: and moreover, I found but little savour in them. The animalcules were now much decreased, and therefore, as the water was also diminished, I poured in well-water, in which were living animalcules. After the lapse of an hour, I examined this water; and whereas I had seen before very few of the animalcules inclining to an oval figure, I now saw many of them, together with animalcules that were twice as long as broad, besides the animalcules that were in the well-water, and a very few animalcules with tails. I added 8 fresh cloves to this water, wondering whether the animalcules in it would then die.

The 4th of September, the animalcules as before, saving that the animalcules with tails were so diminished, that I descried but 2 or 3 of 'em.

The 5th *ditto*, the animalcules inclining to an oval figure were in greater plenty; and I saw a few of those that were twice as long as broad, but none of the animalcules that had been in the well-water, nor of the animalcules with tails.

The 6th *ditto*, I perceived no other animalcules than those tending to an oval.

The 7th of September, saw animalcules which inclined to an oval, without being able to make out any other sort. However, they were decreased rather than increased, and their motion was not quicker, but rather slower.

The 8th of September, the motion of the animalcules even slower, and they were no more plentiful.

The 9th *ditto*, in the morning, at 8 o'clock, the animalcules as before: and because the motion was so slow, I added a little well-water. And in this well-water there were many very little living animalcules. *Ditto*, in the afternoon, at 4 o'clock, I now saw the animalcules that had been in the well-water still alive in plenty in this clove-water; and the other animalcules were now moving more lively. *Ditto*, in the evening at 8 o'clock, the animalcules that had been living in the well-water were now almost all of them dead; so that I was able to see but 2 or 3 alive after several observations.

The 10th *ditto*, at 9 o'clock in the morning, no animalcules seen except those inclining to a round oval figure; but the motion of these was a bit nimbler, and they were no less in number.

The 18th of September. The animalcules inclining to a round oval figure are got less from day to day since the 10th of this month, so that at this time I was able to see only a very few of them; but now I saw some extraordinary tiny animalcules, which looked, through my microscope, no bigger than common sand doth to the naked eye.

The 19th *ditto*, stirring the water around a little, and then examining it, I saw more of the animalcules likened to a round oval than before this date. Along with them I perceived the very little animalcules.

[*Observations on Nutmeg-water.*]

The 13th of July, 1676, I beat some big nutmegs in pieces with a hammer, and put them in 2½ ounces of well-water. This well-water I had divers times examined during the summer till this date, but could yet discover no living creatures in it, save now and then so few and extraordinary small, that I did not see them till I had made several observations.

The 17th *ditto*. Divers observations made since the 13th of the month, but no living creatures perceived therein. And now the nutmegs lay on top, against the surface of the water. The water itself lay fermenting, as if it had been fresh beer: and betwixt the bits of nutmeg lay a lot of round particles of oil, which were very supple. These were for the most part 1000 times smaller[1] than a small sand-grain.

The 19th *ditto*, the fermentation was all done with, and the nutmegs mostly sunken to the bottom.

---

[1] *i.e.*, in bulk: or, in other words, they had a diameter of about one-tenth of that of a small sand-grain—on L.'s scale, about one thousandth of an inch, or 25μ.

The 24th of July, the water was for the most part dried up. I again added well-water thereto; and in this well-water there were now many very little living creatures,[1] which, whenever the well-water came under the water containing the nutmegs, died in a trice.

The 3rd of August. Made divers observations since the last foregoing date, but discovered no living creatures in this water till to-day. The creatures now seen[2] were very few, and so small, that they well-nigh escaped the sight, notwithstanding that one had a very good microscope. And as the water was, for the most part, dried up again, and very many living creatures were at this time present in all the common kinds of water, I poured on some snow-water, in which there were no animalcules.

The 4th *ditto*, the animalcules as before; and they moved among so many various particles, of very near the same bigness as the animalcules themselves, that you would say, 'twas no mere water in which the nutmegs lay; for 'twas made up of soft fluid particles stuck beside one another, much as if you beheld, with your naked eye, the spawn of frogs, or the seed of fishes when it is spent.[3]

The 5th *ditto*, I saw plenty of animalcules, which I can't call long, they looked to me to be round rather; for they were no bigger, through my microscope, than very little sand-grains to one's naked eye; and I must say, that I deem them to be a good three or four times smaller than the thickness of the hair of a mite, or one of the little hairs wherewith the body of a louse is beset.[4]

The 6th *ditto*, the animalcules as before.

The 7th *ditto*, I saw a huge number of exceeding minute animalcules.

---

[1] Probably bacteria and monads.

[2] Bacteria.

[3] L. doubtless observed, on this occasion, bacterial "zoogloea" mixed with particles derived from the macerated nutmegs.

[4] Cf. p. 337 *infra*. The very minute animalcules here mentioned were undoubtedly bacteria.

The 17th *ditto*, I perceived no animalcules ; and as the water was much evaporated away, I added well-water, for want of snow-water.

The 18th *ditto*, no animalcules made out.

The 19th of August, many small animalcules seen again.

The 20th *ditto*, the animalcules as before.

The 21st *ditto*, the small animalcules seen in greater number. I likewise now saw some, though very few, that were a bit bigger. These last were very nearly round, only tending somewhat to an elliptical figure.

The 23rd *ditto*. Besides the said animalcules, I discerned, both now and yesterday, divers animalcules that were twice as long as broad, running to a point before and behind, and of the size of those in the pepper-water ; but their motion was not so quivering. I fancied the cause of this was that this water was thicker.

On the 3rd of September, I could perceive no animalcules. The water being now for the most part evaporated away, I added well-water, wherein were very many little animalcules. I also took a little bit of nutmeg out of the water, and tasting it upon my tongue, found it was still so strong that it surpassed many fresh nutmegs in savour.

The 4th *ditto*, the exceeding very little animalcules now seen alive once more.

The 7th of September, the very little animalcules seen alive, as before ; yet could I discern no animalcules of the sort that were in the well-water ere I put it to the nutmegs. My further observations I have not writ down.[1]

The objection hath divers times been urged against me, that there are, hovering in the air, extraordinary small living creatures, which are hid from our eyes, and can

---

[1] The record of observations ends at this point.

only be discerned by means of surpassing good magnifying-glasses, or telescopes; and these creatures, they say, have been seen in Rome.[1] For my part, notwith standing the manifold observations I have carried out to this end, I have as yet seen no lesser animalcules moving in the air than those which are so big that you can readily make them out with the naked eye. The very little particles which I have commonly found in the air, and which are there in motion, are all earthy particles, which are given off by (so to speak) "dustsome"[2] things. For you can't tear a sheet of paper apieces, but what more than a thousand very tiny fibres break off, and these so light withal, that they can't easily fall upon the earth, owing to the motion that is in the air: you can't draw a comb through the hair of your head, but what various very little particles, which lie or are stuck upon every hair, are set loose and moved in the air; not to mention the wearing away and the breaking off which each several hair suffers in the act of combing. Nor can you so much as rub your hands together, when they are dry, nor stroke your face, without thereby imparting a multitude of tiny scaled-off particles to the air; and 'tis even so with wood, earth, smoke, etc. Such particles as these would seldom fall upon the earth, so long as they be in the sun's rays, or in a light breeze; but on coming out of the sun's rays, and out of the strong motion of the air, they sink towards the earth: and these little bits of dust thus lying still, and not sticking to larger particles that are heavier, may again be set a-moving by the mere motion of the air, or the sun's rays. From what observations I have made hereon, I can't say I ever saw, among the rest, two bits of dust that exactly agreed with one another in shape. But I'll not deny that there can be, in the air, any living creatures which are so small as to escape our sight; I say

---

[1] A rumour, I take it, of the imaginative work of Athanasius Kircher.

[2] *stofligte* MS. L. here invents a word meaning "apt to form dust."

only that I haven't descried them. And furthermore, I am persuaded that they would not be able to remain alive in the air, about our horizon; rather would they be begotten in the clouds, where, in the continual dampness, they could remain alive, and so be conveyed still living to us in mist and rain. I fancy I have even seen something of the sort in the early summer of this year, on two several occasions, when there was a heavy mist here; but I saw the supposed creatures without any motion. And I believe I have now found out a means of performing such observations more exactly and nicely in future.

These observations concerning living creatures, in the liquors spoken of, were indeed deserving of closer attention and description; but for that, there had been need too of a whole man, which my circumstances did not allow of: for I have employed only my spare time upon them.[1]

Much light is thrown on the observations recorded in the foregoing letter by some of the Huygens correspondence. As the relevant MSS. are now accessible in print, and as it would take us too far afield to discuss the position of Huygens as a protozoologist, I shall not now consider this correspondence in detail. It is so important, however, that it cannot here be ignored, and I therefore add the following notes by way of supplement.

Christiaan Huygens never himself published any serious contributions to protozoology: and the records of his own observations, which were made in an attempt to repeat Leeuwenhoek's experiments, remained in manuscript and unknown until only a few years ago. Consequently, his private work[2] had no influence whatsoever upon the progress

---

[1] A few final remarks—having no bearing upon animalcules—are here omitted.

[2] Published for the first time in *Œuvres Compl. de Chr. Huygens*: see particularly Vol. VIII (1899), No. 2148, p. 122; and Vol. XIII, fasc. ii (1916), p. 698 *sq.* So far as I am aware, all that was previously known about Huygens's protozoological work is contained in the fragmentary notes in his *Opuscula Posthuma* (1703) and *Opera Reliqua* (1728). These show only that he was an imitator of L., and give no idea of the originality of his own observations. There is also a reference to the subject in Gregory (1713), however, while contemporary mention was made of his observations in the *Journ. d. Sçav.* for 1678.

of protozoology. Had it been published in his lifetime, it would have assured him a place in the very forefront of the founders of the science. Even at the present moment the excellence and originality of his observations have been largely obscured by his modern editors. In my opinion most of the protozoa described and roughly sketched by Huygens can be easily recognized by any competent protozoologist, yet his editors have not only failed to recognize the majority but have often misidentified common species most ludicrously. As examples, I may note that Huygens's unmistakable account of *Chilodon* (with figures, including a characteristic pair in conjugation) is interpreted as " probably infusoria of the genus *Bursaria* ": his description of *Astasia*, with its characteristic euglenoid movements and " hardly any colour ", is said to suggest the bright green and rigid *Phacus*—" if having hardly any colour be not taken to exclude a slight green coloration " : and so on. But we are here concerned with Leeuwenhoek—not with Huygens—so I shall say no more on this matter now. I hope to deal with Huygens's admirable observations on another occasion.

Whilst Leeuwenhoek's astonishing researches were being considered by the Royal Society, he himself was continuing them and was corresponding with Constantijn Huygens (*pater*) about his discoveries. Sir Constantijn was also in frequent communication with his son Christiaan, at Paris, to whom he reported Leeuwenhoek's findings. Christiaan, at first sceptical, soon repeated and confirmed the experiments: and at the end of 1678 he wrote a most interesting letter,[1] accompanied by a few sketches, to his elder brother Constantijn. In this letter Christiaan gave unmistakable[2] descriptions of *Chilodon*, *Paramecium*, *Astasia*, and *Vorticella*—all found in infusions: and he added " I should much like to know what Leeuwenhoek would say about all this, and whether he has seen anything like them." Evidently the letter was sent to Leeuwenhoek, who wrote to Constantijn Huygens *sen.* about it a little later.[3]

---

[1] Chr. Huygens to Const. Huygens *jun.* 18 Nov. 1678. Printed in *Œuvres Compl.* Vol. VIII (1899), No. 2148, p. 122.

[2] To me they are all unmistakable in this description: and when the notes of 26 July 1678 (published in *Œuvr. Compl.* XIII (ii), 702) are also taken into account, the identifications are surely beyond all doubt.

[3] Leeuwenhoek to Const. Huygens *sen.* 26 Dec. 1678. Letter printed in *Œuvr. Compl.* VIII, No. 2156, p. 140.

Leeuwenhoek here says that he can recognize all the animalcules described by Christiaan, and notes where he had himself observed them previously. But he makes one obvious though natural mistake: he takes Huygens's *Astasia* for the *Dileptus* which he himself discovered, and on which he had observed the cilia. Apart from this, Leeuwenhoek interpreted Huygens's protozoa conformably with my interpretations of his own.

Huygens observed not only the protozoa which Leeuwenhoek discovered in pepper-water, but he also saw and delineated (his fig. F.) the long thread-bacteria so commonly seen in infusions. On these organisms Leeuwenhoek comments:

> These long eels I have seen too. My wonder at these animals, was because one was 3 or 4 times as long as t'other, yet they were always of the very same thickness; and besides, they swam as well backwards as forwards, without my being able to make out any head, or anything that looked like a head. I have already written about all this to the Royal Society at London[1]. . . . .

This is an important passage, as it confirms what Leeuwenhoek had previously said about bacteria. A little later he adds the following remarks, with which we may conclude this first chapter in Protozoology:

> All these animalcules aforesaid I found too in ordinary water, though not so many by a long way as in pepper-water. And in the summer, when I feel disposed to look at all manner of little animals, I just take the water that has been standing a few days in the leaden gutter up on my roof, or the water out of stagnant shallow ditches: and in this I discover marvellous creatures.
>
> And whether I put in the water whole white pepper, black pepper, coarse pounded pepper, or pepper pounded as fine as flour, animalcules always turn up in it, even on the coldest days in winter, provided only that the water doesn't get frozen.
>
> This day [26 December 1678] there are in my pepper-water some animalcules which I judge to be quite 8 times

[1] See p. 140 above.

smaller than fig. A.,[1] on which I can make out the paws too, which are also pleasant to behold, because of their swift motions. The paws of these animalcules are very big, in proportion to their bodies.[2] Besides these animalcules, I discovered in pepper-water, some few weeks since, yet others which I judge to be a good 1000 times less than the animalcule in fig. A: for the circumference of the whole body of one of these extreme small creatures is no bigger than the thickness of a paw of the animalcule in fig. A: and I am persuaded that thirty million of these animalcules together wouldn't take up as much room, or be as big, as a coarse grain of sand.

---

[1] Referring to Huygens's sketch of a small (and unrecognizable) ciliate.

[2] L. probably here refers to the cirrhi on a small hypotrichous ciliate such as *Euplotes*.

CHAPTER 2

EPILOGUE TO LETTER 18. FURTHER OBSERVATIONS ON THE FREE-LIVING PROTOZOA AND BACTERIA

(LETTERS 19, 21, 23, 26, 29*a*, 30, 31, 32, 33, 71, 92, 96)

AS we have already seen, Leeuwenhoek communicated his discovery of the Protozoa and Bacteria not only to the Royal Society but also to Sir Constantijn Huygens. The latter evidently wrote a reply—which is lost—to which Leeuwenhoek rejoined, *inter alia* [1]:

> In order to answer Your Excellency's letter further, I must yet wait 2 or 3 weeks, for the reason that I have to repeat the observations I made some time since (concerning the living creatures in water) with two kinds of water, which, among others, I intend to study every day.

From these words it may be inferred that at the beginning of 1677 Leeuwenhoek was still hard at work on his discoveries. But the Royal Society also did not remain idle or disinterested: the Fellows wanted to know more. Consequently, in an editorial comment upon Leeuwenhoek's observations on the animalcules in pepper-water [2]—wherein he says that he saw "several thousands of the very small animalcules" in a single drop of liquid—Oldenburg remarks [3]: "*This* Phaenomenon, *and some of the following ones seeming to be very extraordinary, the Author hath been desired to acquaint us with his method of observing*, *that others may confirm such Observations as these.*"

---

[1] From *Letter dated 15 February 1677*. To Const. Huygens *sen*. The original Dutch MS. is at Leyden, and has recently been printed in *Œuvr. Compl. de Chr. Huygens* (1899), Vol. VIII, No. 2099, p. 21.

[2] See p. 135 *supra*, 2nd observation on pepper-water: 24 May 1676.

[3] *Phil. Trans.* (1677), Vol. XII, p. 829.

To Oldenburg's inquiries Leeuwenhoek sent the following characteristic reply[1]:

Your very welcome letters of the 12th and 22nd *ultimo*[2] have reached me safely. I was glad to see that Mr. Boyle[3] and Mr. Grew[4] sent me their remembrances: please give these gentlemen, on my behalf, my most respectful greetings. 'Twas also a pleasure to me to see that the other Philosophers[5] liked my observations on water, etc., though they found it hard to conceive of the huge number of little animals present in even a single

---

[1] *Letter 19.* 23 March 1677. MS.Roy.Soc.—The greater part of this letter was translated into English and published in *Phil. Trans.* (1677), Vol. XII, No. 134, pp. 844-846. The original MS., in Dutch, is accompanied by a MS. translation into Latin, concerning which L. makes the following statement in a postscript (in Dutch, which I translate): "Sir, seeing that you are most times hard pressed to find time to translate my observations into the English tongue, and mentioning this to a gentleman who hath divers times been to visit me; this gentleman offered me his services, to translate into Latin such of my observations as I may perchance communicate to you: which offer I did not decline, and I now send you his Latin copy herewith, along with my own letter. I await your answer, and would know if I can serve you by acting in this way in future." Although Oldenburg's translation is said to be "English'd out of Dutch", it appears to me almost certain—from comparison of the three versions—that the English was really rendered from the Latin, and not from the Dutch copy. My own translation—above—is from the latter, written in L.'s own hand. This will explain several slight discrepancies between Oldenburg's version and mine. It must be added that L. himself also printed a considerable extract from this letter, at a later date, in his *Letter 96* (9 Nov. 1695)—published in the Dutch and Latin works.

[2] *i.e.*, February 1677.

[3] The Hon. Robert Boyle (1627-1691)—"Father of Chemistry and brother of the Earl of Cork."

[4] Nehemiah Grew (1641-1712), to whom several of L.'s most interesting letters were addressed, was a Doctor of Medicine (Leyden, 1671) and Secretary of the Royal Society from 1677 to 1679. He was educated at Pembroke Hall, Cambridge, and became a Fellow of the Society in 1671: but he is best known for his botanical work, and his catalogue of the Society's museum. As a botanist he was the rival of Malpighi, and a pioneer in the study of vegetable morphology. His later work is deeply tinctured with religion. (His father, Obadiah Grew, was an ejected minister of the English Church.) For his biography see the *Dict. Nat. Biogr.* and Arber (1913).

[5] *de Heeren Philosophen* MS.—*i.e.*, the Fellows of the Royal Society.

drop of water. Yet I can't wonder at it, since 'tis difficult to comprehend such things without getting a sight of 'em.

But I have never affirmed, that the animals in water were present in such-and-such a number: I always say, that I imagine I see so many.

My division of the water, and my counting of the animalcules, are done after this fashion. I suppose that a drop of water doth equal a green pea in bigness;[1] and I take a very small quantity of water, which I cause to take on a round figure, of very near the same size as a millet-seed. This latter quantity of water I figure to myself to be the one-hundredth part of the foresaid drop: for I reckon that if the diameter of a millet-seed be taken as 1, then the diameter of a green pea must be quite $4\frac{1}{2}$. This being so, then a quantity of water of the bigness of a millet-seed maketh very nearly the $\frac{1}{91}$ part of a drop, according to the received rules of mathematicks (as shown in the margin). This amount of water, as big as a millet-seed, I introduce into a clean little glass tube (whenever I wish to let some curious person or other look at it). This slender little glass tube, containing the water, I divide again into 25 or 30, or more, parts; and I then bring it before my microscope, by means of two silver or copper springs, which I have attached thereto for this purpose, so as to be able to place the little glass tube before my microscope in any desired position, and to be able to push it up or down according as I think fit.

45'
45'
———
225
180
———
2025'
45'
———
10125
8100
———
91 | 125
millet-seeds equal one green pea in bigness (volume).

I showed the foresaid animalcules to a certain Gentleman, among others, in the manner just described; and he judged that he saw, in the $\frac{1}{30}$th part of a quantity

---

[1] In *Letter 96*, L. tells us that his standard "green pea" weighed 8 grains. See p. 214 *infra*.

of water as big as a millet-seed, more than 1000 living creatures. This same Gentleman beheld this sight with great wonder, and all the more because I told him that in this very water there were yet 2 or 3 sorts of even much smaller creatures that were not revealed to his eyes, but which I could see by means of other glasses and a different method (which I keep for myself alone). Now supposing that this Gentleman really saw 1000 animalcules in a particle of water but $\frac{1}{30}$th of the bigness of a millet-seed, that would be 30000 living creatures in a quantity of water as big as a millet-seed, and consequently 2730000 living creatures in one drop of water. Otherwise, I imagine the quantity of water to be of the bigness of a coarse sand-grain; and in this quantity I imagine that I see upwards of 1000 living creatures. Now I take it that the bigness of a coarse grain of sand beareth the following proportion to a drop of water: If the diameter of a sand-grain be 1, then that of a drop of water is more than 10, and consequently a drop of water is more than 1000 times bigger than a sand-grain. Thus there are more than a thousand times a thousand living creatures in a drop of water. 'Tis in such a fashion that I make my uncertain and imaginary reckoning of the animalcules in water: but I guard myself, so far as 'tis possible, against making the number too big, as you can see from the foregoing lines of my letter, wherein I have made the number not half so big as others well might do.

$$\begin{array}{r} 91 \\ 30000 \\ \hline 2730000 \end{array}$$

My counting is always as uncertain as that of folks who, when they see a big flock of sheep being driven, say, by merely casting their eye upon them, how many sheep there be in the whole flock. In order to do this with the greatest exactness, you have to imagine that the sheep are running alongside one another, so that the flock has a breadth of a certain number: then you multiply this by the number which you likewise imagine to make up the length, and so you estimate the size of the whole flock of sheep. And just as the supposed number may differ from the true number by fully 100, 150, or even 200, in a flock of 600 sheep, so may I be even more out of my reckoning in the case of these very little animalcules: for the smallest sort of animalcules,[1] which come daily to my view, I conceive to be more than 25 times smaller than one of those blood-globules which make the blood red; because I judge that if I take the diameter of one of these small animalcules as 1, then the diameter of a blood-globule is at least 3.

These, Sir, are the trifling observations which I have shown to divers curious persons, to their great satisfaction; but the other things that I have seen, and my particular microscope, I cannot yet resolve to make public: which I beg you, Sir, and your fellow philosophers, not to take amiss.

Since sending off my letter[2] concerning the little animals in water, I've not remained idle; but I have continued to examine divers sorts of water, examining even that which was distilled or boiled. During the last sharp spell of cold, when all the little animals had perished, I let the water thaw by the fire; and when it had stood a whole day in my bedchamber, with the fire kindled all the time, I saw, after the lapse of 24 hours (and at another time after 17 hours), that living creatures had come again in the water. Upon this subject I might, indeed, say something further; but I note that my former letter is still under your consideration, so I will spare you more.

To give your Philosophers further assurance, concerning the reality of the multifarious living creatures in even only a very little quantity of water, 'tis my intention, when they appear again in great plenty in the water, to obtain testimony thereof, which I shall then send you.

The foregoing Letter was read at the meeting of the Royal Society on 5 April 1677 [O.S.]; and the observations excited

---

[1] *i.e.*, Bacteria.

[2] Referring to *Letter 18* (p. 117 *supra*).

so much interest that the Secretary (Nehemiah Grew) was ordered to repeat Leeuwenhoek's experiments, for the greater satisfaction of the Fellows.[1]

In a further communication on the same subject—and various others—Leeuwenhoek fulfilled his promise to send the testimony of divers credible eye-witnesses in support of the truth of his statements. To a modern worker it seems somewhat curious that a scientific observer should think of calling in such people as notaries public and ministers of religion to vouch for the accuracy of his observations: but Leeuwenhoek could think of no better method of establishing his *bona fides*, and the result was, no doubt, satisfactory to all parties concerned. It should be remembered that Leeuwenhoek's reputation was not yet firmly established at this early stage in his scientific career, and we know that certain people had already expressed their doubts as to the accuracy of his observations. Among them was Christiaan Huygens, who, writing to Oldenburg in 1675, says: "I should greatly like to know how much credence our Mr Leeuwenhoek's observations obtain among you. He resolves everything into little globules; but for my own part, after vainly trying to see some of the things which he sees, I much misdoubt me whether they be not illusions of his sight; especially when he professes to discover the particles whereof water, wine, and other liquors, are composed."[2] It was this scepticism regarding his researches, apparently, which caused Leeuwenhoek to send those long and detailed extracts from his note-book—which, as already noted, are peculiar to his 18th Letter—to the Royal Society. The disbelievers, therefore, did a signal service to posterity; for they put Leeuwenhoek on his mettle,

---

[1] Cf. Birch, Vol. III, p. 338: "It was ordered, that Dr. Grew should be desired to try what he could observe in the like waters; and that for this purpose an extract should be given him by Mr. Oldenburg of Mr. Leewenhoeck's observations formerly read to the Society."

[2] *Huygens to Oldenburg; 30 January 1675.* MS.Roy.Soc. This letter has lately been published in *Œuvr. Compl. de Chr. Huygens*, Vol. VII, No. 2003, p. 399. The original is in French, and the above is my translation of the passage in question.—Huygens was mistaken in supposing that L. laid claim to having detected the particles (molecules) of which water and other liquids consist—as is abundantly proved by L.'s own statements: see, for example, his letter to Const. Huygens (20 May 1679) translated on p. 187 *infra*.

and thereby enabled us to read today a detailed record of some of the most remarkable and original researches ever executed.

The further communication referred to above is Leeuwenhoek's 21st Letter—according to my reckoning—and the passages in question are as follows [1]:

> In my letter of 23 March, 1677, I demonstrated that one drop of water (which is as big as a green pea) is equal in volume to 92⅛ [2] millet-seeds: and to bring it home to some friends of mine who could not grasp this, I took 6 millet-seeds and stuck them alongside one another with a little pitch. Then, with a pair of callipers, I took the width of the axes of the said millet [3]-seeds, and found the distance between the points was equal to the axis of a big currant; and I remarked that the cube of 6 is 216. Now, said I, let us put an uncertain for a certain quantity; and let us say, that as the currant sinks in water, and the millet-seeds sink likewise in water, they are therefore of like gravity: this being so, then 216 millet-seeds should weigh as heavy as this currant. I then placed the currant in a small but exceeding nice pair of scales, and found that 212 millet-seeds were of equal weight with the currant.
>
> I said also [4] that when I should again have a great number of living creatures in water, I would send you testimonials thereof, for the satisfaction of yourself and the other Philosophers: these I now send you herewith, from eight several Gentlemen, some of whom say that

---

[1] From *Letter 21.* 5 October 1677. To Oldenburg. MS.Roy.Soc. An English abstract was published by R. Hooke in his *Lectures and Collections* (1678), Part II; Letter I, pp. 81-83. (Also reprinted in Hooke's *Lectiones Cutlerianae,* 1679.) Apparently this letter, though sent to Oldenburg, came into Hooke's hands when he succeeded him—after his death—as Secretary of the Society.—This letter is called " [26] Brief 18*B* " by Vandevelde (1922, p. 356), who, as he was unaware of the existence of the original MS., could assign no date to it. My translation is made from the manuscript itself.

[2] This is a mistake. It should be 91⅛ (91·125). See p. 169 *supra.*

[3] In the MS. the word *geerst* (= millet) is here miswritten " *geest* ".

[4] *i.e.*, in his letter of 23 March 1677. See p. 171 *supra.*

they have seen 10,000 living creatures in a parcel of water the bigness of a millet-seed, while others say 30,000 and also 45,000. I have generally counselled these Gentlemen, when giving their testimony, to put down but half the number that they judged they had seen; for the reason that the number of animalcules in so small a quantity of water would else be so big, that 'twould not be credited: and when I stated in my letter of 9 October, 1676, that there were upwards of 1,000,000 living creatures in one drop of pepper-water, I might with truth have put the number at eight times as many. For if there be, as the testimonial saith, 45,000 animalcules in a quantity of water as big as a millet-seed, then there would be 4,140,000 living creatures in a drop of water: and over and above this vast number, I can say that I am able to discern at times even as many other living creatures, which are so little that they were hid from the sight of the Gentlemen who gave their testimony. The first number, when doubled, amounts therefore to 8,280,000 living creatures in one drop of water. This is inconceivable: but let us put it thus, that supposing a coarse grain of sand be divided into 8,000,000 parts, then I do indeed see little living creatures in water which are no bigger than these particles of sand would be. And this being conceived, 'twill not appear so marvellous.

45000
92
———
90000
4050000
———
4140000

The attestations[1] of the eight eye-witnesses have fortunately been preserved with the foregoing letter. There are actually five of them, but one bears three signatures and another two—making eight testimonies in all. One[2] is in

---

[1] Presented at a meeting of the Society on 15 October 1677, and read on November 1 [O.S.]. Cf. Birch, Vol. III, pp. 346, 347.

[2] By Alexander Petrie, son of a more famous father of the same name (*ca.*1594-1662) who was a Scottish divine and minister of the Scottish church at Rotterdam. The father's life will be found in *Dict. Nat. Biogr.*, but I have been unable to discover anything further about the son—the present writer.

English, and is written and signed by the minister of the English church at Delft. It is as follows[1]:

> I underwritten, being willing to give testimony unto that whereof I was an eye-witnesse, do declare that having seen and read Mr Leewenhoecks letter of March 23. 1677. as it is set down in the printed Philosophical Transactions, Numb. 134. p. 844. I was desirous to see a proof of what I found there related; and for my satisfaction, Mr Leewenhoeck did put a litle quantity of water, about the bignesse of a Millet-grain, into a very slender glasse-pipe, on which looking through his Microscope, I did see a very great number of litle animals moving in that water, so many that I could not possibly number them, and to my sight they seemed to exceed the number expressed in his fore-mentioned letter: and moreover, being desirous to see a proof whether those *animalcula* were indeed living animals, Mr Leewenhoeck by adding a very small quantity of vinegar to the same water, and putting it again into the same glasse-pipe, I did see those litle animals in the water, but they did not moove at all (being killed by the vinegar) which I beheld with admiration, that in so small a quantity of water I should see such a vast number of those litle animals. Whereof, being *Testis oculatus*, I was willing at the desire of ingenious Mr Leewenhoeck to confirm the truth of his relation by this testimony written and subscribed by me, in Delft, Aug: $\frac{20.}{30.}$ 1677.
>
> **Alex: Petrie.**
>
> Pastor of the English Congregation in Delft.

The other testimonials are couched in similar terms. There is a long one in Latin, signed by "Benedictus Haan[2] *Pastor*

---

[1] MS. Roy. Soc.

[2] Benedictus Haan (*seu* de Haan) was Lutheran minister successively at Breda (1666), Delft (1675), and Amsterdam (1692). He died in 1702, and is otherwise dimly remembered as the author of sundry verses which, according to van der Aa, "afford very feeble proof of his ability as a poet."

Luther: *Delph*:" and "M. Henricus Cordes[1] *Past. Luth. Hag.*"; and there are two shorter ones in the same language signed respectively by "R. Gordon[2] *Medicinae Studiosus*" and the three following persons: "J. Boogert[3] *J.U.L. et Notar. Publ.*"; "Rob. Poitevin[4] *Doct. m. monspel.*"; "W. V. Burch[5] *J.U.L. et coram curia Hollandiae advt.*" The remaining attestation is short and in Dutch, and is signed "Aldert Hodenpijl."[6]

---

[1] Hendrik Cordes, Lutheran minister at The Hague from 1674 to 1678, was the son of Paulus Cordes (1613-1674), who held a like office at Amsterdam. Hendrik, who died in 1678, is known to students of Spinoza: for his successor was the Colerus (Köhler) who wrote the life of the Jewish philosopher. Colerus (1705), speaking of Spinoza, says: "He had a great esteem for Dr. *Cordes*, my Predecessor; who was a learned and good natured Man, and of an exemplary Life, which gave occasion to *Spinosa* to praise him very often. Nay, he went sometimes to hear him preach, and he esteem'd particularly his learned way of explaining the Scripture, and the solid applications he made of it. He advised at the same time his Landlord and the People of the House, not to miss any Sermon of so excellent a Preacher." See Pollock (1899) p. 395.

[2] This was Sir Robert Gordon (1647-1704), who "travelled much into foreign countries for his improvement, was a man of extensive learning and knowledge, and particularly skilled in mechanics and chemistry." He was son of Sir Ludovick Gordon, of Gordonstoun, Elginshire, and became a Fellow of the Royal Society in 1686. (Cf. Birch, Vol. IV, pp. 454, 455.) Owing to his scientific pursuits he became known in the neighbourhood where he lived as "Sir Robert the Warlock". For his life see the *Dict. Nat. Biogr.*

[3] J. Boogert. The letters *J.U.L.* stand for *Juris Utriusque Licentiatus*—a degree inferior to that of *Doctor*. It is evident, therefore, that he was a lawyer and notary public; and Mr Bouricius tells me further that his forename was Johannes and he was the son of a physician. It is probable that he was the Jan Fransz. Boogert (or Bogaert) mentioned in Boitet (1729, pp. 453, 495) as one of the governors of the reformatory at Delft in 1677, and a governor of the poor-house in 1680. This J. B. died in 1702.

[4] Robert Poitevin, Doct[or] m[edicinae] Monspel[liensis], I cannot trace further: but I find that several other medical men with the same surname also qualified at Montpellier, where other members of this family resided. Perhaps he was the Leeuwenhoeks' family physician. Astruc (1767) makes no reference to him.

[5] W. v[an der] Burch. The words following his name show that he was a barrister; and I think he must have been the Willem Reyersz. v. d. Burch (1627-1712), sometime town-councillor and "*weesmeester*" at Delft, who is referred to in Boitet (1729, p. 90 *et alibi*)—though Mr Bouricius (*in litt.*) considers this doubtful.

[6] Aldert Hodenpijl. Mr Bouricius informs me that he was married to

All these attestations bear out what Leeuwenhoek himself tells us in his letters. But they also tell us that the capillary glass tube containing the animalcules was as thick as a horse-hair [1] (Haan and Cordes), and that it was divided into a large number of measured parts,[2] though it contained but a droplet of water no bigger than a millet-seed. Hodenpijl says the animalcules looked to him as large as lice, or even larger [3]: while Haan and Cordes declare that some of them appeared as big as bugs.[4]

To the testimony of these worthy men we may now add that of Christiaan Huygens, who, at the end of his French version of Leeuwenhoek's observations,[5] added the following remarks of his own [6]: "These are the observations of Mr. Leeuwenhoek. His manner of making them is to introduce the water into very little glass tubes, one third or one quarter of a line in diameter; and these he afterwards applies to his microscopes. He showed me some of these little insects very distinctly, continually tumbling about in the water". We may suppose, accordingly, that Huygens, when he wrote this, had overcome his original scepticism regarding Leeuwenhoek's observations. Indeed, the demonstration of which he here speaks was probably the stimulus which prompted him, soon

---

Judith le Roy, and he has found records of the baptism of three of their children (*circiter* 1668): but he has been able to find out nothing of present interest about him in the Archives of Delft. It seems probable, however, that Aldert H. is identical with *Aalbert* H. who is recorded in Boitet (1729, pp. 519-20) as having been *schutterkoning* (= champion shot) of Delft in 1661, 1665, and 1668. (The discrepancy between "Aldert" and "Aalbert" may be easily accounted for—Mr Bouricius assures me—by the "general slovenliness [*slordigheid*] in writing names at that time".) Why L. sent his testimony I do not know—unless it was because his pre-eminence in shooting guaranteed the excellence of his eyesight.

[1] *ad crassitiem pili equini crasso* MS.

[2] Haan and Cordes say 50 parts, Hodenpijl says 70, and Boogert and his co-signatories say 90. No doubt the discrepancy is to be explained by the circumstance that they recorded L.'s procedure on three different occasions.

[3] *hebbende de groote van een luijs, en sommige grooter* MS.

[4] *apparebant ad magnitudinem cimicis* MS.

[5] See p. 115, note 6.

[6] Published in *Œuvr. Compl. de Chr. Huygens*, Vol. VIII, p. 27. These remarks remained in manuscript until 1899, when this volume was published. The original is in French, and the above is my translation.

afterwards, to make his own remarkable contributions to protozoology.[1]

It cannot be doubted that the "very smallest animalcules," of which Leeuwenhoek himself speaks, were in reality not protozoa but bacteria. The particulars which he records prove this conclusively, and it is hardly necessary to make infusions of pepper—as I have done[2]—to convince oneself of this: while the fact becomes superabundantly clear from Leeuwenhoek's next letter on this subject, which was written at the beginning of 1678 and contains the following remarkable passage[3]:

> I can't help mentioning that I can now make out, very plain and clear, the shape of those little animals of the smallest sort, whereof I said before[4] that I could ascribe no figure to them; and this because of the pleasure that I do take in their manifold delightful structures, and the motions that they make from time to time in the water. Upon the 4th of this present month,[5] when it froze hard, I did fill a small clean glass with pounded pepper to $\frac{1}{3}$ of its height, adding $\frac{2}{3}$ of rain-water, and set it for the first night in my bedchamber. The next day, it[6] being well softened, I put it[7] in my closet; and within thrice 24

---

[1] See p. 163 *supra*.

[2] Cf. also Beijerinck (1913).

[3] From *Letter 23*, 14 January 1678. This letter was written to Robert Hooke, who published an incomplete English version of it in his *Lectures and Collections* (1678), Part II; Letter 2, pp. 84-89. This translation was made by Hooke himself: for in a letter to L., dated 10 March 1682 (MS. unpublished), he says so, and adds: "I have as neere as I could followed the sense of your Expressions though not verbatim."—I translate from the original MS. I may add that this letter serves to confirm my numeration of L.'s early epistles: for it is No. 23 according to my reckoning, and L. himself refers to it in his 113th Letter as "my 23rd". It was read at a meeting of the Society on 24 Jan. 1678 (cf. Birch, III, 380), but is not to be found in the *Phil. Trans.*, nor in the Dutch or Latin editions of the letters. Hooke reprinted his translation in *Lectiones Cutlerianae*, Part V (1679).

[4] *Letter 18*. (See p. 143 *supra*.) The organisms referred to were evidently bacilli.

[5] January, 1678.

[6] *i.e.*, the pepper.

[7] *i.e.*, the glass.

hours I discovered in it[1] so great a many of such inconceivably small creatures, that a man's mind may not contain them all: and in my judgement, the sort that were most plentiful were much more than 1000 times thinner than a hair of one's head, and 3 or 4 times as long as thick. These would oft-times shoot so swiftly forward with the hindmost part of their body, that you might think you saw a pike darting through the water; yet each shoot was, in length, most-times about half a hair's breadth. The figures of the other sorts of creatures, whereof some were even less, I shall pass over, else 'twould take all too long a-writing: I will only say, that in pepper-water, that hath stood somewhat long, I have oft-times seen, among the extraordinary little animalcules, little eels;[2] and the structure and the motions which these had, was as perfect as in big eels. But they were, to my eye, quite a thousand times thinner than a hair off one's head; and if a hundred of these little eels were laid out end to end, the whole length of them would not reach to the length of a full-grown one of those eels that are in vinegar.[3]

Leeuwenhoek's next letter in which we find any mention of protozoa was written in September of the same year (1678). It also contains some observations of whose precise significance I am uncertain: but it is so characteristic, and so clearly reveals his method of working and ways of thinking, that I cannot refrain from quoting it. This is what he there says[4]:

---

[1] *i.e.*, the pepper-infusion in the glass.

[2] Spirilla.

[3] *Anguillula aceti*—the "vinegar-eel"—which L. regarded as really a little fish. Large specimens measure about 1·5 mm. in length: cf. p. 335 *infra*.

[4] From *Letter 26*. 27 September 1678. To Nehemiah Grew. MS.Roy.Soc. Unpublished. (A poor contemporary English MS. translation accompanies the original Dutch MS.) The above is my translation of a part of the letter.—There is an important reference to this epistle in L.'s letters to Magliabechi (*vide* Targioni-Tozzetti, 1745: Epist. I, Vol. II, p. 345); but the observations on the reddening of grass are there referred to the year 1648—which must assuredly be a misreading or misprint for 1678.

But many of the things we imagine, and the natural objects that we inquire into, are very insignificant; and especially so, when we see those little living animals whose paws we can distinguish, and estimate that they are more than ten thousand times thinner than a hair of our beard; but I see, besides these, other living animalcules which are yet more than a hundred times less, and on which I can make out no paws, though from their structure and the motion of their body I am persuaded that they too are furnished with paws withal: and if their paws be proportioned to their body, like those of the bigger creatures, upon which I can see the paws, then, taking their measure at but a hundred times less, it follows that a million of their paws together make up but the thickness of a hair of my beard; while these paws, besides their organs for motion, must also be furnished with vessels whereby nourishment must pass through them.

Because many people, both in the towns and in the open country, are stricken with fever,[1] and because their shoes get very red whenever they walk through the grass in the meadows; the common man concludes that the air is therefore infected, and very fiery. This coming to my ears, I betook myself without the town and examined the dew: but I could find nought in it worthy of remark. However, seeing that my shoes also had got reddened by the grass, I turned my attention to the grass itself, and saw that some of it was studded with reddish dots. Bringing these before my microscope, I saw that they consisted of small globules, whereof upwards of a thousand did not equal the bigness of a small sand-grain. (I find there are various kinds of grass: and among others, one sort that was very rough, which was not contaminated [2].) Inquiring after a reason for these globules being upon the

---

[1] Probably a reference to malaria, and therefore of some interest at the present time.

[2] Marginal note in original.

grass, I observed that they came not out of the air (as was the vulgar opinion), but out of the grass itself: the cause whereof I conceived to be this. The dry cold, that we had some three weeks earlier, caused the death of the extreme tips of some blades of grass; and this was followed by very warm weather, which drove fresh nourishment again upwards through the pores[1] in the grass. But this food-matter, wherewith the pores of the grass were filled, being unable to get out at the top (because the ends or the uppermost pores of the grass were stiff and dried up), burst open the pores in many places where they were most weakened; and thus many globules were squeezed out of them. These globules, lying stuck together upon the outside of the grass, and becoming stiffer on exposure to the surrounding air, took upon themselves a reddish colour; whereas these same globules, when they lie inclosed in the pores, are green.[2] And whenever one happens to strike one's foot against such grass, the said globules are dusted off it, and make one's shoes reddish. But since a red colour is most agreeable with the notion of fire, we must not take it amiss in the common man if he deems the said substance to be a fiery matter: seeing that there are among us physicians (who fancy themselves experienced) who say, when they see blood whose whey-like matter[3] is yellow, that the blood is bilious; or say of black blood, that 'tis burnt: just as if everything yellow were bile; and everything black, burnt.[4]

Meantime the Fellows of the Royal Society[5] had not been wholly idle in the matter of the "little animals." Robert

---

[1] *Pori* MS.

[2] L. evidently confused the red corpuscles on the grass-blades with chloroplasts within them.

[3] *i.e.*, serum.

[4] It is clear from this, and many another passage in L.'s writings, that he had but a poor opinion of the general medical practitioner of his day.

[5] The Fellows (or some of them) would perhaps have taken particular interest in the observations on infusions: for they would recall—unlike

Hooke, who succeeded Oldenburg in 1677 as Secretary, himself repeated the experiments with pepper-water and other infusions. In 1678 he published[1] some account of his observations, which confirmed Leeuwenhoek's findings: and his experiments were also briefly communicated to Leeuwenhoek by letter at the end of 1677. Hooke's published description records that he succeeded in seeing the animalcules—or some like them—described by Leeuwenhoek: "some of these," he says, "so exceeding small, that millions of millions might be contained in one drop of water."[2] A draft of Hooke's unpublished letter is still in possession of the Royal Society; and as it contains several points of interest I will now give it. He wrote[3]:

> The papers you directed to the Lord Brouncker[4] were read at a full meeting of the Royall Society and very kindly accepted by the Members thereof and they have orderd me to returne you both their thanks for soe freely communicating your observations, and also an account of what hath been here done in order to verify your observation concerning the small animalls you have first discovered in Pepper-water.
>
> Having steeped then in Raine water pepper wheat

---

most modern Fellows—that Bacon, whose writings had so profound an influence upon the Society at its inception, had emphasized the need of inquiry into the various substances which produce animalcules by putrefaction. Cf. *Nov. Org.*, Lib. II, cap. 50: "*Etiam materiae diversae putrefactionum, unde animalcula generantur, notandae sunt.*"

[1] See *Lectures and Collections made by Robert Hooke* (1678). Part II, Microscopium. Also reprinted in *Lectiones Cutlerianae* (1679).

[2] *Ibid.*, p. 83. Hooke evidently refers to bacteria—not protozoa.

[3] MS. letter (unpublished)—R. Hooke to Leeuwenhoek, Dec. 1 [?— date partly obliterated], 1677. Roy.Soc.MSS. The original is in English, and I give it exactly as written—only omitting a part at the end which has no bearing upon the subject under consideration. I have merely expanded words which are contracted in the original—for the reader's convenience, and for typographical reasons. The letter is in Hooke's own hand, and is signed "your very great admirer and honorer R.H."

[4] William, second Viscount Brouncker (1620?—1684)—an Irish peer. He was M.D. (Oxford) and a mathematician, and an original Fellow and first President of the Royal Society on its re-foundation in 1662-3.

> barly oats pease and several other graines,[1] and having fitted up some microscopes which had layne a long while neglected, I having been by other urgent occupations diverted from making further inquirys with that Instrument, I began to examine all those severall Liquors and though I could discover divers very small creatures swimming up and down in every one of those steepings and even in Raine it self and that they had various shapes & differing motions, yet I found none soe exceedingly filled and stuffed as it were with them as was the water in which some cornes of pepper had been steeped. Of this the President & all the members present were satisfyed & it seems very wonderfull that there should be such an infinite number of animalls in soe imperceptible a quantity of matter. That these animalls should be soe perfectly shaped & indeed with such curious organs of motion as to be able to move nimbly, to turne, stay, accelerate & retard their progresse at pleasure. and it was not less surprising to find that these were gygantick monsters in comparison of a lesser sort which almost filled the water.

It seems clear that the "gygantick monsters" were protozoa, while those of the "lesser sort" were bacteria. The foregoing lines contain, I believe, the first mention of the discovery of any of these organisms in infusions of wheat, barley, oats, and peas: for none of these are recorded by Leeuwenhoek as having been used in making the "steepings" employed in his own experiments. It is therefore unfortunate that Hooke—so far as I can ascertain—never wrote any further descriptions of the organisms which he discovered.

Rumours of these remarkable discoveries spread, it would appear, into even the highest circles: for in another letter from Hooke to Leeuwenhoek, written a little later, the following passage occurs[2]:

---

[1] At a slightly later date—at a meeting of the Society on 7 March 1678—Hooke also demonstrated the presence of "animalcules" in infusions of aniseeds and coffee. See Birch, Vol. III, p. 391.

[2] MS. letter (unpublished), R. Hooke to Leeuwenhoek, dated 18 April

> The prospect of those small animalls have given great satisfaction to all Persons that have viewed them. His majesty[1] having been acquainted with it, was desirous to see them and very well pleasd with the Observation and mentiond your Name at the same time. I know not whether any of the ways I have here made use of for the Discovery of them may be in any thing like those with which you make your observations. But I have two or 3 other ways which I shall shortly communicate,[2] that doe farr exceed those I have here mentiond.[3]

Some important additional particulars regarding Hooke's observations can be gathered from Birch's *History*. He tells us[4] that at the meeting of the Society held on 1 November 1677 [O.S.]:

> There were produced a great many exceedingly small and thin pipes of glass of various sizes, some ten times as big as the hair of a man's head; others ten times less. These were made, in order to try a conjecture of Mr. Hooke propounded to the Society, that the discoveries, affirmed to be made by Mr. Leewenhoeck, were made by help of

---

1678 (Roy. Soc. MSS.). The original, of which only a part is here copied, is in English. It is written in Hooke's hand and signed "R.H." I again expand the abbreviations in the original, for the reader's convenience.

[1] *i.e.*, King Charles II of England, "Founder" and Patron (*Fundator et Patronus*) of the Royal Society—as he is styled in the *Charta secunda* of 1663.

[2] The communication will be found in Hooke's *Lect. & Collect.* (1678), p. 89 *et seqq.*

[3] This letter from Hooke is referred to by L. at the end of his own *Letter 28*, 25 April 1679, to N. Grew (*Brieven* I, p. 13: first published in Dutch in 1686). As the 28th Letter deals largely with spermatozoa, it has often been erroneously inferred that Hooke demonstrated spermatozoa—not protozoa—to the King. But the correspondence between Hooke and L. affords no grounds for such an inference; and I have been unable to discover any evidence in support of the accepted belief that the Merry Monarch was once entertained at an exhibition of spermatozoa by the Royal Society (or any member thereof). This myth probably originated with Haller (*Elementa* [1765], VII, 523)—as Cole (1930, p. 14) has already noted.

[4] Birch, Vol. III, p. 346.

> viewing with a good microscope such small pipes containing the liquor or water, in which those multitudes of exceedingly small insects or animals wriggling among each other are discovered; for that he alledged, that the said pipes being filled with liquors became themselves as it were magnifying glasses. . . . . . It was therefore ordered, that against the next meeting pepper-water should be provided, and some better microscope than that made use of, that the truth of Mr. Leewenhoeck's assertions might, if possible, be experimentally examined.

Accordingly, at the next meeting, on 8 November 1677, "the first thing exhibited was the experiment charged on Mr. Hooke at the last meeting, of examining pepper-water with better microscopes and thinner and small pipes."[1] But the experiment was not wholly satisfactory, and various objections to the observations were raised by the Fellows present. At the following meeting, however, on November 15, ample confirmation was forthcoming. In the words of Birch:[2]

> The first experiment there exhibited was the pepper-water, which had been made with rain-water and a small quantity of common black pepper put whole into it about nine or ten days before. In this Mr. Hooke had all the week discovered great numbers of exceedingly small animals swimming to and fro. They appeared of the bigness of a mite through a glass, that magnified about an hundred thousand times in bulk; and consequently it was judged, that they were near an hundred thousand times less than a mite. Their shape was to appearance like a very small clear bubble of an oval or egg form; and the biggest end of this egg-like bubble moved foremost. They were observed to have all manner of motions to and fro in the water; and by all, who saw them, they were verily believed to be animals; and that there could be no fallacy in the appearance. They were seen by Mr.

---

[1] Birch, Vol. III, p. 349.

[2] Birch, Vol. III, p. 352.

> Henshaw,[1] Sir Christopher Wren,[2] Sir John Hoskyns,[3] Sir Jonas Moore,[4] Dr. Mapletoft,[5] Mr. Hill,[6] Dr. Croune,[7] Dr. Grew,[8] Mr. Aubrey,[9] and divers others; so that there was no longer any doubt of Mr. Leewenhoeck's discovery.

Leeuwenhoek's next communication on the "animalcules" in infusions was sent to Robert Hooke, and is very brief; but it was accompanied by a copy of a very curious and interesting letter which he had previously written to Constantijn Huygens. In the letter to Hooke he says:[10]

> As I see and hear that you are a man much given to speculation, I have thought fit to send you a copy of a very rough calculation which I set down on paper at the urgent intreaty of Mr. Constantijn Huygens van

---

[1] Thomas Henshaw (1618-1700), barrister and author: Vice-President and an original Fellow of the Society. Cf. *Dict. Nat. Biogr.*

[2] Christopher Wren (1632-1723), artist and famous architect—soon to be President of the Society (1680)—too famous to need further annotation.

[3] John Hoskyns (1634-1705), barrister of the Middle Temple: later Secretary and President of the Society. Cf. *Dict. Nat. Biogr.*

[4] Jonas Moore (1617-1679), mathematician and surveyor. Elected F.R.S. in 1674. He is several times mentioned by Pepys in his *Diary*, and his life is given in the *Dict. Nat. Biogr.*

[5] John Mapletoft (1631-1721), M.D. and D.D., of Trinity College, Cambridge. Elected F.R.S. in 1676. He was an intimate friend of John Locke, and before he became a divine practised medicine in London with Sydenham.

[6] Abraham Hill (1635-1721), Treasurer of the Society, and an original Fellow. Commissioner of Trade in 1689—a business-man of no known scientific attainments.

[7] See p. 48, note 2, *supra*.

[8] See p. 168, note 4, *supra*.

[9] John Aubrey [*seu* Awbrey] (1626-1697), the well-known antiquary; an original Fellow of the Society.

[10] From *Letter* 29*a*. 16 January 1680. MS.Roy.Soc. An English extract from this letter—and its enclosure—was published in Derham's *Philos. Expts. & Obss. of R. Hooke* (1726), p. 55. (The letter is there incorrectly dated Jan. 6.) I translate from the Dutch original.—A contemporary English MS. translation is preserved with the original Dutch MS. in the Roy. Soc. collection, but it has given me no help. The letter was read at the meeting of the Society on 22 Jan. 1680 [O.S.], and discussed at the following meeting on Jan. 29. See Birch, Vol. IV, p. 5.

Zuylichem.[1] And I feel bound to say, furthermore, that last Friday evening I took some pepper-water, in which there were many living animalcules, and mixed it with about a like amount of rain-water, wherein I had put a quantity of pounded ginger: and forthwith examining this mixt water, I found that the animalcules were slow a-moving. Some hours afterwards, examining this water anew, I could perceive no animalcules whatsoever in it: but about twice 24 hours afterwards, I saw very distinctly some animalcules which I judged to be a hundred million times smaller than a sand-grain, but without being able to discern any of those animalcules that had been before in the pepper-water.[2]

The enclosed letter to Constantijn Huygens, dated 20 May 1679, I shall now give in full. The original, from which it was copied, is preserved among the Huygens manuscripts at Leyden[3]—the following being a complete translation of the copy sent to Hooke:

Along with this goeth my calculation, which I confess is quite imperfect, seeing that my estimates were made by the eye alone.

I have oft-times let my thoughts run on the extreme small vessels and sinews[4] wherewith the very little

---

[1] The father of Christiaan Huygens the astronomer and mathematician—not his elder brother. Cf. p. 42, note 2, *supra*.

[2] It is probable that the animalcules in the pepper-water were protozoa of some sort, which were killed when the ginger-water was poured upon them: while the very minute forms which developed in the mixture after 48 hours were evidently a new crop of bacteria.

[3] See Haaxman (1875), p. 136,—where the date is given as 21 May 1679: but L.'s copy, sent to Hooke, is by himself dated May 20, as stated above. The copy was made with his own hand.—The original has recently been printed in full in *Œuvr. Compl. de Chr. Huygens*, VIII, 168-172 (also there dated May 21).

[4] Or "nerves": MS. *senuwen*. *Zenuw* nowadays means a nerve—as it often did to L.—but at an early date it also meant a sinew (tendon), and from what follows this seems to be the correct rendering here. (Cf. the original meaning of Lat. *nervus* and Gr. *νεῦρον*.)

animalcules are furnished withal; and more especially when I have been asked, whether I am able to see the particles of water itself? To which I did often answer, that there be little animals in water that are many million times smaller than a sand-grain; and that these little animals, on which I can discern no feet, must notwithstanding be furnished with instruments for motion; and that these instruments must themselves consist, in part, of blood-vessels which convey nourishment into them, and of sinews which move them; and that through these vessels, moreover, water must also pass. And this being so, we must suppose the particles of the water itself to be so small as to be, for us, inconceivable: and I'm persuaded that no man will ever advance so far in science as to be able to gaze upon the particles whereof water itself consisteth.

I shall here first lay down the proportion which the animalcules bear to a sand-grain, in so far as my eye is able to arrive at it; together with the number of animalcules proportionate to the bigness of a cubic inch.

I usually judge that three or four hundred of the smallest animalcules, laid out one against another, would reach to the length of the axis of a common grain of sand; and taking only the least number (to wit 300), then

$$\begin{array}{r} 300 \\ 300 \\ \hline 90000 \\ 300 \\ \hline 27000000 \end{array}$$

27000000 animalcules together are as big as a sand-grain.

Let's assume that such a sand-grain is so big, that 80 of them, lying one against the other, would make up the length of one inch as BC [Text-fig. 1].

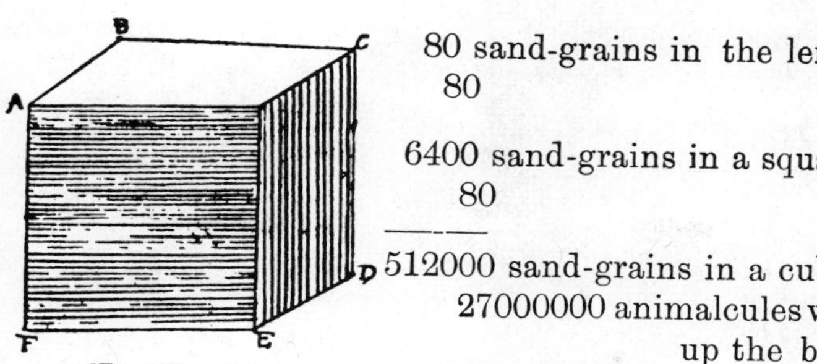

80 sand-grains in the length of one inch.
80

6400 sand-grains in a square inch.
80

512000 sand-grains in a cubic inch.
27000000 animalcules which make up the bigness of a sand-grain.

[Text-Fig. 1.]

amounting to 13824000000000 animalcules in a cubic inch, as ABCDEF.

This number of animalcules is so great, that if one had as many sand-grains, of the bigness aforesaid, then one could lade with them more than 108 of our ordinary sand-lighters; that is, reckoning one *schagt* of sand (which is 144 cubic feet) to every lighter.

I have let my thoughts run likewise on the very little vessels that are in our bodies, and have judged that they are above a thousand times thinner than a hair of one's head; and I have therefore put the proportion of the very little vessels thus in relation to the body, in order to arrive afterwards at the proportion of the vessels in the little animals.

First of all, I sought to know how many hairbreadths are equal to the length of one inch; and having by me a copper rule, whereon the inches are divided into 3 parts, and each of these again into 10 parts (thus altogether, an inch divided into 30 parts), I laid hairs from my periwig upon these divisions; and observing them thus through a microscope, I judged that 20 hairbreadths are equal to $\frac{1}{30}$ of an inch. Consequently, there are 600 hairbreadths in the length of one inch.

Further, I measured, roughly, the thickness of my body above the hips, and judged (taking one thing with another) that the diameter of my body was 8 inches.[1]

[1] If this were approximately correct, then L. was considerably more

Archimedes showeth that as 14 is to 11, so is the square of the diameter to the content of a circle.[1]

14—11—8		
8	704	
64	14	$50\frac{2}{7}$ square inches for my body's thickness.
11		
704		

	600	hairbreadths in a length of one inch.
	33	diameters of the very little vessels in our bodies for one hairbreadth (that is, reckoning the little vessels in our bodies 1089 times thinner than a hair)
gives	19800	little vessels in a length of one inch.
	19800	
gives	392040000	little vessels to a square inch.
	50	square inches for the body's thickness
gives	19602000000	vessels in the thickness of the body.

If we now suppose that the little vessels bear the same proportion to the bodies of the little animals, as those in us do to our bodies; then, in order to compare the very little vessels of the animalcules with the thickness of a sand-grain, the number given above must still be multiplied by 300 (since, as already said, a sand-grain is 300 times thicker than an animalcule).

---

slender than the apparently heavily-built man depicted in his portraits. Moreover, the statement is not easy to reconcile with the later record that at this date he weighed over 11 stone (cf. p. 222 *infra*).

[1] Nowadays we usually find the area of a circle by πr^2; but $^{11}/_{14} \times d^2$ is obviously the same thing, and Prof. D'Arcy Thompson informs me that it is actually in this form that the proposition is found in the *Circuli Dimensio* of Archimedes.—It is highly improbable, of course, that L. had ever studied the writings of this great mathematician.

Consequently, if the thickness of a sand-grain is 1, the vessels in the little animalcules are ——

19602000000
300
5880600000000

And because this number is so exceeding great, I have thought good to express the proportion in terms of a hair's breadth in relation to the circumference of the earth.

	5400	miles[1] for the length of the circumference
	2000	rods for every mile
gives	10800000	rods for the circumference
	12	feet for one rod
gives	129600000	feet for the circumference
	12	inches in one foot
gives	1555200000	inches in the circumference
	600	hairbreadths in one inch
gives	933120000000	hairbreadths for the length of the circumference.

This number of hairbreadths, which is equal to the length of the circumference of the earth, even when again multiplied by 6 will not equal that number aforesaid which represents the proportion of the vessels in the little animals to the thickness of a sand-grain (as we have estimated it above). To sum up, then:

As a sixth of a hair-breadth is:
To a length of 5400 miles:
So is one of the smallest vessels in the smallest animalcules:
To the thickness of a sand-grain (of such size that 80 thereof, lying one against another, equal a length of one inch).

Sir, you have here the wonderful proportions that I

[1] Leeuwenhoek's "mile", consisting of 2000 "rods" of 12 feet, is, as a simple calculation shows, equal to some $4\frac{1}{2}$ English miles. (The English mile = 320 rods, and the English rod = $16\frac{1}{2}$ feet.)

conceive to exist in the secret parts of Nature: and from this appeareth also, that all we have yet discovered is but a trifle, in comparison of what still lies hid in the great treasury of Nature; and how small must be those particles of water[1] which, to all appearance, pass many at a time through such tiny vessels.

I hope that with this I have satisfied your requirements.[2]

I have given the foregoing letter in full for several reasons. In the first place, it serves to illustrate Leeuwenhoek's fondness for simple mathematical deductions; secondly, it shows very clearly that, in the case of his "smallest animalcules", he was dealing with bacteria; and thirdly, it shows the success and failure of the application of his "uniformitarian" principles to microscopic creatures. In his estimate of the size and numbers of the bacteria present in a minute drop of water, he was not mistaken: but when he proceeded to show, by simple arithmetic, the magnitude of the blood-vessels in such organisms, he went ludicrously astray. His education and his century both failed him. His greatness and his littleness are here revealed simultaneously—to those endowed with the accumulated knowledge of the next 250 years. Yet even at the present day Leeuwenhoek's mistaken conclusion may serve as a warning to the biologist with statistical tendencies. It is surely worthy of remembrance, even now, that the most flawless mathematical calculations may sometimes be wholly erroneous.

Leeuwenhoek's next observations on "animalcules" are contained in a further letter to Robert Hooke. After recording some observations of no[3] present interest, the letter ends thus:[4]

---

[1] *i.e.*, the molecules of which water itself is composed.

[2] Referring to Const. Huygens's request that he should put down on paper his calculations concerning the magnitude of the parts of the "little animals" (*vide supra*).

[3] A few words which are perhaps not irrelevant to the present subject will be referred to later (see p. 207 *infra*).

[4] *Letter 30.* 5 April 1680. To R. Hooke. MS.Roy.Soc. Published in *Brieven*, Vol. I (Dutch), and *Opera Omnia*, Vol. I (Latin): also an English abstract in *Phil. Trans.* (1693), Vol. XVII, No. 196, p. 593; but this does not include the passage here quoted.

In the court-yard of my house there stand two vines; and observing their growth to be such, that a moisture dripped from their shoots, I examined this sap on several successive occasions, just to see if I could discover any living creatures in it: and most times I discerned therein divers kinds of living animalcules, whereof one sort was uncommon big in comparison of the others; nay, I even saw some little animals that I had seen aforetime in divers sorts of water. Hereupon I repaired to my garden which lieth within this town, and there too I examined the sap dripping from the vines, but in it I could discover no living creatures, save only a little worm that was of an uncommon bigness,[1] compared with the other animalcules. I betook myself thence to my garden which lieth without the town, and there again examined the sap from several vines, but could discover no living animalcules in it. I cut off pieces from two vine-branches, to make them drip the more, and went to examine the sap again next day, but could find therein nothing living. And I took a new glass phial, and caught the sap in it, and carried it home and examined it; but notwithstanding, I could perceive no living animalcules in it. I am now busy finding out, if 'tis possible, why there be living animalcules in one sap, but none in the other.

A little later Leeuwenhoek addressed another letter on the same subject to Dr Gale,[2] and in it recorded the results of his further experiments and observations on the sap of vines. This letter is as follows:[3]

---

[1] Probably a nematode.

[2] Thomas Gale (1635?—1702), a Doctor of Divinity, was at this time Secretary of the Royal Society—an office to which he was appointed in November, 1679. He was a Fellow of Trinity College, Cambridge, and Professor of Greek in the University from 1662 to 1672. Later (1697) he became Dean of York.—At the beginning of this letter L. says that he is writing to Gale because Hooke had informed him that Gale was become Foreign Secretary, and that he should therefore address his letters to him in future.

[3] *Letter 31.* 13 May 1680. To Thomas Gale. MS.Roy.Soc. Printed

This serves as a continuation of my letter of the 5th of April [1680], wherein I noted how I had observed living animalcules[1] in the sap leaking from the shoots of the vine standing in my court-yard; whereas in the sap which dripped from the vines in my garden, I could discover no living creature. I have divers times turned my thoughts to this matter, and can find no more satisfactory explanation thereof than the following:

The rain-water, which is drawn aloft by the power of the sun, and forms the clouds, is commingled with the seed of these animalcules; and as it had been raining for several days running, before the date of my first observations on vine-sap, the tags of leather, wherewith the branches of the vine were nailed fast against a stone wall, had become quite water-logged; but afterwards there followed a warm sunshine, which caused the vine-branches to drip, and thus the foresaid leathern tags were kept continually wet, by the dripping of the vine upon them; and in this manner not only did divers sorts of animals come forth from this rain-water, but they even (so I imagine) bred in it, and swam along the vine-branches, even to the topmost part of the vine, where the moisture dropped out.

About 24 hours after I had dispatched my observations to Mr. Hooke, the vine-branches in my court-yard stopped dripping, and the weather grew uncommon warm, so that the vine-branches, and the leathers as well, got quite dry: hereafter, it rained near the whole night, then the sun shone in the morning, and it rained afresh in the afternoon: and observing that the leathern tags (with which, as remarked above, the branches of the vine were nailed fast to the wall) were once more soaked through, I

---

in *Brieven*, Vol. I (Dutch), *Opera Omnia*, Vol. I (Latin), and briefly abstracted in English in *Phil. Trans.* (1693), Vol. XVII, No. 196, pp. 593-4,—along with the preceding letter. It was presented at a meeting of the Society on 13 May 1680 [O.S.] (Birch, Vol. IV, p. 37). I translate the whole letter, with the exception of a few words at the beginning and the end.

[1] The MS. says *Dierkens*, but the printed letter has *Dieren* (=animals).

examined the water that lay upon them, and in it I discovered[1] sundry little animals of the biggest sort previously seen in the sap aforesaid, and I saw some of a lesser sort lying dead: and when I examined these animalcules more narrowly, I found that they belonged to two kinds commonly present in ordinary waters.[2] After this time, about the middle of April, it rained a whole day, and the night following; and next morning, when the sun came out, I betook myself to my garden, and [examined][3] the sap dripping from a vine-branch, which I had cut a few days before, in order to make it drip, at the same time tying or binding a strip of wash-leather around it, so that when it rained, the rain-water would stay caught in it, and not readily dry up, and thus get better mixed with the sap that dripped out: and in this water I discovered a few animalcules of the sort already described. I also examined the sap from a second vine, which I had likewise treated in the same way, and herein too I perceived the animalcules. I also visited a third vine, from which I had also previously cut off a branch, so that it would drip;[4] but this one I did not tie round with a leather, and I took the sap that ran down the branch at the place where it was most plentiful (namely, in a fork, where the shoot came off the stem); but I

A A

[TEXT-FIG. 2.]

could perceive no living animalcules in it, though I saw in it, with admiration, many little chrysalises, or pupae, as in Fig. A A [see Text-fig. 2]: and although they were

[1] *gesien* MS. *ontdekt* printed version.

[2] It is obviously impossible to identify these "animalcules", though they were probably protozoa or bacteria of some sort.

[3] A verb is here accidentally omitted from the MS. and also from the Dutch printed version. The sense evidently requires "examined" or "observed"; and as the Latin translator supplied "*examinavi*", I do likewise.

[4] These words (*op dat die druipen soude*) are in the printed version but not in the MS.

more than a million times smaller than a coarse sand-grain, yet could I see very plainly that they were furnished with 5 joints. This appeared very strange to me, as I had formerly convinced myself that no water-animalcules proceed from such structures, and I had never conceived that animalcules of such littleness could live in the air. I took these chrysalises home, and put some of them in the air, to see what would come out of them; but within a few days, they got so dry that their former figure was scarce discernible; and those which I meant to keep in water got lost.

These trifles are all I have to tell you for the time being.[1]

The foregoing characteristic observations upon protozoa (or bacteria) show us an interesting picture of Leeuwenhoek at work—discovering new "animalcules" in new situations, wondering how they make their appearance and multiply in certain liquids, and endeavouring to account for their apparently erratic distribution. Soon afterwards he again attacked the problem of their generation, and sent the following account of his experiments:[2]

When it became known to me that divers opinions have been expressed concerning the generation of little animals; and as I heard, especially, that a certain Gentleman[3] hath writ that no living creature can be generated if the vessel, or bottle, in which any moisture or meat has been put, be tightly stoppered; I had a mind to carry out some trials of this matter.

---

[1] This sentence is in the MS. but not in the printed version.

[2] From *Letter 32*. 14 June 1680. To Thomas Gale. MS.Roy.Soc. Printed in *Brieven*, Vol. I (Dutch) and *Opera Omnia*, Vol. II (Latin). No abstract of this letter was published in the *Phil. Trans.* though the letter is a very remarkable one. It contains, in addition to the observations here related, a description of yeasts obtained from beer—the first microscopic study of these organisms.

[3] Doubtless Francesco Redi, whose celebrated treatise on "the Generation of Insects" first appeared in 1668. L. could know of Redi's work only by hearsay, since he was ignorant of Italian.

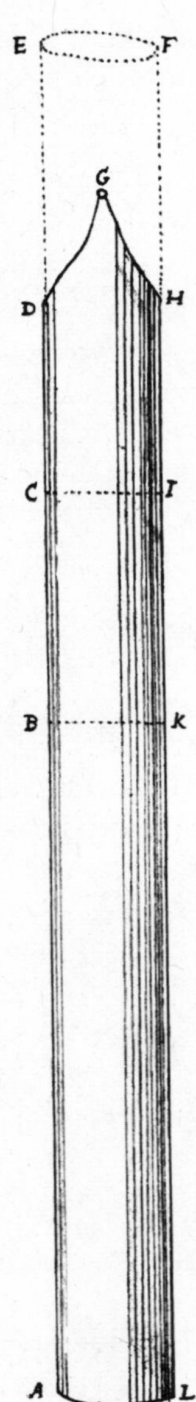

A FIGURE FROM LETTER 32 (14 JUNE 1680)

illustrating the experiment with the pepper-tube. On the left, Leeuwenhoek's original drawing (reduced to $\frac{4}{5}$): on the right, the same figure as improved by the engraver for reproduction in the printed letter (same size).

Accordingly, I took two glass tubes, as ABCDEFHIKL [Plate XXII], which, after they were both closed below at AL, were filled up to BK with pounded pepper, and then to CI with clean rain-water, as soon as it had been collected on May 26[1] in a clean china dish (in which no victuals had been put for quite ten years); then, by the heat of the flame, the glass was fashioned to the figure of ABCDGHIKL, having at its pointed end G a small opening; for I considered that though the glass was now hot, the air within it would presently become equally cold with the air that was outside it; and after the lapse of about a quarter of an hour, I sealed up the aperture at G tight, by means of the flame. I also prepared myself a second glass, treating it likewise, save that in this I left the aperture at G open; in order to ascertain, if 'twere possible, in which water the living animalcules would first turn up. But after it had stood thus for three days, during which time I made divers observations upon it, I judged that if there were already any very little living animalcules in this water, 'twould not be possible for me to discover them, for the reason that the glass was too thick, and because of the many little particles of pepper which lay against the glass inside, so that it was not feasible to carry out such particular observations as the occasion required. On this account, I took a little water out of the second glass, through the small opening at G; and I discovered in it a great many very little animalcules, of divers sorts and moving about among one another, each several sort having its own particular motion. But as the first tube was of a somewhat thinner glass, I left it shut up till the fifth day, and during that time made various observations upon it; but I could discover no living animalcules in it, so I resolved to break the glass open at G, and in breaking it, the air which had thus been shut up for 5 days within it (and which was much

---

Anno 1680.

compressed by the air-bubbles which rose everywhere to the top of the water) escaped with force out of the tube: for which reason I rather fancied that there would be no living creatures in this water. But I found the contrary: for no sooner did I draw some water through the small opening I had made at G, and bring it before my microscope, than I perceived in it a kind of living animalcules that were round, and bigger than the biggest sort that I have said were in the other water, though they were yet so small that it was not possible for me to discern them through the thickness of the glass tube.[1] After this tube had stood thus open for 24 hours, I examined the water again; and I then saw, besides the foresaid animalcules, various other sorts, though they were so small that they were hard to make out.

Still, I bethought me that when that Gentleman aforesaid spake of living creatures[2], he meant only worms or maggots, which you commonly see in rotten meat, and which ordinarily proceed from the eggs of flies, and which are so big that we have no need of a good[3] microscope to descry[4] them.

The whole of the foregoing passage (as printed in Dutch) has recently been copied and learnedly commented upon by Prof. Beijerinck (1913), who himself repeated the experiments. He infers that the "animalcules" which Leeuwenhoek discovered were undoubtedly bacteria—not protozoa—and that among them were probably (as he found in his own experiments) *Bacillus coli*, *Azotobacter*, and *Amylobacter saccharobutyricum.* It was to this last species, he thinks, that the "bigger sort" which were found in the sealed tube probably belonged. Beijerinck also points out that these are the earliest known observations on any anaerobic bacteria: but although

[1] So in the printed version. The MS. has "for reasons already mentioned" (*voor de verhaelde oorsaeken*).

[2] *dierkens* MS. *schepsels* printed version.

[3] *goet* is in printed version, but not in MS.

[4] *bekennen* MS. *beschouwen* printed version.

Leeuwenhoek discovered that organisms could live and multiply under the hemi-anaerobic conditions present in his closed tube, he was unable at that time, of course, to realize the full importance of his discovery. I have also confirmed the foregoing observations, though I made no attempt to determine exactly what species of bacteria were present in the tubes—being satisfied with Prof. Beijerinck's authoritative opinion. I am also satisfied that no protozoa can usually be obtained in experiments such as the above if the procedure described be adhered to.

It seems remarkable that Leeuwenhoek—always a vigorous opponent of the doctrine of spontaneous generation—appears to have made no further study of the very interesting phenomena which the foregoing experiments record. He must have been puzzled, at first, to account for the appearance of bacteria in his sealed tube: but I think his own words supply the explanation which occurred to him, and which apparently satisfied him at that time. In previous letters[1] he makes the suggestion that "animalcules" or their "seeds" are present, or can exist, in rain—being drawn up into the clouds with the water in which they live or are formed, and subsequently scattered when the rain falls. Consequently, he probably imagined that the rain-water introduced into the sealed tube already contained "animalcules"—or "seeds" capable of germinating into "animalcules"—which found sufficient "air" in the tube to enable them to live and breathe and multiply for at least some days. Nearly a hundred years subsequently elapsed before any further light was shed on this subject by the ingenious experiments of Spallanzani, though it was not until much later that the problem was solved—more or less completely—by Pasteur and Tyndall. Redi's famous observations by no means solved the problem of spontaneous generation—as is often lightly stated: and this point is clearly brought out by Leeuwenhoek's experiment, as he himself apparently realized; though he made no attempt—or, at least, recorded none—to push his inquiries any further.

A few months after he had written the foregoing letter to Dr Gale, Leeuwenhoek wrote again to Dr Hooke: and in

---

[1] Cf. *Letter 18* (p. 163) and *Letter 31* (p. 194).

the course of his letter he gave some further details concerning the animalcules in pepper-water. His words are as follows:[1]

> Some days ago I once more poured water upon some pounded pepper; and a few days later, I saw, among others, two kinds of animalcules[2] in it; and moreover, there seemed to be big and little ones of either sort,[3] so that methought the big ones were full-grown, and the little ones their young; and at the same time I imagined that in the biggest sort of these animalcules I could see the young, or maybe their eggs, inside their bodies.[4] And I imagined, besides, whenever I saw two little animals entangled together, either swimming or lying still, that they were a-copulating.
>
> [5] Whereas I suffer many contradictions, and oft-times hear it said that I do but tell fairy-tales about the little animals, and that there are people in France who do not scruple to say that those are not living creatures which I exhibit, and that if such water be boiled, the particles which one imagines to be animals still continue to move; yet notwithstanding, I have demonstrated the contrary

---

[1] From *Letter 33*. 12 November 1680. To R. Hooke. MS.Roy.Soc. Printed in *Brieven*, Vol. I (Dutch), and *Opera Omnia*, Vol. II (Latin). An incomplete English translation was published in *Phil. Collect. of R. Hooke* (1681), No. 3, pp. 51-58. The whole letter was first published in Dutch in 1684 (*Ondervindingen en Beschouwingen*, etc. pp. 1-32): while the full Latin version appeared in 1695 (*Arc. Nat. Det.*).—It should be noted that in the earlier part of this letter—not here translated—L. casually mentions that he "saw some little animalcules swimming" (p. 8, Dutch printed version) among various "globules" which he found in rain-water that he had put in a special piece of apparatus. They were probably protozoa or bacteria; but as no further mention is made of them, they are not identifiable.

[2] Evidently ciliates.

[3] *dat yder soorte groter en kleynder haar vertoonde* printed version (1684) *dat ijder in sijn soort bestonden uijt groote en kleijne dierkens* MS. (1680).

[4] Probably a misinterpretation of the inclusions in food-vacuoles.

[5] The lines following, as far as the calculations on p. 203, have been translated by Hoole (1798) in his Introduction, pp. iv-vi. His rendering is faithful in substance, though not always in diction. In translating L. he allowed himself more latitude than I have done.

to divers distinguished Gentlemen, and I make bold to say, that people who say such things have not yet advanced so far as to be able to carry out good observations.

For my own part, I can say with truth, that the smallest sort of which I shall here speak, I see alive and exhibit as plainly to my eye as one sees, with the naked eye, little flies or gnats sporting in the air, though they may be more than a hundred million times less than a coarse grain of sand ; for not only do I observe their progression, both when they hurry, and when they slow down, but I see them turn about, and stand still, and in the end even die ; and those that are of a bigger sort,[1] I can also see running along as plain as you see mice before your naked eye ; nay, in some I can even see the inward parts of their mouth, as they stick them in and out, and make play with them ; indeed, in one sort I see the very hairs on their mouth, though they themselves are several thousand times less than a sand-grain.

As they'll say 'tis not credible that so great a many of these little animalcules can be comprehended in the compass of a sand-grain, as I have said, and that I can make no calculation of this matter,[2] I have figured out their proportions thus, in order to exhibit them yet more clearly to the eye: Let me suppose, for example, that I see a sand-grain but as big as the spherical body ABGC [Text-fig. 3, p. 202] and that I see, besides, a little animal as big as D, swimming, or running on the sand-grain ; and measuring it by my eye, I judge the axis of[3] the little animal D to be the twelfth part of the axis of the supposed sand-grain, AG ; consequently, according to the

---

[1] From the descriptive details which follow, L. evidently refers here to ciliates.

[2] The beginning of this sentence—up to the point here marked—is worded differently in the MS. and in the printed version. The meaning is, however, identical in the two.

[3] *van* (of) is here omitted from the printed version—by a misprint—but is present in the MS.

ordinary rules, the volume of the sphere ABGC is 1728 times greater than the volume of D. Now suppose I see, among the rest, a second sort of little animals, which

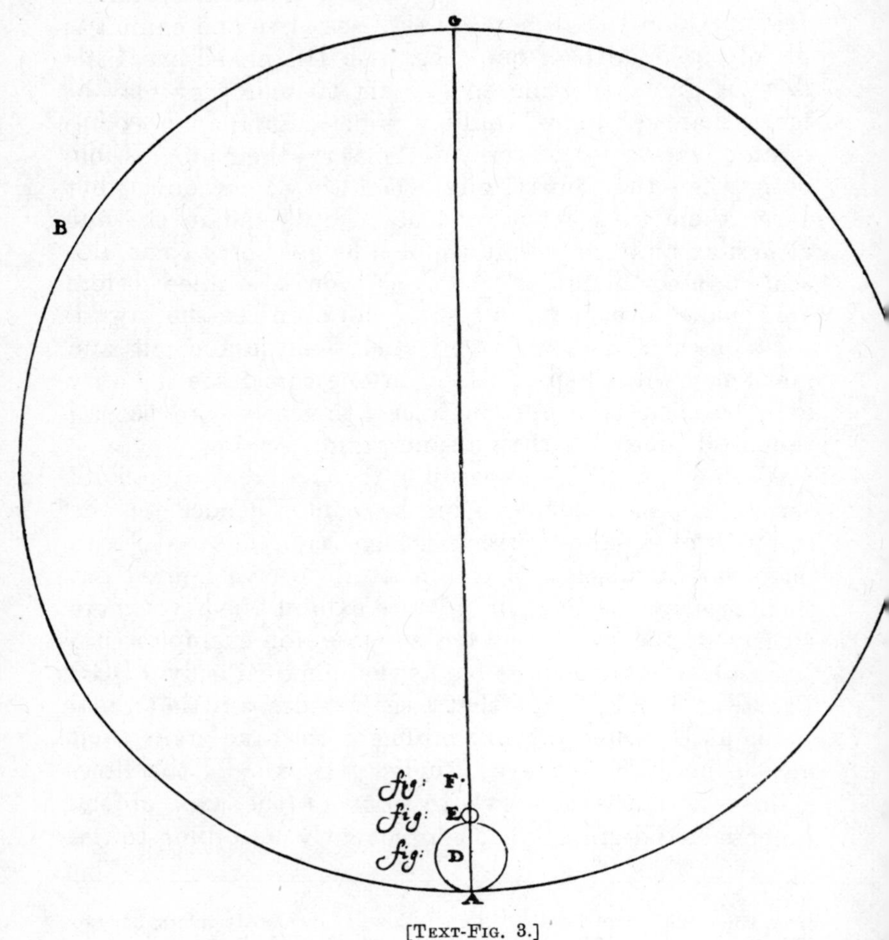

[TEXT-FIG. 3.]

I likewise measure by my eye (through a good glass, giving a sharp image); and I judge its axis to be the fifth part, though I shall here allow it to be but the fourth part (as Fig. E), of the axis of the first animalcule D; and so, consequently, the volume of Fig. D is 64 times greater than the volume of Fig. E. This last number, multiplied by the first number [1728], comes then to 110592, the number of the little animals like Fig. E which are as big (supposing their bodies to be round) as the sphere ABGC. But now I perceive a third sort of little animalcule, like the point F, whereof I judge the axis to be only a tenth part of that of the supposed animalcule E; wherefore 1000 animalcules such as F are as big as one animalcule like E. This number, multiplied [1] by the one foregoing [110592], then makes more than 110 million little animals [like F] as big as a sand-grain.

12	10	4	1728
12	10	4	64
144	100	16	6912
12	10	4	10368
288	1000	64	110592
144			1000
1728			110592000

Otherwise I reckon in this fashion [2]: Suppose the axis of Fig. F is 1, and that of Fig. E is 10; then, since the axis of Fig. D is 4 times as great as that of Fig. E, the axis of D is 40. But the axis of the big sphere ABGC is 12 times that of Fig. D; therefore the axis AG is equal to 480. This number multiplied by itself, and the product again multiplied by the same number, in order to get the volume of ABGC, gives us the result, as before, that more than 110 million living animalcules are as big as a grain of sand:

---

[1] "*vermenigvuldig*," in printed version, is a misprint. The MS. has, correctly, *vermenigvuldigt*.

[2] So in printed version. The MS. has merely *Of anders* (Or otherwise).

axis of Fig. F = 1
axis of Fig. E = 10
4
———
axis of Fig. D = 40
12
———
80
40
———
axis AG = 480
480
———
38400
1920
———
230400
480
———
18432000
921600
———
110592000

However, when I took somewhat coarser sand, as I did when I drew up my estimate, I had to say that 20 axes of the foresaid [biggest] animalcules did but make up one axis of a sand-grain; and again, 5 axes of the lesser animalcule equalled the axis of the first; and further, 10 axes of the smallest creature equalled one axis of the second. In fine, then, according to this calculation, a thousand million living animalcules are as big as a coarse sand-grain (taken from fine scouring sand).

1 = axis F
10 = axis E
5
———
50 = axis D
20
———
1000 = axis AG
1000
———
1000000
1000
———
1000000000

In Leeuwenhoek's next communications we find no further mention of either protozoa or bacteria until we come to his *Letter 71*, which, while recording various other observations, contains the following words:[1]

I have by me the following notes, which I feel constrained to add.

For several days past I have kept in a clean glass, in my closet, some rain-water, gotten from a rain-cistern; in which water there was a little red worm,[2] which I divers times observed, by reason of its curious structure.

In this water, after a day or two, a multitude of little living creatures did propagate themselves, they being of two sorts which you commonly find in fresh or sweet waters. The bigger sort I judged to be so small, that thirty thousand of them together would scarce make up a body as big as a coarse grain of sand.

On several different days I did look upon these little animals,[3] and for so long, that not alone my eyes, but my very hands, got a-weary; and this was simply because I did perceive such a plenty of these little animals, which were coupled together, and so long remained in this posture: and I observed how the bigger sort dragged the little ones along, or swam forward with them, with the help of very plentevous feet, wherewith these animals are furnished withal; so that I was thus able on this occasion to observe the copulation of these little animals clearer than ever before. Nay, I saw them as plain as you can see flying creatures[4] a-copulating before your naked eye.

---

[1] *Letter 71.* 7 March 1692. To the Royal Society. MS.Roy.Soc. Printed in *Brieven*, Derde Vervolg, p. 396 (the passage here translated beginning on p. 423): *Opera Omnia*, Vol. II, p. 239 (1st pagination). A partial English translation was also published in *Phil. Trans.* (1694), Vol. XVIII, No. 213, pp. 194-199; but the passage here given in full is there so abridged that it occupies only 8½ lines (on p. 198).

[2] Evidently a "blood-worm" (larva of *Chironomus*).

[3] The animals referred to are evidently ciliates.

[4] *i.e.* insects—not birds.

These observations caused me to view more nicely the lesser animalcules that were also swimming about in the water, and whereof the number was a good twenty times as many as that of the little animals aforesaid. Some of these animalcules were also coupled; and I saw that these likewise not only stayed long a-copulating, but also that one of the pair, whether it swam through the water or ran upon the glass, dragged the other one forward, or trailed it after itself.

The foregoing passage is of great interest, since it is evidently a record of observations made upon the conjugation or fission of ciliates. In my opinion the evidence is in favour of the view that Leeuwenhoek, on this occasion, witnessed both these phenomena; though it is regrettable that he gave so brief an account of what he saw. I cannot help thinking that what he interpreted as "one animalcule dragging another one along" was a conjugating pair; whereas "one animalcule trailing another behind it" was really an organism dividing transversely into two. Later,[1] as we shall soon see, he described the conjugation of ciliates in unmistakable terms.[2]

In a letter written some 3 years afterwards, Leeuwenhoek mentions the discovery of "animalcules" in a new situation. After describing his observations on the oyster, and its generation, he remarks[3]:

I also paid attention to the ordinary water that is in the shells of oysters; and I discovered therein a great lot of little animalcules, which, in bigness and figure, were like the little animalcules that you generally find in canal-water, rainwater cisterns, and common ditch-water. These animalcules were, in my judgement, above five hundred times smaller than a young oyster.

---

[1] Cf. also the earlier observations in *Letter 33*, p. 200 *supra*.

[2] *Letter 96*, p. 213 *infra*.

[3] *Letter 92*. 15 August 1695. To Frederik Adriaan, Baron van Rhede. Published in *Brieven*, Vijfde Vervolg, p. 114: *Opera Omnia*, Vol. II, p. 511. No MS., and not in *Phil. Trans.*

No doubt these animalcules were protozoa: and it should be mentioned that Leeuwenhoek had recorded a similar observation at an even earlier date. Writing to the Royal Society about fifteen years before, he mentioned[1] that he had found "divers kinds of little living animalcules" in the juice of mussels and oysters: but he gave no further account of them, and it is impossible to ascertain what sort of organisms these were. It should also be noted here, however, that in a much later letter[2] he expressed the opinion that some of the "animalcules" which he thought he saw formerly in the juice of oysters were probably not really organisms at all, but "particles" set in motion by the cilia on the tissues of the mollusc.[3]

Leeuwenhoek's last recorded observations on the "animalcules" in infusions are contained in a letter written several years later, and sent not to the Royal Society but to the Elector Palatine. This very interesting letter runs as follows[4]:

> In my letter of 18 September[5] [1695] I ventured most respectfully to describe how I opened a Freshwater Mussel[6] and took out of it the unborn young mussels,[7]

[1] *Letter 30.* 5 April 1680. To Robert Hooke. MS.Roy.Soc. Published in *Brieven*, Vol. I, p. 33 (1st pagination): *Opera Omnia*, Vol. I, p. 25 (2nd pagination): English abstract in *Phil. Trans.* (1693), Vol. XVII, No. 196, p. 593.

[2] *Letter dated 10 June 1712.* To the Royal Society. MS.Roy.Soc. English version printed in *Phil. Trans.* (1712), Vol. XXVII, No. 336, p. 529. Not published elsewhere, and not numbered by L. himself.

[3] It seems to me probable that L. was here referring to the observations contained in *Letter 30*, and not to those in *Letter 92*, which appears to record a genuine observation of protozoa.

[4] *Letter 96.* 9 November 1695. To the Elector Palatine. Published in *Brieven*, Vijfde Vervolg, p. 156: *Opera Omnia*, Vol. II (*Contin. Arc. Nat.*), p. 30 (2nd pagination). Not translated by Hoole. No MS., and not in *Phil. Trans.* I translate the whole letter, with the exception of a few immaterial words at the beginning and end.

[5] *Letter 95*, printed immediately before the present letter in L.'s published works.

[6] *Veen-Mossel* (literally "fen-mussel") = *Anodonta*: not easily recognizable in the Latin version, where it is called "*concham ex genere earum quae ex fossis capiuntur*." *Veen* means not only a fen, marsh, or bog, but also the *peat* which can be dug out of such places: and consequently Hoole (Vol. I, p. 85 *sq.*) translates *veen-mossel* as "peat-muscle." But Anodon was never known by this name in England—so far as I am aware.

[7] *i.e.*, the "Glochidia" larvae—described and figured in *Letter 95*.

which had developed so far that I judged them to be completely formed, because their shells seemed to be perfect.

I took several thousand of these unborn mussels, and put them in a glazed white earthenware basin, and forthwith poured canal-water upon them, in order to see whether any of these unborn mussels would remain alive and grow bigger.

Having put these little unborn mussels in the water, I viewed them on several successive days, yet I could make out no change in their size. But since, owing to the rain which had fallen plentifully, our canals were filled at that time with no other water than what runs off the land, and which must then flow through our Town, I saw, beyond my expectations, a great many very little living animalcules, of divers sorts and sizes, in this water, a-swimming among the unborn mussels. Amongst others I saw some little worms,[1] having a figure very much like those worms that children void in their stools,[2] but whose thickness I judged to be a quarter of that of a hair off one's head.

Furthermore, I saw some animalcules stuck fast to one another by their long tails[3]; and these animalcules, as well as sundry other sorts, I had never seen before, and their motion was uncommon pleasant to behold.

Further, I saw that these animalcules did increase in numbers from day to day.

At first, after four or five days, I replenished the water, wherein these unborn mussels lay, in such a fashion that I poured off all but about a spoonful[4] of it, and then presently added more canal-water again thereto.

---

[1] Probably free-living nematodes.

[2] Probably meaning the nematode *Oxyuris* (=*Enterobius*) *vermicularis*.

[3] Evidently a colonial Vorticellid (*Carchesium*?). The "animalcule with a tail" is L.'s name for *Vorticella*, already described in *Letter 18* (p. 118). Further observations on the colonial forms are recorded later in the present letter. (See also p. 277 *sq.*, *infra.*)

[4] *op een lepel vol water na* Dutch version *omnem fere aquam* Latin translation.

In these my inquiries, I imagined that the unborn mussels got eaten up by the little animalcules aforesaid; because it oft-times happened that I saw a multitude of little animalcules that had got between the shells of the young mussels, so that I judged, indeed, that I could even see as many as fifty animalcules inside a single young mussel. And during my observations, I observed that the fishy matter in the unborn mussels got less from day to day; nay, to such an extent even, that after the lapse of twelve days, little or no fishy matter was to be discerned between their little shells, which had become all transparent. After this time, too, I could not perceive that the animalcules were increasing in such great plenty.

My notion that the little animals were partly the cause of the unborn mussels being eaten up (though ten thousand of the little animals aforesaid would, for the most part of them, scarce equal in bigness one of the little mussels), was confirmed when I came to inspect the little mussels (at the time when I had placed them in water in a white Delft porcelain basin) after inclosing them in various little glasses[1]; whereupon I perceived that each little mussel inclosed in the little glass, though also lying in water, still had its fishy substance between its shells, notwithstanding that many of them had their shells wide apart, or agape.

I have sometimes been puzzled when beholding the multitude of little unborn mussels which lay inclosed in a big mussel; for I was not able to conceive why our canals, and fens, are not overflowing with mussels, seeing that the water does not run so strong that it could carry the little mussels along with it, while they are still very small; and in the second place, seeing that they are not gathered to serve as food: so that one mussel ought to beget thousands. But now, after discovering how the little

---

[1] As mentioned below, these "little glasses" (*glaasjens*) were capillary glass tubes, such as L. commonly employed in his experiments.

animals aforesaid devoured them, methought this a sufficient reason why freshwater mussels are not found in greater plenty.[1]

After this, I let the water stand for twelve more days, without replenishing it, in order to see whether, if I did so, the animalcules would multiply in greater numbers. But I perceived that the animalcules decreased from day to day; so that by the 8th of October they were indeed grown so few, that where I had before discovered a good hundred of them, I now could scarce see one; and those of the biggest sort, which still remained over, moved forward very slow, and were very thin in the body; and all the little shells of the unborn mussels had so far increased in transparency, that I could make out some hundreds of very little parts, whereof they were composed. And so, from all these observations, I concluded that all the various animalcules had now died for lack of food.

In order to satisfy myself further concerning the plentevous multiplication of the little animalcules, and in so very short a time, I took a parcel of canal-water, somewhat more than a common wine-glass full, and put in it an ordinary mussel, that I had taken out of its shell[2]; and I put this mussel in the water to see, if 'twere possible, whether the animalcules would multiply beyond what they commonly do, owing to the food that they would be able to get from the mussel.

After the mussel had lain for four-and-twenty hours in the water, I took a little of the uppermost part of the water, and examined it through the microscope; and I

---

[1] From these observations one can hardly doubt that L. had got something more than an inkling of the part played by putrefactive micro-organisms in the general oeconomy of nature. To appreciate the novelty of this notion—nowadays commonplace—one must remember that it belongs, historically, to the nineteenth century.

[2] In such an infusion of freshwater mussel many different Protozoa are commonly found, including ciliates (e.g., *Paramecium*) and flagellates (e.g., *Trepomonas*). For this reason it is impossible to determine what particular forms L. was likely to have seen.

saw, to my wonder, a vast number of animalcules. And after the water, with the mussel in it, had stood for twice twenty-four hours, I observed that the number of animalcules was greatly increased. I took a little of this water, and put it in a glass tube, whose diameter was about a fifteenth of an inch, and which was filled for about an inch of its length with the water. In this water I saw a few little animalcules swimming, whereof several thousand together would scarce equal a sand-grain in bigness. These animalcules had a pretty structure, for the round circumference of their bodies seemed to be made up of ten or twelve brighter round pellets, while in the middle of them there seemed to be a little dark spot, somewhat bigger than the pellets. These animalcules generally rotated themselves in their progression (which took place slowly).[1]

When these animalcules had been a little while in the foresaid glass tube, I saw a slender little structure like unto a little branching vein, with seven or eight lesser branches, each several little branch being full a hundred times thinner than a hair off one's head; and at the same time I saw that at the utmost extremity of every little branch, one of the forementioned little animals was firmly fixt, though at first I could discover no motion in 'em. Yet after the lapse of about a minute, I perceived that some animalcules began to move themselves to and fro, whereby each of the thin little branches became bent into divers coils. The longer this motion continued, the stronger it became, till at last the little creature, by its efforts, got loose from the little branch, and swam off; and the same thing came to pass with all the others too, so that the little branching structure was forsaken by all the animalcules that were discernible.[2]

---

[1] Probably ciliates—the bright bodies being food-inclusions, and the dark central spot the meganucleus.

[2] This graphic narrative gives an unmistakable description of *Carchesium*.

From this spectacle, I imagined that the little animals of this kind must have laid their little eggs, or young animalcules, upon the ends of every little branch, and that they had there waxed in bigness, and grown up.

Furthermore, this little branching vein was for the most part clothed with a clearer matter, which I judged was made up of round pellets. Seeing this, it came into my head that all the round particles which I could see might perhaps be really eggs, or young animalcules, and that from these particles, moreover, similar animalcules might presently come forth. After the lapse of another twenty-four hours, I looked upon the little branch again; and I then saw that some animalcules, which had reached their full growth, were fixed anew upon it; and that many of these animalcules were swimming around the little branch, while the roundish particles, that I'd seen on the branch the day before, were much diminished in number.[1]

At a distance of about half an inch from the little vein-branch aforesaid, there lay in the water a little fibre, whereon were also fixed some little animals; and these too were come forth (so I imagined) from the round corpuscles which were likewise fixed to the fibre. These animalcules were increased to such great numbers in the space of twice twenty-four hours, that I now saw quite fifty of them where I had before seen but one.

Now, as we have made sure that, in twice twenty-four hour's time, animalcules appear, which have reached their full growth; and as we imagine that they have come forth from little round particles: therefore, we need not wonder at the multifarious little animalcules which we perceive to be bred in water in only a few days' time (provided only that food be not lacking for them). And who knows but what one sort of these very little water-

---

[1] The observations here recorded were, no doubt, perfectly accurate: but the interpretation which L. put upon them is, of course, incorrect.

creatures may not gobble up another sort, using it as food,[1] just as we see that big fish do? For, an 'twere otherwise, the water would get stuffed full with little animalcules.

One day afterwards I looked at the animalcules again, and saw, to my wonder, that many of 'em were coupled; nay, some of 'em even coupled before my eye; and at the beginning of their copulation they had a wobbling motion, but after coupling swam forward together, and did stay still too, fixt to the glass.[2]

At this time I saw also that the bodies of each animalcule of the pair were of a roundish figure; for no matter how they turned about in swimming forward, they always kept one and the same shape, looking like a little round cluster of grapes, the cluster being stuck together very tight; and as the animalcules swam forward, you saw each of the supposed grapes in motion.

'Twas eventide when I carried out the observations last mentioned; and next day, in the morning, I found that many of the animalcules were dead, and by evening they were so diminished, that I could find but four of them that were still alive: wherefore I concluded, that the little creatures were died off for want of food. After another night had passed, I saw but one animalcule living; and the bodies of all the dead animalcules in the water were so gone to pieces, that I saw nought but little round particles (as they seemed to my eye), which made the water, wherein these little animals had been swimming, all troubled.

---

[1] As the "bigger sort" were, in part, ciliates, while the "smallest sort" were bacteria, L.'s conjecture here was perfectly sound.

[2] This passage proves conclusively that L. observed the conjugation of ciliates. In his earlier observations he had only seen the organisms joined together; and consequently he may have seen ciliates really undergoing fission—not conjugating. But here he says he actually saw them come together, so that there can be no doubt as to the correctness of his interpretation.

Two days after the foregoing discoveries, I again beheld the small parcel of water aforesaid in the glass tube; and as I did so, I saw a huge number of extreme small fishes, or animalcules, which I may call little eels,[1] because in swimming forwards they lashed their bodies like eels do, and so quick that 'twas marvellous. These little fish did mostly stay close beside one another, and round the circumference of the tube, and in vast numbers; and in my judgement their length was equal to the diameter of one of those blood-globules which make the blood red. And they remained alive some seven days, after which time I could make out only one every now and then.

Among these little animals, or little fishes, I did also see a-swimming a few smaller animalcules, whereof I deemed that eight of 'em together were no bigger than the said blood-corpuscle[2]: and now I could no longer discern that little structure that I heretofore likened to a little branching vein, how oft soever I looked for it. These last-mentioned animalcules were so prodigiously increased in two or three days, that 'tis incredible; though by now half the water was evaporated away.

All the water that I have so far spoken of, which I had put in the glass tube, and wherein the foresaid multiplicity of little animalcules were bred, I deemed (to the best of my knowledge) to be no more in bulk than the eighth part of a green pea; but not being content with this my estimate, I went and weighed a like quantity of water, and I found its weight two grains. I did also weigh some peas, and found that a common pea weigheth eight grains.

Through the microscope with which I had carried out the first observations, I imagined I still saw,[3] in water

---

[1] Probably *Spirilla*—certainly bacteria of some sort.

[2] *i.e.*, their diameter was about half that of a red blood-corpuscle. Undoubtedly bacteria.

[3] L., it will be recalled, commonly used a different microscope for each separate observation—the object being more or less permanently fixed and focussed before the lens.

taken from the surface of that wherein the mussel lay, a vast company of living animalcules: but to make sure of this, I made use of a glass of higher magnification, and a different instrument: and I then saw so great a many of such extreme small animalcules,[1] that there's no man living could possibly conceive of them; nay, they were so little, that several millions of them together would not be as big as a coarse grain of sand. Nevertheless, all these animalcules, when I put them in a glass tube, remained alive but a little while.

Moreover, I found that the animalcules in the water that the mussel was in, had increased so much in seven or eight days, that I might well say their number was (to the best of my judgement) quite ten times a hundred thousand more than those in the water before I put the mussel in it.

Regarding this increase of animalcules in water, and in so very short a time, I have oft-times been amazed: and especially, because I chanced to see divers sorts of animalcules, which increased in numbers, without being able to discern any of them that were smaller; all of them being of an equal bigness.[2]

But after observing what I have just related (namely, that there are animalcules which do not take to swimming about till they have reached their full growth, and which soon after are ready to copulate; and therewithal that a full-grown animalcule is produced in one night), I was now, to my great satisfaction, delivered from all those difficulties, that I had for years laboured under, concerning the generation of these little creatures.

When I first discovered, in the year 1675, a great plenty of divers very little animalcules in water, and made these observations known by letter to the Royal

---

[1] Bacteria.

[2] He means that he could detect no young ones of any species.

> Society in London, neither in England[1] nor in France could they accept of my discoveries: nor do they even yet in Germany, as I'm informed.

This remarkable document ends at this point with a couple of extracts from Leeuwenhoek's letters of 23 March 1677 (to Oldenburg) and 5 October 1677 (to Lord Brouncker), which were sent to the Elector Palatine "to give him greater satisfaction concerning the vast numbers of little animalcules that are found in water": but as these letters have already been given fully on earlier pages,[2] it is unnecessary to repeat them here.

With these observations we come to the end of Leeuwenhoek's researches on the free-living Protozoa and Bacteria, in so far as they were made in the XVII Century. Later he made many notable additional observations, but these will be chronicled in a later chapter: and we must now retrace our steps in order to record his equally wonderful discoveries concerning the parasitic Protista.

---

[1] This can hardly be regarded as a fair description of the reception accorded to L.'s earliest observations by the Fellows of the Royal Society.

[2] *Vide* pp. 168 and 173 *supra*. The second letter was originally addressed to Oldenburg, but redirected to Brouncker when L. heard of his death.

CHAPTER 3

THE FIRST OBSERVATIONS ON ENTOZOIC PROTOZOA AND BACTERIA

(LETTERS 7, 33, 34, 38, 39, 75, 110, etc.)

WE have already seen (in Chapter 1) how Leeuwenhoek discovered the free-living Protozoa and Bacteria. We must now chronicle his discoveries in the world of similar " parasitic " organisms.[1]

It will be remembered that Leeuwenhoek first saw protozoa in water in the summer of 1674.[2] He probably first saw a parasitic protozoon—though he had no idea what it was—in the autumn of the same year. Whilst examining the bile of various animals, he hit upon some curious structures which he described, in the course of a rather rambling letter, in the following terms:[3]

> The bile of a cow was examined[4] by me on the 1st instant, and therein I beheld some few globules[5] that floated in the liquid ; but I didn't see them unless I set the bile in a continual motion before my sight, for 'twould else have been impossible for me to perceive the globules in it,

[1] To call all such micro-organisms studied by L. by the opprobrious name of "parasite" is hardly justifiable, for most of the forms which he described cannot be regarded as harmful. They are " parasitic " in a colloquial and unscientific sense only.

[2] See p. 109.

[3] From *Letter 7*. 19 October 1674. To Oldenburg. MS.Roy.Soc. This letter was wholly unpublished until recently, when I first published (Dobell, 1922) the passages given here in revised translation.

[4] *i.e.*, with the microscope.

[5] *clootgens* MS.

because they were so few in the bile that I was examining. But afterwards, examining the bile of another cow, I found that the globules were of a heavier matter than the liquid that they floated in; wherefore I drew off the bile from the bottom of the gall-bladder, and then found that there were[1] many hundred times more globules in this bile than in that which I had taken from the upper part of the gall-bladder; and there were, besides, some corpuscles[2] which, to my eye, looked as big as ants' eggs.[3] These had the figure of an egg,[4] only with this difference, that whereas an egg is more sharply pointed at one end than at the other, yet these corpuscles were equally pointed at both ends: and moreover these corpuscles were composed of globules joined together, and had a yellow colour, except several which were somewhat whitish; but notwithstanding, they were so transparent that you could see the body of one through that of another. And this transparency making me wonder whether they might not, in fact, be little vesicles filled inside with liquid, I fished some of these corpuscles out of the bile with a fine hair; and looking at 'em on the hair, I perceived two which seemed to be pushed in, just as though you had blown up a bladder and then stuck your thumb in it, so as to make a dent in it; whereupon I was the more firmly persuaded that these corpuscles were filled with some sort of humor. Afterwards, on examining more biles from oxen, I found them the same as before; only with this difference, that one bile might be furnisht with more of the oval corpuscles than another.

---

[1] *was* MS.

[2] *deeltgens* MS.

[3] L. means that the objects looked, under his microscope, about as big as "ants' eggs" look to the naked eye. At a later date he published a remarkable account of ants, from which it is clear that he was well aware that the ant's "egg" is not really an egg, but a pupa. See *Letter 58*, 9 Sept. 1687.

[4] *i.e.*, a hen's egg.

In the bile of two calves I find, furthermore, some very little globules floating, and very many irregular particles of divers forms; among others, some like little floating clouds, all consisting of very little globules joined together. On seeing these irregular congealed particles, I judged them to be joined or stuck together through no other cause than because the bile had got cold, and was without motion. In the bile of a third calf there were a few oval corpuscles.

Moreover, in the bile of sucking lambs I find there are very little globules, and some, though very few, bright particles, which are a bit bigger; besides irregular particles, of divers figures, and also composed of globules clumped together.

The bile of a yearling sheep I find to be like that of sucking lambs, only with this difference, that in this bile there are also oval corpuscles of the bigness and figure of those that I remarked in ox-bile.

I have examined the bile of two young rabbits: that of the first was inclined to a purple colour, and in it I beheld very many globules, and irregular particles made up of globules clumped together, which were of various red colours:[1] and this diversity of colour I imagined to be due to no other cause than that some of these compound particles, being made up of more globules, were denser than the rest. In the other bile the irregular particles were fewer, but there were more globules and the colour was a light reddish.

Further, I examined the bile from three old rabbits. The first had a very few small globules, but very many oval corpuscles of a figure like those that, as I have said, I saw in the bile of a cow. In the bile of the two other rabbits there was nought but globules, and irregular

---

[1] Evidently red blood-corpuscles. L. had described these—from his own blood—in another letter written earlier in the same year (*Letter 3*, 7 April 1674). An English abstract of this appeared in *Phil. Trans.* (1674), Vol. IX, No. 102, p. 23.

> particles made up of globules joined together; though the thin matter[1] of one was much thicker and stickier than that of the other, and there were some little clouds floating through it.
>
> . . . .
>
> I have furthermore examined the biles of fowls, turkeys, etc., and in them I also found very little globules floating, and irregular particles composed of globules stuck together.

I think there can be no doubt that the "oval corpuscles"—called *eijronde deeltgens* in the original—which Leeuwenhoek discovered in the gall-bladder of one of his "three old rabbits," were the oocysts of the coccidian *Eimeria stiedae;* while the comparable structures which he found in the bile of sheep and oxen were, equally certainly, the eggs of trematodes.[2] But as I have already discussed this subject in some detail elsewhere,[3] I shall say no more about it here. If my interpretations be correct, then the foregoing extract records the first observations ever made upon the Sporozoa or upon any parasitic protozoon.

It is true that Leeuwenhoek himself did not realize that he had discovered a stage in the life-history of a brand-new kind of parasite: but the same can be said also of others who are now generally credited with the discovery of the Coccidia.[4] The fact remains, none the less, that he saw and described—though his description was not published for nearly 250 years—a coccidial parasite long before all other men.

---

[1] *i.e.*, the liquid part of the bile.

[2] *Fasciola hepatica*—the worm itself—was well known to L.; for the Dutch anatomist Bidloo (1649-1713) dedicated a little memoir to him, in 1698, in which it was described and figured. At a later date, L. himself wrote a letter to the Royal Society on the "Worms observ'd in Sheeps Livers"—of which an English abstract was published in *Phil. Trans.* (1704), Vol. XXIV, p. 1522. The original letter is extant, and is dated 3 Nov. 1703. It was not included in the Dutch or Latin collected works.

[3] See Dobell (1922).

[4] The lesions of hepatic coccidiosis in the rabbit appear to have been first depicted by [Sir] Robert Carswell (1793-1857; Professor of Pathological Anatomy at University College, London) in the year 1838. He regarded them as "the seat of tuberculous matter." The oocysts of *E. stiedae* were first figured and described in print by Dr Thomas Gordon Hake (1809-

Leeuwenhoek's next observations on "animalcules" inhabiting the bodies of other animals were written down in 1680 and printed some few years later. They occur in the course of his description of the spermatozoa of insects—various species of which he dissected in his attempts to study their "seminal animalcules". After recording some findings in flies, he casually adds the following:[1]

> I have also seen, in the summer,[2] in a big horse-fly (which was a female, out of which I pulled many eggs), a lot of small animalcules; though these were not a sixth of the length of the animalcules aforesaid,[3] but a good 10 times thicker.[4] They lay mingled with the thin matter[5] that was in the fly's guts, and moved forwards very quick.

From the size and proportions of the "animalcules" here mentioned, and from their situation, it can hardly be doubted that Leeuwenhoek actually saw on this occasion a protozoon (or possibly a bacterium) in the gut of a horse-fly. The dimensions of the organism are against the bacterial interpretation, but agree very well indeed with the supposition that he saw a *Crithidia* (or *Leptomonas*).[6] If this was so, then we

---

1895; a practising London physician, and English minor poet) in 1839. He interpreted the lesions as "carcinoma", and the oocysts as "a new form of the pus globule." See Dobell (1922).

[1] From *Letter 33*. 12 November 1680. To R. Hooke. MS.Roy.Soc. Published in *Brieven*, Vol. I (Dutch), and *Opera Omnia*, Vol. II (Latin). The full letter first appeared in print (in Dutch) in 1684. An incomplete English translation was published earlier, however, in Hooke's *Phil. Collect.* (No. 3, pp. 51-58; 1681). The passage here translated is on p. 23 of the Dutch printed version.

[2] Presumably 1680.

[3] L. here refers—as the context shows—to the spermatozoa of "the smallest sort of our common house-fly."

[4] On L.'s system this means that they had rather more than thrice the diameter of the fly's spermatozoa.

[5] *i.e.*, liquid or watery material.

[6] These flagellates occur—as is now well known—in many different species of Tabanidae. Several species of *Crithidia* have been described, in recent times, from the intestines of European species of *Tabanus*.—I may add that, forty years ago, Bütschli (1887-89; Vol. III, p. 1101) pointed out that the organisms here described by L. were probably flagellates; but he wrongly dated the observations 1695—the date of publication of the first Latin translation.

have here the first recorded observations ever made upon any protozoa belonging to the important flagellate family of the Trypanosomatidae. But this interpretation, though very plausible, is not absolutely certain; for the details recorded are obviously too scanty to warrant dogmatic deductions. Nevertheless, it can, I think, be concluded—with complete assurance—that Leeuwenhoek observed "parasitic" protists of some sort in the intestine of a horse-fly as early as the year 1680.

We now come to a letter of great historic interest and importance—a letter which has rarely been read aright, but one which records in no uncertain terms the discovery of the intestinal protozoa and bacteria of Man. This letter was written in 1681, and in it Leeuwenhoek discusses a variety of subjects—such as the structure and falling-out of the hair, "blackheads" (*comedones*), clay, and gout: but the only part which here concerns us deals with the discovery of "living animalcules in the excrements." The passages in question run as follows:[1]

> I weigh about 160 pound, and have been of very nigh the same weight for some 30 years,[2] and I have ordinarily of a morning a well-formed stool; but now and then hitherto I have had a looseness, at intervals of 2, 3, or 4 weeks, when I went to stool some 2, 3, or 4 times a day.[3] But

[1] From *Letter 34*. 4 November 1681. To R. Hooke. MS.Roy.Soc. Published in full in *Brieven*, Vol. I (Dutch), and *Opera Omnia*, Vol. I (Latin). The Dutch version first appeared in 1686 (*Ontled. en Ontdekk.*), the Latin [from which the date of the letter was omitted] in 1687 (*Anat. s. Int. Rerum*). An English abstract was published by R. Hooke in *Phil. Collect.* (1682), No. 4, p. 93: and another by Derham in the posthumous *Phil. Expts. and Obss.* of Hooke (1726), p. 61. The letter itself was presented to the Society at their meeting held on 2 Nov. 1681, and read in English translation at the following meeting on Nov. 9 [O.S.]. Cf. Birch, Vol. IV, pp. 99, 101. Part of this letter was also translated by Hoole in his *Select Works* of L.—but not the part with which we are now concerned. I have already translated and commented upon the paragraphs dealing with intestinal protozoa elsewhere (Dobell, 1920).

[2] When he wrote this L. was 49 years old.

[3] The Latin version of this passage is somewhat ambiguous, and has apparently led some readers to suppose that L. frequently suffered from diarrhoea lasting for 2-4 weeks at a stretch. It has even, indeed, given rise to the belief that he suffered from chronic dysentery for 30 years. His own words do not countenance any such conclusions. Cf. Dobell (1920).

this summer[1] this befell me very often, and especially when I partook of hot smoked beef, that was a bit fat,[2] or ham, which food I'm very fond of; indeed, it persisted once for three days running, and whatever food I took, I kept in my body not much[3] above 4 hours; and I imagined (for divers reasons) that I could get myself well again by drinking uncommon hot tea, as hath happened[4] many a time before.

My excrement being so thin,[5] I was at divers times persuaded to examine it;[6] and each time[7] I kept in mind what food I had eaten, and what drink I had drunk, and what I found afterwards[8]: but to tell all my observations here would make all too long a story. I will only say that I have generally seen, in my excrement, many irregular particles of sundry sizes, most of them tending to a round figure, which are very clear and of a yellow colour:[9] these were the ones that make the whole material[10] look yellow to our eye. And there were also, besides, suchlike particles that were very bright and clear, without one being able to discern any colour in them.[11]

I have, moreover, at divers times seen globules that were as big as[12] the corpuscles in our blood, and that each

---

[1] *i.e., anno* 1681.

[2] *dat een weynig vet was.* These words are in the printed version but not in the original MS.—A similar remark is made by L. much later in *Send-brief* XXXIX, 13 July 1717, to J. G. Kerkherdere.

[3] *veel* is here in the printed letter, but not in the MS.

[4] *is gelukt* [=succeeded] MS. *is geschied* [=befell] printed version.

[5] *i.e.*, dilute or watery.

[6] *i.e.*, with the microscope.

[7] *soo nu en dan* MS. *soo nu als dan* printed version.

[8] This word is not in the originals. I add it to preserve the sense.

[9] Probably incompletely digested remains of meat (striated muscle).

[10] *i.e.*, the faeces *en masse.*

[11] Probably fat-droplets.

[12] The Latin version mistranslates *soo groot als* as "bigger than" (*globulos globulis nostri sanguinis majores vidi*).

of them was made up of 6 separate globules :[1] and further, there lay, among all this material, globules whereof 6 of 'em together would make up the bigness[2] of a blood-corpuscle. These last were in such great[3] plenty, that they seemed to form a good third of the whole[4] material: while there were besides many globules which were so small, that six-and-thirty of 'em would make up the bigness of a blood-globule.[5]

All the particles aforesaid lay in a clear transparent medium, wherein I have sometimes also seen animalcules[6] a-moving very prettily ; some of 'em a bit bigger, others a bit less, than a blood-globule, but all of one and the same make. Their bodies were somewhat longer than broad, and their belly, which was flatlike, furnisht with sundry little paws, wherewith they made such a stir in the clear medium and among the globules, that you might e'en fancy you saw a pissabed[7] running up against a wall ; and albeit they made a quick motion with their paws, yet for all that they made but slow progress. Of these animalcules I saw at one time only one in a particle of matter as big as a sand-grain ; and anon, at other times, some 4, 5, or even 6 or 8. I have also once seen animalcules of the same bigness, but of a different figure.[8]

---

[1] At one time L. held the curious belief that each red blood-corpuscle was composed of 6 aggregated smaller "globules". This was an error probably due, I think, to misinterpretation of diffraction-images.

[2] *i.e.*, in volume—not in diameter.

[3] *groote* stands here in the MS. but not in the printed letter.

[4] *gantsche* MS. omitted from printed letter.

[5] *i.e.*, their diameter was between $\frac{1}{3}$ and $\frac{1}{4}$ of that of a human red blood-corpuscle.

[6] The following description—as I have elsewhere tried to show (Dobell, 1920)—is a graphic account of the flagellate *Giardia* (=*Lamblia*) *intestinalis*.

[7] The woodlouse or sow-bug (*Oniscus asellus*). The Latin translation of this passage has given rise to many curious misunderstandings. Cf. Dobell (1920), where "pissabeds" are more fully discussed.

[8] As no other details are given, it is impossible to identify these organisms. Possibly they were *Trichomonas* or *Chilomastix*.

I have also seen a sort of animalcules that had the figure of our river-eels: these were in very great plenty, and so small withal, that I deemed 500 or 600 [1] of 'em laid out end to end would not reach to the length of a full-grown eel such as there are in vinegar.[2] These had a very nimble motion, and bent their bodies serpent-wise, and shot through the stuff as quick as a pike does through the water.[3]

At another time I saw, in 4 several observations, but one animalcule of the sort first spoken of;[4] but at my fourth observation, observing more narrowly than before, I saw a great number of animalcules,[5] each of which I judged to be more than 200 times less than a globule of our blood: for I imagined that I could make out that the length of six diameters of one animalcule couldn't reach beyond the diameter of one blood-globule. But here I speak to those who are versed in geometry, and know full well that if the diameter of one body be 1 and that of another (of like figure) be 6; then the difference in their bulk is as 1 to 216. And I can't forbear to say that I have divers times judged that I have seen, with great delight, in a particle of matter of the bigness of a coarse sand-grain, more than 1000 living animalcules, and these of 3 or 4 sorts, all alive together; nay, you might well have supposed that the whole material consisted of nought but living animalcules. Some people hearing this might

---

[1] The Latin version wrongly says "50 or 60" (*quinquaginta aut sexaginta*), which would—if correct—put a very different complexion on this passage.

[2] *Anguillula aceti*, the "vinegar-eel". Cf. p. 150 *supra*.

[3] From the description here given, it can hardly be doubted that these organisms were spirochaetes. In recent years a vast literature has sprung up on the intestinal species in man; but it must suffice to note here that more than one species occurs in human faeces, and that spirochaetes of some sort are normally present in the intestines of most human beings. This is the first record of their occurrence.

[4] Referring to *Giardia*.

[5] Probably bacteria, but possibly inanimate particles in Brownian movement.

perhaps imagine that these animalcules, because of their extreme littleness, might well get through into our blood; but I conceive that the vessels which conduct the material (out of which blood, fat, etc. is made) are so small, or must pass through such narrow channels, that even if such a little animalcule were divided into more than 1000 parts, 'twould still be too big to get through them.[1]

I have, moreover, examined my excrement when it was of ordinary thickness, and also mixed with clean water, but could then discover no animalcules in it; but whenever the stuff was a bit looser than ordinary, I have still seen animalcules therein, contrary to my expectation. I have, however, also seen in it some particles of food that were not digested; among others, for example, after I had eaten asparagus I saw very prettily its little tubes (off which the soft parts had been all digested away).

At divers times in the summer I have betaken myself into our meadows, and collected the dirt of cows and horses, just as they let it drop; yet I could discover no living animalcules therein, but most of this stuff (setting aside grass-particles which were undigested) was made up of globules, whereof 6 would be as big as a blood-globule, and many lesser globules of which I judged that 36 together would be only as big as a blood-globule; all these lying in a clear medium.

In the month of May,[2] I rode my horse (which is a mare) very hard, for about 1½ hour's going;[3] and on getting back to the stable, she let go her urine; and as the last of this urine looked to me very thick, and was

---

[1] L. means that the channels—in the intestinal wall—through which the ultimate food-particles in the gut pass into the blood-stream are too minute for bacteria to traverse them: and that even if a bacterium were but a tenth of its length, it still would be too big to do so.

[2] Presumably *anno* 1681.

[3] 1½ *ure gaens* MS. The printed version says "an hour and a quarter" (*een en een quart van een ure*). Apart from this discrepancy in the time, it should be noted that L. does not mean that he rode his mare hard for an hour and a half (a pretty strenuous feat), but for a distance equal to that

of an ashen colour, I viewed it[1] through a common microscope, that I had by me; and I found that what gave it the ashen colour were globule-like particles, of sundry sizes, each of 'em made up of still lesser globules stuck together. And these last globules were as big as the globules of our blood, and each of these again consisted of six several globules. I can't describe the first sort of globules better than by likening them to a round bunch of grapes, growing very close together, as it looks to your naked eye; and although the particles were not perfectly round, yet I may call 'em globules, for they were wanting in nothing but that those which were as big as a blood-globule (which I have already described as compound) stuck out a bit on the outside, like each grape does from its bunch.[2] Of this matter I took up a little, and found that besides the globules aforementioned there were yet many others, which had a sixth of the bigness of one of our blood-globules, and also some whereof I judged that 36 of 'em together would only make up the bulk of a blood-globule.[3]

---

which would be covered in an hour and a half by a man on foot. (Cf. note 3 on p. 109 *supra*.) The Latin translator—who copies the time from the printed Dutch version, not the MS.—accordingly renders this phrase (correctly) as "*circiter horam atque horae quadrantem pedestris itineris*. . ."

[1] In an earlier communication (*Letter 33*, 12 Nov. 1680), L. mentions that he examined his own urine, at a time when he was sick, and found in it—in addition to numerous particles—several red blood-corpuscles (cf. p. 12 of Dutch printed version).

[2] This is a hard sentence to translate closely and intelligibly. I give it as near as I can—without improving it too much.

[3] The foregoing observations—though they record the discovery of no new animalcules—appear to me to be of great importance; for they show that L. really recognized living bacteria when he saw them. He did not here—or elsewhere—mistake minute inanimate particles for "animalcules." At first sight it may seem strange that he did not take *all* minute moving particles for living organisms—as would have been indeed excusable. "Brownian movement" was not "discovered" until a century and a half later: but the phenomenon itself must have been frequently witnessed by L. He accounted for it as a consequence of the heat imparted to his microscopic preparations by their proximity to his own body. (He had to hold his microscopes very close to his face, because of the very short focus of his lenses.)

I then bethought me to examine the dirt of hens; and in order to get it clean, I squeezed the dirt out of a fowl's body as soon as it was dead. On viewing it, I saw therein a huge number of little snakes or eels, which I considered to be the fowl's seed; as indeed it was. For the cock was more than half full-grown;[1] and I took it for certain that in squeezing out its dirt, I had compressed its seed-vessels so violently that I squeezed the material out of them too. Afterwards I squeezed the dirt out of the hind end of several young hens, but I didn't discover anything but one living animalcule, which was about as big as a sixth of a blood-globule. The dirt consisted, further, of a clear matter, mixed with very many globules as big as a sixth of a blood-globule. These also looked as though they were composed of 2, 3, 4, 5, or 6 globules stuck together. And there were besides very many wee globules whereof 36 together (so I imagined) would be only as big as a blood-globule.

I also[2] gently pressed the dirt out of two new-killed pigeons, that were about a month old; and in the first I couldn't find any living animalcules at all. But in the dirt from the second pigeon (which was much clearer than the first's) I saw many animalcules;[3] so that I judged there were quite 100 of 'em in a bit as big as a sand-grain. These moved among one another very prettily[4], and were all of one and the same bigness, having the figure of an egg, and being in my judgement as big as a sixth part of one of our blood-globules. Beyond this, the stuff was like what I have described above from hens.

---

[1] *half volwassen* MS. *volwassen* printed version. I follow the MS. because it is difficult to comprehend how the bird could have been "*more* than *full*-grown". The Latin translator evaded the ambiguity by calling the fowl "*major annis gallus*".

[2] *ook* MS. omitted from printed letter.

[3] Bacteria of some sort, in all probability.

[4] *seer aerdig* MS. but the Dutch printed letter says *seer vaardig* [=very quickly]—which is concordantly rendered *expeditissime* in the Latin.

The foregoing quotations—which contain, I believe, all that Leeuwenhoek ever wrote on such subjects—record a series of truly remarkable discoveries; and they prove conclusively that he discovered intestinal protozoa and bacteria in man and several other animals. He here saw, and recognizably described, the flagellate *Giardia*[1] and the Spirochaetes and other Bacteria in his own faeces. He also, I think, must have seen other human intestinal flagellates (possibly *Trichomonas* or *Chilomastix*), though this is uncertain: but he certainly saw bacteria in the excrement of a fowl and in that of a pigeon, though curiously enough he failed to find them in the dung of cattle and horses.

Some of the interpretations which have been put upon Leeuwenhoek's words in this connexion must be read to be believed. As I have commented upon them elsewhere[2] I need say no more about them here. I will only note that the passages just quoted supply all the evidence there is for the statement—frequently met with in the literature—that Leeuwenhoek described the ciliate *Balantidium coli*, and that he himself suffered from dysentery caused by this parasite. Beyond all doubt this is a literary fiction lacking all foundation. Though an Austrian nobleman[3] assures us that Leeuwenhoek could not have seen what he described, and therefore what he saw must have been something totally different; and though a distinguished American medico[4] tells us that when Leeuwenhoek says he had weighed 160 lbs. for 30 years and usually had solid stools, he meant that he had suffered from balantidial dysentery since the age of 30: nevertheless, serious students of protozoology may well rest content with the plain and obvious meaning of his own simple words.

Before we proceed to the next discoveries, it may not be amiss to emphasize the novelty of those just recorded. At the time when the foregoing observations were made, no protozoa or bacteria of any kind were known—except the free-living

---

[1] Cf. Dobell (1920).

[2] Dobell (1920).

[3] Stein (1867), Vol. II, p. 321. Although I exposed Stein's blunders some years ago, I note that a recent German writer (Pritze, 1928) still accepts them. But as he evidently overlooked my paper, and knows nothing of L.'s work, I cannot take his opinions seriously.

[4] Strong (1904).

forms described by Leeuwenhoek himself a few years earlier. No animal or "animalcule" smaller than a worm was known to live inside the body of man: and the existence of hordes of micro-organisms within the bodies of healthy animals was as wholly unsuspected as it was unheard-of.

It is worthy of note, moreover, that neither here nor elsewhere in his writings does Leeuwenhoek associate entozoic protozoa or bacteria with the causation of disease. He found them in normal hosts, and it probably never occurred to him that any of them might have pathogenic properties. Having no medical education, and no preconceived notions regarding "animalcules," he recorded his findings simply and objectively, and it was left to others to elaborate his great discovery into the vast present-day *corpus* of medical protozoology and bacteriology. In a sense, therefore, he missed the great practical implications of his revelation.[1] But it must not be forgotten that the micro-organisms which he studied were all, in all probability, harmless; and consequently he deserves every credit for not speculating in excess of his facts. If every worker on the same subjects during the next 250 years had possessed an equally conservative and scientific spirit, a great deal of unnecessary confusion in our knowledge of "microbes" might have been avoided.

No further observations on entozoic protozoa were recorded until 1683. But in this year Leeuwenhoek wrote another highly interesting letter, in which he described many novel observations on frogs and other animals. He here accurately described, and discussed, the frog's spermatozoa and blood-corpuscles—for the first time; and in the course of his description he interpolated an account of various "animalcules" which he had discovered incidentally. Some of these animalcules were undoubtedly protozoa, but they are so involved

---

[1] Contemporary medical workers, however, were not slow to seize upon the pathological possibilities of L.'s discoveries. For example we find, as early as 1683, that "*the ingenious Fred. Slare* M.D. *and* F.R.S.", commenting upon a "murren" in Switzerland which carried off many cattle, says: "I wish Mr. *Leewenhoeck* had been present at the *dissections* of these infected *Animals*, I am perswaded He would have discovered some strange *Insect* or other in them."—Slare [*alias* Slear] (1647?-1727) was a physician and chemist. He qualified at Oxford in 1680, and became a Fellow of the Royal Society in the same year—just after L. himself.

with the other matters mentioned that it is not always easy to separate them. The passages in question—omitting irrelevant details (duly indicated)—are as follows: [1]

> The first frog that I dissected sat in the road; and it seemed so weak from the cold,[2] that though I gave it a bit of a kick on with my foot, it didn't jump away. When I picked it up and opened it, I found 'twas a female, in whose guts there were worms, which had the shape of those worms that children void in their stools.[3] These worms [4] were about as thick as a hair off one's head.[5]
>
> . . . .
>
> But what most surprised me was, that I observed in the blood (which had run out of the many blood-vessels that I had cut, into the clean [6] dish in which I dissected the frog) a great number of living animalcules,[7] which were about

---

[1] From *Letter 38*, 16 July 1683 [N.S.]. To Christopher Wren. MS.Roy.Soc. Read at a meeting of the Society held on July 18 [O.S.]—not on July 11, as appears (owing to omission of a date) in Birch, Vol. IV, p. 215. Published in *Brieven*, Vol. I (Dutch); *Opera Omnia*, Vol. I (Latin). The Dutch version first appeared in 1685 (*Ontled. en Ontdekk.*), and the first Latin version in the same year (*Anat. et Contempl.*). In both of these the letter is dated correctly: but in the *Op. Omn.* (and in the earlier *Anat. s. Int. Rer.* [1687], which contains a 2nd edition of the Latin letter) it is misdated July 26. A short English translation was published in *Phil. Trans.* (1683), Vol. XIII, No. 152, p. 347; and this was therefore the first version to appear in print. Hoole also translated a part of this letter, but not that which here concerns us. My translation is based primarily upon the original MS.

[2] In a previous (untranslated) paragraph it is noted that these frogs were studied on 1 April 1683, when they were coupling. It is thus certain that the species was *Rana temporaria*—not *R. esculenta*, which breeds later.

[3] Probably meaning *Oxyuris* (=*Enterobius*) *vermicularis*.

[4] The "worms" found in this frog were obviously not protozoa or bacteria but nematodes; and– if the foregoing identification of *Oxyuris* be correct—they were probably *Oxysoma brevicaudatum*, which is very common in *R. temporaria*.

[5] A description of the blood-corpuscles of the frog is here omitted.

[6] *schone* printed version. Not in MS.

[7] When all the particulars related are taken into account—size, host, origin, movements, etc.—I think there can be very little doubt that this "animalcule" was *Trichomonas* (or *Trichomastix* ?) *batrachorum*.

half as long and half as broad as one of the oval blood-corpuscles; all being of one and the same structure. 'Twas no small pleasure to see this sight: for I had let so much time slip by, that the oval blood-corpuscles were sunk down somewhat (owing to their weight) towards the bottom, and then these animalcules made a pretty motion, for as they went a-swimming, they knocked into the blood-corpuscles, and sent them spinning. And I judged that in every particle of blood as big as a sand-grain there were quite 50 animalcules.

The blood aforesaid was very watery, and not pure blood by any means: for as soon as I separated a good bit of the frog's skin from the flesh, some watery juice[1] began to run out of the skin, as well as the flesh; and still more when I opened the belly. And as I had well-nigh bashed in the frog's head, trying to make it keep quiet, methought some watery juice might well have been squashed out of its mouth or stomach too, and from this juice the animalcules might have come; for when I afterwards took blood out of the frog's veins clean, I could discover no animalcules therein; neither when I viewed the watery matter which came from between the skin and the flesh, nor yet in that from the hollow of the belly.[2]

In the foresaid watery matter, I noticed some irregular particles, most of which looked to me round, and were about as big as the globules of our blood. In some of these[3] I could make out that they were composed of 6 lesser globules; and there were besides particles that seemed only about $\frac{1}{6}$ of the bigness of the others. And when I

[1] *i.e.*, lymph.

[2] From the foregoing and succeeding passages it is clear that L. satisfied himself that there were no animalcules in the blood or lymph: and consequently there is no foundation for the statement—sometimes made—that he discovered protozoa in the blood of the frog.

[3] Plasma-cells, from the lymph. The smaller "globules" inside them were doubtless the large basophile granules contained in such cells.

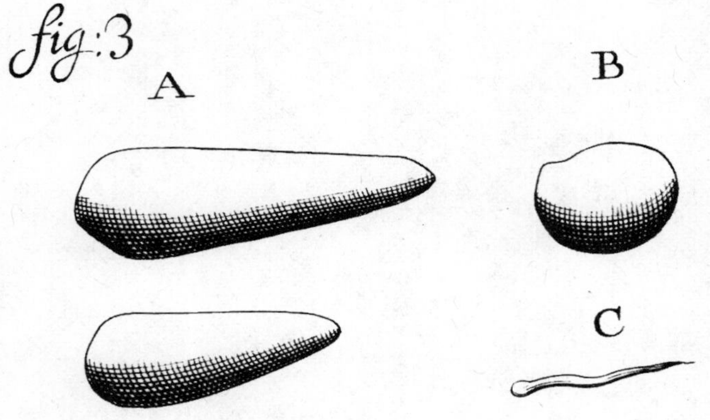

LEEUWENHOEK'S PICTURES OF THE INTESTINAL PROTOZOA OF FROGS
From the engravings in the Dutch edition of *Letter 38* (16 July 1683). × $1\frac{1}{2}$.

Fig. A, *Opalina* (*Cépèdea*) *dimidiata*.
Fig. B, *Nyctotherus cordiformis*.
Fig. C, a larval nematode?

examined the said watery blood of divers frogs, that had run out into the dish (for I took a clean dish for each several frog), a very few animalcules were[1] to be seen in it once more.

Because I couldn't satisfy myself about the animalcules aforesaid, though I was sure they didn't belong to the blood itself, but were gotten into it by accident; in the month of June[2] I continued my observations, and at last I came across some frogs[3] in whose dirt, which I took out of the guts, I beheld an unconceivably great company of living animalcules, and these of divers sorts and sizes. The biggest sort[4] had the shape of Fig. A.[5] Of these I judged there were quite 40 in a quantity of material as big as a grain of sand. The second sort[6] had the figure of B: these were very few in number. The third sort had very near the shape of our river-eels, as Fig. C: these were in even greater plenty than the first. And moreover the whole material was so full of little animalcules, that the very dirt seemed to consist of nothing but little living animals; for the little particles of the dirt itself were so stirred[7] by the motions of the animalcules, that they looked almost as though they were themselves animalcules too.[8] The number of the little animalcules

---

[1] *is* MS.—corrected to *zijn* in printed version.

[2] *Anno* 1683.

[3] The species is not discoverable from this description, but the protozoa found indicate that they were *Rana esculenta*—not *R. temporaria*. L. knew well (and could distinguish) both species. In *Letter 65*, 7 Sept. 1688, he tells us that there are two kinds of frog (*vorsch*) in Holland—the common "*kikvorsch*" [= *R. temporaria*], and the larger "*work*" [= *R. esculenta*] which is "eaten by the French."

[4] *Opalina* (*Cépèdea*) *dimidiata*—without a doubt.

[5] *hadden de fig*: *van. A* MS. *hadden de gedaante van Fig. 3. A.* printed version. See Plate XXIII.

[6] *Nyctotherus cordiformis*: but see below.

[7] *wiert . . . bewogen* MS.—corrected to *wierden . . . bewogen* in print.

[8] This graphic description must appeal to every worker who has studied the intestinal protozoa of frogs, for it vividly describes the usual appearance

last spoken of was so great, that I judged there were several thousand of 'em in every bit of matter as big as a sand-grain.

On seeing this, I took it for certain that the animalcules which I said before were in the blood (which I had taken out of the dish), came to be there only in this way: namely, because the frog, when it was being cut up, voided its dirt into the dish, or because I had unwittingly wounded the guts of the frog, in whose dirt there must have been many animalcules, which got mixed with the blood.

It has been generally allowed that the larger animalcules which Leeuwenhoek here described and figured (his Figs. A and B) were ciliates—which occur so commonly in the guts of frogs. But it is possible, I believe, to identify them more exactly. To anybody familiar with the intestinal fauna of the two common frogs of Northern Europe (*Rana temporaria* and *R. esculenta*), it must be obvious that the abundant long organisms (Fig. A) were *Opalina* (*Cépèdea*) *dimidiata*, while the smaller, scantier, and more rounded creature (Fig. B) was *Nyctotherus cordiformis*. Both of these occur very commonly in *Rana esculenta*,[1] and I therefore infer that the frogs which Leeuwenhoek was studying on this occasion were of this species.[2]

It would have been impossible to determine the exact species of these ciliates before the intestinal protozoa of frogs had been adequately studied. Consequently, most of the early identifications are not worth serious consideration. The first correct determination we owe, I think, to Bütschli, who says

---

of frogs' faeces under the microscope. The "animalcules" responsible for the phenomenon are flagellates (*Trichomonas*, *Trichomastix*, *Chilomastix*, and *Hexamita*), and various motile bacteria.

[1] *O. dimidiata* is well known as the characteristic species of opalinid from this host: *Nyctotherus*, however, is usually described as occurring in *R. temporaria* only. That the above statement is correct I know from my own observations.

[2] The frog in which L. found the worms previously was—as already noted—*R. temporaria*: but there is nothing in his words to prove that the frogs of the second batch were not of the other species. If they were, then the above identification amounts almost to a certainty.

that in Leeuwenhoek's description "Opalinae and Nyctotherus can be recognized with sufficient certainty."[1] No species are indicated, though the two which I have mentioned must, I think, have been intended. Saville Kent, however, had previously identified Leeuwenhoek's Fig. A as *Opalina intestinalis*:[2] but this is highly improbable, because there is no certain record of this species having ever been found in either *R. temporaria* or *R. esculenta*.[3]

Metcalf, who has studied the Opalinidae in greater detail than any other specialist, writes of Leeuwenhoek's observations as follows:[4]

"*Opalina* was first mentioned [?] by Leeuwenhoek in 1685[5] [?]. In his *Opera omnia* (1722) he quotes the earlier record [?] of finding innumerable *animalculae* [*sic*] of various sizes and forms in the foeces [*sic*] of the frog. One of these figured [L.'s Fig. B] seems in all probability to have been *O. ranarum*. Another may have been *O. dimidiata* [L.'s Fig. A]."

From this it seems to me that Metcalf cannot have studied Leeuwenhoek's works or words very carefully, nor does he appear to appreciate the difficulties of his own interpretation. If—as he suggests, and as I am convinced—Fig. A represents *O. dimidiata*, then the smaller rounded form (Fig. B) can hardly have been *O. ranarum*. For this species is at least as large as *O. dimidiata*, and occurs typically in a different host—*R. temporaria*.[6] Consequently, if Metcalf's interpretation were correct, it would leave the small size of Fig. B un-

---

[1] Bütschli (1887-89), Vol. III, p. 1101. The date of the observations is wrongly given, however, as 1687. Cf. also *ibid.*, pp. 1718 and 1721.

[2] Kent (1881-82), Vol. II, p. 562.

[3] *Opalina* (*Protoopalina*) *intestinalis* is a species proper to *Bombinator*—not *Rana*. Cf. Metcalf (1923), p. 51. Kent's error was first noted by Metcalf (1909), p. 319.

[4] Metcalf (1909), p. 319. My comments are interpolated in square brackets for the sake of brevity. In my opinion this single sentence contains at least six mistakes, but it seems unnecessary to do more than indicate them.

[5] In a later work (Metcalf, 1923, p. 438) the date is given as 1865 [!]—presumably by misprint of the first date (1685), which was itself incorrect. Little errors of this sort abound in nearly all discussions of L.'s work.

[6] I know of no certain record of *O. ranarum* having been found in *R. esculenta*, or of *O. dimidiata* from *R. temporaria*. Cf. also Metcalf (1923).

explained, and would necessitate the assumption that Leeuwenhoek found his ciliates not merely in two different frogs, but in frogs of two different species—of which there is no indication whatever in his own writings. But if, on the other hand, it be agreed that Fig. A shows *O. dimidiata*, then the frog was a specimen of *R. esculenta*, and the smaller ciliate was clearly *Nyctotherus*—not an opalinid at all. The figure certainly suggests this strongly,[1] and everything else supports this obvious, natural, and easy interpretation.

When we come to consider Leeuwenhoek's Fig. C, however, we are faced with very grave difficulties. This organism is said to have been like a "river-eel", and to have been abundant in the frog's faeces: and in size it appears, from the figure, to have been longer than a *Nyctotherus*—though the drawings were not made accurately to scale. Elsewhere in Leeuwenhoek's writings we find nematodes (*Anguillula*, etc.), spirilla, and spirochaetes, all likened to "eels": and in the rectal contents of *R. esculenta* we may find not only various species of nematodes, spirilla, and spirochaetes, but also long flexible and actively motile bacilli (*Bacillus flexilis* and similar forms). To determine which—if any—of these Leeuwenhoek may have seen on this occasion, is I think impossible. I must therefore leave Fig. C unidentified, though I am inclined to believe that it depicts a larval nematode.

I conclude, consequently, that Leeuwenhoek discovered and described *Opalina*, *Nyctotherus*, and *Trichomonas* (or *Trichomastix*) in the faeces of frogs, in addition to various other protozoa and bacteria which are not now identifiable.[2]

And now we come to a letter which is, perhaps, as famous as any Leeuwenhoek ever wrote to the Royal Society—the one containing his account of the "animalcules" in the human mouth. This letter is frequently quoted—or rather mis-

---

[1] For example, there is a definite indication of the mouth, and the outline is—to me—quite convincing. The interpretation of Fig. B as *Balantidium coli*—recently put forward by Pritze (1928)—is so outrageous as to deserve no further notice.

[2] I ought perhaps to point out that Prowazek (1913) has identified some of these organisms with *Balantidium coli*. Although he has been copied by others (*e.g.* Pritze, 1928), his interpretation is manifestly absurd. There is no evidence that L. ever saw *any* species of *Balantidium* in the frog, and *B. coli* certainly does not live in this host.

quoted—by bacteriologists, and is usually said to be the first memoir in which bacteria of any sort are mentioned. How far this is true, readers of foregoing quotations can judge for themselves. References to this important epistle, addressed to Francis Aston, *Sec.R.S.*,[1] are almost invariably given incompletely or incorrectly; and this is doubtless due in part—though not altogether—to the fact that many versions of it are extant. Moreover, many different interpretations of the organisms described have been advanced, and this has led to some truly astonishing conclusions. Yet Leeuwenhoek's words are, as usual, plain and straightforward, while the interpretation of his observations appears to me obvious. To anybody familiar with the flora and fauna of the human mouth they surely present no difficulties. I shall therefore give his own words (as well as I can) first, and shall comment upon them afterwards—adding exact references but ignoring many manifestly absurd statements made by other commentators.

The passages in question run as follows:[2]

---

[1] Concerning Francis Aston little is now known. (He is not mentioned in the *Dict. Nat. Biogr.*) He was elected F.R.S. in 1678, and became Secretary in 1681—a post which he suddenly threw up in 1685 (cf. *Rec. Roy. Soc.*, and Weld, I, 302). Afterwards he received a gratuity from the Society (Weld, I, 305), and on his death bequeathed to them his estate at Mablethorpe in Lincolnshire, together with his books and instruments (Weld, I, 428). His portrait now hangs in the apartments of the Society at Burlington House (at the foot of the staircase). For the following additional information I am indebted to Mr H. W. Robinson, Assistant Librarian of the Royal Society: Aston was born about 1644, and died in June or July 1715. He went to Westminster School in 1656, and was King's Scholar in 1660 (aged 16). He entered Trinity College, Cambridge, in 1661, and became Fellow in 1667. (B.A. *Cant.* 1664/5: M.A. 1668.) He travelled abroad for some years, and in his youth was an intimate friend of Isaac Newton.

[2] From *Letter 39.* 17 September 1683. To F. Aston. MS.Roy.Soc. Published in *Brieven*, Vol. I (Dutch), and *Opera Omnia*, Vol. II (Latin). The Dutch version was first printed in 1684 (*Ondervind. en Beschouw.* pp. 1-19), the Latin in 1695 (*Arc. Nat. Det.* pp. 41-53). Both versions are wrongly dated the *12th* of the month ("*den 12 Septemb. 1683*" and "*pridie Iduum Septembris 1683*") apparently through a misreading of the MS. Owing, it would seem, to some oversight, two different English abstracts appeared in the *Phil. Trans.* The first was published in Vol. XIV (1684), No. 159, p. 568 [*bis*—a misprint for *598*]: the second in Vol. XVII (1693), No. 197, p. 646. [The first—published 20 May 1684—is the fuller and better.] Hoole (1798) has given a third—and as far as it goes the best—

I have ere this sent you my observations concerning spittle, which I see have been made public in print in the *Lectures and Collections* published by Mr. Robert Hooke, Secretary of the Roy. Soc., in the year 1678.[1] Since that time I have made divers further observations on my spittle, with the idea that if there be any animalcules lying about in the body, they would get into the mouth, sooner or later, through the spit-ducts; but in what observations I made to this end, I could make out no animalcules there, nor could I say aught else but what I have hitherto writ.

'Tis my wont of a morning to rub my teeth with salt, and then swill my mouth out with water: and often, after eating, to clean my back teeth with a toothpick, as well as rubbing them hard with a cloth: wherefore my teeth, back and front, remain as clean and white as falleth to the lot of few men[2] of my years,[3] and my gums (no

---

partial English translation in *Select Works*, Vol. I, p. 118. Löffler (1887, p. 5) has translated a fragment into German, but he misdates the letter September 14. It was read at a meeting of the Society held on 24 October 1683 [O.S.]: cf. Birch, Vol. IV, p. 219. Various reproductions of the illustrative figures are noted below (p. 244 *et seq.*). They have already given rise to much confusion and misstatement.—Though there are already at least one Dutch, two Latin, and three English versions of this letter in print, I rely upon the original MS. (in L.'s own hand), from which my translation has been made.

[1] A reference to *Letter 23*, 14 January 1678. To R. Hooke. MS.Roy.Soc. English version (incomplete) published in Hooke's *Lect. & Collect.* (1678), part II, Letter 2, p. 84. (Reprinted in Hooke's *Lect. Cutl.* (1679) pt. V.)—This letter contains an account of certain "Globules in the Flegm": but L. had examined saliva still earlier, for in *Letter 4* (1 June 1674, to Oldenburg) he notes that "In clean spit, examined by me in the morning, I find a few very little particles floating in the liquid; whereof I saw some sink to the bottom; as also divers irregular particles, some of which seemed to consist of globules stuck together. And in the spittle that I examined in the afternoon, I found the globules and irregular particles in greater plenty". (MS.Roy.Soc. Partial English translation in *Phil. Trans.* (1674), Vol. IX, No. 106, p. 121.)

[2] *als er weijnig menschen van mijn Jaren sijn* MS. *als weynig menschen . . . gebeurt* printed version.

[3] When he wrote this, L. was approaching his 51st birthday. He tells

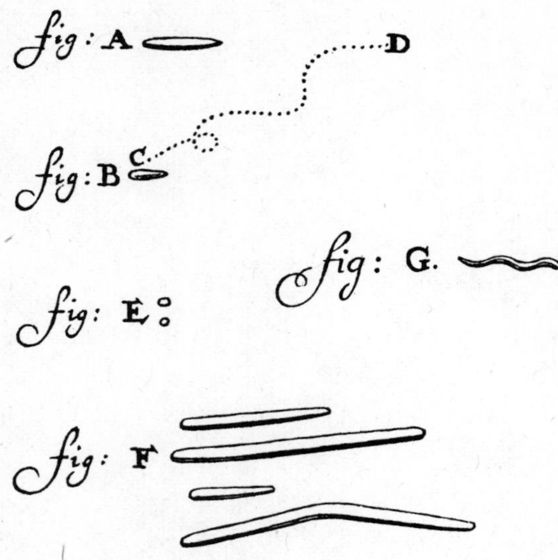

LEEUWENHOEK'S FIGURES OF BACTERIA FROM THE HUMAN MOUTH
(Letter 39, 17 Sept. 1683)

Enlarged (× 1½) from the engravings published in *Arc. Nat. Det.*, 1695.

Fig. A, a motile *Bacillus*.
Fig. B, *Selenomonas sputigena*. C . . . . D, the path of its motion.
Fig. E, Micrococci.
Fig. F, *Leptothrix buccalis*.
Fig. G, A spirochæte—probably "*Spirochaeta buccalis*," the largest form found in this situation.

matter how hard the salt be that I rub them with) never start bleeding. Yet notwithstanding,[1] my teeth are not so cleaned thereby, but what there sticketh or groweth between some of my front ones and my grinders (whenever I inspected them with a magnifying mirror), a little white matter, which is as thick as if 'twere batter.[2] On examining this, I judged (albeit I could discern nought a-moving in it) that there yet were living animalcules therein. I have therefore mixed it, at divers times, with clean rain-water (in which there were no animalcules), and also with spittle, that I took out of my mouth, after ridding it of air-bubbles (lest the bubbles should make any motion in the spittle): and I then most always saw, with great wonder, that in the said matter there were many very little living[3] animalcules, very prettily a-moving. The biggest sort had the shape of Fig. A[4] [Plate XXIV]: these had a very strong and swift motion, and shot through the water (or spittle) like a pike[5] does through the water. These were most always few in number.

The second sort had the shape of Fig. B. These oft-times spun round like a top, and every now and then took a course like that shown between C and D: and these were far more in number.

---

us elsewhere, however, that he sometimes suffered from toothache—to alleviate which he smoked a pipe of tobacco, which generally made him feel very sick. He also tells us later how some of his teeth decayed.

[1] *Nogtans* printed version—omitted in MS.

[2] *beslagen meel* MS. and Dutch printed version "wetted flower" *Phil. Trans.* (1684) "like a mixture of flour and water" Hoole *farinae aqua subactae similem* Latin edition. The 2nd *Phil. Trans.* version (1693) incorrectly calls this soft mealy material (*materia alba*) "a kind of gritty Matter."

[3] *levende* is here in the MS. but not in the printed version.

[4] *hadde de Fig*: *van A.* MS. *was van de Fig*: *A.* printed version.

[5] *een snoek* MS. and Dutch printed version. The Latin translator rendered this—with some justification—*piscis lupus*: which caused Löffler (1887, p. 5) to mistranslate it "*Raubfisch*" (instead of *Hecht*). To "shoot through the water like a pike" is a phrase commonly used by L. to describe any rapidly darting aquatic animalcule.

To the third sort I could assign no figure: for at times they seemed to be oblong, while anon they looked perfectly[1] round. These were so small that I could see them no bigger than Fig. E: yet therewithal they went ahead so nimbly, and hovered so together, that you might imagine them to be a big swarm of gnats or flies, flying in and out among one another. These last seemed to me e'en as if there were, in my judgement, several thousand of 'em in an amount of water or spittle (mixed with the matter aforesaid) no bigger than a sand-grain; albeit there were[2] quite nine parts of water, or spittle, to one part of the matter that I took from betwixt my front teeth, or my grinders.

Furthermore, the most part of this matter consisted of a huge number of little streaks, some greatly differing from others in their length, but of one and the same thickness withal; one being bent crooked, another straight, like Fig. F, and which lay disorderly ravelled together. And because I had formerly seen, in water, live animalcules that had the same figure, I did make every endeavour to see if there was any life in them; but I could make out not the least motion, that looked like anything alive, in any of 'em.

I have also taken spittle from the mouths of two different womenfolk,[3] that I'm sure clean their teeth every day, and examined it as narrowly as I was able to, but could discern therein no living animalcules. But afterwards I examined the same spittle mingled with a little of the matter that I picked out with a needle from betwixt their teeth: and then I discovered as many living

---

[1] *volkomen* is here in the printed text, but not in the manuscript.

[2] *was* MS.—corrected to *waren* in print.

[3] *twee distincte Vrouwspersonen* MS. and Dutch ed. *binarum foeminarum* Lat. ed. "two several women" *Phil. Trans.* (1684) "other Persons" *Phil. Trans.* (1693) "two ladies" Hoole (1798). It is almost certain that these were L.'s own womenfolk—his second wife Cornelia, and his daughter Maria.

ve hadden een seer starcke en vaardige bewegınge, en
schooten door het water, of speeksel, als een snoek door
het water doet. dese waren meest doorgaans weynig int
getal. De tweede soort hadde de fig: van B. dese drayde
haar veeltyts om als een Tol, en namen, soo nu als dan
een cours als met C. en D. is aen gewesen. dese waren
veel meerder int getal. Aen de derde soort en konde
ik geen fig: bekomen, want op de eene tyt schenen
deselve te bestaan uyt een Lang-ront, en op de ander
tyt weder uyt een ront, dese waren soo kleyn, dat
ik deselve niet grooter konde sien als fig: E. en daar
by soo een vaardige ~~bewegınge~~ voortgang, dat deselvige
soo door malkanderen swierden, als of wy ons in
beelden, een groot getal van Muggen of vliegen
door malkanderen te sien vliegen. dese laatste syn
my wel te vooren gekomen, dat ik oordeelde eenige
duysenden, te sien inde quantiteit water, of speeksel
(vermengt met de verhaalde materie) dat niet grooter
was als een sant groote, schoon "datter" wel 9. deelen water, "of speeksel was"
en 1. deel materie ~~was~~, dat ik tusschen myn tanden
of kiesen had uyt genomen. vorders bestont de
meeste materie uyt een over groote menigte van strom-
tgens, de eene veel van den anderen verschillende inde
Lengte, en nogtans van een ende deselve dikte, de eene
krom gebogen, ende de andere regt, als fig: F. die onge-
schikt door malkanderen lagen, en om dat ik voor
desen, dierkens int water heb sien leven, die deselve
fig: hadden, soo heb ik alle devoiren aen gewent, om
te sien, of daar leven in was, Maar ik heb geen
de minste bewegınge, dat na eenig leven geleek, daar
aen

A PAGE OF THE ORIGINAL HOLOGRAPH MS. OF LETTER 39
(17 Sept. 1683: leaf 2 *recto* = page 3),
containing part of Leeuwenhoek's description of the Bacteria in the mouth.
Facsimile. (The first word is [*desel*] *ve*, continued from the previous page.)
This is a good sample of Leeuwenhoek's handwriting at this period.

animalcules, together with the long particles, as hereinbefore related.

I have also examined the spittle of a child about eight years old, and likewise could discover no living animalcules therein; and afterwards the same spittle, mixed with the stuff that I got out from atween the child's teeth: whereupon I perceived as great a many animalcules and other particles as heretofore made mention of.

I didn't clean my teeth (on purpose) for three days running, and then took the stuff that had lodged in very small quantity on the gums above my front teeth; and I mixt it both with spit and with fair rain-water;[1] and I found a few living animalcules in it too.

While I was talking to an old man (who leads a sober life, and never drinks brandy or tobacco,[2] and very seldom any wine), my eye fell upon his teeth, which were all coated over; so I asked him when he had last cleaned his mouth? And I got for answer that he'd never washed his mouth in all his life.[3] So I took some spittle out of his mouth and examined it; but I could find in it nought but what I had found in my own and other people's. I also took some of the matter that was lodged between and against his teeth, and mixing it with his own spit, and also with fair water (in which there were no animalcules), I found an unbelievably great company of living animalcules, a-swimming more nimbly than any I had ever seen up to this time. The biggest sort (whereof there were a great plenty) bent their body into curves in going forwards, as in Fig. G. Moreover, the other animalcules were in such enormous numbers, that all the water (notwithstanding

---

[1] *water* MS. *regen-water* Dutch printed version.

[2] In olden times it was customary to speak of "drinking" tobacco—both in Holland and in England—though it meant "smoking" (as we now say).

[3] Hoole (1798, p. 119)—with his usual squeamishness—purifies these coarse details into more polite observations upon "the teeth of an old gentleman, who was very careless about keeping them clean."

only a very little of the matter taken from between the teeth was mingled with it) seemed to be alive. The long particles too, as before described, were also in great plenty.

I have also taken the spittle, and the white matter that was lodged upon and betwixt the teeth, from an old man[1] who makes a practice of drinking brandy every morning, and wine and tobacco in the afternoon; wondering whether the animalcules, with such continual boozing, could e'en remain alive. I judged that this man, because his teeth were so uncommon foul,[2] never washed his mouth. So I asked him, and got for answer: "Never in my life with water, but it gets a good swill with wine or brandy every day." Yet I couldn't find anything beyond the ordinary in his spittle. I also mixed his spit with the stuff that coated his front teeth, but could make out nothing in it save very few of the least sort of living animalcules hereinbefore described time and again. But in the stuff I had hauled out from between his front teeth (for the old chap hadn't a back tooth in his head), I made out many more little animalcules, comprising two of the littlest sort.

Furthermore, I put some strong wine-vinegar in my own mouth, and then set my teeth, and let the vinegar run betwixt 'em time after time: and after doing so, I rinsed my mouth out thrice with fair water. Afterwards I once more fetched out some of the foresaid stuff from between my front teeth, as well as from between my grinders; and I mixed it divers times both with spittle and with clean rain-water: and most always I discovered in it an unbelievable number of living animalcules, though most of 'em were in the matter I got from between my back teeth, and only a few had the appearance of Fig. A.

---

[1] Hoole (1798) prudishly refrained from translating the observations made upon this disreputable "old gentleman", who, in the *Phil. Trans.* (1684), is called simply—without other descriptive detail—"a good fellow".

[2] *ongemeen vuijl* MS. *buyten gemeen vuyl* printed letter.

I have also put a little wine-vinegar to this stuff mixed with spittle, or with water: whereupon the animalcules fell dead forthwith. And from this I drew the conclusion that the vinegar, when I filled my mouth with it, didn't penetrate through all the matter that is firmly lodged between the front teeth, or the grinders, and killed only those animalcules that were in the outermost parts of the white matter.

In several of the observations aforesaid, I saw on 2 or 3 occasions some very bright transparent particles, whereof many were perfectly round, others having an irregular round figure. These were of divers bignesses, and the biggest of them I judged to be about 25 times bigger than a globule of one's blood[1]: and if they hadn't sunk to the bottom, by reason of their weight, I should have taken them for fat-particles.[2]

I have had several gentlewomen in my house, who were keen on seeing the little eels in vinegar: but some of 'em were so disgusted at the spectacle, that they vowed they'd ne'er use vinegar again. But what if one should tell such people in future that there are more animals living in the scum on the teeth in a man's mouth, than there are men in a whole kingdom? especially in those who don't ever clean their teeth, whereby such a stench comes from the mouth of many of 'em, that you can scarce bear to talk to them; which is called by many people "having a stinking breath", though in sooth 'tis most always a stinking *mouth*. For my part I judge, from myself (howbeit I clean my mouth like I've already said), that all the people living in our United Netherlands are not as many as the living animals that I carry in my own mouth this very day: for I noticed one of my back teeth, up against the gum, was coated with the said matter

---

[1] *i.e.*, they had about thrice the diameter of a human red blood-corpuscle. These were probably squamous cells—the smaller being "salivary corpuscles" (dead leucocytes).

[2] *vet-deeltgens*; *i.e.*, oil droplets.

for about the width of a horse-hair, where, to all appearance, it had not been scoured by the salt for a few days;[1] and there were such an enormous number of living animalcules here, that I imagined I could see a good 1000 of 'em in a quantity of this material that was no bigger than a hundredth part of a sand-grain.[2]

It must be noted here that the illustrations accompanying the foregoing letter differ slightly in each version. The original drawings are, unfortunately, lost: and the best figures—those now reproduced—are in the original Latin edition (*Arc. Nat. Det.*, 1695) and *Opera Omnia*. From the first Dutch edition[3] (1684) Fig. G, a highly important picture, was for some unexplained reason omitted altogether.[4] In the first *Phil. Trans.* version (1684) all the figures appear, but Fig. G has an irregular and unrecognizable shape: while in the second *Phil. Trans.* version (1693) Fig. G again disappears, and the others are reversed.[5]

A plausible explanation of these discrepancies is the following. The figures originally sent by Leeuwenhoek to the Royal Society were badly drawn and poorly engraved, and he was probably dissatisfied with them—especially with Fig. G, which was very bad. When he was about to publish the same pictures himself later in the same year, he resolved to have this figure redrawn, and therefore told the engraver not to copy the original. Then, by an oversight, the letter was printed with the figure missing. Later, discovering his mistake, Leeuwenhoek had a new and improved drawing

---

[1] The Latin version inserts here "*materiam illam inde exemi*" [=so I extracted some of this stuff], but this is not in the Dutch originals.

[2] The sentences in the foregoing paragraph are loosely strung together and ungrammatical in the original: and consequently they are not easy to translate into intelligible English without "improving" beyond recognition. If the reader should find my version inelegant and confused, I would refer him to its prototype—which is much worse.

[3] In the only copy of the 2nd Dutch edition of L.'s works which I have yet seen, the whole letter containing these observations (No. 39) is missing—the copy being otherwise perfect.

[4] It is referred to, however, in the text (both MS. and printed Dutch version).

[5] This is obviously due to the engraver's direct copying of the original drawings on to his plate.

prepared, and this was inserted in the Latin translation which appeared subsequently. The still later omission of Fig. G from the second *Phil. Trans.* version was probably merely a consequence of the great condensation which this very short and faulty translation underwent at the hands of its editors.

Some such explanation would readily account for the variations in the different versions. But in any case, I think, we need not hesitate to accept the final and complete set of drawings published with the Latin letter—drawings which Leeuwenhoek must himself have seen and passed for press. The omission of Fig. G from the Dutch edition was certainly unintentional, as it is referred to in the letterpress.

It is not possible to doubt, after reading the foregoing descriptions and inspecting the pictures, that Leeuwenhoek discovered[1] the bacteria in the human mouth: for he described—and described recognizably—all the most characteristic forms occurring in this situation. To anybody familiar with these organisms his figures speak so clearly that his words are almost superfluous. If I were shown these sketches for the first time, and asked to interpret them, I should be able to say—after only a moment's reflexion—what they probably depict. Fig. A is a *Bacillus*: Fig. B shows the peculiar organism known as "*Spirillum sputigenum*":[2] Fig. E shows some of the *Micrococci* commonly present in the mouth: Fig.

---

[1] I must note that priority for this discovery has been claimed for Hartsoeker; but this is due to a misunderstanding. The true story can be pieced together from L.'s writings and Hartsoeker's own words (1730). Hartsoeker, knowing of L.'s discovery of the spermatozoa, tried to pass it off as his own: but he says that he was ashamed to tell people that he had examined *semen* with the microscope, and therefore told them at first that the "animalcules" which he had found in it were in the *saliva*. But he further says, quite definitely (1730, p. 6), that he never really saw any animalcules in saliva, and he attempts to discredit L.'s discovery. He regarded it as an invention. Consequently, Hartsoeker himself never claimed to have found any organisms in the human mouth, and even denied their existence.

[2] So named by Miller (1890). This organism is not really a *Spirillum* at all, but belongs to the genus *Selenomonas* Prowazek, 1913*a*. I have studied it (in pure culture) but I have seen no accurate description of it.—In the genus *Selenomonas* the flagella arise from the concave surface of the arched or crescentic body—not from its ends, as in *Spirillum*. Their lashing produces the curious whirling motion observed by L. Although the text-books of bacteriology are usually silent on the subject, I can say from my own knowledge that *Selenomonas sputigena* is very common in human mouths—and very difficult to isolate in cultures.

F is the *Leptothrix*[1] always found on the human teeth: and Fig. G is unquestionably a spirochaete—probably the so-called "*Spirochaeta buccalis*".[2] The figures obviously represent bacteria, and include no protozoa; and nowhere but in the mouth is such an assemblage of forms to be found. When Leeuwenhoek's own words are considered in conjunction with these illustrations, the interpretations just advanced must surely be self-evident to everybody who studies the microbes of the human mouth "with the help of a good microscope."

Yet ever since the foregoing observations were recorded they have been misinterpreted—and even questioned and denied—in the most astonishing manner. It is unnecessary to chronicle here all the wild assertions that have been made in this connexion.[3] Two of the most recent comments will serve as illustration:

(i) Singer (1914) reproduces the figures from the *Phil. Trans.* 1684 (misdated by him 1683), and says that figs. A, F, and G [the spirochaete] are all "rod-shaped organisms" [meaning bacilli?]; and that B [*Selenomonas*] is "a flagellated organism" [meaning a protozoon?]. He even recognizes "sarcinae" in Leeuwenhoek's description: but the figure[4] so strangely interpreted is said by Leeuwenhoek himself to represent epidermal scales from the human skin, as seen under a low magnification.

(ii) Wenyon (1926), discussing the *Trichomonas* of the human mouth, says "it is probable that Leeuwenhoek saw the flagellate in the tartar of his own and other people's teeth."[5] Although no reference is given to the passage in

---

[1] *Leptothrix buccalis* Robin, 1853: *Bacillus maximus buccalis* Miller, 1890.

[2] A specific designation commonly ascribed to Cohn. But see Dobell (1912).

[3] I must mention, however, that Robin (1853, pp. 352-354) made a careful study of the Latin versions of *Letter 39*, and correctly identified the *Leptothrix*. He also recognized Fig. B as a "*vibrion*". Beijerinck (1913, p. 10, note) wrongly supposes that Löffler (1887) was the first to direct attention to L.'s pictures of bacteria in the human mouth.

[4] Fig. H—which occurs in the same letter, but is not reproduced here. To my mind this figure bears no resemblance to a *Sarcina* or any other bacterium: and of course no *Sarcina* lives normally in the mouth of man.

[5] Wenyon (1926), Vol. I, p. 656. So far as I am aware, there is no passage in any of L.'s writings which can be plausibly interpreted as an account of the *Trichomonas* of the human mouth.

which *Trichomonas* is supposed to have been described, clear that Wenyon must here refer to one or other of "animalcules" which we have just discussed—but which one, I cannot even guess. To me it is obvious that they were *all* bacteria: but Wenyon takes the view that *none* of them could have been, since he considers that bacteria "were quite beyond the scope of the simple magnifying apparatus used by Leeuwenhoek."[1]

Thus, while Singer finds, in Leeuwenhoek's words and pictures, more bacteria than Leeuwenhoek himself, Wenyon is able to recognize none at all!

Some further researches on the "animalcules" in the human mouth were reported by Leeuwenhoek nine years later. His letter runs as follows:[2]

> In my letter of the 12th[3] of September, 1683, I spake, among other things, of the living creatures that are in the white matter which lieth, or groweth, betwixt or upon one's front teeth or one's grinders. Since that time, and especially in the last two or three years, I have examined this stuff divers times; but to my surprise, I could discern no living creatures in it.

---

[1] Wenyon (1926), p. 3.

[2] From *Letter 75*. 16 September 1692. To the Royal Society. MS.Roy.Soc. Printed in full in *Brieven*, Vol. II, p. 508: *Opera Omnia*, Vol. II, p. 307 (1st pagination). The Dutch version first appeared in 1693 (*Derde Vervolg d. Brieven*), the Latin in 1695 (*Arc. Nat. Det.*, p. 334). No English translation was ever published in the *Phil. Trans.*, and so far as I am aware no English version has yet appeared in print. (Hoole did not translate the relevant passages in this letter.) A German paraphrase—of a fragment only—is given by Löffler (1887, p. 6), who misdates the epistle October 1.—The printed Dutch version follows the original MS. so closely that few annotations are necessary: while the Latin version in *Opera Omnia* (ed. noviss., 1722)—by an unknown hand—is one of the best translations I have ever read. Barring a few trivial misprints, it renders its Dutch prototype with wonderful faithfulness.—The originals of the illustrations are lost; the MS. in the Roy.Soc. collection being accompanied by a proof of the engraved plate sent by L. himself in place of the original sketches.

[3] As noted already (p. 237, note 2), the correct date of this letter—as written by L. himself on the MS.—is not the 12th but the 17th of September.

Being unable to satisfy myself about this, I made up my mind to put my back into the job, and to look into the question as carefully as I could. But because I keep my teeth uncommon clean, rubbing them with salt every morning, and after meals generally picking them with a fowl's quill, or pen; I therefore found very little of the said stuff stuck on the outside of my front teeth: and in what I got out from between them, I could find nothing with life in it. Thereupon I took a little of the stuff that was on my frontmost grinders; but though I had two or three shots at these observations, 'twas not till the third attempt that I saw one or two live animalcules. Yet I could well make out some particles lying about that I felt sure must have been animalcules. This put me in a quandary again, seeing that at and about the time when I wrote to you concerning these animalcules, I never failed to see there was life in them: but though now I used just the very same magnifying-glass and apparatus (which I judged to be that best suited to the purpose), yet I couldn't make out any living creatures at all.

Having allowed my speculations to run on this subject for some time, methinks I have now got to the bottom of the dying-off of these animalcules. The reason is, I mostly or pretty near always of a morning drink coffee, as hot as I can, so hot that it puts me into a sweat: beyond this I seldom drink anything save at mealtimes in the middle of the day and in the evening; and by doing so, I find myself in the best of health. Now the animalcules that are in the white matter on the front-teeth, and on the foremost of the back-teeth, being unable to bear the hotness of the coffee, are thereby killed: like I've often shown that the animalcules which are in water are made to die by a slight heating.

Accordingly, I took (with the help of a magnifying mirror) the stuff from off and from between the teeth further back in my mouth, where the heat of the coffee couldn't get at it. This stuff I mixt with a little spit out of my mouth (in which there were no air-bubbles), and I did all this in the way I've always done: and then I saw, with as great a wonderment as ever before, an unconceivably great number of little animalcules, and in so unbelievably small a quantity of the foresaid stuff, that those who didn't see it with their own eyes could scarce credit it. These animalcules, or most all of them, moved so nimbly among one another, that the whole stuff seemed alive and a-moving.

I again paid the strictest attention I possibly could to the bigness, or at any rate to the length, of the bodies of many of 'em [1]; but mostly to the little animalcules, which looked to me roundish. Afterwards, I took a grain of coarse sand (of the sort of sand that we use here in this country [2] for scouring the pewter, and other household chattels), and I stuck this sand-grain in front of the microscope through which I had seen the animalcules: and I am bound to say, after making careful measurements, which I did by eye, that the diameter of the sand-grain was above a thousand times longer than the diameter of one of the little animalcules which I saw in great numbers. Consequently, then, such a grain of sand was far more than a thousand millionfold bigger than one of the little creatures aforesaid.

Besides, I also saw divers animalcules [3] whose bodies were a bit thicker than the little animals hereinbefore spoken of; but these were quite 5 or 6 times longer than they were thick, and therewithal their body was of equal thickness all along, so that I couldn't make out which was their head, or which their tail end; all the more because when they were a-swimming, which they did very leisurely (and this was their only motion, with a little bending of the body now and then, as it seemed to me), they would go ahead first with one end of the body

---

[1] *de hoe grootheijt of de lengte van veele haar lighamen* MS. . . . *of wel de lengte van veele haar 'er lighamen* Dutch printed version.

[2] *alwaar hier te lande* MS. *waar mede hier te lande* printed version.

[3] Obviously bacilli of some sort, but otherwise unidentifiable.

in front, and anon with the other.[1] These animalcules, as they appeared to me, I have shown in Fig. A. [See Text-fig. 4.]

And I saw, too, sundry animalcules[2] that had very near the same length, and also some a bit longer. These moved their bodies in great bends, in comparison of the first animalcules, and made with their bendings so swift a motion, in swimming first forwards and then backwards, and particularly with rolling round on their long axis, that I couldn't but behold them again with great wonder

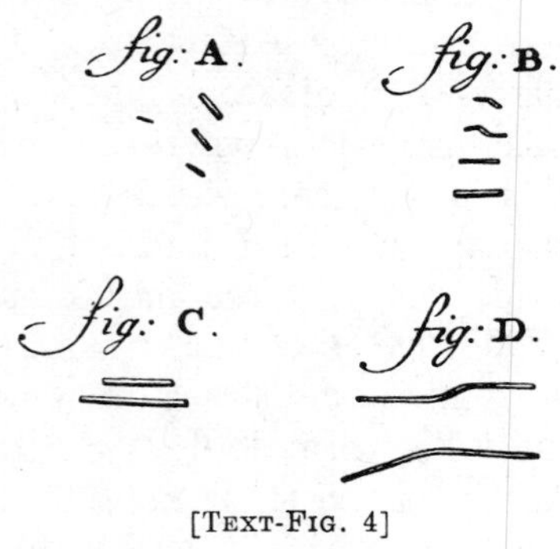

[TEXT-FIG. 4]

and delight: the more so because I hadn't been able to find them for several years, as I've already said. For I saw not alone the nimble motion of their own body; but the little animalcules too, which swam in great plenty round about these animalcules, were shoved off or driven away from them, just as if you imagined you saw a butterfly or moth flitting among a swarm of gnats, so that the gnats were all wafted away by the butterfly's wings. These animalcules I have represented in Fig. B.

---

[1] This very acute observation was made on other bacteria, of course, at a much earlier date—as already noted. It furnishes conclusive proof that the organisms observed were bacteria.

[2] From the following account these were evidently spirochaetes again: but the figures are very poor, and could hardly be identified without L.'s description of the organisms themselves.

Furthermore, I saw animalcules[1] that were of very near the same thickness, but of singular length. These had so little[2] motion that I had most times to confess they might not be living creatures at all; yet when I could keep my eye on them, without getting tired, I could make out that they bent their body very slow, just bending it into a very faint curve, so that they didn't move forward, or very little. These animalcules, as they looked to me, are shown in Fig. C.

Now I also saw yet other animalcules,[3] that were of very nigh the same thickness, but which in length even surpassed those last described. But you seldom saw two of this sort alongside, or floating off in the wet stuff, that were of one and the same length. These animalcules[4] too were[5] in great numbers, whereof some were straight, while others had a kink in them, as shown in Fig. D. But the longer these animals were, the less motion or life could I discern in them: and notwithstanding I could make out no life in 'em, yet I made sure they were living creatures, or had been such when they were in the mouth, and situated on the back teeth, where many are generated.

But we must be still more amazed when we consider how these animalcules can move, and shift 'emselves about, in stuff as thick as this is when it is lodged upon and betwixt the teeth; and how hard and slow it must be for them to get about in such stuff. But when, on the other hand, the said stuff is mixed up with spittle, and by this mixing the animalcules find themselves in a fluid material, many of them feel released, as it were, and never stop moving, so far as the eye can see.

---

[1] ? *Leptothrix*.

[2] *seer weijnig* MS. *soo weynig* printed version.

[3] *Leptothrix*—almost certainly.

[4] *Dierkens* MS. omitted from printed letter.

[5] *sijn* MS. and printed version: apparently a mistake for *waren*. The Latin version has *erant*, and I make the same correction.

It must be confessed that the foregoing observations add little to those made previously. But bacilli, spirochaetes, and *Leptothrix* are again recognizably described—if not recognizably figured: and this letter therefore confirms, to some extent, the earlier one (No. 39). It also gives us a characteristic glimpse of the author and his methods, and for that reason—if for no other—deserves notice.

Various writers have already reproduced the illustrations accompanying this letter, but nobody hitherto appears to have made any attempt to interpret them—apart from noting that they represent "bacteria". This is to be explained, I think, in the usual way: most people merely glance at Leeuwenhoek's figures and do not take the trouble to read his words relating to them, so that his excellent observations have been all too often misunderstood or treated as mere curiosities.[1]

A few further observations on the bacteria about the teeth were interpolated in a letter written to the Royal Society five years later. In the midst of a discussion of the eggs of snails, the germination of wheat, and the spat of oysters, we find the following digression:[2]

> I can't forbear to tell you also,[3] most noble Sirs, that one of the back teeth in my mouth got loose again, and bothered me much in eating: so I decided to press it hard on the side with my thumb, with the idea of making the roots start out of the gum, so as to get rid of the

---

[1] In passing, I may also add that a recent writer (Prescott, 1930) cites the foregoing letter (No. 75) as evidence that "A. von Leeuwenhoek" held the view "that microscopic organisms were produced spontaneously from non-living matter." It is difficult to conceive how anybody who has ever read a word of L.'s writings could make such a mistake: but perhaps Prescott—like many another writer who quotes L.—did not consult the work to which he refers. This would also explain the singular fact that he cites the original Latin edition of the letter (1695) but gives the pagination of the *editio novissima* (1722).

[2] From *Letter 110*. 10 September 1697. To the Royal Society. MS.Roy.Soc. Printed in *Brieven*, Vol. III (*Sevende Vervolg*, 1702); *Opera Omnia*, Vol. III (*Epist. Soc. Reg.*, 1719); and in abbreviated English in *Phil. Trans.* (1697), Vol. XIX, No. 235, p. 790. The passage here translated begins on p. 40 of the Dutch edition, p. 35 of the Latin, and p. 797 of the *Phil. Trans.*

[3] *ook* printed version: not in MS.

tooth; which I succeeded in doing, for the tooth was left hanging to only a small bit of flesh, and I was able to snip it off very easily.

The crown of this tooth was nearly all decayed, while its roots consisted of two branches; so that the very roots were uncommon hollow,[1] and the holes in them were stuffed with a soft matter.

I took this stuff out of the hollows in the roots, and mixed it with clean rain-water, and set it before the magnifying-glass so as to see if there were as many living creatures in it as I had aforetime discovered in such material: and I must confess that the whole stuff seemed to me to be alive. But notwithstanding the number of these animalcules was so extraordinarily great (though they were so little withal, that 'twould take a thousand million of some of 'em to make up the bulk of a coarse sand-grain,[2] and though several thousands were a-swimming in a quantity of water that was no bigger than a coarse sand-grain is), yet their number appeared even greater than it really was: because the animalcules, with their strong swimming through the water, put many little particles which had no life in them into a like motion, so that many people might well have taken these particles for living creatures too.

These were Leeuwenhoek's last recorded observations on the bacteria of the mouth, but there is another reference to bacteria which he saw in a decoction of the "fur" off his own tongue some years later. Although these were obviously putrefactive organisms, and not species proper to the human

---

[1] The original words are *zoo dat selfs de Wortels boven gemeen hol waren.* The Latin translator apparently took this to mean that the *upper parts* of the roots were hollowed out (as is very probable, of course), for he renders these words "*superior utriusque radicis pars admodum erat excavata*": but *boven gemeen* is a common expression with L., and always means "unusually" or "out of the common run of experience." In the *Phil. Trans.* the words "*boven gemeen hol*" are absurdly mistranslated "extraordinary whole".

[2] *de groote van een grof zand* printed letter . . . *geen grof zand* MS.

mouth, I shall quote his words here—as they are not wholly irrelevant in the present context. In an interesting letter written in June, 1708, he said:[1]

> At the latter end of the month of April, 1708, I was again seized with a high fever, which stayed with me for four days, rising higher each night; and as my tongue was again coated with a thick whitish matter, I oft-times removed some of it, which seemed stuck very tight to the parts of the tongue, with a small penknife or with a silver tongue-scraper: and viewing it many times through the magnifying-glass, I could see nought else but what I have described[2] in my previous discoveries. . . .
>
> On two occasions, I took some of the foresaid stuff from my tongue, and put it in a small clean China coffee-cup,[3] and then poured boiling rain-water upon it, and let it seethe a good half hour; with the idea of separating the glue-like matter (wherewith the particles seemed to be stuck to one another) by so doing, in order that I should the better be able to view the parts themselves.
>
> . . . .
>
> Now when the stuff which I had taken off my tongue had lain in the water, in which it was boiled, for about a fortnight,[4] I saw that the water was well-nigh evaporated away; so I poured again a little rain-water, which had stood some days in a clean phial in my closet,[5] into the boiled water aforesaid. And five or six days afterwards,

---

[1] From *Letter dated 29 June 1708*. To the Royal Society. MS.Roy.Soc. Not published in Dutch or Latin editions. English translation (incomplete) printed in *Phil. Trans.* (1708), Vol. XXVI, No. 318, pp. 210-214. I translate from the MS. in L.'s own hand.

[2] A reference to a letter dated *18 Oct. 1707*. MS.Roy.Soc. Incomplete English translation in *Phil. Trans.* (1707), Vol. XXV, No. 312, p. 2456 [misprinted 1456]. Not published in Dutch or Latin.

[3] *een schoon jndiaanse Coffe Copje* MS. "a clean China Coffee-dish" *Phil. Trans.*

[4] *ontrent veertien dagen* MS. "above a Fortnight" *Phil.Trans.*

[5] *op mijn Comptoir* MS. "upon my Desk near the said boil'd Water" *Phil. Trans.* Cf. p. 114 *supra*.

I brought a thin glass tube suddenly with its one open end over the bottom of the porcelain cup, where most of the particles that had come off the tongue lay all of a heap;[1] with the idea that when the water entered the tube, a few particles from the tongue would also be carried upwards into the tube, so that I should thus again be enabled to view the particles off the tongue: in doing which,[2] I saw an inconceivable number of exceeding small animalcules, and these of divers sorts. But far the greatest number was of one and the same bigness, yet this was so little that they could not be discerned but by great attention, through a very good magnifying-glass; and most of these animalcules were abiding[3] where the said matter from the tongue lay, and I took into consideration whether the said creatures might not indeed be getting their food from the particles of the tongue. And when these animalcules had been in the glass tube for about two hours, I perceived that a great many of 'em were dead.

---

[1] *over hoop lagen* MS. In the *Phil. Trans.* the translator transferred the adverb to the glass tube, making L. say that he "hastily turned it *upside down* [my italics] into the bottom of the China Cup."

[2] *in welk doen* MS. "and it happen'd as I wished" *Phil. Trans.*

[3] *haar . . . waren onthoudende* MS. "rendezvous'd" *Phil. Trans.*—a good translation, but not a word that L. would have used.

CHAPTER 4

THE LATER OBSERVATIONS ON FREE-LIVING PROTOZOA

(Letters 122, 125, 144, 147, 149, 150, VII, XXIX)

IN the three preceding chapters we have followed Leeuwenhoek in his multifarious protistological wanderings during the last quarter of the XVII Century. We have yet to consider his equally remarkable excursions into similar unexplored fields at a later date.

At the turn of the century—when he was already an old man, nearing his 70th birthday—he was still, despite his age, at the height of his powers; and during the next few years—between 1700 and 1716—he recorded some of his most interesting protozoological discoveries. These observations were all made on free-living forms found in water.

In a letter written at the very beginning of 1700, Leeuwenhoek gave the first description and picture of *Volvox*. The letter[1] begins with an account of other observations, and describes *inter alia* some gnat-larvae which he had found in ditch-water.[2] It then proceeds :

> I had got the foresaid water taken out of the ditches and runnels on the 30th of August :[3] and on coming

---

[1] *Letter 122*. 2 January 1700. To Sir Hans Sloane. MS.Roy.Soc. Published [Dutch] in *Brieven*, III, 152 (2nd pagination), *Sevende Vervolg* (1702) : [Latin] in *Opera Omnia* (*Epist. Soc. Reg.*), III, 146 (1719) : English translation in *Phil. Trans.* (1700), Vol. XXII, No. 261, p. 509.—Curiously enough, Vandevelde entirely overlooks the fact that this letter contains the first description of *Volvox*.

[2] These observations are also remarkable : for they show that L. had noticed the difference in posture of Anopheline and Culicine larvae in the water—a peculiarity now well known, but generally supposed to have been discovered by recent malariologists.

[3] *Anno* 1698, as appears from the earlier part of the letter.

home, while I was busy looking at the multifarious very little animalcules a-swimming in this water, I saw floating in it, and seeming to move of themselves, a great many green [1] round particles, of the bigness of sand-grains.

When I brought these little bodies before the microscope, I saw that they were not simply round, but that their outermost membrane was everywhere beset with many little projecting particles,[2] which seemed to me to be triangular, with the end tapering to a point: and it looked to me as if, in the whole circumference of that little ball, eighty such particles were set, all orderly arranged and at equal distances from one another; so that upon so small a body there did stand a full two thousand of the said projecting particles.

This was for me a pleasant sight, because the little bodies aforesaid, how oft soever I looked upon them, never lay still; and because too their progression was brought about by a rolling motion; and all the more because I imagined at first that they were animalcules. And the smaller these little bodies were, the greener in colour they appeared to me: whereas contrariwise, in the biggest (that were as big as a coarse grain of sand) no green colour could be made out in their [3] outermost part.

Each of these little bodies had inclosed within it 5, 6, 7, nay, some even 12, very little round globules,[4] in structure like to the body itself wherein they were contained.

While I was keeping watch, for a good time, on one of the biggest round bodies, among the others, in a little water, I noticed that in its outermost part an opening

---

[1] *groene ronde deeltjens* MS. *ronde deeltjens* Dutch printed version "great round particles" *Phil. Trans.* *Groene* (green) is very important; and "great" is an obvious mistranslation or misprint. The Latin version also omits "green"—calling them simply *particulae rotundae*.

[2] *i.e.*, the individual flagellates composing the colony.

[3] *het* MS. *haar* printed version.

[4] *i.e.*, the daughter-colonies.

appeared, out of which one of the inclosed round globules, having a fine green colour, dropt out, and took on the same motion in the water as the body out of which it came. Afterwards, the first round body [1] remained lying without any motion: and soon after a second globule, and presently a third, dropt out of it; and so one after another till they were all out, and each took on its proper motion.[2]

After the lapse of several days, the first round body became, as it were, again mingled [3] with the water; for I could perceive no sign of it.

What also seemed strange to me, was that I [4] could never remark, in all the motions that I had observed in the first round body,[5] that the contained particles [6] shifted their positions; since they never came in contact, but remained lying separate from one another, and orderly arranged withal.

Many people, seeing these bodies a-moving in the water, might well swear that they were little living animals; and more especially when you saw them going round first one way, and then t'other.

Now when a great many of the said round bodies were in a bottle along with many little living animals, I saw that after the space of three days they were all gone, inasmuch as I could then make out none of the said bodies in the bottle.

Moreover, I had put a few drops of water (as shown at CD [Plate XXVI]) in a glass tube (Fig. 1, AB) about

---

[1] *i.e.*, the mother-colony.

[2] *en yder een beweginge aannam.* These words are in the printed version but not in the MS., and were probably added in the proof as an afterthought.

[3] *i.e.*, the mother-colony broke up. The word is *vereenigt* [=united] in the MS., but was changed to *vermengt* [=mixed] in the printed version.

[4] The word *ik*—which is necessary for the sense of this passage—is here present in the MS. but omitted in the printed version.

[5] *i.e.*, the mother-colony.

[6] *i.e.*, the individual flagellates composing the colony.

PLATE XXVI

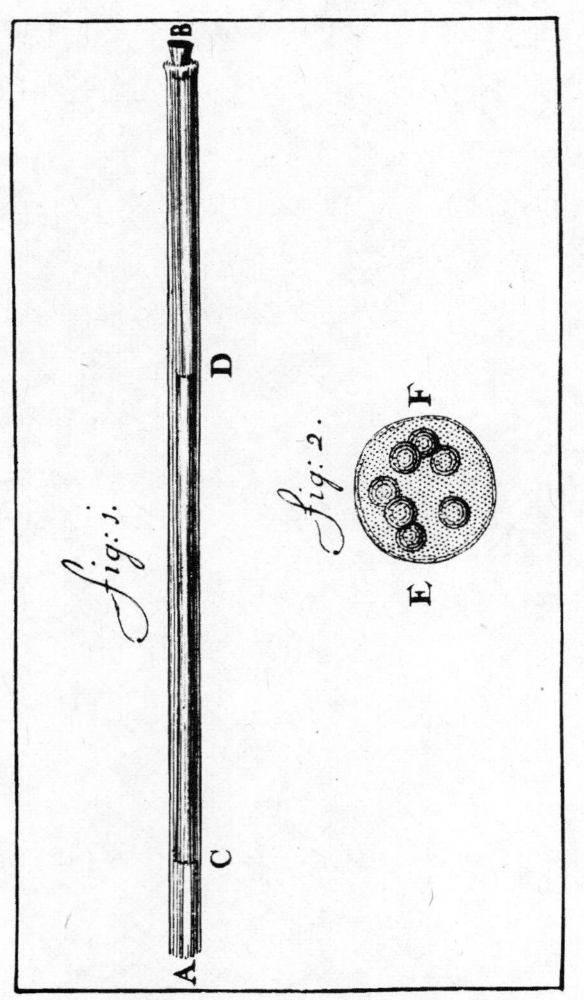

ILLUSTRATIONS TO LEEUWENHOEK'S LETTER ON *Volvox* (No. 122; 2 Jan. 1700).

From the engravings accompanying the Dutch edition.

eight inches long, and of the thickness of the quill of a hen's feather.[1] One end (A) I left open, the other end (B) I plugged with a bit of cork (so that betwixt D and B there was nothing but air), with the idea that[2] when I came to handle the tube, the water wouldn't run out of it. The air being now shut up in the tube, between D and B, cannot remain of the same volume, or extent, but changes at every moment, so to speak; for one can't approach the tube with the hand, the breath, or any part of the body that is a little warmer than the air wherein the tube is lying, without the air in the tube being affected by some part of it; and this warmth brings about an expansion or greater enlargement of the air (in the tube), whereby the water is made to move, being driven from DC towards A: notwithstanding we may perceive no motion in it with our naked eye. And just as the least warmth causes this outward displacement of the air in the glass tube, so likewise warmth readily departs from the tube, whereupon a movement of the water takes place[3] back from C towards B.

In this water were included two of the foresaid round bodies,[4] and these of the biggest sort; and contained in each of them were five little round particles,[5] which inclosed particles were pretty well grown in size: and in a third big body there lay seven round lesser particles. These last were uncommon small.

After the lapse of four days, the said round bodies remaining shut up in the glass tube all this while, I perceived that in two of them the outermost membrane

---

[1] *een schagt van een hoender* [MS. *honder*] *penne* Dutch edition "of a Goose Quill" *Phil. Trans.*

[2] *dat* is here accidentally omitted in the MS., but restored in the printed version.

[3] *aan neemt* MS. *is nemende* printed version.

[4] *i.e.*, mother-colonies.

[5] *i.e.*, daughter-colonies.

(which was become exceeding thin and clear) was [1] burst asunder; and that the ten particles, that were contained within the two big bodies, were moving about in the water, rolling first one way and then the other.

Furthermore I perceived,[2] after the space of five days, that the small particles inclosed in the third large body were not only grown in bigness, but I could also then discern that from inside these small particles other lesser round particles [3] were to come forth. After the lapse of five days more, this third round body was also a bit burst open, and its contained particles were also come out of it: but notwithstanding it was open on one side, it kept on going round in the water, and that as quick as it had done heretofore.

Some days afterwards, I could make out nought but some little bits whereof the bigger bodies had been composed; and soon after, these too went out of sight.

Without a break I continued from day to day to watch these little particles that had issued from the bigger ones; and I always saw that they not only waxed in bigness, but that the particles contained within them got bigger too.

At the end of September,[4] I perceived that the contained particles were not so regularly round as the bigger bodies wherein they were inclosed, and therewithal that some of them were broke apieces; and that the last particles that were come out of the big ones seemed not to be round, and lay without motion against the glass.[5]

---

[1] *waren* MS.—corrected to *was* in printed version.

[2] *dat* (redundant) stands here in the MS., but has been removed in the printed version.

[3] *i.e.*, daughter-colonies within the daughter-colonies. This acute observation gave great support to the doctrine of the "preformationists" at a later epoch, though it was then usually accredited to Spallanzani—who merely repeated and confirmed L.'s observations.

[4] *Anno* 1698.

[5] The whole of the foregoing sentence is inexplicably omitted from the Latin version.

Now these last bigger bodies, when they had unburdened themselves of their contained particles, or when they broke asunder, were quite four times less than those wherefrom they issued: wherefore we may conclude that they had not reached their full growth, or gotten their right food.

We have also noted that the said round bodies agree in their weight with water.[1] This being so, they may be set in motion in the water with the least movement that it receiveth from the air.

I thought fit to have one such body pictured, with its contained particles; as shown[2] in Fig. 2, at EF. In this body, the inclosed round particles (which had so waxed in bigness that they were ready to be cast out) did not lie in such regular order as they did in those before described; and as in this one there was not so continuous a motion, I imagine that this was simply due to the contained particles not all lying at an equal distance from the centre, so that the round body was heaviest on the side where the particle furthest from the centre was placed, whence its motion was somewhat hindered.

For what purpose these round bodies are created we know not. But as I observed that the various round bodies, when mixt with a great many little animals[3] in the big bottle, were all vanished in the space of three days, I did well ponder whether they were not created to serve as food for such little animals.

Now as we see that the oft-mentioned round bodies come into being not of themselves,[4] but by generation, as we know all plants and seeds do (inasmuch as every seed,

---

[1] *i.e.*, have the same "specific gravity" as water. This term was unknown, of course, to L., though the concept was familiar; and I therefore render his words literally and not too "scientifically".

[2] See Plate XXVI.

[3] L. here means mosquito-larvae, crustacea, etc., —not protozoa.

[4] *niet uijt haar selven*—meaning "not spontaneously", or "not by spontaneous generation".

be it never so small, is as it were endowed with its inclosed plant [1]); so can we now be more assured than we ever before were heretofore [2] concerning the generation of all things. For my part, I am fully persuaded that the little round bodies, which are found in the bigger ones, serve as seeds; and that without them these big round bodies couldn't be produced.[3]

In the summer I divers times applied myself to the study of the waters lying around our town, the last occasion being on the 8th of October 1699: but I could satisfy myself no further in this matter.

The remainder of this letter contains no other observations on Protozoa: and the next reference to any of these organisms occurs some five months later, when Leeuwenhoek very briefly mentions and depicts the shell of a Foraminiferan, which he had found in the stomach of a shrimp. He did not, of course, know that it was the shell of a protozoon: but as this is the only mention—so far as I am aware—of any Rhizopod in the whole of his writings, I will quote the passage. After discussing the anatomy of the shrimp, he describes what he had found in shrimps' stomachs, and adds: [4]

In some of their stomachs I also discovered very little snail-shells, which, because of their roundness, I called

---

[1] Demonstrated by L. elsewhere.

[2] *te vooren* . . . *tot nog toe*—redundant in the original.

[3] The foregoing description of *Volvox*, though perfectly intelligible in the original, is somewhat obscured by the circumstance that L. uses the same word (*deeltjens*=particles) throughout to denote the mother-colonies, the daughter-colonies, and the individual flagellates. To make his meaning plain I have therefore substituted "body", "bigger particle", etc., for "particle", where it is necessary to distinguish the "particles" of different categories. The Latin translator took a like liberty with his original, and rendered *deeltjens* by *particulae rotundae*, *particulae majusculae*, *particulae minores*, etc., as occasion required.

[4] From *Letter 125*. 2 June 1700. To Frederik Adriaan, Baron van Rhede: [Dutch] in *Brieven*, 7de Vervolg, p. 196 (1702); [Latin] in *Opera Omnia* (*Epist. Soc. Reg.*), III, p. 186 (1719). No MS., and not in *Phil. Trans.* The Latin translation is wrongly dated *January* 2 (*postridie Kal. Ian.* 1700). An English version of the letter will be found in Hoole (1807), Vol. II, p. 266—the passage cited being on pp. 271-2.

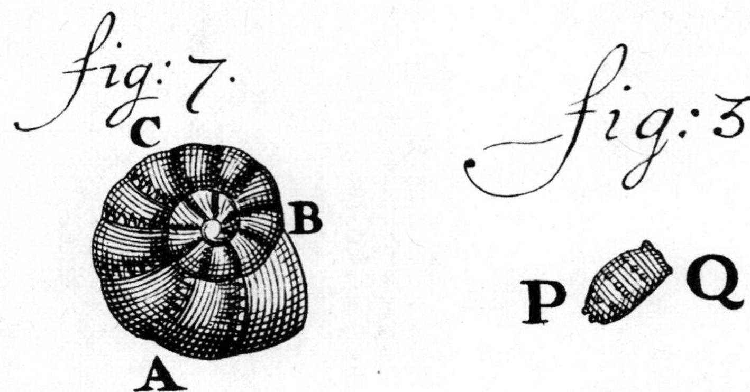

TWO OF LEEUWENHOEK'S FIGURES ILLUSTRATING LETTERS 125 AND 144
Enlarged from the original engravings.

Fig. 7, ABC.—Shell of a Foraminiferan (*Polystomella* ?).
Fig. 3, PQ.—The Ciliate *Coleps*. (The original measures only 6 mm. in length.)

little cockles;[1] and these little shells were no bigger than a coarse sand-grain.

In order to exhibit the pretty structure of these little shells before the eye, I thought 'twould not be amiss to get a drawing made of one of them. Fig. 7, ABC [Plate XXVII] shows one of these little cockles, which I took out of the stomach of a shrimp.

It has been generally agreed that the shell here referred to was that of a Foraminiferan, but different writers have interpreted its species variously. For my part, I feel fairly confident that the picture represents a *Polystomella*.[2]

Leeuwenhoek's next contribution to protozoology is imbedded in a well-known letter dealing chiefly with Rotifers: and the protozoological elements in this epistle have, it seems to me, been hitherto largely ignored or misunderstood. To my mind there can be little doubt that he here left us an unambiguous record of his discovery of three different Protozoa—two Phytoflagellates (*Haematococcus* and *Chlamydomonas*) and a Ciliate (*Coleps*). But I will leave him to speak for himself:[3]

On the 25th of August,[4] I saw that in a leaden gutter,[5] on the front of my house, for a length of about five feet

---

[1] *een slakhoorntje*. Hoole translates "snails", but Sewel (1708) says the word denotes "*a Cockle-shell*"; and from L.'s allusion to their roundness, I take this to be correct. The Latin translator called them *limaces cochleares*.

[2] Cole (1926, p. 13) takes the same view; but Miall (1912, p. 216) identifies the organism as *Nonionina*. Robert Hooke (1665, Obs. XI, p. 80; Scheme V, Fig. X) had previously described and figured a foraminiferan shell—probably *Rotalia*—which he had discovered in sand: but to L. his observation was apparently unknown.

[3] *Letter 144*. 9 Feb. 1702. To Hendrik van Bleyswyk. *Brieven* (7de Vervolg), III, 400; *Op. Omn.* (*Epist. Soc. Reg.*), III, 380. No MS. and not in *Phil. Trans.* Partially translated into English by Hoole (1807), II, 207.—Vandevelde says this letter is a "*Beschrijving van waterdiertjes, wellicht infusoriën*": but neither he nor anybody else appears to have sorted out the various "Infusoria" described, though Bütschli (Vol. II, p. 621) recognized *Haematococcus*.

[4] Presumably *anno* 1701.

[5] John Ray (in 1663) notes as a curiosity that in Holland "the Rain

and a breadth of seven inches, some rain-water had remained standing, which had a red colour; and as it occurred to me that this redness might well be caused by red animalcules (as I had indeed seen come about in muddy ditches), I took a drop or so of this water and looked at it through the microscope; and I discovered a great many animalcules[1] that were red, and others that were green, whereof the biggest looked no bigger through the microscope than coarse sand doth to your naked eye, and others smaller and smaller, each after its kind.

These animalcules were for the most part round, and the green ones were somewhat yellowish in the middle of their bodies.

Their bodies seemed to be composed of particles that presented an oval figure; and therewithal they had short thin instruments which stuck out a little way from the round contour, and wherewith they performed the motions of rolling round and going forward;[2] and when they took a rest, and fixed themselves to the glass, they looked like a pear with a short stalk; but this stalk,[3] on curious examination, was split at the end, or divided into two, and 'twas with these two parts that the animalcules fixed 'emselves fast to the glass.[4]

---

that falls upon the Houses is by Pipes and Gutters conveyed into a Cistern, and there reserved for the uses of the House, as at *Venice* in *Italy*." It would appear, therefore, that gutters were not commonly installed on English houses at that date. (See Ray, 1673; p. 53.)

[1] The description which follows obviously refers to the Phytoflagellate *Haematococcus pluvialis* (=*Sphaerella lacustris*), which is very commonly found in gutters. This is the first account of this organism. The smaller green ones were probably, for the most part, *Chlamydomonas*—equally common in this situation: *vide infra*.

[2] *waar medeze een omwentelende beweginge en voortgang te weeg bragten*: "by means of which they caused a kind of circular motion and current in the water"—Hoole. This mistranslation entirely spoils the sense of this important passage describing the action of the flagella.

[3] Hoole here interpolates "or rather this tail"—which is not in the original, and shows that he did not understand what L. was talking about.

[4] This is a remarkably good observation of the locomotory organs of *Haematococcus*, which possesses two anterior flagella that often adhere to one another for a variable length at their proximal ends.

The smallest animalcules of this sort I judged to have been begotten of the bigger ones.

I did also see yet another kind of animalcules, that were much smaller.[1] These were very clear in the body; but I judged that there must have been quite a hundred of the former sort to every one of the latter.

On the 31st of August, the water was so far dried up (owing to the great heat, which had continued for three days running), that if I pressed my finger on the dirt[2] lying on the lead, little more than a drop of water as big as a sandgrain stuck to it: and though I could discern a few living animalcules, which were transparent, in this water, yet all the green and red ones were dead.

On the 1st of September, the stuff in the leaden gutter was become so thick, that it was like stiff wet clay; and notwithstanding all my efforts, I could discover no living creatures in it of the sort that I had seen before.

At this point Leeuwenhoek leaves *Haematococcus* and goes on to describe the Rotifers which he also discovered in his leaden gutter; but in the course of his description he accurately notes that:

The stuff in the guts of these little animals[3] was most always red, proceeding (as I imagined) from the red animalcules[4] which they use as food: but I also saw afterwards a few of these little animals which hadn't any of the red stuff inside them, particularly the young ones which had not long left their mother's body.

Here follow further observations on Rotifers—including the famous experiment in which Leeuwenhoek found that

---

[1] Possibly bacteria, but obviously unidentifiable from this slight description.

[2] A little later (4 Nov. 1704) L. says—in the words of a contemporary English translator (MS.Roy.Soc.)—" I don't suffer such foul stuf to lye long in my gutter, but twice a year cause the lead to be scowered so clean that it looks just like new ".

[3] *i.e.*, Rotifers.

[4] *i.e.*, *Haematococcus*.

they can "return to life" after desiccation. Whilst relating his experiences, however, he mentions an organism which is almost certainly identifiable—from the figure which he fortunately gives—as the ciliate *Coleps*. He says: [1]

Now divers little animalcules came before the draughtsman's eye, whose structure was very like what is shown in [Plate XXVII] Fig. 3,[2] between P and Q, whose belly was flat, and from which little instruments stuck out, wherewith it effected its progress. And as this animalcule had little round globules in its body, so there were yet many other little animals [3] a-swimming in the water, whose whole body seemed no bigger, under the microscope, than one of these globules in the bigger sort just spoken of.[4]

I have divers times so placed the said animalcules [5] out of water, that they were encompassed by an amount of water not so big as a sand-grain; in order to see whether these little creatures, when all the water round them was evaporated away, and they were lying in nothing but air, would burst asunder, as I had made certain of in other animalcules: [6] and I saw that whenas the water was

---

[1] *Brieven*, III, p. 407: *Op. Omn.* III, p. 387.

[2] In the figure as copied by Hoole (II, Pl. XVI, fig. 35) the resemblance to *Coleps* is largely lost. The original—though very small—shows quite clearly the characteristic barrel-like form (with one side somewhat flattened) of this organism. The expanded anterior end (bearing the terminal mouth), the caudal spines, and even the four girdles of armour-plates, are all clearly indicated. Bütschli noted the resemblance to *Coleps*, but considered the identification as doubtful. To me it appears certain.

[3] Possibly bacteria—or perhaps flagellates.

[4] These two sentences are very clumsily constructed in the original—though their meaning is clear enough—and I have not attempted to improve them.

[5] *de verhaalde dierkens.* It is not absolutely certain that this expression means the organisms just mentioned: it possibly refers to the Rotifers. If it really refers to the Protozoa, then the ensuing words confirm the view that L. was here describing *Coleps*; for this ciliate has a cuirass composed of numerous interlocking platelets, which prevent its bursting when dried.

[6] Cf. *Letter 18*, p. 120 *supra*.

> almost exhaled, and the animalcule could no longer turn and twist itself about in it, it took on an oval figure, and stayed lying thus, without my being able to see that the moisture evaporated away out of the creature's body, for it kept its oval figure.

At this point Leeuwenhoek returns to his experiments with the Rotifers: but in the account of their revivification after drying he notes that he

> also saw two several sorts of little animalcules a-swimming through the water, whereof the least were so little, that many thousands together would not equal a coarse grain of sand in bigness.[1]

After some further remarks on Rotifers he then says:

> Once more we see here the unconceivable Providence, perfection, and order, bestowed by the Lord Creator of the Universe upon such little creatures which escape our bare eye, in order that their kind shouldn't die out.
>
> From these discoveries we can well understand that in all falling rain, carried from gutters into water-butts, animalcules are to be found; and that in all kinds of water, standing in the open air, animalcules can turn up. For these animalcules can be carried over by the wind, along with the bits of dust floating in the air: and on the other hand, animalcules which are a hundred million times and more smaller than a coarse grain of sand, can be borne aloft, along with the water particles, albeit not as high as the clouds, but at least a little way up; and then when the sun goes down, they fall to earth in what we call dew; and they may well be taken up too and carried along by the wind. This is the more probable, since we know that in a storm the sea is so lashed on the shore by the wind, that drops of sea-water are found on trees, running down their trunks, and still salty, more than half-an-hour's journey from the coast. This salt

---

[1] *Lit. cit.*, *Brieven* III, p. 409. These were evidently not Rotifers but Protozoa or Bacteria.

water is judged by the vulgar (though mistakenly) to be the salt evaporated by heat from the sea.[1]

On the said[2] 4th of September, it rained a little while at eventide; yet so much fell, that in the leaden gutter aforesaid there was some water on the 5th and 6th of September: and this water I examined on both days, and discovered, in every drop that I took from the gutter, eight or ten of the animalcules described, though I could not discern a single one of the round green or red creatures that was alive.

On the 6th of September, I put up seven glass tubes, in which I placed some of the dry stuff aforesaid out of the leaden gutter; pouring into some of them boiled, and into others unboiled rain-water.[3] . . . On the 7th of September I viewed the said glass tubes, and beheld with wonder in one of them an inconceivably great number of little green animalcules,[4] all alive, all of which seemed round, as before described, and a-moving among one another; nay, I saw so many that the very water seemed to the naked eye to have a faint green colour: but how curiously soever I examined the other glass tubes, I could find no living green animalcules in them. . . .[5]

On the 9th of September it rained a little; and two or three days later it rained so much, that on the 14th of September there was water to the depth of about a finger's breadth in the leaden gutter. Of this water I took about two drops; and examining it, I saw a great many of the little round animalcules previously made mention

---

[1] *dat door de warme uytwaseminge van de Zee werd voortgebragt.* These words were omitted by Hoole—also most of what follows.

[2] Mentioned earlier, in connexion with Rotifers, in a paragraph not here translated. Apparently *anno* 1701.

[3] I here omit two lines referring to Rotifers.

[4] There can hardly be any doubt that these organisms were *Chlamydomonas.* In similar experiments I have always obtained this flagellate in abundance.

[5] Further observations on Rotifers are here omitted.

of, whereof most had the outermost part of their bodies a pale green, and the middle of the body quite red.[1]

On the 15th and 29th of September, on the 13th and 27th of October, on the 25th of November, and the 9th of December, I continued my observations aforementioned; steeping the said stuff[2] both in new-fallen rain, that was collected in an East-Indian porcelain dish, and in boiled and ordinary rain-water: whereof I kept notes. But as the upshot was always one and the same, I discarded these notes: and I will only say that, on the day last mentioned, I put some boiled water, when it had got nearly cold, with a little of the oft aforementioned dirty stuff, into a glass tube that was sealed off at one end, and stopt with a cork at the other, and carried it about in my pocket: and I found some hours afterwards that not only the big animalcules[3] . . . were swimming in the water, but also many others so small, that they looked through the microscope no bigger than a dot, such as you might make with a pen. And when I had carried this glass tube in my pocket for eight days, these last-mentioned animalcules were so increased that there were some thousands of them, both fixt on the glass and a-swimming in the little quantity of water.

On the 8th of February,[4] when the oft-mentioned stuff had lain for a few days more than five months upon a clean white paper in my closet, I put a little of it into a clean glass tube, and poured boiled rain-water, after it had cooled, upon it: and after the space of about half an hour, I already found one animalcule swimming about in the water, and many others that remained still rounded up; and three hours later I saw various others of this kind, and some small ones of a different make.[5]

---

[1] Undoubtedly *Haematococcus*.

[2] *i.e.*, the dry deposit in the gutter.

[3] There is a reference here to the figures, which shows that these big forms were Rotifers.

[4] Presumably 1702.

[5] Possibly Protozoa.—These observations were referred to again by L. in

Now since we see that these animalcules can lie bedded so long in dry matter, as before described, and then on coming into water can swell out their bodies, and swim off; we may therefore conclude that in all pools and marshes, which have water standing in them in winter, but which dry up in summer, many kinds of animalcules ought to be found; and even though there were none at first in such waters, they would be brought thither by water-fowl, by way of the mud or water sticking to their feet and feathers.[1]

Seeing these wondrous dispensations of NATURE, whereby these little creatures are created so that they may live and continue their kind, our thoughts must be all abashed; and we ask ourselves, Can there even now be people who still hang on to the antient belief that living creatures are generated out of corruption?

About a couple of months after the foregoing lines were written, Leeuwenhoek sent the Royal Society some further observations on the animalcules occurring in rain-water. The following is a translation of the greater part of this letter:[2]

---

his *Letter* XXIX (5 Nov. 1716, to Boerhaave); *Send-brieven*, p. 288 (published 1718). *Vide* p. 297 *infra*.

[1] These remarks recall a well-known passage in *The Origin of Species*, where Darwin discusses the dispersal of organisms by similar means.

[2] MS. *28 April 1702*. To the Royal Society. Not published in Dutch or Latin works. English version (abbreviated) printed in *Phil. Trans.* (1702), Vol. XXIII, No. 279, pp. 1152-1155 [where the date is wrongly given as 1701]. I translate from the original Dutch MS. According to my numeration this is *Letter 147*: but Vandevelde (1924, p. 132), who did not detect the error in the date as printed in the *Phil. Trans.*, calls it "Brief 2 Tr 1 [137a]". The MS. of the English version is extant, along with the Dutch original, in the Royal Society collection, and is in the hand of John Chamberlayne.—Chamberlayne (1666-1723) was a miscellaneous writer and translator—said to have been conversant with 16 languages—who was educated at Oxford (1685) and Leyden (1688). He became a Fellow of the Society in 1702, and translated—as will appear presently—several of L.'s other letters for publication. His best known work—*Magnae Britanniae Notitia*, which went through many editions—was a rescript of a smaller book by his father, Edward C. It contains an interesting account of the Royal Society—among many other things.

On the 19th of September, 1701, it rained a little while about noon, whereupon I caught some of the rain-water, as pure as I was able to, in a clean East-Indian porcelain dish:[1] putting this water then in a glass tube, in order to see whether, in such new-fallen rain, on standing in my closet, any living creatures would turn up.

I examined this water several days running, and discovered therein many little bits of dust, otherwise called particles, such as generally float in the air, consisting of very little bits of burnt wood, or charcoal, wherein I could make out the horizontal and ascending vessels; also a little bit of straw, and many blackish particles which I imagined to be congealed particles out of smoke from the coals that our smiths and brewers burn: and among these was a pretty structure[2] composed of round globules clotted together, just like the little stars that we see in the snow in winter. But I could discover no living creature till the 28th of September, when I discovered some exceeding small animalcules that were fixed to the glass, or anon swam forwards with a quivering motion; which afforded me no unpleasant spectacle.

These animalcules were so small, that I could only make them out by very nice scrutiny; the tube, in which the water was, being so big and thick; but especially because the animalcules seemed to me as clear as glass: but it looked to me as though their bodies were twice as long as the width of their thickest part,[3] the foremost and hindmost parts of their bodies running somewhat to a point.

---

[1] *in een suijvere jndiaanze porsteleijne schootel* MS. "in a fine *China* Bason" Chamberlayne.

[2] *een aardig maaksel* MS. "an odd Phenomenon" Chamberlayne.

[3] *hare lighame twee maal soo lang waren, als deselve op haar dikste sijn* MS. "twice as long as they were big" Chamberlayne.—The organisms were probably flagellates, but are obviously unidentifiable. Their attachment to the glass suggests *Monas vulgaris*, which would also fulfil the other requirements of the description.

Yet from the 10th of October till the 14th of the same month, I could perceive no living creature, how carefully soever I looked. But whereas I had till now always examined only the uppermost part of the water that was in the glass tube, on the 15th of October I inspected very narrowly the bottom of the glass tube (which was four inches long, and had a diameter of a third of an inch): and there I saw very many of the animalcules aforesaid, both fixed upon the glass and swimming forth; and many others sat so still upon the glass, that you might think they were not animalcules at all; but when one of 'em moved, among the crowd, several others next to it did too.

Not being content with these my observations, because I misdoubted me whether there might not well have been some water in this tube previously, and that from this source these animalcules had come, and had remained fixed to the glass, before I poured this rain into the glass tube: in order to satisfy myself hereof, I procured a glass tube that had lain full twenty years shut up in a dry chest, and whereof I was assured that neither the least water, nor anything but air, and what is therewithal contained in it, could have gotten into it.

On the 18th of October it rained in the forenoon, after we had had several days of strong and stormy wind: and I once more caught the rain in the porcelain dish, and after flinging away the first two lots received in it, I poured the third lot of water into the glass tube.

This last water I viewed many times; but how curiously soever I looked, I could make out no living creature in it, though I saw particles stuck to the glass, that agreed in bigness and figure with the animalcules aforesaid: till the 24th of October, when I discovered three animalcules that were running along and swimming forward against the glass, and not in a straight line, but with bendings and turnings as they went along: and the day after, I discovered like animalcules in quite ten different places, both running forward and swimming, and that as plain as if you saw, with your bare eye, those little animals that the common man calls Water-fleas, swimming in the water.[1]

Now there lay against the glass, within the compass of a coarse grain of sand, more than a hundred particles that were of the bigness of the foresaid animalcules, which particles I divers times viewed one day, to discover if possible whether any living creature would come out of them,[2] or turn up thereabouts; but how carefully soever I looked, yet could I discern no living creature among these particles, nor those lying hard by: until the 28th of October, when I saw, among the particles last mentioned, a good five-and-twenty animalcules swimming forwards, as well as running upon the glass: and I did then discern two sorts of animalcules,[3] whereof the smallest appeared to me first shining, and then not shining: and their shininess, so I imagined, was observable whenas they swam with their back or uppermost part of the body turned towards my eye. These last animalcules had a quite different motion, in swimming forward, from those a bit bigger. As regards the particles that were fixed to the glass, I couldn't see any change in 'em.

I examined the said water for several days running, and I saw the smallest animalcules in such great plenty, both coursing upon the glass and swimming, at every spot where I cast my eye, that 'twas amazing: and as I was holding the microscope in one hand, and in the other the glass tube (in which the water, owing to the width of the tube, was set in motion),[4] I invariably perceived that

---

[1] *op het water* MS. "in the ordinary Brooks and Canals" Chamberlayne—a picturesque but inaccurate rendering of the original.

[2] *uijt de selve . . . soude voortkomen* MS. "whether they were living Creatures" Chamberlayne.

[3] Probably protozoa, but not identifiable.

[4] *i.e.*, by the warmth of his hand, producing convection-currents.

when the animalcules were aswimming, and got off somewhat from the glass, they were borne forward, as if they were not strong enough (as you might say) to swim upstream: yet they alone made, as they went ahead, certain windings, while the bits of dust in the water (which were very big in comparison with the animalcules) were swept forward in a straight line.[1]

I have also made sure that, when I put new-fallen rain in a glass tube in which there was never before any moisture, shortly afterwards very many little air-bubbles made their appearance in it, and remained sticking to the glass: but a little while later these air-bubbles were gone.

To satisfy myself further hereof, on the 6th of November I took once more a new glass tube, and examined it through the microscope: but notwithstanding I had very carefully shut it up, and covered it over, I saw that there were yet many very little bits of dust in it. On the 6th of November it rained again, and I caught the rain, as before described, and put it in the glass tube; in order to see whether in this one also the air-bubbles would make their appearance, and whether they would then vanish from sight.

I examined this water divers times, even after it had been four hours in the tube; in which time I could discover not more than two or three air-bubbles, which were on a dried-up mite,[2] out of which the air seemed to issue.

But whereas I had stood the former glass tube upright, and had put another one down somewhat aslant, I now placed this last glass tube lying almost flat, only so that the opening lay a bit higher, lest the water ran out of it,

---

[1] This passage is paraphrased by Chamberlayne, though its import is correctly conveyed. It can hardly be doubted that L. was here able to distinguish the animate from the inanimate particles.

[2] *een uijt gedroogte mijt* MS. "a dry Particle" Chamberlayne. I do not know whether the "mite" should be interpreted literally or metaphorically.

and that the air-bubbles might keep the position that they had at the top of the glass; and after the lapse of ten hours I saw a great many air-bubbles, that were mostly affixed to the said dust-particles. And forasmuch as we know that no dry matter or any other particles, in which air is included, when they get under water can then get the water into them unless the air be first dislodged, so the same held good also for the particles that were in the glass tube.

But what is one to say of this, that some of the air-bubbles were quite a hundred (and others several hundred) times bigger than the particles on which they were stuck?

Next day, in the morning, I perceived no more than four very little air-bubbles, and a few hours afterwards I couldn't find a single one.

I examined this water every day till the 14th of November, but could discover no living creature in it; and the day after, I had the mischance to let my tube drop, so that it was smashed to bits.[1]

It is not possible to identify the organisms mentioned in the foregoing letter, though some of them must certainly have been protozoa. At the end of the year, however, Leeuwenhoek wrote a very important epistle in which he described and figured several freshwater protozoa which are easily recognizable. This letter is so important, indeed, that I must translate almost the whole of it. It is addressed to the Royal Society, and runs as follows:[2]

---

[1] The remainder of this letter deals with other subjects, and is therefore omitted.

[2] *Letter dated 25 December 1702.* To the Royal Society. MS.Roy.Soc. Not printed in Dutch or Latin editions. English translation in *Phil. Trans.* (1703), Vol. XXIII, No. 283, pp. 1304-1311. (The MS. of this translation is also extant, and is in the hand of John Chamberlayne. See p. 270, note 2, *supra.*) According to my numeration this is *Letter 149*. Vandevelde numbers it "Brief 2 Tr 3 [147]".—I have made my translation from the original Dutch MS., but have compared it with Chamberlayne's and note one or two points in which his version differs.

I take the liberty of informing you, Gentlemen, that I have oft heard the common people say that *duckweed*[1], which floats on the water, is generated in the ground underneath.

I could not allow of the truth of this assertion; for whenever I examined duckweed, I always found that one of these plants is produced by another, as with trees and other vegetables.

Whenever I turned my attention to duckweed, I always noticed that it never grows in deep water, even though the water be small and stagnant, and without motion, save such as is imparted to it by the wind[2]; but it is seen in great plenty on broad sheets of water, which are not deep and have little motion, but especially in narrow and shallow ditches.

I have also observed that in ditches wherein there is very little water, the duckweed is very small, in comparison with that which is found on big sheets of water, along the banks, where the water is shallow and has but little motion.

Delfshaven, belonging to our Town, lies about two hours' distant from it; and from here, through a sluice from the River Maas, the water that runs through our town is let in with the flood in summertime, and this water is then as clear as though we had the River Maas itself here.

Now with this running water there is brought in, from time to time, a little duckweed; yet so little, that 'twould take you half an hour to collect thirty little weeds in a pot all at once. I got some of the duckweed scooped out of this water, in an earthen pot, with lots of water, so that their roots might not be hurt.

I took several of these little weeds out of the pot of water

---

[1] *het kroost* MS. (alibi *Eende kroost*)="*Lens palustris*" of the old writers = *Lemna* of modern botanists.

[2] "and that the Wind does it no harm" Chamberlayne. This is a mistranslation.

its roundness two *little wheels*, which displayed a *swift rotation*, as shown in Fig. 3, *a b c*. (The draughtsman, seeing the little wheels going round, and always running round in the same direction, could never have enough of looking at them, exclaiming[1] "O that one could ever depict so wonderful a motion!") These little wheels were as closely beset with teeth, or *cogs*, as the wheel of a watch might be: and when these animalcules had thus performed their motions for some time, they pulled their little wheels into their body again, and their body right into the little case; and soon after they brought a part of their body out of the case again, with the motions aforesaid; and at another time they would stay a long while inside the case, as though shut up in it. But although I had, indeed, formerly discovered such little wheels on other animalcules[2] too, yet their bodies were different from these, and their cases were of a dark nature, so that you couldn't easily make out the animalcules in them; and therewithal they seemed to be composed of pellets.

And I also saw some cases that were several times smaller than that just mentioned, and these[3] were as clear as glass, so that you could see the little creatures lying within them quite distinctly. Fig. 3, *Pdef*, shows the case, with the animalcule *Pdf*, occupying a part of it, as it lay taking a rest. Fig. 3, *ogh*, shows the little case

---

[1] *konde men soo een wonderbare beweginge altijd vertoonen* MS. "O, that he could always see such a wonderful kind of motion" Chamberlayne. I take it that the artist's wish was to be able to portray (*vertoonen*) this motion—not that he might go on looking at it for ever. Regarding the artist himself, see p. 343 *sq.*, *infra*.

[2] *Melicerta ringens.* In later letters (MSS. 4 Nov. 1704, to Roy.Soc., and 28 June 1713) L. gives an admirable description of this rotifer, and describes how it builds its house. See *Phil. Trans.* (1705), Vol. XXIV, p. 1784: also *Letter* VII (Dutch and Latin works) and *Phil. Trans.* (1713), Vol. XXVIII, p. 160.

[3] Evidently not rotifers but tubicolous ciliates (Cothurnidae)—probably the common *Cothurnia cristallina*, though the species cannot be determined from the description and figures.

with the animalcule as it looked when it stuck part of its body (*gh*) out of it, at which time alone you could now and then just make out the two little wheels,[1] because of their exceeding smallness, but only when its body was straightened out, for otherwise it lay drawn up short.

Further, I discovered a little animal[2] whose body was at times long, at times drawn up short, and to the middle of whose body (where I imagined the undermost part of its belly was) a still lesser animalcule of the same make seemed to be fixed fast by its hinder end. Such a little animal, because of its wonderful structure and manner of propagation, I have had drawn, and at least twice as big as it looks to the naked eye when you see it in the water and attached to the root of a bit of duckweed. Fig. 4, ABCDEFG, shows this creature, whereof A is the hind end that it hangs on by, while at CDE are shown its eight[3] horns (though others a bit smaller had six horns), as it looked when it had straightened itself out, for otherwise it can scarce reach to a quarter of this length; and its horns seemed to my eye to be made in so marvellous a manner, that the draughtsman's art isn't competent to portray them, though the artist did his best to draw a small bit of a horn, as shown at KLM in Fig. 5.

In Fig. 4, at BH, is shown a little animal that is coming out of the first one; and formerly, when I saw such a little animal fixed to a bigger one, I imagined that it was only a young animalcule attached by chance to a big one; but by nicer attention to the matter, I saw that it was a reproduction: for I observed that whereas the second animalcule, at the time when I first recognized that it really was one, had only four very short little horns, yet after the lapse of sixteen hours I saw that its

---

[1] A misinterpretation of the peristomial cilia. In *Cothurnia* it is very common to find 2 individuals (the products of fission) in the same house.

[2] *Hydra*—the first description of this organism.

[3] The draughtsman—as will be evident—inadvertently depicted *nine* tentacles instead of eight: cf. Plate XXVIII, fig. 4.

body and its horns had increased in bigness, and four hours later still I saw that it had forsaken its mother.

When I discovered the young animalcule aforesaid, I also perceived that, on the other side of the body of the first animal, there was situated [1] a little round knob, which I did see getting bigger, from time to time, for the next few hours (as shown in Fig. 4, between G and I); and at last it appeared as a little pointed structure, which had so far grown in bigness in the course of thirteen or fourteen hours, that you could make out two little horns upon it. After the lapse of another four-and-twenty hours, this last-mentioned animalcule had four horns, whereof one was small, a second a bit bigger, and the other two much bigger; and these last the little animal stuck out at full length, or pulled in short. And another three hours later this little animal was gone off from his mother. [2]

I tried to trace this reproduction further, and for this purpose took the duckweed away from the animalcule, so that I could follow it better; but next day that animalcule not only lay dead, but its horns and a piece of its hind end were all gone, having rotted off, as you might call it.

Another little animal, that had brought forth two young ones, not only had her body laden with many other

---

[1] *aan de andere zijde . . . een rond knobbeltje zad* MS. I take this last word to be a verb (*zat* = sat). Chamberlayne, however, evidently took it for a substantive (*zaad* = seed), and consequently translates "a round little knob of seed". But I cannot reconcile this interpretation with the construction of the sentence as a whole, and at this period L. always spelt *zaad* (=seed, a frequent word with him) with *aa*—never "*zad*". "A knob of seed" is also an unintelligible expression. Dr A. Schierbeek (*in. litt.*) agrees with my interpretation.

[2] All the foregoing observations on the budding of *Hydra* are very remarkable. No animal which reproduces asexually by budding was known at that date; and the sensation caused by the similar observations of Trembley, and others, nearly half a century later, is in strange contrast with the apparent indifference which greeted L.'s discovery.

animalcules[1] (which are flat beneath, and roundish above, and which I have discovered in most other kinds of water, and which are hardly a thousandth of the size of the animals which they crawl on with their little feet, and cause annoyance to); but a much bigger sort of animalcules[2] whose bodies were roundish, so pestered one of these little animals, not only getting on her body, but also by clinging on to her horns, that in spite of all the struggles she made with her horns and body, she couldn't shake it off; and I noticed afterwards that the little animal had lost one of her horns.[3]

[4] What seemed to me remarkable and wonderful, was that these little animals would oft-times let down their horns so far, that you would think, on seeing them through the microscope, that they were several fathoms long.

At one time or another I let the draughtsman have a look at the horns as they were being stretched out, or anon pulled in; and with me he was forced to exclaim "What wonders are these!" For as the creature pulled in its horns, they became perfectly round, and the closer they got to the head, the thicker they became, and when they were pulled right in, they formed a still bigger round blob.

I charged the draughtsman to draw, as well as he was able to, a small part of a horn when so stuck out, which is here shown in Fig. 6, NOP. On this part are shown

---

[1] Evidently the "common polyp-louse", *Trichodina pediculus*.

[2] The "large polyp-louse", *Kerona*. The ciliates ectoparasitic on *Hydra* were again studied and described at a much later date by Rösel von Rosenhof, Trembley, Baker, and others. This is the earliest account of them.

[3] "in the scuffle" is added here by Chamberlayne—a picturesque addition, but not authorized by L.'s own words.

[4] I have translated the remainder of L.'s remarks on *Hydra* because they are so entertaining: they contain no further observations on protozoa. But *Hydra*, rotifers, and protozoa were all "animalcules" for L., and he did not separate them zoologically; so his views on one sort are illustrative of his notions about all.

the knot-like lumps, which are to be seen also in Fig. 5, KLM. These lumps look to me as though they were made up of seven round globules; to wit, one in the middle, which sticks up a bit above the others, and the rest lying round it in a rosette.

Now if we consider what a lot of instruments must all be contained in a little piece like Fig. 6, in order that it may be not only stretched out, but also drawn in, and moved around, and with as many bends and knots in it too as you might make in a piece of string; so must we wonder all the more at such a contrivance. And who knows but what every knot-like part may not also itself be furnished with yet other organs, whereby they are set in motion. Seeing these things I was put in mind of the knotted threads over which people have spent so much time these last few years:[1] and I said to myself, If the ladies of our country could see such a wonderful and perfect structure, would they not have reason to bewail the time and gifts which they employ in making such a lot of useless knots, in which not the least bit of art or beauty is ever to be seen!

I saw in this water, or on the duckweed, many wonderful animalcules, some of them getting their food from it, and others (as I imagined) using it as a skulking place, to avoid being devoured by little fishes: but the weed seemed only calculated to show off[2] the three sorts of animalcules aforesaid.[3]

. . . .

---

[1] This apparently refers to some kind of macramé-work in which L.'s countrywomen then indulged: but I have been unable to find any other reference to it in contemporary writers.

[2] *maar voor genomen de drie verhaalde dierkens aan te wijsen* MS. I take the above to be L.'s meaning. In his view, everything in nature was created for some purpose; and I suppose he would have said that one of the purposes of duckweed is to accommodate and display animalcules such as *Vorticella*.—The last words of the above sentence were omitted by Chamberlayne—possibly because he could not understand what they meant.

[3] L. here describes the duckweed itself, and its generation, at greater

Whilst observing this last weed, I saw with wonder a great many animalcules[1] swimming in spirals through the water, and they were in such a great number together in so small a space, that they looked like a little cloud, visible to the naked eye, in the water; and animalcules of this sort I have never before seen in other waters, but on the second day they were nearly all gone.

Furthermore, in this water there were so many sorts of animalcules that I had never discovered in any other waters, that I was mazed to see such a diversity of structures; and each too had its own proper motion, wherefore I many times looked upon these delightsome and wondrous little creatures, which quite escape the bare eye.

During these observations, I saw one sort that exceeded many of the others in bigness, which were coupled together,[2] in which act they lay very still against the glass, unless a bigger sort came too near them: and as they lay still, you could leisurely discern those instruments wherewith they can so swiftly move themselves,[3] and even the motions of certain parts in their bodies, from which some would certainly conclude that they saw the circulation of the blood;[4] but I would sooner take it for the chyle[5] in the guts. These animalcules were so big that you could descry them[6] in a glass tube, with clear

---

length. As this part of the letter—though very interesting—is irrelevant to the present subject, I have omitted it, and resume the translation at the point where the animalcules are again referred to.

[1] Probably protozoa, but unidentifiable.

[2] Probably ciliates conjugating. Cf. pp. 200, 205, 206, 213, *supra*.

[3] Cilia, in all probability: but possibly cirrhi.

[4] This reference to the internal "circulation" is puzzling, unless L. actually observed the cyclosis of the food-vacuoles (in non-conjugating individuals) or the rhythmic pulsation of the contractile vacuoles.

[5] A modern reader might perhaps consider *chyle* here to be a mistake for *chyme*: but in L.'s day these terms were often used synonymously. Cf. *Lexicon Medicum* (Blankaart, 1748; p. 192)—"CHYMUS, idem est quod *chylus*".

[6] *i.e.*, with the naked eye.

kleyne Schepsels, die ons bloote oog ontwyken, beschouwde.
Onder dese beschouwinge sag ik een Soort, die boven veel andere in grootheijt uijtstaaken, die te samen gekoppelt waren
in welke doen Sij seer stil tegen het glas bleven sitten, ten
ware een grooter Soort haar niet te na quamen, in welke stil
sitten, men sedig de werktuijgen, waar mede Sij haar vaardig konnen bewegen konde bekennen, en selfs ook de beweginge van eenige deelen in haar Lighaam, waar uijt eenige
wel besluijten soude, dat ze de Circulatie van het bloet
sagen, maar ik wil eer gelooven, dat het de Chijl inde
darm was, dese dierkens waren soo groot, dat men deselve
in een glase Tuba met klaar water sijnde konde bekennen, en onder veel Soorten van dierkens, quamen mij dierkens voor vande groote als Santjens, die van een volkome
maaksel waren, als onse Tuijn Spinnekoppen.
Hier hebt gij Hoog Edele Heeren, mijne aanteekeninge, die ik
int beschouwen van kroost, en kleijne dierkens hebbe gehouden,
in welk doen ik tot mijn selven hebbe geseijt, wat sijnder al
Schepsels die ons onbekent sijn, en hoe weijnig ist dat wij
weten. Ik sal onder tusschen blijven Haar

Hoog Edele Heeren.

Onderdanige Dienaar

Antonij van Leeuwenhoek

LAST PAGE OF THE LETTER ABOUT DUCKWEED

Facsimile (reduced) of original holograph MS. (25 Dec. 1702). This is a good sample of Leeuwenhoek's handwriting and signature during his later life.

water: and among many kinds of creatures, I saw some as big as sand-grains, which had as perfect a structure as our garden spiders.[1]

Here, Gentlemen, you have the notes that I have kept about my observations on duckweed and little animalcules: in making which I said to myself, How many creatures are still unbeknown to us, and how little do we yet understand!

The foregoing letter contains recognizable descriptions of at least five different Ciliates—*Vorticella*, *Carchesium*, *Cothurnia*, *Trichodina*, and *Kerona*—all of which were first observed by Leeuwenhoek. He had, of course, described the Vorticellids at an earlier date, since when others had repeated his observations: and he had also, as we have already seen, previously observed the conjugation of freshwater ciliates—here mentioned again. But the letter is, nevertheless, full of protozoological novelties.

Little more than a month later Leeuwenhoek sent the Royal Society another remarkable letter, which contained a description of the curious colonial flagellate *Anthophysa vegetans*—one of the "iron-protozoa." This letter has been generally overlooked by protozoologists, and nobody hithert[2] appears to have identified the organism described. The identification is, however, easy and certain. Only one interpretation of Leeuwenhoek's description and figures is possible. I will now give a translation of the relevant passages in this highly interesting letter:[3]

---

[1] Probably water-mites.

[2] O. F. Müller, who rediscovered and named this flagellate (*Volvox vegetans* O.F.M., 1786; p. 22, Pl. III, figs. 22-25), was apparently ignorant of L.'s earlier observations.—I am aware that *Anthophysa* is mentioned among L.'s discoveries in the "Leeuwenhoek Film" recently exhibited in Holland: but this mention was taken from my own note (1923), in which I attributed the discovery to L. without specific reference to the letter here translated.

[3] *Letter dated 5 February 1703.* To the Royal Society. MS.Roy.Soc. Not published in Dutch or Latin Works. English translation (almost complete) published in *Phil. Trans.* (1703), Vol. XXIII, No. 286, pp. 1430-1443. The MS. of this translation is preserved along with the Dutch original, and is in the hand of John Chamberlayne. The above is a new translation (from the MS.) of a part of the letter only.—Vandevelde (1924, p. 133) calls this letter "Brief 2 Tr 4 [148]"; but according to my numeration it is *Letter 150.*

At the end of the month of July, 1702, I was standing in front of my dwelling, beside the water[1], which flowed with a gentle stream through our Town, and was very clear, and had almost the colour of the Maas water; when, as the sun shone bright, I saw something moving in it, which seemed to me a-glitter; and so I had a mind to try and find out what this shining matter was.

In order to satisfy myself, I took a glass tube, having very near a foot's length and a finger's width, and after tying a string to it, I let it drop into the water; and when it was nearly half full, I pulled it out of the water and let it fall from a certain height straight down into the water, so that, being right under, the tube got filled with water.[2]

Examining this water with the magnifying-glass, I saw that divers sorts of animalcules were swimming about in it, whereof some were of a structure that I don't remember to have ever before discovered in any waters.

I viewed this water divers times one day, but couldn't discover what occasioned the glittering that it had afore 'twas put in the glass tube.

On the 4th of August, I saw, through a magnifying lens, that in eight or ten places there were particles sticking fast to the glass; so that though all the water, and consequently all the very small particles that were floating in it also, was moved (with a slight motion which I imparted to the tube)[3], yet these particles remained stuck to the glass.

This constrained me to examine them through the microscope, and I saw then that the particles looked like a complete bough off a tree, with its many twigs, as we might see it with the naked eye; some of them differing from others in the number of their twigs.

---

[1] *i.e.*, the canal [in the *Hippolytusbuurt*]: so rendered by Chamberlayne.

[2] This passage is abbreviated by Chamberlayne.

[3] This terminal bracket is not in the MS.—apparently owing to an oversight: and the sentence, which is rather involved and disorderly in the original, I have had to rearrange somewhat in order to make its meaning clear. Chamberlayne's words are a short paraphrase.

Nearly all of these branch-like particles were fixed by their little stalks to the glass, and seemed to have had their beginnings in a little bit of matter that was stuck to the glass.

To satisfy myself further hereof, on the foresaid fourth of August I put some of the water that was flowing along in front of my dwelling into another glass tube, which was rather longer and wider than the first, after flinging away the first and second lots of water that entered the tube.

I examined this water divers times; and after it had stood some thirty hours in the tube, I discovered the bough-like structures as perfect as I have before described them; and among others, one that lay so that the thick stem from which the other branches sprouted seemed right against my eye.

I fixed a microscope before this last-mentioned particle, with the idea of finding out if 'twould grow bigger in the course of time.

After the lapse of another six hours, I couldn't discern that it had increased in bigness; but now I perceived that the extreme tips of the twigs, which were more than twenty[1] in number, were nearly all beset with round transparent globules,[2] whose diameters were quite three times that of the extremities of the topmost twigs.

As I now saw that some transparent animalcules, of the bigness of the round globules just described, were moving about among the twigs, it occurred to me that the round globules also might be animalcules, and that these animalcules had made themselves fast on the extremities of the little twigs aforesaid.[3]

---

[1] *meer dan twintig* MS. Chamberlayne wrongly translates "about twenty".

[2] *bolletjens* MS. Chamberlayne translates "bubbles"—quasi *belletjens*. But I think this somewhat distorts the sense. *Bol* and *bel* are not equivalent, and L. does not use their diminutives indiscriminately.

[3] The flagellates forming the flower-like "heads" of *Anthophysa* do, in fact, frequently break off and swim away.

My opinion hereof was strengthened next day, when I saw, in the morning, after the water had been twice four-and-twenty hours in the tube, that nearly all the round globules that were on the twigs had gotten off them; and that some of these round globules, which I was sure were animalcules, were moving about among the branches, while a very few of them placed themselves again on the twigs, and stayed sitting there motionless for as long as I was busy looking at 'em.

After another twelve hours' time, I could not perceive that the bough-like structure was[1] grown any bigger; but I then saw that a few of the twigs were again beset with round globules, and that an animalcule, which was at least fifty times bigger than one of the globules, was running about on the branches: and forasmuch as the ends of the twigs, whereon this creature had been running, were once more laden with round globules, I concluded (though I could get no ocular proof thereof) that the big animalcule was dropping her young ones there.[2]

On the 6th of August, I took a glass tube that was more than a foot long, and with a diameter of an inch; and this one was sealed up at one end with the flame, lest there might be some doubt whether the foresaid bough-like structure originated from the cork: and after I had rinsed it out once or twice, I put this glass tube in my closet, and viewed it many times, but I discovered no bough-like structures till after the water had stood in the glass tube for about forty hours,[3] when I fastened a magnifying-glass to the tube, to see if the bough-like structures (after I first saw them) would not grow any bigger. But how nicely soever I viewed them, I could make out no change in them.

---

[1] *waren* MS.—a false concord. The observation seems to have been made on one "bough", and I therefore translate accordingly.

[2] This was, of course, an error. The "big animalcule" was probably a ciliate—some of which prey upon *Anthophysa*.

[3] *ontrent veertig uren* MS. Chamberlayne mistranslates this "above 40 hours".

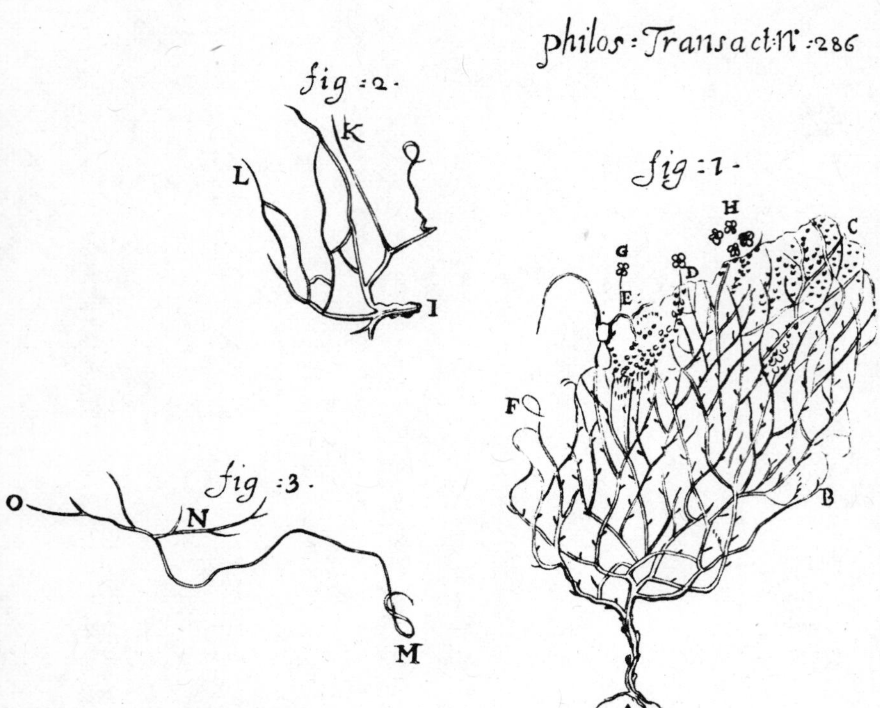

LEEUWENHOEK'S FIGURES OF *Anthophysa vegetans*

From the engravings in *Phil. Trans.* (1703), illustrating his Letter of 5 Feb. 1703. (The original drawings, in red crayon, are reversed.) Slightly enlarged.

And now I also saw that upon the extreme tips of a very few of the branches there were three or four, or sometimes even five, round globules, set beside one another like a rosette; which afforded no unpleasant spectacle. For when one such branch was fastened to the glass by its thick end alone (from which all the other lesser branches sprang), then all the twigs [1] were put in motion by any little movement which you imparted to the water; whereby also some of the aggregated globules, which were set thereabouts, and which you would judge not to be stuck fast upon the utmost twigs, were [2] likewise put in motion: but I assured myself, after divers observations, that they were really fastened thereto, though I could make out no structure whereby they were joined, owing to its exceeding thinness. [3]

I let the water run very slowly out of the glass tube, in order that the branches (which were fastened to the glass by their stem, and whose twigs were kept in continual motion when one handled the tube) might lie against the glass, as the water ran off them, so that my draughtsman [4] would thus be able the better to make a picture of them. [See Plate XXX.]

Fig. 1, ABCDEF, shows the structure described, as it was lying against the glass. A represents the part that you would put down as the root of a plant, whereby alone 'twas fastened to the glass. We see here what a lot of twigs there are on it, which now look rather disorderly ravelled together, though lying free in the water they were not unpleasant to behold: especially because their colour was like that of oaken wood, and in many places they were encrusted with little round

---

[1] *alle de sprankjens* MS. Chamberlayne says "all the five small Twigs"; but this is not in the original, and does not make sense.

[2] I supply *waren*, which is missing in the original—apparently owing to the presence of the same word in the clause immediately preceding.

[3] This sentence is much condensed in Chamberlayne's translation.

[4] Cf. p. 342 *infra*.

granules, just as if they were made up of congealed round particles.[1]

At G, and hard by D, are shown the rosette-like structures which seem to consist of several globules, and whereof some are also indicated at H: and though I couldn't see that the structures shown at H were joined to twigs, yet they always moved about in the water in the same way as the utmost little twigs did.

No sooner was the water poured out of the glass tube, than I forthwith viewed the structure aforesaid: and thereupon I saw swimming, between the twigs called BD and BE, two animalcules as small as each of the globules whereof the structures shown at H are made up: and these animalcules then went on swimming, even in the little water that had not yet evaporated from between the twigs, till my eye wearied with looking at them. During this observation I further saw one of the four globules shown at H break off, and make off as though swimming away, though the distance of its removal was not above a hair's breadth: and this particle which swam off was certainly an animalcule, for it turned and twisted itself round about several times. And in another globule I did also see indeed a little motion ; but it didn't break off from the others, with which it formed the figure of a rosette.

There were, furthermore, many other little bough-like structures which did not lie so orderly: and when the water ran off them, they took on the shapes shown in Fig. 2, IKL, and Fig. 3, MNO.

What are we to say about the fabric of these little boughs, or tree-like growths? We can't suppose that they proceed from a seminal matter in the water: but, with submission to better judgements, we are more satisfied by imagining that they are composed of some substance which, floating in small particles in the water,

---

[1] The stalk of *Anthophysa* is encrusted with brown particles of ferric hydroxide, and this is by no means a bad description of its appearance.

> is clotted together by some kind of mutual attraction. This won't seem strange to us, if we bear in mind that whenever we file a bit of iron it gets rather hot; and if we apply the filed part to the filings, they'll stay hanging chain-wise from it; though in nothing like the way such filings do with a lodestone.

At this point Leeuwenhoek digresses into a description of some chemical experiments. Then, after describing how he dissolved a little metallic silver in dilute nitric acid, he tells us how he witnessed the wonderful branching "tree" which grew in this solution when he dropped into it "a particle of copper of the bigness of a sand-grain." Such "trees" are now familiar to every schoolboy, but in Leeuwenhoek's time they were novelties: nor has their wonder been wholly evaporated away by the work of modern chemists.[1] It is clear, moreover, that Leeuwenhoek saw in the metallic "tree" a physical analogy—suggesting an explanation of its growth—to the "tree" of *Anthophysa*, formed (in part) by the congealed particles of ferric hydroxide: for he adds "I observed with a great deal of pleasure, how the Silver in this clear Water was coagulated into such bodies as are described by the above-mentioned Trees".[2] Nevertheless, while recognizing the resemblances, he confesses that the process of growth is, in both cases, to him "wholly inscrutable".

About 10 years later Leeuwenhoek sent another most interesting letter to the Royal Society—a letter in which he described anew his observations on Rotifers and Vorticellids. After referring to his previous observations on *Melicerta*, and its ciliary mechanism, he says:[3]

---

[1] Cf. Leduc (1911).

[2] Chamberlayne's translation.—L. gives a figure of his "silver tree" which is, I believe, the first ever published. His observations are, apparently, unknown to Leduc and other recent students of similar phenomena.

[3] From *Letter* VII. 28 June 1713. To the Royal Society. MS.Roy.Soc. Published in *Brieven*, IV, 64 (1718); *Epist. Physiol.* (*Op. Omn.* IV), p. 63 (1719). English translation printed in *Phil. Trans.* for 1713 [published 1714], Vol. XXVIII, p. 160. (The MS. of this translation—in an unknown hand—is preserved in the Roy. Soc. collection.) I translate directly from the original MS. in L.'s own hand.

Notwithstanding I have so many times seen such animalcules,[1] and let others see 'em too, yet one can't be satisfied with just looking at[2] so wonderful a structure: chiefly because one can't get clear on how such an unbelievable motion is brought about, and in the second place, as to what purpose this motion was for. For when we see any part of such a creature (that is endowed with motion[3]) moved,[4] we feel sure that this part wasn't made for nothing, but is a necessary part of it; and consequently this wheelwork is of use to the animalcule's body, though we can't call to mind just what use it is.[5]

He then records some further observations on Rotifers—made "at the end of July and the beginning of August [1712]"—and proceeds:

Furthermore, I paid great attention to their revolving toothed wheelwork; and I saw that an incredibly great motion was brought about by the said instrument, in the water round about it, whereby many little particles, that could be made out with the magnifying-glass, were wafted towards the animalcule, while others were carried away from it; whereof some, being borne into the middle of the revolving instrument, were used as food by the animalcule.[6] And other particles, when they got up to it, went off from the animalcule as quick as if it flung them away; seeing which, I came to the conclusion that the cast-off particles were no good to the creature for food.

From this observation we may well conclude that, since

---

[1] Called *Dierkens* throughout in the Dutch printed version, but *Diertjens* in the MS.

[2] *te beschouwen*: these words are in the printed version but not in the MS.

[3] The words in parenthesis are in the MS. but not in the printed version.

[4] *bewegen* MS. *dat bewogen werd* printed version.

[5] *is* printed version *was* MS.

[6] *van het Dierke als tot spys gebruykt wierden* Dutch printed version. The MS. says *het Dierke als tot spijs gebruijkte* (the animalcule used as food).

these animalcules can't *displace 'emselves*[1] in the water, they can't[2] chase after their food, like all[3] other creatures do that are endowed with motion, so that they can get from place to place.[4]

These animalcules,[5] then, and all the others too, that can't shift 'emselves from place to place, either because they are fixt by the tail, or otherwise, must be furnisht with similar instruments, in order to make a stir in the water; whereby they get any stuff that is in the water for their food and growth and for the defense[6] of their body.[7]

And when we observe the animalcules that are fixt by a long tail[8] to something or other, like many that we have discovered on the little roots of duckweed,[9] we see that they don't merely go round in a circle with the extreme part of their body[10] (whereby they make, in proportion to the littleness of their body, a big bustle in the water); but the creatures can also pull their tails together, and that very quick too; so that when they stick their tails out again, they displace the water round about them, and

---

[1] Underlined in MS. but not italicized in printed version.

[2] There are slight verbal differences here between the MS. and the printed version, but they do not affect the sense.

[3] *alle* is in Dutch printed version, but not in MS.

[4] The Latin version adds "whenever they want to" (*quoties libet*): but this is not in the Dutch.

[5] So in MS. The Dutch printed version has "animals" (*Dieren*).

[6] Referring to the pellets with which—as he had just described—*Melicerta* builds its house.

[7] This passage is worded differently in the MS. and in the printed version, but the sense is identical. In the *Phil. Trans.* the two foregoing paragraphs were condensed into a single sentence.

[8] *i.e.* Vorticellids.

[9] Cf. p. 277 *sq.*, *supra*.

[10] L. means that the body of the Vorticellid travels in a circle round the point of attachment of the stalk. The Latin translator apparently misunderstood these words, which he rendered "*extremitates corporis sui in orbem complicant*".

being thus come into *different water*,[1] they can get fresh food out of it.

Now I also saw a very few animalcules [2] (whose bodies were short and thick), that were much bigger than the animalcules that make a little case for their dwelling-place,[3] and these were fixed to the little roots of the duckweed by their hindmost or tail-like part; and notwithstanding they were able to move from place to place, they also made none the less a circular motion with the foremost part of their body: whence I also concluded that such a motion was for no other purpose than to make anything that would serve as food come towards them.[4]

I have ere now asked myself, What is the use of such a toothed wheelwork, like a cogged wheel out of a clock? But if we now let our thoughts run on further, we must decide that such a thing is necessary, if a great stir is to be made in the water: for if it were a round and smooth wheel, it would make little motion in the water; whereas now every tooth that sticks out from the circumference causes a great stir in the water, in comparison with a smooth and even rotation.

This being so, we are faced once more with the mysteries, and unconceivable order, which such tiny creatures (which quite escape one's naked eye) are endowed with.

---

[1] Underlined in MS., but not italicized in printed versions. The phrase is rendered in *Phil. Trans.* "and so bringing fresh Water under them,"—which is incorrect.

[2] Clearly unidentifiable from this meagre description, but probably rotifers.

[3] Referring to *Melicerta* (and the tubicolous ciliates?). The word here translated "dwelling-place" is in the original *huysvesting*, which may mean "edification" in any of the literal or metaphorical senses which this word has in English.

[4] "From whence I concluded, that those Motions serv'd some other purposes than only to draw their Food to 'em." *Phil. Trans.* The translator here completely reversed the sense of L.'s words.

Can anybody doubt, after reading the foregoing words, that Leeuwenhoek had, in 1713, already discovered the chief function of the peristomial cilia ("wheelwork") of *Vorticella*? Surely not. Old Antony knew as well as I do (and everybody else now does) how the Vorticellids, and many other ciliated organisms, capture their food from the surrounding water—though he misconceived the structure of the mechanism. By persistent study he had advanced a long way beyond his original interpretations of 1676,[1] and had at last reached the truth.

The remainder of this letter contains some further observations on "animalcules": and as some of these—though none is exactly identifiable—were undoubtedly protozoa and bacteria, I will now quote what else he here relates:[2]

> At the beginning of the month of August,[3] I was in a garden where there was a pond well stocked with fish; and pretty well all over the water there floated a thin scum, which looked greenish, though you couldn't see any other green-stuff in the water: which seemed to me odd, because in other years[4] I had noticed that the water was very clear in this pond, as it was also in the ditch from which the pond was continually replenished; but I was told that when it rains, the scum goes away.
>
> I went a little aside, all on my own, and took a wooden lath, with which I touched the surface of the water; and putting a little drop of the water in a green wine-glass, I looked at it through a microscope that I had by me: and I discovered in this water so unbelievably many little animalcules, which even through a microscope are scarce discernible, that no one could be made to credit it, unless he got a sight of it for himself; and also divers sorts of

---

[1] Cf. p. 118 *supra*.

[2] The passages which follow begin at the top of p. 68 of the Dutch printed works (Vol. IV, *Send-brieven*).

[3] Presumably *anno* 1712: but from the final paragraph this is not certain.

[4] *op andere jaren* MS. "at other times" *Phil. Trans.*

large animalcules, mixt with very[1] many air-bubbles, of extreme littleness.

A few days[2] afterwards, I asked to have a little of this water brought to my house, in order to examine it more nicely; but I could discover nothing else in it than what I have just related, though I noticed a little later that no *air-bubbles*[3] were to be seen in it.

Now if people rinse beer and wine glasses in such a pond, who can tell how many animalcules may be left in these glasses? whence some of them may even get into our mouths. And this being so, people have no reason to ask me how the little animalcules, which, as I have said many a long year ago,[4] are in the stuff between our teeth, and in *hollow grinders*,[5] are able to get there.

Thus far my notes, which I kept some years ago, and which I have come across within these last few days.

Leeuwenhoek's last recorded observations on protozoa are contained in a letter written in 1716 to Boerhaave.[6] Unfortunately they are mentioned very briefly—being sandwiched in between observations and speculations on spermatozoa. Despite their brevity, however, they are of extreme interest.

After speaking of the spermatozoa of various animals, Leeuwenhoek abruptly interjects the following remarks:[7]

---

[1] The word "very" (*seer*) is in the printed version, but not in the MS.

[2] *Eenige dagen* MS. *Eenige weynige dagen* Dutch printed version.

[3] *Lugtbellen* [underlined] in MS. The printed version has *lugtbolletjes*.

[4] *Vide* p. 238 *sq.*, *supra*. The "animalcules" were, of course, bacteria.

[5] *inde stoffe . . . tussen onse tanden, ende inde* holle kiesen [last two words underlined] MS. "in and about our Teeth" *Phil. Trans.* There are slight verbal differences here between the Dutch printed version and the MS., though the sense does not differ.

[6] Herman Boerhaave (1668-1738), Professor of Botany, Chemistry, and Medicine at Leyden—"a whole Medical Faculty in himself"—is too famous a character to need further annotation. He was elected a Fellow of the Royal Society in 1730. For his life see especially Banga (1868, p. 807) and *N. Nederl. Biogr. Woordenb.* (1924), VI, 127 [a long and excellent article by van Leersum].

[7] From *Letter* XXIX. 5 November 1716. To Boerhaave. Published in *Brieven*, Vol. IV, p. 284; and (in Latin) in *Opera Omnia*, Vol. IV (*Epist. Physiol.*), p. 279. No MS., and not in *Phil. Trans.*—The passage here translated begins on p. 288 of the Dutch edition.

I can't forbear adding here, that I have allowed water-animalcules, mixed with a little earthy matter, to lie dry in my closet for a whole winter: and when I put them again in water, I saw some of them unfold their limbs, which seemed to be wrapped up inside them, and swim about in the water.[1] I have also observèd that animalcules, which really belong to the waters, are to be found in the soil in our meadows;[2] and these animalcules are carried thither, along with particles of water, by strong winds, and come not only from the canals but even from the sea. And notwithstanding that most of these creatures are unable to stand the winter's cold, and so die, yet some of them survive, to propagate their kind: and this has been their lot from the very beginning of things.

Then a few lines further on we strike the following gem:

Now I must tell you that there is, right at the back of my house, a small flat lead, on which the rain-water doesn't dry up for several days after it hath rained. In this water I have many a time seen, among others, some very little roundish animalcules, of divers sizes, and whereof the bodies were round, and having a diameter, when full grown, of about thrice the diameter of one of those globules that make our blood red: and in their bodies you could distinctly make out four round globules. These creatures were so vastly multiplied in a few days, that I was dumbfounded at it.

I was all agog to know how this multiplication might come to pass: and in the end I found out that these animalcules lived for no longer than 30 or 36 hours, and that they then fixed themselves upon the glass, and stopped there without moving: while soon after, their body burst asunder, and lay divided into eight portions:

---

[1] These were probably Rotifers, though some may possibly have been encysted Ciliates.

[2] This is probably a record of the first observations ever made on soil-protozoa.

and these were actually young animalcules, for in five or six seconds some of them swam off.

Inasmuch as one animalcule thus begets 8 little ones, and each of these again brings forth 8: then there would be produced, in the course of 9 days, two hundred and sixty-two thousand one hundred and forty-four animalcules from a single animalcule:

In 36 hours, or 1½ days,........... 8 animalcules
8
in 3 days............64 animalcules
8
in 4½ days..........512
8
in 6 days.........4096
8
in 7½ days.......32768
8
in 9 days....262144 animalcules.

From the size and shape of these animalcules, as well as from their habitat and method of reproduction, it is obvious that they were some common phytoflagellate; and it is highly probable, since no mention is made of their colour, that they were not the forms previously described (to wit, *Haematococcus* and *Chlamydomonas*). I have very little doubt that the description applies to *Polytoma*—of which it is, indeed, so far as it goes, an astonishingly good description.[1] The division of the parent body into 4, and then into 8; the bursting of the enclosing membrane, and the swimming away of the daughter-individuals,—all this was observed and recorded with remarkable accuracy.

How Leeuwenhoek was able to discover, with the limited means at his disposal, the facts which are here so simply set

[1] I am glad to find that Bütschli (Vol. II, p. 621) long ago arrived at the same conclusion.

forth, must remain for ever a marvel. On reading these passages the modern protozoologist, knowing the patience and perseverance needed to make such observations—even with adequate instruments, and with the accumulated information of the next 200 years to help him—can only regard this extraordinary old man,[1] as he regarded his "little animals", with dumbfounded admiration.

—Door Arbeijt en Naarstigheijt komt men tot saaken die men te vooren onna speurlijk agten.
Actum desen 30: April 1698
ANTONY VAN LEEUWENHOEK

[1] L. was 84 years of age when this letter was written—"in the autumn of his life," as he says a little later (cf. p. 88).

ELUCIDATIONS AND ANNOTATIONS

THE following supplementary notes—dealing with very various subjects—are collected together here simply because they are too long to print as footnotes to the foregoing text. They contain much that is important for the student of Leeuwenhoek and his writings, but the reader will please bear in mind that they are notes and explanations only—not full dissertations on the subjects treated. My information has been gathered from many sources during many years, but is still far from complete: and I offer it to fellow-students merely in the hope that it may help them in their own studies. On some matters I could, indeed, say much in addition: but as Father Antony himself would say, "I will spare you more, for 'twould else take all too long a-writing."

(i) LEEUWENHOEK'S NAME

As the curious name "Leeuwenhoek" has, seemingly, at all times been a stumbling-block to foreigners (and has even puzzled Dutch scholars), the following annotations may not be amiss.

LEEUWENHOEK, as a surname, appeared until quite recently to be extinct. I have been unable to find anybody bearing it since the middle of the XVIII Century: but my researches in this connexion were only superficial, and Mr Bouricius has delved deeper and has deservedly been more successful. He has discovered[1] that there are still Leeuwenhoeks living in Holland—"between Oudewater and Gouda." They are, so Bouricius believes,[2] descendants from Antony's uncle[3] Huych [=Hugh]—his father's only brother. (See the Family Tree,

---

[1] Cf. Schierbeek (1929, 1930).

[2] Mr Bouricius's researches—though unpublished—seem to have been very thorough: for Schierbeek (1930), who has seen his notes, says that "the genealogy is completely ascertained" of these present-day Leeuwenhoeks.

[3] "*Oudoom*" [= great-uncle] according to Schierbeek (1930).

p. 18 *supra.*) Nevertheless, it is certain that, at the present day, there can be no Leeuwenhoeks who are directly descended from the great Antony himself: for he was the only son of his father, and none of his male issue outgrew infancy. His sisters married—and so changed their names—while his only surviving daughter remained unmarried.

The literal meaning of the name "Leeuwenhoek" is obvious: for *leeuw* means a lion, and a *hoek* is a corner or angle. (Accordingly, the name was neatly graecolatinized[1]—in Antony's own lifetime—into "*Leogonus*".) That the name itself is probably a place-name seems equally obvious, especially as we find it coupled with *van.* A very plausible derivation has been found recently by Bouricius (1924, 1925). According to him, Antony's forefathers resided in a corner-house by the *Leeuwenpoort* (= Liongate) in the East-End of Delft:[2] and consequently they were, in all probability, known to their neighbours as the family "from the corner of the Liongate" (*van* [den] *Leeuwen* [poorts] *hoek*).

At the present day there is nothing in Delft to connect Leeuwenhoek and his family with the topography of the place. It is true there is his effigy on the railings round the playground of a girls' school in the *Oude Delft*; but this was put there recently in error.[3] And there is also, of course, a modern road called *Antony van Leeuwenhoek singel*—outside the old town, and leading to the railway station.

For the orthography of the name ANTONY VAN LEEUWENHOEK there is good authority. In his early life, however, he signed himself "Antonj Leeuwenhoeck"—the christian name ending with a *long i* (not English *j*) and the surname with *ck*, and without *van.* This is the spelling in all MS. signatures up to and including *Letter 39* (17 Sept. 1683): but *Letters 40, 41*, and *42* are signed "Antonj Leeuwenhoek"—

---

[1] Cf. the panegyric poem prefixed to the first volume of the *Opera Omnia.*

[2] In early days the town of Delft was fortified by walls and moats, communicating with the outside by various "gates" (*poorten*). This enclosure was originally effected about A.D. 1070-1072 by Duke Godfrey of Lorraine, the Hunchback (*Govert mit den bult*, or *den Bultenaer*). Some of these gates are still standing—more or less: but the *Leeuwenpoort* was not one of them. It was an alley near the East Gate (*Oostpoort*), and has now vanished. Cf. Boitet (1729, p. 592), Bouricius (1924, 1925).

[3] See p. 338 *seq.*

still without *van*, but with final *-k* in place of *-ck*. *Letter 43* (5 Jan. 1685) is the first one signed "Antonj van Leeuwenhoek" —with *long i*, with *van*, and with *-k*: and thereafter he appears generally to have written his name thus—that is, for the last 38 years of his life. In the year 1685-6, however, he himself seems to have been in some perplexity regarding his signature: for *Letters 44* (23 Jan. 1685), *46* (13 July 1685), and *48* (22 Jan. 1686) are again signed "Antonj Leeuwenhoek", while *Letter 45* (30 Mar. 1685) is signed "A: v: Leeuwenhoek" and *Letter 47* (12 Oct. 1685) simply "A: Leeuwenhoek."[1] Examples of his signature at different dates are shown in Plates V, X, and XXIX.

In the Dutch published letters, the *long i* of the forename was generally printed as a short *i*—though sometimes as a *y*. It is therefore questionable whether "Antoni" or "Antony" is to be preferred. I adopt the latter spelling as it is conformable with English usage,[2] and because an English *y* is a justifiable equivalent of the *long i*. We have in English no such letter; and a terminal *j* not only appears strange to us, but may even lead—as I can testify from experience—to ludicrous mispronunciation of the name. I may add, for the information of English readers, that the name "Antony" is not accented on the first syllable in Dutch (as it is in English), but on the second: Antóny—not *An*tony.

On the memorial—in the Old Church at Delft—erected to Antony by his daughter Maria, the full name is latinized as *Antonius a Leeuwenhoek* (the form in which it usually appears in the Latin translations[3] of his works). But curiously enough the Dutch inscription on the stone slab covering his grave gives

---

[1] Haaxman (1875, p. 6 note) has already discussed the proper spelling of L.'s name, and adopted the same spelling as I do: but he had seen only a small percentage of the extant MSS.—having consulted none of those in the Roy. Soc. collection—and therefore had not the support (which I can claim) of some 150 autograph signatures. Had he seen these, he would probably have expressed his opinion more emphatically.

[2] Though L.'s chief Dutch biographer—Haaxman (1871, 1875)—also invariably styles him "Antony," Bouricius (1924, 1925), for reasons which are not evident, prefers to call him "Anthony"; while Schierbeek (1930) now names him "Anthoni," and some other recent Dutch writers "Anthonie."

[3] *Antonius de Leeuwenhoek* also occurs, and possibly accounts for some recent writers' miscalling him "*de* Leeuwenhoek" (instead of *van* L.).

his name as "*Anthony van Leewenhoek*"—the *u* having dropped out of the surname, and an *h* and a *y* having crept into the first name. In old Dutch—as in modern English—it is quite usual to find "Anthony" spelled with an *h*. The objection to spelling Leeuwenhoek's name thus is that he never—as far as I know—so spelled it himself.[1]

Authority might thus be found for a variety of spellings: and if importance were attached to the orthographical vagaries of Leeuwenhoek's contemporaries, and of his interpreters and commentators down to the present day, any one of a long list of variant literal combinations might easily be advocated. I will merely note here that in the English versions of his epistles, published in the *Philosophical Transactions*, his surname is spelled in no less than 19 different ways. It appears as Leewenhoeck, Leeuwenhoeck, Leeuwenhoeek, Leewenhook, Lewenhoeck, Leuwenhoek, Leuwenhook, Leevvenhoeck, Leewenhoek, Leeuwenhoek, Leuwenhock, Leuwenhoeck, Leuvenhook, Lewenhoek, Lewuenhoek, Lewuenhoeck, Leewuenhoek, Leewnenhoek, and Leeuenhoek. Most of these spellings, however, are certainly due to misprints or misreadings of his signature.

It is further noteworthy that Leeuwenhoek's name has suffered the most extraordinary mutations, mutilations, and perversions at the hands of foreigners. Germans, for example, commonly call him "Anton von Leuwenhoek"—and pronounce the name as though spelled thus in their own language; while to the French he is generally "Antoine Leuwenhoeck"—if nothing worse. It is almost the rule, moreover, to find his name spelled in several different ways by the same writer—be he English, French, or German. Wrisberg (1765), for example, refers to Leeuwenhoek thrice—calling him (in Latin) "Loewenhoeckius," "Lavenochius," and "Loewenhoeck" on each several occasion. (Examples could easily be multiplied.) But perhaps the most remarkable transformations occur in Italian writings—even in those of his contemporaries and immediate followers. As instances I may cite Vallisneri, who usually called Leeuwenhoek "Lewenoeckio" but on at least one occasion "Le Wenocchio";

---

[1] The name bestowed upon him at his baptism, however, was neither Antony nor Anthoni, but "Thonis." (See Plate III.)

while the illustrious and erudite Spallanzani regularly dubbed him "Levenoecchio". To Buonanni he was just "Lauenoch".

Foreigners generally find great difficulty not only in spelling Leeuwenhoek's name but also in pronouncing it. On the assumption, apparently, that it is some kind of tongue-twister in an unknown and barbarous lingo, they invent and emit noises unintelligible to any Hollander. Some of the more confident commentators, however, tell us how to pronounce the name properly. For example, Richardson (1885) informs us that it should be "pronounced in English fashion Leuvenhock". I do not know why it should ever be pronounced English-fashion—rather than Dutch fashion: nor can I imagine any reason for so singularly mispronouncing a plain Dutch word. Certainly no native of Holland would recognize "Leuvenhock"—pronounced English-fashion—if he were to hear it. But I can assure my fellow-countrymen that the name "Leeuwenhoek" is pure Dutch, and not so difficult to pronounce as it looks; and that no Hollander will misunderstand if it be spoken as though written in English "Laywenhook". This does not—as I am well aware—represent modern Dutch pronunciation exactly; but it is phonetically far better than the common English mispronunciations resembling "Lervenherk" or "Loivenherk" or "Luvenhock". The Dutch diphthong *eeu(w)* is closely similar in sound to *ay-oo* (said quickly) in English: and there is surely no conceivable reason why the Dutch *oe* (exactly equivalent to *oo* in English, and to our own *oe* in the words "shoe" and "canoe") should be pronounced as though it were German, French, Italian, or Latin.

The reader will no doubt recall (see p. 43 *supra*) that Constantijn Huygens—who knew English well—said that Leeuwenhoek's name would be written "according to our orthography" as "Leawenhook". But the phonetic value of *ea* in English is not now constant: it differs widely in different words. Huygens evidently had in mind the modern sound of these vowels in words such as "great" or "break"—not in "real", "seal", "Chelsea", or "bread". (For some judicious comments on this subject see Wheatley's edition of Pepys: preliminary "Particulars", *ad finem.*) In Huygens's time *ea* in most English words "sounded as it still does in 'great'" (Bense, 1925; p. 205). He therefore meant that "Leeuwenhoek" should be pronounced as "Laywenhook" in English—as I have already said.

The Swedish traveller Björnståhl, who visited Leeuwenhoek's tomb in 1774, says that the name should be pronounced "Lewenhuk" (*more germanico*). I am not prepared to dispute this: it is perhaps as near the truth as my own foregoing attempt to imitate the sound in English. But when the same writer adds[1] that the name "Leeuwenhoek" means "*einen Greif*" [*i.e.*, a griffin], I must part company with him. This strange interpretation appears, indeed, to rest upon nothing but an erroneous inference from the mutilated heraldic device on the tombstone covering Antony and his daughter Maria—which still shows a flying eagle bearing a scutcheon, on which the Leeuwenhoek coat-of-arms was formerly emblazoned.[2]

It will be evident, therefore, that there is now no real mystery enshrouding the name "Leeuwenhoek". We know well enough how to spell it, how to speak it, what it means, and where it came from. Any doubts which may still exist about it are, apparently, due to mistakes or misunderstandings manufactured by credulous or incompetent commentators. No profound research is needed to arrive at such a conclusion: it must be obvious to everybody—no matter what his nationality—who devotes more than passing attention to the matter.

(ii) LEEUWENHOEK'S LANGUAGE

Leeuwenhoek's only language was Dutch—not the modern literary language of the Netherlands, nor Old Dutch (properly so called), but the "Nether-Dutch" commonly spoken in the Province of South Holland in the XVII Century. It is a language far removed from that of "Reynard the Fox" (*Vanden Vos Reinaerde*, written *circa* A.D. 1250), and is not even so archaic as the Dutch Bible (which dates from 1637, though—like the English—it contains much earlier elements). Consequently, for any educated Hollander of the present day it is no harder to understand than colloquial English of the same period is nowadays to an educated Englishman.

I have heard it said that Leeuwenhoek's language is more like Cape Dutch—the "*Taal*" or "*Afrikaans*" now

---

[1] *Vide* Björnståhl (1780-84); Vol. V, p. 364 of German translation (1782).

[2] The coat-of-arms proper (now gone) consisted of a *lion* rampant azure, tongued and clawed gules, in a field or. See Haaxman (1875), p. 125, and Morre (1912), p. 15.—The grave was despoiled during the French occupation of Delft.

spoken in South Africa—than modern Dutch: and I have been credibly informed that a certain well-known historian of zoology actually engaged a Boer from Cape Colony (in preference to an educated Hollander) to translate some of Leeuwenhoek's original letters for him, in the belief that he would thus obtain the most accurate English rendering. (I have also been told that the Cape Dutchman declined the task after inspecting the early MSS. He is said to have expressed the opinion that they were really not written in Dutch at all!) So far as I can judge, Leeuwenhoek's speech was very different from modern Afrikaans: but I have no accurate knowledge of this language—what little I know being derived chiefly from perusal of the interesting work of Bosman (1928). In any case it is certainly a mistake to suppose—as I know some people do—that Leeuwenhoek's Dutch is as different from modern Dutch as Chaucer's English is from modern English. Anybody who can read modern Dutch can, with a little patience and practice, easily read Leeuwenhoek's printed letters.

That Leeuwenhoek knew no language but his own is attested by himself and others. For example, he refers in *Letter 2* (*ante*, p. 42) to his lack of education in this respect and Molyneux also comments upon it (*ante*, p. 58). Numerous passages in the published Letters might easily be cited to the same purpose,[1] but perhaps the best testimony is furnished by an unpublished letter written to Oldenburg in 1676. Oldenburg, it appears, had written to suggest that Leeuwenhoek should conduct his future correspondence either in French (which he supposed Leeuwenhoek must know) or in English (for which he imagined a translator could readily be found in Delft, as so many English were then in Holland). Leeuwenhoek answered as follows:[2]

---

[1] *Letter 15* (21 April 1676, to Oldenburg: MS.Roy.Soc.), of which an incomplete translation was published in the *Phil. Trans.* (Vol. XI, No. 127, p. 653. 1676.), is sometimes quoted in evidence. In this letter L. is made to say: "I, *by reason of my unskilfulness in the English Tongue*, could have little more than the contentment of viewing the elegant Cuts" [in Grew's *Anatomy of Trunks*]. But unfortunately the words here italicized (by me) are not in the original MS. They are a gloss by the translator (Oldenburg), and not L.'s own words. Nevertheless, the passage testifies that Oldenburg was aware that L. did not know English.

[2] From *Letter* 13*a*. 22 January 1676. To Oldenburg. Unpublished. MS.Roy.Soc. (The original is in Dutch—the above being my translation.)

Your favour of the 28th December [1675] has reached me safely, from which I see that you doubt not but I have a sufficient knowledge of the French language ; but I must confess, to my sorrow, that I don't know any tongue but the Nether-Dutch, to which I was brought up : but if you write to me in French or Latin, I can manage it all right, as I have friends enough here who can translate it for me. But with English I can't cope, since the death of a certain Gentleman who was well versed in that tongue. I grant you there be plenty of the English nation knocking about everywhere,[1] but not all of them are competent to translate the *Transactions* out of English into Dutch : for when I inquired here for a fit person, I was directed to the chanter of the English Church (who offers his services also for teaching English). This fellow, presuming to do what I wanted, and having translated for me a bit that roused my curiosity, 'twas so lame I could make neither head nor tail of it.

In a slightly earlier letter[2] he also remarks parenthetically ". . . (since I don't understand English, to my sorrow, and there's nobody in this town who has the ability to translate into Dutch for me)". It may be taken as certain, therefore, that Leeuwenhoek could neither speak nor read any language but his own. Consequently—and this must always be remembered—he was never able to detect or correct mistakes committed by the translators of his letters into English and Latin. As these translators were often wholly ignorant of the things which Leeuwenhoek was attempting to describe, their versions should always be read with caution. In all cases of doubt it is necessary to refer—whenever possible—to his own original words.

One of Leeuwenhoek's present-day countrymen,[3] looking

---

[1] Howell, at an earlier date (1622), says " There is no part of *Europe* so hanted with all sorts of Foreigners as the *Netherlands* " (ed. 1705, p. 87).

[2] *Letter 13*. To Oldenburg. 20 December 1675. MS.Roy.Soc. Unpublished.

[3] Becking (1924).

down upon him from the heights of his own wisdom, regards him as a greatly over-rated *dilettante*[1]—"illiterate," "uncultured," "common to a degree"—and even goes so far as to aver that this "*bourgeois satisfait* . . . rather took a pride in the fact that he knew neither French, Latin, English nor German." But I know of no evidence in support of such a statement, and it is clearly contradicted by the words "to my sorrow" (*tot mijn leetwesen*) in the two foregoing extracts. Leeuwenhoek was always ready to confess his ignorance, but he was never proud of it. He would undoubtedly have said that nobody but a fool could pride himself on knowing less than other people.

Although—as already remarked—Leeuwenhoek's language presents few difficulties to his own countrymen, it must be confessed that to foreigners his words often appear at first sight very queer, and occasionally even enigmatic. But this is merely due to certain peculiarities of spelling and speech to which one soon becomes accustomed—peculiarities proper to his age and country, and not eccentricities or comicalities proper to himself. We see exactly comparable features in English of the same period, and inexperienced modern readers apparently tend to regard both as humorous. For example, I have seen people laugh at a grave sentence in Robert Hooke because the word "guess" is spelled "Ghesse": while Saville Kent refers to the "quaint style of diction" of Oldenburg's excellent contemporary English translation of Leeuwenhoek's *Letter 18* merely, I believe, because it was not couched in the current English of 1880. Every serious student of Leeuwenhoek and Hooke must realize at once, however, that there is nothing either "quaint" or "funny" about their phraseology or spellings—any more than there is about Tyndale's English translation of the Gospel, or Spinoza's Dutch writings on religion.

The following few notes are not intended for Leeuwenhoek's learned fellow-countrymen or for professional philologists, but for poor foreign scholars like myself—"illiterate" and "common"—who have no special knowledge of the peculiarities of his language, but who want to read and understand what he himself wrote. I design merely to give a few hints such

---

[1] "dilettant" in Becking's own Italian-Dutch-American-English.

as I should myself have found helpful when I first began to try and read his own writings.

Leeuwenhoek's speech is (*pace* Professor Dr Becking) an interesting example of the Dutch of the transitional period between the language of the Bible and the modern tongue. It preserves not a few genuine old words, and sometimes reflects the troubled history of his time; for we find, interspersed among his homely native vocabulary, numerous foreign intruders—mostly of French origin—which have not taken root in the language, and which will therefore be sought in vain in a modern Dutch-English dictionary. (I may instance the following, which all occur frequently in Leeuwenhoek's early letters: *presentatie*, *superfitie*, *circumferentie*, [*en*]*devoir*, *observeeren*, *imploieren*, *imagineeren*, *continuelijk*.) The interpretation of such words is, fortunately, seldom difficult for an English reader, because we have incorporated their counterparts into our own tongue.

There is a vast difference between the early letters and the last letters—not only in the handwriting but also in the words and wording.[1] The first letters are comparatively archaic, and inscribed in the Dutch character: the last are far more "modern", and written in the "Italian" hand which is now universal. Between these extremes, however, all intermediates occur. I would also note that the spellings and punctuation are more "modern" and uniform in the Dutch printed letters than they are in the original manuscripts. But this is also true of English writings of the same period—so far as I have studied them. "Correct" and uniform spelling seems to be generally due to printers and compositors, rather than to scholars and authors, in all printed languages.

Only the archaic and the irregular spellings likely to trouble present-day foreign readers of Leeuwenhoek's early letters will be noted here. The *genuine archaisms*—as distinct from the variations in spelling characteristic of the erratic orthography of the period—are chiefly the following:

---

[1] I am not concerned here with L.'s *style* of writing, which I can judge only as a foreigner. His own countrymen not seldom speak of it contemptuously—Becking, for instance, and earlier Pijzel (1875), who describes it as "pretty slovenly" (*vrij slordig*).

(1) Vowels

ae is written for *aa* (e.g. *aen*, *daer*, *waer*, *aengaen*, for aan, daar, waar, aangaan).[1]

eij may represent *ei*: as *weijnig* [weinig], *Meij* [Mei], etc.

i, *ij*, and *j* are often interchangeable, and do not always correspond with the modern usage of *i*, *ij*, and *y*. The diphthong *uij* often stands for modern *ui*. Spellings such as the following are thus common: *jk*, *jmagineer*, *duijsent*, *huijs*, *Antonj* [= ik, imagineer, duizend, huis, Antony].

ou is occasionally written for *oe*: e.g. *genouch* [genoeg].

ue often occurs instead of *eu* or *uu*: e.g. *curiues*,[2] *generues*, *figuer* [= curieus, genereus, figuur].

uije may represent *uu*: e.g. *vuijer*, *muijer*, [= vuur, muur].

(2) Consonants

c or *ck* commonly stands for *k* (or sometimes *kk*). Leeuwenhoek regularly wrote *ick* [for ik], *welcke* [welke], *oock* [ook], *malcander* [malkander], *clootgens* [klootjes], *comen* [komen], *druckingh* [drukking], *trecking* [trekking], etc.

ch for *g*. For example *nochtans* [nogtans], *weijnich* [weinig]. The terminal *h* was subject to elision, however, before a following aspirate: thus L. wrote *hollicheijt* [holligheid = holheid].

cx or *ckx* for *ks*. Examples: *sulcx*, *sulckx* [zulks].

d = *dt* = *t*. Examples: *hadt* [had], *edelheijdt* [edelheid], *Engelant* [Engeland], *Hollant* [Holland], *goet* [goed], *huijt* [huid], *zad* [zat].

f = *ff* = *v*. Examples: *halff* [half], *selff* [zelf], *off* [of], *beneffens* [benevens].

g = *j*. Examples: *diertgens* [diertjes], *deeltgen* [deeltje].

gh = *g*. E.g. *langh* [lang], *hoogh* [hoog], *verwonderingh* [verwondering].

---

[1] It may be noted, however, that L. generally spelled the noun *haar* [= Engl. hair] as *hair*—not *haer*. He adopted the latter spelling for the possessive pronoun *haar* [= Engl. her, their].

[2] L. also wrote *curieus* and *curius*. He also wrote *couleur* or *couluer* [for *kleur*] indifferently.

qu = *kw* = *k*. E.g. *quaet* [kwaad], *quaelijck* [kwalijk], *manqueeren* [mankeeren].

s = *z*. Examples of this equivalency are too numerous for selection. Words such as *sijn* [zijn], *dese* [deze], *seer* [zeer] occur copiously on every page of the early manuscripts.

sch and *ssch* sometimes stand for *s* or *ss*. Examples: *wasch* [Du. was = Engl. wax], *volwassche* [volwassen].[1] We even find *sch* = *z* occasionally—as in *schonneschijn* [zonneschijn].

th is occasionally written for *t*. E.g. *voortseth* [voortzet].

x sometimes represents modern *ks*. Example: *exter* [ekster].

The *irregular and capricious spellings*—common in English and Dutch of Leeuwenhoek's period, and of no philological importance—are too numerous to mention. Variants may often be found in the very same sentence. It is perhaps worth noting, however, that certain spellings are phonetically interesting—the omission of letters indicating, for example, that they were commonly not pronounced at that date. Thus, the final *-n* (now silent in Dutch, though still heard in Flemish) in a word like *volwassen* was sometimes unwritten (*volwassche*): while Leeuwenhoek also sometimes wrote *seder* (for *sedert*), *ondecking* (for *ontdekking*), *schilpad* (for *schildpad*), *ert* (for *erwt*) etc. He also occasionally added a consonant where it is properly lacking—as in *pampier* (for *papier*) and *miscroscope* (for *microscoop*). The former is a vulgarism, the latter a mistake. What appears at first sight to be a misspelling is occasionally, however, an earlier form—such as the word *mergen* (A.-S. Mergen), which Leeuwenhoek regularly wrote for *morgen* (= Engl. morning, morrow) in his early letters. *Omme* (for *om*: O.Du. *ombe*) occurs very frequently; while *omtrent* and *ontrent* are one as common as the other.

The only other obsolete usages likely to trouble modern foreign readers are the frequent insertion of the negative adverb *en* in phrases such as "*alsoo ick niet* en *versta* ", "*ick niet* en *can*", "*dat ick daer gansch geen sin uijt* en *conde*

---

[1] *-s* and *-ce* may also represent *-sch(e)*: thus, in *Letter* 13*a* we find "*de france tael* " and " *het frans* " in the same sentence—followed by a reference to " *de engelsche tael* " and " *de engelse kerck* ".

verstaen", etc. etc. (in which *en* is now unnecessary and untranslatable): and the habit which Leeuwenhoek (not alone) had of dividing up his compound words into their constituents—*e.g.*, he commonly wrote *over geset*, *voort comen*, *al hoe wel*, *on na speurlijk*, *door gaens*, etc., where we should now write *overgezet*, *voortkomen*, *alhoewel*, *onnaspeurlijk*, *doorgaans*, and so forth.

Leeuwenhoek's language appears, to me, to be full of philological interest; but I am no philologist, and must therefore content myself with noting some of the more obvious etymological and orthographic peculiarities of his writings. In my study of his manuscripts and printed letters I have been greatly aided not only by his contemporary translators but also by the lexicographers of his own period; and for the information of other students I therefore cite the chief dictionaries and other linguistic works which I have found most useful. Oudemans—the standard authority on Old and Middle Dutch—I have consulted only occasionally, on special points. Hexham, Hannot, and Halma have been of frequent assistance, while Kiliaan and Martinez and Minsheu have sometimes helped me over difficulties. Meijer's *Woordenschat* (1745) contains numerous words which I have found in no other vocabulary: I should have used this valuable book more if I had known of its existence earlier. But my chief help, in translating Leeuwenhoek, has been the great dictionary of Sewel (1708)—a man[1] who possessed a wonderful knowledge of the Dutch and English languages in Leeuwenhoek's time. This dictionary has been my constant aid during the last 17 years, and I can confidently recommend it to anyone who wishes to know the exact Dutch and English equivalents of

[1] Willem Sewel (or William Sewell, as he would now be called in English) was born at Amsterdam in 1654. His grandfather was an Englishman, who married a Dutchwoman and settled in Holland. Sewel visited England as a boy, but lived most of his life in Holland, where he was first a weaver, then a journalist and translator, and finally the greatest of Dutch-English lexicographers. His parents were Quakers; and in addition to his dictionary —which first appeared in 1691, and ran through several editions—he wrote a "History of the Rise, Increase, and Progress" of this sect (published in Dutch, 1717, and in English, 1722). Sewel died in 1720, aged 66. As he regarded himself as a Hollander, he would be pained to learn that his life is now to be found in our *Dict. Nat. Biogr.* but in no Dutch biographical works which I have consulted.

words and phrases current in Sewel's day. For modern Dutch and Dutch-English dictionaries I have relied in the main upon van Dale and ten Bruggencate, though I have frequently referred to other similar works. In common with all students of early English, I have received help at times from the well-known *French Dictionary* of Cotgrave, and Florio's famous Italian-English vocabulary. The English dictionaries—of every period—which I have consulted, are all those to which I have had access: they are therefore far too numerous to mention. (I possess and regularly use more than a dozen.) As several old Dutch-English phrase-books and grammars, and the old Dutch Bible, have given me occasional assistance in arriving at the exact meaning of old-fashioned spellings and expressions, I quote the editions of these which I have used.

REFERENCES.—See, in the general bibliography at the end, the following entries especially: *Anonymus* (1658), de Beer & Laurillard (1899), BIBLIA (1702), Bosman (1928), ten Bruggencate (1920), Cappelli (1912), Cotgrave (1650), van Dale (1884), Florio (1688), Halma (1729), Hannot (1719), Heugelenburg (1727), Hexham, (1658, 1660), Kiliaan (1599), *Kilianus auctus* (1642), Maigne d'Arnis (1890), Martinez (1687), Meijer (1745), Minsheu (1627), Oudemans (1869-1880), Sewel (1691, 1708, 1754).

(iii) LEEUWENHOEK'S MICROSCOPES AND MICROSCOPICAL METHODS

Leeuwenhoek left us no description of the apparatus which he used for making his observations on protozoa and bacteria. As we have already seen, he kept "for himself alone" his "best microscopes" and his "particular manner of observing very small creatures." He never divulged his secret method: though undoubtedly he had a real secret, which enabled him to outstrip all other microscopists for at least a century. But he left many microscopes behind him when he died, and a few of these are still in existence. Consequently, we know something about his apparatus, though we can still only guess how he used it in making his "best observations."

The earliest particular accounts of Leeuwenhoek's microscopes are the descriptions of the instruments bequeathed to the Royal Society.[1] Martin Folkes,[2] who examined Leeuwenhoek's cabinet of microscopes shortly after it reached England, has left the following record[3]:

> The Legacy consists of a small *Indian* Cabinet, in the Drawers of which are 13 little Boxes or Cases, each containing two Microscopes, handsomely fitted up in Silver, all which, not only the Glasses, but also the *Apparatus* for managing of them, were made with the late *Mr. Leeuwenhoek*'s own Hands: Besides which, they seem to have been put in Order in the Cabinet by himself, as he design'd them to be presented to the Royal Society, each Microscope having had an Object placed before it, and the Whole being accompany'd with a Register of the same, in his own Hand-Writing, as being desirous the Gentlemen of the Society should, without Trouble, be enabled to examine many of those Objects, on which he had made the most considerable Discoveries.
>
> Several of these Objects yet remain before the Microscopes, tho' the greater Number are broken off, which was probably done by the shaking of the Boxes in the Carriage. I have, nevertheless, added a Translation of the Register, as it may serve to give a juster Idea of what *Mr. Leeuwenhoek* design'd by this Legacy, and also be of Use, by putting any curious Observer in Mind of a Number of Minute Subjects, that may in a particular Manner deserve his Attention.
>
> The 13 Cases abovemention'd are numbered from 15 to 27 inclusively,[4] corresponding to which is the Register of the Objects, Two to every Case, as follows.

---

[1] See p. 95 *supra*. As is well known, these instruments are now all lost. There is no foundation for the statement of Haeser (1853; Vol. I, p. 562: repeated in 3rd ed. 1881) that they are in the British Museum—nor have they ever been there, so far as I am able to ascertain.

[2] See p. 102, note 4, *supra*.

[3] Folkes (1724), p. 447 *sq.* L.'s own description of his cabinet has already been given on p. 96 *supra*.

[4] Baker (1740, p. 507), commenting on these numbers, says "it neces-

No. 15. Globules of Blood, from which its Redness proceeds.

A thin Slice of Wood of the Lime-Tree, where the Vessels conveying the Sap are cut transversely.

No. 16. [Blank.]

The eye of a Gnat.

No. 17. A crooked Hair, to which adheres a Ring-Worm, with a Piece of the Cuticle.

A small Hair from the Hand, by which it appears those Hairs are not round.

No. 18. Flesh of the Codfish (*Cabeljaeuw*) shewing how the fibres lie oblique to the Membranes.

An Embrio of Cochineal, taken from the Egg, in which the Limbs and Horns are conspicuous.

No. 19. Small Pipes, which compose the Elephant's tooth.

Part of the Crystalline Humour, from the Eye of a Whale.

No. 20. A Thread of Sheeps-Wool, which is broken, and appears to consist of many lesser Threads.

The Instrument, whence a Spider spins the Threads, that compose his Web.

No. 21. A Granade, or Spark made in striking Fire.

The Vessels in a leaf of Tea.

No. 22. The *Animalcula in Semine Masculino*, of a Lamb taken from the Testicle, *Jul.* 24. 1702.

A Piece of the Tongue of a Hog, full of sharp Points.

---

sarily implies there were 14 preceding Boxes, since no Man begins with the Number 15.—— Mr. *Leeuwenhoek*, then, had another Cabinet, that held 14 Boxes before ours in numerical Order, and probably each Box contained a Couple of Microscopes, as our Boxes do."

No. 23. A Fibre of Codfish, consisting of long slender Particles.
Another of the same.

No. 24. A Filament, conveying Nourishment to the Nutmeg, cut transversely.
Another Piece of the same, in which the Figure of the Vessels may be seen.

No. 25. Part of the Bone or Tooth abovementioned, consisting of hollow Pipes.
An exceeding thin Membrane, being that which cover'd a very small Muscle.

No. 26. Vessels by which Membranes receive Nourishment and Increase.
A Bunch of Hair from the Insect call'd a Hair-Worm.

No. 27. The double Silk, spun by the Worm.
The Organ of Sight of a Flie.

. . . .

For the Construction of these Instruments, it is the same in them all, and the *Apparatus*[1] is very simple and convenient: They are all single Microscopes, consisting each of a very small double Convex-Glass, let into a Socket, between two Silver Plates rivetted together, and pierc'd with a small Hole: The Object is placed on a Silver Point, or Needle, which, by Means of Screws of the same Metal, provided for that Purpose, may be turn'd about, rais'd, or depress'd, and brought nearer or put farther from the Glass, as the Eye of the Observer, the Nature of the Object, and the convenient Examination of its several Parts may require.

Mr. *Leeuwenhoek* fix'd his Objects, if they were solid, to this Silver Point, with Glew; and when they were Fluid, or of such a Nature as not to be commodiously

---

[1] The reader will be better able to follow Folkes's description if he here looks at my figure 1 on Plate XXXI, facing p. 328.

view'd unless spread upon Glass, he first fitted them on a little Plate of Talk, or excessively thin-blown Glass, which he afterwards glewed to the Needle, in the same Manner as his other Objects.

. . . .

The Glasses are all exceedingly clear, and shew the Object very bright and distinct, which must be owing to the great Care this Gentleman took, in the Choice of his Glass,[1] his Exactness in giving it the true Figure; and afterwards, amongst many, reserving such only for his Use, as he, upon Tryal, found to be most excellent. Their Powers of magnifying are different, as different Sorts of Objects may require; and, as on the one Hand, being all ground Glasses, none of them are so small, and consequently magnify to so great a Degree, as some of those Drops, frequently us'd in other Microscopes; yet, on the other, the Distinctness of these very much exceeds what I have met with in the Glasses of that Sort.

Folkes gives no figures and no further information of material importance, though he makes the interesting statement that Leeuwenhoek had previously presented to Queen Mary,[2] when she visited him at Delft, "A Couple of his Microscopes, which, as I have been inform'd by one who had them a considerable Time in his Hands, were of the same Sort as these, and did not any ways differ from one of the 13 Cases contain'd in the Drawers of this Cabinet." [3]

---

[1] This is a very shrewd remark. Undoubtedly L. knew a great deal about glass, and he was an expert glass-blower—as his recorded experiments prove. He learnt the art by watching a professional at the fair in Delft, and then practising by himself at home.

[2] Mary II of England, wife of William III of Orange. She died in 1694. Folkes calls her "the late Queen Mary," and clearly did not mean her sister and successor, Queen Anne (died 1714). Halbertsma (1843, p.14) appears to have confused these two Queens when he says that L. was visited by "Anna Maria."

[3] Folkes (1724), pp. 450-1. Nothing else is now known about these instruments, which have long since vanished—like those presented to the Royal Society.

The only other descriptions of the Royal Society's microscopes were given some years later by Henry Baker[1] (1740,[2] 1753), who determined their magnifying powers and—in his second publication—also gave two diagrammatic representations of the instruments. Baker tells us that Leeuwenhoek's microscopes were under his examination for three months,[3] but he found Folkes had already given "such an exact and full Description of their Structure and Uses, as renders any farther Attempt to that Purpose intirely needless."[4] He notes that most of the objects before the glasses were even then (1740) "destroyed by Time, or struck off by Accident; which indeed is no Wonder, as they were only glewed on a Pin's Point, and left quite unguarded. Nine or Ten of them, however, are still remaining; which after cleaning the Glasses, appeared extremely plain and distinct, and proved the great skill of Mr. Leeuwenhoek . . ." He then makes the interesting further remark that Leeuwenhoek's skill was also shown "in the Contrivance of the Apertures of his Glasses, which, when the Object was transparent, he made exceeding small, since much Light in that Case would be prejudicial; But, when the Object itself was dark, he inlarged the Aperture, to give it all possible Advantage of the Light."[5]

But we are chiefly indebted to this verbose amateur for having carefully determined the focal length and magnifying power of every lens in the collection—notwithstanding he

---

[1] Henry Baker (1698-1774) was a Londoner, whose varied activities included dabbling in science. As a boy he was apprenticed to a bookseller, but later he made a fortune by teaching deaf mutes by a secret method of his own. In 1729 he married the youngest daughter of Daniel Defoe. He was elected F.R.S. in 1741, and by his will endowed the "Bakerian Lecture" of the Society. In early life he wrote much poetry and light literature. His chief contributions to science were two popular books on the microscope—mainly compilations, containing little original. In these works, which ran through many editions and were translated into several languages, he drew largely on L.'s letters. Cf. *Dict. Nat. Biogr.* and *Rec. Roy. Soc.*

[2] Though dated 1740, this paper must have been published considerably later: for it contains a reference to the 2nd edition of Baker's *Microscope Made Easy* (1743 : 1st ed. 1742), and he styles himself F.R.S.—to which he was not elected until 12 March 1741.

[3] Baker (1753), p. 434 footnote.

[4] Baker (1740), p. 504.

[5] Baker (1740), p. 504.

"was sensible it must cost much Trouble." "This Task," he says, "I have performed, with as much care and Exactness as I was able." His results were summarized in a table, which I here reproduce in full:[1]

A Table *of the* Focal Distances *of Mr.* Leeuwenhoek'*s* 26 *Microscopes, calculated by an Inch Scale divided into* 100 *Parts; with a Computation of their magnifying Powers, to an Eye that sees small Objects at* 8 *Inches, which is the common Standard.*

Microscopes with the same Focus.	Distance of the Focus.	Power of magnifying the Diameter of an Object.	Power of magnifying the Superficies.
	Parts of an Inch	*Times*	*Times*
* 1.	$\frac{1}{20}$ or $\frac{5}{100}$	160	25600.
1.	$\frac{6}{100}$	133 nearly	17689.
1.	$\frac{7}{100}$	114 nearly	12996.
3.	$\frac{8}{100}$	100	10000.
3.	$\frac{9}{100}$	89 almost	7921 almost.
8.	$\frac{1}{10}$	80	6400.
2.	$\frac{11}{100}$	72 something more.	5184 something more.
3.	$\frac{12}{100}$	66 nearly	4356 nearly.
2.	$\frac{14}{100}$	57	3249.
1.	$\frac{15}{100}$	53 nearly	2809 nearly.
1.	$\frac{1}{5}$	40	1600.
26			

* This largest Magnifier of all is in the Box marked 25. [Note by Baker.]

Baker himself notes regarding these figures: "I have given the Calculations in round Numbers, the Fractions making but an inconsiderable Difference; and I hope any Mistakes I may have made in so nice a Matter will be excused". I must also note—since it has been generally overlooked—that all the magnifications are given for an image-distance (8 inches) which is not the "common standard" now universally adopted (10 inches). Consequently, all Baker's "magnifying powers" represent only $\frac{4}{5}$ of the actual magnification according to modern notation: and therefore the "largest Magnifier", with

[1] Baker (1740), p. 506. The later description (Baker, 1753; p. 436), though that usually quoted, gives far less detail.

a focal length of $\frac{1}{20}$ in., magnified not 160 but 200 diameters according to present-day reckoning—and so on throughout.

After a somewhat lengthy discussion, Baker reaches the conclusion that Leeuwenhoek's best microscopes, with which he made his most considerable discoveries, "must certainly have been much greater Magnifiers than any in our Possession" —a conclusion which was then well founded.

I need not give Baker's illustrations of a Leeuwenhoek microscope—which have often been copied—nor their accompanying description,[1] for more instructive data are now available: but I must here quote some other contemporary records which throw more light on the present subject.

It is well known that Leeuwenhoek left many microscopes with his daughter when he died. Apart from the 26 bequeathed to the Royal Society there were some hundreds of others—though their number is generally misstated. Maria did not sell any of these instruments, but preserved them all her life. After her own death (1745), however, they were put up for auction and dispersed. Copies of the sale-catalogue (1747) are still extant; but the late Professor P. Harting, of Utrecht, possessed a unique example which is of the greatest interest and on which he has left some valuable notes[2]. I shall therefore here translate his words *verbatim*, as they contain information now unobtainable elsewhere. In 1850 he wrote:[3]

> I have in my possession two copies of the catalogue of Leeuwenhoek's microscopes, drawn up for the auction which took place on Monday the 29th of May, 1747. One of these copies was probably used by the notary or auctioneer at the time of the sale, for it is interleaved with white paper on which the names of all the buyers, and the prices fetched by the instruments, are carefully recorded. The catalogue is got up rather more luxuriously than is customary at the present day; for it is printed

---

[1] Baker (1753), pp. 434-436; Plate XVII, figs. VII and VIII. (Dutch edition [1770], pp. 453-456; Pl. XVII, afb. 7 & 8.)

[2] Haaxman (1875), p. 38, has also described this catalogue, but adds nothing material to Harting's account.

[3] *Het Mikroskoop*, Vol. III, p. 41 footnote. I have been unable to discover what happened to Harting's copies of the catalogue after his death.

on heavy writing-paper, while a pretty allegorical copper-plate engraving is placed at the beginning, along with another displaying Leeuwenhoek's portrait. The text is in Dutch and Latin both.

From this catalogue it appears that Leeuwenhoek left no less than 247 completely finished microscopes, each provided with a lens, and generally also with an object; and, in addition to these, 172 lenses merely mounted between little plates—419 lenses in all, therefore. Among these lenses there are three made from so-called "Amersfoort diamond" (rock-crystal pebble)[1]; and of one of the microscopes it is noted that its magnifying-glass is ground from a sand-grain, while the object placed before it is likewise a sand-grain. Two microscopes are specified as having two glasses, another three. It thus appears that Leeuwenhoek also manufactured doublets and triplets[2]; for, with his kind of apparatus, there can obviously be no question of any proper compound microscope. More than half of these microscopes (approximately 160) were mounted in silver. Among the rest there are three made of gold—two of which weighed 10 engels[3] 17 grains, the third 10 engels 14 grains. One of the former was sold for 23 florins 15 stivers, while both the others were bought in. (This is probably the only occasion on which microscopes have been sold by weight.) The remaining microscopes were sold in pairs. The brass ones fetched 15 stivers to 3 florins a pair, the silver 2 to 7 florins. The entire sale realized a sum of 737 florins and 3 stivers.[4] The names of the buyers show that all these

---

[1] *i.e.* quartz. I know of no evidence to show that L. ever made lenses from real diamonds—as is sometimes stated (*e.g.* by Nordenskiöld, 1929; p. 165).

[2] It now seems more probable that these were really double (or triple) *simple* microscopes—*i.e.* 2 (or 3) single lenses mounted in the same frame side by side—like the "double microscope" illustrated by Haaxman (1875) p. 34, fig. 2A.

[3] An *engels* equals 32 grains: see p. 338 *infra*.

[4] About £61. 10*s.* in modern English currency.

microscopes were purchased by Hollanders,[1] and it is therefore surprising that one nowadays so seldom meets with any surviving specimens of Leeuwenhoek's instruments in this country.

Elsewhere Harting has published a list of the objects which Leeuwenhoek left fixed before his magnifying-glasses—as mentioned in the sale-catalogue. Though they include—like Folkes's list—no protozoological or bacteriological items, they seem sufficiently interesting to quote. According to Harting, they were as follows:[2]

Animal Objects

Muscle-fibres of a whale.
„ „ „ codfish.
„ „ the heart of a duck.
Transverse section of the muscles of a fish.
Scales from human skin.
Crystalline lens of an ox.
Blood-corpuscles of a man.
Liver of a pig.
Transverse section of the bladder.
Bladder of an ox.
Papillae from the tongue of an ox.
Hair of sheep.
„ „ beaver.
„ „ elk.
„ „ bear.
„ out of the [human] nose.
Scale of a perch.
„ „ „ sole.
Spinning-apparatus of a spider.
Thread [web] „ „ „
Sting „ „ „
Teeth „ „ „
Eyes „ „ „
Spinning-apparatus of a silk-worm.

[1] The names of all the purchasers (42 in number) have since been printed in Harting (1876), p. 33.

[2] Translated from Harting (1850): *Het Mikroskoop*, Vol. III, p. 465.

Brains of a fly.
Optic nerves of a fly.
Tips of the feet of a fly.
Sting and sheath of a flea.
Feet „ „ „
Eyes of a dragon-fly.
„ „ „ beetle.
Sting of a louse.
Skin „ „ „
Ovipositor „ „ „
Red coral.
Section of oyster-shell.
Embryo oysters in a little [glass] tube.

Vegetable Objects

Transverse and longitudinal sections of elm-wood.
„ „ „ „ „ fir-wood.
„ „ „ „ „ ebony.
„ „ „ „ „ lime-wood.
„ „ „ „ „ oak-wood.
„ „ „ „ „ cinnamon.
„ „ „ „ „ cork.
„ „ „ „ „ rush.
Section of fossil wood.
Germ out of the seed of rye.
Vascular bundles out of a nutmeg.

Mineral Objects

Bits of white marble, rock-crystal, diamond, gold-leaf, gold-dust, silver-ore, saltpetre, crystals, etc.

Harting was fortunately able to examine one of Leeuwenhoek's few surviving lenses carefully: and as his tests are the only recent ones made by an expert—so far as I am aware—I must here note what he found. He reports[1] that the biconvex lens which he studied was "really very good indeed", and proved that its maker had attained "a very high degree of proficiency in grinding extremely small glasses." Its magnifying power was no less than 270 diameters [indicating a focal

---

[1] *Het Mikroskoop* (1850), Vol. III, pp. 43, 44.

length of about 0·9 mm.]: and its resolution was so good that, with suitable illumination, it was capable of resolving the 4th group of lines on a Nobert test-plate (*i.e.*, a scale 10 μ long subdivided into 7 equal parts by parallel lines ruled with a diamond on glass[1]). In Harting's opinion this was probably the optical limit of Leeuwenhoek's lenses: but the lens which he studied was only one of hundreds, and some of the others —now lost—may well have been superior.[2]

Leeuwenhoek himself has—to my knowledge[3]—left us no account of his particular procedure in making and mounting lenses. Others published their methods,[4] but he never did. How to grind and polish lenses for spectacles and telescopes was common property, however, at the time when he wrote; and it seems probable that he worked by the ordinary rules and with the customary apparatus. If you had asked him how to make a very powerful lens, of very short focus, he would doubtless have told you that it could only be made by the usual methods: but as such a glass would be much smaller, and more convex, you would have to do everything on a smaller scale, and pay more attention to details. If you can make a good lens with a focus of 1 foot, then you can—if you take pains, and know your job—make an equally good one with a focus of $\frac{1}{100}$ of an inch. It is more difficult, and takes longer; but that is all. It is a question only of the time and trouble that you are prepared to expend. The general methods of grinding and polishing lenses were no secrets: and when Leibniz asked old Leeuwenhoek why he did not educate a school of younger men in the art, he made the following reply:[5]

---

[1] *Op. cit.*, Vol. I, p. 404.

[2] The lens examined by Harting was in a microscope preserved, at that date, in the physical collection at Utrecht. The instrument now in the zoological collection of the same university is greatly inferior—its lens having a focal length of about $\frac{1}{4}$ in. (*fide* Mayall, 1886).

[3] Crommelin (1929), in his recent admirable essay on lens-grinding [and lens-grinders] in the 17th century, is of the same opinion. On this subject, he says, L. "has left us entirely in the dark".

[4] See especially Manzini (1660).

[5] *Send-brief* XVIII, pp. 168-9 [*Epist. Physiol.* XVIII, p. 167]. Letter dated 28 Sept. 1715. Not in *Phil. Trans.*

To train young people to grind lenses, and to found a sort of school for this purpose, I can't see there'd be much use: because many students at Leyden have already been fired by my discoveries and my lens-grinding, and three lens-grinders have gone there in consequence; to whom the students have repaired, to learn how to grind lenses. But what's come of it? Nothing, as far as I know: because most students go there to make money out of science, or to get a reputation in the learned world. But in lens-grinding, and discovering things hidden from our sight, these count for nought. And I'm satisfied too that not one man in a thousand is capable of such study, because it needs much time, and spending much money; and you must always keep on thinking about these things, if you are to get any results. And over and above all, most men are not curious to know: nay, some even make no bones about saying, What does it matter whether we know this or not?

In addition to Folkes's and Baker's and Harting's descriptions there are many other brief accounts and figures of Leeuwenhoek's instruments. The first picture of his "microscope" is that introduced into Verkolje's mezzotint (1686), in which Leeuwenhoek is depicted holding one in his own hand (see Frontispiece). A similar piece of apparatus is probably meant to be shown in the hands of the allegorical personages represented in two of the engraved titles to his works.[1] Baker (1753) gave, with his description, a couple of poor diagrams which have been copied over and over again—by Hoole (1807) and many others down to Disney (1928) and Bulloch (1930) at the present day. Uffenbach (1754) also pretended to portray "Leeuwenhoek's microscope"; while a small but excellent figure (from an unknown example) was engraved on the title-page of the booklet by van Haastert (1823). Other pictures—sometimes accompanied by descriptions—are to be found in the works of Harting (1850),

[1] See *Ontled. & Ontdekk.* (1686) = *Anat. s. Int. Rer.* (1687): *Vijfde Vervolg d. Brieven* (1696) = *Arc. Nat. Det.* (1695). These engravings should also be found (somewhere or other) bound up in all the Dutch and Latin collective editions of L.'s letters.

Haaxman (1871, 1875), Mayall (1886), Locy (1910, 1925), Sabrazès (1926), and divers other writers. "Leeuwenhoek's microscope" has even appeared in a recent film, in a modern advertisement for a proprietary dentifrice, and in popular periodicals—such as the Dutch illustrated weekly *De Prins*, which lately published (3 January 1925) the best photograph which I have yet seen.

Although Leeuwenhoek made and left many microscopes, nearly all of them have long since disappeared. Not only have those bequeathed to the Royal Society vanished without trace,[1] but even some of the few other examples mentioned by Haaxman and Harting—still surviving in 1875—cannot now be found. According to my friend Professor Crommelin (1929*a*) only 8 specimens in all are now known to exist, 5 of which are in Holland. Of these, 1 is in the Zoological Institute at Utrecht, and 3 others were, until recently, in the private possession of Mr P. A. Haaxman at The Hague: but 2 of the latter have now passed into the Historical Scientific Museum at Leyden, and have thus become the property of the Dutch nation.[2] (All three were exhibited at a congress in Leyden in 1907. Cf. van Leersum, de Feyfer, and Molhuysen, pp. 114, 115.) I am informed that two other genuine instruments are now in Germany—one in a well-known museum, the other in the possession of an optical firm: but I have not yet been able to verify these statements. I have also been told[3] that the late Dr Henri Van Heurck, of Antwerp, had an authentic specimen of Leeuwenhoek's handiwork in his collection which was sold in 1914. The Nachet Collection (Paris) also claims to possess one.[4] Neither in England nor America,

---

[1] There seems to be a general suspicion—probably fostered by some injudicious remarks of Saville Kent (Vol. I, p. 9, footnote)—that Baker, the last man known to have handled these instruments, was in some way responsible for their disappearance. This is entirely unjustifiable: for a search through the Society's records (made on my behalf by Mr A. H. White, our learned librarian) has shown that we still possessed L.'s microscopes long after Baker's death. They vanished from the Royal Society's collection only about a century ago, and the few remaining records appear to incriminate a very different person.

[2] Cf. Crommelin (1929*a*).

[3] By Mr W. E. Watson Baker, who—with his father—valued the collection before the sale.

[4] The Nachet Catalogue, I may remark, is grossly inaccurate in nearly

however, is there any genuine specimen (so far as I have been able to ascertain), though modern facsimile reproductions are now in circulation in both these countries. These copies are accurate, and some of them may before long be passed off as authentic originals. More than one such exact facsimile was made for the late Sir Frank Crisp, who preserved one example in his private collection and presented another to the Royal Microscopical Society of London (on 21 January 1914), in whose rooms it can now be seen.[1] Crisp's own facsimile was sold at Stevens's in London on 17 February 1925, when his collection was auctioned after his death.[2] Other similar reproductions are also in existence. One was recently in California, and a friend of mine (who saw it) states that its owner assured him that he could obtain similar "Leeuwenhoek microscopes" at any time—for a price—from Holland. Be this as it may, there are certainly facsimiles (and forgeries?) now on the market, and prospective purchasers should be on their guard.

Most of the recent descriptions and pictures of "Leeuwenhoek's microscope" are based on the rather poor specimen now preserved in the Zoological Laboratory at Utrecht. The best account and figures[3] of this instrument are, I think, those of Mayall (1886): but as I am not wholly satisfied with his or any other description or pictures (Mayall, apparently, never saw the microscope which he described), I shall here attempt to revise his version with the help of a few drawings of my own. My account is based on personal examination of three genuine specimens, one copy, and a study of all other available data. I must point out, however, that my own figures (Plate XXXI) were not drawn from any actual instrument. They form a composite design—a generalized

---

all its references to L. (see Nachet, 1929). I have not seen the instrument in this collection; but from the description and picture it appears suspiciously like one of the recent copies of the Utrecht example.

[1] Cf. Disney (1928), p. 160. This instrument is evidently a copy of the original now in the Zoological Institute at Utrecht, and most of the other copies appear to have been made from the same example. One such has been figured recently by Becking (1924).

[2] See the *Catalogue* of this sale, Lot 1.

[3] Woodcuts, made directly from photographs. These excellent figures have recently been reproduced (as line blocks) by Disney *et al.* (1928, Plate 1) without acknowledgement.

representation of "a Leeuwenhoek microscope"—embodying all the features common to the extant examples. I have tried to show the mechanism as simply as possible and with the fewest and most easily comprehensible drawings, because I find all previous accounts incomplete, inaccurate, or difficult to understand. Several describers, indeed, do not themselves appear to have grasped the mechanism—either literally or metaphorically. My drawings are based primarily on the microscopes formerly in the possession of Mr P. A. Haaxman (The Hague), whose daughter—Mejuffrouw S. A. E. Haaxman—very kindly permitted me (on 29 June 1923) to take one of these priceless little instruments to pieces, sketch the various parts, and reassemble it. For the accuracy of my description I rely chiefly upon the notes and tracings which I made on this occasion. Unfortunately I have had no opportunity of testing any of Leeuwenhoek's lenses.

All Leeuwenhoek's microscopes had an appearance like that shown in Plate XXXI, fig. 1. Properly speaking, they were not "microscopes" at all, but—as he himself usually called them—simple "magnifying-glasses". Each consisted of a single biconvex lens (not a system of lenses); and the mechanical parts were contrived not to focus this lens upon an object lying on a fixed stage (as in a modern compound microscope), but in order to bring a movable object into the focus of the glass, which was itself fixed. It is important to realize this fundamental point in the design, which is highly original. It should also be emphasized that all these instruments were very small—even smaller than my drawings. They were generally made of the same metal throughout, though different metals were used (brass, copper, silver, and even gold occasionally): and the workmanship and finish were none too good. Leeuwenhoek concentrated his attention upon the optical part of his "microscopes": and when he had succeeded in grinding and polishing and mounting a good lens, he evidently did not think it worth while to spend a lot of time in finishing off its mechanical accessories, which were made just good enough for his purpose.

Fig. 1 (Plate XXXI) shows the whole instrument from the back, as fitted up ready for use. Figs. 2 and 3 illustrate details; and fig. 4 is a diagrammatic longitudinal section. These drawings will, I hope, almost explain themselves—if carefully studied; but I may add the following notes:

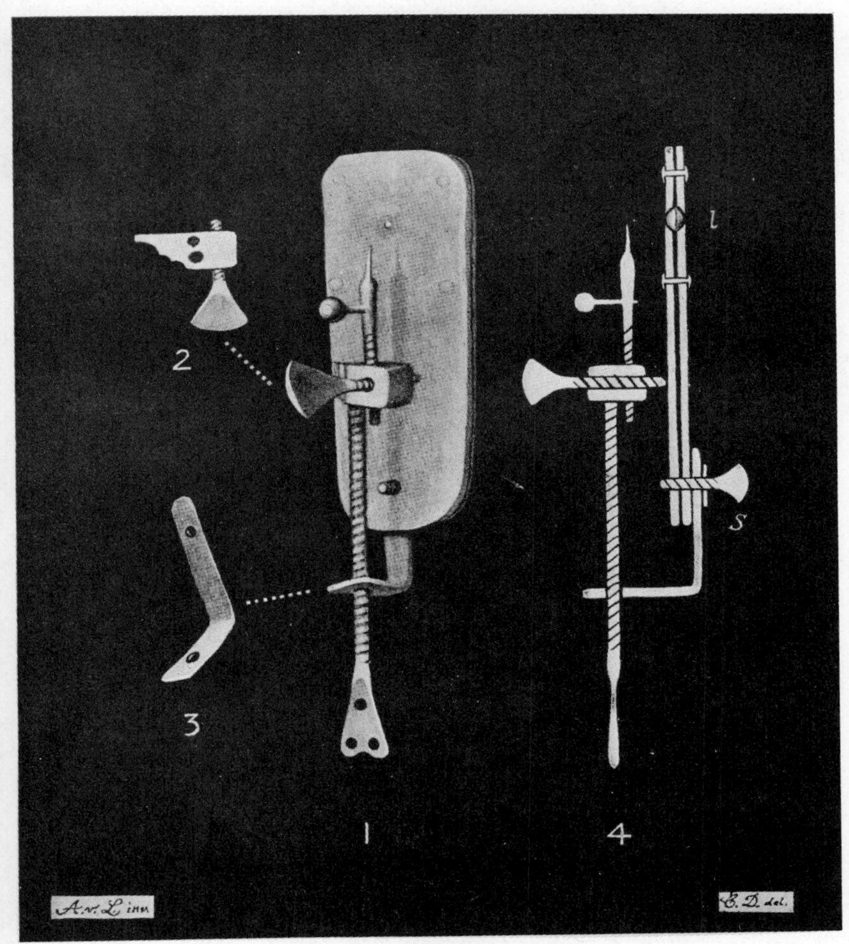

LEEUWENHOEK'S "MICROSCOPE"

For explanation see the text.

The minute biconvex lens (*l*, fig. 4) was mounted between two thin oblong plates of brass (or other metal). Towards one end of each plate, at the same point in the middle line, a concavity was ground or punched and a hole pierced in its centre. When these apertures had been made to coincide exactly, the lens was clamped between the plates, in the concavities (as shown in fig. 4), and secured by four equidistant rivets forming the corners of a square (see fig. 1) with the lens at its centre. In other words, the rivets and the lens—in surface view—formed a quincunx, the lens occupying the central spot.

The two oblong metal plates[1] with the lens thus mounted between them constitute the essential optical part of the instrument. Leeuwenhoek probably kept many of his lenses so mounted, and fixed interchangeable mechanical parts to them as required. These mechanical accessories—for focussing the object before the lens—are shown in the figures and have been well described by Mayall in his *Cantor Lectures* (1886) as follows: "The object is held in front of the lens, on the point of a short rod, the other end of which screws into a small block or stage of brass [whose peculiar shape is shown from above in fig. 2], which is rivetted somewhat loosely on the smoothed cylindrical end of a long coarse-threaded screw [figs. 1, 4] acting through a socket angle-piece [fig. 3] attached behind the lower end of the plates by a small thumb-screw [*s*, fig. 4. Only the projecting end of this screw is visible in fig. 1. It is furnished with a roughly-fashioned metal washer above the angle-piece—shown in section in fig. 4]. The long screw serves to adjust the object under the lens in a vertical direction, whilst the pivoting of the angle-piece [fig. 3] on its thumb-screw [fig. 4, *s*] gives lateral motion. The object-carrier can be turned on its axis, as required, by screwing the rod into the stage [by means of a metal knob, shown in figs. 1 and 4. When the rod is rotated by moving the knob, the object is not only turned on its axis but raised or lowered by the screw passing through the block—thus forming a sort of "fine adjustment" for the "coarse adjustment" provided by the long screw]. For focussing, a thumb-

---

[1] The brass lens-holding plates of the best Haaxman specimen measure approximately 41 mm. by 18 mm.; but their sides are not accurately parallel, and their corners are roughly rounded.

screw passes through the stage near one end [figs. 1, 2, 4], and presses vertically against the plates, causing the stage to tilt up at that end; the fitting of the long screw-carrier (angle-piece [fig. 3]) is such that the stage at the end is sprung down somewhat forcibly on the brass plates, and it is against this pressure that the focussing screw acts."

As we have already heard, the object to be viewed was either stuck directly on to the pin of the object-carrier, or else it was first mounted in some way (*e.g.*, on a small plate of glass or mica, or between two thin glass plates like a modern slide and coverslip, or in a capillary glass tube) and the whole was then fixed and focussed before the lens. A "microscope" of this type, with a lens of very short focus and high magnification, must have been extremely awkward to manipulate. It would be necessary to place the eye almost in contact with the lens, and it is not clear how Leeuwenhoek was able to obtain the requisite illumination. The known *magnifying power* of his best glasses was, of course, sufficient to enlarge objects as small as blood-corpuscles (and even bacteria) to visually perceptible dimensions—a fact which modern workers with the compound microscope seem apt to overlook. With the front lens of my 2 mm. apochromatic objective—having a magnification of about 120 diameters—I can distinctly see (using the light of a clear sky only) bacteria as small as *Bacillus coli* in a stained film. But to see such organisms alive in water, and with sufficient clarity to describe their movements, is another matter. (My own eyesight, I should note, is exceptionally good—probably but little inferior to Leeuwenhoek's.) Yet Leeuwenhoek not only knew how to make lenses of adequate magnifying power and aperture and resolution, and sufficiently free from spherical and chromatic aberration, but he also understood how to obtain the necessary *visibility*. He was able, in some way, to get the indispensable contrast between the object and its background which we now readily obtain by means of central stops, iris diaphragms, or staining.

It appears to me certain, indeed, that Leeuwenhoek cannot have made his extraordinarily accurate observations on bacteria and protozoa by means of the apparatus just described *when used in the ordinary way*. He had unbounded patience and magnificent eyesight—as his works abundantly testify—

but he could not perform miracles. Moreover, there is no reason to suppose that he possessed any apparatus essentially different from that which is now known. (Blanchard's suggestion (1868) that he destroyed his best instruments in his old age "with the idea of continuing to appear to everybody as an incomparable observer", is quite unjustifiable.) All the evidence indicates that it was *the method of using* this apparatus which he "kept for himself alone": his secret lay, as he tells us repeatedly, in his "particular *method* of observing." What can it have been? The answer is—to me—almost certain, though I cannot prove from his own words (since he tried not to give his secret away) that I am right. I am convinced that Leeuwenhoek had, in the course of his experiments, hit upon some simple method of *dark-ground illumination*. He was well aware, as we know, of the ordinary properties of lenses; and he tells us himself that he used concave magnifying mirrors and employed artificial sources of illumination (*e.g.* a candle). Consequently, he may well have discovered by accident—or even have purposely devised—some method which gave him a clear dark-ground image. Such a discovery—possibly inspired by observing the motes in a sunbeam—would at once explain all his otherwise inexplicable observations, without supposing him to have possessed any apparatus other than that which we now know he had. But no hint was ever knowingly given, in all his many letters (so far as I have been able to ascertain), of what his "particular method of observing" may really have been.

Nevertheless, there is, in a very early letter, a remark which seems to me to substantiate my interpretation—though one must, I think, be personally familiar with such things to appreciate it properly. Writing about red blood-corpuscles in 1675, Leeuwenhoek (in reply to criticism) says:[1]

> . . . but I can demonstrate to myself the globules [= corpuscles] in the blood as sharp and clean as one can distinguish with one's eyes, without any help of glasses, *sandgrains that one might bestrew upon a piece of black taffety silk.*[2]

---

[1] From *Letter 9*. 22 January 1675. To Oldenburg. MS.Roy.Soc. Unpublished.

[2] The words I have here interpreted and italicized are, in the original, "*de santgens . . . diemen op een swart sijde taff soude mogen werpen*".

Taffeta (formerly *taffety* or *taffata*—a word of Persian origin) is a name now applied to various coloured fabrics of wavy lustre: but in earlier times it denoted a silken cloth of uniform texture—when black, much used for mourning. It should be remembered that Leeuwenhoek speaks here not only as a microscopist but also as a draper; and he therefore meant that he could see human red blood-corpuscles under his microscope just as clearly as he could see sandgrains scattered on a piece of the smooth black silk he sold in his shop. The more I consider these words, the more am I convinced that nobody could ever have thought of such a simile unless he had seen red corpuscles under dark-ground illumination. Their appearance by transmitted light is wholly different, and could never suggest such a comparison. To my mind these words furnish an almost conclusive proof that Leeuwenhoek's "particular method of observing very small objects" was some simple system of dark-field lighting, used in combination with his ordinary microscopes. It is idle to speculate on *how* he may have achieved this result: it is sufficient to note that such a supposition will easily explain all his otherwise inexplicable observations. (It readily explains, for instance, how he was able to see flagella and cilia and spirochaetes and micrococci with a magnification of only some 200-300 diameters.) But as he himself would say, "I hand this notion over to others."

Leeuwenhoek's apparatus for viewing the circulation in the tail of an eel was fully described and illustrated by himself.[1] It is a peculiar instrument, designed for a special purpose, and not his "microscope" proper—though it has more than once been figured as such by later writers. I need not consider it here. I may note, however, that one of these instruments is now in the Leyden Museum (with some lenses made and mounted for it by himself, and a copy by another maker). Leeuwenhoek's own figures[2] show that he sometimes used the lenses of his "microscopes"—mounted between two oblong metal plates, as already described—in fitting up this

---

[1] *Letter 66.* 12 January 1689. To the Royal Society. Printed in Dutch and Latin works, but not in *Phil. Trans.* The original is preserved among the Boyle MSS. of the Royal Society.

[2] See especially fig. 8, on the plate accompanying this letter.

apparatus. His magnifying-glasses were evidently so designed that they could be used interchangeably for "microscopes" or "enchelyscopes", as occasion required, by adding the appropriate mechanical parts.

I may also note here that Leeuwenhoek was one of the first—if not the very first—to study the structure of solid opaque bodies by means of sections. Some which he cut with his own hand "by means of a sharp shaving razor" are still in existence. They were enclosed in a little packet affixed to an early letter,[1] and have remained intact to the present day. According to his own description, they are (1) "Cork"; (2) "White of a writing pen" [parings from a quill]; (3) "Bits of the optic nerve of a cow, cut crosswise"; (4) "Pith of elder." He added the following suggestions for looking at these objects:

> . . . . I would venture to recommend that, when one of these sections has been brought upon the pin of a microscope, you then hold the microscope towards the open sky, within doors, and out of the sunshine, as though you had a telescope and were trying to look at the stars in the sky through it.

LEEUWENHOEK'S MICROMETRY.—Before the invention of micrometers it was extremely difficult to measure very small objects under the microscope: their size could, indeed, be only estimated, by reference to other objects of known dimensions. On an earlier page[2] we have read Leeuwenhoek's own account of the way in which he assessed the probable magnitude of various animalcules, but a few further notes are necessary.

Leeuwenhoek took the *inch* (of his land and period) as an absolute unit for small measurements. A copper rule,[3] with

---

[1] *Letter 4.* 1 June 1674. To Oldenburg. MS.Roy.Soc. Partly published in English in *Phil. Trans.* (1674), Vol. IX, No. 106, p. 121. L. also sent a copy of this letter to Const. Huygens, and this copy—now in the Leyden library—has recently been printed in its original Dutch by Vandevelde and van Seters (1925).

[2] See p. 201 *seq.*, *supra.*

[3] Referred to on p. 189 *supra.*

the inches subdivided into tenths, was his standard. Fortunately, he had this engraved for one of his later letters,[1] so that it can now be measured. From the picture it appears that his "inch" was approximately 26·15 mm., and therefore slightly greater than the modern English inch (25·4 mm.).[2] His own drawing of a cubic inch (p. 189 *supra*) confirms this determination.

The commonest objects with which Leeuwenhoek compares "animalcules" are a sandgrain, a human red blood-corpuscle, a vinegar-eel, and a millet seed. He also used other more or less verifiable measures, however, such as "a hairsbreadth," "the diameter of a louse's eye," "the bigness of a hair on a louse," etc. I may say a word on each of these.

Sandgrains are Leeuwenhoek's common standard of comparison. At first sight it seems impossible to translate these highly variable structures[3] into exact modern measurements, but it is actually—from the information which he supplies—quite feasible. He generally referred to two kinds of sand—coarse and fine. A *fine sandgrain*, according to the letter translated on p. 188, was about $\frac{1}{80}$ inch in diameter: but elsewhere[4] he states that 100 of his very small sandgrains, laid end to end, equalled about an inch. This seems to be the usual magnitude he had in mind—*i.e.*, about $\frac{1}{100}$ of an inch, or (using his scale) approximately 260 μ. A *coarse sandgrain*, according to his own statement,[5] was about $\frac{1}{30}$ inch in

---

[1] *Send-brief* XXVIII, to Boerhaave. 28 September 1716. Also published in Latin in *Epist. Physiol.* and *Op. Omn.* The plate faces p. 271 of the Dutch edition, and p. 266 of the Latin.

[2] The scale in the figure is 5 inches long, and is accurately delineated. A fair average can therefore be readily obtained for 1 inch. But as the actual engraving was made on copper, and the prints are on paper (which was wetted, and then shrank somewhat), I have made my estimate from 4 different prints in my possession (which differ only very slightly from one another). The mean for 1 inch (here given) is therefore derived from the combined measurements of 20 printed inches.

[3] L. said himself (*Send-brief* XLI, 26 Aug. 1717) that "as big as a grain of sand" is an inaccurate expression, and it would be better to use a millet seed or a mustard seed for comparison.

[4] *Letter 35*, to R. Hooke. 3 March 1682. Published in Dutch and Latin works.

[5] *Letter 42*, to the Royal Society. 25 July 1684. Published in Dutch and Latin works.

diameter, and therefore some 870 μ. These magnitudes seem to agree well with all Leeuwenhoek's inferences—so far as I have been able to check them.

A *Red Blood-corpuscle* (of man) measures about 7·5 μ in diameter, and Leeuwenhoek's frequent choice of this structure as a standard of size has been amply confirmed by all later microscopists. Even today we commonly see an outline of a human erythrocyte inserted among drawings of microscopic organisms as an indication of their relative magnitude.

It may be remarked here that Leeuwenhoek himself had a very good idea of the actual diameter of a red corpuscle, though he could not express it exactly in terms of any micrometric unit: for he notes in one place[1] that he had satisfied himself that 100 diameters of a red corpuscle amounted to something less than that of a coarse grain of sand (which he had just assessed at $\frac{1}{30}$ inch). Consequently, he imagined the diameter of a corpuscle to be rather less than $\frac{1}{3000}$ of an inch—an astonishingly good estimate.[2]

The *Vinegar-Eel* (the nematode *Anguillula aceti*) is assigned various sizes in the text-books. I have cultivated and studied this worm at various times, and find that ordinary large individuals (females) may measure anything from about 1200 μ to 1700 μ in length. "A full-grown eel such as we see in vinegar" is approximately 1·5 mm. long, and this agrees quite well with all Leeuwenhoek's references.

A *Millet Seed* is more difficult to appraise. There are now many kinds of millet (*Panicum miliaceum*)—"a name applied with little definiteness to a considerable number of often very variable species of cereals, belonging to distinct genera and even subfamilies of Gramineae".[3] I have measured

---

[1] *Letter 42*, p. 32 of Dutch edition.

[2] This was pointed out by Harting in 1850 (*Het Mikroskoop*, III, 404), and again by myself (1920)—in ignorance of his earlier annotation. Haaxman (1875, p. 56) makes the absurd mistake of commending L. for estimating the diameter at $\frac{1}{300}$ (instead of $\frac{1}{3000}$) of an inch.

[3] *Encyclopaedia Britannica*, 11th ed. (1911). It is rather surprising that "a millet seed" is still so frequently referred to, as a standard of size, in biological writings (especially text-books). I have asked many people how big a millet seed is, but have never yet found anybody who could tell me even approximately—including one distinguished person who had himself used the expression as a descriptive term.

samples of modern "brown" and "white" millet (commonly sold for bird-seed) and found that the grains averaged 1·8 mm. and 2·17 mm. respectively: but as they are not spherical, their "diameter" is difficult to determine. In one place[1] Leeuwenhoek estimates a green pea to have a diameter equal to 4½ millet seeds, while elsewhere[2] he says that a pea weighs 8 grains. On selecting a few fresh green peas of about this weight (520 mg.) and measuring them, I found their diameters to be rather less than 1 cm. (But here again—as peas are not round—it is impossible to express their diameter, or "axis" as he called it, with precision.) If Leeuwenhoek's millet had a diameter of about $\frac{2}{9}$ of such peas, it must have measured roughly 2 mm. across. This agrees with my estimates from modern millet, and does not seem to disagree with any of his own statements. I assume, therefore, that when he uses "a millet seed" as his standard, he means a spherical body approximately 2 mm. in diameter.

A *Hairsbreadth* is estimated by Leeuwenhoek himself[3] as equal to $\frac{1}{600}$ of an inch (about 43·6 μ on his scale). The hairs measured were plucked from his wig—not his own head—and human hairs are usually much coarser.[4]

The *Eye of a Louse*[5] appears to be rather an indefinite standard of size. I find, however, that it can be estimated approximately. The eyes of *Pediculus humanus corporis* (the louse which Leeuwenhoek particularly studied) have fairly uniform dimensions in both sexes. They are not spherical; but series of measurements made longitudinally and transversely give closely similar mean diameters. The average for "an eye of a big louse" I have found to be about 70 μ—ranging from 64 μ to 80 μ. It can thus be said, with a fair approximation to the truth, that "a louse's eye" has a diameter 10 times that of a human red blood-corpuscle. This is in good agreement with Leeuwenhoek's interpretations.

---

[1] See p. 169 *supra*.

[2] See p. 214 *supra*.

[3] See p. 189 *supra*.

[4] Most of my own hairs, which are unusually fine, have diameters at least twice as great. I have never seen a human hair (from the head) measuring only 43 μ in diameter; but I have made no extensive investigation of this matter—being content with L.'s own statement.

[5] Cf. p. 121 *et alibi*, *supra*.

A *Hair on a Louse* is a less accurate comparison: for the setae on *P. corporis* vary greatly in diameter, in different parts of the body. Moreover, they all taper to a point, so that their sides are not parallel. Large hairs, I find, have a maximum width of about 4 μ: but smaller ones measure only 2·5 μ or even less. "The thickness of the hairs wherewith the body of a louse is beset" I estimate—very roughly—to be something more than 3 μ.

I can add little else to what Leeuwenhoek himself tells us about his micrometry.[1] I may mention in conclusion, however, that he had some correspondence on the subject with Dr James Jurin in the last year of his life. Jurin, in 1718, invented[2] a new method of measuring small objects; and in 1722 he wrote to Leeuwenhoek about it, and persuaded him to try it. Leeuwenhoek did so, and his answering letter was published.[3] Though it is not generally known, Jurin's own draft (in English) of his letter to Leeuwenhoek is still extant. It is an interesting letter, and its present owner[4] has kindly allowed me to read and copy it: but as it has no bearing upon Leeuwenhoek's own methods, I need not print it here.

Finally, I may note that the *weights* mentioned by Leeuwenhoek, in various letters, sometimes furnish clues to his measurements. We could, indeed, exactly determine some of his small measures of length if we knew the exact equivalents of his weights in modern units. We do not know, however, how closely his "grain" or "ounce" agree with modern weights of the same name; though fortunately he recorded his

---

[1] It should be noted that an earlier attempt to evaluate L.'s measurements was made by Muys (1741; p. 332, note 72). His words are worth consideration; but his estimates can hardly be regarded as satisfactory at the present time, so I shall not discuss them here.

[2] See Jurin (1718). His method was simple and ingenious. It consisted in closely winding fine hairs or silver wire on a needle, along a measurable length, and then determining the diameter of the hair (or wire) by counting the number of turns in that length. The diameter of the filament being thus ascertained, it was cut into small bits and strewn among the objects to be measured, whose size was estimated (under the microscope) by comparison. In this way Jurin determined the diameter of a human red blood-corpuscle to be $\frac{1}{3240}$ inch (a very close approximation).

[3] *Phil. Trans.* (1723), Vol. XXXII, No. 377, p. 341 (MS. Roy. Soc. 19 March 1723).

[4] Mr A. K. Totton, a kinsman of Jurin and a former pupil of mine.

own "table of weights" himself, so that we know their relative values. Writing to Tschirnhausen[1] in 1699 he says:[2]

> Over here we divide a pound [*pont*] into 16 ounces [*oncen*], and each ounce into 20 *engels*,[3] and each *engels* into 32 grains [*asen*]; and consequently, then, a grain [*aas*] is $\frac{1}{10240}$ of a pound.

It is thus clear that Leeuwenhoek's "grain" (*aas*), which was $\frac{1}{640}$ of his ounce, can hardly have been identical with our modern grain ($437\frac{1}{2}$ = 1 ounce, or 7,000 = 1 lb. avoirdupois). Wherever I translate "*asen*" as "grains", in the foregoing pages, it is merely for want of any other term; and the reader will therefore please bear in mind that Leeuwenhoek's "grain" was only approximately the weight nowadays called by the same name in English (1 grain = 0·065 gramme). But these are problems for the expert metrologist—not for a poor protozoologist or bacteriologist—and their further discussion is beyond my competence.

(iv) LEEUWENHOEK'S DWELLING

The tragicomical history of Leeuwenhoek's house in Delft has never yet been fully related, but it deserves notice here for several reasons. These are the facts, so far as I have been able to ascertain them. My information is derived chiefly from Soutendam (1875), Haaxman (1875), Harting (1876), Bouricius (1924, 1925), and an anonymous article[4] recently published in the *Wereldkroniek*—supplemented by a few personal observations and inquiries made on the spot in 1923.

In September 1875 an international celebration of "the 200th Anniversary" of Leeuwenhoek's discovery of the "Infusoria" was held at Delft. (Harting [1876] records the events which led up to this congress.) The fixing of the date of the original discovery on September 1675 was, as we now

---

[1] E. W. von Tschirnhausen (1651-1708), the well-known German mathematician.

[2] *Letter 120*, dated ". . . 1699." Published in Dutch and Latin collective works. See p. 131 of Dutch edition.

[3] There is no English equivalent of this word.

[4] See *Anonymus* (1909).

know, incorrect: nevertheless, the "anniversary" was duly celebrated on the date erroneously determined—to the evident satisfaction of all participants. By that time everyone had forgotten where Leeuwenhoek had lived: but the then archivist of Delft (Mr J. Soutendam) endeavoured to find out, and he finally pitched on an old house standing at the corner of *Oude Delft* and the *Boterbrugstraat* (not "*Botersteeg*", as Haaxman called it). An "*astrolabium*" or "*planetarium*" still present by the doorstep (figured by Soutendam, 1875) was taken to confirm his identification of the site—this bit of "scientific apparatus" presumably indicating that the house in question had once been occupied by a man of science. Even at that date (1875), however, the house itself was, by all accounts, much restored and altered.

As Leeuwenhoek's habitation had been thus identified, the "anniversary" celebrations included a visit of the delegates *en masse* to this hallowed spot. The tenant of the house at that time (Mr J. B. A. Muré) received them graciously: he also allowed a stone memorial slab to be affixed to the front of his residence, and bound himself legally to be responsible for its future preservation. (The agreement is printed in Harting, 1876; p. 89.)

So far so good. Some years later, however, the tenant of the house died, and it passed into the hands of a builder at The Hague who inconsiderately ordered it to be demolished. By that date (1892) everybody had, apparently, forgotten all about Leeuwenhoek again: but when the house came to be pulled down, the stone block bearing his name, and the "planetarium" by the steps, were noticed. They were therefore preserved, consecrated with the seal of the municipality, and deposited (on 3 December 1892) in the Municipal Museum at Delft—where they now repose. (The memorial tablet is an oblong block of white marble bearing the words ANTONY VAN LEEUWENHOEK/MDCLXXV—MDCCCLXXV in gilt capitals. The "planetarium" is a decorative iron railing bearing no obvious resemblance to any scientific instrument.) The site occupied by the house was not built on, but was converted into a playground for the girls' school adjoining (the *Meisjeshuis*, erected in 1760); and again everything was forgotten.

Some 17 years later, a local society called "*Delfia*"—concerned with the improvement of the town, and the preservation of its antiquities—realized that something ought to be done to commemorate Leeuwenhoek in the place of his birth, residence, and death. They therefore instituted a competition in which artists were invited to submit designs for a suitable memorial. The winning entry was duly accepted and erected —a bronze shield,[1] showing a bas-relief bust of Leeuwenhoek (modelled on Verkolje's portrait) with a Dutch inscription, executed and signed by J. C. Schultsz. It is still stuck on the railings surrounding the school playground, where it was affixed in 1909. Apart from his tomb, this is still the only monument to Leeuwenhoek in Delft.

But more recent research into the town archives—made by a later and more critical archivist, the late Mr L. G. N. Bouricius—has proved that Leeuwenhoek never lived on the spot where his modern bronze effigy with its false inscription now hangs. His real residence was in a neighbouring street —the *Hippolytusbuurt*—and has long since vanished without trace. Consequently, all the belated local endeavours to commemorate Leeuwenhoek have been futile. It is certain that he never lived on the spot where the delegates were thrilled in 1875, and where his memorial now incongruously stands: nor did he make the supposed discoveries in the year therein alleged. His own house—where he lived and laboured and died—was in a different street, and has long since been destroyed by his forgetful fellow-townsmen. The railings adorning another man's doorstep—now preserved in the Municipal Museum of Delft—are a worthless object which would surely have excited his derision.

Before the celebrations of 1875 were held in Delft, invitations were issued by the organizing committee to every body and everybody likely to be interested. Yet England—almost alone—made no response. The Royal Society, indeed, not only sent no delegate, but even failed to acknowledge their invitation: and England and London and the Royal Society thus placed themselves—to quote Harting (1876)—"on a level with Spain and Portugal and Greece." We ought, undoubtedly, to have taken some part in commemorating Leeuwenhoek's discoveries, with which we were so intimately concerned: yet our disgrace is now, perhaps, mitigated by

[1] Figured in the anonymous article in the *Wereldkroniek* (1909). A plaster cast is also preserved in the Museum at Delft.

the accidental circumstance that no Englishman or Fellow of the Royal Society was present at the farce enacted in 1875 at "Leeuwenhoek's house, where he discovered the Infusoria in 1675". But the whole affair is deplorable, and the less said about it the better.

The comedy of errors associated with "Leeuwenhoek's house" is unhappily paralleled in the history of his birthplace. About ten years ago, Mr Bouricius succeeded in discovering the place where Leeuwenhoek was born—a house in the *Oosteinde* of Delft, at that date still erect but used as a warehouse by a hide-merchant named Roes. Bouricius (1925) published a picture of this building, and with his kind assistance I had it rephotographed in 1926. (See Plate II.[1]) But in February, 1929, Mr Bouricius unfortunately died: and later in the same year, when Dr Schierbeek was about to propose to a Dutch scientific gathering[2] that a commemorative tablet should be placed on the house, he found that it had just been pulled down—to enlarge the playground of another children's school!

It will thus be seen that the house in which Leeuwenhoek was born, the other house in which he lived and worked and traded and died, and even the house in which he is now erroneously supposed to have resided, have all been demolished. Delft, Holland, England, London, the Royal Society, and everyone else in every land, may therefore all be censured for having done nothing to preserve Leeuwenhoek's bodily connexion with the world.

But it is needless to bewail the hard fact that such material relics of Leeuwenhoek's existence have been thus wantonly destroyed. His own works are a *monumentum aere perennius* which no vandal or house-breaker or Fellow of the Royal Society can ever annihilate. For my own part, I feel no sorrow when I reflect that the site of his own dwelling is now occupied by an obscure modern shop: and I almost rejoice that the place where he was born, and the ground

---

[1] This photograph has already been published, unfortunately, by Dr Schierbeek (1930), though it was taken at my expense for the present work. I note this lest I be accused of borrowing his illustration without acknowledgement.

[2] *Genootschap voor Geschiedenis der Genees-, Natuur- en Wiskunde.*

whereon he is wrongly supposed to have lived, are both now open spaces where little Dutch children can play in the sun. I even find something appropriate, poetic, and comforting in these "inscrutable dispensations of Providence."

(v) LEEUWENHOEK'S DRAUGHTSMEN

It is well known that most of the illustrations accompanying Leeuwenhoek's letters were not drawn by his own hand. He tells us himself that he was a poor draughtsman, and therefore employed more skilful artists to make his figures.[1] There are several references to this subject in his published works; but perhaps the most explicit expression is to be found in an early unpublished letter, wherein he says—in answer to Oldenburg's complaint that his drawings were not sufficiently clear—that he *sees* with the utmost clarity all that he describes, but then adds: [2]

> Yet I am to blame, because I can't draw; and secondly, because I am resolved not to let anybody know the method that I use [3] for this purpose: and so I just make only rough and simple sketches with lines, mostly in order to assist my memory, so that when I see them I get a general idea of the shapes: besides, some of the forms I see are so fine and small, that I don't know how even a good draughtsman could trace them, unless he made them bigger.

Many of the original drawings sent with the letters to the Royal Society have been preserved. They are, for the most part, of no great artistic merit, and differ in minor details from the published engravings. This is, in the main, because the originals were usually drawn with red or black chalk, or pencil (exceptionally with ink or in colour), and were often reduced in size by the engraver. All variations are readily explicable by the difference in technique—the soft line made with red crayon on paper being impossible to render exactly by the hard line of the burin on metal. On the whole, the

---

[1] Cf. *Letter 2*, p. 42 *supra*.

[2] Translated from *Letter 11*. 26 March 1675. To Oldenburg. MS.Roy.Soc.

[3] *i.e.*, in handling the microscope—as is evident from the context.

engravers dealt faithfully with their prototypes: and I fancy that the average modern editor, if drawings such as Leeuwenhoek's originals were submitted to him in illustration of a present-day paper, would return them to the author with a note saying that they were "not suitable for reproduction". I have, indeed, been compelled to act on this principle myself: the original drawings, *en sanguine* on discoloured and yellowish paper, illustrating the letters on *Anthophysa* and the protozoa on duckweed, are still extant; but I cannot reproduce them here—for technical reasons—and have had to use the engravings originally made from these drawings instead.

A few "rough and simple sketches"—mostly on the margins of the MSS.—were evidently the work of Leeuwenhoek himself[1]: because careful examination shows that they were drawn with the same pen and the same ink as the accompanying autograph handwriting. They bear out his own statement that he was no artist.

In Leeuwenhoek's letters I have been unable to find any mention of the name of the draughtsman—"*de teijckenaer*", or "the limner" as Hoole always calls him—who made his illustrations for him. (He is frequently mentioned, but never by name.) It is unlikely, indeed, that all the drawings were executed by the same artist, for they were made at intervals during some 50 years; and there is no reason to believe that Leeuwenhoek's longevity was characteristic of all citizens of Delft at that period. It seems to me certain, therefore, that more than one hand must have participated in the illustration of his discoveries.

It is generally supposed that Leeuwenhoek's draughtsmen are unknown. Nevertheless, there is at least one important record bearing on this subject which seems to have been overlooked. In Boitet's book on Delft (1729; pp. 790-91) we are told of a certain Thomas van der Wilt (born 1659[2]), who was "a fine painter and a good poet," and who was a pupil of Johannes Verkolje. It is said by Boitet that he settled in Delft, and there found plenty of work as a portrait-painter and otherwise; and "By his wife *Johanna Biddaff* he had a son,

---

[1] The cube illustrating the argument in the letter to Const. Huygens (p. 189 *supra*) is one of these: and the pepper-tube (Plate XXII) is another.

[2] He died at Delft in 1733 (*fide* Bryan, 1905).

called Willem, who made such progress in drawing, through his father's instruction, that there were few who could match him. Nearly all the plates in the celebrated work of Mr. Leeuwenhoek were marvellously drawn from life by him through magnifying-glasses. . . . . But he died in the flower of his life on 24 January 1727, at the age of 35."

There is no reason to doubt the truth of this story—published only two years after Willem's death in his home town: but it is impossible to believe that Willem van der Wilt drew "nearly all" (*meest alle*) Leeuwenhoek's figures. If he died aged 35 in 1727, he must have been born in 1691 or 1692; and consequently he could have drawn none of the illustrations for the letters written in the XVII Century. He probably made the illustrations of the *Send-brieven*: but he could not have been responsible for any others—save some of those reproduced between 1700 and 1712 in the *Phil. Trans.* The pictures of vorticellids and rotifers published at the beginning of the XVIII Century may perhaps have been drawn by him, and it may well have been Willem who made the recorded remark about their surprising "wheelwork".[1] But he must have been a mere child at the time.

Whilst there is thus good reason to believe that Leeuwenhoek's last letters were illustrated by Willem van der Wilt, there seems to be no direct evidence to show who drew the figures for the earlier ones. Nevertheless, it seems to me probable that some of them may have been drawn by his father Thomas. If we consider all the evidence furnished by Boitet, it appears to me highly suggestive. Very briefly, it is as follows: (1) Thomas van der Wilt was an artist living in Delft at the time when Leeuwenhoek wrote his early letters. (2) His son was employed by Leeuwenhoek to illustrate his later letters. (3) Thomas himself must therefore have been known to Leeuwenhoek.[2] (4) He (Thomas) earned a good living in Delft not only by painting portraits, but also by exercising his artistic abilities in other ways. (5) Thomas's father, though not a native of Delft, was a linen-draper—the trade which Leeuwenhoek himself engaged in. (6) Thomas

---

[1] Cf. p. 279 *supra*.

[2] This is confirmed by the circumstance—mentioned a little later—that Thomas was responsible for some panegyric verses elucidating the allegorical title-page of the *Send-brieven*.

was a pupil of Verkolje—the artist who painted Leeuwenhoek's portrait.

What could be more likely, therefore, than that Leeuwenhoek employed Thomas van der Wilt to draw the pictures for some of his earlier epistles? When all the circumstances are taken into account, this seems to me to be something more than a plausible guess at the identity of one of the original draughtsmen.

But Leeuwenhoek must have known other artists who lived in his native town, and the evidence in favour of Thomas van der Wilt is clearly not conclusive. Among Leeuwenhoek's acquaintances we must include, for example, that incomparable painter Jan Vermeer. He was born in the same year as Leeuwenhoek, in the same place, and at almost the same hour (their baptisms are registered on the same page), and lived and worked all his life in Delft—of which he has left us one of the most beautiful pictures in existence (see Plate VII). Moreover, we know that, on Vermeer's untimely death in 1675, Leeuwenhoek was appointed as his executor.[1]

I must note, in conclusion, that Thomas van der Wilt once painted a portrait of the poet Hubert Poot (1689-1733), who wrote Leeuwenhoek's epitaph; and an excellent engraving of this picture, by Houbraken, was prefixed to Poot's collected *Gedichten* (Delft, 1722)—reproduced here in Plate XVI. I have seen no other specimens of Thomas's artistic work, but according to Boitet and others he also painted the Rev. Mr Gribius—Leeuwenhoek's minister, who announced his death to the Royal Society (see p. 93 *supra*). The only sample of Thomas's poetry which I have seen is the poem explaining the engraved title-page—"*Op de Titel-prent*"—of Leeuwenhoek's *Send-brieven* (1718: not printed in the Latin edition [*Epist. Physiol.*], 1719).

For my part, I accept Boitet's evidence that Leeuwenhoek's later letters were illustrated by Willem van der Wilt, and I incline to the view that some, at least, of the earlier ones were illustrated by his father Thomas. But the subject obviously demands further research, which I must leave to future students possessed of the time and opportunities requisite for pursuing inquiries of this character.

---

[1] *Vide* p. 35 *sq.*, *supra*. It is noteworthy also that L.'s microscopes were ultimately auctioned in the chamber belonging to the artists' Guild of St. Luke—of which Vermeer was sometime "Master"

(vi) THE PORTRAITS OF LEEUWENHOEK

Several "portraits of Leeuwenhoek" are still extant. They were made at various dates by various artists, and the following fragmentary notes upon them may be of interest—information on this subject being somewhat difficult to obtain, and not having been previously collected.[1]

(1) BY JOHANNES VERKOLJE (1650-1693 : lived at Delft 1673 till his death, and is buried there. Cf. v. Riemsdijk, 1921, p. 281). There are two portraits of Leeuwenhoek by this artist :

(*a*) An *oil-painting*. (See Plate XI, opposite p. 49 of the present work.) Dated 1686 (*fide* Moes, 1905). Three-quarter length, showing Leeuwenhoek seated at a table; wearing a golden-brown robe, a wig, a knotted white neckerchief, etc. Head turned to *left* of picture (*i.e.* to his own right), knees to right. On the table a globe, an ink-stand with a quill pen, the sealed diploma of the Royal Society, a small pair of compasses, and a sheet of paper bearing a drawing of a circle and some indistinct figures. (The drawing appears to be that here shown in text-fig. 3, p. 202.) In his right hand he holds another pair of compasses.[2] He is depicted with a fresh complexion and clear blue eyes. An opening at the right in the dark background shows a glimpse of a distant landscape with a winding river ("perhaps the Thames" according to Haaxman—but why not the Maas?).

This painting was formerly in the possession of Dr C. H. W. van Kaathoven of Leyden (Haaxman, 1875, p. 17*n* : Harting, 1876, pp. 117-119). On his death it was purchased (19 June 1879) by the *Rijksmuseum*, Amsterdam, where it now hangs (Room 273, No. 2521). Cf. Moes (1905, p. 12); v. Riemsdijk (1921, p. 281). This is the prototype of most of the published portraits. It has been reproduced in recent times by Crommelin (1926), van Seters (1926), and others, while

[1] Since this was written a short article on the same subject has been published by de Lint (1931)—too late for its contents to be discussed here.

[2] A little *passer* similar to this, and once belonging to L., is still (or was in 1923, when I saw it) in the possession of Mr P. A. Haaxman at The Hague.

Haaxman had it lithographed[1]—by A. J. Wendel, not very successfully—as a frontispiece for his biography (1875).

(*b*) A *mezzotint engraving.* (See the Frontispiece.) This differs from the painting chiefly in the following particulars: the head is turned to the *right*, knees to the left; and Leeuwenhoek holds a *microscope* in his *left* hand (not compasses in his right). The whole picture is, in fact, reversed. On the table, instead of the diploma, there is a spray of oak-leaves with galls[2] on them, and a large magnifying-glass with a handle. A curtain hangs behind the head, and the distant landscape is missing. Below is engraved a Dutch inscription with some verses signed "Constanter" (the pen-name of Constantijn Huygens *pater*). The mezzotint is signed "*J. Verkolje pinx. fec. et exc. A°. 1686.*"[3] (This is important, as it confirms the date of the *painting*.)

Several prints, at least, of this engraving are in existence. Dr van Kaathoven, of Leyden, formerly possessed one, which afterwards passed into the possession of Mr P. M. Beelaerts, who in turn bequeathed it to the town of Delft.[4] (It is now in the *Gemeentemuseum*.) But the best impression which I have seen is in the private collection of Mr George H. Gabb (London), from whose copy my frontispiece has been reproduced.[5] Other reproductions of the mezzotint (from other originals) have previously been published in *Opuscula Selecta Neerlandicorum*, Vol. I (1907); by Locy (1910, p. 79) and Cole (1926, frontispiece); and in the *Deutsche Medizinische Wochenschrift* (1911; No. 22, supplement). This last plate—included in that journal's "*Bildersammlung aus der Geschichte der Medizin*"—is a fine large half-tone reproduction, but bears

---

[1] This poor lithograph has unfortunately been copied (instead of the equally accessible original) by several well-meaning popular writers—such as Baumann (1915) in Holland, and Mrs Williams-Ellis (1929) in England.

[2] *Letter 50*, 14 May 1686 (published in Dutch and Latin works) contains a description of L.'s observations on oak-galls, and its date affords confirmation of the date of the engraving.

[3] Not 1685, as stated by Haaxman (1875, p. 18*n*).

[4] Cf. Haaxman (1875) and Veldman (1898, p. 74). I have seen this impression, which is fairly good.

[5] I am greatly indebted to Mr Gabb for his permission to copy the original in his collection, and for the trouble which he has taken to insure its accurate photographic reproduction.

a ridiculous biographical note (signed "Pagel") on its back. The original picture is therein hesitatingly attributed to "J. Veikolpe", and "Anton" van Leeuwenhoek is called a "well-known precursor of Robert Koch, in so far as the discovery of the infusoria is due to him."

It seems obvious that Verkolje first made his portrait of Leeuwenhoek in oils, and shortly afterwards (in the same year) himself engraved it in *mezzotinto.* The artist evidently copied his own painting directly on to the copper plate (which accounts for the figure being reversed in the printed engraving), and in doing so made several minor alterations or improvements—appropriately substituting a microscope for the compasses originally held in the hand, but failing to notice that he ultimately made Leeuwenhoek appear left-handed! The mezzotint by Verkolje is probably the best of all portraits of Leeuwenhoek: and that it was an excellent likeness is attested by the verses written on it by Const. Huygens.

There are several references to this mezzotint by Leeuwenhoek himself in unpublished passages in his letters. Apparently the Royal Society wrote, about the beginning of 1694, to ask him for his portrait. In his reply he says:[1]

> I haven't any of my pictures; and furthermore, the plate has been printed off, and the plate-maker, who was also the printer and painter,[2] is dead. But if I can get one at our approaching annual fair, at which time many art-dealers come to our town, I'll not neglect to let you have what you ask for.

Later in the same year he wrote again:[3]

> I couldn't find any copies of my portrait, in mezzotinto,[4] for sale by any of the printsellers at our annual fair: but at last I've gotten six copies from a bookseller in another

---

[1] Translated from *Letter of 26 May 1694.* To R. Waller. MS.Roy.Soc. Unpublished.

[2] Referring to Verkolje, who died in the previous year.

[3] From *Letter 84.* 14 September 1694. To R. Waller. MS.Roy.Soc. Published in Dutch and Latin printed works, but with the passage here translated entirely omitted. Not in *Phil. Trans.*

[4] *inde swarte konst* MS.

> town, which I dispatched a fortnight ago to London by Skipper *Richart Houlatson*, with the address: *For the Secretarij of the Roijall Societij at Gresham Colledge*,[1] without any further inscription.

The Royal Society failed to acknowledge the receipt of these letters and pictures (and also of other letters from Leeuwenhoek received at that time), and two years later we find him writing again[2]:

> When I learnt that several Fellows were wishful to have two or three copies of my portrait, printed in mezzotinto, . . . I couldn't remain idle, but made every effort to satisfy them; and finally I obtained six prints (as the plate had been printed off). These mezzotintos, as also my Latin book, I sent to London, and addressed them, as I've been wont to do, to Gresham Colledge: to all which letters I got no answer . . .

What happened to these six prints is not now known. They have all disappeared from the Royal Society's collection, and the Society now possesses only a single mutilated copy of the mezzotint acquired at a much later date.

All the well-known engraved portraits of Leeuwenhoek are derived from Verkolje's oil-painting. The best-known, and most often reproduced, is the excellent copperplate engraving by A. de Blois prefixed to the Dutch and Latin collective works (*Brieven* and *Opera Omnia*). It first appeared as a frontispiece to the *Vervolg der Brieven* (1687), with a Dutch inscription: afterwards, with Latin lettering, in *Arcana Naturae Detecta* (1695). Various copies of this copy have also been made—in line, stipple, mezzotint, and by modern photographic processes. At least one early engraving was

---

[1] The words "For . . . Colledge" are thus in English in the MS. (The rest, of course, is in Dutch.)

[2] From *Letter 102*. 10 July 1696. To the Royal Society. MS.Roy.Soc. Published—with omission of the passage here translated—in the Dutch and Latin printed works: English extract in *Phil. Trans.* (1696), Vol. XIX, No. 221, p. 269 (from which the passage is also absent). This letter actually contains a protest against the Society's failure to acknowledge 8 of L.'s communications (*Letters 77* to *84*)—a discourtesy which caused him to start sending his observations to other people instead.

reproduced in colours. The best copper-engraving (copied from de Blois) is that by A. Smith,[1] prefixed to Hoole's *Select Works* (Vol. I, 1798): but another good one—probably copied from Smith's, but with the head turned to the right (as in the original mezzotint)—was made by J. Chapman and published by G. Jones in 1813. All these reproductions show Leeuwenhoek's head only, in an oval frame with more or less added decoration.

Regarding Anker Smith's engraving (in Hoole) the following points should be noted. Although it bears an extract from a Dutch letter printed in 1696, and is marked "*Painted by I. Verkolje*", it was almost certainly copied from the engraving by de Blois accompanying the Latin *Arc. Nat. Det.* The oval frame bears the words: "ANTONIUS A LEEUWENHOEK DELPHENSIS, R.S.S. AET. LXIII. MDCXCV." Both age and year are entirely wrong, and consequently this circumscription has already led to misunderstanding. I can only suppose that Smith (or Hoole) wrongly took the date of the *Arc. Nat. Det.* (1695) as that in which de Blois's engraving was made; and that the age of 63 was then inferred from this error. Anyway, there can be no doubt that Smith's engraving was ultimately derived from an original made in 1686 (not 1695), which portrayed Leeuwenhoek at the age of about 54 (not 63).

Verkolje's portraits have been copied and recopied over and over again, and terribly travestied and perverted in the process. The die of Leeuwenhoek's own seal[2] was admirably incised from the mezzotint: the modern bronze effigy[3] of himself, now suspended in *Oude Delft*, is also based—less successfully—on Verkolje's originals. Moreover, there are contemporary tiles and pottery of Delft-ware bearing Leeuwenhoek's supposed simulacrum "after Verkolje" (a very long way after). I have seen two samples of these—a plate and a plaque—now in the *Rijksmuseum*; and Haaxman and Harting mention others. I have also seen a present-day descendant of Verkolje's pictures—showing "the man who

---

[1] Anker Smith (1759-1819), a once celebrated engraver of small plates for book-illustration. He was elected A.R.A. in 1797.

[2] Cf. p. 360.

[3] Cf. p. 340 *supra*.

first saw a microbe"—in an English children's magazine,[1] and a comic reconstruction recently (1931) used to advertise an American proprietary tooth-paste in India: but the last stage in degradation has surely been reached in the caricature imprinted on the covers of the current American *Abstracts of Bacteriology* (Vol. I issued in 1917) and some other publications of the Society of American Bacteriologists.

(2) By Nicolaes Maes (1632-1693: from 1673 to 1693 at Amsterdam, where he died and was buried). According to C. H. de Groot (1916: Vol. VI, pp. 530-531) there are two portraits of Leeuwenhoek by Maes. The first (No. 202, *de G.*) is an oil-painting now in the National Gallery, London (1921 Catalogue, No. 2581). This picture was formerly owned by Mr George Salting, the Australian art-collector, and was bequeathed to the Nation in 1910. It is undated, and depicts an old man "in full face. His right hand is raised, grasping his robe. He has long hair, a moustache, and a pointed beard on his wrinkled face. [He wears a black robe and a white shirt.] At the back is a curtain, with a column in shadow to the right" (de Groot). This is a very fine painting, but it is certainly no portrait of Leeuwenhoek. It shows a man totally unlike the sitter for Verkolje's portraits, and there is no evidence whatsoever that it depicts our Antony. In 1923 I called the attention of the then Director of the National Gallery (Sir Charles Holmes) to this misidentification: and on looking into the matter for himself he agreed that "there is no just ground for identifying the portrait . . . as a portrait of Leeuwenhoek." He informed me further that the picture was first labelled "Anthony van Leeuwenhoek, F.R.S." *after* it left the Salting Collection—by whose authority is not now known.[2] Its label has consequently now been changed to "*Portrait of a Gentleman*". De Groot blundered badly when he accepted this painting as a portrait of Leeuwenhoek.

According to de Groot there is also another portrait (likewise undated) by Maes. It is described as follows: "202*a*. Anthoni van Leeuwenhoek.—In a dark red coat trimmed with fur. His long hair falls on his shoulders. 28 inches by 24 inches. *Sale.*—Lady Anna Chandos-Pole and others,

---

[1] See *Anonymus* (1927).

[2] Letters dated 8 & 10 May 1923.

London, July 19, 1914. No. 106" (de Groot, 1916: Vol. VI, p. 531). Whether this is a genuine portrait or not I do not know. I have been unable to trace it further. I can only add that according to *Art Prices Current*, 1913-1914 (Vol. VII, pp. 307, 505), the picture was not the property of Lady Chandos-Pole, but belonged to Maj.-Gen. Sterling, of 249 Knightsbridge, London, and was sold at Sotheby's on 29 April 1914 for £46: while later in the same year (10 July 1914—not 19 July, as stated by de Groot) it is said[1] to have been resold at Christie's for £120. 15*s*.

Notwithstanding the allegations of de Groot and others, there seems to be still no satisfactory evidence to prove that any portrait of Leeuwenhoek was ever painted by Maes: but the matter obviously needs further investigation.

(3) BY ADRIAEN VAN OSTADE (1610-1685: born at Haarlem, where he worked and died). See Moes (1905; Vol. II, p. 12) No. 4415 (1): de Groot (1910; Vol. III, p. 410) No. 876.—De Groot calls this a "*Portrait of Anthonie van Leeuwenhoek* (1632-1722), physicist and surgeon of Haarlem",[2] and he describes the picture thus: "He sits, turned three-quarters left, and leans his left arm on the table and his right hand on his hip. He wears a black costume with a white collar and brown gloves. In front of him are a book and a celestial globe. Signed in full at the foot of the globe, and dated 1665; panel, 8½ inches by 7 inches." This portrait is stated to have been sold in Paris on 2 May 1865 (*Sale* H. de Kat, No. 63). I have been unable to find it. I may note, however, that what appears to be a copy in black chalk, by A. Delfos, is preserved in the Municipal Museum at Delft. It is a poor portrait (if it be one) and bears little resemblance to the authentic pictures of Leeuwenhoek, though the face recalls many of the peasants portrayed in Ostade's other paintings.

Adriaen van Ostade was no portrait-painter (and in my opinion a very poor artist): and at present I am not convinced that he ever attempted to paint a portrait of Leeuwenhoek—or, if he did, that it is now in existence.

---

[1] It is also there said to represent "Lieuvenhoch, the father of the Microscope"!

[2] There are 5 obvious errors in these dozen words.

(4) By Cornelis de Man (1621-1706: born, worked, and died at Delft). According to Moes (1905; Vol. II, p. 12) there is—or was—a portrait of Leeuwenhoek by this artist, dated 1681, in the "*Anatomie-Kamer te Delft.*" When I visited the town in 1923 I was unfortunately unable to find it: and subsequent inquiries made through the late archivist (Mr Bouricius), and the late Prof. Beijerinck, have been equally fruitless.

(5) By Jan Vermeer (1632-1675, of Delft). There is no authentic record of any portrait of Leeuwenhoek having ever been painted by this great master. Nevertheless, it has recently been stated by Lucas (1922, p. 8) that Leeuwenhoek, "the inventor of the microscope," was "probably his model for the three or four scientific pictures". (By "scientific pictures" Lucas means those paintings by Vermeer showing a "Geographer" or "Astronomer" at work.) I have not seen the originals of any of these (nor had Lucas when he wrote), but I have studied good photographic reproductions of them all. There are four, and they appear to me to portray as many different people. No two are alike, and none bears any recognizable likeness to Leeuwenhoek—as we know him from Verkolje's authentic portraits. I am entirely at a loss to understand how anyone can seriously suggest that Vermeer's "Geographers" and "Astronomers" all represent the same person—and that person Leeuwenhoek. The suggestion becomes still more perplexing when we find that Lucas (*op. cit.*, p. 20) also accepts as genuine the spurious "portrait" by Maes[1]—which in no way resembles any of the people depicted by Vermeer or Verkolje.

I must call attention, however, to some curious points which came to my notice whilst seeking evidence (not given by him) for Lucas's statements. The very fine painting by Vermeer known as "The Geographer," now in the *Städelsches Institut* at Frankfort,[2] shows a man poring over a map or chart, and with a pair of compasses in his right hand. Behind his head there is a globe, and some other maps are also in the

---

[1] See above, p. 351.

[2] There is an excellent reproduction in colour in "Jan Vermeer of Delft" (*Portfolios of Great Masters*), published by Halton & Truscott Smith, Ltd. London, 1925.

picture—a couple loose on the floor, one framed on the wall. This is one of the few of Vermeer's pictures which is signed *and dated.* The date, painted on the wall behind, is MDCLXVIIII (*i.e.*, 1669—not 1668, as stated by more than one writer on Vermeer). Now this is the very year in which Leeuwenhoek was appointed surveyor.[1] Moreover, the globe in the picture is apparently a *celestial* (not terrestrial) globe, and is very like that shown in both of Verkolje's portraits. Leeuwenhoek must surely have possessed a similar one. In Verkolje's oil-painting, furthermore, Leeuwenhoek is shown holding a pair of compasses in his right hand [2]—just like Vermeer's "Geographer". The framed map on the wall has only an artistic import: it has no "scientific" significance, being simply a decoration—introduced into many of Vermeer's other pictures which have no connexion with geography.

There is no authority for calling this picture "The Geographer"—a modern label. Suppose we call it "The Surveyor"? This title seems equally appropriate; and we might then suppose that Vermeer was inspired to paint it by seeing Leeuwenhoek at work on ground-plans and surveys in preparation for his qualifying examination in 1669! But all this is mere guesswork, though the coincidences just noted are curious—if nothing more. "The Geographer" himself is not much like Leeuwenhoek; and there is no evidence, as I have already remarked, that Vermeer ever painted his portrait.

(6) BY JAN GOEREE (1670-1731: designer, engraver, and poet. Known also as *Gouré*).—In the engraved title-page of Leeuwenhoek's last published letters (*Send-brieven* and *Epist. Physiol.*) there is inset a little oval portrait circumscribed "ANTONIVS LEEUWENHOEKIVS DELPHIS NATVS MDCXXXII". It is supported by a fat female angel blowing a trumpet, and somewhat overclouded by other allegorical accessories. The first state of this plate (in the Dutch edition) is lettered at foot "Te DELFT by ADRIAAN BEMAN, 1718." and in the left bottom corner "*J. Goeree sculpt: Direx.*" The second state (Latin edition) bears the words "DELPHIS apud ADRIANUM BEMAN, 1719."—with the same signature.

---

[1] Cf. p. 34 *supra*.

[2] See Plate XI, facing p. 49.

I formerly attached but little importance to this small detail—believing it to be on a level with the rest of the engraved title. But a few years ago Dr W. H. van Seters, of Leyden, when collecting material for the "Leeuwenhoek Film" (which has now been exhibited on various occasions: cf. Kaiser, 1924), rediscovered[1] an old design above which Leeuwenhoek once wrote a motto and his name. Dr van Seters kindly sent me a photograph of this drawing (included in the film), which reveals several points of interest. Leeuwenhoek's signature (undoubtedly genuine) is there dated 30 April 1698. It is written at the top of the page, and is followed by a large allegorical drawing illustrating his motto[2] ("*Door Arbeijt en Naarstigheijt*"). But this drawing was evidently added later, as it is signed "*J. Goeree del: 1707.*" Moreover, it bears, as a pendant, the miniature portrait of Leeuwenhoek incorporated later in the engraved titles of his last letters. This picture was therefore probably made in 1707—not at the date of publication of the *Send-brieven* (1718). Careful study of the engraving has also convinced me that it was made with considerable care, and under Goeree's own supervision—as the words "*sculpt: Direx.*" indicate. I therefore now regard this portrait (shown in my Plate XII) as a genuine and conscientious attempt, by fairly competent artists, to delineate Leeuwenhoek as he appeared in his 75th year. In any case, this is the only known portrait of him in his later life which can make any pretence to authenticity.

In conclusion, I must mention three glyptic representations of Leeuwenhoek. The first is the profile portrait on the silver medal awarded to him in 1716 by the University of Louvain (see p. 80). This has already been depicted by van Loon and Haaxman. The medal is now in the *Gemeentemuseum* at Delft; and as it was struck during his lifetime, its

---

[1] It was exhibited at the Leeuwenhoek Celebration in 1875, and was described by Harting (1876, p. 120). I think the picture was very probably intended as a title-page for the projected edition of L.'s letters (following No. 146 and preceding the *Send-brieven*) which was never published in Dutch or Latin.—According to de Lint (1931) the original is now in the collection of Dr J. van der Hoeven at Eefde [near Zutphen]. It is reproduced in *Opusc. Select. Neerland.*, Vol. IX, Pl. III (1931).

[2] Given in full on p. 299 *supra*.

maker may well have had Leeuwenhoek himself as a model. The portrait is therefore worth consideration. The second carved likeness is the white marble medallion on his tomb (see p. 100, and Plate XV). This was made after his death, and was probably modelled on the silver medal. It has less interest, therefore, as a portrait. The third representation is that on the "Leeuwenhoek Medal," awarded every ten years by the Royal Academy of Sciences of Amsterdam to persons who have distinguished themselves as microbiologists.[1] This medal is of gold, valued at *f.* 300 (about £25), and has been described and figured by Harting (1876). The portrait which it bears is, however, a modern fake; and its historico-iconographical value is consequently *nil*.

(vii) LEEUWENHOEK'S "FIRST 27 UNPUBLISHED LETTERS"

As Leeuwenhoek's own collective editions of his works—both Dutch and Latin—begin with a letter called "No. 28", dated 25 April 1679, it has generally been assumed that all his earlier letters (No. 1—No. 27) have been lost. But this is not so: most of them have been preserved among the Royal Society MSS., and many have been printed in English or Latin (generally abbreviated) in the early volumes of the *Philosophical Transactions*.

I have discussed these letters in some detail in an article about to appear in *Opuscula Selecta Neerlandicorum*, Vol. IX, so I need not repeat what I have there said.[2] But as my numeration differs entirely from that of Vandevelde—who previously attempted to arrange and number them without consulting the original manuscripts—and as I have made frequent references to these letters in the foregoing pages, I give here a tabular synopsis for the reader's convenience and guidance.

---

[1] The first award was made to C. G. Ehrenberg in 1875. The later recipients have been Ferdinand Cohn (1885), Louis Pasteur (1895), M. W. Beijerinck (1905), David Bruce (1915), and F. d'Herelle (1925).

[2] Since these lines were written, the article has appeared in print: see Dobell (1931).

LEEUWENHOEK'S "FIRST 27 LETTERS"

Letter No.	Addressed to	Date	Roy. Soc. MS.	Published in *Phil. Trans.*
1	H. Oldenburg	? [Transmitted by de Graaf 28 Apr. 1673]	[No MS.]	Vol. VIII, No. 94, pp. 6037-6038. **1673**. [Extracts, in English.] Vol. VIII, No. 97, pp. 6116-6118. **1673**. [Figures, with description in English.]
2	H. Oldenburg	15 Aug. 1673	L.1. 1	Vol. IX, No. 102, pp. 21-23 and 23-25 [in 2 parts]. **1674**. [Extracts, in English.]
3	H. Oldenburg	7 Apr. 1674	L.1. 2	Vol. IX, No. 102, pp. 23-25. **1674**. [Combined with part of *Letter 2*. Extracts only, in English.]
3a	H. Oldenburg	16 Apr. 1674	L.1. 3	Unpublished
4	H. Oldenburg	1 June 1674	L.1. 4	Vol. IX, No. 106, pp. 121-128. **1674**. [Part only—in English.]
5	H. Oldenburg	6 July 1674	L.1. 5	Vol. IX, No. 106, pp. 128-131. **1674**. [Extracts only—in English.]
6	H. Oldenburg	7 Sept. 1674	L.1. 7	Vol. IX, No. 108, pp. 178-182 [misprinted 821]. **1674**. [Incomplete English translation.]
6a	H. Oldenburg	7 Sept. 1674	L.1. 6	Unpublished
7	H. Oldenburg	19 Oct. 1674	L.1. 8	Unpublished
8	H. Oldenburg	4 Dec. 1674	L.1. 9	Vol. X, No. 117, pp. 378-380. **1675**. [Extracts in English.]
9	H. Oldenburg	22 Jan. 1675	L.1. 10	Unpublished
10	H. Oldenburg	11 Feb. 1675	L.1. 11	Unpublished
11	H. Oldenburg	26 Mar. 1675	L.1. 13	Unpublished
12	H. Oldenburg	14 Aug. 1675	L.1. 15	Vol. X, No. 117, pp. 380-385. **1675**. [Extracts, in English.]
13	H. Oldenburg	20 Dec. 1675	L.1. 16	Unpublished
13a	H. Oldenburg	22 Jan. 1676	L 1. 16*a*	Unpublished
14	H. Oldenburg	22 Feb. 1676	L.1. 17	Unpublished
15	H. Oldenburg	21 Apr. 1676	L.1. 18	Vol. XI, No. 127, pp. 653-656. **1676**. [Incomplete English translation, with notes (by Nehemiah Grew).]
16	H. Oldenburg	29 May 1676	L.1. 20	Unpublished
17	R. Boyle ..	28 July 1676	[With Boyle MSS.]	Unpublished
18	H. Oldenburg	9 Oct. 1676	L.1. 22	Vol. XII, No. 133, pp. 821-831. **1677**. [Incomplete English translation.]

SYNOPSIS OF LEEUWENHOEK'S "FIRST 27 LETTERS"—*continued*

Letter No.	Addressed to	Date	Roy. Soc. MS.	Published in *Phil. Trans.*
18a	H. Oldenburg	30 Oct. 1676	L.1. 24	Unpublished
19	H. Oldenburg	23 Mar. 1677	L.1. 25	Vol. XII, No. 134, pp. 844-846. **1677.** [Incomplete English translation.]
20	H. Oldenburg	14 May 1677	L.1. 27	Vol. XII, No. 136, pp. 899-905. **1677.** [English translation. A full Latin translation of this letter was published later in Derham's *Philos. Expts. & Obss. of R. Hooke* (1726), pp. 65-74.]
21	H. Oldenburg	5 Oct. 1677	L.1. 29	[Not in *Phil. Trans.* English extracts published in R. Hooke's *Lect. & Collect.* (1678), Part II, Letter 1, pp. 81-83: reprinted in his *Lect. Cutlerianae* (1679).]
21a	Viscount Brouncker	16 Oct. 1677	L.1. 32	Unpublished
22	Viscount Brouncker	... Nov. 1677	[No MS.]	Vol. XII, No. 142, pp. 1040-1043. **1679.** [Full letter, in Latin.]
23	R. Hooke ..	14 Jan. 1678	L.1. 33	[Not in *Phil. Trans.* English extracts published in Hooke's *Lect. & Collect.* (1678), Part II, Letter 2, pp. 84-89: reprinted in his *Lect. Cutlerianae* (1679).]
24	N. Grew ..	18 Mar. 1678	L.1. 34	Vol. XII, No. 142, p. 1044. **1679.** [Abstract, in Latin.]
25	N. Grew ..	31 May 1678	L.1. 36	Vol. XII, No. 140, pp. 1002-1005. **1678.** [Two extracts, in English.] Vol. XII, No. 142, p. 1045. **1679.** [Latin summary of another part of letter.]
26	N. Grew ..	27 Sept. 1678	L.1. 38	Unpublished
27	N. Grew ..	21 Feb. 1679	[No MS.]	Unpublished [This letter is mentioned by L. in his letters dated 13 June 1679 (No. 28*a*, unpublished), 13 Oct. 1679 (No. 28*b*, unpublished), and 25 Apr. 1679 (No. 28—published in Dutch and Latin printed works). It was apparently lost in transmission.]

Addendum.—All the Letters marked "Unpublished" in the foregoing list have now (with the exception of the last, which still remains lost) been printed in full in Vol. IX of *Opuscula Selecta Neerlandicorum*, Amsterdam, 1931. This volume has appeared too late for its contents to be considered in the present work.

In addition to the information given in this table, I must note the following points:

(1) Leeuwenhoek sent a complete copy of his *Letter 4* (1 June 1674, to Oldenburg) to Const. Huygens, and the MS. is preserved at Leyden. This copy has recently been printed by Vandevelde and van Seters (1925).

(2) *Letter 19* (23 March 1677) and *Letter 21* (5 Oct. 1677) are quoted extensively by Leeuwenhoek himself, in his own language, in his *Letter 96* (9 Nov. 1695, to the Elector Palatine) printed in the Dutch works—with Latin versions, of course, in the corresponding Latin editions.

(3) *Letter 22* (Nov. 1677) is quoted, almost entire, in its original Dutch, by Leeuwenhoek in his *Letter 113* (17 Dec 1698, to Harmen van Zoelen—published in the collective editions): and a complete English translation of it (made but not published by myself) has now appeared in the recent work of Cole (1930).

(4) Finally, I must note that the printed *Catalogue* of the Royal Society MSS., compiled many years ago by the youthful Halliwell-Phillipps (1840), is not free from errors; and accordingly its entries relating to the Leeuwenhoek MSS. are not to be accepted as invariably accurate.

(viii) LEEUWENHOEK'S SEALS

Seals on old manuscripts are often important for purposes of identification: how important they may sometimes be, I know from the following incident. Recently, Carbone (1930) believed that he had discovered a new Leeuwenhoek letter among the *Magliabechi MSS.* in the National Library at Florence. This document was among the genuine letters of Leeuwenhoek addressed to the Florentine scholar, but was unsigned. Carbone reproduced it in facsimile—including the seal (enlarged). From its contents it was at once evident to me that this letter (written in Latin, and dated 2 May 1692 from Hanover) could not possibly have been written by Leeuwenhoek. I guessed immediately, however, that it was written by Leibniz: and on comparing it with Leibniz's extant letters to the Royal Society, I found that the corrections throughout were apparently made in his handwriting, and that *the seal was one which he used.* A seal is often as good as a signature (for no man lent his seal-ring to others), and I therefore felt satisfied that the letter was written by Leibniz and not by Leeuwenhoek. This I was soon able to confirm by discovering that the manuscript in question had actually been published previously as a genuine Leibniz letter by Targioni-Tozzetti (1746, pp. 119-122).

Leeuwenhoek's own seals have never yet been described. At various periods of his life he sealed his letters with at least three different ones—usually of red wax, but occasionally of black. Most of the extant impressions are imperfect—the seals having generally been broken, of course, in opening the letters. The following notes are put together from the available fragments. They may assist future students in identifying his writings, but are as incomplete and imperfect as their originals.

(1) Most of the early epistles are sealed with the monogram shown in Plate XXXII (upper figure). This is taken from an almost perfect impression on *Letter* 3*a* (16 April 1674)—stamped from an oval die measuring approximately 16 mm. by 14 mm. The letters APL presumably stand for A[ntony] P[hilipszoon] L [eeuwenhoek] ; the rest of the device I cannot interpret with any confidence. Above, there appears to be an arabic numeral 4: below, connected by a vertical line, the roman figure xx or (more probably) xxv can be read.

(2) Another early seal—which I am unable to reproduce—was a heraldic device, all extant impressions of which are more or less fractured or indistinct. The die was apparently oval, about 17 mm. by 16 mm., with a slightly beaded border. The available examples show a small shield, bearing four raised vertical lines, surmounted by a helmet. On the field behind are various irregularly distributed plumules (?), but no lettering or other recognizable figures. This seal is affixed to several early signed and authentic letters to the Royal Society (including No. *13*, 20 December 1675, from which an extract is here translated). The armorial bearings I have been unable to identify. I can only add that an identical scutcheon with four vertical lines is several times figured by Boitet (1729) as the coat-of-arms of the Uttenbroek family—a family with which Leeuwenhoek is not known to have been connected.

(3) Nearly all the later letters, when sealed, bear a portrait of Leeuwenhoek himself. The die used for this seal (see Plate XXXII, lower figure) was evidently cut with very great care and precision, and the various impressions—in red (rarely

TWO OF LEEUWENHOEK'S SEALS

Enlarged. For description see the text.

in black) wax—show an astonishing amount of detail when closely studied. The seal was obviously copied from Verkolje's mezzotint portrait of Leeuwenhoek (1686): it shows his bewigged head, as there depicted, with a curtain behind, and even reproduces such *minutiae* as his little moustache. Most impressions, however, are faulty or badly fractured. The best (from which my figure here is reproduced) is on Maria's letter to the Royal Society.[1] I judge the original die to have measured—outside its beaded border—approximately 21 mm. by 18 mm. But I cannot be sure, as most impressions are so imperfect. (The specimen figured by Carbone (1930) is extremely poor.)

This seal cannot have been used by Leeuwenhoek before 1686, when Verkolje made his mezzotint. It may therefore possibly help to date some of his undated letters in future. The artist who cut the die is not known; but he must have been extremely skilful, for his work reveals—on careful study of good impressions—a degree of accuracy in reproducing minute detail which is really remarkable. Unfortunately, the dies of all the seals are now lost.

SIMPLEX SIGILLUM VERI

---

[1] See p. 98 *supra*. There are two seals on this letter, but only one is perfect. The other is distorted by a slip in impressing the wax.

ENVOY: LEEUWENHOEK'S PLACE IN PROTOZOOLOGY AND BACTERIOLOGY

A FEW years ago I called Leeuwenhoek "Father of Protozoology and Bacteriology", and I now repeat this title—which has since been adopted by others—on the title-page of the present work. I do this designedly, because in my opinion he alone deserves this designation. In my opinion (which has not been formed too hastily) he was the first man who ever saw living protozoa and bacteria under a lens, and by correctly interpreting and describing his observations he created the modern disciplines of Protozoology and Bacteriology. Consequently, his relation to these sciences is that of "father" or "only begetter".

Nevertheless, there are still some people who dispute Leeuwenhoek's claim to the discovery of the Protozoa and the Bacteria, while there are others who bestow upon him titles which he does not deserve—as he himself would freely have confessed. He has already been styled "Father" and "Founder" of Micrography by Blanchard (1868) and Vandevelde (1922)—to mention no other authors: though it is obvious that Pierre Borel and Henry Power and Robert Hooke and Marcello Malpighi have all at least as good a right to the title. Launois (1904) obviously goes rather too far when he calls Leeuwenhoek one of the "Fathers of Biology": there is more evident justification for those who regard him as the "Father" of Histology or Cytology or Haematology [1]—or even as just the First Milk-Analyst.[2] Almost every writer who discusses Leeuwenhoek's work regards him, apparently, as "father" of his own speciality—some strangely misinformed but enthusiastic authors even hailing him as "the Inventor

---

[1] Sabrazès (1926).

[2] Wynter Blyth (1903).

of the Microscope".[1] Many such claims are manifestly absurd; yet his own right to be regarded as the Father of Protozoology and Bacteriology is, I believe, real and indisputable.

The discovery of the microscope is still in dispute, but I need not discuss the subject here. Its invention is intimately bound up with that of the telescope, and the rival claims of Italy and Holland in this connexion have been ably defended in recent times by Govi (1888), and Harting (1850) and de Waard (1906)[2] respectively. The question has also been critically considered lately by Singer (1921) and Disney (1928). For present purposes it will suffice to note that one form of the microscope (*i.e.*, the *compound* microscope, to which the name is properly applied) was probably devised in Holland in the first decade of the XVII Century (not earlier), while immediately afterwards another form was independently discovered in Italy. But Leeuwenhoek probably knew nothing of all this, and it is unnecessary to argue here about the priority of Zacharias Janssen, Lipperhey, Drebbel, Galileo, or any other possible "inventor of the microscope". Leeuwenhoek did not use a microscope, but only a simple lens; so that the invention of the compound instrument (which occurred before he was born) has no bearing whatsoever upon his own work or discoveries.

The discovery of simple lenses is, however, also a subject of dispute. It is now known, from the profound researches of the French scholar Martin (1871), that the ancients knew nothing about magnifying-glasses—notwithstanding the confident assertions of Dutens and many another more recent writer. Our Roger Bacon[3] (*circa* 1214-1294) had at least a glimmering of the properties and possibilities of lenses, but the first were probably made, and used as spectacles, about

---

[1] Even since these lines were written I have read a paper (Chapman, 1931) in which it is said that L.'s observations "have earned for him the title of 'The Father of Microscopy'."

[2] This excellent and fully documented work appears to have been overlooked by all recent writers on the history of the microscope—including Singer and Disney.

[3] Cf. Bridges (1914). In this connexion the reader may also consult with profit the recent historical analyses by Singer (1921) and Disney *et al.* (1928). The literature dealing with Bacon is too vast to cite here.

the year 1300 in Italy—their popularization "for the help of poor blind old men" being chiefly due to the pious and private labours of the monk Alessandro de Spina of Pisa. The actual inventor of spectacles, however, is said to be a Florentine—Salvino d'Armato degl'Armati.[1] Friar Bacon and his brethren in Italy were probably the originators of simple lenses; and the unknown people who first wore spectacles and used ordinary magnifying-glasses—for assistance in reading or for personal amusement—are the real "precursors" of Leeuwenhoek as a "microscopist".[2]

According to Govi (1888), the word "microscope" (*microscopio*) was invented by Giovanni Fabri[3]—one of the earliest members of the *Accademia dei Lincei*—who first used it in a letter to Federigo Cesi dated 13 April 1625. The first pictures made with the aid of this instrument are usually supposed to be those of the bee and weevil interpolated by Francesco Stelluti (1630) in his Italian translation of the poems of Persius. The first "micrography" is the *Century of Microscopic Observations* by Pierre Borel,[4] published in Latin at The Hague in 1656: but it was soon followed by the similar work of Henry Power[5] (1663-4) and the more celebrated *Micrographia* of Robert Hooke (1665)—both written in English and printed in London.

The writings of Stelluti and Borel and Power and Hooke all antedate anything that Leeuwenhoek ever published. But when he wrote his first letters he had probably never heard of any of these authors: and as he could read neither English nor Latin nor Italian, they could have afforded him

---

[1] Cf. Redi (1678), Mensert (1831), Harting (1850), Pansier (1901), etc.

[2] I cannot refrain from mentioning here a remarkable fantasy recently published by our greatest living English poet and novelist—an unhistorical story revealing more than superficial historical knowledge. I refer to Rudyard Kipling's "The Eye of Allah", printed in his volume entitled *Debits and Credits* (8°. London, 1926).

[3] Fabri or Fabro, in Italian. His real patronymic was Faber, and he was descended from a family of this name who came from Bamberg in Bavaria. Cf. Carutti (1883, pp. 25, 39), etc.

[4] Pierre Borel, *alias* Petrus Borellus (1620-1689), a French physician, antiquary, and philologist. Cf. *Nouv. Biogr. Gén.*, VI, 697.

[5] Henry Power (1623-1668), M.D. Educated at Christ's College, Cambridge, and practised as a doctor at Halifax. He was one of the first Fellows of the Royal Society—having been elected in 1663.

little help—even had he seen their works. Moreover, there are no descriptions of protozoa or bacteria in any of these publications—so far as I have been able to ascertain. I have studied them all with care, but have sought information on such organisms in them in vain. I believe they contain none, and nobody (to my knowledge) has yet proved that they do Nobody now claims that Fabri or Stelluti or Power or Hooke discovered the Protozoa or the Bacteria: but a half-hearted claim has recently been made for Borel by Singer (1915), so I cannot altogether ignore it here.

Borel (1656) tells us that "worms" *are said to be found* in the blood of people suffering from "fever",[1] though he makes no claim to have seen such things himself. Yet Singer says[2] that to him "It seems . . . highly probable that he caught a glimpse of infusoria and possibly bacteria, for he assures us that all decomposing material swarms with similar worms." Singer gives no exact reference to the passage on which he relies, but apparently alludes to Borel's *Observatio de Sanguine*; in which he does *not* give any such assurance, but merely says *it is probable* that worms would be found in every decomposing material *if attention were paid to it*.[3] The whole passage is clearly hypothetical. As a prophecy it may have some interest for helminthologists: for the protozoologist or bacteriologist it is obviously without significance. Something more than a misreading or mistranslation of Borel's words is surely needed to prove that he forestalled Leeuwenhoek.

Another claim to priority in the discovery of the Bacteria has been put forward for the German Jesuit priest Athanasius Kircher (1602-1680)—well known as a voluminous and reckless writer on all manner of subjects.[4] I do not pretend to have

---

[1] *Certò etiam refertur, in sanguine febricitantium vermes reperiri.*

[2] Singer (1915), p. 338. Singer's references to Borel are not always easy to follow. In two places, indeed, he appears to confuse Borel's work of 1656 with his earlier publication of 1653. But this—so far as I can discover—contains only one trivial reference to the use of the "engyscope" [= microscope], having no bearing on the present subject. Borel's later observation (1656*a*, p. 198) on "whale-like insects in human blood"—to which Singer also alludes—cannot conceivably refer to either protozoa or bacteria.

[3] *quare verisimile est idem in omni re, dum putrefit, contingere, si animadvertatur* (Borel, 1656; Obs. III, p. 8).

[4] Cf. *Nouv. Biogr. Gén.*, XXVII, 769, and *Allg. Dtsch. Biogr.*, XVI, 1.

read all his works (which is probably impossible and would certainly be unprofitable), but only some parts of those which deal with biological topics. In none of them can I find any evidence whatsoever to indicate that he ever saw or described either a protozoon or a bacterium. But others believe that they have been more fortunate, so I must briefly consider their findings.

The first person to credit Kircher with the discovery of the Bacteria was, I believe, Friedrich Löffler (1887), who opens his work on the history of bacteriology with a quotation from the *Scrutinium Pestis* (1658)[1] wherein Kircher says: "That air, water, and earth are swarming with countless insects, is so certain that it can even be proved by ocular demonstration. It has hitherto also been known to everybody that worms swarm out of rotting bodies: but only after the wondrous invention of the Microscope did it become known that all decomposing things swarm with an innumerable brood of worms invisible to the naked eye: which even I myself would never have believed, had I not proved it by repeated experiment over many years."[2]

Now this passage contains no obvious reference to any organisms other than worms or insects—well known to everybody at the time when Kircher wrote: yet for reasons unexplained Löffler alleges that it "announces . . . the discovery of a new world of living creatures"—by which he means, presumably, the Bacteria. But does it? Surely not. The assumption is so far-fetched, indeed, that Löffler felt constrained to add that "Kircher was unable to give any more accurate data regarding these worms;" and he then made an irrelevant reference to the *Ars Magna Lucis et Umbrae* (1646). Any ordinary person would conclude that Kircher never described bacteria for the simple reason that he never saw them—and because Leeuwenhoek had not then

---

[1] Löffler actually quotes (in German translation) from an edition of 1671, but gives no exact reference to the passage. I have not seen this edition, but it appears to be a reprint of the first Leipzig edition (1659), which I possess. In this the passage quoted (from Cap. VII, § II) is on p. 69. I have to thank Dr Singer for kindly lending me his own copy of the original edition of 1658.

[2] I translate from the original dog-latin of Kircher (1658)—not from Löffler.

published his discoveries. The organisms which Leeuwenhoek discovered were, for those times, of a "Stupendious Smalness";[1] and there is good reason to believe that Kircher possessed no instruments capable of showing any objects of the order of magnitude of common bacteria.

Singer (1914), however, has recently reasserted Löffler's claims, and has attempted to support them with translated quotations from Kircher's "Experiments" with rotting flesh, leaves, and wood. These are really too ridiculous to quote.[2] It is obvious—from Kircher's own words—that he saw nothing but maggots, mites, and nematodes, such as anybody possessed of a simple low-power magnifying-glass can nowadays perceive. I have consulted all the passages on which Löffler and Singer rely, and have repeated some of Kircher's so-called experiments: and I have even read a considerable part of the *Scrutinium Pestis* and of the *Ars Magna*, and have made long search in Buonanni's *Micrographia Curiosa* (1691) and *Musaeum Kircherianum* (1709). But the results have been incommensurate with my labours. To me the *Scrutinium Pestis* appears as a farrago of nonsensical speculation by a man possessed of neither scientific acumen nor medical instinct.[3] Kircher obviously had no conception of a *real* experiment—in the Baconian and modern sense. It is easy enough, of course, to tear a line here and there from his voluble writings, and to use it as evidence on his behalf: but if such lines be considered in their context they have a very different complexion. For instance, some recent authors have inferred that Kircher's remarks about rats dying and decomposing at a time of plague show that he realized the relation of these rodents to plague-

---

[1] Grew (1701), p. 12.

[2] About ten years ago I had some correspondence with Dr Singer on this matter, and I then attempted to convince him of the error of his views. From his last letter to me on the subject I gather that he is no longer prepared to defend Kircher's claim to the discovery of either the Bacteria or the Protozoa, and that he now accepts my interpretations.

[3] Kircher—who was a priest with no biological or medical training—had obviously derived most of his "knowledge" from wide reading, and it seems to me not unlikely that in his vague references to "worms" occurring in the blood of sick people he was merely harking back to the speculations of antiquity: for example, to the well-known passage where Pliny says "*nascunturque in sanguine ipso hominis animalia exesura corpus*" (*Hist. Nat.*, lib. XXVI, cap. xiii; ed. Genevae 1582, p. 488).

epidemics. I wish such authors would also explain, in modern terms, what Kircher meant when he recorded further how plague could arise likewise from a rotting mermaid.

For my part, I cannot regard Kircher as anything more than the veriest dabbler in Science. His own writings appear to me unscientific in the highest degree, and I can find no evidence that he ever saw—even by chance—a protozoon or a bacterium through his "smicroscope." His writings appear, consequently, to furnish no evidence whatsoever to prove that he forestalled Leeuwenhoek. But as I have already said, I have not read all his works. I can therefore only beg his supporters (if any there still be) to adduce some solid passage—which I have hitherto been unable to discover in his vast publications—to prove that he ever saw a protozoon. (Discussion of his "discovery" of the Bacteria may well be postponed until it has been demonstrated that he observed these larger organisms.) I am aware, of course, that Garrison [1] calls Kircher "the earliest of the microscopists" and says that he was "undoubtedly the first to state in explicit terms the doctrine of a 'contagium animatum' as the cause of infectious diseases": but I submit that these statements also have not yet been substantiated, and I cannot conceive that they ever will be. Microscopists and *contagium animatum* both existed before Kircher began to write.

This brings us to another line of argument against Leeuwenhoek's originality—the argument from the doctrine of *contagium vivum*.[2] It is as certain as anything historic ever can be that Kircher was not the first exponent of this idea: and there can be no doubt that the part played by "animalcules" in the causation of diseases was foreshadowed long before either Kircher or Leeuwenhoek was born.[3] Some of the oldest known authors appear to have been familiar with the

---

[1] Garrison (1921), p. 250.

[2] In this connexion the paper by Singer (1913) should be mentioned, though I must confess that I have been unable to verify many of his statements and references.

[3] I do not deny, of course, that Kircher formulated a "doctrine of *contagium animatum*"—and possibly more explicitly than his predecessors: but I do deny that it had any more objective basis than similar earlier guesses. The doctrine had no concrete foundation before L.'s discovery of *real* "animalcules."

concept of a living "contagion" or infective agent—invisibly floating in the air at the time of epidemic pestilences, and comparable with some kind of "insect". Malaria, for example, was all too well known in classical times, and even rustic writers such as Varro[1] (116-27 B.C.) and Columella (*floruit ca.* A.D. 50) guessed that the "insects" abounding in marshes have some causal connexion with "fever".[2] (The ancients even used mosquito-nets as a prophylactic.) At a much later date Lancisi (1718) developed a more coherent and modern theory of malarial infection: yet even in his hands it remained nothing but an ingenious speculation.[3] The true aetiology of malaria has become known only in the last fifty years. In Leeuwenhoek's day both the malarial parasite and its mode of transmission by the mosquito were still wholly unknown to mankind, and the guesses of his predecessors and contemporaries have really no bearing upon his own discoveries. Nobody before Leeuwenhoek ever saw a living protozoon, and

---

[1] Marcus Terentius Varro (who was no mere husbandman) is particularly noticeable because of his antiquity. He is frequently cited, but seldom correctly. In all his extant works there appears to be but one passage bearing on the aetiology of malaria: and as most editions of his writings are rare, and as the passage in question is very short, I may quote it here. Discussing sites appropriate for a country house, Varro notes certain places to be avoided (such as the banks of a river—apt to be too cold in winter and unhealthy in summer) and then adds: "Attention should also be paid to any marshy places thereabouts; both for the same reasons, and because [they dry up,] certain minute animals grow there, which cannot be detected by the eye, and which get inside the body from the air, through the mouth and nostrils, and give rise to stubborn distempers." (*Advertendum etiam siqua erunt loca palustria, et propter easdem causas, et quod [arescunt,] crescunt animalia quaedam minuta, quae non possunt oculi consequi, et per aera intus in corpus per os, ac nares perveniunt, atque efficiunt difficilis morbos.*) Cf. Varro, lib. I, cap. XII (*Script. Rei Rust.*, ed. 1543, p. 54 *recto*). The words in square brackets should probably be omitted—*arescunt* being a MS. misreading or dittography of the word following.—Since writing the foregoing note I find there is now an excellent English edition of Varro by Storr-Best (1912): nevertheless, I let my own translation of the passage stand.

[2] The references to malaria in the Latin classics are mostly collected in the recent posthumous work of Celli (1925), while the Greek literature has been ably reviewed by Jones (1909).

[3] Lancisi actually refers to L.'s discoveries in order to prove the existence of such extremely minute animalcules as he himself postulated. Cf. *op. cit.* p. 46.

all early speculations about the relation of "insects" to malaria belong properly to the prehistory of entomology—not to that of protozoology.

The whole history of bacteriology has recently been so admirably written by Bulloch (1930) that I can add nothing to his account of its origins.[1] He has shown quite clearly that real bacteriology (like real protozoology) began with Leeuwenhoek's discoveries, though it was preceded by a long period of speculation on the causes of contagious diseases. Some early writers, it is true, made astonishing guesses at the existence of bacteria—particularly Fracastoro (1478 or 1483—1553), whose hypothetic "*seminaria*" bear a remarkable resemblance to modern "germs" or "microbes".[2] But nobody before Leeuwenhoek ever saw a bacterium with his own eyes. Nebulous though ingenious notions about invisible living organisms floated in the air for some thousands of years: but it required the untutored genius of a Leeuwenhoek to condense them—single-handed and with only his own little home-made "microscopes"—into the concrete realities of present-day laboratories and text-books of bacteriology.

Another point should not be overlooked in this connexion. When Leeuwenhoek announced his discovery of the "animalcules" in various waters and infusions, it was universally regarded as something entirely new. Yet the earlier writings of Kircher and others had already been public property for some years. Why, then, were contemporary "philosophers" astounded at Leeuwenhoek's "discoveries"—if they were not real discoveries? And why did some contemporary and later critics dispute his observations? Why did no author of his time—including Kircher, who was still alive and busy writing—claim priority? It is surely strange, to say the least, that nobody before Löffler in 1887 ever connected Leeuwenhoek's concrete discoveries of 1676 with Kircher's random speculations and "experiments" of 1658.

---

[1] I may note, however, that I have studied most of the early writings mentioned in this fine and accurate work: but as I agree entirely with its conclusions, and as it has an authority far beyond anything to which I can pretend, I shall here dispense with all other references to the subject.

[2] I cite the work of Fracastoro because I have devoted particular attention to his writings, owing to their great historic interest. On Fracastoro see also C. and D. Singer (1917).

All Leeuwenhoek's contemporaries regarded him as unquestionably the discoverer of his "little animals". But his discoveries were soon confirmed by Hooke—as we have already seen—and by several other "philosophers". In the last decade of the XVII Century the work of Buonanni[1] (1691) appeared, containing the first pictures of free-living ciliates, but reaffirming the doctrine of spontaneous generation—a small advance and a big step backwards at the same time. Of much greater importance were the papers by King[2] (1693) and Harris[3] (1696), who both saw and described a variety of free-living protozoa and bacteria—frankly in imitation of Leeuwenhoek, but adding new facts and some original speculations. Of far less value, protozoologically, were the notes by Gray[4] (1696, 1697), who observed protozoa with his ingenious "water-microscope" but gave only a slight account of what he saw. These five men—Hooke, Buonanni, King, Harris, and Gray—must all be regarded as belonging to the first generation of protozoologists.

But by far the greatest scion of this generation still remains unknown to us by name. In two anonymous English publications[5] which appeared in the *Phil. Trans.* in 1703 are to be found some amazingly good figures of free-

---

[1] Filippo Buonanni, *alias* Philippus Bonannus (1638-1725), an Italian Jesuit priest.

[2] Sir Edmund King (1629-1709), M.D.; physician to Charles II, whom he attended during his last illness. He was elected F.R.S. in 1666.

[3] The Rev. John Harris (1667?-1719), D.D., rector of Winchelsea in Sussex, F.R.S. (1696). Author of *Lexicon Technicum* (1704).

[4] Stephen Gray (?-1736) was a physicist, who published a number of papers in the *Phil. Trans.* He was not made a Fellow of the Society until 1732.

[5] See *Anonymus* (1703, 1703*a*). The first paper consists of extracts from several letters written in 1702 and "communicated by Sir C. H." [= Sir Charles Holt, not a Fellow]: the second comprises two other letters (1703) from "a Gentleman in the Country", communicated by "Mr. C." [probably John Chamberlayne]. All these letters were really written by the same person, whose identity I have vainly endeavoured to discover. The letters themselves are not in the Society's archives or the British Museum (so far as I have been able to ascertain), and all the documents relating to them appear to have been destroyed. In view of their great interest, I have made repeated attempts to discover their authorship; but every clue has proved unavailing, and I fear that "The Gentleman in the Country" covered up his tracks on purpose—in order to remain anonymous for ever.

living protozoa and bacteria, and diatoms[1]—confirming and amplifying many of Leeuwenhoek's findings and accompanied by a commentary, light-hearted and conversational, which shows nevertheless remarkable insight and ability. The pictures were far ahead of anything previously published, and are sufficient alone to establish their draughtsman as Eldest Son of the Father of Protozoology.

Only one other protozoologist of Leeuwenhoek's period deserves notice here—Louis Joblot (1645-1723), a Frenchman. His observations were first published in 1718,[3] and attracted little notice at the time: but his book is, in fact, the first special treatise on the Protozoa, and it contains descriptions and figures of many forms not previously described. A recent writer[4] has tried to show that Joblot was not merely a follower of Leeuwenhoek, but actually his equal—an independent co-discoverer of the Protozoa. But such a suggestion is manifestly groundless. There is no evidence that Joblot studied the Protozoa as early as the time when their discovery was announced by Leeuwenhoek; and the appearance of his book in the next century—only five years before they both died—definitively assigns his publication to a later generation. In Joblot's writings there is no direct reference to Leeuwenhoek's discoveries, but much internal evidence of imitation.[5]

I have already had occasion to note[6] that Leeuwenhoek himself made no application of his discovery of "microbes" to medical doctrines of contagion. He discovered protozoa and bacteria not only in waters and infusions but also in the

---

[1] *Tabellaria*—the first account and figures of this organism. Most of the other figures are equally easily recognizable.

[2] On Joblot see especially Fleck (1876), Cazeneuve (1893), Boyer (1894), Konarski (1895), Brocard (1905), and Dobell (1923). I may note here that the work of Sturm (1676), cited by Ehrenberg and others as containing contemporary observations on "infusoria", really deals only with insects and nematodes—not with protozoa. It should not be quoted in this connexion.

[3] This work is now very rare, and is better known from the much later and comparatively common edition of 1754.

[4] Konarski (1895).

[5] Cf. Dobell (1923).

[6] See p. 230 *supra*.

bodies of living animals—including man : but he never in his writings suggested, so far as I am aware, that his discovery of such "animalcules" threw any light upon the aetiology of morbid infections or furnished, for the first time, an objective basis for the old speculations regarding the existence of "living germs" of diseases—*seminaria morborum*, *contagium vivum*, *contagium animatum*, and the like. Yet this application of his findings was immediately made by others. Within a few months of the appearance of his *Letter 18*, announcing the discovery of the "little animals" in all manner of liquids, we find "an observing person in the country" writing to the editor of the *Philosophical Transactions* as follows[1]: "Mr. *Leewenhoecks* Microscopical Discoveries are exceeding curious, and may prompt us to suspect, that our Air is also vermiculated, and perhaps most of all in long Calms, long-lasting Eastern Winds, or much moisture in Spring-time, and in seasons of general Infections of Men or Animals."

As soon as this possible connexion between demonstrable "animalcules" and hypothetic infectious "germs" was suggested, it became almost commonplace : its theoretical implications and its obvious practical applications were henceforth recognized. Yet nobody made any real use of them during the next century and a half. Mankind possessed the necessary data, and was inspired—as usual—by the appropriate ideas : but the course of history has shown that both knowledge and notions arrived prematurely. We should not blame Leeuwenhoek, therefore, for making discoveries before they could be appreciated properly either by himself or by the world at large. Rather should we censure, I think, those modern writers who do not take his work into consideration when discussing present-day problems. To me it is incomprehensible how one author in my lifetime could have defended a thesis on *Parasitology in the XVI and XVII Centuries*,[2] and another could have written a book on *The Discovery of the Microbic*

---

[1] See *Anonymus* (1677). Cf. also the words of Slare (1683), quoted already on p. 230.

[2] Rémignard (1902). This dissertation—approved by the great Raphael Blanchard—contains only two ridiculous references to L. The first (p. 55) merely alludes to the fact that he did not discover *Demodex*, while the second (p. 63) informs us that he believed in the spontaneous generation of frogs.

Agents of Disease,[1] and yet could both have ignored all Leeuwenhoek's discoveries entirely. His work undoubtedly has an important bearing on the history of both these subjects.

Notwithstanding such present-day neglect, Leeuwenhoek's discoveries were utilized by contemporary theorists. I may mention particularly Benjamin Marten,[2] who published in 1720 (three years before Leeuwenhoek died) a most curious treatise to which attention has recently been directed by Singer (1911). In this book Marten, by assuming that tuberculosis is caused by invisible "*animalcula*" like those discovered by Leeuwenhoek, develops a theory of the pathogenesis of this disease remarkably similar to current conceptions. In many a passage, if one substitutes "*Bacillus tuberculosis*" for "*animalcula*" his statements are in close agreement with the views expressed in modern bacteriological and pathological works. As a prognostication, or even as a mere *tour de force*, Marten's book is notable: but he himself never saw the tubercle bacillus, and his writings had no influence on the history of bacteriology.

In recent times a claim to recognition has also been made for the French physician J.-B. Goiffon (1658-1730), of Lyons. Mollière (1886) calls him "*un précurseur des théories microbiennes*" on the strength of a dissertation on the plague which he published in 1722. In this Goiffon propounds the theory that plague is caused by an invisible virus (*vénin*)—probably some kind of "insect"[3]—which floats in the air and penetrates into the blood either through the pores of the skin or else through the mouth or nose. But Goiffon never attempted to see such "insects" himself, and makes no mention of the real "animalcules" already well known at that date (through the discoveries of Leeuwenhoek

---

[1] Grober (1912). This German writer's ignorance of L.'s existence was possibly feigned, and due to a false patriotism: for though his book bears evidence of considerable learning, its author had apparently never even heard of Pasteur also.

[2] Marten was a London physician about whom very little seems to be known. His book is excessively rare, and I am indebted to Dr Charles Singer for the loan of his own copy—the only one which I have studied. There is another, however, in the British Museum.

[3] In one place he actually conceives of it as possessing wings!

and his imitators). His own speculations are not particularly prescient or original, and appear to have but little relation to modern conceptions. I regard Goiffon's dissertation as historically negligible: in any case, it was without influence upon the course of bacteriology or protozoology.

I cannot omit to mention, in the present connexion, an extraordinary effort in pseudo-microbiology published just after Leeuwenhoek's death by a French quack doctor. This charlatan, who wrote under the initials "M.A.C.D.", pretended to discover the "insects" responsible for all diseases, and to cure his patients by eradicating them by secret methods.[1] He claimed to be following the system of an English physician who had learned of it in Persia: and he gave a comical description—accompanied by the crudest cuts—of no less than 91 absurdly-named "little insects" which cause as many complaints. This imposture was exposed by Vallisneri,[2] in a posthumously published letter which is not generally known. I need make no further reference to it: I mention it only because certain learned authors have apparently taken this obvious bit of charlatanry for a serious contribution to microbiology or for genuine satire.[3] It was certainly neither.

There is no need, for present purposes, to trace in detail the history of our knowledge of Leeuwenhoek's "little animals" down to modern times. We are here concerned merely with the beginnings of protozoology and bacteriology: yet to see them as beginnings we must cast our eye also upon the later historical landmarks. As everyone knows, scant progress was made in the century following Leeuwenhoek's death; though it is worth noting that the first scientific

---

[1] See M.A.C.D. (1726, 1727). I quote him (as is customary) under these initials, though his real name, according to Vallisneri (1733), was Boil. From the "*Privilège du Roy*" at the end of his work, where the author is referred to as "*le sieur* A.C.D.", it seems that the initial M. stands for *Monsieur*. Consequently, he ought properly to be catalogued as "D. . ., A.-C."

[2] See Vallisneri (1733), Vol. III, p. 218. It is here explained how "Mr A. C. D." was able to impose upon his patients by showing them the "insects" in their blood or urine through a trick microscope—which apparently exhibited the object mounted before it, but really showed protozoa out of an infusion.

[3] Cf. Lesser (1738), Ehrenberg (1838), Bulloch (1930), etc.

names[1] were assigned to protozoa by John Hill[2] in 1752, and that the first serious systematic treatment of both protozoa and bacteria was attempted in 1773 by O. F. Müller[3]—revising and amplifying the inadequate account of these organisms given by Linnaeus[4] (1758, 1767). These three writers—an Englishman, a Dane, and a Swede—were all very remarkable men, in very different ways; yet they had this in common that they all respected Leeuwenhoek. Even the cavalier Hill—a bitter critic of the Royal Society and all its works (which he nevertheless copied[5] freely for his own profit)—was forced to allow his merits. In one place he says, for example, "Even *Lewenhoeck* the Father, as he may be called, of this Branch of Observation, is not without his Mistakes, tho' there are many more in Proportion in all that have followed him".[6]

Hill was an amateur microscopist, and he made no original contributions of value to protozoology: but though Linné was a professional naturalist, he had equally little knowledge of the Protozoa—notwithstanding he made the first attempt to classify the micro-organisms known in his day. But Müller was a systematist with a good working knowledge of the "Infusoria."[7] He applied Linné's system to organisms which he had himself seen and studied: and he was, withal, an

---

[1] They were pre-Linnaean and not binominal: yet some of them—such as *Paramecium*—are still current.

[2] Much has already been written about "Sir" John Hill (1716-1775), though nobody has yet duly appraised his contributions to protozoology. Cf. especially the *Dict. Nat. Biogr.*, T. G. Hill (1913), and Woodruff (1926).

[3] Otto Friderich Müller (1730-1784). Cf. *Dansk Biogr. Lex.*, XI, 594. The most recent estimate of him (chiefly as a botanist) is that of Christensen (1922, 1924). Bütschli fully appreciated his protozoological works, but no other recent student of the protozoa has attempted to assess or even interpret all his extremely important observations on these organisms.

[4] Carl von Linné (1707-1778). For his life see especially Daydon Jackson (1923).

[5] As an instance I may note that most of Hill's figures of protozoa (1752) were boldly copied without acknowledgement from the anonymous writer of 1703—from the *Phil. Trans.* which he so affected to despise!

[6] Hill (1752*a*), p. 94.

[7] Müller's "*Animalcula Infusoria*" were a motley crew of microscopic creatures, comprising not only all the protozoa and bacteria then known, but also worms, rotifers, algae, and other organisms.

excellent observer. His wrong interpretations were inevitable at the time when he wrote: and when we remember that he made his observations mostly with the aid of simple lenses of English manufacture (probably much inferior to Leeuwenhoek's), we can now only admire his accuracy. In my view, Müller was one of the great protozoologists of all time. He was also, for his period, a good bacteriologist—familiar at first hand with many bacteria—though he nowhere considers the possibility that any micro-organisms may be causally connected with disease.

Linnaeus's views regarding protozoa and bacteria, and their relation to infectious diseases, are not easily ascertained. In the *Systema Naturae* (ed. X, 1758) he grouped all the known protozoa in his Class VERMES and its last order ZOOPHYTA. Apart from a few Foraminifera and Vorticellidae—placed under molluscs and polyps respectively—all the Protozoa which he recognized were comprised in the single genus *Volvox*, containing only two species. In his 12th edition, however, he elaborates this system somewhat, and assigns all the "animalcules" then known to three ill-defined genera—*Volvox*, *Furia*, *Chaos*. All the "infusoria" described in "the books of micrographers" (including Leeuwenhoek) are lumped together in a single species "*Chaos infusorium*": but as an appendix he adds 6 doubtful kinds of "living molecules" which he leaves to his followers to elucidate.[1] The list is so curious, in many ways, that I must quote it here:[2]

α. The *contagion* of eruptive fevers?
β. The *cause* of paroxysmal fevers?
γ. The *moist virus* of syphilis?
δ. *Leeuwenhoek's* spermatic animalcules?
ε. The aery mist *floating in the month of blossoming*?[3]
ζ. *Münchhausen's septic agent* of fermentation and putrefaction?

Dr Bulloch—who quotes the foregoing list in its original

---

[1] "*obscurae . . . moleculae vivae . . . posteris relinquendae.*"

[2] I translate the original Latin into English in order to be consistent: but all students of the history of protozoology and bacteriology are doubtless familiar with Linné's own words.

[3] Meaning, of course, the month of May—which the Dutch also prettily call *Bloeimaand*.

Latin—justly remarks (1930, p. 22) that it "is surprising to find Linné, 30 years after Leeuwenhoek's death, placing in the same class spermatozoa and the 'ethereal clouds in the time of flowering'"; and he and others have been puzzled by Linné's "*aethereus nimbus*" (ε, *supra*). But it is probably, I think, merely a reference to the anonymous English author of 1677.[1]

Linnaeus himself doubted whether all the then known protozoa[2] and bacteria (as we now call them) might not really be stages in the development of fungi, and he questioned their relation to diseases. Similar vague suggestions were mooted in the dissertations of some of his pupils (Boström, 1757; Nyander, 1757; Roos, 1767): but what Linnaeus himself believed I cannot discover. I think he had no definite ideas; for though he was certainly not blind to the possibility that "microbes" may cause diseases, he was also sceptical and unable to make up his mind. In his own thesis for his degree (1735) he argued that "intermittent fevers" are caused by drinking water contaminated with clay, though in 1757 he apparently approved Boström's thesis contending that the cause was "bad air" or faulty sanitation. Yet at the same time he envisaged the existence of "*exanthemata viva*" (cf. Nyander), and ten years later (cf. *Syst. Nat.*, and Roos, 1767) was seemingly still sitting on the fence. In my view, Linné and his pupils never understood Leeuwenhoek's "little animals," and all their attempts at systematization merely created confusion. Their works are of great historic interest, however, in showing how far professional biologists and medicos had profited by Leeuwenhoek's "amateur" labours a century after he announced his first discoveries.

The only other authors of this period who call for passing notice here are three Germans—of very different merits. First, Rösel von Rosenhof,[3] a miniature-painter who published some admirable descriptions and figures of protozoa in 1755: secondly,

---

[1] Quoted on p. 373 *supra*.

[2] The name "Protozoa" was first used by Goldfuss (1817): but his group so named included not only the "Infusoria" but also "Lithozoa", "Phytozoa", and "Medusae".

[3] August Johann Rösel von Rosenhof (1705-1759). His life by Kleemann, his son-in-law, is prefixed to the fourth volume of his *Insecten-Belustigungen*. Cf. also Miall (1912), p. 293 *sq*.

Ledermüller,[1] a lawyer and amateur microscopist: thirdly, the physician Wrisberg[2]—better known as an anatomist and obstetrician—who published a dissertation on "*Animalcula Infusoria*" in 1765. The work of Ledermüller (1760-1765) is really almost negligible, so far as the Protozoa are concerned. It is chiefly remarkable for being constantly misquoted as the first publication in which the indefinite term "Infusoria" was employed[3]: but so far as I have been able to discover, the word occurs nowhere in Ledermüller's long-winded writings. It was really first used, I believe, by Wrisberg in the booklet just mentioned, which—though always cited as a classic—contains little of protozoological importance or novelty.

The much-quoted English works of Adams[4] (1746) and Baker[5] (1742, 1743, 1753, etc.) are of no account. Both were copyists and compilers, who drew largely upon Leeuwenhoek's publications for their own purposes. Baker's books, however, enjoyed a great vogue among the amateurs of his day, and were translated into several foreign languages. In the opinion of Harting (1876)—which seems well founded—the Dutch translations of his popular works on the microscope were, indeed, responsible for a sudden revival of interest in Leeuwenhoek in Holland: for it is a singular fact that on his death Leeuwenhoek was not only almost immediately forgotten by the learned world but even by his own countrymen, and the memory of his achievements has therefore undergone periodic resuscitations both at home and abroad.

The latter half of the XVIII Century was enlivened by the classical controversy between Spallanzani[6] and Needham

---

[1] Martin Frobenius Ledermüller (1719-1769). For his life see the recent sketches by Willnau (1921, 1926).

[2] Heinrich August Wrisberg (1739-1808). His life will be found in the *Allg. Dtsch. Biogr.* and Hirsch's *Lexikon*.

[3] Bütschli—usually so accurate—appears to be responsible for the origin of this erroneous statement. Ledermüller actually spoke only of "infusion animalcules" in the vernacular ("*Infussions Thierlein*"; *op. cit.* Vol. I, p. 88).

[4] George Adams, the elder (?-1773): mathematical instrument-maker to George III. See *Dict. Nat. Biogr.*

[5] Henry Baker, F.R.S. See note 1 on p. 318 *supra*.

[6] The *Abate* Lazzaro Spallanzani (1729-1799)—too great and famous an ornament of Italian science to require annotation here. (But the reader may consult with profit the recent note by Bulloch, 1922.)

(supported by Buffon)[1] on the subject of spontaneous generation. This dispute is too familiar for reconsideration here: and I need only note that Spallanzani successfully defended Leeuwenhoek's position—though he paid little attention to his Dutch predecessor—and was able to support their mutual belief by many admirable new experiments. But despite his great experimental skill and instinctive appreciation of scientific principles, Spallanzani possessed no real knowledge of protozoa or bacteria. Most of the organisms which he studied can now be recognized only with difficulty, or not at all, from his descriptions. Spallanzani was a great experimentalist and physiologist, but no morphologist or systematist. Needham's contributions, however, to all branches of protozoology and bacteriology may not unfairly be now assessed as *nil*. He may have been a good Catholic, but he was a hopelessly bad protozoologist and bacteriologist.

Although the middle of the XVIII Century produced numerous confirmations of Leeuwenhoek's protozoological discoveries, they were not—at that time—usually so regarded: they were rather considered as novelties. Nevertheless, Antony's marvellous researches on the multiplication of *Volvox* and other phytoflagellates were extended by the work of Trembley[2] (1744*a*, 1747), de Saussure[3] (1769), Ellis[4] (1769), and Corti[5] (1774)—two Genevese, an Englishman, and an Italian. Germany, soon afterwards, also contributed her share to protozoology through the work of Gleichen[6] (1778),

---

[1] John Turberville Needham (1713-1781), a British catholic priest who spent most of his life in France and Belgium. Elected F.R.S. in 1747.

[2] Abraham Trembley (1700-1784), sometime tutor to the sons of William Bentinck, English resident at The Hague. Later he came to England, and was elected F.R.S. in 1743.

[3] Horace Bénédict de Saussure [*seu* Desaussure] (1740-1799), naturalist and celebrated Alpinist. For his life see especially Senebier (1801). He was elected F.R.S. in 1788.

[4] John Ellis (1710 ?-1776), government agent in the West Indies, and author of the well-known work on Corallines. Elected F.R.S. in 1754.

[5] Bonaventura Corti (1729-1813), a catholic priest. Professor of Natural History at Reggio, and a friend of Spallanzani. One of the earliest students of the Cyanophyceae, and the discoverer of *Spirulina*.

[6] Baron Wilhelm Friedrich von Gleichen-Russworm (1717-1783).

who re-examined the organisms in infusions, and of Eichhorn[1] (1775, 1783), who discovered the first heliozoon (*Actinosphaerium*). But Holland's only representatives during this period were Job Baster (1759), who recorded some trifling observations on vorticellids, and Martinus Slabber (1778) who rediscovered, redescribed, and first depicted *Noctiluca*.[2] Yet it is a remarkable fact that—apart from Müller, who was in this connexion mainly a nomenclator and systematist—nobody arose anywhere for more than a century following Leeuwenhoek's death who can now fairly be called a bacteriologist. For 150 years from the date of their discovery the Bacteria were strangely neglected. Mankind remained inexplicably blind to their importance, and almost to their very existence.

From the standpoint of protozoology and bacteriology the first quarter of last century is a blank. At the end of this barren period, however, a revival of interest in Leeuwenhoek's "little animals" set in—a revival which led, with gradually increasing momentum, to the enthusiastic development of our modern sciences. It is now difficult to place oneself in the position of a zoologist or physician a hundred years ago: progress in our knowledge of all "microbes" has since been so rapid and so revolutionary. In 1832, Bory de St.-Vincent[3] had just published his reclassification of the "Infusoria"—which he needlessly renamed "Microscopica"[4]—and Ehrenberg[5] was busy cataloguing the booty collected in his travels: his monumental monographs were just germinating in the form of

---

[1] Johann Conrad Eichhorn (1718-1790), pastor of the Church of St Catharine at Danzig.

[2] *Noctiluca*, one of the chief organisms causing phosphorescence on the surface of the sea, was discovered by the Englishman Joseph Sparshall, of Wells in Norfolk, whose observations were recorded by Baker (1753, p. 402 *sq.*).

[3] Colonel J. B. Bory de St.-Vincent (1778-1846), soldier, politician, traveller, and naturalist. For his life, works, and correspondence see Lauzun (1908).

[4] "*Microscopiques*." I believe Bory borrowed this term—as he did so much else—from Müller (1773, p. 4: "microscopica *dicuntur, quod unice lenticulae amplificantis ope videntur*").

[5] Christian Gottfried Ehrenberg (1795-1876), of Berlin. The fullest biography is that of Laue (1895). See Dobell (1923*a*) for further references.

tentative preliminary papers.[1] His huge final treatise of 1838, together with its comparatively small but devastating corrective by Dujardin[2] in 1841, forms the real foundation of modern Protozoology. But the first experimental work on transmissible microbic diseases was probably that published in the same period by Bassi[3] (1835), while the first on any protozoal infection came much later from Pasteur (1870). Both of these experimenters studied, singularly enough, no well-known maladies of man, but certain obscure "epidemics" of silkworms—"*moscardino*" and "*pébrine*" respectively.[4]

It is not my purpose now to trace the history of Protozoology and Bacteriology during the last hundred years, so I shall leave the subject at the moment when our modern sciences commenced. The authors I have mentioned, and the works which they performed, are chronicled merely to remind the reader of certain salient events which cannot be overlooked if we would see Leeuwenhoek in his true perspective and proportions.

Of Leeuwenhoek's discoveries in sciences other than Protistology I am not competent to speak. I observe, however, that he is usually most praised by those most qualified to judge. Those authors who decry his observations generally reveal themselves, at the same time, ignorant of himself and his works. As an instance I may cite the opinions expressed by certain botanical writers. Two careful Dutch authors—van Hall (1834) and Bolsius (1903)—find much that is original and admirable in Leeuwenhoek's studies of plants: but the more famous German botanist Sachs (1875), whose knowledge of Leeuwenhoek was obviously not profound, says that "on the whole, all his numerous communications, in comparison

---

[1] I possess and have studied all of these, though I do not cite them here.

[2] Félix Dujardin (1801-1860), Professor of Zoology at Rennes. For his life see Joubin (1901). I have also studied—though I do not cite—the earlier works of this admirable protozoologist.

[3] Agostino Bassi (1773-1856), of Lodi. See his *Opere* (1925), recently reprinted and edited, with a remarkable introduction by the late Prof. B. Grassi; who sums up his review with the statement that "it is proved that parasitology, like many other branches of knowledge, had its cradle in our own Italy: foreigners have merely recognized and perfected it." Nevertheless, no Italian saw protozoa or bacteria before the year 1674.

[4] *Moscardino* is now supposed to be caused by a fungus (*Botrytis*) and *pébrine* by a protozoon (*Nosema*)—both of doubtful systematic status.

with Malpighi's pleasing clarity and Grew's systematic thoroughness, create a painful impression of superficiality and amateurishness."[1] A similar opinion of Leeuwenhoek's work in general has, moreover, been recently expressed by one of his own compatriots (Becking, 1924), who sees in him merely "a pair of eyes, a pair of hands, directed by other minds. For when his own mind tried to direct, he could produce nothing but chaos." This is surely a strange estimate of the almost wilfully independent Leeuwenhoek I know—who certainly produced something very different from chaos when he discovered the Protozoa and the Bacteria! But even for these discoveries Becking allows Leeuwenhoek little credit: he avers that "although he was the first to see bacteria, yeasts and protozoa, we can not look upon him as the founder of microbiology." Despite his obviously great knowledge[2] of Leeuwenhoek, and his own distinction in other branches of learning, I am unable to judge of Becking's competence in protozoology—since he has not (to my knowledge) contributed as yet anything to the advancement of that science. His evaluation of Leeuwenhoek may, however, be contrasted with that of the only man of our times who possessed a profound knowledge both of the Protozoa themselves and of protozoological history. He not only respected and admired Leeuwenhoek's work, but he even dedicated one of his own most important memoirs to his memory.[3]

Other biologists have already honoured Leeuwenhoek in their own peculiar way by naming various organisms after him. It is true no protozoon or bacterium or other "little animal"

---

[1] Sachs (1875), p. 264; translated. I have good reasons for believing that these words were actually plagiarized from an earlier and less-known author.

[2] Becking writes as one who knows all about L., and he says that "the uncritical praise of his commentators and biographers can only be ascribed to an insufficient knowledge of his works and that of his contemporaries." Considering Becking's greater knowledge, I confess that at first I found it difficult to understand how he could refer to L. as "a humble lens-grinder", who was "a patrician's son" and "had many children", etc. But such obvious misstatements of fact are to be explained, doubtless, by his conviction that "What really matters in a biography is not the so-called biographical datum." I differ from him in believing that accurate data are the *sine qua non* of any biography.

[3] Bütschli (1876).

of his own discovering now bears his name:[1] yet it has been bestowed—more or less permanently—upon a minute moth,[2] a tiny mite,[3] and an insignificant Australian flowering plant[4] . . . "*cum rerum Natura nusquam magis quam in minimis tota sit.*"

My personal estimate of Leeuwenhoek is based upon a study of his own works. I admit that I have not yet examined his numerous writings sufficiently, but I have read enough to realize that those people who ridicule him are generally ignorant, and usually reveal their own incompetence in the very act of denouncing his. Whilst professing to show us his faults they unintentionally pillory themselves. Leeuwenhoek and his disciples have now no need even to contradict statements such as "this physician described many things that he never saw," or "his assertions . . . sufficiently prove that he saw less through his microscope with his eyes than with his imagination:"[5] and nowadays we only laugh when we read this pronouncement by the self-appointed judge of the Royal Society—"*Lewenhoeck* . . . had the good fortune to be one of the first People who worked at microscopical Observations, but we are to acknowledge at the same Time, that he has had the Honour of having stocked the Philosophical Transactions with more Errors than any one Member of it, excepting only his Successor in Peeping, Mr. *Baker.*"[6]

---

[1] The name "*Pandorina leuwenhoekii*", proposed by Bory de St-Vincent (1826, p. 22), is an invalid synonym of *Volvox globator* Linnaeus: while the same author's "*Esechielina leuwenhoekii*" (1826, p. 78) has been engulfed in the synonymy of *Rotifer vulgaris*.

[2] *Oecophora leeuwenhoekella* [Tineidae] F. v. P. Schrank, 1802. For the various spellings of the specific name see Sherborn (1927). Cf. also *Isis* (1839), p. 192.

[3] Genus *Leeuwenhoekia* Oudemans, 1911.

[4] *Levenhookia pusilla* Brown, 1810. In proposing the genus, Robert Brown says (in Latin) that he dedicates it "to the memory of the most famous micrographer, in whose works there are many most beautiful observations on the structure of vegetables." Brown's spelling of the generic name is curious, and is evidently an attempt to reconcile Dutch orthography with Latin and with English pronunciation. Later emendations (such as "*Leevenhokia*" van Hall, 1834) can hardly be regarded as improvements.

[5] Jourdan (1822), *Biogr. Méd.*, V, 561.

[6] John Hill (1751), p. 156. The reference is to Henry Baker (see p. 318 *supra*), one of Hill's pet aversions.

At all times the name of Leeuwenhoek has been mentioned with respect by those who have really made his acquaintance. Even general historical writers[1] are sometimes aware that he was one of the phaenomena of the XVII Century: and even in his own lifetime his claims to recognition were conceded by biological and medical authors. Leeuwenhoek was no "physician" or "surgeon", as he has so often been ridiculously styled: nevertheless, he was already called "celebrated" in Roukema's *Dictionary of Famous Physicians* as early as 1706, and he now has a whole section to himself in Banga's *History of Medicine and its Practitioners in Holland* (1868) and in Hirsch's *Biographical Lexicon of Distinguished Doctors of all Times and Peoples* (1886). The great and learned Leibniz paid attention to his discoveries, which were not without influence upon his own philosophy: indeed, the abstract "monads" of the *Monadology* are not altogether unrelated to Leeuwenhoek's concrete "animalcules".[2] But to trace Leeuwenhoek himself through all the misunderstandings and misquotations and muddles of the multitudinous authors who have utilized his discoveries for their own ends, is a task beyond my competence; and for my present purpose it is, fortunately, unnecessary.

Leeuwenhoek will be finally judged by his own writings, and not by anything that other people say he wrote. He has left us a great mass of records—both published and unpublished—from which we can now extract what we please. I have endeavoured to recover from them all his observations on the Protozoa and the Bacteria, and to set in order his inchoate and uncorrelated findings in a manner which may fairly convey their import and importance to present-day students. To me his words, when judicially weighed in the scales of contemporary and recent knowledge, prove conclusively that he was the first protozoologist and the first bacteriologist. He has had thousands of followers and imitators, and was preceded by a few prophetic precursors; but his own true place in Protozoology and Bacteriology appears to me incontro-

---

[1] For example, Hallam in his *Literature of Europe* (published first in 1837-9).

[2] Leibniz also mentions L. in his *Théodicée* (published in 1710). His correspondence with L. is discussed by Ehrenberg (1845): but the first author who appears to have realized Leibniz's intellectual debt to L. is Rádl (1905).

vertible. He was the originator of everything we now know about " microbes ", and of all that will ever be known about these organisms. To say that he is " not the founder of microbiology . . . although he was the first to see bacteria, yeasts, and protozoa " may sound very knowing, and may satisfy those who seek paradox and literary effect : but every workaday bacteriologist and protozoologist knows that it is sheer nonsense. One might equally well say that Columbus did not discover the New World because he left no account of New York.

In the foregoing pages I have done my best to portray Leeuwenhoek and to chronicle some of his great discoveries anew in his own words. If I have also attempted to represent other leading figures in the historic scene wherein he himself appears, it is because I realize that he can be recognized in his true character only when the other actors are ranged beside him on the stage. It is not for me, or any other living man, to design or paint the scenery or to dress the players or even to clap or hiss their exits and their entrances. I can but strive to discharge with fidelity the humbler office of the man who manipulates the limelight—whose duty is to show, in just illumination, the performers in a drama which I neither did nor ever could compose, and of whose intricate plot I have but the roughest working knowledge.

I have always endeavoured to regard Leeuwenhoek objectively and dispassionately, but I am conscious that I have not always succeeded : for whenever I listen to his talk about " little animals " I am carried away by the unintentional eloquence of his discourse. He speaks an ungrammatical and old-fashioned language which is not my mother-tongue, and which I have learned painfully and as yet imperfectly : but he also echoes a language which I hear oftener than any other—that of the " little animals " themselves. I have spent all my working life trying to understand them, but I still know no more than old Antony knew—just enough, in fact, to inspire me with the enthusiasm to continue listening and labouring, but never enough to feel satisfied with my interpretations. I have unbounded admiration for Leeuwenhoek because he heard and interpreted things that I, unaided, could never have discovered, and hit on problems—during quiet nights in his own private closet—of which neither he nor I can ever know the final solution.

One of Leeuwenhoek's own countrymen has recently called me his "greatest living admirer."[1] I am proud to admit the accusation, and this book gives some of the grounds for my conceit. But the foregoing pages are not meant as an appeal to the reader's emotions—only to his reason. "How Dogmatical soever my Assertions may seem to be, yet do I not affect the unreasonable Tyranny of obtruding upon the Faith of any. He that speaketh Reason, may be rather satisfied, in being understood, than believed."[2] Consequently, if my poor labours succeed in robbing me of a title which I hold but temporarily and precariously, they will not have been wholly in vain; and I shall be the first to rejoice when I am deposed from a position which I do not deserve, cannot maintain, and have never sought.

> As I aim at nothing but Truth, and, so far as in me lieth, to point out Mistakes that may have crept into certain Matters; I hope that in so doing those I chance to censure will not take it ill: and if they would expose any Errors in my own Discoveries, I'd esteem it a Service; all the more, because 'twould thereby give me Encouragement towards the Attaining of a nicer Accuracy.[3]

---

[1] Dr W. H. van Seters, as reported in the *Nieuwe Rotterdamsche Courant* of 13 July 1926 (Nr. 83, blz. 6).

[2] Nehemiah Grew (1672), last lines of Preface.

[3] Translated from L.'s *Letter 135* (25 Dec. 1700): published in *Brieven*, Sevende Vervolg, p. 307.

A SHORT LIST OF LEEUWENHOEK'S WRITINGS

THERE is still no complete edition of all Leeuwenhoek's letters: and of those already published there are so many versions that specific reference to any particular passage is often a matter of grievous difficulty. The bibliographies already printed by Gronovius (1760), Pritzel (1872), and many others, are so incomplete and otherwise imperfect as to be almost worthless. But a committee of experts has lately been formed in Holland with the object of printing or reprinting all Leeuwenhoek's extant writings; and we may therefore hope that the material for a full and accurate bibliography will shortly be collected and collated, and placed at the disposal of the public.

In the meantime, since I have not the leisure or learning —still less the funds—of the Dutch committee, but owe it to my readers to give the sources of my own information, I can only offer the following record of those writings which I have myself consulted. For the present work I have had to study every available manuscript and publication in order to collect the passages relating to protozoa and bacteria, and I have therefore had to catalogue every discoverable letter and collate all its versions. But my own private list of Leeuwenhoek's writings, so compiled, is still far too faulty to print here—and also far too long: and moreover this is obviously not the place to publish such a compilation. I therefore give now only the briefest indication of my sources for the assistance of fellow-students.

MANUSCRIPTS

The Leeuwenhoek Manuscripts in the possession of the Royal Society: 4 volumes, containing also numerous translations, drawings, and other relevant material. Imperfectly catalogued by Halliwell-Phillipps (1840). Referred to, here throughout, as "*Roy. Soc. MSS.*" Together with a few letters among the *Boyle MSS.* and elsewhere in the Society's archives, and including fragments and copies of letters addressed to others, they amount approximately to 200. At present I cannot enumerate them more exactly. (Their number is grossly overstated by most previous authors, who apparently count originals and translations and printed proofsheets as "original manuscripts".) As these manuscripts form the basis of the present work, I may add the following notes upon them:

The *Roy. Soc. MSS.* (mostly Dutch) were very incompletely and imperfectly printed in the form of extracts or abstracts, in English or Latin, in contemporary numbers of the *Philosophical Transactions* and Hooke's *Philosophical Collections* (which replaced the *Transactions* between Vol. XII, 1678-9, and Vol. XIII, 1682-3). These periodicals contain approximately 120 printed "extracts" from Leeuwenhoek's letters, though the "extracts" do not represent exactly the same number of original letters. The printed versions will all be found in *Phil. Trans.* Vol. VIII (1673) to Vol. XXXII (1723) inclusive [none in Vols. XVI and XXX], and are indexed—more or less accurately—by Maty (1787). Similar "extracts" from 2 letters were included in Hooke's *Lectures and Collections* (1678)—reprinted in his *Lectiones Cutlerianae* (1679)—and of 3 others in his posthumous *Philosophical Experiments and Observations* edited by Derham (1726).

Many of these manuscripts were published in full, however, in Leeuwenhoek's printed Dutch and Latin collective works, and 14 of the previously wholly unpublished early Dutch letters have just appeared in *Opuscula Selecta Neerlandicorum*, Vol. IX (1931): while two of the letters sent to the Royal Society, together with a fragment of *Letter 116*, have passed somewhat mysteriously into the *Sloane MSS.* now preserved in the British Museum. (I say 'mysteriously' because the honourable Sir Hans Sloane, M.D., had no obvious right to incorporate any of Leeuwenhoek's original letters, addressed to him as Secretary of the Society, in his own private collection.)

Other surviving manuscripts of Leeuwenhoek are known to me only through more or less recently printed versions or descriptions. I have not yet been able to study all the originals, but note their existence here for the help of others:

The Leeuwenhoek Manuscripts in the Huygens Collection at Leyden (University Library). Eight in number, and now printed in *Œuvres Complètes* of Chr. Huygens (see especially

Vol. VIII; 1899) or by Vandevelde and van Seters (1925). Also partially printed or abstracted by Snelleman (1874), Haaxman (1871, 1875), Vandevelde (1924*a*). [Some of the MSS. known to Haaxman (1875) have seemingly since disappeared. They were apparently removed by a former librarian, who claimed them as his private property.] A complete list of these MSS., with 5 others (one published) which I have not been able to trace further, is given by Harting (1876, pp. 121-3).

The Leeuwenhoek Manuscripts in the National Library at Florence. These letters (about 15) were all addressed to Magliabechi,[1] and have been partly printed by Targioni-Tozzetti (1745) and Carbone (1930). [The latter erroneously includes among them a letter written by Leibniz,[2] and previously published as such by Targioni-Tozzetti (1746).]

Four [*? three*] *Leeuwenhoek Manuscripts in the Municipal Museum at The Hague.* They are discussed, and their contents described, by Servaas van Rooijen (1905).

Manuscript of a Letter (dated 3 [? 13] March 1716) *to Leibniz.* Preserved among the *Leibniz MSS.* at Hanover (*fide* Ehrenberg, 1845), together with drafts of 3 letters from Leibniz to Leeuwenhoek. [This letter—*Send-brief* XX—was published in full in L.'s Dutch and Latin collected works.]

PUBLICATIONS

No serious attempt has yet been made by any bibliographer to collect and collate all Leeuwenhoek's numerous printed letters. His published writings have been, indeed, the despair of all authors who have had occasion to refer to them; and I do not, therefore, pretend to describe or enumerate all their many versions here.

Leeuwenhoek himself published in his lifetime 165 letters (not counting letters contained within letters): and to these

---

[1] Antonio Magliabechi (1633-1714), a Florentine scholar of prodigious learning. This remarkable man—of poor parentage—became librarian to Duke Cosmo III of Tuscany: and though he published nothing during his lifetime he is said to have been himself "a walking library" (including the dust and cobwebs, apparently). L. wrote to him because he had heard that he was then the most learned man in Italy: and he also dedicated to him his Latin edition entitled *Arcana Naturae Detecta* (1695).

[2] Cf. p. 46, note 1, and p. 359 *supra*.

he assigned numbers—in chronological order. He published them, however, in two separate series—the first numbered with arabic numerals, the second with roman. But the first series began with No. 28[1] (not No. 1) and ran to No. 146, and thus consisted of 119 letters in all: while the later series (46 letters) was consistently numbered from I to XLVI. This, in itself, is apt to cause confusion: but the difficulty of collation is increased because the letters were not originally published always in strict chronological order, and were frequently, on their first issue, not numbered at all. Their seriation can therefore be determined only by their dates, or by the numbers assigned to them in later issues, editions, or translations.

All the letters originally printed in Dutch, under Leeuwenhoek's supervision, were translated into Latin and printed in that language; but the Dutch and Latin versions were not issued simultaneously.[2] (As a rule—but not invariably—the Dutch versions preceded the Latin.) Furthermore, the letters —whether in Dutch or in Latin—generally made their appearance a few at a time in the form of a brochure with a common title: while a little later another collection would appear—often printed for a different publisher and with a different title—and in this some of the earlier letters were often incorporated. The final complete collections of Leeuwenhoek's letters were made up of these earlier partial collections—of various issues—and new editions; and, in the case of the Latin translations, sometimes of entirely new versions corrected and amended almost beyond recognition.

The following is a short list of the chief printed versions —both Dutch and Latin—which I have myself been able to study, together with a few notes [in square brackets] which may be serviceable to others. The arrangement is chronological (for either language), and the names of publishers are given in parenthesis after the place and date of publication. Numbers are prefixed merely for convenience of present reference, and have no other significance.

---

[1] Cf. p. 356 *supra*, and Dobell (1931).

[2] By far the best list is that given in Harting (1876, pp. 132-139): but this publication is itself so rare that few authors can nowadays refer to it. My own copy was most generously presented to me by the late Prof. M. W. Beijerinck—after I had for years vainly attempted to obtain one through booksellers.

I. Dutch Editions

1. *Ondervindingen en Beschouwingen der onsigtbare geschapene waarheden, vervat in verscheydene Brieven, geschreven aan de Wijt-beroemde Koninklijke Societeit in Engeland.* 4°. Leyden, 1684 (van Gaesbeeck). [pp. viii + 8 + 32. Contains *Letters* 32 & 33, *unnumbered* and paged separately. Figs. engraved in text.]

2. *Ondervindingen en Beschouwingen der onsigbare geschapene waarheden, waar in gehandeld werd vande Eyerstok* [enz. enz.]. 4°. Leyden, 1684 (van Gaesbeeck). [pp. ii + 21 + 19. Contains *Letters* 37 & 39, *unnumbered* and separately paged. Figs. engraved in text.]

   (*a*) Another edition of *Letter* 37 entitled : *Antony van Leeuwenhoeks 37ste Missive, Geschreven aan de Heer Cristopher Wren.* 4°. [Lugd. Bat. 1696 ?] [No preliminary leaves : paged 1-20 (not 21, as in orig. ed.), and with different make-up.]

3. *Ondervindingen en Beschouwingen der onsigbare geschapene waarheden, waar in gehandelt wert vande Schobbens inde Mond* [enz.]. 4°. Leyden, 1684 (van Gaesbeeck). [pp. iv + 24. Contains *Letter* 40 : *unnumbered,* with figs. engraved in text.]

   (*a*) Another edition, entitled : *Antoni van Leeuwenhoeks* 40ste *Missive, Geschreven aan de Heer Francois Aston.* 4°. [Lugd. Bat. 1696 ?] [No preliminary leaves : pp. 1-24, identical with 1st ed.]

4. *Ondervindingen en Beschouwingen der onsigbare geschapene waarheden, waar in gehandeld werd over het maaksel van't Humor Cristallinus* [enz.]. 4°. Leyden, 1684 (van Gaesbeeck). [pp. ii + 26. Contains *Letter* 41 : *unnumbered,* with figs. engraved in text.]

   Later edition : see No. 17.

5. *Ontledingen en Ontdekkingen van de onsigtbare Verborgentheden ; vervat in verscheyde Brieven, geschreven aan de Wyd-vermaarde Koninklijke Wetenschap-soekende Societeyt tot Londen in Engeland.* 4°. Leyden, 1685 (Boutesteyn). [pp. 88, but mispaginated 79-94 from p. 72 to end. Contains *Letters* 38, 42, 43 ; *unnumbered,* and with continuous pagination. All figs. engraved in text.]

   (*a*) Another edition [? 2nd] dated 1691. [*non vidi.*]

   (*b*) Another edition [? 3rd] dated 1698. Same title and publisher, but with *letters numbered.*

6. *Ontdekkingen en Ontledingen van Sout-figuren van verscheyden Souten : van Levendige Dierkens in de Mannelyke Saden de Baarmoeder ingestort ; ende van de Voort-telinge* [enz.]. 4°. Leyden, 1685 (Boutesteyn). [pp. 76. Contains *Letters* 44 & 45 ; *unnumbered,* and with continuous pagination.]

   (*a*) Second edition, *ibid.* 1696 : with *letters numbered* (but 45 misnumbered 46.)

7. *Ontledingen en Ontdekkingen van het Begin der Planten in de Zaden van Boomen* [enz.]. 4°. Leyden, 1685 (Boutesteyn). [pp. 78. Contains *Letters* 46 & 47 : *unnumbered,* and with continuous pagination.]

   (*a*) Another [? 2nd] edition, *ibid.* 1697. Letters likewise unnumbered.

8. *Ontledingen en Ontdekkingen van levende Dierkens in de Teel-deelen van verscheyde Dieren, Vogelen en Visschen ; van het Hout met der selver meningvuldige Vaaten* [enz.]. 4°. Leyden, 1686 (Boutesteyn). [Engraved title (dated 1685) + pp. 40 + 35. Contains *Letters* 28, 29, 30, 31 ; and 34, 35, 36—each series continuously paginated separately. Letters all *unnumbered*.]
   (*a*) Second edition, *ibid*. 1696. Letters *numbered*.

9. *Ontledingen en Ontdekkingen van de Cinnaber naturalis, en Bus-poeder ; van het maaksel van Been en Huyd* [enz.]. 4°. Leyden, 1686 (Boutesteyn). [pp. 110. Contains *Letters* 48, 49, 50, 51, 52 : *unnumbered*, and with continuous pagination.]
   (*a*) Another edition ; Leyden, 1713 (Langerack)—with letters still unnumbered.

10. *Vervolg der Brieven, geschreven aan de Wytvermaarde Koninglijke Societeit in Londen*. 4°. Leyden, 1687 (Boutesteyn). [pp. viii + 155. With engraved portrait. Contains *Letters* 53-60 : all except the first (53) *numbered*, and with continuous pagination.]
   (*a*) Second edition, *ibid*. 1688.
   (*b*) Another [? 3rd] edition, *ibid*. 1704.

* In the preliminary pages the publisher gives a *list of all L.'s letters from No.* 28 *to No.* 52, with their dates, publishers, titles, and contents (but not dates of publication).

11. *Den Waaragtigen Omloop des Bloeds, Als mede dat De Arterien en Venae Gecontinueerde Bloed-vaten zijn, Klaar voor de oogen gestelt. Verhandelt in een Brief, geschreven aan de Koninglyke Societeit tot Londen*. 4°. Delff, 1688 (Voorstad). [pp. ii (title-p.) + 1-30 : 1 folding plate. Contains *Letter* 65 only—*numbered*.]

12. *Natuurs Verborgentheden Ontdekt : zijnde een Tweede Vervolg der Brieven, geschreven aan de Koninglijke Soçieteit tot Londen*. 4°. Delff, 1689 (Voorstad). [pp. ii (titlepage) + 157-350 (mispaginated after p. 260). Contains *Letters* 61-67, all *numbered*.]
   (*a*) Second edition ; Delft, 1697 (Kroonevelt).

13. *Derde Vervolg der Brieven, geschreven aan de Koninglyke Societeit tot Londen*. 4°. Delft, 1693 (van Kroonevelt). [pp. viii + 351-531. Contains *Letters* 68-75 : all *numbered*, and continuously paginated.]

14. *Vierde Vervolg der Brieven, geschreven aan de Wytvermaarde Koninklijke Societeyt in London*. 4°. Delft, 1694 (van Kroonevelt). [pp. ii (titlepage) + 533-730. Contains *Letters* 76-83 : all *numbered*, and continuously paginated.]

15. *Vijfde Vervolg der Brieven, geschreven aan verscheide Hoge Standspersonen en Geleerde Luijden*. 4°. Delft, 1696 (van Krooneveld). [Engraved title (dated 1696), pp. vi + 172 + x (Blad-wyser). Contains *Letters* 84-96 : all *numbered*, and with continuous pagination.]

16. *Sesde Vervolg der Brieven, geschreven aan verscheide Hooge Standspersonen en Geleerde Luijden*. 4°. Delft, 1697 (van Krooneveld). [pp. iv + 173-342 + x (Blad-wyser & Druk-feilen). Contains *Letters* 97-107 : all *numbered* and continuously paginated.]

17. *A. van Leeuwenhoeks 41ste Missive, Geschreven aen de Koninklijke Societeit tot Londen* [enz.]. 4°. Delft, 1698 (van Kroonevelt). [pp. ii + 26. Apart from title, and preliminary page in former, identical with Gaesbeeck's ed. of 1684 (No. 4).]

18. *Sevende Vervolg der Brieven, waar in gehandelt werd, van veele Opmerkens en verwonderens-waardige Natuurs-Geheimen.* 4°. Delft, 1702 (van Krooneveld). [pp. vi + 452 + xxii (Blad-wyser). Contains *Letters* 108-146 : all *numbered*, and continuously paginated.]

19. *Send-Brieven, zoo aan de Hoog-edele Heeren van de Koninklyke Societeit te Londen, als aan andere Aansienelyke en Geleerde Lieden* [enz.]. 4°. Delft, 1718 (Beman). [Engraved title with portrait inset (dated 1718), pp. xiv + 460 + xxviii (Register & Druk-fouten). Contains *Letters* I-XLVI, *numbered* and continuously paged.]

20. BRIEVEN [seu WERKEN]. 4°. 4 vols. (or sometimes 5). Various dates, publishers, and places.—The final Dutch collective edition of all L.'s published letters. Contains *Letters* 28-146 and I-XLVI, and is variously made up of the several separate issues already listed—bound together. With 2 portraits, engraved titles, and numerous engraved figs. in text and on inserted plates. Perfect copies, composed of first editions throughout, and with all the plates, are now extremely rare. The following is a short description of the only one (my own) which I have yet seen :

Deel I—Made up of Nos. 1, 2, 3, 4, 5, 6, 7, 8, 9 : thus containing *Letters* 28-52. With engraved title dated 1685 (1st state, with Dutch lettering "*Ontdeckte Onsigtbaar-heeden*").

Deel II = Nos. 10, 12, 13, 14. *Letters* 53-83. With engraved portrait prefixed (de Blois, after Verkolje : 1st state, with Dutch lettering).

Deel III = Nos. 15, 16, 18. *Letters* 84-146. Engraved title dated 1696 (2nd state, with Dutch lettering).

Deel IV = No. 19. *Letters* I-XLVI (*Send-brieven*), with engraved title dated 1718 (1st state, with Dutch lettering at foot), having Goeree's portrait inset.

II. LATIN EDITIONS

21. *Anatomia et Contemplatio Nonnullorum Naturae invisibilium Secretorum Comprehensorum Epistolis Quibusdam Scriptis ad Illustre Inclytae Societatis Regiae Londinensis Collegium.* 4°. Lugd. Batavorum, 1685 (Boutesteyn). [pp. 78. Contains *Letters* 43, 42, 38—in this order—with all figs. engraved in text. Letters *unnumbered* : continuous pagination. Excessively rare first Latin edition. My own copy is the only one which I have seen. No copy in British Museum, or hitherto discovered in any library in Britain.]

22. *Anatomia Seu interiora Rerum, Cum Animatarum tum Inanimarum* [sic], *Ope & nebeficio* [sic] *exquisitissimorum Microscopiorum Detecta, variisque experimentis demonstrata* [etc.]. 4°. Lugduni Batavorum, 1687 (Boutesteyn). [pp. vi + 64 (mispaginated 58) + 260 (mispaginated 258). Two parts—each continuously paged—

containing respectively *Letters* 43, 42, 38, and *Letters* 28, 29, 30, 31, 34, 35, 36, 46, 47, 44, 45, 48, 49, 50, 51, 52 (in this order). All letters *unnumbered*. Figs. partly engraved in text, and partly inserted as separate plates. With engraved title of No. 8, but Dutch words erased.]

23. A Second Issue of the preceding (No. 22) with the misprints "*inanimarum*" and "*nebeficio*" in title corrected to *inanimatarum* and *beneficio*. Same date, place, and publisher. [In the copy in my possession—the only one which I have collated—the first part (*Letters* 43, 42, 38) is paged 3-78, and is a reprint of these pages in No. 21 (not 22). The mispagination of Part II is also partially corrected.]
   (*a*) *Editio novissima, prioribus emendatior* [retranslation, with letters still unnumbered]. 4°. Lugd. Bat., 1722 (Langerak).

24. *Continuatio Epistolarum, Datarum Ad longe Celeberrimam Regiam Societatem Londinensem*. 4°. Lugduni Batavorum, 1689 (Boutestein). [pp. viii (title & indices) + 124. Contains *Letters* 53-60, in order; with continuous pagination but *unnumbered*.]
   (*a*) Second edition; Lugd. Bat. 1696 (Boutestein).
   (*b*) Third edition; Lugd. Bat. 1715 (Du Vivie, Haak, & Langerack). Letters unnumbered.
   (*c*) Another [? 4th] edition, Lugd. Bat. 1730 (Langerak). Letters unnumbered.

25. *Arcana Naturae Detecta*. 4°. Delphis Batavorum, 1695 (Krooneveld). [Engraved portrait and title (same as No. 15, but with Latin lettering and dated 1695) + pp. vi + 568 + xiv (index & emendanda). Contains *Letters* 32, 33, 37, 39, 40, 41, 61-92, with continuous pagination. Letters 32-41 *unnumbered*: 61-92 *numbered*.]
   (*a*) Second edition; Lugd. Bat. 1696 (Boutestein).
   (*b*) Third edition; Lugd. Bat. 1708 (Boutestein).
   (*c*) *Editio novissima, auctior et correctior*; Lugd. Bat. 1722 (Langerak).

26. *Continuatio Arcanorum Naturae detectorum, qua continetur quicquid hactenus ab Auctore lingua Vernacula editum, & in linguam Latinam transfusum non fuit*. 4°. Delphis Batavorum, 1697 (Kroonevelt). [pp. ii + 192 + viii (index). Contains *Letters* 93-107: all *numbered*, and with continuous pagination.]
   (*a*) Reprint, with new titlepage, Lugd. Bat. 1722 (Langerak).

27. *Epistolae ad Societatem Regiam Anglicam, et alios Illustres Viros Seu Continuatio mirandorum Arcanorum Naturae detectorum* [etc.]. 4°. Lugduni Batavorum, 1719 (Langerak). [Portrait + pp. xvi (title & index) + 429 + x (2nd index). Contains *Letters* 108-146, all *numbered* and continuously paged. Lat. transl. of No. 18.]

28. *Epistolae Physiologicae Super compluribus Naturae Arcanis* [etc.]: *hactenus numquam editae*. 4°. Delphis, 1719 (Beman). [Engraved title, with portrait inset (same as No. 19, but with Latin lettering at foot, and dated 1719); pp. xx (title, dedication, & summary) + 446 + xxvi (index & errata). Contains *Letters* I-XLVI; all *numbered*, and paged continuously. Latin translation of No. 19.]

29. OPERA OMNIA, *seu Arcana Naturae, ope Exactissimorum Microscopiorum Detecta, experimentis variis comprobata, Epistolis, ad varios illustres Viros, ut et ad integram, quae Londini floret, sapientem Societatem . . . datis.* 4°. 4 vols. Lugduni Batavorum, 1722 (Langerak).—This is the Latin equivalent of No. 20, and contains all the *Epistolae* from 28 to 146 and I-XLVI. It is made up of various editions and issues, and most copies which I have collated are imperfect. The usual arrangement is as follows (though many other collections are to be found):

Vol. I = Nos. 23*a* (part i), 22 (ii), 24*b*. [Engraved title of No. 25, general title, and 12 other preliminary pages (*carmen panegyricum, lectori typographus, & index*): pp. 1-64 + 1-260: *Index triplex* [pp. xxiv]: title, pp. vi (*praemonitio ad lectorem & index*) + 1-124. Contains, therefore, *Letters* 43, 42, 38; 28, 29, 30, 31, 34, 35, 36, 46, 47, 44, 45, 48, 49, 50, 51, 52; 53-60.]

Vol. II = Nos. 25*c* & 26*a*. [Engraved title of Nos. 8 & 22, with new Latin lettering; new titlepage + pp. xiv (*index*) + 1-515; *Index* (pp. xxiii + *errata*); new titlepage + *Index argumentorum* (pp. viii) + pp. 1-192 + *Index* (pp. viii). Contains, therefore, *Letters* 32, 33, 37, 39, 40, 41, 61-92; and 93-107.]

Vol. III = No. 27. [Portrait + title with engraved device + pp. xiv (*index* 1) + pp. 1-429 + x (*index* 2). Containing *Letters* 108-146.]

Vol. IV = No. 28. [Containing *Letters* I-XLVI.]

* All these volumes contain numerous figures engraved in the text and on large and small inserted plates—identical with those of No. 20.

In addition to the foregoing publications, I must record the following—issued in Leeuwenhoek's lifetime but not by himself. [All the original MSS. appear to be lost.]

The Letters addressed to Petrus Rabus.—Pieter Rabus (1660-1702; Dutch author, poet, and critic) published in the last decade of the XVII Century a literary review entitled "*De Boekzaal van Europe*" (8°. Rotterdam). Two volumes were issued yearly—separately paged—from 1693 to 1700: and in those published between 1693 and 1697 Rabus not only reviewed those works of Leeuwenhoek which appeared contemporaneously, but he also printed several of his letters addressed to himself. As these are not to be found elsewhere, and as they are not correctly cited by van der Aa or others, I add exact references here. Apart from reviews, and letters printed elsewhere, Rabus published—more or less completely—six of L.'s letters which are otherwise unknown. To wit:

1. A letter dated 27 Oct. 1693. *Boekzaal v. Europe* 1693 (ii), pp. 554-5. [Extract only.]
2. Letter dated 21 May 1695. *Ibid.*, 1695 (i), pp. 532-6. [Extract.]
3. Letter undated. *Ibid.*, 1695 (ii), pp. 96-9.

4. Letter dated 10 Sept. 1695. *Ibid.*, 1695 (ii), pp. 258-261.
5. Letter dated 1 June 1696. *Ibid.*, 1696 (i), pp. 522-5. [Incomplete.]
6. Letter dated 23 July 1696. *Ibid.*, 1696 (ii), pp. 144-151.

* There is nothing of protozoological or bacteriological importance in this otherwise interesting correspondence.

The Letters to Magliabechi, partly published by Targioni-Tozzetti (1745), have already been noted under " Manuscripts " (p. 390)—together with several other letters more recently printed in whole or in part.

The only extensive (though very incomplete) *English Translation* of Leeuwenhoek's works is the bowdlerized version of the Rev. Samuel Hoole (1798, 1807), to which a fuller reference will be found in the ensuing general bibliography (p. 410).

Hy sprack oock van de boomen;
van den cederboom aen, die op den
Libanon is, tot op den ysop die aen
den wandt uytwast: hy sprack
oock van het vee, ende van het
gevogelte, ende van de kruypende
dieren, ende van de visschen.

—I. Kon. iiij. 33.

OTHER REFERENCES AND SOURCES

THE following list contains all the works referred to in the foregoing text, and also a number of other publications upon which I have relied for information—or which I have had to read—but to which no specific allusion is made elsewhere. Annotations are added where they appear needful.

Various national and general biographical dictionaries, of which I have naturally made considerable use, have been cited throughout by abbreviated titles. They are as follows (other articles or publications being given, as a rule, under their individual author's or editor's name):

Allg. Dtsch. Biogr. = *Allgemeine Deutsche Biographie.* 8°. 56 vols. (with supplements). Leipzig. 1875-1912.

Biogr. Ital. Ill. = *Biografia degli Italiani Illustri,* ed. E. de Tipaldo. 8°. 10 vols. Venezia. 1834-1845.

Biogr. Méd. = *Biographie Médicale: Dictionaire des Sciences médicales,* ed. A. J. L. Jourdan. 8°. 7 vols. Paris. 1820-1825.

Biogr. Nat. Belg. = *Biographie Nationale . . . de Belgique.* 8°. 22 vols. Bruxelles. 1866-1920.

Dansk Biogr. Lex. = *Dansk Biografisk Lexikon,* ed. C. F. Bricka. 8°. 19 vols. Kjöbenhavn. 1887-1905.

Dict. Nat. Biogr. = *Dictionary of National Biography,* ed. Leslie Stephen and Sidney Lee. 8°. 70 vols. (with supplements). London & Oxford. 1885-1927.

N. Nederl. Biogr. Woordenb. = *Nieuw Nederlandsch Biografisch Woordenboek,* ed. P. C. Molhuysen, P. J. Blok, & Kossmann. 8°. 8 vols. Leiden. 1911-1930.

Nouv. Biogr. Gén. = *Nouvelle Biographie Générale* (seu *Universelle*), ed. F. Hoefer. 8°. 46 vols. Paris. 1855-1866.

AA, A. J. VAN DER (1852-1878). *Biographisch Woordenboek der Nederlanden.* 8°. 21 vols. Haarlem. [L. in vol. XI (1865), pp. 280-283.]

ADAMS, G. (1746). *Micrographia Illustrata, or the Knowledge of the Microscope Explain'd* [etc.]. 4°. London. [L.'s observations much quoted, and many of his figures reproduced.]

ADAMS, G. (1798). *Essays on the Microscope* [etc.]. 2nd ed. by F. Kanmacher. 4°. London. [Second-hand description of L.'s "single microscope," p. 7.]

AGNEW, D. C. A. (1886). *Protestant Exiles from France, chiefly in the reign of Louis XIV ; or, The Huguenot Refugees and their Descendants in Great Britain and Ireland.* (3rd ed.) Fol. 2 vols. London. [Printed for private circulation.]

ANDRY, N. (1700). *De la Génération des Vers dans le Corps de l'Homme.* 8°. Paris. [Another edition, 12°. Amsterdam, 1701. 3rd ed., 8°. 2 vols. Paris, 1741. Engl. transl. 8°. London, 1701.]

Anonymus (1658). *The Dutch-Tutor* [etc.]. 8°. London.

Anonymus (1662). *Wilhelmus en Mauritius van Nassouw, Prince van Oranjen. Haer Leven en Bedryf.* 12°. Amsterdam.

Anonymus (1677). " Letter to the Publisher " from " an observing person in the country." *Phil. Trans.*, vol. XII, No. 136, p. 889.

Anonymus (1679). *Receuil d'Experiences et Observations sur le Combat, qui procede du mélange des corps. Sur les Saveurs, sur les Odeurs, Sur le Sang, Sur le Lait, &c.* 12°. Paris. [No. 3, pp. 221-262, is a French transl. of L.'s letters on blood and milk in *Phil. Trans.* The translation is attributed to " Mr. Mesmin " by Rotermund (1810) and Hoefer (1860).]

Anonymus (1695). *Register (verstrekkende te gelijk voor een kort Inhoud) van alle de Werken van de Heer Antoni van Leeuwenhoek.* 4°. Leiden. [Anonymously compiled index to the early letters—by " *een Beminnaar der Natuurlijke-weteschappen.*" In 2 parts.]

Anonymus (1703). An Extract of some Letters sent to Sir. *C. H.* relating to some Microscopical Observations. *Phil. Trans.*, vol. XXIII, No. 284, p. 1357.

Anonymus (1703*a*). Two Letters from a Gentleman in the Country, relating to Mr. *Leuwenhoeck's* Letter in *Transaction*, No. 283. *Phil. Trans.*, vol. XXIII, No. 288, p. 1494.

Anonymus (1710). *Les Delices de la Hollande.* 12°. 2 vols. La Haye.

Anonymus (1880). *Herdenking van Jan Swammerdam's 200-jarige Sterfdag, op 17 Februari 1880.* 8°. Amsterdam. (*Genootschap tot Bevordering van Natuur-, Genees-, en Heelkunde.*)

Anonymus (1909). Een gedenkteeken voor Antony van Leeuwenhoek. *Wereldkroniek* (Rotterdam), 10 April 1909, p. 26.

Anonymus (1923). Antony van Leeuwenhoek (1632-1723). *J. Amer. Med. Assoc.*, LXXXI, 1613. [Worthless.]

Anonymus (1927). The living world no man had seen and how its gates were opened. *My Magazine* (London), XXIII, 561. [An account of L. written for children. Worthless.]

ARBER, A. (1913). Nehemiah Grew 1641-1712. *Makers of British Botany*, pp. 44-64. [See OLIVER (1913).]

ASTRUC, J. (1767). *Mémoires pour servir à l'Histoire de la Faculté de Medecine de Montpellier.* 4°. Paris.

BAAN, J. VAN DER (1874). Antonie van Leeuwenhoek. *De Navorscher* (Amsterdam), Jaarg. XXIV (N.S. VII), p. 100.

BACON, F. (1889). *Novum Organum,* ed. T. Fowler. 8°. Oxford. [First published 1620.]

BAER, K. E. VON (1864). Johann Swammerdam's Leben und Verdienste um die Wissenschaft. *Reden . . . und kleinere Aufsätze vermischten Inhalts,* I, 1. [Whole work in 3 vols., 1864-1873. 8°. St. Petersburg. Lecture delivered in 1817.]

BAKER, H. (1740). An account of Mr. Leeuwenhoek's microscopes. *Phil. Trans.*, XLI, (No. 458) 503.

BAKER, H. (1742). *The Microscope made Easy.* 8°. London. [Dutch transl. *Het Microscoop gemakkelyk gemaakt.* Amsterdam, 1744.]

BAKER, H. (1743). *An Attempt towards a Natural History of the Polype.* 8°. London.

BAKER, H. (1753). *Employment for the Microscope.* 8°. London. [Dutch transl. *Nuttig Gebruik van het Mikroskoop.* 2 ed. Amsterdam, 1770.]

BAKKENES, H. C. VAN (1873). Antonie van Leeuwenhoek. *De Navorscher* (Amsterdam), Jaarg. XXIII (N.S. VI), p. 594.

BANGA, J. (1868). *Geschiedenis van de Geneeskunde en van hare Beoefenaren in Nederland* [enz.]. 8°. 2 vols. Leeuwarden. [L. in vol. II, pp. 609-614.]

BARROW, J. (1896). *The Life of Peter the Great.* 8°. Edinburgh. [1st ed. New York, 1845. New ed. with notes, London, 1874.]

BASSI, A. (1925). *Opere . . . scelte e pubblicate a cura del Comitato Nazionale per la ristampa.* 8°. Pavia.

BASTER, J. (1759). *Natuurkundige Uitspanningen, behelzende eenige waarneemingen, over sommige Zee-planten en Zee-insecten* [etc.]. 4°. Haarlem. [Also published in Latin: *Opuscula subseciva . . .* Same form, date, and place.]

BAUMANN, E. D. (1915). *De Dokter en de Geneeskunde.* 8°. 2 vols. Amsterdam. [Nederl. Kultuurgeschk. Monogr. IV & V. For L. see vol. II, p. 24. Trivial.]

BECKING, L. B. (1924). Antoni van Leeuwenhoek, immortal dilettant (1632-1723). *Scientific Monthly* (New York), XVIII, 547.

BEER, H. DE & LAURILLARD, E. (1899). *Woordenschat. Verklaring van woorden en uitdrukkingen.* 8°. 's-Gravenhage.

BEIJERINCK, M. W. (1913). De infusies en de ontdekking der bacteriën. *Jaarb. Kon. Akad. Wetensch.* (Amsterdam), pp. 1-28 [separate].

BENSE, J. F. (1925). *Anglo-Dutch Relations from the Earliest Times to the Death of William the Third.* 8°. The Hague.

BIBLIA, *dat is De gantsche H. Schrifture . . . door Last der Hoogh-Mog: Heeren Staten Generael . . . uyt de Oorspronckelicke talen in onse Nederlandtsche tale over geset* (1702). Gr. fol. Te Dordrecht en t'Amsteldam.

BIDLOO, G. (1698). *Brief . . . aan Antony van Leeuwenhoek; wegens de dieren, welke men zomtyds in de lever der Schaapen en andere beesten vind.* 4°. Delft. [Also in Latin, 4°. Lugd. Bat. 1698. Reprinted in B.'s *Opera Omnia*, Lugd. Bat. 1715. English transl. in Hoole's *Select Works* of L., vol. I, part 2 (1798). The Dutch edition is extremely rare.]

BIRCH, T. (1756-9) *The History of the Royal Society of London for Improving of Natural Knowledge, from its First Rise.* 4°. 4 vols. London.

BJÖRNSTÅHL, J. J. (1780-84). *Resa til Frankrike, Italien, Sweitz, Tyskland, Holland, Ängland, Turkiet, och Grekeland . . . efter des Död utgifven af* C. G. Gjörwell. 8°. 6 vols. Stockholm. [German transl. (C. H. Groskurd). Leipzig & Rostock, 1780-83.]

BLANCHARD, E. (1868). Les premiers observateurs au microscope. Les travaux de Leeuwenhoek. *Rev. d. Deux Mondes*, XXXVIII année (2de période), T.76, p. 379 (15 juillet 1868).

BLANCHARD, R. (1889, 1890). *Traité de Zoologie Médicale.* 8°. 2 vols. Paris.

BLANKAART [=BLANCARDUS], S. (1748). *Lexicon Medicum* . . . J. H. Schulz auct. et emend. . . . denuo recog. M. G. Agnethler. 8°. Halle. [1st ed. Amsterdam, 1679.]

BLEYSWIJCK, D. VAN (1667). *Beschryvinge der Stadt Delft.* 4°. 2 vols. Delft.

BLYTH, A. WYNTER (1903). *Foods: their Composition and Analysis.* 5th ed. (with M. Wynter Blyth). 8°. London. [L. referred to on pp. 26, 27, 190. The author's other "researches" on L. are recorded by Richardson (1885).]

BOEKE, J. (1920). Leeuwenhoek en Mendel. *Vragen des Tijds* (Haarlem), Jaarg. 46, p. 303. [Trivial. Contains no material information beyond that given in my note of 1915.]

BOEKE, J. (1923). Anthony van Leeuwenhoek. 24 October 1632—27 Augustus 1723. *Vragen des Tijds* (Haarlem), Jaarg. 49, p. 317. [Contains nothing noteworthy—except the erroneous date of L.'s death.]

BOITET, R. [Publisher & Editor] (1729). *Beschryving der Stadt Delft,* behelzende een zeer naaukeurige en uitvoerige verhandeling van deszelfs eerste oorsprong, benaming, bevolking, aanwas, gelegenheid, prachtige en kunstige gedenkstukken en zeltzaamheden . . . door verscheide Liefhebbers en Kenners der Nederlandsche Oudheden. Fol. Delft.

BOLSIUS, H. (1903). Antoni van Leeuwenhoek et Félix Fontana. Essai historique et critique sur le révélateur du noyau cellulaire. *Mem. Pontif. Accad. Rom. Nuovi Lincei*, XX, 287.

BONNET, C. (1779-1783). *Œuvres d'Histoire naturelle et de Philosophie.* 8°. 18 vols. Neuchatel.

BOREL [= BORELLUS], P. (1653). *Historiarum, et Observationum Medicophysicarum, Centuria prima* [*& secunda*]. 12°. Castris. [Extremely rare. Not in the British Museum. Consists of pp. xxiv + 1-240. Century II has a separate title, but pagination is continuous.]

BOREL [= BORELLUS], P. (1655-6). *De vero telescopii inventore, cum brevi omnium conspiciliorum historia . . . Accessit etiam Centuria observationum micrococspicarum.* 4°. Hagae-Comitum. [The word "*microscopicarum*" is misprinted as above throughout: while the place of publication (The Hague) is called *Hagae-Comitis* on the separate title of the *Centuria.*]

BOREL [= BORELLUS], P. (1656*a*). *Historiarum, et Observationum Medicophysicarum, Centuriae IV* [etc.]. 8°. Parisiis. [Not to be confused with the 2 preceding works. Contains, in addition to the 200 observations published in 1653 (Centt. I & II), 200 additional ones (Centt. III & IV)— in all 384 pp.]

BORY DE ST.-VINCENT [J. B.] (1826). *Essai d'une Classification des Animaux Microscopiques.* 8°. Paris. [xii + 104 pp. From *Encyclopédie Méthodique* (1824), Tom. II, *Hist. Nat. des Zoophytes.* This separate issue (containing some new matter) is now extremely rare—only 100 copies having been printed. Cf. Lauzun (1908), p. 281. I possess a copy signed by the author.]

BOSMAN, D. B. (1928). *Oor die Ontstaan van Afrikaans.* 2de ed. 8°. Amsterdam.

BOSTRÖM, A. (1757). Febris Upsaliensis. *Amoen. Acad.*, No. LXXVII. vol. V, p. 18. Holmiae (1760).

BOURICIUS, L. G. N. (1924). Anthony van Leeuwenhoek en zijn dochter. *Nieuwe Rotterdamsche Courant*, 13 Dec. (Avondblad B.) & 14 Dec. (Ochtendblad B.) 1924.

BOURICIUS, L. G. N. (1925). Anthony van Leeuwenhoek de Delftsche natuuronderzoeker (1632-1723). *De Fabrieksbode* (Delft), 44 Jaarg., No. 10 (7 Maart 1925). [Offprint, 3 pp. Important, but no copy yet traced in any English library.]

BOYER, J. (1894). Joblot et Baker. *Rev. Scientif.*, XXXI ann. (4 sér., T. I), p. 283.

BRACHELIUS, A. (1666). *Historia Nostri Temporis* . . . overgezet door L.v.B. 8°. Amsterdam.

BREDIUS, A. (1885). Iets over Johannes Vermeer (" de Delftsche Vermeer"). *Oud-Holland* (Amsterdam), III, 217. [Cf. also *ibid.* (1910), XXVIII, 61.]

BREWERTON, E. W. (1930). Entoptic phenomena. *Proc. Roy. Soc. Med.*, XXIV, (Sect. Ophthalm.) 45.

BRIDGES, J. H. (1914). *The Life and Work of Roger Bacon.* 8°. London.

BROCARD, H. (1905). *Louis de Puget, François Lamy, Louis Joblot. Leur action scientifique d'après de nouveaux documents.* 4°. Bar-le-Duc. [Privately printed.]

BROWN, R. (1810). *Prodromus Florae Novae Hollandiae et Insulae Van-Diemen.* 8°. London. [Genus *Levenhookia*, p. 572.]

BROWNE, SIR THOMAS (1642). *Religio Medici.* 8°. London. [Facsimile ed., London, 1883.]

BRUGGENCATE, K. TEN (1920). *Engelsch Woordenboek.* 9 ed. 8°. 2 vols. Groningen & Den Haag.

BRYAN, M. (1903-5). *Dictionary of Painters and Engravers.* (Revised by G. C. Williamson.) 4°. 5 vols. London.

BÜTSCHLI, O. (1876). Studien über die ersten Entwicklungsvorgänge der Eizelle, die Zelltheilung und die Conjugation der Infusorien. *Abhandl. Senckenb. naturf. Gesellsch.*, X, 213.

BÜTSCHLI, O. (1880-1889). Protozoa, in : Bronn's *Klass. u. Ordn. d. Thier-Reichs.* Bd. I (3 vols.). 8°. Leipzig & Heidelberg.

BULLOCH, W. (1922). L'Abbate Spallanzani, 1729-1799. *Parasitology*, XIV, 409.

BULLOCH, W. (1930). History of Bacteriology. *A System of Bacteriology in Relation to Medicine*, vol. I, pp. 15-103. 8°. London. (*Medical Research Council.*)

BUNYAN, J. (1678). *The Pilgrim's Progress from This World to That which is to come : Delivered under the Similitude of a Dream* [etc.]. 8°. London. [Facsimile replica, London (Noel Douglas), 1928.]

BUONANNI [= BONANNUS], F. (1691). *Observationes circa Viventia, quae in rebus non viventibus reperiuntur. Cum Micrographia curiosa* [etc.]. 4°. Romae. [See especially p. 175 *sq.* (description and first figs. of *Colpoda*) : p. 218 : p. 273 (reference to " Joannes Leeuuenhoek," whose observations on bacteria in the mouth B. was unable to confirm). Plates copied in part from Hooke and others.]

BUONANNI, F. (1709). *Musaeum Kircherianum* [etc.]. Fol. Romae.

BURNET, G. (1753). *History of his own Time.* 8°. 4 vols. London. [First ed. 1723-1734.]

CANDOLLE, A. DE (1885). *Histoire des Sciences et des Savants depuis deux siècles* [etc.]. (2 éd.) 8°. Genève-Bale-Lyon.

CAPPELLE, J. P. VAN (1821, 1827). *Bijdragen tot de Geschiedenis der Wetenschappen en Letteren in Nederland.* 8°. 2 vols. Amsterdam & Haarlem.

CAPPELLI, A. (1912). *Dizionario di Abbreviature latine ed italiane.* 8°. Milano.

CARBONE, D. (1930). Contributo alla storia della microbiologia. *Boll. Ist. Sieroterap. Milanese,* fasc. VIII-IX, pp. 1-37 [reprint].

CARSWELL, R. (1838). *Pathological Anatomy. Illustrations of the Elementary Forms of Disease.* Fol. London.

CARUS, J. V. (1872). *Geschichte der Zoologie bis auf Joh. Müller und Charl. Darwin.* 8°. München. [*Gesch. d. Wissensch. in Deutschland,* Bd. XII. " Anton von Leeuwenhoek," pp. 394, 399-400.]

CARUTTI, D. (1883). *Breve Storia della Accademia dei Lincei.* 8°. Roma.

CASTLEMAIN, Earl of (1671). *A Short and True Account of the Material Passages in the late War between the English and Dutch.* 8°. London.

CATALOGUE *of the Collection of Antique Microscopes* formed by the late Sir Frank Crisp, Bart. . . . sold at Stevens's Auction Rooms . . . February 17th, 1925. 8°. London.

CAZENEUVE, P. (1893). *La génération spontanée d'après les livres d'Henri Baker et de Joblot* (1754). Mémoire présenté à l'Acad. des Sci., Belles-Lettres et Arts de Lyon. 8°. Lyon. [Brochure, 24 pp. A slightly modified version published in *Rev. scientif.* (1894), XXXI ann. (4e sér., T.I), p. 161.]

CELLI, A. (1925). Storia della malaria nell'Agro Romano. *Mem. R. Accad. Lincei,* (ser. 6) vol. I, fasc. iii, pp. 73-467. [Opera postuma.]

CHALMOT, J. A. (1798-1800). *Biographisch Woordenboek der Nederlanden.* 8°. Amsterdam. [Only first 8 vols. seen (? all published).]

CHAMBERLAYNE, J. (1723). *Magnae Britanniae Notitia : or, The Present State of Great Britain ; with divers Remarks upon the Antient State thereof.* [26th ed. of *Angliae Notitia,* by E. Chamberlayne (1669).] 8°. London.

CHANTAVOINE, J. (1926). *Ver Meer de Delft. Biographie critique.* 8°. Paris.

CHAPMAN, A. CHASTON (1931). The yeast cell : what did Leeuwenhoeck see ? *J. Inst. Brewing,* XXXVII, 433. [Reproduces part of L.'s *Letter 32* (14 June 1680) to T. Gale.]

CHARANTE, N. H. VAN (1844). *Dissertatio historico-medica inauguralis de Antonii Leeuwenhoeckii meritis in quasdam partes anatomiae microscopicae.* 8°. Lugd.-Bat.

CHRISTENSEN, C. (1922). Otto Friderich Müller, specielt som Botaniker. *Naturens Verden*, VI, 49.

CHRISTENSEN, C. (1924). *Den danske Botaniks Historie.* Vol. I. 8°. Köbenhavn. [O. F. Müller, pp. 135-149. Bibliography, pp. 62-7.]

COLE, F. J. (1926). *The History of Protozoology.* Two lectures delivered before the University of London at King's College in May 1925. 8°. London.

COLE, F. J. (1930). *Early Theories of Sexual Generation.* 8°. Oxford.

COLERUS [= KÖHLER], J. (1705). *Korte, dog waaragtige Levens-beschryving, van Benedictus de Spinosa.* Amsterdam. [Reprint. 's-Gravenhage, 1880.]

COLLOT D'ESCURY (1844). *Holland's Roem in Kunsten en Wetenschappen*, VII, 61. [Whole work in 7 vols. 8°. 's-Gravenhage & Amsterdam. 1824-1844. Contains nothing of any value on L.]

CORNISH, J. (1780). *The Life of Mr. Thomas Firmin, Citizen of London.* 12°. London.

CORTI, B. (1774). *Osservazioni Microscopiche sulla Tremella* [etc.]. 8°. Lucca.

COTGRAVE, R. (1650). *A French-English Dictionary* (ed. Howell). Fol. London.

CREPLIN, F. C. H. (1847). Ueber Anton von Leeuwenhoeck's Leben und Verdienst. *Isis* (Leipzig), Heft XI, p. 915. [German transl. of Halbertsma (1843), with a few trifling notes.]

CROMMELIN, C. A. (1925). *Instrumentmakerskunst en proefondervindelijke natuurkunde.* 8°. Leiden. [Rede uitgesproken . . . aan de Rijksuniversiteit, 12 Mei 1925. L.'s "circulation-microscope", pp. 18-19.]

CROMMELIN, C. A. (1926). *Beschrijvende Catalogus der Historische Verzameling van Natuurkundige Instrumenten in het Natuurkundig Laboratorium der Rijks-Universiteit te Leiden.* 8°. Leiden.

CROMMELIN, C. A. (1929). *Het lenzen slijpen in de 17e eeuw.* 8°. Amsterdam.

CROMMELIN, C. A. (1929*a*). Het Nederlandsch Historisch Natuurwetenschappelijk Museum. *Oudheidkundig Jaarboek.* [Offprint, pp. 1-16.]

CROSE, J. DE LA (1693). *Memoirs for the Ingenious . . . in Miscellaneous Letters.* Vol. I [all published]. 4°. London.

CUVIER, G. (1841-1845). *Histoire des Sciences Naturelles, depuis leur origine jusqu'à nos jours . . . publiée par M. Magdeleine de Saint-Agy.* 8°. 5 vols. Paris. [For L. see especially vol. II, pp. 407-410, 478-9.]

DALE, J. H. VAN (1884). *Nieuw Woordenboek der Nederlandsche Taal.* 3 ed., door J. Manhave. 8°. 's-Gravenhage & Leiden.

DAVAINE, C. (1860). *Traité des Entozoaires.* 8°. Paris.

DE TONI, G. B. (1923). Nella ricorrenza del II centenario della morte di Antonio van Leeuwenhoek. Frammenti Cestoniani inediti. *Arch. Stor. Sci.* (Roma), IV, 224.

DISNEY, A. N., with HILL, C. F., & WATSON BAKER, W. E. (1928). *Origin and Development of the Microscope* [etc.]. 8°. London. [Including Catalogue of Microscopes in the collection of the Royal Microscopical Society of London.]

DOBELL, C. (1909). Researches on the intestinal protozoa of frogs and toads. *Quart. J. Microsc. Sci.*, LIII, 201.

DOBELL, C. (1911). The principles of protistology. *Arch. Protistenk.*, XXIII, 269.

DOBELL, C. (1912). Researches on the spirochaets and related organisms. *Arch. Protistenk.*, XXVI, 117.

DOBELL, C. (1915). Mendelism in the Seventeenth Century. *Nature* (London), XCIV, 588. [Note on L.'s first record of Mendelian dominance.]

DOBELL, C. (1920). The discovery of the intestinal protozoa of man. *Proc. Roy. Soc. Med.*, XIII, (Sect. Hist. Med.) 1.

DOBELL, C. (1922). The discovery of the Coccidia. *Parasitology*, XIV, 342.

DOBELL, C. (1922*a*). Protozoology, in : *Encyclop. Brit.*, 11th ed., suppl. vol. III, p. 186. (12th ed., vol. XXXII.)

DOBELL, C. (1923). A protozoological bicentenary : Antony van Leeuwenhoek (1632-1723) and Louis Joblot (1645-1723). *Parasitology*, XV, 308.

DOBELL, C. (1923*a*). C. G. Ehrenberg (1795-1876). A biographical note. *Parasitology*, XV, 320.

DOBELL, C. (1931). The "first 27 unpublished letters" of Antony van Leeuwenhoek. *Opusc. Select. Neerland.* (Amsterdam), vol. IX, p. xli.

DOBELL, C. & O'CONNOR, F. W. (1921). *The Intestinal Protozoa of Man.* 8°. London.

DRYANDER, J. (1798-1800). *Catalogus Bibliothecae Historico-naturalis Josephi Banks.* 8°. 5 vols. London.

DUJARDIN, F. (1841). *Histoire Naturelle des Zoophytes. Infusoires.* 8°. Paris.

DUTENS, L. (1766). *Recherches sur l'Origine des Découvertes attribuées aux Modernes.* 8°. 2 vols. Paris. [3rd ed. 4°. London, 1796. Also in English : *An Inquiry into the Origin of the Discoveries attributed to the Moderns.* 8°. London, 1769.]

EDMUNDSON, G. (1922). *History of Holland.* 8°. Cambridge.

EHRENBERG, C. G. (1838). *Die Infusionsthierchen als vollkommene Organismen.* Fol. Leipzig.

EHRENBERG, C. G. (1845). Rede zur Feier des Leibnitzischen Jahrestages über Leibnitzens Methode, Verhältniss zur Natur-Forschung und Briefwechsel mit Leeuwenhoek. [Lecture delivered 3 July 1845. 4°. 16 pp.] Berlin. *Kgl. Akad. Wissensch.*

EICHHORN, J. C. [1775]. *Beyträge zur Natur-Geschichte der kleinsten Wasser-Thiere* [etc.]. 4°. Danzig.

EICHHORN, J. C. (1783). *Zugabe zu meinen Beyträgen* [etc.]. 4°. Danzig.

ELLIS, J. (1769). Observations on a particular Manner of Increase in the Animalcula of vegetable Infusions [etc.]. *Phil. Trans.*, LIX, 138.

ELSHOLTIUS [= ELSHOLZ], J. S. (1679). De microscopiis globularibus. *Miscellanea Curiosa, sive Ephemerides . . . Academiae Naturae Curiosorum.* Ann. IX (1678-9), Obs. cxv, p. 280. Vratislaviae & Bregae [1680].

EVELYN, J. (1827). *Memoirs,* edited by W. Bray. 8°. 5 vols. London. [New ed. Including *Diary,* 1641-1706 ; *Correspondence,* etc.]

FLECK, F. LE SUEUR (1843). *Dissertatio historico-medica inauguralis de Antonii Leeuwenhoeckii meritis in quasdam partes anatomiae microscopicae.* 8°. Lugd.-Bat.

FLECK, [J. M.] (1876). Quels sont les premiers observateurs des Infusoires ? *Mém. Acad. Metz,* LVI ann. (3e sér., IV ann.), p. 651.

FLORIO, J. (1688). *Vocabolario Italiano & Inglese* (ed. Torriano & Davis). Fol. London.

FOLKES, M. (1724). Some account of Mr. Leeuwenhoek's curious Microscopes, lately presented to the Royal Society. *Phil. Trans.,* XXXII, 446. [No. 380, for Dec. 1723.]

FONTENELLE, [B.] DE (1709). *Histoire du Renouvellement de l'Académie Royale des Sciences en M.DC.XCIX.* 12°. Amsterdam.

FOSTER, M. (1901). *Lectures on the History of Physiology during the Sixteenth Seventeenth and Eighteenth Centuries.* 8°. Cambridge. [A masterly work, which unfortunately deals very inadequately with " Anton van Leeuenhoek."]

FRACASTORO, G. (1554). *De Sympathia et Antipathia Rerum.* Item *De Contagione, et Contagiosis Morbis, et eorum Curatione.* 8°. Lugduni. [1st ed. published 1546. French transl. of *De Cont.* by L. Meunier. 8°. Paris, 1893—with Latin text below.]

FRACASTORO, G. (1584). *Opera Omnia.* (3rd ed.) 4°. Venetiis. [1st ed. published 1555.]

FRACASTORO, G. (1830). *Syphilis sive Morbus Gallicus,* ed. L. Choulant. 8°. Lipsiae. [An excellent edition of the poem first published in 1530.]

FULTON, J. F. (1930). *Selected Readings in the History of Physiology.* 8°. London. [On pp. 68-75 a mangled version of L.'s *Letter 65,* from the English translation in *Opusc. Select. Neerl.,* vol. I (1907).]

GABLER : *Latijnsch-Hollandsch Woordenboek over de Geneeskunde en de Natuurkundige Wetenschappen.* 3rd ed. (B. Eisendrath). 8°. Leiden [n.d.].

GARRISON, F. H. (1921). *An Introduction to the History of Medicine* [etc.]. 8°. Philadelphia & London. (3rd ed., revised.)

GEYSBEEK, P. G. WITSEN (1821-1827). *Biographisch Anthologisch en Critisch Woordenboek der Nederduitsche Dichters.* 8°. 6 vols. Amsterdam.

GLEICHEN, gen. RUSSWORM, W. F. VON (1778). *Abhandlung über die Saamen- und Infusionsthierchen, und über die Erzeugung* [etc.]. 4°. Nürnberg.

GODIN (1729-1734). *Table Alphabétique des Matières contenues dans l'Histoire et les Memoires de l'Académie Royale des Sciences* [1666-1730]. 4°. 4 vols. Paris.

GOIFFON, [J. B.] (1722). Dissertation sur la peste [etc.], in : *Relations et Dissertation sur la Peste de Gevaudan.* 8°. Lyon. [pp. 35-188, + *corrigenda* (4 pp.).]

GOLDFUSS, G. A. (1817). *Ueber die Entwicklungsstufen des Thieres.* 8°. Nürnberg. [A work of great rarity. The name "Protozoa" occurs only in the diagram at the end, though it is used in its German form (*Protozoen*) on pp. 18 & 21 of the text.]

GOSCH, C. C. A. (1870-1878). *Udsigt over Danmarks zoologiske Literatur.* 8°. 3 vols. (in 4). Kjöbenhavn.

GOVI, G. (1888). Il microscopio composto inventato da Galileo. *Atti R. Accad. Sci. Fis. Nat.* (Napoli), vol. II (ser. 2), ann. 1888. [Engl. transl. in *J. Roy. Microsc. Soc.* (London), IX, 574. 1889.]

GRAAF, R. DE (1677). *Opera Omnia.* 8°. Lugd. Bat. [Another ed., 1678. Ed. nov. 1705, Amsterdam.]

GRAY, S. (1696). Several Microscopical Observations and Experiments. *Phil. Trans.*, vol. XIX, No. 221, p. 280.

GRAY, S. (1696*a*). A Letter from . . . , giving a further Account of his Water Microscope. *Phil. Trans.*, vol. XIX, No. 223, p. 353.

GRAY, S. (1697). A Letter from . . . Concerning making Water subservient to the viewing both near and distant Objects [etc.]. *Phil. Trans.*, vol. XIX, No. 228, p. 539.

GREEN, J. REYNOLDS (1914). *A History of Botany in the United Kingdom from the earliest times to the end of the 19th century.* 8°. London & Toronto.

GREGORY, D. (1713). *Catoptricae et Dioptricae Sphericae Elementa.* 12°. Edinburgh. [1st ed. 1695. Also in English : *Elements of Catoptrics and Dioptrics* [etc.]. 8°. London, 1715.]

GREW, N. (1672). *The Anatomy of Vegetables begun.* 8°. London.

GREW, N. (1701). *Cosmologia Sacra* [etc.]. Fol. London. [With fine portrait as frontispiece.]

GROBER, J. [1912]. *Die Entdeckung der Krankheitserreger.* 8°. Leipzig. [Voigtländers Quellenbücher, Bd. 30.]

GRONOVIUS, L. T. (1760). *Bibliotheca Regni Animalis atque Lapidei, &c.* 4°. Lugd. Bat. [Incomplete but much-copied bibliography of L.'s works on pp. 157-161.]

GROOT, C. H. DE (1910, 1916). *A Catalogue raisonné of the Works of the most eminent Dutch Painters of the Seventeenth Century.* [Transl. & ed. E. G. Hawke.] 8°. London. Vols. III (Ostade) and VI (Maes).

HAASTERT, I. VAN (1823). *Anth. van Leeuwenhoek, vereerend herdacht in eene korte levensschets en lofdicht, uitgesproken in een letter- en wetenschaplievenden kring te Delft, den 26 Augustus 1823.* 8°. Delft : P. de Groot. [39 pp. (the poem occupying last 7). Title-p. with engraving of L.'s microscope. Extremely rare. No copy found in England. Unimportant.]

[HAAXMAN, P. A.] (1923). Antony van Leeuwenhoek. 24 October 1632—26 Augustus 1723. *De Nieuwe Courant* (Rotterdam), Feuilleton, No. 157 ; 7. vii. 23 : and 2 following Nos. [Unimportant. Contains nothing new except a somewhat fanciful account of my interview with the writer's daughter—at which he was not present.]

HAAXMAN, P. J. (1871). Het leven van een groot natuuronderzoeker. Antony van Leeuwenhoek. Geschetst uit zijne brieven en andere bescheiden. *Nederl. Tijdschr. v. Geneesk.*, VII Jaarg. (2 deel), p.1.

HAAXMAN, P. J. (1875). *Antony van Leeuwenhoek. De Ontdekker der Infusorien.* 1675-1875. 8°. Leiden: S. C. van Doesburgh. [pp. viii + 140, with portrait and text-figs. Revised edition of preceding. The only serious attempt yet made to write L.'s biography. Fundamentally important, and now very rare.]

HADFIELD, R. (1920). Introductory address . . . read at the Symposium on *The Microscope: its Design, Construction & Application.* (London, 14 Jan. 1920.) 8°. London. [42 pp. + 13 figs. & portraits. Contains many misstatements about L. and the history of the microscope.]

HAESER, H. (1853-1865). *Lehrbuch der Geschichte der Medicin und der epidemischen Krankheiten.* (2nd ed.) 8°. 2 vols. Jena.

HAESER, H. (1875-1882). *Lehrbuch der Geschichte der Medicin und der epidemischen Krankheiten.* (3rd ed.) 8°. 3 vols. Jena. [For L. see vol. ii (1881), esp. p. 296.]

HAKE, T. G. (1839). *A Treatise on Varicose Capillaries . . . With an account of a new form of the pus globule.* 4°. London. [Very rare. Quoted by many who have never seen it.]

HALBERTSMA, H. (1843). *Dissertatio historico-medica inauguralis de Antonii Leeuwenhoeckii meritis in quasdam partes anatomiae microscopicae.* 8°. Daventriae: J. de Lange. [pp. viii + 72. 2 Pl. Important. Now very rare.]

HALBERTSMA, H. (1862). Ontleedkundige aanteekeningen. VI. Johan Ham van Arnhem, de ontdekker der spermatozoiden. *Versl. & Mededeel. d. Kon. Akad. v. Wetensch.* (Amsterdam). Afd. Natuurkunde, XIII, 342.

HALL, H. C. VAN (1834). Verhandeling over Antoni van Leeuwenhoek, en zijne verdiensten voor de plantkunde. *Tijdschr. v. natuurl. Geschiedenis & Physiol.* (Amsterdam), I, 163.

HALLAM, H. (1847). *Introduction to the Literature of Europe, in the Fifteenth Sixteenth, and Seventeenth Centuries.* (3rd ed.) 8°. 3 vols. London. [First published 1837-9.]

HALLER, A. VON (1757-1766). *Elementa Physiologiae corporis humani.* 4°. 8 vols. Lausanne & Berne.

HALLER, A. VON (1774, 1777). *Bibliotheca Anatomica.* 4°. 2 vols. Tiguri. [List of L.'s works in vol. I, pp. 606-613.]

HALLIWELL [-PHILLIPPS], J. O. (1840). *Catalogues of the Miscellaneous Manuscripts and of the Manuscript Letters in the Possession of the Royal Society.* 8°. London.

HALMA, F. (1729). *Woordenboek der Nederduitsche en Fransche Taalen.* 2 ed. 4°. Amsterdam & Utrecht.

HAMILTON, A. (1890). *Memoirs of the Count de Grammont.* Transl. by Walpole, with notes by Scott and others. 8°. London. [First French ed. 1713.]

HANNOT, S. (1719). *Nieuw Woordboek der Nederlantsche en Latynsche Tale . . . merkelyk vermeerdert en verrykt door* D. van Hoogstraten. 2 ed. 4°. Dordrecht, Utrecht, & Amsterdam.

HARRIS, D. FRASER (1921). Anthony van Leeuwenhoek the first bacteriologist. *Scientific Monthly* (New York), XII, 150. [Worthless.]

HARRIS, J. (1696). Some Microscopical Observations of vast Numbers of *Animalcula* seen in Water. *Phil. Trans.*, vol. XIX, No. 220, p. 254. [Observations dated 1694 and 1696.]

HARRIS, J. (1704). *Lexicon Technicum : or, an Universal English Dictionary of Arts and Sciences.* Fol. London. [Contains many interesting and instructive articles (*e.g.* MICROSCOPE), and a finely engraved portrait of the author.]

HARTING, P. (1848-1854). *Het Mikroskoop, deszelfs gebruik, geschiedenis en tegenwoordige toestand.* 8°. 4 vols. Utrecht.

HARTING, P. (1868). *Christiaan Huygens in zijn leven en werken geschetst.* 8°. Groningen.

HARTING, P. (1876). *Gedenkboek van het 8sten September 1875 gevierde 200-jarig Herinneringsfeest der ontdekking van de mikroskopische wezens, door Antony van Leeuwenhoek.* 8°. 's-Gravenhage & Rotterdam.

HARTSOEKER, N. (1730). *Cours de Physique accompagné de plusieurs piéces concernant la physique qui ont déja paru, et d'un Extrait Critique des lettres de M. Leeuwenhoek.* 4°. La Haye. [Chez Jean Swart ; " par feu Mons. H." *Ext. crit.* pp. 1-66 (paged separately) at end. Fontenelle's *Eloge* of H. reprinted at beginning—17 pp., unnumbered.]

HEUGELENBURG, M. (1727). *Klein Woordenboek, zijnde een kort en klaar onderwijs in de Nederlandze Spel, en Leeskonst.* Sm. 8°. Rotterdam.

HEXHAM, H. (1658, 1660). *A Copious Englisg* [sic] *and Netherduytsch Dictionarie. / Het Groot Woordenboek : gestelt in't Neder-duytsch, ende in't Engelsch.* 4°. Rotterdam.

HILL, J. (1751). *A Review of the Works of the Royal Society of London* [etc.]. 4°. London.

HILL, J. (1752). *An History of Animals* [etc.]. Fol. London. [Vol. III of Hill's " Compleat Body of Natural History." For " the lesser animals, called, Animalcules," see Pt. 1, Bk. 1 : 12 pp. + 1 plate.]

HILL, J. (1752*a*). *Essays in Natural History and Philosophy* [etc.]. 8°. London.

HILL, T. G. (1913). John Hill 1716-1775. *Makers of British Botany*, pp. 84-107. [See OLIVER (1913).]

HIRSCH, A. (1884-1888). *Biographisches Lexikon der hervorragenden Aerzte aller Zeiten und Völker.* 8°. 6 vols. Wien & Leipzig. [In vol. III (1886), p. 651, a short and poor article on L. signed ' Pagel.']

HOEFER, F. (1860). Art. " Leuwenhoek ou Leeuwenhoek (Antoine van)." *Nouv. Biogr. Gén.*, vol. XXXI, col. 13.

HOEFER, F. (1872). *Histoire de la Botanique de la Minéralogie et de la Géologie.* 8°. Paris. [Note on L., p. 190.]

HOEFER, F. (1873). *Histoire de la Zoologie depuis les temps les plus reculés jusqu'à nos jours.* 8°. Paris. [" Leuwenhoek," pp. 200-204.]

HOOKE, R. (1665). *Micrographia : or some Physiological Descriptions of Minute Bodies made by Magnifying Glasses. With Observations and Inquiries thereupon.* Fol. London.

HOOKE, R. (1678). *Lectures and Collections.* 4°. London.

HOOKE, R. (1679). *Lectiones Cutlerianae, or a Collection of Lectures: Physical, Mechanical, Geographical, & Astronomical* [etc.]. 4°. London.

HOOKE, R. (1705). *Posthumous Works:* see WALLER.

HOOKE, R. (1726). *Philosophical Experiments and Observations* . . . publish'd by W. Derham, F.R.S. 8°. London.

HOOLE, S. (1798, 1807). *The Select Works of Antony van Leeuwenhoek, containing his Miscroscopical* [sic] *Discoveries in many of the Works of Nature.* 4°. 2 vols. London. [Also several later issues, bearing the imprints of different publishers.—An excellent and scholarly translation (as far as it goes), but with all letters rearranged without reference to their originals, and with omission of all passages "which to many Readers might be offensive": consequently, of little use to the student of protozoa and bacteria, and worthless to the student of spermatozoa—all reference to which is carefully castrated.]

HOWELL, J. (1645-1655). *Epistolae Ho-Elianae.* 8°. 4 vols. London. [Used: 7th ed. 1 vol. London. 1705.]

HUYGENS, Christiaan (1703). *Opuscula Posthuma* [etc.]. 4°. Lugd. Bat.

HUYGENS, Christiaan (1728). *Opera Reliqua.* 4°. 2 vols. Amstelodami. [Observations on protozoa mentioned in vol. II, *Dioptrica,* pp. 173-6.]

HUYGENS, Christiaan: *Œuvres Complètes, publiées par la Société Hollandaise des Sciences.* 4°. 16 vols. La Haye, 1888-1929. [A magnificent modern work, edited and issued by the *Hollandsche Maatschappij der Wetenschappen* of Haarlem: still in progress.]

HUYGENS, Constantijn. *De Briefwisseling van* . . . (1608-1687), ed. J. A. Worp. 4°. 6 vols. [*Rijks Geschiedkundige Publicatien* vols. 15, 19, 21, 24, 28, 32. 1911-1917.] 's-Gravenhage.

INDEX-CATALOGUE OF THE LIBRARY OF THE SURGEON-GENERAL'S OFFICE, UNITED STATES ARMY. (Series I-III) 46 vols. 1880-1931. Washington.

ISRAËLS, A. H. & DANIËLS, C. E. (1883). *De Verdiensten der Hollandsche Geleerden ten opzichte van Harvey's Leer van den Bloedsomloop.* 8° Utrecht.

JACKSON, B. DAYDON (1923). *Linnaeus (afterwards Carl von Linné). The Story of his Life* [etc.]. 8°. London.

JAEGER, F. M. (1919). *Historische Studiën.* 8°. [*in forma* 4°.] Groningen & Den Haag.

JAEGER, F. M. (1922). *Cornelis Drebbel en zijne Tijdgenooten.* 8°. Groningen.

JOBLOT, L. (1718). *Descriptions et Usages de plusieurs nouveaux Microscopes . . . avec de nouvelles observations* [etc.]. 4°. Paris. [1 vol. in 2 parts.]

JOBLOT, L. (1754). *Observations d'Histoire naturelle, faites avec le Microscope* [etc.]. 4°. Paris. [2 vols. in 1. Vol. II dated 1755. A 2nd edition (posthumous) of the preceding, with additions by the publisher.]

JONES, W. H. S. (1909). *Malaria and Greek History*. 8°. Manchester. [Publications of the University of Manchester. Historical Series No. VIII.]

JORISSEN, T. (1873). *Mémoires de Constantin Huygens* [etc.]. 8°. La Haye.

JOUBIN, L. (1901). Félix Dujardin. *Arch. Parasitol.*, IV, 5.

JOURDAN, A. J. L. (1822). Art. "Leeuwenhoeck (Antoine)." *Biogr. Méd.*, V, 561.

JUNIUS, H. [= A. DE JONGH](1588). *Batavia*. 4°. Ex Officina Plantiniana [Antwerp].

JURIN, J. (1718). De motu aquarum fluentium. *Phil. Trans.*, XXX, 748.

KAISER, L. (1924). Antony van Leeuwenhoek-film. *Nederl. Tijdschr. v. Geneesk.*, Jaarg. LXVIII, (2 Helft) p. 3061.

KENT, W. SAVILLE (1880-1882). *A Manual of the Infusoria*. 8°. 3 vols. London.

KILIANUS, C. [= Cornelis KILIAAN] (1599). *Dictionarium Teutonico-Latinum*. 8°. Antwerp.

KILIANUS AUCTUS, *seu Dictionarium Teutonico-Latino-Gallicum* [etc.]. (1642). 8°. Amsterdam.

KING, E. (1693). Several Observations and Experiments on the *Animalcula*, in Pepper-water, &c. *Phil. Trans.*, vol. XVII, No. 203, p. 861.

KIRCHER, A. (1646). *Ars magna Lucis et Umbrae*. Fol. Romae. [2nd ed. Amstelodami, 1671.]

KIRCHER, A. (1658). *Scrutinium physico-medicum contagiosae Luis, quae Pestis dicitur* [etc.]. 4°. Romae. [Another edition 12°. Lipsiae. 1659.]

KNICKERBOCKER, W. S. (1927). *Classics of Modern Science* (*Copernicus to Pasteur*). 8°. New York. [Contains (pp. 62-6) an alleged reprint of L.'s original "observations on animalculae" [*sic*]—really copied from the worthless *Abridgement* of 1809, and not from the *Phil. Trans.*]

KONARSKI, W. (1895). Un savant Barrisien précurseur de M. Pasteur: Louis Joblot (1645-1723). *Mém. Soc. Lettres, Sciences & Arts, Bar-le-Duc*. (3 sér.) IV, 205.

KRUIF, P. DE (1926). *Microbe Hunters*. 8°. New York. [L. pp. 3-24.]

LANCISI, G. M. (1718). *De Noxiis Paludum Effluviis eorumque Remediis*. 4°. Coloniae Allobrogum. [= Geneva. 1st ed. published 1717.]

LAUE, M. (1895). *Christian Gottfried Ehrenberg, ein Vertreter deutscher Naturforschung im neunzehnten Jahrhundert*. 8°. Berlin.

LAUNOIS, P. E. (1899). Les origines du microscope.—Leeuwenhoek.—Sa vie.—Son œuvre. *C.R. Assoc. Française pour l'Avancement d. Sciences*. (Conférences de Paris.) [Extrait] pp. 1-17. [Unimportant. Based chiefly on Blanchard (1868).]

LAUNOIS, P. E. (1904). *Les Pères de la Biologie*. 8°. Paris. [*Leeuwenhoek —sa vie—son œuvre*, pp. 3-36: virtual reprint of preceding.]

LAUZUN, P. (1908). *Correspondance de Bory de St-Vincent*. 8°. [Agen.] [Contains also an excellent biography and portrait.]

L[EDERMÜLLER], M. F. (1756). *Physicalische Beobachtungen derer Saamenthiergens, . . . mit einer unpartheyischen Untersuchung und Gegeneinanderhaltung derer Buffonischen und Leuwenhoeckischen Experimenten.* 4°. Nürnberg. [Trivial.]

LEDERMÜLLER, M. F. (1758). *Versuch zu einer gründlichen Vertheidigung derer Saamenthiergen; nebst einer kurzen Beschreibung derer Leeuwenhoeckischen Mikroskopien* [etc.]. 4°. Nürnberg. [Unimportant. The description of L.'s microscopes is taken from Baker (1740) though attributed to Cuff, the London microscope-maker.]

LEDERMÜLLER, M. F. (1760-1765). *Mikroskopische Gemüths- und Augen-Ergötzung.* 4°. 3 vols. (with supplements). Nürnberg.

LEDUC, S. (1911). *The Mechanism of Life.* [Engl. transl. by W. D. Butcher.] 8°. London.

LEERSUM, E. C. VAN, DE FEYFER, F.M.G., & MOLHUYSEN, P. C. (1907). *Catalogus van de Geschiedkundige Tentoonstelling van Natuur- en Geneeskunde . . . te Leiden 27 Maart—10 April* 1907 [enz.]. 8°. Leiden.

LEEUWEN, C. VAN (1663). *School-Boeck der Wynroeyeryen, waer inne geleert wordt het Meeten van alle Soorten van Vaten,* [etc.]. 4°. 2 vols. Amsterdam.

LEIBNIZ, G. W. (1842). *Œuvres,* ed. M. A. Jacques. 8°. 2 vols. Paris. [*Théodicée* in vol. ii, p. 1. Reference to L. on p. 120. Work first published in 1710 at Amsterdam.]

LEIBNIZ, G. W. (1912). *La Monadologie,* ed. H. Lachelier. 8°. Paris. [French original version. First published in German 1720.]

LESSER, F. C. (1738). *Insecto-Theologia* [etc.]. 8°. Franckfurt & Leipzig.

LESSER, [F. C.] (1742). *Théologie des Insectes . . . traduit . . . avec des remarques de Mr.* P. LYONNET. 8°. 2 vols. La Haye.

LEUCKART, R. (1863). *Die menschlichen Parasiten.* Vol. I. 8°. Leipzig & Heidelberg.

LEUCKART, R. (1879). *Die Parasiten des Menschen.* (II Aufl.) Vol. I. 8°. Leipzig & Heidelberg.

LINNAEUS, C. (1735). *Dissertatio medica inauguralis in qua exhibetur Hypothesis nova de Febrium Intermittentium Causa* [etc.]. 4°. Harderovici. [Reprinted in *Amoen. Acad.*, vol. X, pp. 1-22. 8°. Erlangiae. 1790.]

LINNAEUS, C. (1758-9). *Systema Naturae.* (10 ed.) 8°. 2 vols. Holmiae. [Protozoa in vol. 1. See especially pp. 820, 821.]

LINNAEUS, C. (1767). *Systema Naturae.* (12 ed.) 8°. 3 vols. Holmiae. [Whole work dated 1766-1768. Protozoa in tom. I, pars 2 (1767), pp. 1324-1327.]

LINT, J. G. DE (1931). De portretten van van Leeuwenhoek. *Opusc. Select. Neerland.* (Amsterdam), vol. IX, p. lix. [In Dutch and English.]

LOCY, W. A. (1901). Malpighi, Swammerdam and Leeuwenhoek. *Pop. Sci. Monthly* (New York), LVIII, 561. [Worthless.]

LOCY, W. A. (1910). *Biology and its Makers.* 8°. New York.

LOCY, W. A. (1925). *The Growth of Biology.* 8°. New York & London.

LÖFFLER, F. (1887). *Vorlesungen über die geschichtliche Entwickelung der Lehre von den Bacterien.* I Theil, bis zum Jahre 1878 [all published]. 8°. Leipzig.

LOON, G. VAN (1731). *Beschryving der Nederlandsche Historipenningen.* Vol. IV (Boek III), p. 223. [Whole work in 4 vols. Fol. 's-Graavenhaage, 1723-31.]

LUCAS, E. V. (1922). *Vermeer of Delft.* 8°. London.

M. A. C. D. (1726). *Systême d'un Medecin anglois sur la cause de toutes les especes de maladies* [etc.]. 8°. Paris. [pp. viii + 34 + vi.]

M. A. C. D. (1727). *Suite du Systême d'un Medecin anglois, sur la guerison des maladies* [etc.]. 8°. Paris. [pp. 22 + ii.]

McKERROW, R. B. (1914). Notes on bibliographical evidence for literary students and editors of English works of the Sixteenth and Seventeenth Centuries. *Trans. Bibliogr. Soc.* (London), vol. XII, (reprint) pp. 1-102.

MAIGNE D'ARNIS, W. H. (1890). *Lexicon Manuale ad Scriptores mediae et infimae Latinitatis.* 8°. Paris.

MALPIGHI, M. (1687). *Opera Omnia Botanico-Medico-Anatomica.* 4°. Lugd. Bat.

MALPIGHI, M. (1743). *Opera Posthuma.* Fol. Venetiis.

MANZINI, C. A. (1660). *L'Occhiale all'Occhio. Dioptrica pratica.* 4°. Bologna.

MARTEN, B. (1720). *A New Theory of Consumptions: more especially of a Phthisis, or Consumption of the Lungs* [etc.]. 8°. London.

MARTIN, B. (1764). *Biographia Philosophica* [etc.]. 8°. London.

MARTIN, T. H. (1871). Sur les instruments d'optique faussement attribués aux anciens par quelques savants modernes. *Bull. Bibliograf. & Stor. Sci. mat. & fis.* (Roma), IV, 165.

MARTINEZ, M. (1687). *Dictionarium Tetraglotton Novum* [Lat.-Gr.-Gall.-Belg.]. Ed. noviss., auct. A. Montano. 8°. Amsterdam.

MATY, P. H. (1787). *A General Index to the Philosophical Transactions, from the first to the end of the seventieth volume.* 4°. London.

MAYALL, J. (1886). *Cantor Lectures on the Microscope.* 8°. London. [*Soc. for Encouragement of Arts, Manufactures, and Commerce.* Also published in the Society's *Journal.* French transl. in *J. MicrSogr.* (1887), vol. XI. Lectures delivered Nov. 23—Dec. 21, 1885.]

MAYOR, J. E. B. (1875). *Bibliographical Clue to Latin Literature.* 8°. London & Cambridge.

MEIJER, L. (1745). *Woordenschat* verdeelt in 1. Bastaardt-Woorden. 2. Konst-Woorden. 3. Verouderde Woorden. [10th ed.] 16°. Amsterdam.

MENSERT, W. (1831). *Verhandeling aangaande de Uitvinding, het Gebruik en het Misbruik der Brillen.* 8°. Amsterdam.

METCALF, M. M. (1909). Opalina. Its anatomy and reproduction, with a description of infection experiments and a chronological review of the literature. *Arch. Protistenk.*, XIII, 195.

METCALF, M. M. (1923). The Opalinid Ciliate Infusorians. *Smithsonian Inst., U.S. Nat. Mus.* Bull. 120. 8°. Washington.

MIALL, L. C. (1911). *History of Biology*. 8°. London.

MIALL, L. C. (1912). *The Early Naturalists: their Lives and Work* (1530-1789). 8°. London. [L. on pp. 200-223. Contains many errors.]

MILLER, W. D. (1890). *The Micro-organisms of the Human Mouth*. 8°. Philadelphia.

MINSHEU, J. (1627). *Ductor in Linguas. / The Guide into Tongues*. (2nd ed.) Fol. London. [1st ed. 1617.]

MOES, E. W. (1897, 1905). *Iconographia Batava*. 4°. 2 vols. Amsterdam. [*Vide* vol. II, p. 12. No. 4415.]

MOLLIÈRE, H. [1886]. *Un Précurseur Lyonnais des Théories Microbiennes. J.-B. Goiffon et la nature animée de la peste*. 8°. Bale-Lyon-Genève.

MOLYNEUX, T. (1685). See BIRCH (1757), vol. IV, p. 365.

MOLYNEUX, W. (1692). *Dioptrica Nova. A Treatise of Dioptricks*, &c. Fol. London.

MONPART (1903). Les maîtres d'autrefois: Leeuwenhoek. *Journ. de la Santé* (Paris). 20e Ann. No. 1023 (16 Aug.), pp. 121-2. [Worthless. No copy found in England.]

MORE, SIR THOMAS: *The Utopia* [etc.] edited by G. Sampson, with introduction and bibliography by A. Guthkelch. 8°. London. 1910.

MORRE, G. (1912). *Description of the Principal Tombs in the Old Church at Delft*. (5th ed.) Delft. [Brochure, 15 pp.]

MORRE, G. (1919). Bijzonderheden omtrent Antony van Leeuwenhoek. *De Gids* (Amsterdam), Jaarg. 83, vol. IV, p. 336.

MORTREUX, E. (1924). Art. LEEUWENHOEK in: *N. Nederl. Biogr. Woordenb.*, VI, 922. [Very poor account.]

MOTLEY, J. L. (1856). *The Rise of the Dutch Republic: a History*. 8°. 3 vols. London. [New ed. *Chandos Classics*, London. n.d.]

MOTLEY, J. L. (1860-1867). *History of the United Netherlands*. 8°. 4 vols. The Hague. [New ed. London, 1869.]

MOUNTAGUE, W. (1696). *The Delights of Holland: or, A Three Months Travel about that and the other Provinces* [etc.]. 8°. London.

MÜLLER, O. F. (1773-4). *Vermium terrestrium et fluviatilium, seu Animalium Infusoriorum, . . . succincta Historia*. 4°. 2 vols. (in 3). Havniae & Lipsiae.

MÜLLER, O. F. (1786). *Animalcula Infusoria fluviatilia et marina* [etc.]. Opus posthumum, ed. O. Fabricius. 4°. Hauniae.

MUYS, W. G. (1741). *Investigatio Fabricae, quae in partibus musculos componentibus extat*. 4°. Lugd. Bat. [Originally dated 1738, but date altered by publisher. Contains numerous references to L., and the earliest biographical note on Johan Ham of Arnhem —co-discoverer with L. of the spermatozoa (p. 288, note 2). Cf. also Halbertsma (1862).]

NABER, H. A. *De Ster van 1572 (Cornelis Jacobsz. Drebbel) (1572-1634)*. 8°. Amsterdam. [*Wereldbibliotheek*, Nr. 54. n.d.]

NACHET, A. (1929). *Collection Nachet. Instruments scientifiques et livres anciens. Notice sur l'invention du microscope et son évolution*. 8°. Paris.

NÄGLER, K. [1918]. *Am Urquell des Lebens. Die Entdeckung der einzelligen Lebewesen von Leeuwenhoek bis Ehrenberg.* 8°. Leipzig. (Voigtländers Quellenbücher, Bd. 92.) [Not dated. Untrustworthy.]

NATIONAL GALLERY. CATALOGUE OF THE PICTURES 1921. 8° London.

NEEDHAM, T. (1745). *An Account of some New Microscopical Discoveries* [etc.]. 8°. London. [There were two different issues of this work. The other is entitled: "*New Microscopical Discoveries; Containing Observations,* . . . [etc.]"; same date and printer. Contents identical.]

NEEDHAM, T. (1749). A Summary of some late Observations upon the Generation, Composition, and Decomposition of Animal and Vegetable Substances. *Phil. Trans.*, XLV, 615. [Also published separately, with new title-page: *Observations upon* . . . *Substances.* 4°. London. pp. 1-52.]

NEEDHAM, [T.] (1750). *Nouvelles Observations microscopiques* [etc.]. 12°. Paris.

NEEDHAM, T. (1769). See REGLEY.

NIEUWENHUIS [G.] (1859). *Woordenboek van Kunsten en Wetenschappen* . . . *door Nederlandsche Geleerden.* Vol. V, p. 347. [Whole work in 10 vols. Fol. Leiden, 1855-1868.]

NOORDENBOS, T. U. (1839). *Dissertatio medica inauguralis, sistens Historiam criticam Aetiologiae Scabiei* [etc.]. 8°. Groningae.

NORDENSKIÖLD, E. (1929). *The History of Biology.* [Transl. by L. B. Eyre.] 8°. London.

NUTTALL, G. H. F. (1921). Notes bearing on Leeuwenhoek, Redi, [etc.] whose portraits have appeared in *Parasitology*, vol. XIII. *Ibid.*, p. 398. [Portraits facing p. 1 of vol.]

NYANDER, J. C. (1757). Exanthemata viva. *Amoen. Acad.*, No. LXXXII, vol. V, p. 92. Holmiae (1760).

OBREEN, F. D. O. (1881-2). Iets over den Delftschen schilder Johannes Vermeer. *Arch. v. Nederl. Kunstgeschiedenis* (Rotterdam), IV, 289.

OLIVER, F. W. (1913) [editor]. *Makers of British Botany. A Collection of Biographies by Living Botanists.* 8°. Cambridge.

OPUSCULA SELECTA NEERLANDICORUM DE ARTE MEDICA. 8°. 9 vols. Amsterdam (*Nederlandsch Tijdschrift voor Geneeskunde*), 1907-1931. [Vol. I contains L.'s *Letter 65*: vol. IX, 14 of his early (previously unpublished) letters to the Royal Society—with English translations and other relevant matter.]

ORNSTEIN, M. (1928). *The Rôle of Scientific Societies in the Seventeenth Century.* 8°. Chicago.

OSBORNE, D. (1652-1654). *Letters*, edited by E. A. Parry. 8°. London, 1888. [New ed. London, *n.d.*] Also ed. I. Gollancz. 8°. London, 1903. *King's Classics* series [suppressed].

OUDEMANS, A. C. (1869-1880). *Bijdrage tot een middel- en oudnederlandsch Woordenboek.* 8°. 7 vols. Arnhem.

OUDEMANS, A. C. (1911). Acarologische aanteekeningen. XXXVI. *Ber. Nederl. Entomol. Ver.* ('s-Gravenhage), III, 137. [*Leeuwenhoekia* nov. gen., p. 138.]

PANSIER, P. (1901). *Histoire des Lunettes.* 8°. Paris.

PARS, A. (1701). *Index Batavicus, of Naamrol van de Batavise en Hollandse Schrijvers.* 4°. Leiden.

PASTEUR, L. (1870). *Études sur la Maladie des Vers à Soie.* 8°. 2 vols. Paris.

PASTEUR, L. (1922). Fermentations et générations dites spontanées. *Œuvres* réunies par Pasteur Vallery-Radot, T. II. 8°. Paris.

PEPYS, S. (1660-1669). *Diary,* edited by H. B. Wheatley. 8°. 8 vols. London, 1928. [First published (10 vols.) 1893-1899. Cf. also Tanner (1925).]

PHILLIPS, L. B. (1871). *The Dictionary of Biographical Reference.* 8°. London.

PIJZEL, E. D. (1875). Antony van Leeuwenhoek. *De Gids* (Amsterdam), XXXIX Jaarg. (3e ser. XIII), p. 105.

PLIETZSCH, E. (1911). *Vermeer van Delft.* 8°. Leipzig.

PLIMMER, H. G. (1913). The President's Address: " Bedellus Immortalis." *J. Roy. Microsc. Soc.* (London), p. 121. [Largely a plagiarism of the equally worthless article by Richardson (1885).]

PLINIUS SECUNDUS, C. (1582). *Historiae Mundi libri* XXXVII. Fol. Genevae. [Generally known as *Historia Naturalis.* See also Engl. transl. by Holland, 2 vols. fol. London, 1601; and by Bostock and Riley, 6 vols. 8°. London, 1855-7.]

POLLOCK, F. (1899). *Spinoza: his Life and Philosophy.* (2nd ed.) 8°. London.

POOT, H. (1722). *Gedichten.* 4°. Delft. [*Gedrukt by R. Boitet voor den Autheur.* Contains (pp. 267, 275, 436) 3 poems to L.; and Poot's portrait by T. v. d. Wilt, with his verses thereon (p. 442).]

POWER, H. (1663-4). *Experimental Philosophy, in Three Books: Containing New Experiments Microscopical, Mercurial, Magnetical.* 4°. London.

PRESCOTT, F. (1930). Spallanzani on spontaneous generation and digestion. *Proc. Roy. Soc. Med.,* XXIII, (Sect. Hist. Med.) 37.

PRITZE, F. (1928). Beiträge zur Kenntnis des Balantidium coli. *Zs. Parasitenk.* (*Zs. wiss. Biol.* Abt. F), I, 345.

PRITZEL, G. A. (1872). *Thesaurus Literaturae Botanicae.* 4°. Lipsiae. [Incomplete bibliography of L., p. 179.]

PROWAZEK, S. VON (1913). Zur Kenntnis der Balantidiosis. *Arch. f. Schiffs- u. Tropenhyg.* (Beih.), XVII, 5. [Cf. also article " Infusoria-Ciliata " in Prowazek's *Handb. d. path. Protozoen* (1914), Lief. vi, p. 858.]

PROWAZEK, S. VON (1913*a*). Zur Parasitologie von Westafrika. *Zbl. Bakt.* (I) Orig., LXX, 32. [*Selenomonas* n.g., p. 36.]

RABUS, P. (1693-1700). *De Boekzaal van Europe.* 8°. Rotterdam. [Contains 6 letters of L. not published elsewhere.]

RÁDL, E. (1905, 1909). *Geschichte der biologischen Theorien.* 8°. 2 vols. Leipzig. [See especially vol. I, p. 103.]

RAY, J. (1673.) *Observations Topographical, Moral, & Physiological; Made in a Journey through part of the Low-Countries, Germany, Italy, and France* [etc.]. 8°. London. [2nd ed., with additions, 2 vols. 1738.]

RAY, J. (1704). *The Wisdom of God manifested in the Works of the Creation.* 4th ed. 8°. London.

RAY, J. (1713). *Three Physico-Theological Discourses* [etc.]. 3rd ed. 8°. London.

RAY, J. (1718). *Philosophical Letters between the late learned Mr. Ray and several of his Ingenious Correspondents, Natives and Foreigners* (ed. W. Derham). 8°. London.

RECORD OF THE ROYAL SOCIETY OF LONDON (1912). 3rd ed. entirely revised and rearranged. 8°. London. [*edidit* A. Geikie.]

REDI, F. (1668). *Esperienze intorno alla Generazione degl' Insetti.* 4°. Firenze.

REDI, F. (1678). *Lettera intorno all'invenzione degli occhiali* [etc.]. 4°. Firenze. [14 pp.]

REDI, F. (1684). *Osservazioni intorno agli Animali Viventi che si trovano negli animali viventi.* 4°. Firenze.

REDI, F. (1809-1811). *Opere.* 8°. 9 vols. Milano. [*Ediz. Class. Ital.*, vols. CLXIX-CLXXVII.]

REGLEY, L'ABBÉ (1769). *Nouvelles Recherches sur les Découvertes microscopiques, et la Génération des Corps organisés* . . . traduit de l'Italien de M. l'Abbé Spalanzani . . . avec des notes . . . par M. de Needham. 8°. Londres & Paris.

RÉMIGNARD, H. (1902). *La Parasitologie aux XVIe et XVIIe Siècles.* Thèse, Fac. Méd. Paris. 8°. (80 pp.)

RICHARDSON, B. W. (1885). Antony Van Leeuwenhoek, F.R.S., and the origin of histology. *The Asclepiad* (London), II, 319. [Privately printed. Inaccurate and misleading.]

RICHARDSON, B. W. (1900). *Disciples of Aesculapius.* 8°. 2 vols. London. [Contains (vol. I, p. 108) a modified version of the foregoing paper.]

RIEMSDIJK, B. W. F. VAN (1921). *Catalogus der Schilderijen . . . in het Rijks-Museum te Amsterdam.* 8°. Amsterdam.

RIX, H. (1893). Henry Oldenburg, first Secretary of the Royal Society. *Nature* (London), XLIX, 9.

ROBERTSON, A. (1922). *The Life of Sir Robert Moray, Soldier Statesman and Man of Science* (1608-1673). 8°. London. ["First President of the Royal Society."]

ROBIN, C. (1853). *Histoire naturelle des Végétaux Parasites qui croissent sur l'homme et sur les animaux vivants.* [Avec atlas de 15 pl.] 8°. Paris.

RÖSEL VON ROSENHOF, A. J. (1746-1761). *Die monatlich-herausgegebenen Insecten-Belustigungen.* 4°. 4 vols. Nürnberg. [New ed., ed. Kleemann: 5 vols. 1792. The observations on protozoa are all in vol. III, supplement (1st ed. 1755).]

ROGERS, J. E. T. (1886). *Holland.* 8°. London. [*Story of the Nations* series.]

ROOIJEN, A. J. SERVAAS VAN (1904). Anthoni van Leeuwenhoek door Leuven's hoogeschool gehuldigd. *Album der Natuur* (Haarlem), 12 afl. (Sept.) p. 380.

ROOIJEN, A. J. SERVAAS VAN (1905). Brieven van Antony van Leeuwenhoek. *Album der Natuur* (Haarlem), 2 afl. (Nov.) p. 57.

ROOS, J. C. (1767). Mundus invisibilis. *Amoen. Acad.*, No. CXLVI. Vol. VII, p. 385. Holmiae [1769].

ROSENHEIM, O. (1924). The isolation of spermine phosphate from semen and testis. *Biochem. J.*, XVIII, 1253. [Identifies the crystals discovered by L. in human semen.]

ROTERMUND, H. W. (1810). *Fortsetzung und Ergänzungen zu C. G. Jöchers allgemeinem Gelehrten-Lexico.* Vol. III, col. 1486. [Incomplete list of L.'s works, with a few notes.]

ROUKEMA, R. (1706). *Naam-Boek der beroemde Genees- en Heelmeesters van alle eeuwen.* 8°. Amsterdam. [Reference to L. on p. 203.]

SABRAZÈS, [J.] (1926). Leeuwenhoek et les débuts de l'hématologie. *Æsculape* (Paris), XVI [N.S.], 90.

SACHS, J. (1875). *Geschichte der Botanik vom 16. Jahrhundert bis 1860.* 8°. München. (*Gesch. d. Wissensch. in Deutschland*, Bd. XV.) [" Anton van Leeuwenhoek," pp. 262-4.]

SAUSSURE, H. B. DE (1769). Letter of 28 Sept. to Bonnet, printed in Bonnet's *Œuvres*, vol. XV, p. 475 : also quoted by Spallanzani, *Œuvres* (ed. Senebier), vol. I, p. 172.

SCHELTEMA, P. (1886). *Het leven van Frederik Ruijsch.* [Dissertation, Leyden.] 8°. Sliedrecht.

SCHIERBEEK, A. (1923). *Van Aristoteles tot Pasteur : leven en werken der groote biologen.* 8°. Amsterdam.

SCHIERBEEK, A. (1927). Nieuws uit het leven van Leeuwenhoek. *Nieuwe Rotterdamsche Courant*, 20 July 1927, Avondbl. A, p. 2 (6de Internat. Congr. v. d. Geschiedenis v. d. Geneeskunde).

SCHIERBEEK, A. (1929). Neues aus dem Leben Leeuwenhoeks. *VI Congr. Internat. Hist. Méd.* (Leyde-Amsterdam, 18-23 juillet 1927), pp. 82-87. [Anvers : De Vlijt.]

SCHIERBEEK, A. (1929*a*). [Over A. v. Leeuwenhoek. Vergadering der Genootschap voor Geschiedenis der Genees-, Natuur- en Wiskunde te Gorinchem, 20 Oct. 1929.] *Nieuwe Rotterdamsche Courant* (Avondbl. A), 22 Oct. 1929.

SCHIERBEEK, A. (1930). Een paar nieuwe bijzonderheden over van Leeuwenhoek. *Nederl. Tijdschr. v. Geneesk.*, LXXIV, 3891.

SCHILL, J. F. (1887). Antony van Leeuwenhoek's Entdeckung der Microorganismen. *Zool. Anz.*, X, 685.

SCRIPTORES REI RUSTICAE (1543). *Libri de re rustica.* 8°. Parisiis. [2 vols. in 1. Book I, Cato & Varro : II, Columella.]

SCRIVERIUS, P. (1609). *Batavia Illustrata.* 4°. Lugd. Bat.

SENEBIER, J. (1801). *Mémoire historique sur la Vie et les Ecrits de Horace Bénédict Desaussure.* 8°. Genève.

SETERS, W. H. VAN (1926). Antony van Leeuwenhoek (1632-1723). (Lecture delivered as an introduction to the representation of the Leeuwenhoek film.) *Lectures on Physics and Physiology for American Students* : Leiden University, July 1926. 8°. Leyden. [*Vide* pp. 48-52.]

SEWEL, W. (1691). *A New Dictionary English and Dutch. / Nieuw Woordenboek der Engelsche en Nederduytsche Taale.* 4°. Amsterdam.

SEWEL, W. (1708). *A Large Dictionary English and Dutch* [etc.]. / *Groot Woordenboek der Engelsche en Nederduytsche Taalen* [enz.]. 4°. Amsterdam.

SEWEL, W. (1754). *A compendious Guide to the Low-Dutch Language* [etc.]. / *Korte Wegwyzer der Nederduytsche Taal.* 2 ed. 12°. Amsterdam.

SHERBORN, C. D. (1902—). *Index Animalium.* 8°. Cambridge.

SINGER, C. (1911). Benjamin Marten, a neglected predecessor of Louis Pasteur. *Janus* (Haarlem), XVI, 81.

SINGER, C. (1913). *The Development of the Doctrine of Contagium Vivum, 1500-1750. A Preliminary Sketch.* London. [Brochure, 15 pp. Privately printed.]

SINGER, C. (1914). Notes on the early history of microscopy. *Proc. Roy. Soc. Med.*, VII, (Sect. Hist. Med.) 247.

SINGER, C. (1915). The dawn of microscopical discovery. *J. Roy. Microsc. Soc.*, p. 317.

SINGER, C. (1921). Steps leading to the invention of the first optical apparatus. *Studies in the History and Method of Science*, vol. II, p. 385. 8°. Oxford.

SINGER, C. & SINGER, D. (1917). The scientific position of Girolamo Fracastoro [1478 ?-1553], etc. *Ann. Med. Hist.*, I, 1.

SINIA, R. (1878). *Johannes Swammerdam in de Lijst van zijn Tijd.* (Akad. Proefschr., Leiden.) 8°. Hoorn.

SLABBER, M. (1778). *Natuurkundige Verlustigingen* [etc.]. 4°. Haarlem. [*Noctiluca* depicted in Pl. 8, figs. 4 & 5 ; and Vorticellids on a zoaea in Pl. 5.]

SLARE, F. (1683). A further confirmation of the above mentioned *Contagion* [described in a Letter from Dr. Wincler, 22 Dec. 1682] etc. *Phil. Trans.*, vol. XIII, No. 145, p. 94.

SNELLEMAN, J. F. (1874). Antony van Leeuwenhoek. 1675—Infusoriën—1875. *Album der Natuur* (Haarlem), Jaarg. 1874, p. 357.

SOUTENDAM, J. (1875). Antony van Leeuwenhoek. *Eigen Haard* (Haarlem), No. 37, p. 308.

SPALLANZANI, L. (1769). See REGLEY.

SPALLANZANI, L. (1776). *Opuscoli di fisica animale e vegetabile* [etc.]. 8°. 2 vols. Modena. [Also French transl. by J. Senebier. 8°. 3 vols. Pavia & Paris, 1787.]

SPALLANZANI, L. (1825-6). *Opere.* 8°. 6 vols. Milano.

SPINOZA, B. DE (1882-3). *Opera* ed. J. van Vloten & J. P. N. Land. 8°. 2 vols. Hagae Comitum.

SPRAT, T. (1667). *History of the Royal Society of London, for the Improving of Natural Knowledge.* 4°. London. [2nd ed. 1702 : 3rd ed. 1722.]

STEIN, F. (1854). *Die Infusionsthiere auf ihre Entwickelungsgeschichte untersucht.* 4°. Leipzig.

STEIN, F. VON (1859, 1867, 1878, 1883). *Der Organismus der Infusionsthiere.* Fol. 3 vols. (in 4). Leipzig.

STELLUTI, F. (1630). *Persio Tradotto in verso sciolto . . .* 4°. Roma. [Microscopic delineations of Bee (p. 52) and Weevil (p. 127).]

STIRLING, W. (1902). *Some Apostles of Physiology.* Fol. London. [Privately printed. For L. see p. 37.]

STORR-BEST, Ll. (1912). *Varro on Farming.* 8°. London.

STRONG, R. P. (1904). The clinical and pathological significance of *Balantidium coli*. *Dept. of Interior, Bur. of Govt. Labs., Biol. Lab.* Bull. No. 26. 8°. Manila.

STURM, J. C. (1676). *Collegium Experimentale, sive Curiosum* [etc.]. 4°. Norimbergae. [= Pars prima (pars secunda publ. 1685). See pp. 138-150. Contains no observations on protozoa or bacteria —only worms, insects, etc.]

SWAMMERDAM, J. (1669). *Historia Insectorum Generalis, ofte Algemeene Verhandeling van de Bloedeloose Dierkens*. 4°. Utrecht. [Latin ed., transl. Henninius, 1682.]

SWAMMERDAM, J. (1737, 1738). *Bybel der Natuure, . . . of Historie der Insecten. / Biblia Naturae; sive Historia Insectorum.* Fol 2 vols. Leyden.

SWAMMERDAM. See also SINIA (1878) and *Anonymus* (1880).

TANNER, J. R. (1925). *Mr Pepys. An Introduction to the Diary together with a Sketch of his Later Life*. 8°. London.

TARGIONI-TOZZETTI, G. (1745). *Clarorum Belgarum ad Ant. Magliabechium nonnullosque alios Epistolae*. 8°. 2 vols. Florentiae.

TARGIONI-TOZZETTI, G. (1746). *Clarorum Germanorum ad Ant. Magliabechium nonnullosque alios Epistolae*. 8°. Vol. I. [All published ?] Florentiae.

TEMPLE, W. (1693). *Observations upon the United Provinces of the Netherlands*. (6th ed. corrected and augmented). 8°. London.

TEMPLE, W. (1709). *Memoirs of what past in Christendom, from the War begun* 1672. *to the Peace concluded* 1679. 8°. London.

THOMSON, T. (1812). *History of the Royal Society, from its Institution to the End of the Eighteenth Century*. 4°. London.

THORPE, E. (1921). *History of Chemistry*. 8°. [2 vols. in 1.] London.

TREMBLEY, A. (1744). *Mémoires, pour servir à l'Histoire d'un genre de Polypes d'eau douce, à bras en forme de cornes*. 4°. Leide.

TREMBLEY, A. (1744*a*). Translation of a Letter from . . . with Observations upon several newly discover'd Species of Fresh-water Polypi. *Phil. Trans.*, vol. XLIII, No. 474, p. 169.

TREMBLEY, A. (1747). Observations upon several species of small water insects of the *Polypus* kind . . . *Phil. Trans.*, vol. XLIV, (Appendix) p. 627.

TREVELYAN, G. M. (1926). *History of England*. 8°. London.

TREVIRANUS, G. R. (1816). *Vermischte Schriften anatomischen und physiologischen Inhalts*. (Göttingen.) Vol. I. [Contains various allusions to L., *e.g.* pp. 122, 145.]

TYNDALL, J. (1881). *Essays on the Floating-Matter of the Air in relation to Putrefaction and Infection*. 8°. London.

UFFENBACH, Z. C. VON (1753-4). *Merkwürdige Reisen durch Niedersachsen Holland und Engelland*. 8°. 3 vols. Ulm-Memmingen-Frankfurt-Leipzig. [Ed. J. G. Schelhorn. For L. see vol. III, pp. 349-360.]

VALLISNERI, A. (1721). *Istoria della Generazione dell'ucmo, e degli animali, se sia da' vermicelli spermatici, o dalle uova* [etc.]. 4°. Venezia.

VALLISNERI, A. (1733). *Opere Fisico-mediche stampate e manoscritte . . . raccolte da Antonio suo figliuolo.* Fol. 3 vols. Venezia.

VANDEVELDE, A. J. J. (1922). De brieven 1 tot 27 van Antoni van Leeuwenhoek, (Delft 24 October 1632 † 26 Augustus 1723). Den stichter der micrographie. *Versl. & Mededeel. Kon. Vlaamsche Acad.* (Gent), Jaarg. 1922, pp. 323-359.

VANDEVELDE, A. J. J. (1922*a*). De brieven 28 tot 52 van Antoni van Leeuwenhoek, (2e bijdrage tot de studie over de werken van den stichter der micrographie). *Ibid.*, pp. 645-690.

VANDEVELDE, A. J. J. (1922*b*). De brieven 53 tot 75 van Antoni van Leeuwenhoek. 3e bijdrage tot de studie over de werken van den stichter der micrographie. *Ibid.*, pp. 1019-1056.

VANDEVELDE, A. J. J. (1922*c*). De brieven 76-107 van Antoni van Leeuwenhoek. (4e bijdrage tot de studie over de werken van den stichter der micrographie.) *Ibid.*, pp. 1093-1132.

VANDEVELDE, A. J. J. (1923). De brieven 108 tot 146 van Antoni van Leeuwenhoek. 5e bijdrage tot de studie over de werken van den stichter der micrographie. *Ibid.*, Jaarg. 1923, pp. 84-116.

VANDEVELDE, A. J. J. (1923*a*). De send-brieven van Antoni van Leeuwenhoek. 6e bijdrage tot de studie over de geschriften van den stichter der micrographie. *Ibid.*, pp. 350-400.

VANDEVELDE, A. J. J. (1923*b*). Antoni van Leeuwenhoek herdacht. Bij den tweehonderdsten verjaardag van zijn overlijden, 26 Augustus 1723. *Ibid.*, pp. 560-581.

VANDEVELDE, A. J. J. (1924). De 2e en 3e Engelsche reeksen der brieven van Antoni van Leeuwenhoek. (7e bijdrage tot de studie over de werken van den stichter der micrographie.) *Ibid.*, Jaarg. 1924, pp. 130-148.

VANDEVELDE, A. J. J. (1924*a*). Over eenige handschriften der brieven van Antoni van Leeuwenhoek. 8e bijdrage tot de studie over de werken van den stichter der micrographie. *Ibid.*, pp. 285-300.

VANDEVELDE, A. J. J. & VAN SETERS, W. H. (1925). Over eenige handschriften der brieven van Antoni van Leeuwenhoek. 9e bijdrage tot de studie over de werken van den stichter der micrographie. *Ibid.*, Jaarg. 1925, pp. 1-35 [offprint].

VANZYPE, G. (1921). *Jan Vermeer de Delft.* (Nouv. éd.) Fol. Bruxelles & Paris.

VELDMAN, H. S. (1898). *Catalogus van den Historischen Atlas van Delft en Delfland.* 8°. Delft.

WAARD, C. DE (1906). *De Uitvinding der Verrekijkers.* 8°. 's-Gravenhage. [Het Microscoop, pp. 293-304.]

WALLER, R. (1705). *The Posthumous Works of Robert Hooke, M.D., S.R.S.* [etc.]. Fol. London. [With biography.]

WARD, N. (1698-1703). *The London Spy.* Ed. A. L. Hayward. 8°. London. [1927.]

WELD, C. R. (1848). *A History of the Royal Society, with Memoirs of the Presidents.* 8°. 2 vols. London.

WENYON, C. M. (1926). *Protozoology : a Manual for Medical Men, Veterinarians and Zoologists.* 2 vols. 8°. London.

WHEWELL, W. (1857). *History of the Inductive Sciences.* (3rd ed.) 8°. 3 vols. London.

WILDEMAN, M. G. (1903). *Archaeography of Delft Curiosities.* 8°. Delft.

WILKINS, J. (1708). *Mathematical and Philosophical Works.* 8°. London.

WILLIAMS-ELLIS, A. (1929). *Great Discoverers.* 8°. London. (British Broadcasting Corporation. Broadcast to Schools: Story III, 1 Feb. 1929.) [Worthless and misleading account of L. on p. 13.]

WILLNAU, C. (1921). *Ledermüller. Erzählung.* 8°. Leipzig.

WILLNAU, C. (1926). *Ledermüller und v. Gleichen-Russworm. Zwei deutsche Mikroskopisten der Zopfzeit.* 8°. Leipzig. [Brochure, 24 pp.]

WOLF, A. (1927). *The Oldest Biography of Spinoza.* 8°. London.

WOODRUFF, L. L. (1926). The versatile Sir John Hill, M.D. *Amer. Nat.*, LX, 417.

WORP, J. A. (1917). See HUYGENS, Constantijn.

WRISBERG, H. A. (1765). *Observationum de Animalculis infusoriis Satura.* 8°. Goettingae.

ZAHN, J. (1685-6). *Oculus artificialis teledioptricus, sive Telescopium.* Fol. Herbipoli. [Compilation. Contains nothing original.]

ACKNOWLEDGEMENTS

THIS book has been so long a-writing, has taken me on so many unexpected quests, and has brought me into contact with so many problems and such divers people (both living and dead), that I now find it difficult to record—or even, I fear, to remember—all the help which I have received from others in the course of its compilation. Almost everybody I know has contributed—wittingly or unwittingly, directly or indirectly—something towards its fulfilment: and with negligible exceptions every person whose aid I have sought has willingly furnished me with information or material. It is impossible, therefore, to mention here by name all the friends and colleagues, all the fellow-students and distant co-workers whom I have never met in the flesh, all the librarians and antiquarian booksellers and editors and publishers, who have given me their unstinted assistance at all times. Consequently, I can only beg them, one and all, to accept now this general acknowledgement of my indebtedness.

But there are some special helpers whose names I cannot omit to mention specifically. My debt to my two "Brothers" I have attempted to repay by dedicating this volume to them. Without their fraternal encouragement it would never have been written, and I therefore owe them both more than I can express—big brother D'Arcy for his unattainable example and incomparable scholarship in wider fields, little brother Paul for his equal enthusiasm on common ground. Next after these I would mention my old friend Mr A. Hastings White, Librarian (now, alas! in only a consultant capacity) to the Royal Society, whose knowledge of everything connected with the Society has been of incalculable assistance. I have never sought his aid in vain, and he has always placed his own vast learning at my disposal most liberally.

I am further indebted, in no small degree, to several good friends in Holland. That great bacteriologist, the late

Professor M. W. Beijerinck of Delft, with characteristic unselfishness gave me aid both material and spiritual. The late Mr L. G. N. Bouricius, Archivist of Delft until his untimely death on 21 February 1929, also supplied me with much valuable information, and never failed to satisfy my frequent inquiries to the utmost of his ability. Dr W. H. van Seters of Leyden, who recently produced the "Leeuwenhoek Film," most kindly communicated—unasked—all his own incidental findings, together with several original photographs and a full copy of the captions. Dr E. P. Snijders—formerly stationed in Sumatra, now Professor at Amsterdam—has given me not only valuable advice but also a magnificent specimen of the old Dutch Bible (1702): while Dr A. Schierbeek, at The Hague, has rendered the kindest assistance in innumerable ways during the last ten years. To all these unseen Dutch friends and fellow-students of Leeuwenhoek I owe a debt which I can never acknowledge sufficiently. They have all given me—a foreigner unknown to them personally—their most generous help. Dr C. A. Crommelin, now Professor of Physics at Leyden, has been equally helpful: but I mention him separately because he is, happily, not only still a living student and admirer of Leeuwenhoek but also one whose hand I have actually shaken. I would also record that the Netherlands Society of Sciences, at Haarlem, have aided me by the gift of two important volumes of the *Complete Works of Huygens*, which they are editing and publishing on so sumptuous a scale.

Among my own countrymen who have given me continued support I must mention particularly Professor William Bulloch, F.R.S., and Professor F. J. Cole, F.R.S. The first—as all real students everywhere know—possesses an unrivalled knowledge of the history of bacteriology (and of medicine in general): the second is now our only living authority on the history of zoology. Both have given me the benefit of their own solid learning on countless occasions. If I have not profited by it, the fault is mine.

To the Council of the Royal Society I am beholden for granting me the facilities necessary to undertake this work; and to the Trustees of the National Gallery and the Directors of the Rijks-Museum and the Mauritshuis for permission to reproduce the pictures shown in four of my plates.

Finally, I wish to acknowledge my deep personal obligation

to my friend Mrs Mabel Selle, who has accurately typed the greater part of this book: for without her expert aid I could never have sent my original troublesome and repeatedly corrected and revised manuscript to press at the appointed hour. To my English printers and publishers, Messrs. Bale and Danielsson, I am indebted no less: for they have invariably met my tiresome typographical and other requirements in the most sympathetic and magnanimous manner.

For mistakes I alone am responsible, and to those who will point them out I shall ever be grateful. I have done my best; yet I know all too well "*Het en kan niet wesen, datter geen ergernissen en komen: doch wee hem door welcken sy komen*—It is impossible but that offences will come, but wo unto him through whom they come" (St Luke xvii, 1).

FINIS

INDEX

* This Index covers the whole of the foregoing work—text, notes, and bibliography. It is a key to the book as a whole, and furnishes clues to all the information contained in it—with its sources—and an indication of all the chief persons and genera of animals and plants mentioned.

** Here, as elsewhere in all notes throughout, the abbreviation "L." stands for ANTONY VAN LEEUWENHOEK.

A CATALOGUE OF SELECTED DOVER BOOKS IN ALL FIELDS OF INTEREST

A CATALOGUE OF SELECTED DOVER BOOKS IN ALL FIELDS OF INTEREST

THE ART DECO STYLE, ed. by Theodore Menten. Furniture, jewelry, metalwork, ceramics, fabrics, lighting fixtures, interior decors, exteriors, graphics from pure French sources. Best sampling around. Over 400 photographs. 183pp. 8³/8 x 11¼.
22824-X Pa. $4.00

THE GENTLEMAN AND CABINET MAKER'S DIRECTOR, Thomas Chippendale. Full reprint, 1762 style book, most influential of all time; chairs, tables, sofas, mirrors, cabinets, etc. 200 plates, plus 24 photographs of surviving pieces. 249pp. 9⁷/8 x 12¾.
21601-2 Pa. $5.00

PINE FURNITURE OF EARLY NEW ENGLAND, Russell H. Kettell. Basic book. Thorough historical text, plus 200 illustrations of boxes, highboys, candlesticks, desks, etc. 477pp. 7⁷/8 x 10¾.
20145-7 Clothbd. $12.50

ORIENTAL RUGS, ANTIQUE AND MODERN, Walter A. Hawley. Persia, Turkey, Caucasus, Central Asia, China, other traditions. Best general survey of all aspects: styles and periods, manufacture, uses, symbols and their interpretation, and identification. 96 illustrations, 11 in color. 320pp. 6¹/8 x 9¼.
22366-3 Pa. $5.00

DECORATIVE ANTIQUE IRONWORK, Henry R. d'Allemagne. Photographs of 4500 iron artifacts from world's finest collection, Rouen. Hinges, locks, candelabra, weapons, lighting devices, clocks, tools, from Roman times to mid-19th century. Nothing else comparable to it. 420pp. 9 x 12.
22082-6 Pa. $8.50

THE COMPLETE BOOK OF DOLL MAKING AND COLLECTING, Catherine Christopher. Instructions, patterns for dozens of dolls, from rag doll on up to elaborate, historically accurate figures. Mould faces, sew clothing, make doll houses, etc. Also collecting information. Many illustrations. 288pp. 6 x 9.
22066-4 Pa. $3.00

ANTIQUE PAPER DOLLS: 1915-1920, edited by Arnold Arnold. 7 antique cut-out dolls and 24 costumes from 1915-1920, selected by Arnold Arnold from his collection of rare children's books and entertainments, all in full color. 32pp. 9¼ x 12¼.
23176-3 Pa. $2.00

ANTIQUE PAPER DOLLS: THE EDWARDIAN ERA, Epinal. Full-color reproductions of two historic series of paper dolls that show clothing styles in 1908 and at the beginning of the First World War. 8 two-sided, stand-up dolls and 32 complete, two-sided costumes. Full instructions for assembling included. 32pp. 9¼ x 12¼.
23175-5 Pa. $2.00

A HISTORY OF COSTUME, Carl Köhler, Emma von Sichardt. Egypt, Babylon, Greece up through 19th century Europe; based on surviving pieces, art works, etc. Full text and 595 illustrations, including many clear, measured patterns for reproducing historic costume. Practical. 464pp.
21030-8 Pa. $4.00

EARLY AMERICAN LOCOMOTIVES, John H. White, Jr. Finest locomotive engravings from late 19th century: historical (1804-1874), main-line (after 1870), special, foreign, etc. 147 plates. 200pp. 11³/8 x 8¼.
22772-3 Pa. $3.50

VICTORIAN HOUSES: A TREASURY OF LESSER-KNOWN EXAMPLES, Edmund Gillon and Clay Lancaster. 116 photographs, excellent commentary illustrate distinct characteristics, many borrowings of local Victorian architecture. Octagonal houses, Americanized chalets, grand country estates, small cottages, etc. Rich heritage often overlooked. 116 plates. 11 3/8 x 10. 22966-1 Pa. $4.00

STICKS AND STONES, Lewis Mumford. Great classic of American cultural history; architecture from medieval-inspired earliest forms to 20th century; evolution of structure and style, influence of environment. 21 illustrations. 113pp. 20202-X Pa. $2.00

ON THE LAWS OF JAPANESE PAINTING, Henry P. Bowie. Best substitute for training with genius Oriental master, based on years of study in Kano school. Philosophy, brushes, inks, style, etc. 66 illustrations. 117pp. 6 1/8 x 9 1/4. 20030-2 Pa. $4.00

A HANDBOOK OF ANATOMY FOR ART STUDENTS, Arthur Thomson. Virtually exhaustive. Skeletal structure, muscles, heads, special features. Full text, anatomical figures, undraped photos. Male and female. 337 illustrations. 459pp. 21163-0 Pa. $5.00

AN ATLAS OF ANATOMY FOR ARTISTS, Fritz Schider. Finest text, working book. Full text, plus anatomical illustrations; plates by great artists showing anatomy. 593 illustrations. 192pp. 7 7/8 x 10 3/4. 20241-0 Clothbd. $6.95

THE HUMAN FIGURE IN MOTION, Eadweard Muybridge. More than 4500 stopped-action photos, in action series, showing undraped men, women, children jumping, lying down, throwing, sitting, wrestling, carrying, etc. "Unparalleled dictionary for artists," American Artist. Taken by great 19th century photographer. 390pp. 7 7/8 x 10 5/8. 20204-6 Clothbd. $12.50

AN ATLAS OF ANIMAL ANATOMY FOR ARTISTS, W. Ellenberger et al. Horses, dogs, cats, lions, cattle, deer, etc. Muscles, skeleton, surface features. The basic work. Enlarged edition. 288 illustrations. 151pp. 9 3/8 x 12 1/4. 20082-5 Pa. $4.00

LETTER FORMS: 110 COMPLETE ALPHABETS, Frederick Lambert. 110 sets of capital letters; 16 lower case alphabets; 70 sets of numbers and other symbols. Edited and expanded by Theodore Menten. 110pp. 8 1/8 x 11. 22872-X Pa. $2.50

THE METHODS OF CONSTRUCTION OF CELTIC ART, George Bain. Simple geometric techniques for making wonderful Celtic interlacements, spirals, Kells-type initials, animals, humans, etc. Unique for artists, craftsmen. Over 500 illustrations. 160pp. 9 x 12. USO 22923-8 Pa. $4.00

SCULPTURE, PRINCIPLES AND PRACTICE, Louis Slobodkin. Step by step approach to clay, plaster, metals, stone; classical and modern. 253 drawings, photos. 255pp. 8 1/8 x 11. 22960-2 Pa. $4.50

THE ART OF ETCHING, E.S. Lumsden. Clear, detailed instructions for etching, drypoint, softground, aquatint; from 1st sketch to print. Very detailed, thorough. 200 illustrations. 376pp. 20049-3 Pa. $3.50

JEWISH GREETING CARDS, Ed Sibbett, Jr. 16 cards to cut and color. Three say "Happy Chanukah," one "Happy New Year," others have no message, show stars of David, Torahs, wine cups, other traditional themes. 16 envelopes. 8¼ x 11.
23225-5 Pa. $2.00

AUBREY BEARDSLEY GREETING CARD BOOK, Aubrey Beardsley. Edited by Theodore Menten. 16 elegant yet inexpensive greeting cards let you combine your own sentiments with subtle Art Nouveau lines. 16 different Aubrey Beardsley designs that you can color or not, as you wish. 16 envelopes. 64pp. 8¼ x 11.
23173-9 Pa. $2.00

RECREATIONS IN THE THEORY OF NUMBERS, Albert Beiler. Number theory, an inexhaustible source of puzzles, recreations, for beginners and advanced. Divisors, perfect numbers. scales of notation, etc. 349pp. 21096-0 Pa. $2.50

AMUSEMENTS IN MATHEMATICS, Henry E. Dudeney. One of largest puzzle collections, based on algebra, arithmetic, permutations, probability, plane figure dissection, properties of numbers, by one of world's foremost puzzlists. Solutions. 450 illustrations. 258pp. 20473-1 Pa. $2.75

MATHEMATICS, MAGIC AND MYSTERY, Martin Gardner. Puzzle editor for Scientific American explains math behind: card tricks, stage mind reading, coin and match tricks, counting out games, geometric dissections. Probability, sets, theory of numbers, clearly explained. Plus more than 400 tricks, guaranteed to work. 135 illustrations. 176pp. 20335-2 Pa. $2.00

BEST MATHEMATICAL PUZZLES OF SAM LOYD, edited by Martin Gardner. Bizarre, original, whimsical puzzles by America's greatest puzzler. From fabulously rare Cyclopedia, including famous 14-15 puzzles, the Horse of a Different Color, 115 more. Elementary math. 150 illustrations. 167pp. 20498-7 Pa. $2.00

MATHEMATICAL PUZZLES FOR BEGINNERS AND ENTHUSIASTS, Geoffrey Mott-Smith. 189 puzzles from easy to difficult involving arithmetic, logic, algebra, properties of digits, probability. Explanation of math behind puzzles. 135 illustrations. 248pp. 20198-8 Pa. $2.75

BIG BOOK OF MAZES AND LABYRINTHS, Walter Shepherd. Classical, solid, and ripple mazes; short path and avoidance labyrinths; more —50 mazes and labyrinths in all. 12 other figures. Full solutions. 112pp. 8⅛ x 11. 22951-3 Pa. $2.00

COIN GAMES AND PUZZLES, Maxey Brooke. 60 puzzles, games and stunts — from Japan, Korea, Africa and the ancient world, by Dudeney and the other great puzzlers, as well as Maxey Brooke's own creations. Full solutions. 67 illustrations. 94pp. 22893-2 Pa. $1.25

HAND SHADOWS TO BE THROWN UPON THE WALL, Henry Bursill. Wonderful Victorian novelty tells how to make flying birds, dog, goose, deer, and 14 others. 32pp. 6½ x 9¼. 21779-5 Pa. $1.25

DECORATIVE ALPHABETS AND INITIALS, edited by Alexander Nesbitt. 91 complete alphabets (medieval to modern), 3924 decorative initials, including Victorian novelty and Art Nouveau. 192pp. 7¾ x 10¾. 20544-4 Pa. $3.50

CALLIGRAPHY, Arthur Baker. Over 100 original alphabets from the hand of our greatest living calligrapher: simple, bold, fine-line, richly ornamented, etc. —all strikingly original and different, a fusion of many influences and styles. 155pp. 11⅜ x 8¼. 22895-9 Pa. $4.00

MONOGRAMS AND ALPHABETIC DEVICES, edited by Hayward and Blanche Cirker. Over 2500 combinations, names, crests in very varied styles: script engraving, ornate Victorian, simple Roman, and many others. 226pp. 8⅛ x 11. 22330-2 Pa. $5.00

THE BOOK OF SIGNS, Rudolf Koch. Famed German type designer renders 493 symbols: religious, alchemical, imperial, runes, property marks, etc. Timeless. 104pp. 6⅛ x 9¼. 20162-7 Pa. $1.50

200 DECORATIVE TITLE PAGES, edited by Alexander Nesbitt. 1478 to late 1920's. Baskerville, Dürer, Beardsley, W. Morris, Pyle, many others in most varied techniques. For posters, programs, other uses. 222pp. 8⅜ x 11¼. 21264-5 Pa. $3.50

DICTIONARY OF AMERICAN PORTRAITS, edited by Hayward and Blanche Cirker. 4000 important Americans, earliest times to 1905, mostly in clear line. Politicians, writers, soldiers, scientists, inventors, industrialists, Indians, Blacks, women, outlaws, etc. Identificatory information. 756pp. 9¼ x 12¾. 21823-6 Clothbd. $30.00

ART FORMS IN NATURE, Ernst Haeckel. Multitude of strangely beautiful natural forms: Radiolaria, Foraminifera, jellyfishes, fungi, turtles, bats, etc. All 100 plates of the 19th century evolutionist's Kunstformen der Natur (1904). 100pp. 9⅜ x 12¼. 22987-4 Pa. $4.00

DECOUPAGE: THE BIG PICTURE SOURCEBOOK, Eleanor Rawlings. Make hundreds of beautiful objects, over 550 florals, animals, letters, shells, period costumes, frames, etc. selected by foremost practitioner. Printed on one side of page. 8 color plates. Instructions. 176pp. 9 3/16 x 12¼. 23182-8 Pa. $5.00

AMERICAN FOLK DECORATION, Jean Lipman, Eve Meulendyke. Thorough coverage of all aspects of wood, tin, leather, paper, cloth decoration —scapes, humans, trees, flowers, geometrics —and how to make them. Full instructions. 233 illustrations, 5 in color. 163pp. 8⅜ x 11¼. 22217-9 Pa. $3.95

WHITTLING AND WOODCARVING, E.J. Tangerman. Best book on market; clear, full. If you can cut a potato, you can carve toys, puzzles, chains, caricatures, masks, patterns, frames, decorate surfaces, etc. Also covers serious wood sculpture. Over 200 photos. 293pp. 20965-2 Pa. $2.50

THE JOURNAL OF HENRY D. THOREAU, edited by Bradford Torrey, F.H. Allen. Complete reprinting of 14 volumes, 1837-1861, over two million words; the sourcebooks for Walden, etc. Definitive. All original sketches, plus 75 photographs. Introduction by Walter Harding. Total of 1804pp. 8½ x 12¼.
20312-3, 20313-1 Clothbd., Two vol. set $50.00

MASTERS OF THE DRAMA, John Gassner. Most comprehensive history of the drama, every tradition from Greeks to modern Europe and America, including Orient. Covers 800 dramatists, 2000 plays; biography, plot summaries, criticism, theatre history, etc. 77 illustrations. 890pp. 20100-7 Clothbd. $10.00

GHOST AND HORROR STORIES OF AMBROSE BIERCE, Ambrose Bierce. 23 modern horror stories: The Eyes of the Panther, The Damned Thing, etc., plus the dream-essay Visions of the Night. Edited by E.F. Bleiler. 199pp. 20767-6 Pa. $2.00

BEST GHOST STORIES, Algernon Blackwood. 13 great stories by foremost British 20th century supernaturalist. The Willows, The Wendigo, Ancient Sorceries, others. Edited by E.F. Bleiler. 366pp. USO 22977-7 Pa. $3.00

THE BEST TALES OF HOFFMANN, E.T.A. Hoffmann. 10 of Hoffmann's most important stories, in modern re-editings of standard translations: Nutcracker and the King of Mice, The Golden Flowerpot, etc. 7 illustrations by Hoffmann. Edited by E.F. Bleiler. 458pp. 21793-0 Pa. $3.95

BEST GHOST STORIES OF J.S. LEFANU, J. Sheridan LeFanu. 16 stories by greatest Victorian master: Green Tea, Carmilla, Haunted Baronet, The Familiar, etc. Mostly unavailable elsewhere. Edited by E.F. Bleiler. 8 illustrations. 467pp.
20415-4 Pa. $4.00

SUPERNATURAL HORROR IN LITERATURE, H.P. Lovecraft. Great modern American supernaturalist brilliantly surveys history of genre to 1930's, summarizing, evaluating scores of books. Necessary for every student, lover of form. Introduction by E.F. Bleiler. 111pp. 20105-8 Pa. $1.50

THREE GOTHIC NOVELS, ed. by E.F. Bleiler. Full texts Castle of Otranto, Walpole; Vathek, Beckford; The Vampyre, Polidori; Fragment of a Novel, Lord Byron. 331pp. 21232-7 Pa. $3.00

SEVEN SCIENCE FICTION NOVELS, H.G. Wells. Full novels. First Men in the Moon, Island of Dr. Moreau, War of the Worlds, Food of the Gods, Invisible Man, Time Machine, In the Days of the Comet. A basic science-fiction library. 1015pp.
USO 20264-X Clothbd. $6.00

LADY AUDLEY'S SECRET, Mary E. Braddon. Great Victorian mystery classic, beautifully plotted, suspenseful; praised by Thackeray, Boucher, Starrett, others. What happened to beautiful, vicious Lady Audley's husband? Introduction by Norman Donaldson. 286pp. 23011-2 Pa. $3.00

SLEEPING BEAUTY, illustrated by Arthur Rackham. Perhaps the fullest, most delightful version ever, told by C.S. Evans. Rackham's best work. 49 illustrations. 110pp. 7⅞ x 10¾. 22756-1 Pa. $2.00

THE WONDERFUL WIZARD OF OZ, L. Frank Baum. Facsimile in full color of America's finest children's classic. Introduction by Martin Gardner. 143 illustrations by W.W. Denslow. 267pp. 20691-2 Pa. $2.50

GOOPS AND HOW TO BE THEM, Gelett Burgess. Classic tongue-in-cheek masquerading as etiquette book. 87 verses, 170 cartoons as Goops demonstrate virtues of table manners, neatness, courtesy, more. 88pp. 6½ x 9¼. 22233-0 Pa. $1.50

THE BROWNIES, THEIR BOOK, Palmer Cox. Small as mice, cunning as foxes, exuberant, mischievous, Brownies go to zoo, toy shop, seashore, circus, more. 24 verse adventures. 266 illustrations. 144pp. 6⅝ x 9¼. 21265-3 Pa. $1.75

BILLY WHISKERS: THE AUTOBIOGRAPHY OF A GOAT, Frances Trego Montgomery. Escapades of that rambunctious goat. Favorite from turn of the century America. 24 illustrations. 259pp. 22345-0 Pa. $2.75

THE ROCKET BOOK, Peter Newell. Fritz, janitor's kid, sets off rocket in basement of apartment house; an ingenious hole punched through every page traces course of rocket. 22 duotone drawings, verses. 48pp. 6⅞ x 8⅜. 22044-3 Pa. $1.50

PECK'S BAD BOY AND HIS PA, George W. Peck. Complete double-volume of great American childhood classic. Hennery's ingenious pranks against outraged pomposity of pa and the grocery man. 97 illustrations. Introduction by E.F. Bleiler. 347pp. 20497-9 Pa. $2.50

THE TALE OF PETER RABBIT, Beatrix Potter. The inimitable Peter's terrifying adventure in Mr. McGregor's garden, with all 27 wonderful, full-color Potter illustrations. 55pp. 4¼ x 5½. USO 22827-4 Pa. $1.00

THE TALE OF MRS. TIGGY-WINKLE, Beatrix Potter. Your child will love this story about a very special hedgehog and all 27 wonderful, full-color Potter illustrations. 57pp. 4¼ x 5½. USO 20546-0 Pa. $1.00

THE TALE OF BENJAMIN BUNNY, Beatrix Potter. Peter Rabbit's cousin coaxes him back into Mr. McGregor's garden for a whole new set of adventures. A favorite with children. All 27 full-color illustrations. 59pp. 4¼ x 5½. USO 21102-9 Pa. $1.00

THE MERRY ADVENTURES OF ROBIN HOOD, Howard Pyle. Facsimile of original (1883) edition, finest modern version of English outlaw's adventures. 23 illustrations by Pyle. 296pp. 6½ x 9¼. 22043-5 Pa. $2.75

TWO LITTLE SAVAGES, Ernest Thompson Seton. Adventures of two boys who lived as Indians; explaining Indian ways, woodlore, pioneer methods. 293 illustrations. 286pp. 20985-7 Pa. $3.00

THE MAGIC MOVING PICTURE BOOK, Bliss, Sands & Co. The pictures in this book move! Volcanoes erupt, a house burns, a serpentine dancer wiggles her way through a number. By using a specially ruled acetate screen provided, you can obtain these and 15 other startling effects. Originally "The Motograph Moving Picture Book." 32pp. 8¼ x 11. 23224-7 Pa. $1.75

STRING FIGURES AND HOW TO MAKE THEM, Caroline F. Jayne. Fullest, clearest instructions on string figures from around world: Eskimo, Navajo, Lapp, Europe, more. Cats cradle, moving spear, lightning, stars. Introduction by A.C. Haddon. 950 illustrations. 407pp. 20152-X Pa. $3.00

PAPER FOLDING FOR BEGINNERS, William D. Murray and Francis J. Rigney. Clearest book on market for making origami sail boats, roosters, frogs that move legs, cups, bonbon boxes. 40 projects. More than 275 illustrations. Photographs. 94pp. 20713-7 Pa. $1.25

INDIAN SIGN LANGUAGE, William Tomkins. Over 525 signs developed by Sioux, Blackfoot, Cheyenne, Arapahoe and other tribes. Written instructions and diagrams: how to make words, construct sentences. Also 290 pictographs of Sioux and Ojibway tribes. 111pp. 6⅛ x 9¼. 22029-X Pa. $1.50

BOOMERANGS: HOW TO MAKE AND THROW THEM, Bernard S. Mason. Easy to make and throw, dozens of designs: cross-stick, pinwheel, boomabird, tumblestick, Australian curved stick boomerang. Complete throwing instructions. All safe. 99pp. 23028-7 Pa. $1.50

25 KITES THAT FLY, Leslie Hunt. Full, easy to follow instructions for kites made from inexpensive materials. Many novelties. Reeling, raising, designing your own. 70 illustrations. 110pp. 22550-X Pa. $1.25

TRICKS AND GAMES ON THE POOL TABLE, Fred Herrmann. 79 tricks and games, some solitaires, some for 2 or more players, some competitive; mystifying shots and throws, unusual carom, tricks involving cork, coins, a hat, more. 77 figures. 95pp. 21814-7 Pa. $1.25

WOODCRAFT AND CAMPING, Bernard S. Mason. How to make a quick emergency shelter, select woods that will burn immediately, make do with limited supplies, etc. Also making many things out of wood, rawhide, bark, at camp. Formerly titled Woodcraft. 295 illustrations. 580pp. 21951-8 Pa. $4.00

AN INTRODUCTION TO CHESS MOVES AND TACTICS SIMPLY EXPLAINED, Leonard Barden. Informal intermediate introduction: reasons for moves, tactics, openings, traps, positional play, endgame. Isolates patterns. 102pp. USO 21210-6 Pa. $1.35

LASKER'S MANUAL OF CHESS, Dr. Emanuel Lasker. Great world champion offers very thorough coverage of all aspects of chess. Combinations, position play, openings, endgame, aesthetics of chess, philosophy of struggle, much more. Filled with analyzed games. 390pp. 20640-8 Pa. $3.50

DRIED FLOWERS, Sarah Whitlock and Martha Rankin. Concise, clear, practical guide to dehydration, glycerinizing, pressing plant material, and more. Covers use of silica gel. 12 drawings. Originally titled "New Techniques with Dried Flowers." 32pp. 21802-3 Pa. $1.00

ABC OF POULTRY RAISING, J.H. Florea. Poultry expert, editor tells how to raise chickens on home or small business basis. Breeds, feeding, housing, laying, etc. Very concrete, practical. 50 illustrations. 256pp. 23201-8 Pa. $3.00

HOW INDIANS USE WILD PLANTS FOR FOOD, MEDICINE & CRAFTS, Frances Densmore. Smithsonian, Bureau of American Ethnology report presents wealth of material on nearly 200 plants used by Chippewas of Minnesota and Wisconsin. 33 plates plus 122pp. of text. 6⅛ x 9¼. 23019-8 Pa. $2.50

THE HERBAL OR GENERAL HISTORY OF PLANTS, John Gerard. The 1633 edition revised and enlarged by Thomas Johnson. Containing almost 2850 plant descriptions and 2705 superb illustrations, Gerard's Herbal is a monumental work, the book all modern English herbals are derived from, and the one herbal every serious enthusiast should have in its entirety. Original editions are worth perhaps $750. 1678pp. 8½ x 12¼. 23147-X Clothbd. $50.00

A MODERN HERBAL, Margaret Grieve. Much the fullest, most exact, most useful compilation of herbal material. Gigantic alphabetical encyclopedia, from aconite to zedoary, gives botanical information, medical properties, folklore, economic uses, and much else. Indispensable to serious reader. 161 illustrations. 888pp. 6½ x 9¼. USO 22798-7, 22799-5 Pa., Two vol. set $10.00

HOW TO KNOW THE FERNS, Frances T. Parsons. Delightful classic. Identification, fern lore, for Eastern and Central U.S.A. Has introduced thousands to interesting life form. 99 illustrations. 215pp. 20740-4 Pa. $2.50

THE MUSHROOM HANDBOOK, Louis C.C. Krieger. Still the best popular handbook. Full descriptions of 259 species, extremely thorough text, habitats, luminescence, poisons, folklore, etc. 32 color plates; 126 other illustrations. 560pp. 21861-9 Pa. $4.50

HOW TO KNOW THE WILD FRUITS, Maude G. Peterson. Classic guide covers nearly 200 trees, shrubs, smaller plants of the U.S. arranged by color of fruit and then by family. Full text provides names, descriptions, edibility, uses. 80 illustrations. 400pp. 22943-2 Pa. $3.00

COMMON WEEDS OF THE UNITED STATES, U.S. Department of Agriculture. Covers 220 important weeds with illustration, maps, botanical information, plant lore for each. Over 225 illustrations. 463pp. 6⅛ x 9¼. 20504-5 Pa. $4.50

HOW TO KNOW THE WILD FLOWERS, Mrs. William S. Dana. Still best popular book for East and Central USA. Over 500 plants easily identified, with plant lore; arranged according to color and flowering time. 174 plates. 459pp. 20332-8 Pa. $3.50

AUSTRIAN COOKING AND BAKING, Gretel Beer. Authentic thick soups, wiener schnitzel, veal goulash, more, plus dumplings, puff pastries, nut cakes, sacher tortes, other great Austrian desserts. 224pp. USO 23220-4 Pa. $2.50

CHEESES OF THE WORLD, U.S.D.A. Dictionary of cheeses containing descriptions of over 400 varieties of cheese from common Cheddar to exotic Surati. Up to two pages are given to important cheeses like Camembert, Cottage, Edam, etc. 151pp. 22831-2 Pa. $1.50

TRITTON'S GUIDE TO BETTER WINE AND BEER MAKING FOR BEGINNERS, S.M. Tritton. All you need to know to make family-sized quantities of over 100 types of grape, fruit, herb, vegetable wines; plus beers, mead, cider, more. 11 illustrations. 157pp. USO 22528-3 Pa. $2.00

DECORATIVE LABELS FOR HOME CANNING, PRESERVING, AND OTHER HOUSEHOLD AND GIFT USES, Theodore Menten. 128 gummed, perforated labels, beautifully printed in 2 colors. 12 versions in traditional, Art Nouveau, Art Deco styles. Adhere to metal, glass, wood, most plastics. 24pp. 8¼ x 11. 23219-0 Pa. $2.00

FIVE ACRES AND INDEPENDENCE, Maurice G. Kains. Great back-to-the-land classic explains basics of self-sufficient farming: economics, plants, crops, animals, orchards, soils, land selection, host of other necessary things. Do not confuse with skimpy faddist literature; Kains was one of America's greatest agriculturalists. 95 illustrations. 397pp. 20974-1 Pa. $2.95

GROWING VEGETABLES IN THE HOME GARDEN, U.S. Dept. of Agriculture. Basic information on site, soil conditions, selection of vegetables, planting, cultivation, gathering. Up-to-date, concise, authoritative. Covers 60 vegetables. 30 illustrations. 123pp. 23167-4 Pa. $1.35

FRUITS FOR THE HOME GARDEN, Dr. U.P. Hedrick. A chapter covering each type of garden fruit, advice on plant care, soils, grafting, pruning, sprays, transplanting, and much more! Very full. 53 illustrations. 175pp. 22944-0 Pa. $2.50

GARDENING ON SANDY SOIL IN NORTH TEMPERATE AREAS, Christine Kelway. Is your soil too light, too sandy? Improve your soil, select plants that survive under such conditions. Both vegetables and flowers. 42 photos. 148pp. USO 23199-2 Pa. $2.50

THE FRAGRANT GARDEN: A BOOK ABOUT SWEET SCENTED FLOWERS AND LEAVES, Louise Beebe Wilder. Fullest, best book on growing plants for their fragrances. Descriptions of hundreds of plants, both well-known and overlooked. 407pp. 23071-6 Pa. $3.50

EASY GARDENING WITH DROUGHT-RESISTANT PLANTS, Arno and Irene Nehrling. Authoritative guide to gardening with plants that require a minimum of water: seashore, desert, and rock gardens; house plants; annuals and perennials; much more. 190 illustrations. 320pp. 23230-1 Pa. $3.50